The Organization of Information

Recent Titles in
Library and Information Science Text Series

Library of Congress Subject Headings: Principles and Application, Fourth Edition
Lois Mai Chan

Developing Library and Information Center Collections, Fifth Edition
G. Edward Evans and Margaret Zarnosky Saponaro

Metadata and Its Impact on Libraries
Sheila S. Intner, Susan S. Lazinger, and Jean Weihs

Organizing Audiovisual and Electronic Resources for Access: A Cataloging Guide, Second Edition
Ingrid Hsieh-Yee

Introduction to Cataloging and Classification, Tenth Edition
Arlene G. Taylor

Library and Information Center Management, Seventh Edition
Robert D. Stueart and Barbara B. Moran

The Collection Program in Schools: Concepts, Practices, and Information Sources, Fourth Edition
Kay Bishop

Children's Literature in Action: A Librarian's Guide
Sylvia Vardell

The School Library Media Manager, Fourth Edition
Blanche Woolls

Young Adult Literature in Action: A Librarian's Guide
Rosemary Chance

Introduction to Library Public Services, Seventh Edition
G. Edward Evans and Thomas L. Carter

Internet Technologies and Information Services
Joseph B. Miller

THE ORGANIZATION OF INFORMATION

Third Edition

Arlene G. Taylor and Daniel N. Joudrey

Library and Information Science Text Series

LIBRARIES UNLIMITED

A Member of the Greenwood Publishing Group

Westport, Connecticut • London

Library of Congress Cataloging-in-Publication Data

Taylor, Arlene G., 1941–
The organization of information / Arlene G. Taylor and Daniel N. Joudrey. — 3rd ed.
p. cm. — (Library and information science text series)
Includes bibliographical references and index.
ISBN 978-1-59158-586-2 (alk. paper) — ISBN 978-1-59158-700-2 (pbk. : alk. paper)
1. Information organization. 2. Metadata. I. Joudrey, Daniel N. II. Title.
Z666.5.T39 2009
025–dc22 2008037446

British Library Cataloguing in Publication Data is available.

Library of Congress Catalog Card Number: 2008037446
ISBN: 978-1-59158-586-2
978-1-59158-700-2 (pbk.)

First published in 2009

Libraries Unlimited, 88 Post Road West, Westport, CT 06881
A Member of the Greenwood Publishing Group, Inc.
www.lu.com

Printed in the United States of America

The paper used in this book complies with the Permanent Paper Standard issued by the National Information Standards Organization (Z39.48–1984).

10 9 8 7 6 5 4 3 2 1

CONTENTS

LIST OF FIGURES

PREFACE

The preface to the first edition of this book began as follows:

> As I began work on the ninth edition of *Introduction to Cataloging and Classification* I became more and more aware that another work was needed that would precede the cataloging text. Core courses in many schools of library and information science now include a course in organizing information. These courses typically cover much more than cataloging and classification. They discuss the concept of organization and its role in human endeavors; many kinds of retrieval tools, such as bibliographies, indexes, finding aids, catalogs, and other kinds of databases; encoding standards, such as MARC, SGML, various SGML DTDs, and XML; creation of metadata; all kinds of controlled vocabularies, including thesauri and ontologies, as well as subject heading lists; classification theory and methodology; arrangement and display of metadata records and physical information-bearing packages; and system design. *The Organization of Information* addresses this need, leaving *Introduction to Cataloging and Classification* as a textbook for courses devoted to the specifics of cataloging and classification.[1]

This statement is as true now as it was when it was written ten years ago. Changes have come in degree, however. More schools of library and information science now include organizing information as a core course. Encoding standards, metadata standards, and systems continue to evolve, and new ones have been developed. New information organizing concepts (or some would say old concepts with new names) have become useful additions to the discussion of organization of information—concepts such as information architecture, knowledge management, tagging, and taxonomies.

The goal of the third edition remains to enable students, practicing librarians, and others interested in organizing information to understand the theory, principles, standards, and tools behind information organization in all types of environments. As with the first two editions there is still more about libraries than about other types of environments. This is at least partly because the weight of history means that there are many centuries of accumulation of theory, principles, and practice behind organization of information in libraries, while archives have not quite two centuries of accumulation, and the other environments have only decades, or in some cases, less than a decade, of history.

In order to accomplish the book's goal effectively, it was necessary to make some rather major changes in the structure of the work. The first three chapters continue to cover the same concepts as in the first and second editions but with extensive updating. Chapter 1 looks at our basic human need to organize and how it is approached in various contexts. A new section discusses indexing and abstracting, and all other sections have been updated. Chapter 2 is concerned with the formats and functions of basic retrieval tools. The sections on indexes, archival finding aids, and museum databases have been significantly expanded. In Chapter 3, we ask, "How did we arrive at this state of organization?" and we discuss the history of basic principles that have developed over the centuries. In this edition, there are amplifications of a few of the historical occurrences that were treated more briefly in earlier editions.

In response to the growing importance of the omnipresent concept of *metadata,* the chapter introducing metadata has been moved forward in the third edition to Chapter 4. It has been restructured and updated, and a large section on metadata models has been added. "Encoding Standards," now Chapter 5, still deals with syntaxes used to format records, but it is expanded to give much more attention to XML and XML schemas and includes a discussion on the future of MARC. The new Chapter 6, "Systems and System Design," (formerly Chapter 5) has been updated. The concepts discussed here permeate and underlie discussion of concepts in later chapters. New concepts covered include discovery interfaces to information systems and next generation catalogs.

Chapters 7 and 8 continue discussion of metadata, covering descriptive metadata in depth in Chapter 7, and covering access points and authority control in Chapter 8. New metadata standards included are DACS (*Describing Archives: A Content Standard*), CCO (*Cataloging Cultural Objects*), and CDWA (*Categories for the Description of Works of Art*). The impending replacement of *Anglo-American Cataloguing Rules, Second Edition* (AACR2) with *RDA: Resource Description and Access* is discussed. There is also more discussion of the International Federation of Library Associations and Institutions' (IFLA) *Functional Requirements for Bibliographic Records* (FRBR). Chapter 8 "Access and Authority Control" has been restructured to reflect more closely the arrangement of Chapter 7. Chapter 8 now begins with expanded discussion of bibliographic relationships and authority control, including the roles of authority work and authority files. Whereas in the second edition Chapter 8 covered only standards for creation of names found in AACR2, this chapter in the third edition includes, as well, standards and guidelines found in IFLA's *Functional Requirements for Authority Data* (FRAD), *International Standard Archival Authority Record for Corporate Bodies, Persons, and Families* (ISAAR (CPF)), Encoded Archival Context (EAC), DACS, CCO, CDWA, and VRA (Visual Resources Association) Core. All sections of both chapters have been updated.

Subject approaches to organizing information are covered in Chapter 9, "Subject Analysis," Chapter 10, "Systems for Vocabulary Control," and Chapter 11, "Systems for Categorization." These are updated and rewritten from the second edition. It seems useful to expand on the challenges and concepts involved in determining the *aboutness* of an information resource; this enlarged and restructured treatment is covered in Chapter 9. Chapter 10 discusses, first, the concepts involved in creating controlled vocabularies, which are then followed by discussion of applying controlled vocabularies, including descriptions of several of the most used existing vocabularies. Issues related to *tagging* have been added to the chapter's coverage of natural language approaches to subject analysis. Chapter 11 covers theory of categorization and how this translates into classification. It includes a new section on the nature of categories and classifications, as well as a section on *clustering*.

One method of determining aboutness continues to be covered in Appendix A: An Approach to Subject Analysis; this appendix has been updated and new material added. Because arrangement and display of information is so important to users' retrieval of information, two new appendices are devoted to these issues: Appendix B: Arrangement of Physical Information Resources in Libraries, and Appendix C: Arrangement of Metadata Displays.

NOTE

1. Arlene G. Taylor, *The Organization of Information* (Englewood, Colo.: Libraries Unlimited, 1999), p. xvii.

ACKNOWLEDGMENTS

Many people have contributed to the existence of this book. To begin naming is always a danger, because one risks inadvertently omitting someone who actually contributed greatly. I would like to try, though, to acknowledge at least some of them. First, I again acknowledge my mentor and cataloging professor, Kathryn Luther Henderson, Professor Emerita, Graduate School of Library and Information Science, University of Illinois at Urbana/Champaign, who inspired me to understand the "why" behind all the practices involved in cataloging. This approach has assisted me greatly in making all the transitions that have been necessitated by the move from a paper environment to an electronic environment during the course of my career.

For this edition, the person who has made such immeasurable contributions that it is difficult to enumerate them all is Dr. Daniel N. Joudrey, Assistant Professor, Graduate School of Library and Information Science, Simmons College. He began the revising process for half the chapters of this edition; although we have both done much of the rewriting of the entire work, working together in concert, catching each other's errors and assisting each other with clearer ways of writing. Without his expertise and major time commitment, this edition would have been considerably delayed.

Other people have made extremely useful contributions. Dr. Jerry D. Saye, Professor, School of Library and Information Science, University of North Carolina at Chapel Hill, has generously shared his office space and good conversation on the Chapel Hill campus while I have worked on this edition. Dr. Judith Jablonski, freelance indexer, and formerly at the School of Information Sciences, University of Pittsburgh, wrote new material about indexing and abstracting to be included in Chapters 1 and 2. Dr. Murtha Baca, Head, Getty Vocabulary Program and Digital Resource Management, Getty Research Institute, edited and made many suggestions for my draft material concerning information organization in the world of museums and art. Numerous other colleagues have called to my attention one point or another that needed improvement. I hope that I managed to incorporate all of these, and I am extremely grateful to all these colleagues for their attention to detail and for caring enough to try to assist in the improvement of this text. I am also grateful to all the colleagues who have adopted the book as a text and have passed on to me the favorable comments of students who find it readable and helpful in understanding this material.

All the students I have ever taught can take credit for contributing, because they have been my "guinea pigs" in the process of explaining theory and mixing it with practice. In addition, over the years, many colleagues, too numerous to mention individually, have contributed to my understanding, first, of cataloging, and then, of broader organizing issues. I wish them to know how much I appreciate their input.

I would like to thank the ALA committee who chose the first edition of this book to receive the 2000 ALA/Highsmith Library Literature Award. The encouragement gained from that recognition has provided impetus needed to keep working when I might rather have taken some time off.

I truly appreciate the staff of Libraries Unlimited for their work in producing the book. Dr. Sue Easun, Acquisitions Editor, has been empathetic with my time problems through two hip replacements and has encouraged me to keep going. Emma Bailey, Assistant Manager, kept the project moving along and helped immensely by being a sounding board when issues arose. Mary Cotofan, of Apex CoVantage, oversaw the copyediting and typesetting stages. I thank all for their help in bringing this book to production.

And finally, I wish to thank my family. My children, Dr. Deborah Dowell, M.D., and Jonathan Dowell, Esq., J.D., have recently made clear how proud they are of me and my accomplishments, and have told me of how they have always bragged to their friends about me. I am proud of them, too, and wish them to know that their acceptance of my mothering style (i.e., being a busy professional and expecting them to take on increasing levels of responsibility for themselves as they became able) has meant a great deal to me through the years. And last, but absolutely not least, I thank my husband, Dr. A. Wayne Benson, whose love, understanding, wordsmithing skills, and culinary skills have assisted and sustained me through many deadlines. He really does, as I said in the dedication to the second edition, make life easier and much more enjoyable.

Arlene G. Taylor
Chapel Hill, NC

ACKNOWLEDGMENTS

I would like to thank the many people who have played a role in the development and writing of this work. First and foremost, I am indebted greatly to Dr. Arlene G. Taylor, without whom, I would not have the opportunities that I have today. She has been my teacher, my mentor, my friend, and now my writing partner. She has been generous, supportive, and encouraging since the moment I met her in the fall of 1998, and she is still all of those things today. She has been an inspiration, especially in my goals to become a great teacher, a respected scholar, an active and engaged faculty member, and a conscientious, thoughtful author. It has been an honor and a pleasure to work with her on this book.

I would also like to thank my brilliant and magnanimous colleagues at Simmons College's Graduate School of Library and Information Science, my wonderful and collegial home in academia. I especially want to thank my generous, encouraging dean, Dr. Michèle Cloonan. Her support has allowed me to spend the time that was needed to work on this all-encompassing project. I would also like to thank Dr. Pat Oyler and Dr. Candy Schwartz, my GSLIS mentors, who are always willing to discuss, help, and listen. I would like to thank Dr. Jeanette Bastian for our discussions of archives, Dr. Rong Tang for our discussions of integrated library systems, and Dr. Sheila Denn for our discussions about database design. I thank them for their time, their thoughts, and their friendship; I value them greatly.

I would like to thank the students that I have taught at Simmons. I have learned a great deal from them regarding where to add material to this book, where material could be dropped, what is immediately clear, and what is difficult to grasp. Through their questions and comments, they have added to this book immeasurably.

On a personal note, I would like to thank my parents, Linda and John Joudrey; my grandparents, Gerry and Bob Shaw; and my remarkable niece, Brittany Feldmeier. I thank them for their love, encouragement, and confidence in me. Finally, I would like to thank my partner and best friend, Jesús Alonso Regalado, without whom, I could not have done this. I thank him for his love, his support, his faith, his *almost* saint-like patience, and his ability to put up with me during my craziest moments (such as when I am writing). He inspires me with his knowledge, his dedication, and his complete and total love of librarianship and bibliography. He *is* the best librarian I have *ever* known. I thank him for coming into my life, because when he did, that is when I really began to live.

Daniel N. Joudrey
Cambridge, Massachusetts

CHAPTER 1

ORGANIZATION OF RECORDED INFORMATION

Merriam-Webster's Collegiate Dictionary gives several senses in its definition of *organize*. The one we are interested in is "to form into a coherent unity or functioning whole: INTEGRATE." And secondarily, we use *organize* in the sense of "to arrange elements into a whole of interdependent parts."[1] This book, then, is dedicated to explaining the process of forming unity and arranging elements as carried out by people who work in places that accumulate information resources for the use of humankind, both immediately and for posterity.

This chapter gives an overview of the field of the organization of recorded information. Terms used here, that might not be readily familiar to persons new to the field of information organization, will be explained in later chapters. In the meantime the reader may find definitions of most unfamiliar terms in the glossary of this book.

THE NEED TO ORGANIZE

There seems to be a basic drive in humans to organize. Psychologists tell us that babies' brains organize images into categories such as *faces* or *foods*. Small children do a lot of organizing and matching during play. As we grow, humans develop more sophisticated cognitive abilities to categorize, to recognize patterns, to sort, to relate, and to create groups of things and ideas. Cognitive scientist Steven Harnad has even said, "Cognition is categorization."[2] With some individuals the need to organize is much stronger than with others. Those who operate on the maxim "A place for everything and everything in its place" cannot begin to work until the work surface is cleared and stray objects have been put in place. That is, such a person has to be organized before beginning a new project. But even those whose workspaces appear to be cluttered or chaotic have some organization in their heads. Such persons usually have some idea, or perhaps certain knowledge, of what is in the various piles or collections of stuff. Regardless of one's personal style, however, human learning is based upon the ability to analyze, organize, and retrieve data, information, and knowledge; to recognize patterns; to compare experiences, concepts, and ideas; and to process the relationships among all of these.

Why do we organize? We organize to understand the world around us. We organize to save time. We organize so that we can bring similar things together into groups. Most of all, we organize because we need to retrieve. Kitchens are organized so that cooking equipment is easily accessible and foodstuffs and spices can be used as needed. Items in a newspaper are organized into specific sections so that similar stories are presented together. Personal music collections are organized so that we can find just the right song when we need it. Workplaces are organized so that documents are retrievable and work can be done. Learning processes are organized so that relationships among ideas can be used to assist the learner in recalling the learned material.

Retrieval of information is dependent upon its having been organized. Information is needed in all aspects of life—for example, for health reasons, to understand each other, to learn about one's relationships, to fix things that are broken, or simply to expand our knowledge. Some of this information has already been assimilated and is in one's knowledge reserve, while other information has to be sought. If this information is not organized, it is difficult, if not impossible, to find. So we have many tools that are organized to aid in the process of finding information that we need: telephone books, directories, dictionaries, encyclopedias, bibliographies, indexes, catalogs, museum registers, archival finding aids, and databases, among others.

Organization of information also allows us to save for posterity copies of all kinds of works that result from human endeavors (e.g., books, art works, sound recordings, films, correspondence, government documents, etc.). Libraries, archives, museums, and other cultural institutions have been doing this for many years and have now moved into the online world of the Internet. Although some examples occasionally may come from the "dot com" world, generally this book is not concerned with the organization of information, resources, or materials in commercial enterprises and other profit-driven ventures that may have put together collections of items for the purpose of sale, rather than collecting items in order to benefit humanity and our collective knowledge reserve.

THE NATURE OF INFORMATION

Consider the following terms: *understanding, data, knowledge, wisdom,* and *information.* If you were asked to place these terms in order, how would you do it? Would you rank them from the lowest level of thinking to the highest? From the highest to the lowest? In alphabetical order? In some other way? Clifford Stoll, in his book *Silicon Snake Oil: Second Thoughts on the Information Highway,* discussed these words that we use to indicate different levels of comprehension of symbols.[3] His order, indicating symbols from the least meaningful to the most meaningful, is: data, information, knowledge, understanding, wisdom. Which of these are we organizing in libraries, museums, archives, and other such institutions? There is a running argument between those who believe we are organizing information and those who believe we are organizing knowledge. The authors' bias is evident from the title of this book. It seems to us that we can use our knowledge to write a book, but until you read that book, understand it, and integrate it into your own knowledge, it is just information. That is why we believe we organize information—so that others can find it, read or otherwise absorb it, and use it to add to their own reserve of knowledge. Notice that in the preceding sentences, we said that you read, understand, and then integrate the information into your own knowledge. So there is some question about Stoll's putting understanding *after* knowledge. Perhaps the two concepts are intertwined. You need to have some understanding in order to incorporate something into your knowledge, but you must have a certain amount of knowledge in order to understand new things.

According to several dictionaries, *knowledge* exists in the mind of an individual who has studied a subject, understands it, and perhaps has added to it through research or other means. The same dictionaries indicate that *information* is the communication or reception of knowledge. Such communication occurs in great part through the recording of the knowledge in some fashion. People write, speak, compose, paint, sculpt, and attempt to communicate their knowledge to others in many other ways. This book, for example, is a representation of the authors' knowledge; but it is not a complete representation of our knowledge of the subject. It is, no doubt, an imperfect representation, in the sense that some concepts may not be explained as clearly as we truly understand them. However, it is not a representation of the reader's knowledge until the reader has read it, processed it, and understood it. That is, it is information that can be placed into a scheme of organization from which it can be retrieved for study by those interested in increasing their knowledge of the subject. Thus, we have chosen to use the term *information* rather than *knowledge* as our expression of what we believe we organize when organizing for the benefit of others. This is not a rejection of *organization of knowledge,* however. The knowledge existing in the brains of people is being harnessed in many situations. Authors work on organizing their own knowledge every time they write. The knowledge of reference librarians is used in an organized way when they assist patrons in answering questions. The phrase *knowledge management,* discussed below, has come into use in the administration of organizations. And, in recent years, some information professionals have begun to refer to classification schemes as *knowledge organization systems* (KOS).

The Nature of the Organization of Recorded Information

As mentioned earlier, this book addresses the organization of recorded information, as other means are necessary to organize information that has only been spoken, heard, or thought about. Recorded information, however, includes much more than just text. Video and audio recordings, images, cartographic representations, and Web pages are all examples of recorded information that go beyond text. Therefore, instead of using words such as *book* or *item* to refer to describable units of information, the term *information resource* is used in this book. Despite the various forms in which information may be recorded, all information resources have some basic attributes or properties in common, such as *title, creator,* and *topic.* These attributes (and others) are recorded to help organize information; collectively, these attributes can be referred to as *metadata.* Metadata, in its most informal but most prevalent definition, is "data about data." This means that the attributes used to describe an information resource are metadata about that resource. Metadata is discussed throughout this book, particularly in Chapter 4, and specific aspects of metadata are addressed in Chapters 7–11.

Ronald Hagler, in his book *The Bibliographic Record and Information Technology,* identified six functions of bibliographic control.[4] *Bibliographic control* (increasingly referred to as *information organization*) is the process of describing information resources and providing name, title, and subject access to the descriptions, resulting in records that serve as surrogates for the actual items of recorded information. These surrogate records (sometimes called *entries, bibliographic records,* or simply *metadata*) are then placed into information retrieval tools, where the records act as pointers to the actual information resources. The descriptions found in the records provide users with enough information to determine the potential value of the resources without actually having to view the items directly. Surrogate records are stored in a variety of retrieval tools including bibliographies, catalogs, indexes, finding aids, museum registers, bibliographic databases, and search engines. Hagler's listing reflects the purpose of his book—that is, the emphasis is upon the work of librarians. However, the list, presented and enlarged below, with wording altered to be inclusive of all recorded information, reflects the major activities involved in the organization of recorded information.

1. *Identifying the existence of all types of information resources as they are made available.*

A book may be published or a Web site may be established, but if no one knows of its existence except the parties involved in its creation, it will be of no informational use to anyone. Existence and identity can be made known in many ways: publishers' announcements, e-mail announcements, reviews, and subject-related listings, to name a few. Most publishers create catalogs listing their products along with abstracts for them. Reference tools such as *Books in Print* are products of this activity. Some online journals send regular e-mail announcements, outlining contents, to let readers know when a new issue is available. Some news organizations allow people to sign up to receive e-mail announcements about new information available at the organization's Web site or about how to order recordings of special programs, and so on.

2. *Identifying the works contained within those information resources or as parts of them.*

In the majority of cases, one information resource is equal to one intellectual, literary, or artistic work. However, a collection of short stories or a group of images may be considered to be an information resource as a whole, or each individual story or artistic work may be considered an information resource. It depends upon how much *granularity* is desired in the level of the description. A Web site that is about a famous person may have individual digitized works by the person, biographical material, accounts of the person written by contemporaries, accounts of events contemporary to the person's life-span, and other parts. The writings about the person and the events may be important works in their own right and may need to be identified separately.

3. *Systematically pulling together these information resources into collections in libraries, archives, museums, Internet communication files, and other such depositories.*

The activity of creating collections has been thought of traditionally as the province of institutions such as libraries, archives, and museums. But collections have always been created in many other situations: for example, personal collections made up because of an intense interest in a particular kind of information, office collections of internal information and information needed to carry out the work of the office, university departmental collections of materials needed for teaching in a particular discipline, and so forth. Now that it is easy to make these collections known publicly, lists are being provided at Web sites.

In recent years, collections often include electronic resources not held or owned locally. Many institutions purchase the right to allow their users to search a resource online. Some resources are accessible only online. Others are also available in print. Part of the process is determining whether such resources need to be added to one's collection in some permanent way. Most institutions wish to collect in a purposeful way. Unless a collection is well organized, it can be difficult to determine which new works will enhance the collection. Developers of collections rely on organized metadata to avoid adding something already owned.

4. *Producing lists of these information resources prepared according to standard rules for citation.*

Lists created in the process of describing information resources include bibliographies, indexes, library catalogs, archival finding aids, museum registers, and Web directories. These are important to the retrieval of individual information resources, because if one is looking for a known item—especially a tangible one that has a physical location—it is necessary to find it listed somewhere. Lists of resources may be in print or electronic form.

5. *Providing name, title, subject, and other useful access to these information resources.*

The successful retrieval of information resources through lists depends on the inclusion of sufficient metadata. The activity that adds the most value to the usefulness and retrieval potential of a collection is the provision of authority-controlled name, title, and subject access points to the descriptions of the information resources. An *access point* is a name, word, or phrase, chosen by a cataloger or indexer and placed in a particular field in a record that describes a resource. It may then be used to obtain that record from a retrieval tool or other organized system. *Authority control* is most often practiced by using a unique character string to represent each name, work, or subject, in order to achieve consistency within the catalog or other retrieval tool. It also involves creating explicit relationships between different names, works, or subjects. Keyword access can be provided more or less automatically and "on-the-fly"—that is, any information in electronic form can be found by searching for a word that appears in the electronic resource. However, as the size of the collection being searched increases, results of keyword searches become less and less satisfactory because of information overload. More satisfactory retrieval comes from being able to search for names, titles, and subjects that have been created under authority control, usually by humans. If a person has been identified by different forms of name, and if that name is brought under authority control, then a search for one form of the name will retrieve information resources related to the person regardless of which form of name appears in a particular resource. If a work has been given different titles in various manifestations, a search for one of the titles will retrieve all. If a system uses controlled vocabulary, a search for a subject word with more than one meaning (which encompasses most English words) will allow differentiation among the various meanings and will direct users to broader, narrower, and related terms. It will also bring together, under one term, all the synonymous terms that may be used to express a concept. Authority-controlled access is of little use, however, unless systems are designed to take advantage of it. Therefore, a major part of organizing information is designing systems for searching and display that will allow information-seekers to find easily what they need and want.

6. *Providing the means of locating each information resource or a copy of it.*

Location of information resources has been, for at least a century, a value added by institutions with collections. The catalogs or other lists created in these institutions give information on the physical location of the information resource. In many library online catalogs, circulation information is available so that if an item has been taken out of the library, that information is made available to the patron. Bibliographic networks (e.g., OCLC) allow one to find out which locations physically own a particular item. Many library, museum, and archival retrieval tools are available on the Web. One can learn from these which locations own an item, whether it is on loan at a particular location (usually a library, as archives and museums generally do not circulate items from their collections), and often whether an item is on order and when it is expected to arrive.

Traditionally, bibliographies and indexes have not given location information. Bibliographies list information resources that exist somewhere, but seldom tell where. Indexes give the larger resource in which a smaller work being listed can be found (e.g., the journal in which an article can be found), but do not give the physical location of the larger resource. All of this is still true for tangible resources, but in lists that include electronic resources found on the Internet, it is now common to give the direct location (e.g., in the form of the URL). However, the instability of URLs makes it difficult to keep them current.

In order to accomplish Hagler's six functions of bibliographic control, adequate and sufficient metadata is needed. Without this metadata, information resources could not be made known to the world, smaller works could not be identified, collections could not be created, lists could not be produced, access could not be granted, and locating the items would be impossible. Metadata is necessary in order to meet these and other functions as well. Metadata, however, will not look the same in all cases. There are differences in how metadata is created for different types of materials, in different environments, among different communities, and in different contexts.

ORGANIZATION OF INFORMATION IN DIFFERENT CONTEXTS

There are many contexts in which there is a desire to organize information so that it will be retrievable for various purposes and so that at least some of it will be kept for posterity. The ones to be discussed here are libraries of all types, archives, museums, the Internet, digital libraries, information architecture, indexing and abstracting, records management, and knowledge management.

Libraries

We consider libraries first because they have the longest tradition of organizing information for the purpose of retrieval and for posterity. As mentioned earlier, the process begins with collections. Collections in libraries are created through the process called *collection development.* Collections of tangible information resources are developed most often in three ways: (1) librarians learn about existence of new works through reviews, publishers' announcements, requests from users of the library, and the like, and then order appropriate materials; (2) gifts are given to the library; (3) approval plans, worked out with one or more vendors, bring in new items according to pre-selected profiles. Less frequently, but still practiced in some academic and research libraries, collection development librarians or bibliographers may take resource-buying trips to purchase special materials, particularly difficult-to-find foreign language materials. And, of course, journals keep adding to a collection's size unless subscriptions are dropped.

When materials are organized into collections, physical entities have to be arranged in some fashion. They may be placed on shelves in the order in which they arrive, or they may be placed in some more meaningful order. They could be placed in alphabetical order, the way that fiction and biography sections are arranged in many public and school libraries. Most resources, however, are arranged by classification.

Classification of materials is part of the process of cataloging, which is usually the first activity to occur following the receipt of new resources. Cataloging individual resources involves creating a description of the physical item; choosing certain names and titles to serve as access points for getting to the description in the catalog; doing authority work on those names and titles; doing subject analysis of the content of the resource; choosing subject headings and classification notations to represent the subject analysis; and creating call numbers (location devices), usually by adding a Cutter number to the classification notation to make a unique set of letters and numbers to identify a particular physical item.

The description, choice of name and title access points, and authority control for names and titles are accomplished in most libraries in the United States and in many other countries through reference to a set of rules called *Anglo-American Cataloguing Rules* (AACR).[5] These rules have been revised multiple times, and currently are being revised again. This time there is an effort to align the design of these rules with the conceptual models for bibliographic and authority data that have been developed by the International Federation of Library Associations and Institutions (IFLA): *Functional Requirements for Bibliographic Records* (FRBR)[6] and *Functional Requirements for Authority Data* (FRAD).[7] The new rules, scheduled to be published in 2009, are called *RDA: Resource Description and Access.*[8]

Subject analysis of resources is performed by persons who have learned to determine the subject matter (or the *aboutness*) of a work. Subject headings that reflect the analyzed aboutness are chosen through reference to a list of controlled vocabulary terms, such as *Library of Congress Subject Headings* (LCSH).[9] Classification notations are chosen from a standard classification schedule, such as the *Library of Congress Classification* (LCC).[10] Most records thus created are encoded with the MAchine Readable Cataloging (MARC)[11] format so that they can be displayed in the Integrated Library Systems (ILS) that most libraries have.

The process of cataloging just described is often referred to as *original cataloging*. Fortunately, it is not necessary for every information resource in every library to be cataloged originally in that library. Because libraries frequently acquire copies of the same items, or decide to catalog the same Web resources, their catalogers can share metadata by adapting a copy of the original cataloging record created by another library for their own catalogs, a process commonly called *copy cataloging*. This is related to the idea of *cooperative cataloging*—the working together by independent institutions to share network memberships or to create cataloging that can be used by others.

Once items have been chosen, received, and added into the catalog, the physical items have to be processed so that they can be housed in the collection. This involves removing or adding book jackets, placing security strips in or on items, placing call number labels and barcodes on the items, sending an item to the conservation/preservation department if it is an older item that is not in good shape, and so forth.

The two major results of the cataloging process are (1) the arrangement of collections and (2) the creation and maintenance of the catalog that provides the major access to the collections. The catalog is able to show what exists in the collection written by certain authors, having certain titles, or on certain subjects. It also collocates (i.e., brings together) all of the works of an author and all the editions of a work, and all works on a subject, even though they might not be brought together in the collection.[12] Finally, the catalog provides some kind of location device to indicate where in the collection the item will be found, assuming it is not circulating to a user.

Before online catalogs existed, typically the library's main card, book, or microform catalog was supplemented by other catalogs. Catalogs for departmental libraries, serial record holdings, special formats catalogs, and shelflists containing location information for specific copies of an item were the most common. Today, all of these have been incorporated into one database in most online catalogs. In addition, most online catalogs are part of integrated systems, which means that circulation information can accompany each catalog record.

Until recently the online catalog continued to contain records only for items physically held by the library system. As libraries have entered into cooperative relationships, this principle of showing "what the library has" has eroded. In union catalogs that contain records from more than one library, the concept was expanded to "what at least one of the cooperating libraries has." More recently, the addition of records for Web-accessible resources has meant that a number of catalogs now contain records for "what the library can provide access to" as well. Portals accessible from online catalogs provide users with a way to locate all the information content that they have the authority to access. The portal server presents an authentication screen to the user; if the user name and password are accepted, the user can have access to whatever resources are allowed by the user's status. An academic institution, for example, may have licenses for its users to access many different online databases. Formerly, one had to learn the access protocol for each database and enter a different user ID and password. Through the controlled access of a portal, an authorized user may be able to search these databases by just clicking to enter them, and may even be able to search several of them at once. A library portal may have access links for local resources, remote resources, reference help, and personal patron information, for example. Local resources may be divided into books, journals, databases, digital collections, and course reserves, and all of these may be accessible through searching the catalog. Reference help may include online reference tools, links to online search engines, and a virtual reference desk with either real-time or e-mail access to a reference librarian. Personal patron information may include lists of materials borrowed, saved searches, and personalized alerts.

Online catalogs also can be gateways to outside systems such as bibliographic networks (e.g., OCLC) that can show where an information resource may be found if it is not in the local catalog. The item can then be requested through *interlibrary loan* (ILL). In addition, bibliographic and full-text databases may be accessed from a catalog gateway. Many of these have become document delivery systems. A major addition to online catalogs has been access to the Web. Many libraries are cataloging Internet resources that seem to be important for the users of that catalog, and a URL in a catalog record can be hyperlinked to the Web for immediate access to the resource.

An influence on the organization process in libraries is found in the reference process. Libraries are organized so that information can be retrieved. In the reference process the success of the organization is tested. If it is found to be difficult to use, some of the organization process must be redone. Administrative services in libraries also must be concerned with the organization of information. Administrators are responsible for technological decisions that directly affect the organization of the recorded information in that setting. Administrators' decisions also affect the future, in which chaos will result if the activities and processes of information organization are not supported.

Archives

Libraries became more and more standardized throughout the twentieth century, with many information resources in a library being duplicates of resources in another, but this is not the situation in archives. Archives usually consist of unique items. Therefore, it once was thought that standardization was unnecessary. Archives could not take advantage of previously created metadata (i.e., use metadata records created by other agencies) because they were not describing materials that were also owned elsewhere. More recently, however, archives have seen significant standardization in their descriptive practices.

Archives preserve records of enduring value that document organizational or personal activities accumulated in the course of daily life and work. Organizational records consist of such things as annual reports, correspondence, personnel records, and the like. Personal records might consist of such things as correspondence, manuscripts, and personal papers, or perhaps a collection of memorabilia or a scrapbook. Even though materials in archives often are thought to be old, this is not necessarily so. Further, archival materials can be in many different formats: texts, graphic images, sound recordings, moving image recordings, on paper, or in analog or digital forms.

Archival materials have been organized for centuries. Unlike library materials, archival materials are arranged and described in groups. Until the last few decades, each archives chose its own way to organize the information, particularly regarding level of control and depth of description. There have been several major schools of thought through the years as to how organization of archival information should be done. The one that seems to have prevailed states that the basic principle of organization is *respect des fonds,* which means that archival materials created and/or collected together should be kept together in their original order without mixing in records or materials from other creators or collections. The concept of *respect des fonds* comprises two sub-principles: provenance and original order. *Provenance* is the originator (i.e., the corporate body or individual) that created, gathered, and/or maintained the collection before it was sent to the archives. The term provenance is also used to show the ownership history of a particular artifact or collection of archival information. *Original order* is the sequence in which the originator of an archival collection kept or created the collection. This may or may not be evident in the collection. If the original order has been lost or the collection was never truly organized by the creator or collector, then an archivist may need to construct a logical order for the collection. While looking at original order, sub-groupings (called *series*) among the materials may be identified. The description of the collection will reflect the arrangement of the groups. Most archives keep the contents of individual collections within the archives as a whole in original order, and the collections are maintained according to provenance.

Standardization and cooperation have come to the archival world in part because of increased interest in research involving documents and archival collections housed all over the world. In addition, interest has grown—especially in the academic community—in making extensive descriptions of archival collections accessible over the Web and in entering abbreviated descriptions of archival collections into the same databases with library catalog records.

Descriptions of archival materials can take different forms. An *accession record* summarizes information about the source of the collection, gives the circumstances of its acquisition (which are more fully treated in the donor file), and briefly describes the physical data and contents for a collection. A *finding aid* gives detailed notes of the historical and organizational context of the collection and continues by describing its content, providing an inventory outlining what is in each box. It may also contain subject headings, authority-controlled access points, and physical details such as the presence of brittle or fragile materials. A separate record also may be created to describe the collection's finding aid for inclusion in a library catalog.

Archival materials are generally housed in boxes kept in closed stacks, accessible only to staff. There is no public browsing and so the arrangement of the individual archival collections does not need to be classified as is usually true in a library with open stacks. Any classification given, in any case, would be so broad as to be almost useless, due to the varied nature of each collection.

In the 1980s, when the archival world became interested in placing records for finding aids into library catalogs, a MARC format for archival and manuscript control (AMC) was developed (MARC-AMC). Despite some lingering problems, the format continues to be used to code archival catalog records (now with the name *mixed materials* instead of AMC). In the last decade, the Encoded Archival Description (EAD)[13] standard has been used to encode finding aids so that they can be displayed on the Web.

The organization of archival information is necessary for use, whether that use is for administrative, historical, or personal reasons. It is also useful for archives that wish to mount exhibits, perhaps in an academic setting, for example, or on the Web. If collections are well organized and documented, an exhibitor can use this to find appropriate additions to the exhibit.

Museums (Art and Object Collections)

Although libraries and archives may contain some visual materials (notably photographs, but also slides, art prints, and the like), the collections of museums, art galleries, and other institutions that collect artifacts and objects of material culture consist primarily of visual material in two- or three-dimensional form. These collections traditionally have been organized for internal use only. Recently, however, research needs, institutional mandates, and general public interest have led such institutions to think about organizing their collections in ways that libraries and archives have for many years. Metadata schemas, such as *Categories for the Description of Works of Art* (CDWA);[14] controlled vocabularies, such as the Library of Congress's *Thesaurus for Graphic Materials* (TGM),[15] the Getty vocabularies,[16] and *Iconclass*[17] (a classification system for describing the narrative and iconographic content of visual works); and content standards, like *Cataloging Cultural Objects* (CCO),[18] have emerged in the last few decades as a response to museums' needs to better organize and disseminate their collections' information.

Museum art works or artifacts are usually acquired through an institution's acquisitions department. As is done in archives, accession records are created, although the practice in natural history museums differs somewhat. In natural history museums, artifacts are acquired largely from fieldwork, and a preliminary field record is made; if it is decided to keep the objects in the collection, accession records are created. In some cases, groups of similar objects are described as a single lot that is given a single accession number. Curating of individual objects, which may not happen for some time, results in departmental-level catalog records with their own numerical sequences. In museums other than the natural history type, items are registered after being accessioned. Registration is a process much like cataloging in libraries. The records created by a museum, historical society, or special collections registrar's department serve as a catalog in that they establish organizational control over the art works and artifacts.

In museums, as in archives, the provenance of an object or a collection of objects is important information and is essential in determining the name and other elements describing that particular object. Both provenance and physical condition of the object must appear with all other information about the object in the catalog or registration record. An aspect of creating records for museum objects and art that is very different from creating records for text is that the objects are often imperfectly known at the time of accessioning and registering. There may be an accumulation of information over time, some of which may be conflicting or contradictory.

Description of visual material is often more difficult than description of textual material. There is more reliance on the perceptions of the person doing the describing. Often there are no words associated with items at all; it is necessary for the describers of such items to use their own words. A single record may have many more fields than does the usual library catalog record. Some fields that are typically needed for art objects that are not used in libraries are: materials, technique(s), provenance, exhibition history, installation considerations, and appraised value. Even with additional fields, it is not possible to anticipate all of the uses a researcher might find in works of art or artifacts. A street scene from a century ago may be useful to historians, architects, urban planners, cultural historians, medical researchers, sociologists, students of photography, or others. Systems have been developed that start with queries that use the text of the description; then query results allow the searcher to browse surrogate images.

Another key difference in cataloging works of art and material culture, as opposed to bibliographic items, resides in the very definition of *work*. The FRBR model, developed for bibliographic items, does not apply in every way to many or even most types of works collected by museums, historical societies, and similar collecting institutions. Murtha Baca and Sherman

Clarke have examined how FRBR does and does not apply to works of art, architecture, and material culture, and discuss some of the implications for descriptive cataloging.[19]

Subject analysis is also more difficult for visual materials—an image does not tell in words what it is about, nor does the title of a visual work always clearly convey what the work is about. Additionally, the line between description and subject analysis is harder to draw. One might describe a work of art as being a painting of a woman in a blue dress holding and looking at a baby—this is a description. But if one gives the subject of the work as "Mary and Jesus," one has crossed the line into interpretation (unless this in the title of the work given by the artist). And if one uses a description like "maternal love," one is definitely interpreting.

A perceived barrier to shared metadata about museum objects has been the fact that museums hold unique objects. This is perhaps less true of natural history collections than other museum and art collections; although each specimen of a bug or bird is unique, each represents a class of organisms that can be identified to the genus and species level. There would have to be copy-specific notes, but this does not preclude the idea of reusing metadata for cooperative access. However, as was true of libraries when cooperative cataloging was first introduced, museum curators fear a loss of individual control and a diminished level of detail. Until the recent advent of initiatives like AMICO,[20] ARTstor,[21] and, OCLC's WorldCat,[22] museums had been reluctant to give up their local terminology and idiosyncratic ways of organizing their information in order to participate in union catalogs or federated retrieval tools. This is now changing. Chapter 7 describes some cooperative museum projects that are currently under way.

Besides their major collections, museums can also have archives, records management programs, and libraries. A museum library may contain published materials that document or relate to the museum collections. As with archival materials, museum collections are accessible only to staff. Much of the collection is stored behind the scenes while only some of it is on display at any one time. Behind the scenes, the items are numbered in a way so that they can be retrieved as needed. Persons responsible for the exhibits must make heavy use of the system of organizational control. In addition, these collections are increasingly being used for research by persons with diverse research needs.

The Internet

The Internet has been likened to a library where all the books have been dumped on the floor and there is no catalog. For many years, efforts have been made to find a way to gain some control over the Internet; however, one cannot yet say that it is organized. There is so much change so fast that efforts begun may be out of date in a few months.

Several different approaches are being taken in the attempt to organize the Internet. Libraries have attempted to use traditional means of organization. Some librarians, for example, have compiled bibliographies of Web sites. Some of these bibliographies eventually have become portals or gateways to the Internet. INFOMINE is an example of a portal created by cooperating librarians from several academic libraries.[23] At its Web site, INFOMINE is described as a "virtual library of Internet resources," although it includes databases, resources on CD-ROM, electronic texts, and other such resources. The system is operated by a team of librarians who create metadata. The system also has automatic and semi-automatic metadata generation of records retrieved by Web crawlers.

Librarians have been part of the team of people who have been working on a metadata standard called the *Dublin Core,* a set of 15 metadata elements used to describe Web resources. In the late 1990s, OCLC established a way for libraries to catalog online resources cooperatively and to have ready access to a database of metadata describing important Web resources. This system is available through OCLC's Web interface for cataloging—called Connexion. In Connexion, cataloging can be done either in traditional MARC/AACR2 format or in Dublin Core format. An important feature of Connexion, with regard to organizing the Internet, is its provision for the development of pathfinders for certain subjects.

Much work on organizing and searching the Internet has been done by persons other than librarians. Search engines, for example, have been developed by computer scientists and programmers. Most people appreciate search engines, even though they may be frustrated that the search engines are not more selective and precise. Most programs or agents (e.g., robots, spiders, etc.) sent out to find sites to add to the indexes of search engines are able to index text only; graphics and pictures can be recognized as such, but cannot be interpreted unless they have accompanying text or labels. In addition to that, these programs cannot analyze a site's purpose, history, policies, and so forth. In order to improve the situation, work on various kinds of metadata for Internet resources is ongoing and important; appropriate information could be gleaned by robots from metadata that has been added to a site by its author or by someone trained in describing and analyzing information resources, although at this time, misuse of metadata (e.g., addition of keywords that are popular words but have nothing to do with the content of the site) has kept most search engines from making use of it. Properly used, though, metadata can include information about non-textual parts of a site, information about the site's purpose and history, information about the contents of the site, and the like.

There is software that automatically classifies and indexes electronic documents, but automated tools categorize information differently than people do. Many information institutions have great interest in this type of software, but the results so far have been less than stellar. Until these systems improve greatly, they will not be used as more than tools to make suggestions to human indexers and catalogers. The search site Yahoo! categorizes Web resources by broad subject areas using human indexers. Before Google began to dominate Internet retrieval, the directory approach to organizing Web sites had been popular (although it was not completely successful as a classification). Though cataloging and classification requires expert intellectual effort, there is recognition that at least some of the work must be automated if there is any hope of keeping pace with the ever-increasing amount of online information. OCLC has developed products and has sponsored research projects, the outcomes of which have been improved library classification schemes, cataloging productivity tools, and new proposals for the creation and maintenance of metadata.[24] Researchers for INFOMINE have developed systems to automatically assign classification notations and subject headings.[25]

Although some believe that organizing the Internet is impossible, the parts that are important for retrieval and for posterity *will* be brought under organizational control. It is human nature, and the principles learned over centuries of organizing print information can be used alongside automated processes and tools to help organize electronic resources. The current effort to create the Semantic Web, wherein data on the Web will be defined semantically and linked to relevant data for the purpose of more effective discovery of information, is a case in point, as are the recent developments of tagging and folksonomies. These grassroots efforts, once again, are a clear demonstration of the basic human desire to organize information.

Digital Libraries and Archives

The Internet has given us the means for making digital libraries accessible. Digital libraries vary greatly in content and methods of organization; all have some kind of organization, although not necessarily traditional library organization. In the early 1990s, the definition of a digital library was a matter of debate. There were many different types of experiments that were referred to as digital libraries that would not be considered to be digital libraries today. For example, at the simplest level were collections of links to resources related to a particular subject; sometimes, such collections (really bibliographies) were coordinated among individual librarians at cooperating institutions in such a way that a particular library would agree to cover certain subject areas, and then the locations of all the collections of URLs were brought together on reference Web pages at each institution. But the phrase *digital library* came to mean collections in which a site provides digitized information resources with an architecture and a service for the retrieval of such resources. By the mid-1990s, it was recognized that a digital library must contain an organized collection; it is not exclusively a set of pointers to other material; and it must be created for a particular audience, group of users, or community. Today, one example of a digital library usually found in an academic setting is the institutional repository—an online system that collects, manages, disseminates, and preserves digital resources related to the intellectual activity of an academic community.

Moving into the twenty-first century, Christine Borgman stated: "Digital libraries are an extension, enhancement, and integration both of information retrieval systems and of multiple information institutions, libraries being only one. The scope of digital libraries' capabilities includes not only information retrieval but also creating and using information."[26] She emphasized that digital libraries are for communities of users and that they are really extensions of the physical places where resources are selected, collected, organized, preserved, and accessed, including libraries, museums, archives, and schools.[27] This is echoed in a white paper sponsored by Sun Microsystems that defines a digital library as "the electronic extension of functions users typically perform and the resources they access in a traditional library."[28] The authors liken the use of the phrase *digital library* to the use of *horseless carriage* and state that digital library technologies are becoming essential enablers of the provision of information services, extending and enhancing the traditional provision of these services in society.[29]

During the 1990s many experimental digital library projects were funded by such agencies as the U.S. National Science Foundation and the U.K. Joint Information Systems Committee. They worked to remove technical and distance barriers from the provision of access to all kinds of information and irreplaceable artifacts. The British Library's "Electronic Beowulf Project" digitized the eleventh-century manuscript of *Beowulf.* Elsewhere, specialized cameras with filters (developed by Eastman Kodak for the space program) were used to create images of the Dead Sea Scrolls and to reveal characters in those manuscripts that were previously invisible due to deterioration. Audio recordings of historic speeches or exotic sounds from nature, along with video clips from television and movies, advanced geospatial data renderings, and so forth, can now be accessed by students and researchers from their desktops. These new capabilities were collected into digital libraries and organized. Issues of digitization, rights management, preservation, and metadata encoding were addressed.

The first digital libraries were custom developments, as there were not yet any off-the-shelf software packages. For example, the University of California at Berkeley has had several projects that have contributed to digital library innovations. One project created specifications for encoding electronic finding aids for special collections and archives. This project was the basis for what has become the Encoded Archival Description (EAD).[30] Another project was the Making of America II project, which proposed a standard encoding for digital objects. This evolved into the Metadata Encoding and Transmission Standard (METS).[31]

Another example is Cornell University, which has been recognized for having undertaken an aggressive digitization program, digitizing such items as primary sources of nineteenth-century American culture and history, audio recordings of rare birdcalls, and works drawn from the university library's rare book collection. The digital library program has established a central repository for all these digitized resources with the aim of supporting the total lifecycle of those resources.[32]

An example of a cooperative project was a program of the museum community that resulted in the Art Museum Image Consortium (AMICO). As museums increased their digitizing projects, they found that they needed help with the increasing amounts of time required to meet demand from students and researchers. AMICO's digital library includes multimedia objects that portray fully documented works of art from member institutions. AMICO members dissolved their collaboration in 2005, but the site remains online for archival purposes.[33]

A successful project that began early in the history of digital libraries and is ongoing is the American Memory digital library of the Library of Congress.[34] It began with a pilot program in 1990 and has grown into one of the most well known digital collections in the world. From the beginning, this digital library has been a collaborative effort, with public, research, and academic libraries, museums, historical societies, and archival institutions digitizing American history collections and making them available on the American Memory site.

As the emphasis has shifted from experimentation to mainstream implementation, focus has changed to emphasize standardization, organization, usability, and production of commercially available packages to be used by institutions just entering the digital library arena. Several library automation companies offer digital library solutions, and some multimedia management technology companies offer packages that include distance education course development (with inclusion of the means to create digital library support for a course or set of courses). For example, Ex Libris offers "DigiTool," a package, working in conjunction with an integrated library system, that includes the means to facilitate cataloging, managing, sharing, searching, and retrieval of digital collections.[35] Other such products are Digital Library offered by SirsiDynix[36] and Digital Imaging from VTLS.[37] There is also independent software that libraries can use to build their own digital libraries. One such product is Greenstone, produced by the New Zealand Digital Library Project, and developed and distributed in cooperation with UNESCO.[38] Greenstone is open-source software that integrates many different document formats and different types of metadata.

Organization of digital libraries is being accomplished with tools such as metadata schemas, XML encoding, user tagging, taxonomies, and so forth. These are described in later chapters of this book. Provision of access to digital libraries is increasingly through portals that give access through a unified user interface to disparate sets of information sources. Portals are described more fully above in the libraries section.

Information Architecture

Just as architects must determine the needs of the people who will use a space and then create a pattern that will fulfill those needs in order to design buildings or other structures that will serve people's needs in addition to being beautiful, so must information architects determine the uses to which information will be put and create patterns for paths to finding needed information in addition to creating attractive interfaces to the information. Information architecture, then, is much more than Web design, but its development and emergence as a field or discipline is closely associated with the creation of Web sites. Andrew Dillon defines *information architecture* (IA) as "the term used to describe the process of designing, implementing and evaluating information spaces that are humanly and socially acceptable to their intended stakeholders."[39] He says he purposely leaves the definition "open so that we cover the organizational, blueprinting, and experience aspects, and allow for IA roles to cover these aspects."[40] Peter Morville and Louis Rosenfeld define *information architecture* as:

- The structural design of shared information environments.
- The combination of organization, labeling, search, and navigation systems within web sites and intranets.
- The art and science of shaping information products and experiences to support usability and findability.
- An emerging discipline and community of practice focused on bringing principles of design and architecture to the digital landscape.[41]

Then they jokingly ask, "Were you expecting a single definition?"[42] There is still disagreement in this emerging field about what is covered, but there does appear to be some agreement upon a desire to manage documents and provide easy access to information based upon an understanding of users' needs and behaviors, including interface and navigation systems as well as useful and pleasing graphic design.

Some information architects reject the notion that information architecture is a new approach to the information organization that has been practiced in libraries, archives, and museums for a long time. But the parallels are striking. Librarians have long understood the necessity of selectively acquiring information resources and then organizing them in ways that will aid users in gaining access to them as needed (even though one may not know all future uses to which the information may be put). Morville and Rosenfeld suggest that one way to explain to family and friends what an information architect does is to say: "I'm an information architect. I organize huge amounts of information on big web sites and intranets so that people can actually find what they're looking for. Think of me as an Internet librarian."[43]

Morville and Rosenfeld identify the following stages that the process of information architecture must go through: research, strategy, design, implementation, and administration.[44] *Research* includes a review of background materials, gaining an understanding of the goals and business context, examining the existing information architecture, content, and intended audiences, and finally conducting studies necessary to explore the situation. *Strategy* arises from contextual understanding developed in the first phase and defines the top levels of the site's organization and navigation structures, while also considering document types and the metadata schema. *Design* involves creating detailed blueprints, a metadata schema, and the like, to be used by graphic designers, programmers, content authors, and the production team. *Implementation* is where designs are used in the building, testing, and launching of the site—organizing and tagging documents, troubleshooting, and developing documentation occur in this phase. *Administration* involves the continuous evaluation and improvement of the site's information architecture.[45] The strategy and design stages are the ones that require a thorough understanding of the theoretical underpinnings of information organization, including understanding of metadata; provision of access points with all the attendant relationships among them; subject approaches by categories, classification, and/or alphabetical tags; and the system design that will allow display of results in a logical and usable fashion (i.e., the principles covered in the rest of this book).

Indexing and Abstracting

Indexing and abstracting are two approaches to distilling information content into an abbreviated, but comprehensive, representation of an information resource. Indexing has a long and changing tradition in terms of what it is, who has done it, why it is done, and how it is done. The history of abstracting is less volatile, and has evolved in the twentieth and twenty-first centuries into decided formats with targeted audiences.

Indexing

Indexing is the process by which the content of an information resource is analyzed, and the aboutness of that item is determined and expressed in a concise manner. Indexing is also concerned with describing the information resource in such a way that users are aware of the basic attributes of a document, such as author, title, length, and the location of the content. Indexing typically concerns textual items only; although image indexing is a growing area of practice. There are three basic types of indexing: back-of-the-book indexing, database indexing, and Web indexing.

In traditional *back-of-the-book indexing*, the index is a list of terms or term phrases arranged alphabetically with locator references that make it possible for the user to retrieve the desired content. Language of the indexing terms is typically derived from language of the text—thus the kind of indexing done in this context is referred to as derived indexing. A good book index will also include second-level entries (i.e., subheadings), variant entries (i.e., multiple entry points), and cross-references. Book indexing is primarily done by freelance specialists who contract with publishers, although some publishers maintain an in-house indexing staff.

In *database indexing* (sometimes referred to as *journal* or *periodical indexing*), each database item is represented by a set of descriptor terms and, in some instances, a classification code. Database indexing normally uses a controlled vocabulary or thesaurus from which the indexer selects or assigns the appropriate terms. The scope and number of descriptor terms assigned to an item is determined by the editorial policies of the publisher of the given database, and in-house or specially trained indexers usually perform the indexing.

Web indexing (or *Internet indexing*) is a type of indexing still very much in development, in terms of both its jargon and its actual practice. Currently, Web indexing falls into the following categories:

- **Back-of-the-book style indexing**—often referred to as *A–Z Indexing*, which uses encoded index links within the Web site;
- **Subject trees indexing**—essentially classification, which categorizes Web sites and supplies them with keywords for searching (e.g., Yahoo!); and,

- **Search engine indexing**—more accurately described as the automatic indexing of Web sites in which: (1) Web sites are searched based on user query terms, (2) an index of the words found and where they were found is maintained, and (3) future searching on these same queries uses the saved indexes.

Because of the varieties of Web indexing, *who* does Web indexing is a question that applies primarily to the A–Z style of Web indexing. Freelance contractors, often book indexers who have expanded their repertoire of services, create A–Z Web indexes. Subject tree indexing may also be contracted; although Yahoo! and others have in-house indexers. Different types of indexes are described more fully in Chapter 2.

A number of software tools have been created that can be used to generate indexes. They use a variety of techniques, the efficacy of which depends upon variables such as cost, time constraints, type and size of files to be indexed, and individual preferences. The American Society for Indexing (ASI) lists several types of tools used for indexing.[46] These include:

- Standalone or dedicated tools, which allow the creation of back-of-the-book indexes from page-numbered galleys;
- Embedded indexing tools, which allow insertion of index entries as invisible text in electronic files;
- Tagging and keywording tools, which allow indexing codes (instead of invisible text) to be embedded in electronic text; and allow creation of hard-coded jumps, similar to Web links; these rely on the words used by the author of the text, not indexers' concepts;
- Automated indexing software, which accompanies most word-processing software, and builds concordances or word lists directly from texts, using the language of the authors (again, not true indexes that include key concepts that may not use the author's words)
- Free-text and weighted-text searching tools, which allow the assignment of values to words and phrases.

Abstracting

Abstracting is a process that consists of analyzing the content of an information resource and then writing a succinct summary or synopsis of that work. Typically abstracting is done for an academic publication or a professional journal. The length, style, and amount of detail in an abstract may vary depending on its intended audience. An abstract is not a review of the work, nor does it evaluate or interpret the work that is being abstracted. Although it contains key words and concepts found in the larger text, the abstract is an original document rather than an excerpted passage. Technically, an abstract is the summary text; in practice, a complete abstract consists of both the title of the abstracted work and the summary text.

Abstracting is done by both authors and specially trained information professionals. Scholarly journals often require that an abstract accompany the articles that authors submit for publication. The rubrics provided by journal publishers can be inconsistent or vague, and the quality of published abstracts can suffer as a consequence. Abstracts are also written by professionals, either in-house or contractors to the publishers. Editorial policies are employed to guide abstractors in this instance; policies are not all the same but are designed in response to specific audience needs.

Abstracts have a number of uses in information organization and retrieval. Users needing to stay abreast of a field or given topic can do so by reviewing abstracts published in that area. Beginning researchers or researchers seeking to master a given area of literature find that reviewing abstracts instead of full texts saves time. Abstracts aid in the decision of which articles need to be read in full versus which can be skimmed or skipped altogether. In a related fashion, because it is sometimes the practice to publish English-language abstracts for non-English language articles, the user can decide from reading the abstract if it is cost- and time-effective to have a translation made of the full article. Librarians and other information professionals find that the use of abstracts assists in the speed and utility of patron literature searches. And database indexers, who typically index only using the title and abstract of a text, require that the abstract be well written and accurate.

Records Management

Records management is the terminology applied to the control of the explosion of information in offices and other administrative settings. It has its roots in the office filing systems that developed throughout the twentieth century. These systems have been highly affected by developments in technology—typewriters, photocopiers, and computers (starting with sorters and collators)—and the use of computers in this context has sometimes been referred to as data administration. Records management systems are often related to archives, as that is where an organization's records may be deposited when their useful operating life has passed.

As was true in other parts of our society, records management originally involved the keeping, filing, and maintaining of paper records. It was a simpler time, but also a frustrating time, because usually only one copy of a record was filed in only one place. The file labels of one records manager were not necessarily logical to the next. As information began being entered and stored in electronic files, access points (the file labels) became invisible. This was not an immediate problem as long as the people who developed the electronic files documented what was contained in them. The situation became more complicated when powerful personal computers began to allow persons to store and file their own information on their desktops. A problem of continuity developed when these personal files were abandoned.

For many years various operations were automated, each with its own system. For example, payroll, general ledger, accounts payable, inventories, and other such systems were automated separately. During the 1990s, integration of these systems took place with the result that the systems had many redundant data fields with little documentation of their content. These fields seemed to be meant to contain the same information, but what was actually there was often different (e.g., name given in full in the payroll file, but middle name shortened to an initial in the faculty file).

In 2001 the International Organization for Standardization (ISO) published a standard for records management.[47] It defines records management as the "field of management responsible for the efficient and systematic control of the creation, receipt, maintenance, use and disposition of records."[48] Further, in describing records systems characteristics, the standard states:

> A records system should
>
> a) routinely capture all records within the scope of the business activities it covers,
> b) organize the records in a way that reflects the business processes of the records' creator,
> c) protect the records from unauthorized alteration or disposition,
> d) routinely function as the primary source of information about actions that are documented in the records, and
> e) provide ready access to all relevant records and related metadata.[49]

There have now been developed a number of commercially available records management systems that track and store records, provide security and auditing functions, have content management and user identity modules, and more. An example of such a system is one called Oracle.[50]

Records managers have dealt with their information explosion by using principles of information organization. The units that need to be organized in the administrative environment are such things as directories, files, programs, and at another level, such things as field values. Organization can be by system (e.g., payroll, budget) or by type of record (e.g., person names, registration records). Records managers must keep track of information that crosses system boundaries (e.g., person names cross boundaries when the same names are entered into several different files). There must be methods for handling concepts that have the same names but different purposes (e.g., the concept of *part time* can have different definitions in a university depending upon whether one is talking about payroll, faculty, graduate students, or undergraduate students).

Keeping all these things straight is often done through a process called *data modeling*. It can either be used as a precursor to database design or as a way to integrate the myriad systems developed over time by persons who are no longer with the corporate body. Data modeling designs a system using a series of related models. The process begins by developing a conceptual model of the records management activity in the particular setting; then a logical model is developed that includes more detail; and finally, the logical model is translated into a physical data model that can be implemented as a records management system. If the data model is updated and adjusted to fit changes in the conceptual model, it can serve for a long time as the basis for information organization in a business or other type of organization. Designing records management systems is addressed in part 2 of the ISO standard.

Organization of records in a person's individual office is another matter. A major factor in one's personal office organization seems to be how particular information resources are, will be, or have been used. For example, if an item is to be referred to in order to write a letter in the immediate future, it will be located at hand; items that have just been completed may be filed. Also, the form of the information resource can be a determining factor: books may be shelved, while papers relating to the books may be placed in file folders. In one's electronic information store, it is usually necessary to develop electronic folders, subfolders, and so forth, if one hopes to be able to find a particular file again in the future. While the search engines in personal computers are often helpful in retrieving individual files, sometimes they cannot narrow a search enough to be helpful, and a structured, hierarchical, browsable folder system may be the most efficient way to retrieve a document. An importance of office organization is that some such office collections will be deposited in archives for posterity.

Knowledge Management

Everyone has heard the phrase "Knowledge is power." Originally, the phrase applied to individuals and implied that persons who increased their knowledge would be able to increase their power in society. During the 1980s it came to be understood that the same thing applied to organizations. At that time, there was much downsizing of organizations in order to reduce overhead and increase profits. In the process it became obvious that the organizations lost important knowledge as employees left and took their accumulated years of knowledge with them. In the same period there was much technological development that was seen at first as a way to save costs by replacing human workers. Again, though, the knowledge held and applied by humans was not all replaced by machines. For an organization to survive, knowledge is brought to bear in the challenges the organization faces. Management of that knowledge increases its power.

The idea of passing on knowledge gained in a work setting has existed for centuries. Apprentices learned various trades by working alongside masters. Children often followed parents into family businesses. More recently, there have been people known as *mentors.* Also, a person leaving a job was often asked to train the replacement person before leaving. The concept known as *knowledge management* (KM) came into being as an attempt to capture employees' knowledge with advanced technology so that the knowledge could be stored and shared easily. As people became overwhelmed with the increased availability of information through rapid technological developments, knowledge management took on the additional role of coping with the explosion of information. This same technology makes possible global sharing of the "managed knowledge" among dispersed subgroups of an organization.

Managing knowledge requires a definition of *knowledge,* a concept that has been discussed by philosophers for years without complete resolution. It has been characterized in several ways—for example, as residing in people's minds rather than in any stored form; as being a combination of information, context, and experience; as being that which represents shared experience among groups and communities; or as a high value form of information that is applied to decisions and actions. R. D. Stacy makes the following observation:

> Knowledge is not a "thing," or a system, but an ephemeral, active process of relating. If one takes this view then no one, let alone a corporation, can own knowledge. Knowledge itself cannot be stored, nor can intellectual capital be measured, and certainly neither of them can be managed.[51]

However, Morville and Rosenfeld posit: "Knowledge managers develop tools, policies, and incentives to encourage people to share what they know."[52]

Dave Snowden notes that knowledge management started in 1995 with the popularization of ideas about tacit knowledge versus explicit knowledge put forward by Ikujiro Nonaka and Hirotaka Takeuchi.[53] Nonaka and Takeuchi postulated that tacit knowledge is hidden, residing in the human mind, and cannot be easily represented via electronics; but it can be made explicit to the degree necessary to accomplish a specific innovation.[54] They described a spiral process of sharing tacit knowledge with others through socializing, followed by listeners internalizing the knowledge, and then new knowledge being created, in turn, to be shared. Snowden says that it does not follow that all knowledge in people's minds could or should be made explicit. However, early knowledge management programs "attempted to disembody all knowledge from its possessors to make it an organizational asset."[55] Software programs were created and are being used for this purpose. For example, Knowledge Base Software from Novo Solutions claims to provide a training tool for new employees, centralize and retain employee knowledge, and create and update categorized and searchable knowledge management articles, among other things.[56] Lotus software from IBM claims to "create, organize, share, and manage business content to provide the right information to the right people" and to "gather and exchange information through professional networks and build communities of experts to help execute tasks faster."[57] These and other such programs work to accomplish the following objectives: to create knowledge repositories, to improve knowledge access, to enhance the knowledge environment, and to manage knowledge as an asset.

M. C. Vasudevan, Murali Mohan, and Amit Kapoor observe that knowledge management in an enterprise often involves: identifying, selecting, and cataloging information resources that are pertinent to the enterprise's needs; identifying information flow patterns among individuals and among groups (e.g., finding out who asks what questions, learning what information is obtained from which sources, determining what types of information are not easily available or accessible); and designing and developing user-friendly systems for accessing the enterprise's knowledge base.[58]

Core issues of concern to people in the information organization business are those of describing, classifying, and retrieving what has been stored. In the context of knowledge management, this means that the organization's knowledge must be sorted out, labeled (i.e., described), and classified into different subjects or groups if it is to be retrieved when needed. Most knowledge management so far has consisted of *content* management, which tends to focus on knowledge that has been made explicit without necessarily knowing what tacit knowledge is still "unmanaged." In order to move into the next generation of knowledge management, Snowden says we must recognize that knowledge can only be volunteered, not forced out. There is always more than can be told, and most important, human knowledge is contextual—that is, knowledge is triggered by circumstance. Snowden believes that the next stage of knowledge management requires understanding the *context* as well as the content.[59]

CONCLUSION

This chapter discusses basic needs to organize, defines information organization, and presents an overview of a number of different kinds of organizing contexts. The following chapters discuss in more detail the processes that have been developed for the organization of information, those that are being worked on, and the issues that affect their implementation.

NOTES

All URLs accessed September 2008.

1. *Merriam-Webster's Collegiate Dictionary & Thesaurus,* Electronic ed., v. 2.5. (Springfield, MA: Merriam-Webster, Inc., 2000).

2. Steven Harnad, "To Cognize is to Categorize: Cognition is Categorization," in *Handbook of Categorization in Cognitive Science,* eds. Henri Cohen and Claire Lefebvre (Amsterdam: Elsevier, 2005), pp. 20–45.

3. Clifford Stoll, *Silicon Snake Oil: Second Thoughts on the Information Highway* (New York: Doubleday, 1995), p. 193.

4. Ronald Hagler, *The Bibliographic Record and Information Technology,* 3rd ed. (Chicago: American Library Association, 1997), p. 13.

5. *Anglo-American Cataloguing Rules, Second Edition, 2002 Revision,* prepared under the direction of the Joint Steering Committee for Revision of AACR (Ottawa: Canadian Library Association; Chicago: American Library Association 2002). [and earlier editions]

6. International Federation of Library Associations and Institutions, IFLA Study Group, *Functional Requirements for Bibliographic Records: Final Report,*

(München: Saur, 1998). Also available: http://www.ifla.org/VII/s13/frbr/frbr.pdf or http://www.ifla.org/VII/s13/frbr.htm.

7. International Federation of Library Associations and Institutions, Working Group on FRANAR, "Functional Requirements for Authority Data: A Conceptual Model." Available: http://www.ifla.org/VII/d4/franar-conceptual-model-2ndreview.pdf.

8. Joint Steering Committee for Development of RDA, "RDA: Resource Description and Access Prospectus." Available: http://www.collectionscanada.gc.ca/jsc/rdaprospectus.html.

9. *Library of Congress Subject Headings,* 13th– eds. (Washington, D.C.: Library of Congress, Office for Subject Cataloging Policy, 1990–)

10. For information about LCC, see Library of Congress Cataloging and Acquisitions, "Classification." Available: http://www.loc.gov/aba/cataloging/classification.

11. Library of Congress, Network Development and MARC Standards Office, "MARC Standards." Available: http://www.loc.gov/marc/.

12. Charles A. Cutter, *Rules for a Dictionary Catalog,* 4th ed. (Washington, D.C.: Government Printing Office, 1904; reprint, London: The Library Association, 1962), p. 12.

13. "EAD: Encoded Archival Description," Version 2002 Official Site, Library of Congress. Available: http://www.loc.gov/ead/.

14. "Categories for the Description of Works of Art," edited by Murtha Baca and Patricia Harpring, The Getty. Available: http://www.getty.edu/research/conducting_research/standards/cdwa/.

15. Library of Congress, Prints & Photographs Division, "About the Thesaurus for Graphic Materials." Available: http://memory.loc.gov/pp/tgmhtml/tgmabt.html.

16. The Getty, "Learn about the Getty Vocabularies." Available: http://www.getty.edu/research/conducting_research/vocabularies/. This site includes links to: "The Art & Architecture Thesaurus" (AAT), "Getty Thesaurus of Geographic Names" (TGN), and "Union List of Artist Names" (ULAN).

17. *Iconclass: An Iconographic Classification System* (Amsterdam: North-Holland Pub. Co., 1974–1981). Now available on the Web: http://www.iconclass.nl.

18. Murtha Baca, Patricia Harpring, Elisa Lanzi, Linda McRae, and Ann Whiteside, on behalf of the Visual Resources Association, *Cataloging Cultural Objects: A Guide to Describing Cultural Works and Their Images* (Chicago: American Library Association Editions, 2006). Partial availability on the Web: http://vraweb.org/ccoweb/cco/index.html.

19. Murtha Baca and Sherman Clarke, "FRBR and Works of Art, Architecture, and Material Culture," in *Understanding FRBR: What It Is, and How It Will Affect Our Retrieval Tools,* edited by Arlene G. Taylor (Westport, Conn.: Libraries Unlimited, 2007), pp. 103–110.

20. AMICO: Art Museum Image Consortium. Available: http://www.amico.org/.

21. ARTstor Images for Education & Scholarship. Available: http://www.artstor.org/index.shtml.

22. OCLC, "WorldCat: Window to the World's Libraries." Available: http://www.oclc.org/worldcat/.

23. "INFOMINE: Scholarly Internet Resource Collections," University of California, Riverside. Available: http://infomine.ucr.edu/.

24. "Automatic Classification Research at OCLC." Available: http://www.oclc.org/research/projects/auto_class/default.htm.

25. "INFOMINE: Scholarly Internet Resource Collections, Current Research and Development Projects," University of California, Riverside. Available: http://infomine.ucr.edu/projects/index.shtml.

26. Christine L. Borgman, *From Gutenberg to the Global Information Infrastructure: Access to Information in the Networked World* (Cambridge: MIT Press, 2000), p. 48.

27. Ibid., p. 42.

28. *Digital Library Technology Trends* (Santa Clara, Calif.: Sun Microsystems, 2002), p. 3. Available: http://www.lib.buu.ac.th/webnew/libtech/digital_library_trends.pdf.

29. Ibid., p. 35.

30. "EAD: Encoded Archival Description," Version 2002 Official Site, Library of Congress. Available: http://www.loc.gov/ead/.

31. *Digital Library Technology Trends,* p. 26.

32. Cornell University Library, "Registry of Digital Collections." Available: http://rdc.library.cornell.edu/.

33. AMICO: Art Museum Image Consortium. Available: http://www.amico.org/.

34. Library of Congress, "American Memory." Available: http://memory.loc.gov/ammem/index.html.

35. Information available at Ex Libris' Web site: http://www.exlibrisgroup.com/category/DigiToolOverview.

36. SirsiDynix, "Digital Archive." Available: http://www.sirsidynix.com/Solutions/Products/digitalarchive.php

37. VTLS, "Digital Imaging." Available: http://www.vtls.com/products/digital_imaging.

38. Greenstone Digital Library Software. Available: http://www.greenstone.org/.

39. Andrew Dillon, "Information Architecture in JASIST: Just Where Did We Come From?" *Journal of the American Society for Information Science and Technology* 53, no. 10 (2002): 821. Also available: http://www.gslis.utexas.edu/~adillon/Journals/IA%20ASIST%20intro.pdf.

40. Ibid.

41. Peter Morville and Louis Rosenfeld, *Information Architecture for the World Wide Web,* 3rd ed. (Sebastopol, Calif.: O'Reilly, 2007), p. 4.

42. Ibid.

43. Ibid., p. 8.

44. Ibid., p. 231.

45. Ibid., p. 232.

46. American Society for Indexing, "Software Tools for Indexing." Available: http://www.asindexing.org/site/software.shtml.

47. International Organization for Standardization, *Information and Documentation: Records Management* (Geneva, Switzerland: ISO, 2001). ISO 15489. Pt. 1. General. Pt. 2. Guidelines.

48. Ibid., pt. 1, p. 3.

49. Ibid., pt. 1, p. 8.

50. Oracle. Available: http://www.oracle.com.

51. R. D. Stacy, *Complex Responsive Processes in Organizations: Learning and Knowledge Creation* (New York: Routledge, 2001), as quoted in Dave Snowden, "Complex Acts of Knowing: Paradox and Descriptive Self-Awareness," *Bulletin of the American Society for Information Science and Technology* 29, no. 4 (April–May 2003): 24.

52. Morville and Rosenfeld, *Information Architecture,* p. 11.

53. Snowden, "Complex Acts of Knowing," p. 23.

54. Ikujiro Nonaka and Hirotaka Takeuchi, *The Knowledge-Creating Company* (Oxford: Oxford University Press, 1995).

55. Snowden, "Complex Acts of Knowing," p. 23.

56. Novo Solutions, "Customer Support & Knowledge Management Solutions." Available: http://www.novosolutions.com/knowledge-base-software/.

57. IBM, "Lotus Software." Available: http://www-01.ibm.com/software/lotus/.

58. M. C. Vasudevan, Murali Mohan, and Amit Kapoor, "Information System for Knowledge Management in the Specialized Division of a Hospital," in *Knowledge Organization, Information Systems and Other Essays: Professor A. Neelameghan Festschrift,* eds. K. S. Raghavan and K. N. Prasad (Chennai, India: Ranganathan Centre for Information Studies, 2006), pp. 247–261. [On p. 248, the authors acknowledge indebtedness for their ideas to: Hsinchun Chen, *Knowledge Management Systems: A Text Mining Perspective* (Tucson, Ariz.: Knowledge Computing Corp., 2001); and, L. J. Haravu, *Knowledge Management: Paradigms, Challenges and Opportunities* (Bangalore, India: Sarada Ranganathan Endowment for Library Science, 2002).]

59. Snowden, "Complex Acts of Knowing," p. 24.

SUGGESTED READINGS

General

Gladwell, Malcolm. "The Social Life of Paper: Looking for Method in the Mess." *The New Yorker,* March 25, 2002. Available: http://www.newyorker.com/archive/2002/03/25/020325crbo_books.

Hider, Philip, with Ross Harvey. *Organising Knowledge in a Global Society: Principles and Practice in Libraries and Information Centres.* Rev. ed. Wagga Wagga, NSW, Australia: Centre for Information Studies, Charles Sturt University, 2008. Chapter 1: Definitions and Introductory Concepts, and Chapter 2: Standards for Bibliographic Data.

Organization of Information in Libraries

Crawford, Walt. "The Card Catalog and Other Digital Controversies: What's Obsolete and What's Not in the Age of Information." *American Libraries* 30, no. 1 (January 1999): 52–58.

Hagler, Ronald. *The Bibliographic Record and Information Technology.* 3rd ed. Chicago: American Library Association, 1997. Chapter 1: "The History and Language of Bibliography."

Taylor, Arlene G. "Cataloging in Context." In *Introduction to Cataloging and Classification.* 10th ed. Westport, Conn.: Libraries Unlimited, 2006, pp. 3–24.

———. "The Information Universe: Will We Have Chaos or Control?" *American Libraries* 25, no. 7 (July–August 1994): 629–632.

Taylor, Arlene G., and Daniel N. Joudrey. "Cataloging." In *Encyclopedia of Library and Information Sciences,* 3rd ed., edited by Marcia J. Bates and Mary Niles Maack. New York: Taylor & Francis, 2009.

Organization of Information in Archives

Ellis, Judith, ed. *Keeping Archives.* 2nd ed. Port Melbourne, Australia: Thorpe, in association with the Australian Society of Archivists, 1993.

Fox, Michael J., and Peter Wilkerson. *Introduction to Archival Organization and Description: Access to Cultural Heritage.* Los Angeles: The Getty Research Institute, 1998.

Miller, Fredric. "Archival Description." In *Reference Services for Archives and Manuscripts,* edited by Laura B. Cohen. Binghamton, N.Y.: Haworth Press, 1997, pp. 55–66.

Roe, Kathleen D. *Arranging & Describing Archives Manuscripts.* Chicago: Society of American Archivists, 2005.

Organization of Information in Museums (Art and Object Collections)

Bearman, David. "Functional Requirements for Collections Management Systems." *Archival Informatics Technical Report* 1, no. 3 (Fall 1987): 1–87.

Bierbaum, Esther Green. "Records and Access: Museum Registration and Library Cataloging." *Cataloging & Classification Quarterly* 9, no. 1 (1988): 97–111.

Buck, Rebecca A., and Jean Allman Gilmore, eds. *The New Museum Registration Methods.* Washington, D.C.: American Association of Museums, 1998.

Organization of Information in the Internet

Berners-Lee, Tim, James Hendler, and Ora Lassila. "The Semantic Web." *Scientific American* 284, no. 5 (May 2001): 34–38, 40–43. Also available: http://www.sciam.com/article.cfm?id=the-semantic-web.

Lynch, Clifford A. "Future Developments in Metadata and their Role in Access to Networked Information." In Jones, Wayne, Judith R. Ahronheim, and Josephine Crawford, eds. *Cataloging the Web: Metadata, AACR, and MARC 21.* (ALCTS Papers on Library Technical Services and Collections, no. 10.) Lanham, Md.: Scarecrow Press, 2002, pp. 183–187.

Oder, Norman. "Cataloging the Net: Can We Do It?" *Library Journal* 123, no. 16 (October 1, 1998): 47–51.

———. "Cataloging the Net: Two Years Later." *Library Journal* 125, no. 16 (October 1, 2000): 50–51.

Organization of Information in Digital Libraries

Arms, William Y. *Digital Libraries.* Cambridge: MIT Press, 2000.

Borgman, Christine L. *From Gutenberg to the Global Information Infrastructure: Access to Information in the Networked World.* Cambridge: MIT Press, 2000, Chapter 2: "Is It Digital or Is It a Library?", Chapter 5: "Why are Digital Libraries Hard to Use?", and Chapter 6: "Making Digital Libraries Easier to Use."

Digital Library Technology Trends. Santa Clara, Calif.: Sun Microsystems, 2002.

Hodge, Gail. *Systems of Knowledge for Digital Libraries: Beyond Traditional Authority Files.* Washington, D.C.: Digital Library Federation, Council on Library and Information Resources, 2000.

Lynch, Clifford. "The Battle to Define the Future of the Book in the Digital World." *First Monday* 6, no. 6 (June 2001). Available: http://www.firstmonday.org/issues/issue6_6/lynch/index.html.

Lynch, Clifford A. "Future Developments in Metadata and their Role in Access to Networked Information." In Jones, Wayne, Judith R. Ahronheim, and Josephine Crawford, eds. *Cataloging the Web: Metadata, AACR, and MARC 21.* Lanham, Md.: Scarecrow Press, 2002, pp. 183–187.

Information Architecture

Dillon, Andrew. "Information Architecture in JASIST: Just Where Did We Come From?" *Journal of the American Society for Information Science and Technology* 53, no. 10 (2002): 821–823. Available: http://www.gslis.utexas.edu/~adillon/Journals/IA%20ASIST%20intro.pdf.

Morville, Peter, and Louis Rosenfeld. *Information Architecture for the World Wide Web.* 3rd ed. Sebastopol, Calif.: O'Reilly, 2007.

Robins, David. "Information Architecture, Organizations, and Records Management." *Records and Information Management Report* 17, no. 3 (March 2001): 1–14.

Wyllys, R. E. "Information Architecture." Reading prepared for Information Technologies and the Information Profession, Graduate School of Library & Information Science, University of Texas at Austin, 2000, updated June 28, 2003. Available: http://www.ischool.utexas.edu/~wyllys/ITIPMaterials/InfoArchitecture.html.

Indexing and Abstracting

Cleveland, Donald B., and Ana D. Cleveland. *Introduction to Indexing and Abstracting.* 3rd ed. Englewood, Colo.: Libraries Unlimited, 2001.

Hedden, Heather. *Indexing Specialties: Web Sites.* Medford, N.J.: Information Today, for The American Society of Indexers, 2007.

Smith, Sherry, and Kari Kells. *Inside Indexing: The Decision-Making Process.* Bend, Ore.: Northwest Indexing Press, 2005. Web site about the book: http://www.insideindexing.com.

Witty, Francis J. "The Beginnings of Indexing and Abstracting: Some Notes Towards a History of Indexing and Abstracting in Antiquity and the Middle Ages." *The Indexer* 8 (1973): 193–198.

Records Management

Atherton, Jay. "From Life Cycle to Continuum: Some Thoughts on the Records Management-Archives Relationship," *Archivaria* 21 (Winter 1985–86): 43–51.

Clayton, Mark. "Library Stacks? No, That's My Office." *Christian Science Monitor* (July 16, 2002). Also available: http://www.csmonitor.com/2002/0716/p16s01-lehl.html.

Ince, A. Nejat, Cem Evrendilek, Dag Wilhelmsen, and Fadil Gezer. *Planning and Architectural Design of Modern Command Control Communications and Information Systems: Military and Civilian Applications.* Boston: Kluwer Academic, 1997, pp. 90–98.

Kwasnik, Barbara H. "How a Personal Document's Intended Use or Purpose Affects Its Classification in an Office." In *Proceedings of the 12th Annual International ACM SIGIR Conference on Research and Development in Information Retrieval.* New York: ACM, [1989], pp. 207–210.

Mullins, Craig. *Database Administration: the Complete Guide to Practices and Procedures.* Boston: Addison-Wesley, 2002.

Shepherd, Elizabeth, and Geoffrey Yeo. *Managing Records: A Handbook of Principles and Practice.* London: Facet Publishing, 2003.

Weldon, J. L. "A Career in Data Modeling." *Byte* 22, no. 6 (June 1997): 103–106.

Knowledge Management

Bhatt, G. D. "Knowledge Management in Organization: Examining the Interactions between Technologies, Techniques, and People." *Journal of Knowledge Management* 5, no. 1 (2001): 68–75.

Snowden, Dave. "Complex Acts of Knowing: Paradox and Descriptive Self-Awareness." *Bulletin of the American Society for Information Science and Technology* 29, no. 4 (April–May 2003): 23–28. Available: http://www.asis.org/Bulletin/Apr-03/BulletinAprMay03.pdf (this version is extracted and condensed from one that first appeared in *Journal of Knowledge Management* 6, no. 2 [May 2003]: 100–111).

Wallace, Danny P. *Knowledge Management: Historical and Cross-disciplinary Themes.* Westport, Conn.: Libraries Unlimited, 2007.

CHAPTER 2

RETRIEVAL TOOLS

This chapter discusses retrieval tools, which are basic building blocks in the organization of recorded information, addressing the following questions: Why do we need retrieval tools? What are the basic retrieval tools, their formats, and their functions?

THE NEED FOR RETRIEVAL TOOLS

Retrieval tools are systems created for retrieving information. They are designed to help users find, identify, select, and obtain information resources of all types. They contain records that act as surrogates for information resources. That is, each *surrogate record* (also called a *description* or *metadata*) gives enough information, such as author, title, and date of creation, so that it can serve as a short representation for and facilitate access to an individual information resource in a collection. Surrogate records are arranged and retrieved by *access points*. An access point can be a name, title, or subject term chosen by an indexer or a cataloger. In online systems an access point can be almost any word in a record if keyword searching of every word (that is not a stopword) is allowed.

Retrieval tools are essential as basic building blocks for a system that will organize as much of the world's recorded information as possible. A dream of being able to provide access to all recorded information has existed since 1892, when Paul Otlet and Henri LaFontaine organized a conference to create Universal Bibliographic Control (UBC). They wanted to create a central file that would include surrogate records particularly for scientific articles in all the scientific journals of the world. The magnitude of the undertaking meant that new techniques different from conventional library practice had to be developed. As UBC evolved throughout the twentieth century, it came to mean that each country of the world would be responsible for creation of surrogate records for its information resources and would share those surrogate records with all other countries. The concept was extended also to authority control of the headings for names and titles used as access points. A program of the International Federation of Library Associations and Institutions (IFLA) combined the ideals of UBC with the concept of making the records machine readable. The many retrieval tools that have been developed as a result of Otlet and LaFontaine's dream have brought us closer to UBC.

THE BASIC RETRIEVAL TOOLS, THEIR FORMATS, AND THEIR FUNCTIONS

The basic retrieval tools discussed in this chapter are:

- bibliographies
  - pathfinders
- catalogs
- indexes
- finding aids
- registers
- search engines and directories

Databases and bibliographic networks have distinct roles in housing retrieval tools. They are discussed in Chapter 6, which addresses the topics of systems and system design.

Bibliographies

Bibliographies basically are lists of information resources. Bibliographies are essential to scholars and to those involved professionally with books and other sources of information (e.g., collectors, dealers, librarians), and are also useful sources of information for all serious readers. They bring together lists of sources based on subject matter, on authors, by time periods, and the like (see the more detailed list of these below). Some bibliographies include *annotations,* that is, brief reviews indicating the subject matter and/or commenting on the usefulness of the information resource.

Bibliographies can be attached to a scholarly work and consist of the information resources that were consulted by the author of the work, or they can be completely separate entities—works in their own right. Each information resource represented in the list has a short *description* (not to be confused with *annotation* or *abstract*). A typical description includes author, title, edition, publisher, place, and date of publication for a book or other such whole entity. For a part of a work (such as a journal article or a poem), one typically includes author, title, name of the larger work, volume (if applicable), date, and page numbers or other part designation. Some descriptions also include physical characteristics.

In a bibliography each description usually appears in only one place, most often under the author (first author if more than one) of the work. This is an example of a retrieval tool that generally provides only one access point. In a bibliography that is arranged only by authors' names, for example, other attributes such as titles, second or later authors, and subjects are not access points (i.e., users who only know the title, the name of a second or later author, or the subject of a work will not easily be able to retrieve the item from the bibliography). The descriptions may be constructed according to various styles, one of which is chosen by the creator of the bibliography. Examples of some of the styles are:

- **APA (American Psychological Association)**[1]
  Mitchell, T. R., & Larson, J. R., Jr. (1987). *People in organizations: An introduction to organizational behavior* (3rd ed.). New York: McGraw-Hill.

- **Chicago Manual of Style**[2]
  Mitchell, Terence R., and James R. Larson, Jr. *People in Organizations: An Introduction to Organizational Behavior.* 3rd ed. New York: McGraw-Hill, 1987.

- **MLA (Modern Language Association)**[3]
  Mitchell, Terence R., and James R. Larson, Jr. *People in Organizations: An Introduction to Organizational Behavior.* 3rd ed. New York: McGraw-Hill, 1987.

- **Science (Scientific Style and Format)**[4]
  Mitchell TR, Larson JR, Jr. 1987. People in Organizations: An Introduction to Organizational Behavior. 3d ed. New York: McGraw-Hill.

- **Turabian**[5]
  Mitchell, Terence R., and James R. Larson, Jr. *People in Organizations: An Introduction to Organizational Behavior.* 3rd ed. New York: McGraw-Hill, 1987.

- **Style Manual (U.S. Government Style Manual)**[6]
  Mitchell, Terence R., and James R. Larson, Jr. *People in Organizations: An Introduction to Organizational Behavior.* 3rd ed. (New York: McGraw-Hill, 1987).

Each bibliography has a particular focus or arrangement. The most common are:

- **Subject:** bibliographies gathering together publications or other information resources that are all about a particular subject (e.g., *The New Press Guide to Multicultural Resources for Young Readers*).[7]

- **Author:** bibliographies of all or some of the works of a particular author and sometimes including sources about the author (e.g., *A Bibliography of Jane Austen*).[8]

- **Language:** bibliographies of textual entities in which the text is a certain language (e.g., *An Extensive Bibliography of Studies in English, German, and French on Turkish Foreign Policy, 1923–1997*).[9]

- **Time period:** bibliographies listing all works that came to light in a particular time period (e.g., *British Women Writers, 1700–1850: An Annotated Bibliography of Their Works and Works About Them*).[10]

- **Locale:** bibliographies listing all information resources created in a particular location. This could be a large locale such as a whole continent, or a smaller locale such as a country, region, state, city, or community (e.g., *Area Bibliography of Japan*).[11] It could also be an institution, such as a bibliography of all the works of the faculty in a particular university.

- **Publisher:** bibliographies listing all of the products of a particular publisher (e.g., *The Stinehour Press: A Bibliographical Checklist of the First Thirty Years*).[12]

- **Form:** bibliographies listing information resources that appear in a certain form, format, or genre (e.g., videocassettes, electronic resources, poetry, biographies, etc.). These are virtually always combined with one of the other foci (e.g., *Maps and Mapping of Africa: A Resource Guide*).[13]

Two or more of these foci are often combined in bibliographies. For example, the title above that illustrates *language* is a combination of language, subject, and time period; the one illustrating *time period* is a combination of subject, locale, and time period; and the one illustrating *form* is a combination of form and locale.

Pathfinders

A *pathfinder* is a special kind of bibliography in libraries that is truly meant to be a retrieval tool. Pathfinders are subject bibliographies with a special function in the library world. While most bibliographies do not indicate whether a location actually has an item or not, pathfinders focus on the resources available in a defined setting for a user who wishes to pursue research in a specific subject area. In addition to the list of relevant resources, the pathfinder may also include specific instructions on how to search the local catalog, locally-accessible databases, and specific reference resources related to the specific subject area. For example, it may include a list of subject headings related to the topic that may be used in the catalog. Reference librarians have created pathfinders for decades, although some creators of electronic pathfinders seem to think the idea originated in electronic form.

OCLC has a facility for creating pathfinders for Web resources, which, of course, are not dependent upon being found in a particular setting. This has allowed easy sharing of pathfinders among libraries and has facilitated sharing of responsibility for creating pathfinders.

Catalogs

Catalogs provide access to individual items within collections of information resources (e.g., physical entities such as books, videocassettes, and CDs in a library; artists' works in an art museum; Web pages on the Internet; etc.). Each information resource is represented by a description of the resource that is somewhat longer than a bibliography description. The descriptions are assigned one or more access points. As mentioned earlier, an access point can be almost any word in a record when keyword searching is used; however, the term *access point* is usually applied to a particular name, title, or subject that is listed on the record separately from the description. An access point is constructed in a certain order (e.g., surname followed by forename or forenames), and it is maintained under authority control. *Authority control* is the process of bringing together all of the forms of name that apply to a single name; all the variant titles that apply to a single work; and relating all the synonyms, related terms, broader terms, and narrower terms that apply to a particular subject heading.

The descriptions in a catalog are constructed according to a standard style selected by a particular community (e.g., *Anglo-American Cataloguing Rules, Second Edition* (AACR2) for libraries; *Describing Archives: A Content Standard* (DACS) for archives; the Dublin Core for Internet resources; etc.). Several different standards for description are discussed in more detail in Chapter 7.

Purposes of Catalogs

Catalogs have traditionally served two main groups. One group is employees of the institution, who need to retrieve information resources, or who need to retrieve information about those resources (i.e., metadata). For example, the catalog is used by collection development librarians in their process of discovering what the library already owns or does not own before selecting new materials; another such use is by the employee of a museum who is looking for objects to place in an exhibit.

The most commonly understood use for a catalog, though, is use by patrons of the institution who wish to borrow material or make use of it on the premises. If such users have a known work in mind, they may search for it in the catalog by author or title (called *known-item searching*). Users might also try searching by keyword if they only remember certain words of the title or some other attribute. If users know they want works by a particular author, they may search under the author's name. If users do not know of a particular work but are searching for something on a particular topic, they may use a subject heading search or a subject keyword search. In online catalogs, keyword searches are often appropriate for helping a person find a record that looks like it might be on the user's topic. Once a potentially useful record is found, the user can identify in that record an authority-controlled subject heading for the topic or a classification notation for the topic. One may then do a search for the subject heading or the classification notation in the catalog (often by clicking on the heading or classification). Alternatively, one may go to the location of the classification notation in the stacks to determine if there are pertinent works shelved with the one that has been identified.

A number of attempts have been made through the years to identify purposes of catalogs. Charles Cutter presented his "objects" of a catalog in his *Rules for a Dictionary Catalog* more than a century ago. He was speaking only of library catalogs in which books were represented, but if these "objects" are broadened to archives, museums, and other collecting institutions, they still seem to represent what catalogs are supposed to do. Cutter said that a catalog should be able:

1. To enable a person to find a book of which either
   - (A) the author
   - (B) the title
   - (C) the subject

   is known.
2. To show what the library has
   - (D) by a given author
   - (E) on a given subject
   - (F) in a given kind of literature.
3. To assist in the choice of a book
   - (G) as to its edition (bibliographically).
   - (H) as to its character (literary or topical).[14]

Seymour Lubetzky worked in the mid-twentieth century to simplify cataloging rules, and he posited that the cataloging code should be reconstructed "in accordance with deliberately adopted objectives... and well considered principles."[15] He then stated that:

> The first objective is to enable the user of the catalog to determine readily whether or not the library has the book he wants.... The second objective is to reveal to the user of the catalog, under one form of the author's name, what works the library has by a given author and what editions or translations of a given work.[16]

Lubetzky's work was the basis for the Paris Principles, adopted at the International Conference on Cataloguing Principles in Paris in 1961. The second of the principles was for "Functions of the Catalogue" and stated:

> The catalog should be an efficient instrument for ascertaining:
>
> 2.1 whether the library contains a particular book specified by
>
> (a) its author and title, *or*
>
> (b) if the author is not named in the book, its title alone, *or*
>
> (c) if author and title are inappropriate or insufficient for identification, a suitable substitute for the title; and

2.2
(a) which works by a particular author *and*
(b) which editions of a particular work are in the library.[17]

In 1998, IFLA published *Functional Requirements for Bibliographic Records* (FRBR), which identifies four generic user tasks that the bibliographic record is intended to support. These four tasks have been built on the work of Cutter, Lubetzky, and the Paris Principles, and essentially represent the four main functions of a catalog:

- to find entities that correspond to the user's stated search criteria...
- to identify an entity...
- to select an entity that is appropriate to the user's needs...
- to acquire or obtain access to the entity described....[18]

The fourth user task in FRBR actually is an addition to the functions identified by Cutter, but it was recognized by several writers in the late twentieth century that a catalog differs from certain other retrieval tools in that it facilitates physically locating the information resources that are represented by surrogate records in the catalog.[19]

Another important purpose served by catalogs has traditionally been to act as an inventory of the collection—that is, to provide a record of what is owned. Often a *shelflist* has been used to accomplish this purpose. A shelflist includes one copy of every record in a catalog arranged in the order in which the information resources, objects, and so forth, are arranged on the shelf. Originally, shelflists were literally in the order of items on the shelf, starting a new sequence with each change in format, or change in collection location, or change in size. Later, shelflists often were arranged by classification notation regardless of format or other categorization. This is the way the concept works in online catalogs. The purpose of serving as an inventory is still there, but the mental image of a shelflist with arrangement as it is on the shelf is lost. Another way in which the shelflist concept becomes somewhat fuzzy is when electronic resources are added to a catalog. Institutions often purchase the right to make remote information resources accessible to their users. In some cases, these resources may not be available for purchase, and in others the institution may simply forgo purchasing the resource outright for budgetary reasons. With paper serials in a library, the library has always had control of how many years of back issues were kept. With Internet resources, whether right to access has been purchased or not, there is no control over how long the information will be available online, its location, its accuracy, or changes in its content.

A *union catalog* is a variation of the concept that a catalog represents just the holdings of one institution. A union catalog represents the holdings of more than one institution or collection. A union catalog of a main library and its branches, for example, shows items that may be held in one or more branches in addition to those held in the main library. The location information indicates where an item is held. A union catalog of a consortium of institutions works the same way; location information shows which items are housed in which of the cooperating institutions. The ultimate union catalog is the one maintained by the largest bibliographic network, OCLC (see description in Chapter 6), where each information resource has one master record, and associated with the record is a holdings record that shows the holding symbol of each member of the network that has cataloged the resource through OCLC or has asked that its symbol be added to the record.

Forms of Catalogs

Catalogs can appear in different forms and can have different arrangements. The formats discussed here are:

- book
- card
- microform
- OPAC (Online Public Access Catalog)

Book Catalogs. Book catalogs originally were just handwritten lists. After the invention of printing with moveable type, book catalogs were printed, but not always in a discernible order. Eventually, entries were printed in alphabetical or classified order, but book catalogs were very expensive and could not be reproduced and updated often. In the early 1900s, book catalogs were almost completely replaced with card catalogs that could be updated as soon as the cards could be filed and were relatively inexpensive to maintain and create. Book catalogs had a brief renaissance in the 1960s and 1970s when (1) computers again made it easy and less expensive to produce book catalogs; (2) large card catalogs became unwieldy; and (3) rapid growth of new libraries and new branches made it desirable to have multiple copies of catalogs. But in order to keep a book catalog up-to-date, supplements were usually produced, resulting in multiple look-ups for one search. In addition, it was usually three to six months before supplements were produced, meaning that new materials were not represented in the catalog during that time.

Online catalogs have replaced both book and card catalogs in most situations, but book catalogs are still used for catalogs of exhibits, artists' works, subject archives, and so forth. Book catalogs provide a way to make the contents of special collections known to users in many locations. For example, book catalogs of historical societies are popular acquisitions by collectors of genealogical materials. This use, though, may be replaced by availability of such catalogs on the Web. Book catalogs also still exist in some libraries and archives as the only retrieval tool available to access older materials, because some institutions have chosen not to convert all of the catalog records for rarely used items into machine-readable form for the online catalog.

An advantage of book catalogs over online catalogs has been that book catalogs are compact and portable and can be consulted anywhere they can be carried. However, with laptop computers and wireless technology, online catalogs are now equally accessible. Another advantage is that glancing over a page of book catalog entries is relatively fast, and some people prefer this to paging through screen after screen of online responses.

Card Catalogs. Card catalogs were popularized in the United States by Library of Congress (LC) cards, first made available for sale in 1901, and by H. W. Wilson cards, which began production in 1938 in response to the needs of small libraries. (Both have now ceased card production.) Technological advances encouraged further use of the card catalog. First, typewriters made handwritten cards unnecessary. Offset printing was used by LC for its cards. Then photocopying allowed the local creation of whole card sets from one master card. Finally, the advent of computer printing made it possible to have customized cards made either locally or at a distant facility. When created at a distance, the cards often were shipped to the receiver in boxes already alphabetized and ready to file.

Because of the influence of LC cards, card catalogs and the order of information on cards in libraries have been standardized for many decades. Users of card catalogs could go from library to library, using catalogs with confidence that they would be able to use distant catalogs with as much ease as their local ones, although the filing arrangement of those catalogs often differed from library to library.

Online catalogs have replaced most card catalogs in the United States, but some libraries, archives, and museums still have card catalogs, especially small institutions or those where there has been only minimal conversion of data to machine-readable form. In many other countries there are more card catalogs, and in some, card catalogs are still the predominant form.

Microform Catalogs. The creation of computer output microform catalogs became possible in the 1960s. They are produced on either microfiche or microfilm and require a microform reader in order to be able to use them. They are produced like book catalogs, but because they do not have to be reproduced on paper and be bound, they can be completely reproduced with new additions every three months or so without having to go through the supplement stage. Due to unpopularity, microform catalogs were replaced rather quickly by online catalogs. It has been found that users will use microfilm if that is the only way to get the information they need, but most people find the readers hard to use and difficult to read.

OPACs. Online Public Access Catalogs (OPACs) are the predominant form of catalog in the United States and in a number of other countries today. In these catalogs, records are stored on a local or remote server. The records are displayed only as needed. There is much flexibility in the look of the displays. Online catalogs have not yet been standardized, although in two or more institutions that have purchased the same system, the displays may look somewhat similar. Writers in the field have long called for standardization, so that patrons can move from catalog to catalog or search multiple catalogs from the same location and find records displayed in the same manner, but this has yet to happen.[20] In recent years, dissatisfaction with online catalogs has been expressed by many in the library and information professions. This frustration—that the online catalog is still difficult to use—is intensified by comparisons to Internet search engines such as Google that are relatively easy to use. At times, this discontent has led some to question the long-term prospects for the online catalog. If catalog vendors respond by improving arrangements of displayed responses (e.g., according to the hierarchy of work, expression, manifestation, and item, as suggested by FRBR), online catalogs may again be seen as providing something not available in search engines and then may survive.

Arrangements within Catalogs

The records within catalogs must be arranged in some fashion or they are unusable. In card catalogs, records are arranged by being filed in a certain order. In book and COM catalogs, records are arranged by being printed one after another in a particular order. Records in OPACs are arranged internally within the database either in sequence of order of entry into the system or in random order. So the arrangement discussed here applies to the arrangement of the displayed responses to search queries in the case of OPACs. (For more information about arrangement of metadata displays, see Appendix C.)

In general, there are three basic arrangements that make sense to users, although there are many variations. Catalog records can be in classified order, in alphabetical order, or in chronological order. Within the basic order, display of records can be further subarranged in one of these same orders, or others.

Classified. Classified catalogs usually have more than one section. In what is considered to be the main section of the catalog, the arrangement or display is in the order of the classification scheme used in that institution. That is, this section is arranged in subject order, where the subject is represented by a classification notation, rather than by subject terminology. There can be as many classification notations assigned to a single record as there are subject concepts in the information resource. Classified catalogs have the advantage that users can look at records for broader and narrower concepts at the same place they are looking for records on a specific concept. In a way, it is similar to browsing in the stacks with a classification notation, except that in the case of the classified catalog, each information resource is represented by several notations signifying all of its concepts, not just one notation as is true of items in the stacks.

As it is nearly impossible for anyone to know all the classification notations relating to a subject, there should be a section of the catalog that lists verbal representations of all topics and gives the notation for each topic. In some situations this function is provided by placing a copy of the classification scheme at the catalog. Most classification schemes include an index of topics in alphabetical order. And, of course, there are users who want to search for authors and/or titles, so there are other sections of the catalog for these. In book, card, or microform catalogs, these subject-term, author, and title sections are arranged in alphabetical order. In OPACs they are word-searchable and the order of displays varies.

Classified catalogs have traditionally been used in European and other countries where several languages are spoken and represented in the setting. The classified subject section of the catalog can include records for every language represented, with several languages being interfiled at the same classification notation. The sections of the catalog that give access to subject terms, authors, and titles can be in the language(s) appropriate to the clientele. The United States has not traditionally felt the need for this approach. Among the reasons the concept is being reconsidered today is that access to catalogs on the Internet is global, and a classified catalog can hold and display records in any language with classification notations that are universal. If indexes to a classified catalog are made in many languages, access can be gained through any one of the many languages. In addition, it makes browsing and broadening and narrowing of searches easy, which is especially helpful for inexperienced online users.

Alphabetical. Early American catalogs were arranged by broad subject categories in alphabetical order. With a collection consisting of a few books, there was little need for elaborate classification or arrangement. As catalogs grew, the broad categories needed to be subdivided, so somewhat narrower categories were created and placed alphabetically within each broad category. For example, if the broad category were domestic animals, the subcategories under it might be cats, cows, dogs, horses, mules, and so forth. These were called *alphabetico-classed catalogs*. As subject categories multiplied, it became more difficult to predict the subject category and where it would be found. It began to make sense to place all subcategories in alphabetical order regardless of class. Charles Cutter was instrumental in the development of what he called the *dictionary catalog*. He recommended alphabetical arrangement with authors, titles, and subjects all interfiled in the same file.

The dictionary card catalog was the standard for the first half of the twentieth century. Later, catalogs in large libraries became complicated to file new cards into because of size and the complexity of filing rules that seemed to grow as the catalogs grew. Early filing rules had reflected the influence of the classified catalog and presorted catalog entries into categories. Cutter recommended alphabetical filing, but names and titles beginning with a word that could also be a subject (e.g., Glass) were supposed to be filed in the order: personal name, geographic entity, corporate body, subject heading, title, e.g.:

Glass, Richard	[personal name]
Glass Mountains (Tex.)	[geographic entity]
Glass Art Society	[corporate body]
Glass	[subject heading]
Glass art	[subject heading]
Glass menagerie	[title]

It can be seen that these are not alphabetical and it is easy to see how complicated such an arrangement was in large catalogs. Attempts to break up the large files resulted in *divided catalogs*. They were sometimes divided into two files and sometimes into three files. If there were two files, they were divided so that authors and titles were in one and subjects were in the other. In three files, the division was authors, titles, and subjects. In the author/title/subject arrangement, records for works *about* a person were often filed in the subject file, while records for works the person *wrote* were filed in the author file. However, it was considered useful to keep records for works by and about a person together, so sometimes all *names* were placed in one file rather than just authors being placed in that file. The divided catalog was easier and less expensive for the keepers of the catalog, but assumed that users knew the difference among author, title, and subject entries, which was not always the case.

With the development of OPACs in the 1980s, the divided catalog was moved online. One usually had to search either by author or by title or by subject. In this case, though, it was seldom possible to retrieve works both by and about a person in the same search. In some ways, the sophistication that had been achieved in card catalogs was abandoned. For example, one could not have criticisms of a work displayed with editions of that work, and at first there were no references from unused forms of names and topics to the authorized forms. Many catalogs still do not allow searches for works both by and about a person, both editions of a work and its criticisms, or other more sophisticated searching, although efforts are being made to improve this situation.

Chronological and Other. Displays of search results today are not always in alphabetical order, although searches for specific authors or titles generally bring up alphabetical displays. However, subject and keyword search display results are sometimes in chronological order, usually latest first, although when choice of arrangement is given, both chronological order and reverse chronological order may be offered. In some systems, search results, particularly those from a keyword search, may be displayed according to some form of relevancy ranking (relevancy as defined by that system). Many online catalogs now allow users a choice of the order in which the results are to be displayed (e.g., alphabetically by author or by title), or a choice of how retrieved responses are to be grouped (e.g., by format). Improvements of this type are gradually being added to online catalogs.

Indexes

Indexes are retrieval tools that provide access to the analyzed contents of information resources (e.g., articles in journals, short stories in collections, papers in conference proceedings, etc.). Although back-of-the-book indexes provide access to the analyzed contents of one work, they are not retrieval tools in the sense defined in this chapter; they are prepared at the time of publication of the work, not at a later time in an effort to provide bibliographic control. They do, however, aid with retrieval of the information found in the text at hand. Some Web sites also have indexes that function very much like back-of-book indexes, but instead of page locator references, each entry links directly to an HTML anchor within the site being indexed. On the Web these are called *A–Z Indexes* (to distinguish them from search trees and search engines; see discussion below). A–Z indexing employs specialized software (such as HTML Indexer™ and XRefHT32).[21] Like book indexes, an A–Z Web index should contain properly identified second-level entries, variant entries, and cross-references.

Indexes that are retrieval tools in the sense discussed in this chapter are separate from the information resources being analyzed. Database indexes (also called *journal indexes* or *periodical indexes*) are the longest-lived examples of indexes as retrieval tools. Such indexes often do not have authority control of names. A name such as Lois Mai Chan can be entered into the same index at different times as Chan, L.; Chan, LM; Chan, L. M.; Chan, Lois M; Chan, Lois Mai, and even Mai Chan, Lois. They do usually maintain authority control over subjects. Indexers tend to use hierarchical controlled vocabularies (called *thesauri*) for the topical terms they wish to bring out in the index. A thesaurus contains systematized language that subsumes narrower terms under broader terms and provides a structure of relationships between related terms.

Unlike catalogs, indexes are not limited to what is available in a local setting or a particular collection, and they do not usually give location information as such. They do give, as part of the surrogate record, the larger resource in which the smaller work can be found. Especially with print indexes, it may then be necessary for a user of the index to search a catalog for the location of the larger work. In some online indexes, there exists the capacity to link to online catalogs to allow users to see quickly if their library owns the larger work. If the larger work is not found in the local catalog, the user may have to search a union catalog or take a request to Interlibrary Loan (ILL). Online indexes increasingly have links to online versions of articles.

Indexing can be carried out by people or by machines or by a combination of both. Database indexing is still mostly completed by specially trained indexers, although they may have some machine-assistance. Indexes can be found in print form or in machine-readable form, most of the latter being found online. Some print versions are arranged in alphabetical dictionary fashion, with entries for authors, titles, and subjects interfiled. (See Figure 2.1.). Others reflect a divided arrangement, having an author/title part separate from the subject index. Online indexes have interfaces that dictate how they are searched and how results are displayed. (See Figures 2.2 and 2.3.) As with OPACs, there is no standardization from index to index. OPACs, at least, have the standardization that comes from using the *Anglo-American Cataloguing Rules*, 2nd ed. (AACR2), whereas there

Archives
See also
Local history and records
Manuscripts
Carr, D. A Community Mind [As generated and maintained by our cultural institutions] bibl f *Public Libr* v41 no5 p284-8 S/O 2002
. . .
Automation
See also
Online catalogs
Retrospective conversion
Brown, A. J. E. and others. When Images Work Faster than Words: The Integration of Content-Based Image Retrieval with the Northumbria Watermark Archive. bibl f diag il *Restaurator* v23 no3 p187-203 2002
Gilliland-Swetland, A. J. Popularizing the finding aid: exploiting EAD to enhance online discovery and retrieval in archival information systems by diverse user groups. (In Ecoded Archival Description on the Internet. Haworth Information Press 2001 p199-225) bibl f tab
Needham, L. The development of the online archive catalogue at the University of Birmingham using CALM 2000. il *Program* v36 no1 p23-9 2002

Figure 2.1. Sample entries from the printed version of the index *Library Literature & Information Science: 2002.* (Source: *Library Literature & Information Science: 2002,* New York: H. W. Wilson, 2003, p. 27.)

is no such standard commonly used by every index. The National Information Standards Organization (NISO) tried to update Z39.4–1984, "Basic Criteria for Indexes,"[22] but committees could not come to agreement with the American Society for Indexing, and so Z39.4 was withdrawn in 1996. An international ISO standard, which the British and others have adopted, was published in 1996.[23]

Another difference between catalogs and indexes is that indexes tend to be created by for-profit organizations, such as H. W. Wilson, or professional societies, such as the American Chemical Society. Often there is a charge for using the online versions directly. The print versions are sold, usually to libraries, or libraries pay for the right to allow their patrons to use the indexes online without the charge. Some libraries have both print and online access, although there seems to be a trend to continue only with the

In Database: Library Lit&Info Science

TITLE: Popularizing the finding aid: exploiting EAD to enhance online discovery and retrieval in archival information systems by diverse user groups
AUTHOR(S): Gilliland-Swetland,-Anne-J
SOURCE: In: Encoded Archival Description on the Internet Haworth Information Press, 2001. p. 199-225
DESCRIPTORS: Archives-Automation; Archives-Cataloging; End-user-searching
DOCUMENT TYPE: Book-Chapter

Figure 2.2. Short view of Gilliland-Swetland entry from Figure 2.1 as it appears in the online index for *Library Literature & Information Science.*

In Database: Library Lit&Info Science

TITLE: Popularizing the finding aid: exploiting EAD to enhance online discovery and retrieval in archival information systems by diverse user groups
AUTHOR(S): Gilliland-Swetland,-Anne-J
SOURCE: In: Encoded Archival Description on the Internet Haworth Information Press, 2001. p. 199-225
PUBLICATION YEAR: 2001
PHYSICAL DESCRIPTION: bibl f tab
ISBN: 0789013975
LANGUAGE OF WORK: English
DESCRIPTORS: Archives-Automation; Archives-Cataloging; End-user-searching
DOCUMENT TYPE: Book-Chapter
UPDATE CODE: 20021105
ACCESSION NUMBER: 200201016100

Figure 2.3. Long view of Gilliland-Swetland entry from Figure 2.1 as it appears in the online index for *Library Literature & Information Science.*

online versions. In any case, the index often is cataloged so that the whole index can be found through the catalog.

Most of the indexing just discussed is performed by humans. However, as early as the 1950s, people began working on automatic indexing that would rely on the power of computers to perform repetitive tasks at high speed. The first such method, introduced by Hans Peter Luhn in 1958, became known as KWIC (*Key Word In Context*) indexing. In a KWIC index, titles are arranged so that each of the words in a title appears once in alphabetical order in the center of a page, with all other words to the left or right of the center word printed in the order in which they appear in the title (so that the alphabetized word is "in context").

KWIC

Introduction to	**Cataloging** and Classification.
Introduction to Cataloging and	**Classification.**
	Introduction to Cataloging and Classification.

An adaptation of the KWIC method is known as KWOC (*Key Word Out of Context*), which prints the words in the left-hand margin instead of in the middle of the page, and the title is printed to the right or beneath the keyword.

KWOC

Cataloging	Introduction to Cataloging and Classification.
Classification	Introduction to Cataloging and Classification.
Introduction	Introduction to Cataloging and Classification.

Another type, KWAC (*Key Word Alongside Context*), is a combination of the KWIC and KWOC.

KWAC

Cataloging and Classification. Introduction to
Classification. Introduction to Cataloging and
Introduction to Cataloging and Classification.

The current application of automatic indexing is in two types of Web indexing: subject tree indexing and automatic indexing of Web sites (i.e., search engines).

Subject tree indexes are directories to Web sites and Web content arranged by categories and subcategories. They are developed by companies (such as Yahoo! and Google) as guides for users to locate information on the Internet more efficiently. Unlike formal classification schemes such as the *Library of Congress Classification* and the *Colon Classification,* subject tree indexes have a small number of categories that are more global in nature. The goal of a subject tree index is quick retrieval rather than the collocation of knowledge. Subject tree indexes, when first developed, were created by a cadre of trained professionals using an in-house classification scheme. With the advance of information technology, it is the person submitting the site via an online registration form who often decides what category or categories fit their site. In a sense, then, subject tree indexes are accomplished by both human indexing and automatic indexing.

A search engine is sometimes referred to as an index but, more accurately, a search engine creates lists of terms which are referred to as indexes. A *search engine* is a computer program that searches Web page documents for specified keywords via a program called a *spider*. The list of documents is returned to an internal database and placed in order by the indexing program according to the words or concepts contained in the document. With the development of metadata schemes such as the Dublin Core and the use of other encoded metadata tags, search engine indexing will become increasingly more accurate for users (if search engines begin to make use of the metadata found on the Web). Search engines are described more fully below.

Finding Aids

Finding aids (sometimes called *inventories*) are descriptions of archival collections that tend to be somewhat longer than typical catalog records, index entries, and citations in bibliographies. Archives usually maintain control over entire collections (not individual pieces) of archival materials from personal or corporate sources. Thus a finding aid describes a collection, not a single letter or record within that collection. While some finding aids are not publicly accessible, this is becoming increasingly rare as archives add more finding aids to the Web. (See Figure 2.4.) The finding aid, itself a retrieval tool, is often described in a catalog record; that is, a surrogate record to describe the finding aid (which is itself a surrogate for the archival collection) is created to provide name, title, and subject access points for it in the catalog. The content standard, *Describing Archives: A Content Standard* (DACS), is used to create both finding aids and MARC-based catalog records.

A finding aid may be a brief or quite lengthy description, depending upon the size of the archival collection, the complexity of its organization, and the level of granularity desired in the description. Because the materials in archives are different from the types of information resources found in other institutions, the types of metadata recorded in a finding aid are considerably different from that found in catalogs or indexes. The following types of information are found in a typical finding aid:

- **Provenance**—including creator, title, dates, and biographical or administrative history;
- **Physical extent and condition**—including the amount (number, volume, and linear or cubic feet), and statement of the collection's condition;

Finding Aid to The Albert Einstein Archives

. . .

Finding aid written in English.

Description of the Collection
Reference Code

IsJJNL Arc 4° 1576

Title of the Collection

The Albert Einstein Archives

Dates of the Collection

1712, 1859-60, 1869, 1871, 1878-1887, 1891-present (bulk 1901-1955)

Location of the Collection

The Department of Manuscripts & Archives
The Jewish National & University Library
The Hebrew University of Jerusalem

Extent and medium of the Collection

c. 55,000 items (56 meters)

Name of creator

Einstein, Albert (1879-1955)

Short Description of the Collection

This collection contains the personal papers of Albert Einstein (1879-1955) and supplementary material collected at the Albert Einstein Archives. The material documents the life and career of Albert Einstein. The collection includes the manuscripts of Einstein's scientific and non-scientific writings, his correspondence with scientific colleagues and non-scientific contemporaries, his general correspondence as well as his personal documents and family correspondence. The collection also includes non-textual materials such as photographs, sound recordings and film footage.

Language/scripts of the Material

Material chiefly in German and English; some material in French, Italian, Russian, Yiddish, Hebrew, and other languages. Small amount of the material in German is in Gothic script.

. . .

Figure 2.4. First part of a finding aid found on the Web at: http://www.alberteinstein.info/finding_aid/.

- **Scope and content notes**—including a narrative description of the nature of the collection, what is included, the extent and depth of the collection, gaps in the collection, types of materials, and access points for names and subjects;
- **Order and structure**—including a description of how the collection is arranged and organized, and detailed container lists;
- **Administrative information**—including location, conditions of use, restrictions, processing, citation, acquisition and accession, repository, and conservation information.

Registers and Other Museum Databases

Registers constitute a primary control tool for museums. A register may also be called an *accession log*. It functions like a catalog, although it has additional kinds of access points. The process of registration in a museum is much like the process of cataloging in a library. During the process, the registrar identifies the object, the donor, any associations (e.g., having belonged to a particular person), any information needed for insurance purposes, and so forth. An identification number is assigned. The accession record becomes the basis for one or more files that help provide organization of the museum's content.

Additionally, museums provide databases for public access on the Web. For example, the Pitt Rivers Museum in Oxford, England has an objects database and a photos database. One can search each database by filling in fields in a search record. The objects database (also called the *Objects Collection Catalogue*) search has boxes for such things as name of the object, country the object is from (a pop-up box in this field lists the current United Nations list of country names), cultural group from which the object comes, material made from, when collected, and so forth. The photo database (also called the *Photographs Collection Catalogue*) search has, in addition to the same fields as for objects, boxes for such things as activity depicted, event depicted, person shown, photographer, photographic process, image dimensions, date of photograph, and so forth. It is suggested that users should not try to search more than three separate fields in the database at one time.[24]

An example of a different approach is that found at the site for the Guggenheim Museum. A selection from the Guggenheim collection is available online with scanned representations and descriptions of the selected pieces of art. One may search the collection records by one of seven directories: artist, title of work, date, movement, medium, concept, or museum. Each directory lists the possibilities A–Z. Or one may search by typing a word in the search box and receiving a list of all records that contain that word.[25] As time goes along, we may see more consistency among presentations of retrieval tools on museum Web sites.

Search Engines and Directories

Search engines are tools developed for computer systems, particularly the Internet, to find instances of requested words or phrases that can be found in the documents covered by the scope of the tool. They were developed for the purpose of searching full text documents (or indexes of those documents) for particular words or phrases. They may or may not provide results that are as intellectually satisfactory as the results from other retrieval tools, but users often report satisfaction because they find *something* related to what they were searching for and find it fast. But most users do not know if what they found is authentic, authoritative, or the best that is available on their topic. Searches for known items or for specific names are sometimes less satisfactory than searches for topical information. Search engines have become more sophisticated, but there are still drawbacks, such as no distinction among homographs and no connections for synonyms. Google[26] is one of the most sophisticated both in giving searching assistance (e.g., asking, "Did you really mean to search for...?" in response to a misspelled word) and in display of results.

Some search engines are used to search only a particular resource, such as the Web site for an organization such as OCLC. Other search engines are for searching the whole Internet (although only a small percentage of the Internet is actually searched by each one). Using a program called a *spider* (also known as a *crawler, robot,* or *agent*), each search engine automatically collects information from Web resources and places it into a database of records or in a full-text index that is similar to a concordance. The spider is typically programmed to go onto the Web to retrieve and download copies of certain target Web pages and everything linked to them, everything linked to the links, and so on. A massive collective index—created from the spider's database—is what is searched when users enter terms into the search box.

Obviously, not every Web page on the Internet has been indexed. Some resources may be indexed by only a few search engines—thus, a variety of responses can be had when searching different engines for the same concept. In addition, not every search engine indexes every type of material available on the Internet. It has only been in recent years that resources in PDF and PowerPoint format have become searchable on the Web. In some cases, resources may be password-protected, and as a result, they may not be indexed in a search engine because they are not accessible to the crawler.

In other cases, some resources may be indexed and returned as search results, despite being restricted—a fact that the searcher may discover only after trying to access the information.

Displays of search results are usually arranged according to *relevance,* which can be calculated in various ways. A search engine may calculate relevance by giving different weightings to factors such as how many search terms are found in each Web page or file; how often each term is found in a page or file; whether the terms are in proximity or dispersed; whether the terms are in the head of the document, or buried further down in its body; and how common (or unique) a particular search term is. Search engines continue to strive for more sophisticated methods of calculating relevance and for displaying results. For example, Google uses a formula that includes not only common factors such as word placement and frequency, but also Web site popularity (i.e., how often a page is linked to by other Web pages) as a factor in ranking search results. Google and the other search engines are continuously updating, refining, and testing their algorithms and formulas in their quests to improve the Internet searching experience. With the development of metadata, search engines had the promise of developing more sophisticated information retrieval techniques, but due to metadata misbehavior (e.g., including popular terms that have no relationship to the site being described), most search engines do not take user-supplied metadata into consideration in their relevance ranking.

Alternatives to search engines include directories and subject gateways. Yahoo!,[27] for example, employs human indexers in the creation of its directory. Humans add subject terms and categorize the records into a hierarchical subject tree index. Searching can be done by browsing or "drilling" down through the categories or by keyword searching. Some Internet directories are organized according to traditional library classification (e.g., Cyberstacks),[28] but most are created anew by the persons who devise the directory. Comparison of the categories used by different directories will show that the hierarchies can be quite different from directory to directory. Once the first place to look for Web sites, directories have waned in popularity considerably in recent years due to the ascendancy of the search engine. In fact, when going to their Web site today, not only is the Yahoo! directory no longer the first page one encounters, there is not even a direct link to it on the homepage. In order to use the directory, one either has to go to an entirely different URL[29] or to find the link for "more options" that is attached to their search engine.

Subject gateways are similar to directories but with a focus on a particular subject area. These are often constructed by academic libraries, sometimes working in groups, or by associations/organizations interested in a subject area and dedicated to providing information on the subject. Examples of the latter are "The Gateway to Educational Materials (GEM)"[30] and the United States Department of Health and Human Services' "DHHS Data Council: Gateway to Data and Statistics."[31]

CONCLUSION

A century ago Charles Cutter stated that catalogs should enable people to find books for which titles, authors, or subjects were known; should show what was available in a library by a particular author, on a particular subject, or in a kind of literature; and should assist in the choice of a book by its edition or character. A century later, Cutter's "objects" are still quite appropriate, except that they have been expanded to all kinds of information resources beyond just books in libraries, and to a number of different kinds of retrieval tools beyond catalogs. This chapter has discussed the major retrieval tools used in the organization and retrieval of recorded information. The surrogate records that make up a retrieval tool must be created and encoded, either by humans or automatically by software programs (created by humans). Chapters 7 through 11 address creating records for retrieval tools. But first, in the next chapter, a historical look at the development of organizing processes through a number of centuries serves to give us a perspective on where we have been, where we are now, and how far we might go.

NOTES

All URLs accessed September 2008.

1. *Publication Manual of the American Psychological Association,* 5th ed. (Washington, D.C.: American Psychological Association, 2001).

2. *Chicago Manual of Style,* 15th ed. (Chicago: University of Chicago Press, 2003).

3. Joseph Gibaldi, *The MLA Style Manual and Guide to Scholarly Publishing,* 3rd ed. (New York: Modern Language Association of America, 2008).

4. Council of Science Editors, *Scientific Style and Format: The CSE Manual for Authors, Editors, and Publishers,* 7th ed. (Reston, Va.: Council of Science Editors in cooperation with the Rockefeller University Press, 2006).

5. Kate L. Turabian, *A Manual for Writers of Research Papers, Theses, and Dissertations,* 7th ed. (Chicago: University of Chicago Press, 2007).

6. U.S. Government Printing Office, *Style Manual,* 29th ed. (Washington, D.C.: U.S. Government Printing Office, 2000).

7. Daphne Muse, ed., *The New Press Guide to Multicultural Resources for Young Readers* (New York: New Press; distributed by W. W. Norton, 1997).

8. David Gilson, *A Bibliography of Jane Austen* (Winchester, England: St. Paul's Bibliographies, 1997).

9. Mustafa Aydn and M. Nail Aikan, *An Extensive Bibliography of Studies in English, German, and French on Turkish Foreign Policy, 1923–1997* (Ankara, Turkey: Ministry of Foreign Affairs, Center for Strategic Research, 1997).

10. Barbara J. Horwitz, *British Women Writers, 1700–1850: An Annotated Bibliography of Their Works and Works About Them* (Lanham, Md.: Scarecrow Press, 1997).

11. Ria Koopmans-de Bruijn, *Area Bibliography of Japan* (Lanham, Md.: Scarecrow Press, 1998).

12. David Farrell, *The Stinehour Press: A Bibliographical Checklist of the First Thirty Years* (Lunenburg, Vt.: Meriden-Stinehour Press, 1988).

13. John McIlwaine, *Maps and Mapping of Africa: A Resource Guide* (New Providence, N.J.: Zell, 1997).

14. Charles A. Cutter, *Rules for a Dictionary Catalog,* 4th ed. (Washington, D.C.: Government Printing Office, 1904; reprint, London: The Library Association, 1962), p. 12.

15. Seymour Lubetzky, *Cataloging Rules and Principles: A Critique of the A.L.A. Rules for Entry and a Proposed Design for Their Revision* (Washington, D.C.: Processing Dept., Library of Congress, 1953), p. 36.

16. Ibid.

17. International Conference on Cataloguing Principles, Paris, 9th–18th October, 1961, *Report* (London: International Federation of Library Associations, 1963), pp. 91–96. Also available in: *Library Resources & Technical Services* 6 (1962), pp. 162–167; and *Statement of principles adopted at the International Conference on Cataloguing Principles, Paris, October, 1961,* annotated ed., with commentary and examples by Eva Verona (London, IFLA Committee on Cataloguing, 1971); and A. H. Chaplin and Dorothy Anderson, eds. *Report/ International Conference on Cataloguing Principles, Paris, 9th–18th October 1961* (London: IFLA International Office for UBC, 1981).

18. *Functional Requirements for Bibliographic Records: Final Report,* IFLA Study Group on the Functional Requirements for Bibliographic Records (Munchen: Saur, 1998), p. 82. A 2008 update is available: http://www.ifla.org/VII/s13/frbr/index.htm.

19. See, for example, Arlene G. Taylor, "Cataloging in Context," in Bohdan S. Wynar and Arlene G. Taylor, *Introduction to Cataloging and Classification,* 8th ed. (Englewood, Colo.: Libraries Unlimited, 1992), p. 8.

20. For more about standardization in online systems as well as more about OPACs, see Chapter 5.

21. David M. Brown, "Introducing HTML Indexer™," Brown, Inc. Available: http://www.html-indexer.com; Tim Craven, "Tim Craven—Freeware: XRefHT32," University of Western Ontario. Available: http://publish.uwo.ca/~craven/freeware.htm.

22. *American National Standard for Library and Information Sciences and Related Publishing Practices—Basic Criteria for Indexes, ANSI Z39.4–1984* (New York: American National Standards Institute, 1984).

23. International Organization for Standardization, *Information and Documentation: Guidelines for the Content, Organization and Presentation of Indexes,* ISO 999:1996 (E), (Geneva: ISO, 1996). Excerpts available: http://www.collectionscanada.gc.ca/iso/tc46sc9/standard/999e.htm.

24. Pitt Rivers Museum, "Online Databases and Catalogues." Available: http://www.prm.ox.ac.uk/databases.html.

25. Guggenheim Museum, "Selections from the Collection." Available: http://www.guggenheimcollection.org/index.html.

26. Google. Available: http://www.google.com.

27. Yahoo! Available: http://www.yahoo.com.

28. Cyberstacks. Available: http://www.public.iastate.edu/~CYBERSTACKS/homepage.html.

29. Yahoo! Directory. Available: http://dir.yahoo.com/.

30. Digital Learning Commons, "Gateway to Educational Materials—GEM." Available: http://www.learningcommons.org/educators/library/gem.php.

31. United States, Department of Health and Human Services, "DHHS Data Council Gateway to Data and Statistics." Available: http://www.hhs-stat.net/.

SUGGESTED READINGS

Buckland, Michael K. "What is a 'Document'?" *Journal of the American Society for Information Science* 48, no. 9 (September 1997): 804–809. Also available: http://people.ischool.berkeley.edu/~buckland/whatdoc.html.

Cleveland, Donald B., and Ana D. Cleveland. *Introduction to Indexing and Abstracting.* 3rd ed. Englewood, Colo.: Libraries Unlimited, 2001. Chapter 1: "Introduction," Chapter 2: "The Nature of Information," Chapter 3: "The Organization of Information," and Chapter 5: "Types of Indexes and Abstracts."

Fox, Michael J., and Peter Wilkerson. *Introduction to Archival Organization and Description: Access to Cultural Heritage.* Los Angeles: The Getty Research Institute, 1998.

Gilster, Paul. *Digital Literacy.* New York: Wiley, 1997.

Levy, David M. "Cataloging in the Digital Order." In *Digital Libraries '95: The Second Annual Conference on the Theory and Practice of Digital Libraries, June 11–13, 1995, Austin, Texas.* Available: http://www.csdl.tamu.edu/DL95/papers/levy/levy.html.

Library of Congress. "Manuscript Division Finding Aids Online." Available: http://www.loc.gov/rr/mss/f-aids/mssfa.html.

Markey, Karen. "The Online Library Catalog: Paradise Lost and Paradise Regained?" *D-Lib Magazine* 13, no. 1/2 (2007). Available: http://www.dlib.org/dlib/january07/markey/01markey.html.

Matthews, Joseph R. "The Value of Information: the Case of the Library Catalog." *Technical Services Quarterly* 19, no. 2 (2001): 1–16.

"Report of the Working Group on Standards for Archival Description." *American Archivist* 52 (Fall 1989): 440–461.

Rowley, Jennifer, and Richard Hartley. *Organizing Knowledge: An Introduction to Managing Access to Information.* 4th ed. Aldershot, England; Burlington,

Vt.: Ashgate, 2008. Chapter 9: "Organizing Knowledge in the Digital Environment."

Society of American Archivists, Committee on Finding Aids. *Inventories and Registers: A Handbook of Techniques and Examples*. Chicago: Society of American Archivists, 1976.

Taylor, Arlene G. *Introduction to Cataloging and Classification*. 10th ed., with the assistance of David P. Miller. Westport, Conn.: Libraries Unlimited, 2006. Chapter 1: "Cataloging in Context" and Chapter 19: "Processing Centers, Networking, and Cooperative Programs."

CHAPTER 3

DEVELOPMENT OF THE ORGANIZATION OF RECORDED INFORMATION IN WESTERN CIVILIZATION

It is often said that you can't tell where you're going until you know where you've been. This chapter looks at where we've been and addresses these questions: How did we arrive at this state of organization? What basic principles of organization have been developed over the last several centuries? Practices and ways of organizing that we now take for granted were once thought of for the first time by intelligent and serious scholars, just as we are coming up with innovative ideas for today's organization that will be taken for granted in the next decades.

INVENTORIES, BIBLIOGRAPHIES, CATALOGS, AND CODIFICATION

Antiquity

One of the oldest lists of books we know about appears on a Sumerian tablet found at Nippur from about 2000 B.C.E. Sixty-two titles are recorded on this tablet of which twenty-four are titles of currently known literary works. We don't know what purpose the list served. Its use may or may

Much of the material in the first half of this chapter is based on Ruth French Strout, "The Development of the Catalog and Cataloging Codes," *Library Quarterly* 26, no. 4 (October 1956): 254–275.

not have resembled that of a catalog. However, the fact that the Sumerians were indefatigable writers makes it hard to believe that they had no catalogs. They seem to have kept everything: history books, medical prescriptions, love poems, business invoices, school children's homework assignments, and the first-known letter home from a student who threatens to drop out of school unless his parents fork over more money for a suitable wardrobe.

Through the archaeological discoveries of excavations of ancient civilizations, we know that tablets and other resources were used to inscribe titles of books, but we don't know for what purpose. They might have been ownership tags (e.g., the ones that had the names of the king and queen and a title on each small plaque), or they might have been relics of something like a bibliography or a catalog. There are more remnants of early records from Babylonia than from Egypt, probably due to the fact that Babylonians wrote on clay tablets, while Egyptians wrote on papyrus.

Around 1500 B.C.E., the Hittites evidently saw the need to convey bibliographic information as part of a written work. Their tablets bore colophons that identified the number of the tablet in a series, its title, and often the name of the scribe. (A *colophon* is a set of data at the end of a "document" that gives varying kinds of bibliographic data. It might give information usually found on a title page, and, in items after the invention of printing with moveable type, it gives such information as date of printing, printer, typeface used, etc.)

Around 650 B.C.E., people in the city of Nineveh had developed a library in which they seem to have taken great care to preserve order and authenticity. The "documents" bore elaborate colophons, but there is no evidence of anything like a catalog.

Two of the great libraries of antiquity were in Pergamum and Alexandria—two active centers of Greek civilization. Later writings have referred to *Pinakes* from both libraries. *Pinakes* is plural of *pinax,* a word that means tray or dish. It is thought that such trays had slightly raised edges and that wax could be poured in the middle; when hardened, the wax could be written in with a stylus. If this was indeed the medium, it is no wonder that no remnants have survived. Writers have quoted from the Pinakes of Alexandria, which was created by Callimachus. The work may have been a catalog, or it may have been a bibliography of Greek literature. Callimachus has been given credit as being the first cataloger of whom we have knowledge.[1]

There are a few generalizations about bibliographic practices of the time that can be drawn from quotations of scholars who quoted from Callimachus's work. For example, a few general categories were considered to be a sufficient subject approach. Callimachus's subjects were epic and other non-dramatic poetry, drama, law, philosophy, history, oratory, medicine, mathematical science, natural science, and miscellanea. A scholar would go to the general subject and then look for the author being sought. The arrangement of entries under the general subject was sometimes classified, sometimes chronological, and sometimes alphabetical, although the Greeks never arrived at a strictly alphabetical arrangement. They sometimes grouped entries by initial letter, but there are no examples of arrangement by any letter past the first one. This probably indicates that their lists were not nearly as long as ours.

Greek civilization seems to have given us the basis for our Western idea that "main entry" ought to be "the author." This kind of entry has not appeared in any work that has survived from early Eastern civilizations. Even today in Asian countries the traditional entry for a book is its title. A Japanese librarian of one author's acquaintance once observed that the principle of author entry goes along with democracy, since it rests upon belief in the importance of the individual.

Little information is available about Roman libraries. From sources that mention them, there is evidence that there was some way of finding a designated book when it was requested. This was probably through "fixed location." One story goes that if a nobleman got into an intellectual argument, he would send a servant to the library to retrieve a certain book that would prove his point.

Middle Ages

We know that during the Middle Ages in Europe there were church and monastery libraries. There was no demand for books, and knowledge was not sought in any way that would require the use of catalogs. Through copying by monks, a system was set up by which the monastery became the sole keeper, manufacturer, and finally, list maker of books through many centuries.

One of the earliest listings of the holdings of a medieval library was dated in the eighth century. It was written on the final flyleaf of a book and consisted of a list of brief titles with authors added to some of them. It probably served as an inventory record and may have represented the shelf arrangement, although there were no location symbols accompanying the titles. This list was typical of most of the so-called catalogs of the following centuries—the briefest sort of inventories recorded in the most casual places.

From the ninth through the thirteenth centuries, the libraries continued to produce lists that seemed to be inventories. One list, which specified that its purpose was for inventory, stated that the library contained 246 volumes. It would be quite unrealistic to expect libraries of this size to feel any need for catalogs. Even after libraries grew to the size of 600 or 700 volumes, lists were still inventories. Occasionally such a list would use author entries, but in no discernible order. A few listed works contained in each volume, and the number of volumes to a work. (Books into which works were copied were often bound blank pages. Works were copied into them in the order in which the scribe picked them up. Several works could be copied into one bound blank volume, but it might take several bound volumes to copy a very long work.) In a few lists there was a subject arrangement, but it was very broad, often using only two categories: biblical and humanistic. At least one list from the thirteenth century added some unusual descriptions in designating books variously as "useless," "legible," "old," and "good," but we do not know whether they were used as an aid in identification for inventory or to help the reader by pointing out which books could be easily read.

Toward the end of the thirteenth century, someone whose identity is not known started a project that might be considered a milestone in the history of catalogs. This was the compilation of the *Registrum Librorum Angliae,* a union list of holdings of English monastery libraries in which, in a quite modern way, each library was assigned a number for coding purposes. The *Registrum* was never finished. There are evidences of later attempts to compile continuations of it, although no finished version has survived.

European Renaissance

The fourteenth century brought some improvements, and a few lists of this period might be called shelflists. The outstanding list of the fourteenth century is from St. Martin's Priory at Dover, dated 1389. In fact, it may be the first of the lists that could be justly designated a catalog. It is divided into three sections. The first is a listing by call number, a number representing fixed location even to the placing of the individual volume. The second section of the catalog, likewise arranged by call number, gives the contents of each volume, with the paging and opening words for each work included. The third part is a landmark in the development of cataloging: a catalog of analytical entries and an alphabetical listing, but with entries of the usual medieval type—some under author, others under title followed by author, with still other entries beginning with such words as *book, part,* or *codex,* obviously with no importance attached to the entry word. (An *analytical entry* is an entry made for each of the works in a volume, as opposed to making only one entry for the entire volume.)

College libraries began in the fourteenth century but did not bring any innovations to the development of bibliographic control. The earliest lists from college libraries revert to the primitive inventories of the preceding centuries. This is possibly explained by the fact that college library book collections were small; it was not unusual for a college library at that time to have only one hundred books.

The main new practice from the fifteenth century was the use of references. In one catalog, the references were not separate entries but were appended to a sort of contents note pointing out in what other place in the library a certain item might be found (e.g., "which seek in the 96th volume of theology"). In the catalog of St. Augustine's Abbey, Canterbury, though, references reached the status of separate entries. A typical example is: "The Meditations of Bernard, not here because it is above in the Bible which was given by W. Wylmynton."

In the middle of the fifteenth century came an event that challenged everything about bibliographic control—the invention of printing. Suddenly, instead of unique manuscript copies of works, there were identical duplicates of many works. A new breed of people came into being for the task of listing the works available—people we might now call "bibliographers."

Toward the close of the fifteenth century, German bibliographer and librarian Johann Tritheim stands out as having taken an important step in the development of bibliographic control. He not only compiled a bibliography in chronological order, which was unusual enough for his time, but he also appended to this an alphabetical author index. It is difficult to understand why such a simple and useful device had not always been used; yet it took centuries of compiling book lists to reach this degree of accomplishment.

From Inventories to Finding Lists to Collocating Devices

Following the precedent set by Tritheim, bibliographers in the sixteenth century continued to take the lead in making improvements. One of these, Konrad Gesner, published an author bibliography in 1545 and a subject index in 1548, and in the process set a new standard of excellence. He continued to use forenames of authors for entry words, according to the tradition of the time, but he recognized the possible inconvenience of this practice and so he prefixed to his bibliography an alphabetical list of authors in which the names were inverted. In addition, his main listing included references from variant spellings of names to the accepted entry form (e.g., "Thobias, see Tobias"). Gesner included in his work (titled the *Pandectarum*) the suggestion that libraries use copies of his bibliographies as their catalogs by inserting call numbers beside entries that represented their holdings, thus providing themselves with both an author and a subject catalog.

In 1595, Andrew Maunsell, an English bookseller, compiled his *Catalog of English Printed Books* and in the preface stated his rules for entry.

He advocated the entry of personal names under surnames rather than forenames. He set up the principle of uniform entry for the Bible, which, prior to Maunsell's collocating them, had been entered under whatever the title page said (e.g., Holy Bible, The Word of God, Bible, etc.). He insisted that one should be able to find a book under three types of entries—the author's surname, the subject, and the translator. These were radical and sudden advances in the development of bibliographic control.

By the beginning of the seventeenth century, catalogs were beginning to be looked upon as finding lists rather than inventories. Early in the century, Sir Thomas Bodley offered to build up the Oxford University Library, which had been destroyed by fire some fifty years before. Bodley took a great interest in the catalog because he expected that it would be useful in his acquisitions program; he wanted the catalog to tell him if the library already owned a work. He insisted upon a classified catalog with an alphabetical author index arranged by surname, and he also wanted analytical entries.

In 1697 Frederic Rostgaard published a discourse on cataloging in which he called for subject arrangement subdivided at once chronologically and by size of volume. For the preceding century, size of volume had been a traditional way of dividing catalogs. Rostgaard proposed a printed catalog, with the spread of two facing pages divided into four parallel columns, each column to contain books of a certain size, arranged so that books of various sizes that had been published on a certain subject within the same year would come directly opposite each other in parallel columns. He recommended an alphabetical index of subjects and authors to be placed at the end of the catalog, with authors entered by surname. The word order of titles as found on the title page was to be preserved. His final suggestion was that his rules not be followed when it seemed best to arrange things differently.

As the eighteenth century began, bibliographic control seemed to have hit a plateau that did not change for most of the century. Catalogs were sometimes classified and sometimes alphabetical; indexes were considered useful, though by no means necessary; some catalogs were still divided according to the size of books; authors were now always entered under surname and were often arranged chronologically; the wording of the title page had assumed a certain degree of prestige and was now being transcribed literally and without being paraphrased; imprints were included; bound-with notes were used; references were quite common; and some analytical entries were used in most catalogs.

In 1791 following the French Revolution, the new French government sent out instructions for cataloging the collections of the libraries that had been confiscated throughout the country. Here we have the first instance of a national code. Libraries were directed to make card catalogs—apparently the first appearance in history of a card catalog. It was introduced, not because someone thought it would be a convenient form, but because, with wartime shortages, it was a practical way of using available materials. Confiscated playing cards were to be used for the purpose—aces and deuces were to be reserved for the longest titles. (Playing cards of the time were blank on the back, rather than having pictures. They were also larger than today's cards.) There was no theory or philosophizing in this code. The title page was to be transcribed on the card and the author's surname underlined for the filing word. If there was no author, a keyword in the title was to be underlined. A *collation* was added that was to include number of volumes, size, a statement of illustration, the material of which the book was made, the kind of type, any missing pages, and a description of the binding if it was outstanding in any way. (This elaborate collation was partly for the purpose of identifying valuable books that the government might offer for sale in order to increase government revenue.) After the cards were filled in and put in order by underlined filing word, they were to be strung together by running a needle and thread through the lower left corners to keep them in order.[2] Here we have a number of procedures that have continued to the present. This code, coming at the end of the eighteenth century, makes a good stepping-stone to the extensive cataloging developments of the nineteenth century.

Period of Codification

The nineteenth century brought a period of much argument over the relative virtues of classified and dictionary catalogs, not only among librarians, but also among readers and scholars in general and even in reports to the House of Commons of Great Britain. Feelings ran very high on the subject, and rather emotional arguments were made, "from the statement that classified catalogs and indexes were not needed because living librarians were better than subject catalogs, to the opinion that any intelligent man who was sufficiently interested in a subject to want to consult material on it could just as well use author entries as subject, for he would, of course, know the names of all the authors who had written in his field."[3]

What was needed was a person who could persuade others of the value of cataloging and subject analysis. That person turned out to be Anthony Panizzi, a lawyer and a political refugee from Italy who was appointed assistant librarian at the British Museum in 1831. When he was appointed Keeper of the Printed Books in 1837, there was much objection. One history book states that it was because "firstly, Panizzi was an Italian by birth, and it was felt that only an Englishman should be in charge of one of our national institutions; secondly, it was said that Panizzi had been seen in the streets of

London selling white mice."[4] No further explanation is given. Another writer, though, gives this account: "Meetings were held against the 'Foreigner' and one of the speakers made an open statement that Panizzi had been seen in the streets of London selling white mice: had it been a few years later, possibly the distinctive title of organ-grinder would have been added."[5]

In 1836 a committee of the House of Commons was charged with inquiry into the management and affairs of the British Museum. One of the "affairs" was the state of catalogs and cataloging. During hearings on the topic, witnesses came to testify for and against the catalogs. Many of the witnesses became quite vehement about one or another sort of entry. Panizzi was able again and again to persuade the committee members to accept his views.

Panizzi wrote his views into a cataloging code known as the "91 Rules" and gained official approval for it in 1839, although he had to give up his concept of "corporate main entry" in order to get approval. Panizzi's code shows that we had at last arrived at "modern" cataloging, because he tried to deal with many of the same problems we are still arguing about today.

Halfway through the nineteenth century, cataloging in the United States began to warrant attention. Until this time American cataloging had been generally a century behind European cataloging. For example, of the three catalogs printed at Harvard, one had been divided into three alphabets according to the size of books; all three contained only very brief records; and none provided a subject approach.

In 1850 Charles C. Jewett published a code for the catalog of the Smithsonian Institution. With this code Americans began to have influence in cataloging. Jewett acknowledged his debt to Panizzi and varied in only a few instances from the instructions in the "91 Rules." Jewett is given credit for extending the principle of the corporate author further than Panizzi had. Research now shows that Jewett copied his rule from Panizzi's original draft, which had a rule for corporate bodies as authors but which did not appear in the "91 Rules" because Panizzi was forced by the British Museum trustees to drop his rules for entry under corporate author.[6] So what Jewett actually did was to bring the concept of corporate authorship to public attention.

Jewett's philosophy of the purpose of a code was this: "*Uniformity* is, then, imperative; but, among many laborers, can only be secured by the adherence of all to rules embracing, as far as possible, the minutest details of the work."[7] In light of this philosophy, it is interesting to observe that the second edition of Jewett's rulebook contains only 39 rules on pages 29–64 with pages 67–90 devoted to examples. The title of Jewett's book, *On the Construction of Catalogues of Libraries, and Their Publication by Means of Separate, Stereotyped Titles,* makes it clear that Jewett was addressing more than just rules for cataloging. The first part of the volume is devoted to his plan to create a stereotyped plate of each title cataloged, to store the plates, and to use them over and over for production of printed catalogs. Stereotyping was a relatively new method of printing, using a metal copy of the typeset image. Jewett planned to have the plates numbered in the order in which they were printed and to keep them in alphabetical order in shallow drawers. The numbers could be used by libraries to indicate which titles were owned by each, and then a catalog could be produced for a library by pulling out the plates for titles owned by that library. Also, a union catalog could be produced from the plates. Jewett's plan was never implemented. Apparently, he was technologically a bit ahead of his time.[8]

When Charles Cutter published his *Rules for a Printed Dictionary Catalogue* in 1876, he strengthened the concept that catalogs not only should point the way to an individual publication, but should also assemble and organize literary units. That is, they should be collocating devices. This was not an entirely new principle: Maunsell had used the heading "Bible"; Panizzi had strengthened it by introducing corporate and government entries; and Jewett had given further support by use of real names rather than pseudonyms. But it was Cutter who actually stated it as a formal principle.

Cutter was also the first to make rules for subject headings as a way to gain subject access to materials through the catalog. And he was the last to incorporate into one set of rules instructions for the description of items, guidelines for subject headings, and rules for filing entries. At the end of the nineteenth century, each of these areas (i.e., description, subject headings, and filing) took on lives of their own and followed separate paths of development. We will now follow the first two paths separately. (Filing arrangement is discussed in Appendix C: Arrangement of Metadata Displays.)

TWENTIETH CENTURY

Description

In the area of description, the twentieth century was an era of codes. The British and the Americans collaborated on a code published in 1908. Its importance lies in its being the first international cataloging code, and in the extent of its rapid and widespread adoption and use by all types and sizes of libraries in the two countries.

In the 1920s, four prominent American librarians helped with writing the Vatican Code, which was published in Italian in 1931. It was quickly accepted by catalogers in many countries as the best and most complete code in existence, but because it was in Italian, most Americans could not use it.

The British and Americans began cooperative work toward a new edition of the 1908 code in the 1930s, but the outbreak of war ended this cooperation. The American Library Association (ALA) proceeded independently in producing its preliminary second edition in 1941. This code was published in two parts: one for entry and heading, and one for description of books. It was widely attacked on the grounds of complexity and too extensive enumeration of cases. The most famous attack was that of Andrew Osborn in his article titled "The Crisis in Cataloging."[9] He discussed four principal theories of cataloging: the legalistic (cataloging with a rule for everything, and an authority to settle any question at issue), the perfectionistic (cataloging performed so well the first time that it is done once and for all), the bibliographic (cataloging made into a branch of descriptive bibliography with extremely detailed physical descriptions and notes), and the pragmatic (cataloging according to the needs of particular types of libraries and/or users). He called for both the cataloging process and the rules governing it to become pragmatic, with simple rules supplemented by cataloger judgment. Osborn's article is one of the classic statements in cataloging theory, and certainly, one of the historical turning points in code development.

In response to all the criticism, the ALA Division of Cataloging and Classification undertook revision of the first part (entry and heading) of the 1941 code. In 1949 the revision was published as the *A.L.A. Cataloging Rules for Author and Title Entries.* The *Rules for Descriptive Cataloging,* published by the Library of Congress (LC) was substituted for the second part (description of books) of the 1941 rules. The ALA portion of the 1949 rules again was criticized as being a continuation of Osborn's "legalistic" characterization. In 1951 ALA commissioned Seymour Lubetzky to do a critical study of cataloging rules. Lubetzky said cataloging should be done according to principles, and he drafted a code based on principles. It was welcomed by progressives, but conservatives began worrying about probable costs of changes.

An International Conference on Cataloguing Principles was held in Paris in 1961, at which a draft statement of principles, based on Lubetzky's code, was submitted. The international participants agreed to adopt these principles and to work in their various countries for revised rules that would be in agreement with the accepted principles. These principles, often referred to as the *Paris Principles* (or *IFLA Principles*) are important because, for the first time, there was multinational agreement upon which to base future international developments.

The Americans and the British again cooperated on a new set of cataloging rules, and in 1967 published the *Anglo-American Cataloging Rules* (although it had to be published in separate North American and British versions because of inability to come to agreement on some points). These rules were based on the Paris Principles, although they deviated in some respects.

In 1974 the International Federation of Library Associations (IFLA) issued the *International Standard Bibliographic Description* (ISBD), produced as a means for the international communication of bibliographic information. ISBD's objectives were to make records from different sources interchangeable, to facilitate their interpretation against language barriers, and to facilitate the conversion of such records to machine-readable form.

AACR2, the second edition of the *Anglo-American Cataloguing Rules,* was published in 1978 to incorporate ISBD, to bring non-book materials into the mainstream, to take into account machine processing of bibliographic records, to reconcile the British and American texts, and to conform more closely to the Paris Principles. Four major national libraries (United States, Canada, Great Britain, and Australia) agreed to standard interpretation and implementation of AACR2, and many other countries have now adopted it for national use. Revised editions of AACR2 were published in 1988 and 1998. These were mainly cumulations of changes incurred in the process of "continuous revision." A significant revision of AACR2 was published in 2002, with updates distributed in 2003, 2004, and 2005. Updates for AACR2 have ceased, as efforts are now focused on the creation of a new descriptive cataloging content standard, *RDA: Resource Description and Access,* which is scheduled to be published in 2009.

Subject Access

Verbal Subject Access

For centuries philosophers worked on classifying knowledge; Callimachus, Plato, Aristotle, and Bacon are among the most famous. Librarians tried to adapt these classifications for use with books by assigning letters and/or numbers to the concepts classified by the philosophers. Other than this, there was not much interest in subject access in libraries before Charles Cutter. As already mentioned, Cutter included a section of guidelines for subject headings in his *Rules for a Dictionary Catalog.*

The *A.L.A. List of Subject Headings* was first published in 1885, and the preface stated that it was to be considered an appendix to Cutter's *Rules for a Dictionary Catalog.* It was based on headings found in five major catalogs of the time, including the Boston Athenaeum and the Harvard subject index. A second revised edition was published in 1905 with the statement that "further changes are not to be expected for many years."[10] However, new terminology became necessary rapidly, and interleaved and annotated editions became unwieldy. Many librarians asked for the list of subject headings that were appearing on LC cards, and so in 1914 the first edition of *Subject Headings Used in the Dictionary Catalogues of the Library of Congress* was published. This list rapidly replaced the ALA List. The title of LC's list was changed to *Library of Congress Subject Headings* (LCSH) in 1975. LCSH has appeared in multiple editions in its printed version, and from 1988 to 2007, a new edition was published every year. The next edition is due in 2009. LCSH is updated weekly in its online version.

The *Sears List of Subject Headings* (*Sears*) was first published in 1923 as *List of Subject Headings for Small Libraries.* It was prepared by Minnie Earl Sears in response to demands for a list of subject headings that was more suitable to the needs of the small library than the ALA or the LC lists. Recognizing the need for uniformity, Sears followed the form of the LC subject headings—she eliminated the more detailed ones and simplified some terminology. *Sears* continues to be published for small libraries in print. It is expected to be made available on the Web by 2009.

Classification

Meanwhile, classification had developed at LC from arrangement by size in the early 1800s to arrangement by the 18 broad categories of the Bacon-d'Alembert system in 1814 when the Library burned. To reestablish it, Thomas Jefferson sold Congress his library, which was classified using 44 main classes based on his interpretation of the Bacon-d'Alembert system. By the end of the century it was clear that the rapidly growing collection needed more detail in classification.

Melvil Dewey, in 1876, issued anonymously the first edition of his classification. He divided all knowledge into 10 main classes, with each of those divided again into 10 divisions, and each of those divided into 10 sections—giving 1,000 categories into which books could be classified. Like its predecessors, it was enumerative in that it listed specific categories one by one. In later editions he added decimals so that the 1,000 categories could be divided into 10,000, then 100,000 and so on. He also introduced the first hints of "number building," or "faceting," when he made tables for geographic areas and for forms of material. (*Faceting* comprises small notations that stand for subparts of the whole topic and are strung together to create a complete classification notation. This is discussed further in Chapter 11.) Notations from these tables could then be added in numerous places to show a certain subject category as being relevant to a particular geographic area or being presented in a particular form.

When LC decided it must improve over Jefferson's classification, *Dewey Decimal Classification* (*DDC*) was in its fifth edition, and Cutter had begun his own enumerative classification scheme, called the *Expansive Classification.* This scheme began with letters of the alphabet, expanded with second letters, and then expanded further with numbers. LC representatives talked with Dewey to convince him to allow them to adapt his scheme, but ran afoul of his intransigence. They did not adopt Cutter's classification directly, but created their own scheme based upon his main class structure.

The *Universal Decimal Classification* (UDC) was developed in 1895 by two Belgian lawyers, Paul Otlet and Henri LaFontaine. UDC was based on the DDC (then in its fifth edition), but was, with Dewey's permission, expanded by the addition of detailed subdivisions and the use of symbols to indicate complex subjects. Why Otlet and LaFontaine were able to get Dewey's permission when LC was not is unclear; but it may have been because UDC was not at the outset intended as a library classification, but as a means to organize documents (see more about this below). UDC expanded Dewey's "standard subdivisions" to about a dozen generally applicable "auxiliaries," which could be joined together as needed in the form we now call "faceting."

During the twentieth century, faceted classification became of interest because it allows the classifier to express all aspects of an interdisciplinary subject in the same classification notation. This type of classification is also referred to as *analytico-synthetic.* The term *facet* was first used with this meaning by S. R. Ranganathan in his *Colon Classification* (called "Colon" because of its use of the "colon" punctuation mark as a major facet indicator) in the early 1930s. As mentioned earlier, Dewey had already provided for some "number building," and *Library of Congress Classification* (LCC) even included a few such facets (although developed only class by class and not applicable through the entire scheme). Ranganathan introduced the fully faceted approach by means of classification notations constructed entirely from individual facets in a prescribed sequence from the most specific to the most general. The work of Ranganathan inspired many librarians and information scientists in the second half of the twentieth century, most notably a group of classificationists in Great Britain collectively known as the Classification Research Group (CRG). The CRG's work led to the revision of the *Bliss Bibliographic Classification,* the creation of the *Preserved-Context Indexing System* (PRECIS), and the development of several faceted classifications used in particular disciplines and industries.

Most classification systems have been used, beginning in the late 1800s, as the base upon which to create call numbers to be used for the physical arrangement of books and other resources on shelves in stacks. Arrangement of physical information resources is discussed in Appendix B.

Special Materials

Archives

U.S. developments in bibliographic control of special materials (i.e., archives, museums) have nearly all come since the turn of the twentieth century. European archival practice stemmed from working with public archives (e.g., land grants, laws, etc.). Archival materials were kept because of legal and other administrative value. The concept of *provenance* emerged in France about 1840, and the concept of *original order* came from the Prussians shortly thereafter.[11]

As in libraries, the first archival catalogs were lists and then inventories. In early archival practice in the United States, material was collected for its artifactual value. It was often cataloged at the item level without any concern for provenance or original order. Thus, the context in which the archival record was originally created was lost. This practice lasted in the United States through the mid-1930s, when European ideas began to influence U.S. practice and when the National Archives and the Society of American Archivists were formed. Early cataloging codes in the United States (e.g., Cutter, AACR) dealt with cataloging manuscripts, but at the item level. In 1983, publication of *Archives, Personal Papers, and Manuscripts* (APPM) brought the library and archival traditions together. APPM is based on ISBD and AACR2, but also includes archival principles. A special MARC format was developed (called MARC-AMC). It has now been incorporated with the other special MARC formats in the process of "format integration." Today, *Describing Archives: A Content Standard* (DACS) is the descriptive standard used in the creation of finding aids and MARC records for archival collections.

Museums (Art and Object Collections)

As in libraries and archives, museums began first with lists and later expanded to include inventories. *Museum documentation* or *museum registration* is terminology that often has been applied to cataloging of art and artifacts. It is a system that provides an indispensable record of information associated with objects for research. Museums are now joining the library and archives communities in codification of descriptive practice. The Internet has spurred this action because of the demand from researchers for access to pictures and textual descriptions of artifacts and art. Museums have recently developed standard means for creating surrogate records (e.g., *Cataloging Cultural Objects* [CCO]). Libraries with these kinds of collections use AACR2's chapters for cataloging realia and graphics, and then enter these descriptions into a MARC format.

Subject Access to Special Materials

Subject access to special materials follows the needs of the user communities. For verbal subject access, archivists use LCSH and the *Art & Architecture Thesaurus* (AAT). The museum community has developed specialized lists and thesauri (often called *lexicons*). Museums also use the AAT. The collective nature of archival description does not lend itself to the use of classification. Some collections of art and artifacts are classified, however. Some natural history museums classify specimens of organisms that can be identified to the genus and species level. Two other examples include the American Museum of Natural History, which uses Romer's classification of vertebrae, and art collections with Christian iconographic themes that use *Iconclass,* developed in the Netherlands.

Mechanization of Bibliography

Automation first entered the information organization picture in the 1870s when the typewriter was introduced into libraries. Typewriters were highly controversial at first because they were so noisy. Many libraries were one-room affairs with the cataloger sitting at a table in the back. Patrons, who had been used to the quiet of the cataloger creating handwritten cards, found the clacking of the typewriter annoying. Some librarians objected, too, because typed cards were not esthetically pleasing compared to cards written in "library hand," a method of writing in which the letters were carefully formed to be completely readable.

The Documentation Movement

The trend to mechanize bibliography began with the Documentation Movement in Europe in the 1890s. The nineteenth century brought the development of professional organizations and the growth of scientific research, both of which created a dramatic increase in the number of published journals. Paul Otlet and Henri LaFontaine spearheaded a movement for bibliographic control in libraries to go beyond books to provide access to parts of books, articles in journals, research documents, brochures, catalogs, patents, government records, archives, photographs, and newspapers. The goal of the Documentation Movement was to capture, record, and provide access to all information in all formats for the improvement of science.

A conference organized by Otlet and LaFontaine was held in Brussels in 1892, with a focus on the creation of Universal Bibliographic Control (UBC). The magnitude of the undertaking necessitated an entirely new body of techniques different from conventional library practice for organization, subject analysis, bibliographic description, and annotation. This quest for new techniques of bibliographic control naturally led to a search for new technology. The concept of documentation was transported to the United States in the 1930s, and in 1937 the American Documentation Institute was formed. In 1938 the International Federation for Documentation was established and was devoted almost exclusively to the promotion of *Universal Decimal Classification* (UDC). From its inception, UDC was not intended as a library classification, but rather as a means to organize and analyze *documents,* a term then defined to include such things as journal articles, scientific papers, patents, and the like, but not books or journals.

An important technological advance for the documentation field was the development of microphotography by Eastman Kodak in 1928. This was seen as a means of collecting, storing, and accessing vast quantities of information, and it was predicted that microfilm would supplant the conventional book.

World War II had an impact on the mechanization of bibliographic control in two ways. First, it created an immediate scientific information explosion, as the U.S. government's imperative was to "get the bomb first." Scientific research was conducted rapidly and in secrecy, with a critical need for immediate dissemination of research results from lab to lab. This heightened the government's awareness of the need for bibliographic control and brought with it government funding to develop a mechanized process. Second, as the outcome of the war shifted in favor of the Allies, huge quantities of German scientific literature were confiscated. This material needed immediate bibliographic control in order to be useful. Microfilms were made and distributed through a committee attached to the Office of Strategic Service. The distribution was under the direction of Frederick Kilgour, who later started OCLC. At the same time, the Central Information Division of the Office of Strategic Service was working on the subject analysis of documents using IBM punched card equipment. The war itself was the impetus for many technological advances; some of these advances could now be applied to organizing and accessing the hoards of scientific and technical literature that also were an outgrowth of the war.

In 1945 Vannevar Bush opened the way for a new era in documentation and information science with his article "As We May Think." Bush developed the idea of *memex,* a "device in which an individual stores all . . . books, records and communications, and which is mechanized so that it may be consulted with exceeding speed and flexibility."[12] Using the medium of microfilm (in 1945, remember), Bush described in detail the hypertext-based scholar's workstation of today. Memex was based on the concept of *associative indexing,* similar to human thought process, where items are linked together and any item can immediately lead to the access of other related information. Bush even predicted new forms of encyclopedias where information could be coded and connected to pertinent articles. A man of vision, Bush believed that science should implement the ways in which we produce, store, and consult the record of the human race.

The 1950s and 1960s saw many and varied attempts at mechanization using the current technology. Calvin Mooers coined the phrase "information retrieval" in 1950. He and other information scientists of the day, such as Ralph Shaw and Mortimer Taube, worked on developments such as the "Rapid Selector," designed to provide subject access to microfilm by a method that used holes punched in the sides of the film. Another technique used a knitting-type needle to access subjects on punched cards. Taube was especially concerned with the linguistic problems of documentary analysis and retrieval.

In 1957, *Sputnik,* the first artificial satellite launched into space from Earth, pushed information needs to the forefront of the scientific community once again. There was increased interest in improving access to recorded knowledge in both the government (National Science Foundation, National Library of Medicine, Library of Congress, etc.) and the private sector (IBM, General Electric, Kodak, RAND Corp., etc.). The field of documentation became the field of information science with a great deal of money made available for research and development. The 1960s saw a period of tremendous technological advances in communication and information processing. The computer became established as the means of storing massive amounts of data and providing high-speed access. In 1968 the American Documentation Institute changed its name to the American Society for Information Science (ASIS) and changed its name again in 2000 to American Society for Information Science & Technology (ASIS&T). By the late 1960s, the use of machines for the retrieval of information was solidly entrenched in the information science community—a community that had developed quite separately from libraries until this point.

Library Automation

In the late 1960s, two developments changed the face of bibliographic control forever. At the Library of Congress, Henriette Avram engineered the creation of the MARC format, enabling the machine readability of bibliographic records. And Fred Kilgour started OCLC and was its first director. To the astonishment of all who knew him, he left his position as associate director of the Yale University Library to run the Ohio College Library Center. He had a vision and the ambition to carry it out. With the development of the MARC format, OCLC was able to provide cataloging information via cable and terminal to all its member libraries, which in turn were able to put their original cataloging online for the use of all other members. In 1977 another major network came into being particularly to serve research libraries—the Research Libraries Information Network (RLIN), which in 2006 was absorbed into OCLC.

CONCLUSION

We see here the coming together of the information science track and the library science track, which had previously developed separately. There seems often to be a very wide gulf between information science and library science (e.g., jokes are cracked about information science being library science for men), but both are interested in and working on the organization of information, as we see in the chapters that follow.

NOTES

All URLs accessed September 2008.

1. For more information about Callimachus's work, see Rudolf Blum, *Kallimachos: The Alexandrian Library and the Origins of Bibliography* (Madison: University of Wisconsin Press, 1991).

2. Joseph Smalley, "The French Cataloging Code of 1791: A Translation," *Library Quarterly* 61, no. 1 (January 1991): 1–14.

3. Ruth French Strout, "The Development of the Catalog and Cataloging Codes," *Library Quarterly* 26, no. 4 (October 1956): 268.

4. Dorothy May Norris, *A History of Cataloguing and Cataloguing Methods, 1100–1850* (London: Grafton, 1939), p. 206.

5. Louis Fagan, *The Life of Sir Anthony Panizzi,* 2nd ed., reprint (New York: Burt Franklin, 1970), p. 134. (Originally published 1880.)

6. Personal communication with Michael Carpenter. For further information about the drafts of Panizzi's rules, see Michael Carpenter, "The Original

73 Rules of the British Museum: A Preliminary Analysis," *Cataloging & Classification Quarterly* 35, no. 1/2 (2002): 23–36.

7. Charles Coffin Jewett, *On the Construction of Catalogues of Libraries, and Their Publication by Means of Separate, Stereotyped Titles,* 2nd ed. (Washington, D.C.: Smithsonian Institution, 1853), p. 18.

8. Elaine Svenonius, *The Intellectual Foundation of Information Organization* (Cambridge, Mass.: The MIT Press, 2001), p. 79.

9. Andrew Osborn, "The Crisis in Cataloging," in *Foundations of Cataloging: A Sourcebook,* eds. Michael Carpenter and Elaine Svenonius (Littleton, Colo.: Libraries Unlimited, 1985), pp. 90–103. Also available in *Library Quarterly* 11, no. 4 (October 1941): 393–411.

10. *A.L.A. List of Subject Headings,* 2nd ed., rev. (Boston: American Library Association Publishing Board, 1905), vi.

11. Ernst Posner, "Some Aspects of Archival Development since the French Revolution," *American Archivist* 3, no. 2 (April 1940): 159–172, esp. 167–168.

12. Vannevar Bush, "As We May Think," *Atlantic Monthly* 176 (July 1945): 101–108. Also available: http://www.theatlantic.com/doc/194507/bush.

SUGGESTED READINGS

Baker, Nicholson. "Discards." *New Yorker* 70, no. 7 (April 4, 1994): 64–86.

Berner, Richard C. "Historical Development of Archival Theory and Practices in the United States." *Midwestern Archivist* 7, no. 2 (1982): 103–117.

Burke, Frank G. "Archives: Organization and Description." In *World Encyclopedia of Library and Information Services,* 3rd ed. Chicago: American Library Association, 1993, pp. 63–68.

Bush, Vannevar. "As We May Think." *Atlantic Monthly* 176 (July 1945): 101–108. Also available: http://www.theatlantic.com/doc/194507/bush.

Carpenter, Michael. "The Original 73 Rules of the British Museum: A Preliminary Analysis." *Cataloging & Classification Quarterly* 35, no. 1/2 (2002): 23–36.

Denton, William. "FRBR and the History of Cataloging." In *Understanding FRBR: What It Is and How It Will Affect Our Retrieval Tools,* edited by Arlene G. Taylor. Westport, Conn.: Libraries Unlimited, 2007, pp. 35–57.

Dunkin, Paul S. *Cataloging U.S.A.* Chicago: American Library Association, 1969. Chapter 1: "Mr. Cutter's Catalog" and Chapter 2: "The Prophet and the Law: Codes After Cutter."

Fishbein, Meyer H. "Archives: Records Management and Records Appraisal." In *World Encyclopedia of Library and Information Services,* 3rd ed. Chicago: American Library Association, 1993, pp. 60–63.

Harris, Michael H. *History of Libraries in the Western World.* 4th ed. Metuchen, N.J.: Scarecrow Press, 1995.

Hopkins, Judith. "The 1791 French Cataloging Code and the Origins of the Card Catalog." *Libraries & Culture* 27, no. 4 (Fall 1992): 378–404.

Humbert, de Romans. *Regulations for the Operation of a Medieval Library.* St. Paul: Associates of the James Ford Bell Library, University of Minnesota, 1980.

Jackson, Sidney L. *Libraries and Librarianship in the West: A Brief History.* New York: McGraw-Hill, 1974.

Lancaster, F. W. "Whither Libraries? or Wither Libraries." *College & Research Libraries* 39, no. 5 (September 1978): 345–357; reprinted in *College & Research Libraries* 50, no. 4 (July 1989): 406–419.

Osborn, Andrew D. "The Crisis in Cataloging." In *Foundations of Cataloging: A Sourcebook,* edited by Michael Carpenter and Elaine Svenonius. Littleton, Colo.: Libraries Unlimited, 1985, pp. 90–103.

Reynolds, Dennis. *Library Automation: Issues and Applications.* New York: Bowker, 1985. Chapter 4: "History: The Public Catalog."

Russell, Beth M. "Hidden Wisdom and Unseen Treasure: Revisiting Cataloging in Medieval Libraries." *Cataloging & Classification Quarterly* 26, no. 3 (1998): 21–30.

Smalley, Joseph. "The French Cataloging Code of 1791: A Translation." *Library Quarterly* 61, no. 1 (January 1991): 1–14.

Stoll, Clifford. *Silicon Snake Oil: Second Thoughts on the Information Highway.* New York: Doubleday, 1995, pp. 197–203.

Strout, Ruth French. "The Development of the Catalog and Cataloging Codes." *Library Quarterly* 26 (October 1956): 254–275.

Taylor, Arlene G. "Cataloguing." In *World Encyclopedia of Library and Information Services.* 3rd ed. Chicago: American Library Association, 1993, pp. 177–181.

Taylor, Arlene G. *Introduction to Cataloging and Classification.* 10th ed. Westport, Conn.: Libraries Unlimited, 2006. Chapter 2: "Development of Cataloging Codes."

CHAPTER 4

METADATA

In the preceding chapters, we have referred briefly to the concept of metadata in numerous contexts. Now, we will go into greater detail about metadata and its types, forms, characteristics, and uses. We will look at some conceptual models that shape the metadata creation process and at how metadata helps to meet the objectives of information retrieval tools. We will look at some useful metadata management tools and then we will discuss metadata in the context of traditional cataloging.

Metadata is commonly described as "data about data." This definition assumes that an information resource (a book, a map, a blog, a photo on Flickr, an online video, etc.) is a form of data. A description of the attributes, characteristics, and contents of that resource would also be data; hence the definition "data about data." This definition represents the very broadest level of the concept. In a cursory survey of terminology usage, numerous definitions can be found, ranging from the aforementioned "data about data" to more complex, lengthier definitions. What they all have in common is the notion that metadata is structured information that describes the attributes of information resources for the purposes of identification, discovery, selection, use, access, and management.

FOLDOC: Free On-Line Dictionary of Computing defines metadata as "definitional data that provides information about or documentation of other data managed within an application or environment.... Meta-data may include descriptive information about the context, quality and condition, or characteristics of the data."[1] This definition implies that metadata includes not only descriptive information such as that found in traditional retrieval tools for the purpose of resource discovery, but also information necessary for the management, use, and preservation of the information resource (e.g., data about where the resource is located, how it is displayed in an electronic environment, its ownership and relationships, its quality and condition, etc.).

Even among information professionals, metadata concepts can be complex and confusing. This is due in part to the multifaceted nature of the topic and in part to the overly broad, pervasive "data about data" definition. With that as a primary description, it is no wonder that many refer to any number of interrelated concepts as "metadata." Discussions about metadata may be about any one (or any combination) of the following conceptual components:

- **Information resources**—specifically their identifying attributes;
- **Content standards**—rules or best practices used to create descriptions of resources;
- **Metadata elements**—individual units of information (fields for specific attributes) required to describe resources;
- **Metadata schemas**—sets of metadata elements created by particular communities or for particular types of resources;
- **Metadata records**—documented descriptions of (or surrogates for) information resources; and
- **Encoding formats**—syntaxes used to convert resource descriptions into machine-readable form.

While in theory we may discuss any or all of these as distinct conceptual components, in practice the divisions among them are not quite so clear. At times, the concepts are so intertwined that efforts to separate them only result in more confusion. An example to illustrate this can be found in the MARC bibliographic format. While many consider MARC to be nothing more than an encoding format, others refer to it as a metadata schema. The confusion stems from MARC's exhibiting properties of both encoding formats and metadata schemas, and on closer examination, it even acts as a content standard by dictating the values of certain data elements in the record (particularly the MARC control fields). So, it is not surprising that there are misunderstandings about metadata.

It is important to remember that the term *metadata* may mean different things to different communities. The information resources found in libraries are quite different from those found in museums, historical societies, repositories of scientific data sets, or on the Web. Differences in the nature, characteristics, and uses of the resources may require diverse approaches to the description of the items and the metadata created. Different types of information professionals (and non-professionals of all types) will therefore have different notions of what metadata entails. For example, when librarians, who are mostly familiar with the bibliographic data found in a catalog, speak of metadata, they often have a different notion of the concept than someone who designs databases or works with complex geospatial information.

THE BASICS OF METADATA

Metadata may be divided into three broad categories: *administrative metadata, structural metadata,* and *descriptive metadata.*[2] These categories are somewhat fluid, however. It is important to remember that the boundaries among them are not fixed and their definitions are not standardized or precise. Individual metadata elements may fit into more than one of these categories (e.g., a unique identifier may be considered useful as descriptive, administrative, *and* structural metadata). In addition, these three categories are not necessarily the only ways to classify metadata. Some authors have named five categories, while some Web sites have identified as many as eleven metadata types. Because there is no formal taxonomy of metadata concepts, what one author might refer to as *technical metadata,* another might call *structural metadata* or *administrative metadata.* The three categories employed in this text reflect the most prevalent usage today. Some additional categories are included as subtypes of administrative metadata including: technical, rights, preservation, and meta-metadata. Each is addressed later in this chapter. For a broad division of these types, see the table on page 92.

Another way of looking at metadata is to consider its level of complexity. Metadata can be classified into three levels. The first is the simple format, in which the metadata is really no more than data extracted from the resource itself. This is reflected by the search engine approach to organizing the Web through automated indexing techniques. The second level is the structured format. This includes formal metadata element sets that have been created for the general user. This level of metadata may have a basic template for metadata creation and does not require professional-level description. The use of HTML Meta Tags reflects this level of complexity. The third level of metadata is the rich format. Information professionals in libraries, archives, and museums tend to use this third level to manually create comprehensive, meticulously detailed descriptions. They are more complex in nature and combine metadata elements with encoding and content

Type	Definition	Typical Elements	Examples
Administrative Metadata	Supports management, decision-making, preservation, rights management, metadata management, and record keeping.	• Acquisition • Condition • Digitization information • File size • Metadata creation data • Preservation actions • Responsibility • Storage requirements • Usage information • User tracking	• PREMIS • Schema for Rights Declaration • NISO Technical Metadata for Digital Still Images • Dublin Core Administrative Components
Structural Metadata	Is the technical information that is needed to ensure that a digital information resource functions properly, displays onscreen, and can be navigated by users.	• Behavior • File sequencing • Next page • Previous page	• METS • Page-turners
Descriptive Metadata	Describes the identifying characteristics and intellectual contents of information resources for the purposes of discovery, identification, selection, and acquisition.	• Contributors • Coverage • Creator or Author • Date • Series • Subject • Title	• ISBD • AACR2/RDA and MARC • Dublin Core • GEM • HTML Meta Tags

standards. Examples of rich formats are found in bibliographic records that are created using AACR2 and MARC and in online finding aids created using DACS and EAD. In recent years, the need for such comprehensive, rich descriptions has been questioned by those interested in developing more cost-effective approaches to metadata creation, often advocating for greater use of automatically-generated metadata whenever possible. Others, however, are convinced that this will result in a reduction of the quality of the metadata produced and are opposed to making radical changes in metadata-creation processes.

Metadata can be used to describe information resources at various levels of *granularity*. It can be created for individual information resources, for discrete components of those resources, or for established collections comprising multiple resources. In other words, metadata could be used to describe:

- a single Web page, which may contain text, images, one or more multimedia files, or any combination of these;
- an individual digitized video clip embedded on that Web page, or one of the other components; or,
- the entire Web site that contains the Web page with the video clip, as well any number of other Web pages that are part of the site.

Different communities may choose to describe their information resources at different levels of granularity. Some communities might describe resources at any or all of these levels, depending on the type of resource, the community's approach to organizing information, and the needs of their users. For example, libraries typically describe printed books on the individual resources level, i.e., one book equals one metadata record. However, archival materials are traditionally described with less granularity, usually at the collection level. Digital libraries may combine or alternate between collection-level and item-level descriptions, based on the nature of a particular collection, the size of the collection, and the users of the collection. In other words, a digital library might describe individual objects (e.g., a digitized map), individual collections (e.g., a collection of 700 digitized maps), or both.

Metadata may be found in various places and in different forms. For example, the metadata for a Web page or an electronic document may be part of the document itself, embedded directly in the header as *meta tags*. Metadata found in this form may be viewed by looking at the HTML or XML encoding for the document, and it may or may not be indexed by an Internet search engine. Metadata may also be found "wrapped" into a digital object's complex packaging. The descriptive metadata may be one small section of a multi-file digital object (such as a digitized music album comprising ten tracks, cover photos, liner notes, searchable lyrics, etc.), and may only be searched and viewed within the content management system used to house the digital repository. Metadata may also be viewed as a surrogate record that is separate from the information resource that it describes. These records may be held in various retrieval tools to allow users to browse or search for the records, instead of trying to navigate through each individual resource in the collection. For electronic documents, there may or may not be direct links to the individual resources from their surrogate records, depending on the nature of the resource, the institution, and the sophistication of the retrieval tool. Because metadata is usually created in the electronic environment (e.g., in an online catalog, in an XML database, or on the Web), the term is rarely applied to records found in paper tools.

METADATA SCHEMAS

In order for it to be used to its full potential, metadata cannot consist of unstructured descriptions of resources; it must be standardized and controlled. Without formal structure or rules, metadata description is no better than keyword access. The basic units of metadata are the element and the schema. *Metadata elements* are the individual categories or fields that hold the individual pieces of a resource description. Typical metadata elements include title, creator, unique identifier, creation date, subject, and the like. *Metadata schemas* are sets of elements designed to meet the needs of particular communities. While some schemas are general in nature, most are created for specific types of information resources or for specific purposes. Specific schemas have been designed to manage government, geospatial, visual, educational, and other types of resources. As a result, schemas can vary greatly. They differ in the number of data elements, in the use of mandatory and repeatable elements, in encoding requirements, and in the use of controlled vocabularies, among other things. While most schemas focus on descriptive elements to support resource discovery and identification, some contain elements to support administrative and structural purposes. Much to the chagrin of students and information professionals alike, it is simply not possible to create a perfect, one-size-fits-all metadata schema that will suffice for the various needs of different communities. Diversity in metadata is both desirable and unavoidable. The goal is to find ways for these different communities to share their useful, meaningful metadata.

According to Sherry Vellucci, there are three characteristics found in all metadata schemas. They are: (1) semantics, (2) syntax, and (3) structure.[3] *Semantics* refers to meaning, specifically the meaning of the various metadata elements. Semantics help metadata creators understand, for example, what the element *coverage* or the element *date* means in a given schema. *Syntax* refers to the encoding of the metadata. This may be the MARC format for bibliographic records or an XML schema or XML DTD for other types of metadata. Stuart Weibel writes that syntax allows us to "take a set of metadata assertions and pack them so that one machine can send them to another, where they can be unpacked and parsed.... Syntax is arranging the bits reliably so they travel comfortably between computers."[4] *Structure* refers to the data model used to shape the way that metadata statements are expressed. Weibel states, "structure is the specification of the details necessary to layout [sic] and declare metadata assertions so they can be embedded unambiguously in a syntax. A data model is the specification of this structure."[5] The structure of metadata should not be confused with *structural metadata* (described later in this chapter), which refers to the organization of the resource being described. Structure, in this context, is referring to the expression of metadata statements, e.g., whether the metadata conforms to the Resource Description Framework (see below).

The semantics of a metadata schema do not necessarily dictate the content placed into the elements. This is the province of content standards, application profiles, or metadata models (metadata structure). These are used to dictate things such as how dates will be formatted within metadata elements or how a personal name will be entered. For example, an application profile might state that all dates are to be recorded using the YYYY-MM-DD format or a content standard may require names to be entered with family name first, followed by a comma, and then by the remainder of the name. *Controlled vocabularies* also may be used to standardize the contents of elements such as *subject* or *resource type*. Controlled vocabularies are lists of words in which certain terms are chosen as preferred, and their synonyms act as pointers to the preferred terms, thereby limiting the range of values that can be entered into a particular metadata element. If tools such as content rules and controlled vocabularies did not exist, information retrieval would be less effective.

METADATA CHARACTERISTICS

In order for metadata to be as useful as possible in meeting the diverse needs of information users, some special metadata characteristics require attention. They are *interoperability, flexibility,* and *extensibility.*[6] *Interoperability* refers to the ability of various systems to interact with each other no matter the hardware or software being used. Achieving interoperability helps to minimize the loss of information due to technological differences. Interoperability can be divided into semantic, syntactic, and structural interoperability. *Semantic interoperability* refers to ways in which diverse metadata schemas express meaning in their elements. In other words, does the element *author* in one schema mean the same thing as *creator* in another schema? *Syntactic interoperability* refers to the ability to exchange and use metadata from other systems. Syntactic interoperability requires a common language or encoding format (e.g., can a MARC record be used and understood in an XML environment?).

Structural interoperability refers to how metadata statements are expressed. Is the metadata understandable by other systems? Are both systems using an entity-relationship model or are the basic models different? Without interoperability on all three levels, metadata cannot be shared effortlessly, efficiently, or profitably.

Flexibility refers to the ability of "metadata creators to include as much or as little detail as desired in the metadata record, with or without adherence to any specific cataloging rules or authoritative lists."[7] Some information professionals seek to create metadata schemas with great flexibility that leave decisions about how much detail to include in the description to the individual institution or community through the use of content standards or application profiles (described later in this chapter). *Extensibility* refers to the ability to use additional metadata elements and *qualifiers* (element refinements) to meet the specific needs of various communities. Qualifiers help to refine or sharpen the focus of an element or might identify a specific controlled vocabulary to be used in that element. An example of extensibility can be found in the education community. In order to meet their specific needs, a standard element set was extended by adding *instructional method* and *audience* as elements (described further later in this chapter). There is a note of caution about extensibility, however. As extensibility increases, interoperability can decrease, because as the schema moves further away from its original design (through additional elements or qualifiers), it becomes less understandable to other systems. This trade-off must be considered carefully before being implemented.

CATEGORIES OF METADATA

As mentioned above, there are three broad categories of metadata: administrative, structural, and descriptive. Until recently, most discussions of metadata focused solely on descriptive metadata. It is only within recent years that administrative and structural metadata needs have been recognized, or at least acknowledged, as metadata issues.

Administrative Metadata

If an institution creates a digital resource, where is it held? How is it stored? What type of object is it? Who decides what it is called and when it needs to be updated? How are these processes accomplished? How did the object come into the collection? Was it born digital? Was it digitized in-house, by a vendor, or by another organization? Who can access it and for what purposes? These questions can be answered with administrative metadata.

Administrative metadata is created for the purposes of management, decision making, and record keeping. It provides information about the technical, preservation, and storage requirements of digital objects. Administrative metadata assists with the monitoring, accessing, reproducing, digitizing, and backing up of digital resources. It includes information such as:

- **hardware and software requirements** (e.g., creation software; creation hardware; operating system)
- **acquisition information** (e.g., when the resource was created, modified, and/or acquired; administrative information about the analog source from which a digital object was derived)
- **ownership, rights, permissions, legal access, and reproduction information** (e.g., what rights the organization has to use the material; who may use the material and for what purposes; what reproductions exist and their current status)
- **use information** (e.g., use and user tracking; content reuse; exhibition records; what materials are used, when, in what form, and by whom)
- **file characteristics** (e.g., file size, bit-length, format, presentation rules, sequencing information, running time, file compression information)
- **version control** (e.g., what versions exist and the status of the resource being described; alternate digital formats, such as HTML or PDF for text, and GIF or JPG for images)
- **digitization information** (e.g., compression ratios; scaling ratios; date of scan; resolution)
- **authentication and security data** (e.g., inhibitor, encryption, and password information)
- **preservation information** (e.g. integrity information; physical condition; preservation actions; refreshing data; migrating data; conservation or repair of physical artifacts)

Some administrative metadata elements, particularly technical metadata such as file sizes and compression rates, may be generated automatically when the object is created or digitized; other elements, however, need to be recorded manually.

Unlike most descriptive metadata, administrative metadata is not standardized. As of this time, there is no single administrative metadata schema that has been adopted widely among institutions. The metadata captured for management purposes, such as who makes decisions and their contact information, tends to be repository-specific and is stored in a variety of forms, in a variety of places. While there is no ubiquitous general administrative metadata schema, some schemas have been created to address specific sub-types of administrative metadata, e.g., Preservation Metadata: Implementation Strategies (PREMIS)[8] and NISO Metadata for Images in XML Schema (MIX)[9] for technical metadata for digital images.

As stated above, administrative metadata may be described as having several subtypes. These include: technical metadata, preservation metadata, rights and access metadata, and meta-metadata. Each of these is discussed below.

Technical Metadata

If an information institution receives a digital resource, would they know what it is? What it can do? Could they make it work? Without technical metadata, they might not be able to make use of the object.

According to PREMIS, "Technical metadata describes the physical rather than intellectual characteristics of digital objects."[10] Basic technical information is needed in order to understand the nature of the information resource, the software and hardware environments in which it was created, and what is needed to make the resource accessible to users. Technical metadata describes the characteristics, origins, and life cycles of digital documents, and is key to the preservation of the resource for future use. Because technical metadata is format specific, different schemas are used for different resource types (e.g., a video on YouTube requires different technical metadata than a digital image in Flickr because they work in different ways and have different characteristics). While some of the metadata elements may overlap, technical metadata is not the same thing as structural metadata. The biggest difference between the two is that structural metadata is primarily machine-readable and machine-processable, while technical information is for humans to read and understand.

Preservation Metadata

Technology changes rapidly. Data files from just a few years ago—our WordStar documents and VisiCalc spreadsheets—are now old and no longer functional. They have been lost because there were no plans to keep the data usable and no real understanding of how quickly technology changes. With this in mind, we must consider how much more we are willing to lose.

Will the Word documents and Access databases we create today be usable in 200 years? What about 20 years? Or 10 years, even? If we are going to save this information from oblivion, we must consider a number of questions. Should we preserve the look and feel of the software, or are we concerned with content only? One hundred years from now, will users still know what a *.jpg* or a *.tiff* is? Without documentation, will they be decipherable? When we preserve an information resource, how do we determine which version of that resource needs to be preserved? In other words, how do we determine the best version? These questions are preservation metadata concerns.

In recent years, the Library of Congress, OCLC, the Research Libraries Group (RLG), the National Library of Australia, and others have launched preservation metadata initiatives. Preservation metadata is the information needed to ensure the long-term storage and usability of digital content. It may include information about reformatting, migration, emulation, conservation, file integrity, and provenance. Typical preservation metadata elements might include: structural type, file description, size, properties, software and hardware environments, source information, object history, transformation history, context information, digital signatures, and checksums. In 2008, the second version of the *PREMIS Data Dictionary for Preservation Metadata*[11] was published; it is the standard used in the United States for preservation metadata.

Rights and Access Metadata

Who can access an information resource and for what purposes? Who can make copies? Who owns the material? Are there different categories of information objects in the collection? Are there different categories of users who can access different combinations of those objects?

Rights and access metadata is information about who has access to information resources, who may use them, and for what purposes. It deals with issues of creators' intellectual property rights and the legal agreements allowing users to access this information. In rights and access metadata, information about parties, contents, and transactions can be found. Typical rights metadata elements include: access categories, identifiers, copyright statements, terms and conditions, periods of availability, usage information, and payment options. An example of a rights metadata schema is the Open Digital Rights Language schema.[12]

Meta-Metadata

Not only can metadata track administrative data about the information resource, it can also track administrative information about the metadata. So, if metadata is "data about data," then the "data about the data about data" is *meta-metadata.* Meta-metadata is important for ensuring the authenticity of the metadata and tracking internal processes. While some meta-metadata resides within some types of descriptive records (e.g., the record creation information and modification dates in a MARC record), other meta-metadata must be tracked in other ways. Few schemas for meta-metadata exist, but in 2003 the Dublin Core Metadata Initiative's Administrative Metadata Working Group approved the "AC-Administrative Components,"[13] a metadata element set to describe and manage metadata. This schema created by Hytte Hansen and Leif Andresen is loosely based on an administrative metadata element set proposed four years earlier. AC focuses on elements that describe attributes of the metadata record, changes and updates, and information for the interchange of records. Its elements include: handling, action, database, contact, affiliation, and transmitter, among others.

Structural Metadata

If an information organization receives a digital object, one that it had no part in creating, could the object be opened? If the digital object were a complex, multi-file entity, would the pieces fit together? Would patrons be able to use the resource? Without structural metadata—probably not.

Structural metadata refers to the "makeup" or structure of the digital object, dataset, or other information resource that is being described. It is the data needed to ensure that a digital resource functions properly and can be used and navigated by the patron. It refers to how individual related files are bound together to create a working digital object, how the object can be displayed on a variety of systems, and how it can be stored and disseminated. It deals with what the resource is, what it does, and how it works. Structural metadata captures the following kinds of information: document types and their structures; file types; object behaviors or functionality; associated search protocols; hierarchical relationships; sequencing and grouping of files; parent objects; paging information; associated files; and so forth.

Structural metadata can be included in the headers or bodies of some types of electronic documents, but in most metadata schemas, structural elements are not well represented. For most schemas—which focus on descriptive metadata—it is simply unnecessary or inappropriate for the type of resource being represented. For example, with a single digital image, extensive structural metadata is not needed, but once that image becomes part of a complex multimedia object that must operate as a single resource, structural metadata becomes necessary. Sometimes, structural metadata is referred to as *display metadata* and sometimes it is mistakenly conflated with *technical metadata,* which was discussed in the *administrative metadata* section above.

Implementations of Structural Metadata

The use of structural metadata is not new, but the terminology used to describe it is. An early, successful implementation of structural metadata is the page-turner model. A page-turner is used for materials with contents that must be ordered in a definite sequence. It provides structure for the contents to be displayed and for the user to navigate through the information resource as one normally pages through a book. The page-turner may allow the user to navigate through the resource on more than one level, that is, at a chapter level and at a page level. The page-turner uses structural metadata to bind together individual images of pages to form a complete object (again, this may be on the level of the e-book, a volume of a set, or a chapter). It may also use the structural metadata to associate a text file with each of those individual pages, so that the intellectual contents of the page image are searchable. Structural metadata can also associate these images with thumbnail images of the pages, images of greater or lesser resolution, HTML- or XML-formatted pages associated with the Web interface (though this may be done on-the-fly), a separate image file (or files) for an illustration on the page, or some other file or link. Some other early examples of structural metadata schemas include the Electronic Binding DTD (Ebind)[14] and the Making of America II project (MOA2),[15] both of which have since been replaced by METS.

METS (Metadata Encoding & Transmission Standard). The best example of structural metadata is found in the Metadata Encoding & Transmission Standard (METS), developed as an initiative of the Digital Library Federation and maintained by the Library of Congress Network Development and MARC Standards Office.[16] METS is an XML schema for encoding structurally complex digital objects into a single document that includes descriptive, administrative, and structural metadata. It provides metadata aimed at managing, preserving, displaying, and exchanging digital objects in a digital library environment. While descriptive and administrative metadata are included in METS documents, the primary focus of the schema is on the structure of digital objects. It is extensible and modular in its approach.

A METS document comprises seven components.

- **the METS header**
- **descriptive metadata**
- **administrative metadata**

- **the file section**
- **the structural map**
- **structural links**
- **behavior metadata**

The METS header contains meta-metadata such as the creator of the METS document and the date of creation. For the descriptive and administrative metadata sections, METS does not define the elements to be included. It allows the creators to choose from a number of extension schemas. For example, the repository might choose to use Dublin Core metadata or traditional cataloging data expressed in XML for the descriptive metadata section. The administrative metadata section can be divided into four subgroupings: technical, intellectual property rights, source, and provenance metadata. For these areas, PREMIS and MIX have been endorsed as extension schemas that may be used to complete the section. Both administrative and descriptive metadata can be held internally or externally, i.e., the metadata can be included inside a METS document or the METS object can point to a separate metadata record outside of the METS document. Both approaches can be used within the same METS document. The file section lists all of the files used to create the digital object. Files may be divided into hierarchically subordinate subgroups. For example, in a digital object that consists of images accompanied by text, there might be file groups for the thumbnail images, for the master images, for TEI encoded text (see Chapters 5 and 7), and for PDF versions. The structural map specifies the ways in which all of the files fit together to create the digital object. The map is hierarchically structured and allows the user to navigate from one part of the digital object to another, e.g., from track one to track five on a digitized sound recording. The structural links section keeps a record of the hyperlinks and lateral relationships among individual files in the structural map. The behavior section describes how the object is to function or perform. As of 2008, METS 1.7 is the current version, but improvements will continue to be made as more implementations occur worldwide. Examples of METS documents can be seen at the Library of Congress's METS Web site.[17]

Descriptive Metadata

Descriptive metadata is a record of the identifying characteristics of an information resource and the analysis of its contents for the purposes of discovery, identification, selection, and acquisition. It includes the following kinds of information:

- **identifying data** (e.g., title; author; date of creation or publication; information regarding the analog source from which a digital object is derived)
- **intellectual organization data** (e.g., information placed under authority control; headings to provide collocation with related works, names, subjects, etc.; identification of relationships among entities)
- **intellectual access data** (e.g., subject headings; classification; categorization)

Chapters 7–11 cover various aspects of descriptive metadata in more depth.

METADATA MODELS

In recent years, as more and more metadata schemas have been developed, there has been a growing interest in developing shared visions of metadata and information resources and in maximizing interoperability. In order to achieve these goals, several metadata models have been designed. *FOLDOC* states that a *model* is "a description of observed behaviour, simplified by ignoring certain details. Models allow complex systems to be understood."[18] Merriam-Webster defines it as, "a description or analogy used to help visualize something... that cannot be directly observed."[19] Models may be used for several reasons, including specifying a broad conceptual framework for the entire bibliographic universe or prescribing specific structural requirements for metadata descriptions. In this section, we discuss three metadata models: the Functional Requirements for Bibliographic Records (FRBR), the Resource Description Framework (RDF), and the Dublin Core Abstract Model (DCAM).

Functional Requirements for Bibliographic Records (FRBR)

In 1998, the International Federation of Library Associations and Institutions (IFLA) published *Functional Requirements for Bibliographic Records.*[20] This report and the conceptual model it details are often referred to as FRBR, which is pronounced *Ferber* by some and as the initials *F.R.B.R.* by others. The report is an attempt to apply an entity-relationship model[21] to the various components of the bibliographic universe. It is important to point out that FRBR is a conceptual model; it is not a system design, a record structure, a content standard, or an encoding format. It is a model that enumerates the entities found in the bibliographic universe, and gathers those entities into groups based on the functions or roles of those entities. FRBR identifies the attributes or characteristics associated with each entity, as well as relationships that exist among and within the entity groups. In addition, the conceptual model identifies several tasks that users perform while using information retrieval tools and bibliographic data. These user tasks inform the entire model, helping readers to remember the reasons why the bibliographic universe is organized. The model maps each entity's attributes and its relationships to the user tasks. Finally, FRBR makes recommendations regarding a minimal set of required elements to be included in bibliographic records. Ultimately, the FRBR model identifies four user tasks, three groups of entities, and myriad attributes and relationships among the entities. Some of these are addressed in the sections that follow. In addition, another IFLA report, *The Functional Requirements for Authority Data* (FRAD),[22] is mentioned. FRAD, like FRBR, is an attempt at modeling the bibliographic universe; but instead of focusing on bibliographic records, FRAD is concerned with authority data and the concepts related to authority control. It is an extension of the FRBR model, adding more entities, attributes, relationships, and user tasks. For more information about authority control and FRAD, please see Chapter 8.

User Tasks

One of the primary purposes of creating metadata is to help users find the information resources they might need. It is advantageous then, when creating metadata, to look at the objectives that users may have when approaching an information retrieval system, so that their goals and needs may be met. The following is FRBR's list of user tasks. Upon examination, it becomes clear that these tasks are related closely to both Cutter's "objects" of the catalog[23] and the Paris Principles mentioned in Chapter 2.[24] FRBR states that users approach an information system in order to accomplish the following activities:[25]

- **To Find**—Users approach retrieval systems to search for information resources that meet certain criteria. They may wish to find the articles published by *Cataloging & Classification Quarterly* in 2008, books about Ranganathan, or DVDs containing Sondheim musicals held by the Boston Public Library.

- **To Identify**—The metadata records found in retrieval tools help users to recognize the appropriate entities and information resources. This may involve distinguishing among similar entities or identifying an item that corresponds to a citation in a bibliography. For example, a user may wish to find the works by Michael Gorman on cataloging. The user will depend upon the system to (1) collocate all of the works by each author named Michael Gorman, and (2) distinguish the Michael Gorman who wrote about cataloging from the Michael Gorman who wrote about religious views on abortion.
- **To Select**—Systems help users to choose information resources that are appropriate for their needs. This may involve attributes such as content, format, language, edition, or system requirements. For example, a user may need a copy of *Hamlet* in Catalan, but not one in Spanish, Basque, or English.
- **To Obtain**—Users approach systems in order to acquire or gain access to information resources. Users depend on the system to provide call numbers, the names of journals containing articles sought, or URLs for direct access to resources.

In addition to these four objectives, Elaine Svenonius adds a fifth:

- **To Navigate**—This objective takes into account the information-seeking behavior of some users who may not be able to articulate completely their information needs, but will instead use the structure of the information system to find the information they are seeking.[26]

The navigation task depends heavily on the information system being able to identify and to take advantage of the relationships that exist among information resources; this can only happen if those relationships are represented in metadata descriptions.

Reflecting its orientation toward authority data, FRAD includes another type of user in its model: *metadata creators.* This addition supplements "general" users of bibliographic data (e.g., patrons in a library, information seekers of all kinds, etc.). Consequently, the user tasks identified in FRAD are somewhat different. The first two tasks are identical to those in FRBR (i.e., *to find* and *to identify*). The second two, however, are quite different. These are *to contextualize* and *to justify,* tasks performed by those creating authority data. According to FRAD, contextualization is to "place a person, corporate body, work, etc. in context; clarify the relationship between two or more persons, corporate bodies, works, etc.; or clarify the relationship between a person, corporate body, etc. and a name by which that person, corporate body, etc. is known."[27] Justification refers to documenting the process of placing names and titles under authority control.

In order to meet the needs of all users, patrons as well information professionals, metadata should be created with these user tasks in mind. Additionally, the metadata created should include descriptions of various entities of interest in the bibliographic universe, their attributes, and the relationships among those entities.

FRBR Entities and Attributes

In the FRBR model, three groups of entities are identified. The first group comprises the "products of intellectual or artistic endeavours"[28] that are named and described in bibliographic records. These products are *works, expressions, manifestations,* and *items.* These four entities are related hierarchically. The first entity, *work,* is the top, most general level of the hierarchy. It is an abstract concept that exists primarily in the mind of the creator; there is no single physical object associated with it. It can be described as the artistic or intellectual vision of the creator. The second level, *expression,* is a realization of a work in the form of text, numbers, sounds, and so on. *Expression* is also an abstract, content-related entity with no particular physical carrier. In order for a work and its expression to take material form, it must be embodied in the third entity, *manifestation.* The fourth level, *item,* represents a single exemplar or instance of a manifestation. The item is the individual copy of an information resource.

Each of the Group 1 entities has its own set of attributes associated with it. Attributes help users to find, identify, select, obtain, and navigate among information resources in retrieval tools. Some examples of attributes are found in the following table.

Group 1 Entity	Typical Attributes
Work	Title of Work, Form of Work, Audience, etc.
Expression	Title of Expression, Language of Expression, Extent, etc.
Manifestation	Title of Manifestation, Statement of Responsibility, Form of Carrier, Publisher, Date, etc.
Item	Item Identifier, Provenance of Item, Access Restrictions, etc.

Although some of the attributes may seem repetitive, the values of those attributes may not be identical among the four levels of the Group 1 entities. For example, the title of a work, the title of an expression, and the title of a manifestation may be the same or they may be different based on the language of the expression, title changes over time, the inclusion or exclusion of introductory words, or other variations.

The second group contains entities responsible for the creation, production, dissemination, and ownership of Group 1 entities. In this group, FRBR includes *persons* and *corporate bodies;* a third entity, *families,* has been added by FRAD after consulting with the archival community. The FRBR and FRAD models establish that persons, corporate bodies, and families create works, realize expressions, produce manifestations, and own or provide access to items. This framework reflects the entity-relationship model very well. The concept of *creator,* an element typically found in most metadata schemas, is *not* described as an attribute of a work, but instead is recognized as a separate entity that is connected to a work (or expression, manifestation, or item) through a specific kind of relationship (i.e., a *created by* relationship).

Group 3 entities are those which can be the subjects of works. These include: *concepts, objects, places,* and *events.* Concepts are abstract ideas, objects are physical objects, places are types of locations, and events are types of occurrences. Group 3 also includes all of the other entities in the FRBR model, because works can be about other works, expressions, manifestations, and even individual items. Works also can be about persons, families, and corporate bodies.

In addition to the three groups of entities identified in FRBR, FRAD has identified five additional entities specifically related to authority data. These entities include *name, identifier, controlled access point, rules,* and *agency.* Like the FRBR entities, the FRAD entities have attributes and relationships associated with each of them. More information about FRAD entities can be found in Chapter 8.

FRBR Relationships

The final major component in an entity-relationship model is the existence of relationships among the various entities. FRBR and FRAD identify some widely applicable, general relationships among the entities, as well as some specific types of bibliographic relationships that can exist. General relationships include:

- the hierarchical relationships among works, expressions, manifestations, and items, i.e., a work *is realized though* one or more expressions, which *are embodied in* one or more manifestations, which *are exemplified in* items

- the relationships among Group 1 entities and persons, corporate bodies, or families, i.e., *created by, realized by, produced by,* and *owned by* relationships
- the subject relationships among Group 1 entities and those in groups 1, 2, and 3.

The more specific types of bibliographic relationships represented in FRBR have been influenced greatly by Barbara Tillett's taxonomy of bibliographic relationships[29] and Richard Smiraglia's research focusing on derivative bibliographic relationships (see discussion in Chapter 8).[30] The FRBR relationships include:

- **Work-to-work relationships**—These are relationships that exist between two separate works. This includes successor, supplement, complement, summarization, adaptation, transformation, and imitation relationships. Examples include sequels, concordances, indexes, librettos, digests, paraphrases, dramatizations, and parodies.
- **Whole/part relationships**—These are relationships that have some sort of component aspect. These can be independent or dependent whole/part relationships. Examples include the relationship between a chapter and the whole work, between a book and the series of which it is a part, or between one article and the journal in which it is published.
- **Expression-to-expression relationships**—These can reflect the relationship between two expressions of the same work or between expressions of different works. The former includes abridgements, revisions (e.g. revised editions), translations, and arrangements; the latter group is identical to the work-to-work relationships listed above.
- **Manifestation-to-manifestation relationships**—These include reproduction relationships (e.g., reprints, microfilms, facsimiles) and alternate relationships (e.g., simultaneously published editions, multiple formats).

- **Item-to-item relationships**—These include reproduction and reconfiguration relationships (e.g., binding changes, extracts).

In addition to those enumerated in the FRBR model, FRAD identifies several additional types of relationships that are applicable to authority data.

The FRBR and FRAD models have played pivotal roles in IFLA's development of the latest set of international cataloging principles.[31] These principles and the FRBR and FRAD models have also been influential in the development of *RDA: Resource Description and Access,* the replacement for the *Anglo-American Cataloguing Rules, Second Edition, 2002 revision.* RDA is expected to be published in 2009.[32]

Resource Description Framework (RDF)

Because no one-size-fits-all metadata schema exists, the metadata community quickly came to realize that multiple descriptions for a single information resource might be created. The Warwick Framework,[33] developed at the Second Dublin Core Metadata Workshop in 1996, is a model for pulling together distinct packages of metadata that are related to the same information resource into a single container. Referred to as *container architecture,* this conceptual model allows different communities to create, maintain, and share their metadata. The Warwick Framework still guides the development of the Dublin Core, but its greatest impact was as an evolutionary step in the development of the first iteration of the Resource Description Framework (RDF), a metadata specification developed by the World Wide Web Consortium (W3C) in 1999, whose basic metadata model helps to promote structural interoperability.[34]

According to the W3C:

> The Resource Description Framework (RDF) is a language for representing information about resources in the World Wide Web. It is particularly intended for representing metadata about Web resources, such as the title, author, and modification date....RDF can also be used to represent information about things that can be identified on the Web, even when they cannot be directly retrieved on the Web...RDF is intended for situations in which this information needs to be processed by applications, rather than being only displayed to people. RDF provides

> a common framework for expressing this information so it can be exchanged between applications without loss of meaning.[35]

RDF-structured metadata enables the exchange and reuse of metadata in ways that are semantically unambiguous; in other words, RDF allows machines to "understand" what is being "said" by the metadata. This is accomplished by communicating metadata statements in the form of *triples*. RDF statements (i.e., triples) contain three components: a subject, a predicate, and an object. In the model, a subject is any resource that can be uniquely identified by a Uniform Resource Identifier (URI). Resources have properties, and properties have values. The property is the predicate in the RDF statement and the object is its value, which can be a string of characters or a URI for another resource.[36] If the value is another resource, then that resource also can have properties, which can have values, some of which could be yet other resources. There is no limit to the number of connections that may exist among various entities. Figure 4.1 is a simple illustration of the connections

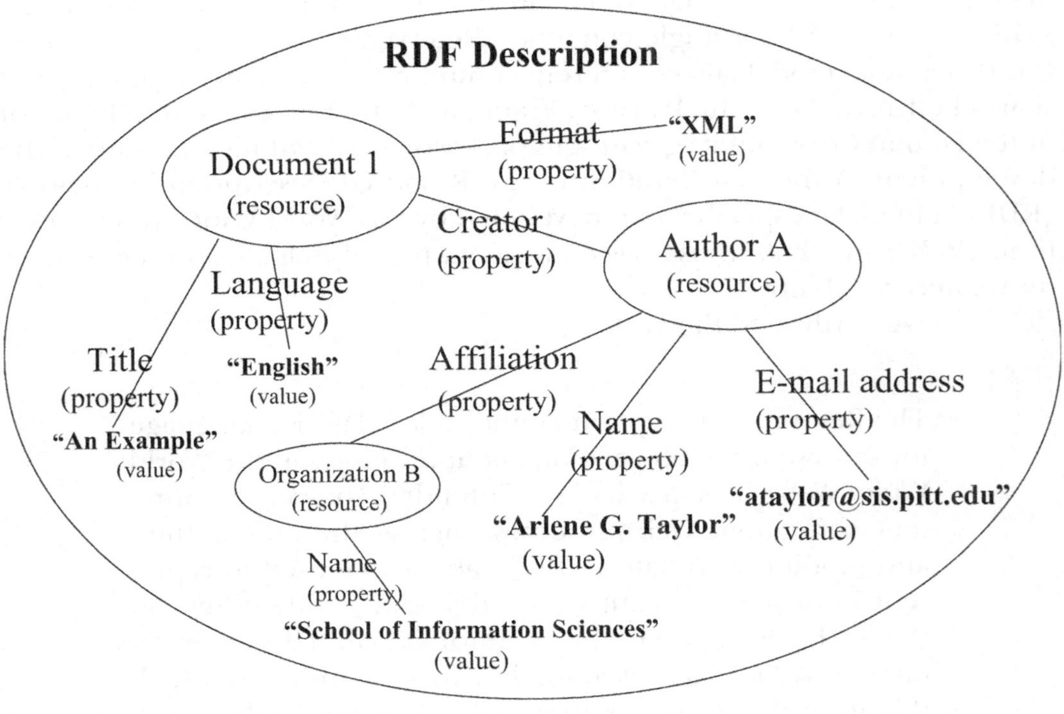

Figure 4.1. Basic conceptual RDF model.

that can exist using the RDF model. In this illustration, a resource, called *Document 1,* has properties named *Format, Creator, Language,* and *Title.* Each property has a value. For example, the value of the *Creator* property is another resource called *Author A.* This resource has properties named *Affiliation, Name,* and *E-mail.* The value of the *Affiliation* property is yet another resource called *Organization B.*

In order for this model to be useful, however, it must be expressed concretely. RDF may be encoded in XML[37] or in some other markup language such as Notation3[38] or the Terse RDF Triple Language (Turtle).[39] Using XML, an RDF description identifies the fact that it is using RDF, identifies the namespaces to be used for the property names, and provides the description. For example, the *Arlene G. Taylor Home Page* is a resource on the Web. It has a creator and that creator's name is Arlene G. Taylor. These facts can be expressed in a simple RDF statement or they can be expressed graphically as seen in Figure 4.2.

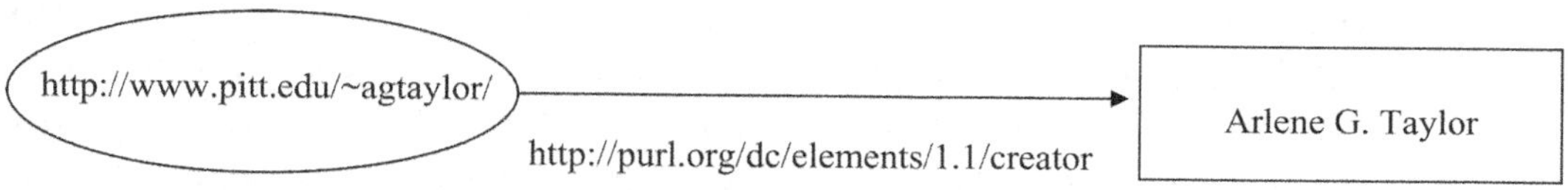

Figure 4.2. A simple RDF statement using Dublin Core.

The subject of the metadata statement is represented by the unique identifier for the Web page, the predicate is a creation relationship (expressed in any number of ways; here it is using Dublin Core), and the object is the name of that creator. Most RDF descriptions, however, are more complex than that. The statement in Figure 4.2 contains only one subject, predicate, and object. This does not reflect the true nature of metadata description. Using RDF triplets, a more complete description of this resource, could look like this:

SUBJECT	PREDICATE	OBJECT
http://www.pitt.edu/~agtaylor/	http://purl.org/dc/elements/1.1/creator	"Arlene G. Taylor"
http://www.pitt.edu/~agtaylor/	http://purl.org/dc/elements/1.1/title	"Arlene G. Taylor Home Page"
http://www.pitt.edu/~agtaylor/	http://purl.org/dc/elements/1.1/publisher	"University of Pittsburgh"
http://www.pitt.edu/~agtaylor/	http://purl.org/dc/elements/1.1/format	"text/html"

Or, it could be encoded in XML as:

```
<?xml version= "1.0"?>
<rdf:RDF
  xmlns:rdf = "http://www.w3.org/1999/02/22-rdf-syntax-ns#"
  xmlns:dc = "http://purl.org/dc/elements/1.1/">
<rdf:Description rdf:about = "http://www.pitt.edu/~agtaylor/">
  <dc:creator> Arlene G. Taylor </dc:creator>
  <dc:title> Arlene G. Taylor Home Page </dc:title>
  <dc:publisher> University of Pittsburgh </dc:publisher>
  <dc:format> text/html </dc:format>
  <dc:language> en </dc:language>
</rdf:Description>
</rdf:RDF>
```

In this XML-encoded example, the first two lines say that this description is in XML, using RDF as the metadata structure. The next two lines identify the fact that the tags come from both the RDF and Dublin Core namespaces with the URIs for those namespaces. The remainder is the description of the resource followed by the required closing tags. This description also can be translated into a full graphic representation as seen in Figure 4.3.

RDF is considered one of the major building blocks in the vision for the Semantic Web, an idea first articulated in 1997 by Tim Berners-Lee, the man who is credited with inventing the World Wide Web.[40] The Semantic Web is intended to provide more structure to the Web that will allow computers to deal with its content in meaningful ways. It is intended that information will be defined in such a way that its meaning or semantics can be discernible, shared, and processed by automated tools as well as by people. Berners-Lee and colleagues give an example of a brother and sister needing to coordinate their schedules with a certain kind of physical therapy specialist who is also covered by a particular insurance plan so that one of them can take their mother to this specialist. The Semantic Web allows their automated agents to work together to find the right place at a time one of them has available, all within a few minutes.[41] Berners-Lee and colleagues state, "For the semantic web to function, computers must have access to structured collections of information and sets of inference rules that they can use to conduct automated reasoning."[42] The RDF metadata model provides this structure. Several groups within W3C are working toward realization of the Semantic Web, including several working on RDF-related specifications.[43]

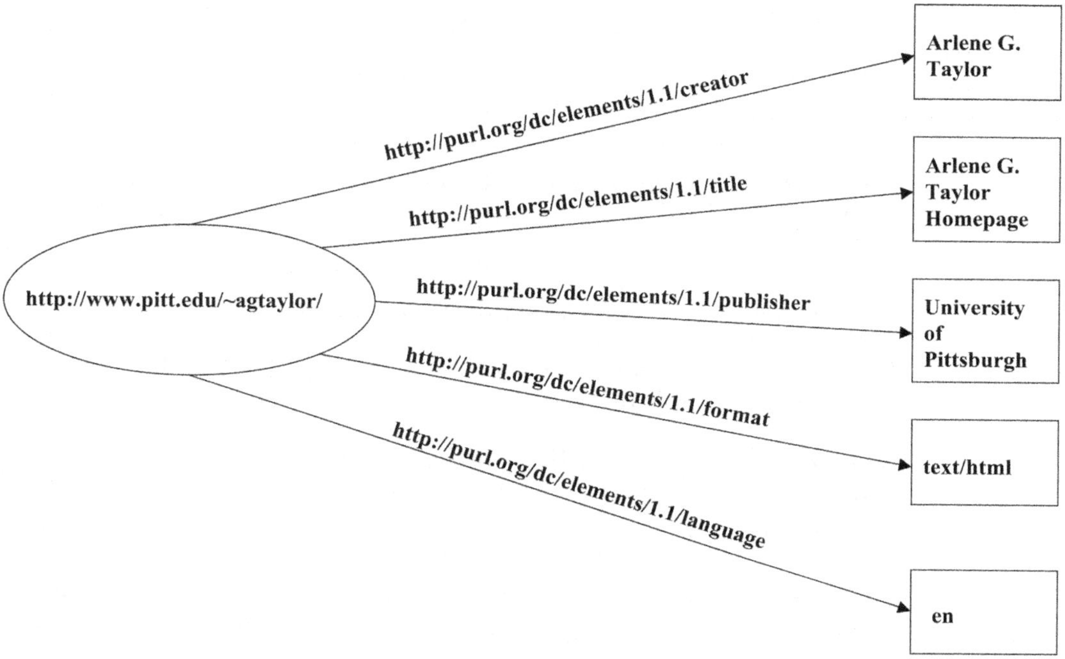

Figure 4.3. Graphical representation of the RDF description.

DCMI Abstract Model (DCAM)

The Resource Description Framework has influenced the DCMI Abstract Model, published in 2007 by the Dublin Core Metadata Initiative (DCMI). The primary purpose of the model is to "specify the components and constructs used in Dublin Core metadata."[44] By specifying these, it will allow for better communications about metadata and more interoperability across information environments. It describes how the syntax-independent model's entities are related in order to create complete metadata structures. The abstract model comprises three related information models: a resource model, a description set model, and a vocabulary model. The three information models contain entities of various types. The DCMI Resource Model includes entities such as *resources, properties,* and *values.* The resource model is described entirely by a few simple statements about relationships between these entities.

The abstract model of the resources described by *descriptions* is as follows:

- Each *described resource* is described using one or more *property-value pairs.*

- Each *property-value pair* is made up of one *property* and one *value.*
- Each *value* is a *resource*—the physical, digital or conceptual entity or *literal* that is associated with a *property* when a *property-value pair* is used to describe a *resource.* Therefore, each *value* is either a *literal value* or a *non-literal value:*
  - A *literal value* is a *value* which is a *literal.*
  - A *non-literal value* is a *value* which is a physical, digital or conceptual entity.
- A *literal* is an entity which uses a Unicode string as a lexical form, together with an optional language tag or datatype, to denote a resource.[45]

The DCMI Resource Model states that Dublin Core metadata consists of statements describing resources and each description refers to properties and values (a second resource). This is similar to the resource-property-value model found in RDF. The DCMI Description Set Model includes entities such as *description sets, descriptions, statements, properties,* and *values,* and the DCMI Vocabulary Model includes *vocabularies, terms, properties, classes, vocabulary encoding schemes,* and *syntax encoding schemes.* These allow for metadata descriptions to be made up of multiple descriptive statements for the same resource. Terms used to articulate the values of a property can be prescribed from certain controlled vocabularies. For more about the DCMI Abstract Model, consult the latest version on the Dublin Core Web site.

METADATA MANAGEMENT TOOLS

As metadata applications have become more common and more schemas flourish, tools and systems have been developed to help deal with this proliferation of information. Some of these tools and systems are application profiles, metadata registries, crosswalks, harvesting projects, and templates for metadata creation.

Application Profiles

As stated earlier, there is no one-size-fits-all metadata schema. Different schemas have been developed for different purposes, different communities, and different materials. All of these schemas have strengths and weaknesses. When looking for a metadata schema to meet the needs of a particular institution, a community, or a particular project, it is sometimes discovered that no one schema satisfies all of the metadata requirements, but that parts of different, existing schemas would work well *if* they could be combined in a new way. A mechanism to allow metadata creators to use various elements from different schemas is the *application profile.*

An application profile, according to Priscilla Caplan, is a formally developed specification that limits and clarifies the use of a metadata schema for a particular user community. "Whether informal guidelines or formal profiles, additional rulesets are generally needed to supplement metadata schemes as published."[46] Application profiles, therefore, are documents that describe a community's recommended best practices for metadata creation. They contain metadata elements drawn from one or more namespaces. A *namespace* is a formal collection of element types and attribute names; it is the authoritative place for information about the metadata schema that is maintained there. The namespace allows metadata elements to be unambiguously identified and used across communities, promoting semantic interoperability.

The elements selected for an application profile may be a small subset of the elements from a single schema, or they may be elements drawn from two or more schemas combined together. An application profile is a formal way to declare which elements from which namespaces are used in a particular application or project or by a particular community. An example is the application profile proposed by the Dublin Core Education Working Group (DC-ed) for describing educational resources. It proposes adding to the 15 basic DC elements two domain-specific elements (*audience* and *instructional method*) in the DC-ed namespace, and also proposes various element refinements (*conformsTo, educationLevel,* and *mediator*) to be used with these added elements.[47]

Application profiles, unlike metadata schemas, do not create or introduce new metadata elements; they simply mix and match existing elements from various schemas, if one schema is not sufficient. Application profiles may also specify what values are permitted by selecting a controlled vocabulary to be used in certain elements in the record. This is done to instill some consistency in certain fields so that similar resources can be retrieved together. Application profiles may also refine the definitions of elements by using qualifiers to make them semantically narrower or more specific. For example, an application profile may specify that *Audience* will be used as an additional metadata element, that a particular list of values (terms) should be used for the *Type* element, and that *Date* may be made more specific with the element refinement *dateSubmitted.*

Metadata Registries

Another tool helpful to the metadata creator is the metadata registry. A registry is a database used to organize, store, manage, and share metadata schemas. Registries provide information about the schemas and their elements, controlled vocabularies, application profiles, definitions, and relationships, using a standard structure as outlined in ISO/IEC 11179–3:2003, "Information Technology–Metadata Registries (MDR)—Part 3: Registry Metamodel and Basic Attributes."[48] Metadata registries, once they become more widely implemented, will help greatly to improve interoperability among metadata schemas. A problem is that few registries exist at this time. It is expected that in the future, they will be used to exchange information, clarify meaning and usage, and prevent duplication of effort. It is hoped that metadata registries may be a source of machine-understandable information about schemas to support activities and agents on the Web. An existing example is the National Science Digital Library (NSDL) Metadata Registry.[49]

Crosswalks

Crosswalks, too, are tools used to achieve interoperability, specifically semantic interoperability. Without that one-size-fits-all schema, crosswalks are needed so that users and creators understand equivalence relationships among metadata elements in different communities. Crosswalks help us see, for example, that the 700 field in a MARC record for personal name added entries (usually for second and third named authors, editors, illustrators, translators, etc.) is roughly equivalent to the *Contributor* field in a Dublin Core record. According to Margaret St. Pierre and William LaPlant, "A crosswalk is a specification for mapping one metadata standard to another. Crosswalks provide the ability to make the contents of elements defined in one metadata standard available to communities using related metadata standards."[50] They go on to observe that creation and maintenance of a crosswalk is difficult and susceptible to error. One needs expertise in each metadata schema included in the crosswalk. But because each standard is developed by experts in a particular field with inherent specialized terminology, persons with expertise in several standards are rare. A key difficulty in creating and maintaining crosswalks is the element-mapping process. The mapping might not be too difficult if the schemas are relatively simple, are for the same types of materials, or have many overlapping concepts. It is far more complex, however, when the mapping is cross-domain, is between schemas of different levels of complexity, or is between schemas with great semantic differences. Generally, the more metadata schemas that are included in the crosswalk, the more difficult it is to do the mapping.

It is important to remember that the conversion process, via crosswalks, from one schema to another lacks precision. Few metadata crosswalks provide round-trip conversion with no loss of data. Some data are lost in one direction or the other (or both). However, until technology is developed that allows machines to understand the meaning of various metadata elements, crosswalks are the best tools we have for semantic interoperability. An example of a crosswalk is "Dublin Core Metadata Element Set Mapping to MODS Version 3."[51] It is a typical example of a situation where just one element of one schema (in this case Dublin Core) is equivalent to more than one element in the other (MODS). Suggestions are given as to which default MODS element may need to be used when converting a Dublin Core record to MODS. The Metadata Advisory Group of the MIT Libraries lists a number of other crosswalks available on the Web.[52]

Harvesting Tools and Templates

Other tools currently in use include harvesting technologies, which involve automated agents that go out on the Web to harvest metadata at a minimal level of complexity. This information is stored and retrieved as needed. The most widely known harvesting project is the Open Archives Initiative Protocol for Metadata Harvesting (OAI-PMH) in which data providers expose their metadata in the form of Dublin Core-based XML documents for collection by harvesters.[53] This metadata, once collected, can then be added into large, searchable metadata indexes.

In addition, metadata creation tools, software, and templates (i.e., forms with blank fields that serve as patterns for different metadata schemes) are among the instruments available to improve productivity and consistency. Some of these are commercial products, while others, such as a number of Dublin Core templates can be found on the World Wide Web free of charge.[54] Templates and harvesting often are used together—that is, an option in completing a template may be to begin by harvesting data from the Web site to be described.

METADATA AND CATALOGING

In recent years, some have debated whether *metadata* was a new concept in the electronic age or whether it was simply a repackaging of activities performed in libraries for centuries. Some definitions of metadata refer exclusively to electronic materials, but the term is not necessarily restricted to digital objects and Web resources only. Many authors like to point out that the library profession has been creating metadata for millennia. Even the earliest Sumerian lists contained metadata in some form. Some authors equate creating metadata for electronic resources with the cataloging of books. Some consider cataloging to be a subset of activities under the broader concept of metadata creation.

Parallels between the two processes certainly exist. The basic objectives of metadata creation and cataloging (i.e., providing descriptions of and access to items) are alike. The processes used to create the descriptions are also similar; both focus on recording the attributes that allow users to identify and select the information resources that most closely meet their needs. Electronic and analog materials share many characteristics. Both generally have titles, creators, creation dates, subject matter, and publication sources of some sort. There are enough similarities between the two activities and the information resources treated by them to see that a relationship exists between metadata creation and cataloging.

While there are parallels, differences are also claimed. Some feel the dissimilarities are too great to equate metadata with cataloging. Stefan Gradmann states that the differences lie in:

- who creates the metadata (nonprofessionals);
- why it is created (resource discovery, not just description);
- the process (more efficiently produced); and
- the materials described (electronic resources).[55]

It is puzzling that these are presented as distinctions. Unfortunately, the ideal of having authors create their own metadata is not coming to pass, but it is not just professional catalogers who are picking up the slack. For at least three decades, much cataloging has been done by people called *paraprofessionals*. Cataloging, too, is about resource discovery. That is why there has been such an emphasis on access points for names and subjects with a concentration on authority control for these. Classification has provided yet another way for users to discover resources by finding them alongside other materials on the same subject. With respect to Gradmann's third difference, *the process*, cataloging has become more efficient in recent years with the advent of computers. Finally, the conventions of cataloging have always been expanded to apply to information resources in new formats (digital or otherwise), as seen in the latest version of the *Anglo-American Cataloguing Rules*.[56] In many ways, it appears that metadata creation is just a reinvention and/or extension of traditional cataloging.

Most of the objections raised to the comparison tend to focus on certain characteristics of electronic resources. Electronic resources have particular differences that must be considered. These differences are important to acknowledge, even though they do not negate the relationship between cataloging and metadata creation. The first of these is more a perceived difference than a real one. It is the degree to which there is difficulty in determining what is an information resource. There has always been some difficulty in deciding what is a "catalogable unit," but the cataloging world has had centuries to develop standards and practices. For the most part, one physical item has been equated with one bibliographic record. However, there are still questions about when to provide a single record for multiple items (e.g., serials, multivolume sets) and when to provide multiple records for just one item (e.g., anthologies of short stories, articles in journals). Now we have the same problem for digital resources. What is a describable unit on the Web or in a digital library? Do we create metadata for a single Web page or for the entire site that contains it? Do we describe a digital image or a collection of digital images? This returns us to the granularity issues mentioned earlier. In addition, with a digital image, what exactly is being described? Should the metadata describe the digital image only? Should it describe both the digitized photo and the original physical photograph? If both are in the collection, should there be one record or two?

An obvious difference between analog and electronic resources is that remote-access electronic resources have no physical carriers, unlike books, maps, or videotapes. A key feature of traditional cataloging is the physical description of the item in hand (e.g., 280 p. : ill. ; 26 cm. *or* 1 videocassette (15 min.) : sd., col. ; 3/4 in.). Except, perhaps, for indications of illustrative matter, color, and sound, a physical description of a Web site seems fairly unnecessary. There are, of course, electronic resources that are accessed by means of a physical carrier. Those resources, whether they are held in a cassette, CD-ROM, or magnetic disk, all have physical characteristics that may be of importance to patrons attempting to identify which items best meet their information needs. So, it is apparent that not all electronic resources are the same, and must be described somewhat differently.

Another distinction between electronic and analog resources relates to the concept of edition. For some electronic resources, like commercial software, it is obvious when a new edition or version has been released. But for others, like Web sites, it is not so obvious. Web sites can be ephemeral and/or unstable. Some Web sites simply disappear without a trace. Others can, and do change often. While some sites may have relatively stable content, others are updated frequently. Unlike most tangible information resourcess, where updated information necessitates a new physical carrier, an updated Web site can be difficult to detect. This is complicated by the fact that the old site is generally gone for good. If a Web page is slightly altered, does that make it a new edition? Probably not, but at what point does a new resource or a new edition emerge? At what point is new metadata required? When changes occur, it is not always obvious whether the metadata for that Web site should also change. Library cataloging, in an attempt to address these issues, has chosen to treat Web pages as *integrating resources,* a category that also includes some loose-leaf publications and databases. Some consider this solution as ingenious, while others see it as less than ideal.

Location information also differs. When metadata records and information resources are both encoded and accessible online, the encoded nature of the metadata records allows users to locate and access an information resource almost simultaneously. Therefore, special attention must be paid to location/access metadata for electronic resources. URLs are far more likely to change than are call numbers in an average library, and keeping them up-to-date may be time-consuming and difficult.

The last major difference between analog and electronic resources that we will discuss is structural. Compared to the structure of an analog resource, the structure of a digital object can be very complex. For example, a digitized book requires more and different types of metadata than does a physical book sitting upon a shelf. In order for it to be found and used, the physical book, for the most part, requires only descriptive metadata (such as title, author, and subject) and some kind of call number, with some administrative metadata thrown in for good measure. The digital object, however, requires extensive structural metadata in order for the object to be displayed and to function properly in an online environment. This is *in addition* to the necessary descriptive metadata about the digitized resource and any original analog equivalent that may exist, as well as any required administrative metadata (such as technical, preservation, rights, and meta-metadata). Of the differences between electronic and analog resources, this is the one that has the greatest impact on activities related to organizing information resources. It is the strongest argument in favor of distinguishing between metadata creation and cataloging, although it is only applicable to a portion of electronic resources.

CONCLUSION

This chapter has provided a simple introduction to metadata issues. While many see metadata creation as little more than the activities of traditional library cataloging applied to some new formats, there are some additional considerations required in this new environment of digital resources. The complexity, quantity, and variety of information required to organize digital resources is often greater than those for traditional resources, and at times, new approaches are needed. It is important to remember, though, that the ultimate purpose for both cataloging and metadata creation is to allow users to navigate information systems to find, identify, select, and obtain the information they need. In addition, it is important that we are careful in the terminology we use when discussing metadata. Although the conceptual components discussed throughout this chapter are highly intertwined, it can be helpful to try to specify the type of information we are referring to when we use the term *metadata*. One person's metadata may be another person's content standard.

NOTES

All URLs accessed September 2008.

1. Denis Howe, ed., "FOLDOC: Free On-line Dictionary of Computing." Available: http://foldoc.org/. The definition given is for the hyphenated "meta-data," which, FOLDOC says, is not to be confused with "Metadata," a term coined by Jack E. Myers, who used the term in a brochure for a product, and registered it as a U.S. trademark. This distinction is not typical in the LIS field.

2. These categories of metadata are described in detail later in this chapter and in Chapter 7.

3. Sherry L. Vellucci, "Metadata and Authority Control," *Library Resources & Technical Services* 44, no. 1 (2000): 33–43.

4. Stuart Weibel, "Metadata: Semantics; Structure; Syntax," in "Weibel Lines: Ruminations on Libraries and Internet Standards." Available: http://weibel-lines.typepad.com/weibelines/2008/02/metadata-semant.html.

5. Ibid.

6. Vellucci, pp. 36–37.

7. Ibid., p. 36.

8. "PREMIS: Preservation Metadata Maintenance Activity," Library of Congress. Available: http://www.loc.gov/standards/premis/.

9. "MIX: NISO Metadata for Images in XML Schema, Technical Metadata for Digital Still Images Standard Official Web Site," Library of Congress. Available: http://www.loc.gov/standards/mix/.

10. *PREMIS Data Dictionary for Preservation Metadata,* Version 2.0, Library of Congress, p. 24. Available: http://www.loc.gov/standards/premis/v2/premis-dd-2-0.pdf.

11. Ibid., pp. 1–4.

12. "The ODRL Initiative," Open Digital Rights Language Initiative. Available: http://odrl.net/.

13. Jytte Hansen and Leif Andresen, "AC-Administrative Components: Dublin Core DCMI Administrative Metadata," Dublin Core Metadata Iniative. Available: http://dublincore.org/groups/admin/ or http://www.bs.dk/standards/AdministrativeComponents.htm.

14. "Digital Page Imaging and SGML: An Introduction to the Electronic Binding DTD (Ebind)," Berkeley Digital Library SunSITE. Available: http://sunsite.berkeley.edu/Ebind/.

15. The Making of America II Project. Available: http://sunsite.berkeley.edu/moa2/.

16. "METS: Metadata Encoding & Transmission Standard: Official Web Site," Library of Congress. Available: http://www.loc.gov/standards/mets/.

17. Ibid.

18. Denis Howe, ed., "FOLDOC: Free On-line Dictionary of Computing." Available: http://foldoc.org/.

19. Merriam-Webster Online. Available: http://www.merriam-webster.com/.

20. International Federation of Library Associations and Institutions, IFLA Study Group, *Functional Requirements for Bibliographic Records: Final Report* (München: Saur, 1998). Available: http://www.ifla.org/VII/s13/frbr/frbr.pdf or http://www.ifla.org/VII/s13/frbr/frbr.htm.

21. Entity-relationship models were first proposed by Peter Chen in 1976 in the context of database design. For more information see, Peter Pin-Shan Chen, "The Entity-Relationship Model: Toward a Unified View of Data," *ACM Transactions on Database Systems* 1, no. 1 (1976): 9–36.

22. International Federation of Library Associations and Institutions, Working Group on FRANAR. "Functional Requirements for Authority Data: A Conceptual Model." Available: http://www.ifla.org/VII/d4/franar-conceptual-model-2ndreview.pdf.

23. Charles A. Cutter, *Rules for a Dictionary Catalog*, 4th ed. (Washington, D.C.: Government Printing Office, 1904; reprint, London: The Library Association, 1962), p. 12.

24. International Conference on Cataloguing Principles, Paris, 9th–18th October, 1961). *Report.* (London, International Federation of Library Associations, 1963), pp. 91–96. Also available in: *Library Resources & Technical Services* 6 (1962), pp. 162–167; and *Statement of principles adopted at the International Conference on Cataloguing Principles, Paris, October, 1961,* annotated ed., with commentary and examples by Eva Verona (London: IFLA Committee on Cataloguing, 1971); and A. H. Chaplin and Dorothy Anderson, eds. *Report/International Conference on Cataloguing Principles, Paris, 9th–18th October 1961* (London: IFLA International Office for UBC, 1981).

25. International Federation of Library Associations and Institutions, IFLA Study Group, "Functional Requirements for Bibliographic Records."

26. Elaine Svenonius, *The Intellectual Foundation of Information Organization* (Cambridge, Mass.: MIT Press, 2000), pp. 18–19.

27. International Federation of Library Associations and Institutions, Working Group on FRANAR. "Functional Requirements for Authority Data."

28. International Federation of Library Associations and Institutions, IFLA Study Group, "Functional Requirements for Bibliographic Records."

29. Barbara B. Tillett, "Bibliographic Relationships," in *Relationships in the Organization of Knowledge,* edited by Carol A. Bean and Rebecca Green (Dordrecht: Kluwer Academic Publishers, 2001), pp. 19–35.

30. Richard P. Smiraglia, "Authority Control and the Extent of Derivative Bibliographic Relationships" (PhD diss., University of Chicago, 1992).

31. International Federation of Library Associations and Institutions, Meeting of Experts on an International Cataloguing Code. "Statement of International Cataloguing Principles" April 10, 2008 version. Available: http://www.ifla.org/VII/s13/icc/imeicc-statement_of_principles-2008.pdf.

32. Joint Steering Committee for Development of RDA, "RDA: Resource Description and Access." Available: http://www.collectionscanada.gc.ca/jsc/rda.html.

33. For more discussion of the Warwick Framework, see: Susan S. Lazinger, *Digital Preservation and Metadata: History, Theory, Practice* (Englewood,

Colo.: Libraries Unlimited, 2001), pp. 193–195; Carl Lagoze, "The Warwick Framework: A Container Architecture for Diverse Sets of Metadata," *D-Lib Magazine* 2 (July/August 1996). Available: http://www.dlib.org/dlib/july96/lagoze/07lagoze.html.

34. In this section, we are primarily concerned about the conceptual model rather than full implementations of RDF. Since the original version of RDF was published, the framework has been expanded considerably to include specific recommendations on syntax and vocabulary. Describing the full range of RDF activities and applications is beyond the scope of this book.

35. W3C, "RDF Primer." Available: http://www.w3.org/TR/rdf-primer/.

36. Ibid.

37. W3C, "RDF/XML Syntax Specification (Revised)." Available: http://www.w3.org/TR/rdf-syntax-grammar/.

38. W3C, "Notation 3 (N3): A Readable RDF Syntax." Available: http://www.w3.org/DesignIssues/Notation3.html.

39. Dave Beckett, "Turtle—Terse RDF Triple Language." Available: http://www.dajobe.org/2004/01/turtle/.

40. Tim Berners-Lee, "Realising the Full Potential of the Web." Available: http://www.w3.org/1998/02/Potential.html; and Tim Berners-Lee, James Hendler, and Ora Lassila, "The Semantic Web," *Scientific American* 284, no. 5 (May 2001): 34–38, 40–43. Also available: http://www.sciam.com/article.cfm?id=the-semantic-web.

41. Berners-Lee, Hendler, and Lassila, "The Semantic Web."

42. Ibid.

43. W3C, "Semantic Web Activity Statement." Available: http://www.w3.org/2001/sw/Activity.

44. Andy Powell, Mikael Nilsson, Ambjörn Naeve, Pete Johnson, and Thomas Baker, "DCMI Abstract Model," Dublin Core Metadata Initiative. Available: http://dublincore.org/documents/abstract-model/.

45. Ibid.

46. Priscilla Caplan, *Metadata Fundamentals for All Librarians* (Chicago: American Library Association, 2003), p. 7.

47. DC-Education Application Profile Task Group, "DC-Education Application Profile," Dublin Core Metadata Initiative. Available: http://dublincore.org/educationwiki/DC_2dEducation_20Application_20Profile.

48. Available for purchase: http://www.iso.ch/iso/en/.

49. National Science Digital Library, "NSDL Registry." Available: http://metadataregistry.org/.

50. Margaret St. Pierre and William P. LaPlant, "Issues in Crosswalking Content Metadata Standards," NISO. Available: http://www.niso.org/publications/white_papers/crosswalk/.

51. Library of Congress, Network Development and MARC Standards Office, "Dublin Core Metadata Element Set Mapping to MODS Version 3." Available: http://www.loc.gov/standards/mods/dcsimple-mods.html.

52. MIT Libraries, Metadata Advisory Group, "Metadata Reference Guide: Metadata Mappings (Crosswalks)." Available: http://libraries.mit.edu/guides/subjects/metadata/mappings.html.

53. Open Archives Initiative, "Open Archives Initiative Protocol for Metadata Harvesting." Available: http://www.openarchives.org/pmh/.

54. Templates can be found through the Dublin Core Metadata Initiative Web site. Available: http://dublincore.org/.

55. Stefan Gradmann, "Cataloging vs. Metadata: Old Wine in New Bottles?" *International Cataloguing and Bibliographic Control* 28, no. 4 (1999): 88–90.

56. *Anglo-American Cataloguing Rules, Second Edition, 2002 Revision,* prepared under the direction of the Joint Steering Committee for Revision of AACR (Ottawa: Canadian Library Association; Chicago: American Library Association, 2002).

SUGGESTED READINGS

Baca, Murtha, ed. *Introduction to Metadata.* 2nd ed. Los Angeles, Calif.: Getty Research Institute, 2008.

Caplan, Priscilla. *Metadata Fundamentals for All Librarians.* Chicago: American Library Association, 2003. Chapter 16: "Administrative Metadata," Chapter 17: "Structural Metadata," and Chapter 18: "Rights Metadata."

Federal Geographic Data Committee (FGDC). "What Are Metadata?" Available: http://www.fgdc.gov/metadata.

Hillmann, Diane, and Elaine L. Westbrooks, eds. *Metadata in Practice.* Chicago: American Library Association, 2004.

Hodge, Gail. *Understanding Metadata.* Bethesda, Md.: National Information Standards Organization, 2004. Available: http://www.niso.org/publications/press/UnderstandingMetadata.pdf.

International Federation of Library Associations and Institutions. "Digital Libraries: Metadata Resources." Available: http://www.ifla.org/II/metadata.htm.

International Federation of Library Associations and Institutions, IFLA Study Group. *Functional Requirements for Bibliographic Records: Final Report.* München: Saur, 1998. Also available: http://www.ifla.org/VII/s13/frbr.pdf or http://www.ifla.org/VII/s13/frbr/frbr.htm.

International Federation of Library Associations and Institutions, Working Group on FRANAR. "Functional Requirements for Authority Data: A Conceptual Model." Available: http://www.ifla.org/VII/d4/franar-conceptual-model-2ndreview.pdf.

Intner, Sheila S., Susan S. Lazinger, and Jean Weihs. *Metadata and Its Impact on Libraries.* Westport, Conn.: Libraries Unlimited, 2006. Chapter 1: "What Is Metadata?" and Chapter 2: "Metadata Schemas and Their Relationships to Particular Communities."

Jones, Wayne, Judith R. Ahronheim, and Josephine Crawford, eds. *Cataloging the Web: Metadata, AACR, and MARC 21.* (ALCTS Papers on Library Technical Services and Collections, no. 10.) Lanham, Md.: Scarecrow Press, 2002.

Lazinger, Susan S. *Digital Preservation and Metadata: History, Theory, Practice.* Englewood, Colo.: Libraries Unlimited, 2001. Chapter 1: "Why Is Digital Preservation an Issue?" and Chapter 2: "What Electronic Data Should Be Preserved?"

Maxwell, Robert L. *FRBR: A Guide for the Perplexed.* Chicago: American Library Association, 2008.

"Metadata Standards, Crosswalks, and Standard Organizations." In "Cataloger's Toolbox." Memorial University of Newfoundland Libraries. Available: http://staff.library.mun.ca/staff/toolbox/standards.htm.

Smiraglia, Richard P., ed. *Metadata: A Cataloger's Primer.* New York: Haworth Information Press, 2005.

Taylor, Arlene G., ed. *Understanding FRBR: What It Is and How It Will Affect Our Retrieval Tools.* Westport, Conn.: Libraries Unlimited, 2007.

Vellucci, Sherry L. "Metadata and Authority Control." *Library Resources & Technical Services* 44, no. 1 (January 2000): 33–43.

Zeng, Marcia Lei, and Jian Qin. *Metadata.* New York: Neal-Schuman, 2008.

CHAPTER 5

ENCODING STANDARDS

Metadata must be encoded in order for it to be used, processed, and manipulated in our increasingly electronic information environment. If surrogate records are not converted to electronic form, they cannot be stored and retrieved in online retrieval tools or on the Web. This chapter addresses several ways to encode metadata and surrogate records. These include the MARC (MAchine-Readable Cataloging) format as well as various markup languages derived from SGML (Standard Generalized Markup Language). The MARC format is the encoding standard used to create bibliographic records stored in library catalogs. It is a mature standard that has been in use for more than three decades. SGML, developed as a meta-language for encoding electronic texts, came into use after 1986. SGML and its by-products have since been adapted for encoding surrogate records as well as electronic documents. Various applications of SGML have been created over the years including HTML (Hypertext Markup Language) and XML (Extensible Markup Language). Specific DTDs (Document Type Definitions) and XML schemas also have been designed to encode data for individual communities or document types. All of these standards may be used to store, share, and retrieve metadata in retrieval tools or to manage and structure documents on the Web or in other electronic environments.

In the minds of many information professionals, metadata content and encoding for the content are inextricably entwined. Metadata records can be created by first determining the descriptive content and then encoding the content manually afterward, or by filling in the blanks in a metadata record template comprising the various codes. Each of the encoding standards discussed in this chapter acts a kind of container. It is sometimes helpful to think of encoding or syntax as a bucket or a package that does little more than hold the precious metadata content. It can be thought of as a way of carrying the metadata from one place to another. The metadata content held in the container may be guided by a separate descriptive standard, or in a few rare cases, by the encoding standard itself. For example, the metadata entered into a MARC record is usually controlled by outside descriptive cataloging rules (e.g., AACR2), by the conventions of a thesaurus (e.g., *Library of Congress Subject Headings*), and by the rules of a classification scheme (e.g., *Dewey Decimal Classification*); there are, however, some MARC 21 fields for which the rules for content appear only in the MARC 21 standard itself (e.g., the MARC 21 field 007 gives specific codes for certain materials, such as microforms or motion pictures). Although some metadata standards include both encoding and content specifications, in this book, encoding standards are discussed separately before covering the creation of metadata content. This is an attempt to show that creating content and encoding metadata are not the same processes. In other words, the same content can be coded with any one of several different encoding standards (i.e., the same metadata could be held in different containers). It is also helpful to understand the shapes and sizes of containers before starting to fill them. Creation of metadata content is covered in Chapters 7–11.

ENCODING OF CHARACTERS

Before addressing the encoding of records, it may be useful to say a few words about how computers are able to handle the very basic level of the characters that make up content that appears as a record. Each letter of an alphabet, each numeral, and each symbol in every language that exists has to be represented by a code, because, fundamentally, computers just deal with numbers. They store letters and other characters by assigning a code to each one. An ISO standard, ISO/IEC 10646, *Universal Multiple-Octet Coded Character Set* (UCS) is the first standardized character set with the purpose of including all characters in all written languages of the world (including all mathematical and other symbols). Unicode is an American industry counterpart that is kept compatible with UCS. Unicode is overseen by the Unicode Consortium and was named for its aim to embrace three characteristics: *universality,* covering all modern written languages; *uniqueness,* with no duplication of characters even if they appear in more than one language; and *uniformity,* with each character being the same length in bits.[1] UCS/Unicode provides a unique 16-bit (or 31-bit) unit of encoding for every character in every modern language. Before UCS/Unicode, there were a multitude of different encoding systems for the display of characters, such as ASCII and EBCDIC.

ENCODING OF RECORDS

In order for metadata to be accessible, it must be conveyed to users through some type of information retrieval tool. Now that our retrieval tools are primarily online, metadata is usually created in electronic form. Although some print retrieval tools are still used, even those are created using electronic means. Metadata records are encoded into electronic form by assigning tags, numbers, letters, or words (i.e., codes) to discrete pieces of information in the description. For example, a primary author's personal name is given the tag "100" in MARC coding; or in an XML schema, such as TEI, it is preceded with "**<author>**" and is followed by "**</author>**." Such encoding is often referred to in metadata schemas as the *syntax* of the schema.

Surrogate records are encoded in order to be able to provide users access to the contents of those surrogate records. Encoding allows for the setting off of individual parts of the record (called *fields* or *elements*) for specific purposes. This enables the creation of software programs that allow the indexing and searching of only certain fields. For example, if a user wishes to search only for personal authors, the catalog will narrow the search to a stockpile of metadata that had been coded as either 100 or 700 in MARC-based surrogate records. As noted above, the same result is achieved in some XML schemas by placing a name between opening and closing **<author>** tags.

Encoding also is used to provide for display. In a similar manner to the searching of only certain fields, programs can be written so that each field will display in a certain position on the screen according to the wishes of those creating the display. For example, when a TEI **<author>** tag or a MARC 100 or 700 field is used to identify the name of a person who is the author of an information resource, that author's name can be displayed at the top of the record or after the title, and can be displayed with a particular label or not.

Another use for encoding is to allow many languages and scripts to be displayed and searched in the same file. Languages that are in the Roman alphabet have always been able to be interfiled, although filing them alphabetically was sometimes a problem (see discussion of filing issues in Appendix C: Arrangement of Metadata Displays). Languages in other scripts had to be *Romanized* in order to interfile them in the paper world. Online, however, if the display of non-Roman scripts is provided for, record encoding allows for identification of the fields of the surrogate record regardless of the language or script.

Encoding also is used for data transmission. Institutions that collect information resources tend to have their own online systems into which they place encoded surrogate records for their resources. When these information resources are duplicates of those found in other institutions' online systems, cooperative arrangements are made to exchange surrogate records. This *cooperative cataloging* means that each institution does not have to create every record for every resource from "scratch." Shared, standardized encoding allows such exchanges of records to occur among institutions around the world.

There are a number of standards in use for encoding metadata. The examples discussed here are:

- MARC (MAchine-Readable Cataloging)
  - MARC 21
  - UNIMARC (UNIversal MARC)
- SGML (Standard Generalized Markup Language)
  - HTML (HyperText Markup Language)
  - XML (Extensible Markup Language) and its DTDs (Document Type Definitions) and Schemas
    - → TEI (Text Encoding Initiative) Schema
    - → EAD (Encoded Archival Description) DTD and Schema
    - → ONIX (Online Information eXchange) DTD and Schema
    - → MARCXML Schema and MODS (Metadata Object Description Schema)

MARC (MAchine-Readable Cataloging)

In the 1960s, the Library of Congress created the MARC (MAchine-Readable Cataloging) format as a way to share bibliographic data among libraries. The MARC communications format (see Figure 5.1) is used for encoding metadata and transmitting it from one system to another. It is

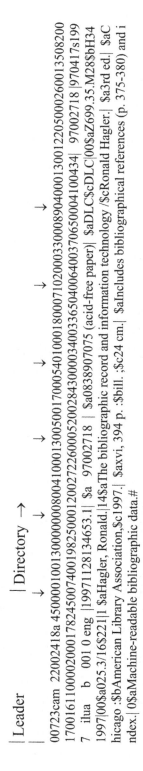

```
| Leader                | Directory →
|                       ↓          ↓          ↓          ↓          ↓          ↓
00723cam  22002418a 4500001001300000008004100013005001700054010001800071020003300089040001300122050002600135082001700161100002000178245007400198250001200272260005200284300003400336504006400370650004100434|   97002718 |970417s1997   ilua    b   001 0 eng  |19971128134653.1|  $a   97002718  |  $a0838907075 (acid-free paper)|  $aDLC$cDLC|00$aZ699.35.M28$bH34 1997|00$a025.3/16$221|1 $aHagler, Ronald.|14$aThe bibliographic record and information technology /$cRonald Hagler.|  $a3rd ed.|  $aChicago :$bAmerican Library Association,$c1997.|  $axvi, 394 p. :$bill. ;$c24 cm.|  $aIncludes bibliographical references (p. 375-380) and index.| 0$aMachine-readable bibliographic data.#
```

Figure 5.1. Record in the MARC communications format. Directory is divided into 12-character segments as shown by the arrows at the top of the record. Directory continues through line two and for the first 18 characters of line three. In each 12-character segment, the first 3 characters are the MARC tag for the field represented, the next 4 characters give the length of the field, and the last 5 characters give the starting position for that field in the portion of the record that follows the directory.

primarily used in libraries, although it has been used in some museums and archives over the years.

The MARC format comprises several components, including:

- a leader,
- a directory, and
- an assortment of content fields, including:
  - control fields,
  - code and number fields, and
  - variable data fields.

The leader is somewhat like the leader on a roll of film. It identifies the beginning of a new record and contains 24 alphanumeric characters that identify, among other things, the character coding scheme (e.g., UCS/Unicode) and the kind of information resource that is being described. The record directory contains a series of fixed-length segments (each twelve characters long) that identify the field tag, length, and starting position of each field in the record. The following is a single segment from Figure 5.1:

↓ ↓ ↓
245007400198

The segment is conveying that the 245 field (the title and statement of responsibility) is 74 characters long and it begins at the 198th character position in the record. The MARC directory was a major contribution to the information science world. Instead of containing only fixed-length fields, which was common in databases in the 1960s, the directory allowed for variable-length fields, which are now prevalent in databases.

The MARC format identifies three types of data fields: control fields, code and number fields, and variable data fields. *Control fields* carry alphanumeric data elements; they are used for processing machine-readable bibliographic records. In MARC 21 these field tags begin with two zeros (i.e., 00X fields). Control fields are used for such data as fixed-length descriptive data, Library of Congress (LC) control numbers, and codes for date and time of latest transaction. Some control fields are referred to as fixed fields, but one of these (the 008 field) is often called *the fixed field* and is displayed differently from other fields in some online systems.

The *code and number fields* make up the 0XX fields (i.e., 01X-09X). They contain standard numbers, classification numbers, and other codes.

Several of these fields have subfields that are fixed in length. Examples of code and number fields are the 020 field for International Standard Book Numbers (ISBN), the 022 for International Standard Serial Numbers (ISSN), the 041 for Language Codes, the 050 for Library of Congress call numbers, and the 082 field for Dewey Decimal Classification Numbers.

Variable data fields (1XX-8XX) carry alphanumeric data of variable length. These fields contain traditional cataloging data, but also may carry additional information, such as playing time, URLs, and linking entries. Variable data fields often have quite a few subfields in order to achieve greater granularity in encoding. Variable fields include, for example, the 245 for title statements, the 100 for primary authors (personal names), the 300 for descriptions of the physical formats of resources, and the 5XX fields, which contain an assortment of notes.

When records are received in the MARC communications format, each system displays records according to its own programming. OCLC puts the fixed field at the top and uses abbreviations to interpret the various codes that make up the 008 field. LC displays the fixed field as a long string of alphanumeric characters in the 008 position without abbreviations or separations. Local systems have a staff display that is quite different from the network systems' displays. The public interface to the catalog (OPAC), generally does not display the fixed field at all (except in implementations that allow a MARC view). System displays also vary in such things as spacing before and after subfield codes, placement of indicators, and the like (see Figures 5.2 and 5.3).

Number and code fields and variable data fields are made up of tags, indicators, and subfield codes. Tags are the three-digit numbers (from 001 to 999) that designate the kind of content that will be entered into the field. A convention is followed in which all fields beginning with the same first digit are identified as a group. The groups are:

1XX	Main entry fields
2XX	Title and edition fields
3XX	Physical description fields
4XX	Series fields
5XX	Notes fields
6XX	Subject fields
7XX	Added entry and linking fields
8XX	Series added entry and holdings data fields
9XX	Local data fields

LC Control Number: 97002718

000 00994pam 2200253 a 450
001 706941
005 19971128134653.1
008 970417s1997 ilua b 001 0 eng
010 __ |**a** 97002718
020 __ |**a** 0838907075 (acid-free paper)
040 __ |**a** DLC |**c** DLC |**d** DLC
050 00 |**a** Z699.35.M28 |**b** H34 1997
082 00 |**a** 025.3/16 |**2** 21
100 1_ |**a** Hagler, Ronald.
245 14 |**a** The bibliographic record and information technology / |**c** Ronald Hagler.
250 __ |**a** 3rd ed.
260 __ |**a** Chicago : |**b** American Library Association, |**c** 1997.
300 __ |**a** xvi, 394 p. : |**b** ill. ; |**c** 24 cm.
504 __ |**a** Includes bibliographical references (p. 375-380) and index.
650 _0 |**a** Machine-readable bibliographic data.

Figure 5.2. Formatted display of the record in Figure 5.1, as displayed in the Library of Congress Online Catalog.

OCLC 36909449

Books		**Rec stat**	p	**Entered**	19970417			**Replaced**	20010523		
Type	a	**ELvl**		**Srce**		**Audn**		**Ctrl**		**Lang**	eng
BLvl	m	**Form**		**Conf**	0	**Biog**		**MRec**		**Ctry**	ilu
		Cont	b	**Gpub**		**LitF**	0	**Indx**	1		
Desc	a	**Ills**	a	**Fest**	0	**DtSt**	s	**Dates**	1997,		

010		97-2718
040		DLC ‡c DLC ‡d UKM ‡d NLC
020		0838907075 (acid-free paper)
020		0888022808 (Canada)
050	00	Z699.35.M28 ‡b H34 1997
082	00	025.3/16 ‡2 21
100	1_	Hagler, Ronald.
245	14	The bibliographic record and information technology / ‡c Ronald Hagler.
250		3rd ed.
260		Chicago : ‡b American Library Association, ‡c 1997.
300		xvi, 394 p. : ‡b ill. ; ‡c 24 cm.
504		Includes bibliographical references (p. 375-380) and index.
650	_0	Machine-readable bibliographic data.

Figure 5.3. Formatted display of the record in Figure 5.1, as displayed by OCLC.

These groupings mean, for example, that all of the 6XX fields are somehow related to subject access (e.g., 600 is for a personal name used as subject; 610 is for a corporate name used as subject; 650 is for a topical subject, etc.).

Indicators consist of two positions following a tag. These positions contain coded information interpreting or supplementing the data in the field. The number of indicators depends on the individual tag. For some fields, no indicators are used, so the indicator positions are empty. In other fields, one or two of the indicators may be defined and used. Each indicator position is independent of the other. An example in MARC 21 is the indicators for the title field. The first indicator in the 245 tells us whether a title added entry is needed.[2] The second indicator tells us how many characters should be skipped over (counting a blank space as one character) to get to the first word in the title that is *not* an article.

> **245 14 $a The quality of Chinese records in the OCLC database : $b a proposal for rule-based validation / $c principal investigators, Edie Rasmussen and Marcia Lei Zeng.**

In this example, the second indicator is "4" because the title begins with the article "the" and we want the title to be arranged with *Q* titles as "Quality," not with *T* titles as "The."

A subfield code consists of a delimiter and a letter or number. The purpose of subfield codes is to introduce a greater level of granularity into MARC encoding; they identify elements in a field that might require separate treatment. Delimiters are unique characters that indicate the beginning of a particular subfield. The delimiter may be represented differently depending on the system: ‡ or $ or |, for example. The lowercase letter or number that follows the delimiter is a data element identifier. For example, in the 245 example above, subfield *a* identifies the title proper, subfield *b* identifies the subtitle or other title information, and subfield *c* identifies the statement of responsibility (e.g., the authors). The subfield letters and numbers have different meanings from field to field. The following are subfield codes: $a, $b, $2, and so forth. (It should be noted that in some systems, most notably OCLC, the $a code of the first element in a field is not shown by the system.) These components are identified in the example provided in Figure 5.4.

MARC 21

MARC 21 (named "21" for the twenty-first century) came into being in 2000 as a result of agreement between the United States and Canada

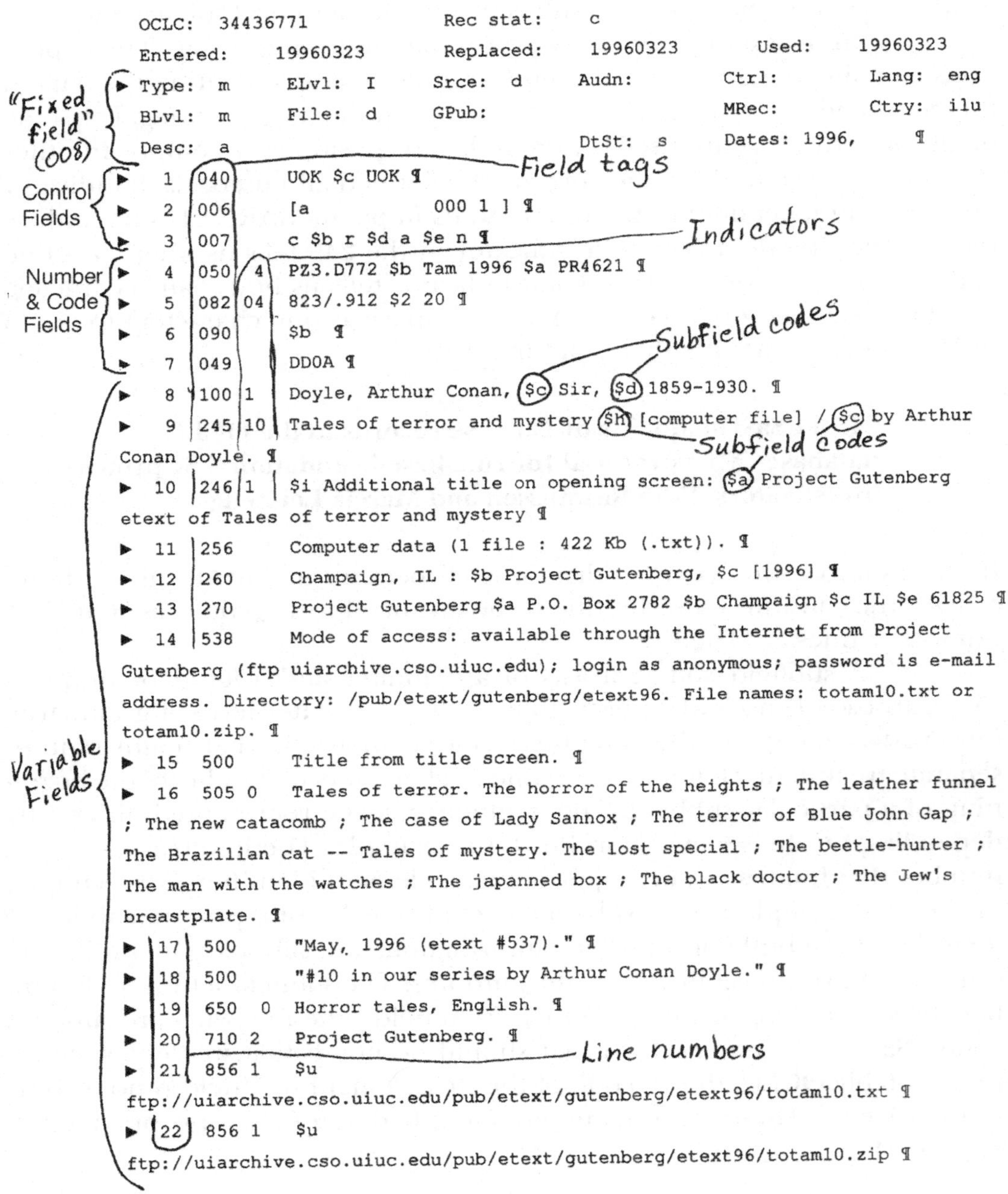


```
OCLC:  34436771              Rec stat:    c
Entered:    19960323         Replaced:    19960323       Used:    19960323
▶ Type:  m      ELvl:  I     Srce:  d     Audn:        Ctrl:        Lang:  eng
  BLvl:  m      File:  d     GPub:                     MRec:        Ctry:  ilu
  Desc:  a                                DtSt:  s     Dates: 1996,      ¶
▶  1  040        UOK $c UOK ¶
▶  2  006        [a           000 1 ] ¶
▶  3  007        c $b r $d a $e n ¶
▶  4  050   4    PZ3.D772 $b Tam 1996 $a PR4621 ¶
▶  5  082  04    823/.912 $2 20 ¶
▶  6  090        $b  ¶
▶  7  049        DDOA ¶
▶  8  100  1     Doyle, Arthur Conan, $c Sir, $d 1859-1930. ¶
▶  9  245  10    Tales of terror and mystery $h [computer file] / $c by Arthur
Conan Doyle. ¶
▶ 10  246  1     $i Additional title on opening screen: $a Project Gutenberg
etext of Tales of terror and mystery ¶
▶ 11  256        Computer data (1 file : 422 Kb (.txt)). ¶
▶ 12  260        Champaign, IL : $b Project Gutenberg, $c [1996] ¶
▶ 13  270        Project Gutenberg $a P.O. Box 2782 $b Champaign $c IL $e 61825 ¶
▶ 14  538        Mode of access: available through the Internet from Project
Gutenberg (ftp uiarchive.cso.uiuc.edu); login as anonymous; password is e-mail
address. Directory: /pub/etext/gutenberg/etext96. File names: totam10.txt or
totam10.zip. ¶
▶ 15  500        Title from title screen. ¶
▶ 16  505 0      Tales of terror. The horror of the heights ; The leather funnel
; The new catacomb ; The case of Lady Sannox ; The terror of Blue John Gap ;
The Brazilian cat -- Tales of mystery. The lost special ; The beetle-hunter ;
The man with the watches ; The japanned box ; The black doctor ; The Jew's
breastplate. ¶
▶ 17  500        "May, 1996 (etext #537)." ¶
▶ 18  500        "#10 in our series by Arthur Conan Doyle." ¶
▶ 19  650  0     Horror tales, English. ¶
▶ 20  710 2      Project Gutenberg. ¶
▶ 21  856 1      $u
ftp://uiarchive.cso.uiuc.edu/pub/etext/gutenberg/etext96/totam10.txt ¶
▶ 22  856 1      $u
ftp://uiarchive.cso.uiuc.edu/pub/etext/gutenberg/etext96/totam10.zip ¶
```

Figure 5.4. Components of a MARC record.

to merge their national MARC formats (USMARC and CAN/MARC), compromising on the differences between them. In 2004, the British Library adopted MARC 21 as its cataloging format, and that same year, the German National Library announced it also would be moving to MARC 21. The first MARC format was developed at the Library of Congress in 1968 under the leadership of Henriette Avram. It was identified simply as MARC until other versions were developed in the 1970s, and then the first version was referred to as LC-MARC. Finally, the name USMARC came to distinguish it from more than twenty other national versions (e.g., UKMARC, RUSMARC, IBERMARC, etc.).

MARC 21 is based on ANSI standard Z39.2, *American National Standard for Bibliographic Information Interchange* (1971, revised 1985).[3] The international version is ISO 2709:1996, *Information and Documentation—Format for Information Exchange*.[4] MARC 21 records may be encoded with either an 8-bit encoding called MARC-8 or with the Unicode UTF–8 encoding rules, using a subset of UCS/Unicode until all systems can accommodate the full UCS/Unicode set of characters.[5]

MARC 21 actually has five formats for different types of data. These include the following:

- **Bibliographic format**—for encoding bibliographic data in records that are surrogates for information resources (see Figures 5.2–5.4)

- **Authority format**—for encoding authority data collected in authority records created to help control the content of those surrogate record fields that are subject to authority control (see Figures 8.11 and 10.2)

- **Community information format**—for encoding data in records that contain information about events, programs, services, and the like, so that these records can be integrated with bibliographic records (see Figure 5.5)[6]

- **Holdings format**—for encoding data elements in holdings records that show the holdings and location data for information resources described in surrogate records

- **Classification data format**—for encoding data elements related to classification numbers, the captions associated with them, their hierarchies, and the subject headings with which they correlate

LEADER	00000nam 2200000 a 4500
001	196
100	[CONTACT NAME GOES HERE]
245	Kane County Audubon Society
270	Meeting place: Peck Farm
270	Kaneville Road
271	Geneva, IL
272	60134
273	[PHONE NUMBER GOES HERE]
276	Kane County Audubon Society
276	513 S. 13th Ave.
276	St. Charles, IL 60174
307	Meetings: 2nd Wednesday at 7:00 p.m., September through May
520	An organization interested in the study of birds and birding and local flora and fauna.
650	Hobby/Special Interest Clubs
700	[CONTACT NAME GOES HERE]
701	[PHONE NUMBER GOES HERE]
856	State of Illinois Audubon website: http://www.illinoisaudubon.org

Figure 5.5. MARC Community Information Format as used in the Gail Borden Public Library District in Elgin, Illinois.

UNIMARC

UNIMARC (UNIversal MARC)[7] was developed in 1977 as a vehicle for interchange of MARC records between national bibliographic agencies. The most recent version includes updates made in 2005. It conforms to ISO 2709, as does MARC 21. UNIMARC calls for use of ISO character set standards, but also allows parties to agree on the character set to be used, when exchanging records.

The proliferation of national MARC formats necessitated development of UNIMARC. At first it was thought that UNIMARC would act only as a conversion format. In this capacity, it requires that each national agency create a translator to change records from UNIMARC to the particular national format and vice versa. When a translator is in place, records can be converted to UNIMARC to be sent to other countries, and records received from other countries can be translated from UNIMARC to the national format. In addition to this use, a few national agencies that did not already have a MARC format have adopted UNIMARC as the standard in their countries.

Differences between UNIMARC and MARC 21 are immediately apparent upon looking at the list of code blocks beginning with 0, 1, 2, etc. For example, the 1xx fields are *coded information* rather than *main entry* fields, and the 2xx block is a *descriptive information* block in which a title field is designated 200, rather than 245 as in MARC 21. Also, the second indicator of the 200 field is blank and therefore does not tell how many characters to skip for an article. UNIMARC also allows for embedded fields (e.g., an authority record number may appear at the beginning of an access point field). It de-emphasizes main entry in the 7xx block, where 700 is for Personal Name–Primary Intellectual Responsibility, but if the concept of main entry does not exist or is not distinguished in a source format, then 701 is used for all personal names.

The Future of MARC

In recent years, some information professionals—particularly those working with digitized resources—have expressed dissatisfaction with the limitations of the MARC format. They have suggested that librarians should be developing an XML-based encoding format for its bibliographic metadata in order to remain current and relevant in today's information environment. Others have defended the MARC standard, stating that it has more than met its purpose over the years and continues to be relevant. As with most standards, there are both strengths and weaknesses associated with MARC. Strengths include the fact that MARC is a mature standard. It has been in existence for 40 years, and it is well understood and well tested. It has been widely adopted by libraries around the world. Millions of records have been created in the last four decades and are available to those libraries through bibliographic networks. MARC has long been established as the format used in integrated library systems (ILS), and as of yet, few ILSs process information in other encoding formats (ILSs are discussed in Chapter 6).

Weaknesses include the fact that MARC is virtually unknown outside of libraries. This limits the ability of non-MARC information institutions to use the bibliographic data created by libraries. Some believe this marginalizes librarians and library metadata in the wider Web-based information environment. Others find MARC's size limitations and its inability to convey hierarchical or complex relationships among entities to be problematic. Some dislike MARC's inability to embed related objects in the record (e.g., book covers), and see this as symptomatic of MARC's antiquated data structure. Many have suggested that an XML schema should replace MARC. Others have suggested that instead of arguing over MARC versus XML, we should be discussing MARC *and* XML (which is indeed being accomplished—see discussion below) in order to take advantage of the interoperability of XML, without giving up the established content designation structure of MARC. At this writing, the future of MARC seems assured for at least the next few years; but as technology continues to advance, MARC's age and limitations become more apparent.

SGML (Standard Generalized Markup Language)

SGML is a metalanguage—that is, a language for describing markup languages. It is an international standard for document markup and conforms to ISO 8879:1986, *Information Processing—Text and Office Systems—Standard Generalized Markup Language (SGML)*.[8] Unlike the MARC family of encoding languages, it does not contain a predefined set of tags that can be used to mark up documents, nor is it a standard template for producing particular types of documents. Instead, it is a set of guidelines for designing hardware–independent markup languages. Markup languages describe the structures of documents, so that documents may be interchanged across computer platforms (both text and markup are encoded in the same character set, e.g., Unicode or ASCII text). They allow documents to be represented in such a way that the document structure may be identified independently from the content. *Document structure* means coding that says: this piece of text is the title, this content is the first chapter, this string of characters is a section heading, these lines comprise a paragraph, this is a quoted statement, and so on. Or, for surrogate records, the coding says: this is a title element, this is a creator element, this is a publisher element, and so forth. It is said that SGML is flexible enough to define an infinite number of markup languages.

SGML defines data in terms of entities (or things or objects), elements, and attributes (or properties). An entity is a "thing" (or information resource) to be encoded (e.g., a document, a part of a document, a surrogate record). An element is a particular component in the entity, such as a title, a chapter title, a section heading, a paragraph, a publisher name, a classification number, and so forth. An attribute gives particular information about an element (e.g., specifying that the text should be printed in italics, giving the name of the thesaurus from which a subject term has been taken, etc.). The relationships between entities, elements, and attributes are described using SGML.

SGML prescribes markup that consists of delimiters and tags. Delimiters are defined symbols (e.g., <, >, </, "), and are used to construct tags (e.g., **<author>** is a tag). Tags usually appear before and after an element in the form: **<tag>**element**</tag>** (e.g., **<author>**Edward Gaynor**</author>**). Attribute values are delimited by "..." or '...' (e.g., **<quote lang = 'spa'>**¿Que pasa?**</quote>**). Tags may be nested hierarchically. An example of a nested set of tags from TEI (described below) is:

```
<fileDesc>
        <titleStmt>
                <title>...</title>
                <author>...</author>
        </titleStmt>
        <publicationStmt>...</publicationStmt>
</fileDesc>
```

Because SGML is not itself a markup language, it requires users either to define a Document Type Definition (DTD) at the beginning of a document or to declare a particular external DTD as the one being followed. DTDs are discussed further below.

HTML (HyperText Markup Language)

HTML,[9] a somewhat straightforward SGML application, was developed for the creation of Web pages. It is a basic markup language that allows almost anyone to be a Web author. It defines the content, the layout, and the formatting of Web documents. It provides for creation of simple structure, enables display of images, and provides for establishing links between documents. Users of an HTML-encoded document can navigate through the text itself if internal links have been made, or can move from one text to another with external links. In HTML 4.01 there are specific provisions for elements that can be used to describe properties of a document (e.g., title, expiration date, a list of keywords, etc.), making it possible to encode metadata. XHTML[10] is a reformulation of HTML 4 as an XML application, with three DTDs corresponding to the ones defined by HTML 4. They are:

- **XHTML 1.0 Strict**—to be used to obtain very clean structural markup that does not include any markup for layout; layout instructions should be handled by using a style sheet
- **XHTML 1.0 Transitional**—to be used to take advantage of XHTML features including style sheets but making small adjustments so that older browsers which cannot understand style sheets can still read the pages
- **XHTML 1.0 Frameset**—to be used in creating pages that partition a browser window into two or more frames

A major benefit of migrating to XHTML is in being conformant to XML, while still having the content be able to be displayed correctly by older browsers. At the time of this writing, HTML 5 is being drafted by a W3C working group to replace both HTML 4.01 and XHTML.[11]

Today, it is rare to find metadata encoded in HTML. In the early years of the Web, the creation and insertion of *META tags* in the headers of HTML documents was encouraged by the W3C. Although specific metadata elements were not defined in the HTML standard, page creators could use any metadata element set as long as a URI could be provided for that set in the generic META tags. The Dublin Core Metadata Initiative also encouraged Web page designers to insert Dublin Core metadata into their documents headers as part of the Web page creation process. Much to the disappointment of many information professionals, however, the make-your-own-metadata approach never really caught on with most creators of Web content; or when it did, it often involved mischief or malfeasance (e.g., attempts to fool search engines into directing users to an irrelevant page through misrepresentations of the content). By 2002, no existing search engine gave any credence to the keyword META tags found in Web documents.[12]

As the Web has grown, HTML has been criticized as being too simplistic to provide for many desirable Web applications. HTML, in general, is used to create simple Web documents with coding primarily focused on the display aspects of the design (HTML is not particularly good at representing complex document structures). To achieve this, some believed that full support of SGML on the Web was the answer. SGML, however, is fairly complex and has features that make the programming involved complicated and lengthy. Plug-ins were developed to supplement HTML, but they require the user to download the plug-in and install it. The Java language has enhanced HTML functionality, but a person has to be able to program in order to create a Web page with it. XML, a subset of SGML, has been developed as an answer to these problems.

XML (Extensible Markup Language)

XML (ISO 8879) is touted by its developers as being just as easy to use on the Web as HTML but at the same time being as powerful as SGML.[13] Unlike HTML, XML focuses on structural markup and leaves issues of display to style sheets instead. In addition, because XML was developed some years after SGML, it incorporates techniques needed for multimedia files, such as the ability to identify the format used to encode an illustration. It is essentially a version of SGML that can be used on the Web. Its components are the same: entities, elements, and attributes. XML, however, allows, but does not require a Document Type Definition (DTD).

A DTD is an SGML or XML application. A DTD defines, with its own notation, the structure of a particular *type* of document. It gives advance notice of what names and structures can be used in a particular document type, so that all documents that belong to a particular type will be alike. It could be thought of as like a template for a particular type of document. A DTD defines:

- the elements that might be part of that particular document type
- element names and whether they are repeatable
- the contents of elements (in a general way, not specifically)
- what can be omitted
- tag attributes and default values
- names of permissible entities

For example, a DTD for a memo might have the following lines:

```
<!DOCTYPE memo [
<!ELEMENT memo (to, from, date, subject?, para+) >
<!ELEMENT to (#PCDATA) >
<!ELEMENT from (#PCDATA) >
...etc.] >
```

This DTD is stating that a *memo* includes a *to* element, a *from* element, and a *date* element; it includes one or more paragraphs, as indicated by the plus sign; and it may or may not include a *subject* element, as per the question mark. It also states that the *to* and *from* elements are made up of alphanumeric character strings (#PCDATA).

In the XML environment, there is an alternative to DTDs known as *XML schemas.* Schemas have evolved as richer forms of DTDs, which define the content and semantics of documents, in addition to their structure. An XML schema differs from a DTD in being expressed in the XML syntax itself and in following XML rules. Therefore, a developer does not have to learn another notation, and the software does not have to have a different parser. An XML schema can also define shared vocabularies with links to the namespaces in which those vocabularies reside, which cannot be part of an XML DTD. In short, an XML Schema defines:

- elements and attributes that can appear in a document
- parent-child relationships among elements
- the order and number of child elements
- whether an element is empty or can include text
- data types for elements and attributes
- default and fixed values for elements and attributes[14]

An XML Schema for a memo would be written in XML and look like XML tagging:

```
<xs:element name = "memo">
<xs:complexType>
<xs:sequence>
<xs:element name = "from" type = "xs:string"/>
<xs:element name = "to" type = "xs:string"/>
etc.,...
</xs:sequence>
</xs:complexType>
</xs:element>
```

This XML schema is stating that this document is a *memo;* it is made up of multiple elements in a particular sequence, which includes *from* and *to* elements, which are made up of textual strings.

An XML DTD or XML schema may be created for only one document, in which case it may be contained at the beginning of the text, but creating a DTD or schema is time-consuming. It makes more sense to create DTDs or schemas that can be used for many documents. These exist separately from the texts that refer to them. Many DTDs and schemas have been created and are in general use. A few of these are discussed below as examples. They are:

- **TEI Schema**—for encoding literary texts
- **EAD DTD and Schema**—for encoding archival finding aids
- **ONIX DTD and Schema**—for encoding publishers' records
- **MARCXML Schema** and **MODS**—for encoding MARC 21 records in XML

TEI (Text Encoding Initiative) Schema. When it was created in the late 1980s, TEI[15] was designed as an SGML DTD, but over the years it has evolved first into an XML DTD, and then in the latest version, TEI 5, into an XML schema. TEI was created to overcome the difficulty of having multiple encoding schemes being used to encode old, literary, and/or scholarly texts. Once encoded, the documents could not be exchanged easily. TEI makes features of a text explicit in a format that allows the processing of that text by different programs running on different machines. The text can be represented exactly as it appears in its original printed form (in the case of encoding text from books). Texts can be exchanged for research purposes (e.g., textual analysis). TEI can also be used for newly created documents, especially in cases where authors have a particular vision of how the text should look. TEI was originally created for texts in the humanities but is no longer limited to those texts. The guidelines provide a framework that can be used to describe many kinds of texts. TEI Lite[16] is a subset of TEI in much the same way as XML is a subset of SGML. TEI Lite may be considered to contain a core set of tags from TEI. The structure of the first part of a TEI Header is shown below.

```
<teiHeader>
  <fileDesc>
    <titleStmt>...</titleStmt>
    <editionStmt>...</editionStmt>
    <extent>...</extent>
    <publicationStmt>...</publicationStmt>
    <seriesStmt>...</seriesStmt>
    <notesStmt>...</notesStmt>
    <sourceDesc>...</sourceDesc>
  </fileDesc>
  <!—remainder of the TEI Header here—>
</teiHeader>
```

For an example of a complete TEI Header, see Figure 5.6.

EAD (Encoded Archival Description) DTD and Schema. EAD[17] is an XML DTD or schema for encoding finding aids used in archives and libraries. As with other DTDs and schemas, EAD does not specify intellectual content but defines the encoding designations. It eases the ability to exchange finding aids among institutions and allows users to find out about collections in distant places. Version 2002 of the EAD DTD functions both as an SGML and an XML DTD, as well as an XML schema. It conforms to all

```
<?xml version="1.0" encoding="UTF-8" ?>
<TEI.2>
<teiHeader>
<fileDesc>
    <titleStmt>
        <title>The Child in the House: An Electronic Edition</title>
        <author>Walter Pater</author>
        <sponsor> <name id="CETH">Center for Electronic Texts in the Humanities
        (CETH)</name></sponsor>
        <respStmt><resp>Digitized, proofed, edited and encoded in TEI SGML by </resp> <name
        id="piez">Wendell Piez</name> </respStmt>
    </titleStmt>
    <extent>6200 words in <gi>text</gi>; approximately 41K bytes uncompressed.</extent>
    <publicationStmt>
        <distributor><address><addrLine><name>Center for Electronic Texts in the
        Humanities</name></addrLine><addrLine>169 College Avenue</addrLine><addrLine>New
        Brunswick NJ 08903</addrLine></address> </distributor>
        <availability><p id="ch0.01">Freely available for non-commercial use when distributed with
        this header intact.</p></availability>
        <date value="1995">November 1995</date>
    </publicationStmt>
    <sourceDesc><bibl id="MS">
        <author>Walter Pater</author>
        <title>Miscellaneous Studies</title>
        <edition>Library Edition</edition>
        <pubPlace>London</pubPlace>
        <publisher>Macmillan and Co.</publisher>
        <date value="1910">1910</date></bibl>
    </sourceDesc>
</fileDesc>
<encodingDesc>
    <projectDesc><p>This text is prepared as a dual-purpose TEI pilot: to implement the TEI Lite DTD with
    SoftQuad Author/Editor and WordPerfect 6.1 SGML edition SGML-aware editors running on a PC
    platform); and to assess application of the TEI preparatory to developing documentation for TEI markup
    procedures.</p></projectDesc>
    <tagsDecl><rendition>The TEI tag <gi>sic</gi> appears where a doubtful reading occurs in the Library
    Edition and may be rendered with its "corr" [correction] attribute in square brackets. The <gi>foreign</gi>
    tag appears for foreign words printed in Italics in the original text, and can be so
    rendered.</rendition></tagsDecl>
    <refsDecl><p id="ch0.05">The text of "The Child in the House" is designated with the unique ID "ch" to
    distinguish it from other works of Pater in a Collected Electronic Edition. The paragraphs of this text are
    designated with ID attributes, providing unique identifying codes, in the form "chX.Y", where X is 0 (for
    paragraphs in the header) or 1 (for paragraphs in the text body), and Y is the Arabic number of the
    paragraph.</p><p id="ch0.06">Empty <gi>pb</gi> [page break] elements also appear at the beginning of
    every page occurring in the Library Edition. The "ed" attribute is specified as MS (MS designating the
    volume <title>Miscellaneous Studies</title> in the Library Edition); the appropriate page number appears as
    the "n" attribute, with a code in the form "MS.N" appearing as the "id" attribute. This information is
    encoded so as to provide external references to the most commonly available complete print edition of Pater's
    works, and not strictly for encoding of cross-references within an electronic edition; for these, the
    aforementioned paragraph coding, or an extension of it, may be used.</p></refsDecl>
</encodingDesc>
<profileDesc>
    <langUsage><language id="Eng">British English</language> <language
    id="Deu">German</language> <language id="Fra">French</language> <language
    id="La">Latin</language></langUsage>
</profileDesc>
</teiHeader>
```

Figure 5.6. TEI Lite encoded record. TEI Lite coding is in bold. (This is only the Header of a TEI-encoded document.)

SGML/XML specifications. The minimum set of EAD tags required for an online finding aid include the following elements:

```
<ead>
        <eadheader>
                <eadid>...</eadid>
                <filedesc>
                        <titlestmt>
                                <titleproper>...</titleproper>
                        </titlestmt>
                </filedesc>
        </eadheader>
        <archdesc level = "fonds">
                <did>...</did>
                <dsc type = "combined">...</dsc>
        </archdesc>
</ead>
```

For a more complete example of an EAD-encoded document, see Figure 5.7.

ONIX (Online Information eXchange) DTD and Schema. ONIX[18] is a standard format that publishers can use to distribute electronic information about their books and other publications. In the online environment, it replaces the information that would be found if one were looking at the jacket cover or the container (and it often contains even more metadata about the item). ONIX covers both the content of elements (see Chapter 7) and the encoding of the metadata. XML was chosen because it is optimized for data exchange between computers, the tags are human-readable, and XML software is inexpensive enough even for small publishers. The latest version at this writing is Release 2.1 revision 03, which adds new elements to support international usage. ONIX 2.1 revision 03 comprises five parts:

- **Product Record Format specification**—a comprehensive guide to the complete ONIX for Books data element set, for all senders or receivers of book industry product information in ONIX format.
- **XML Message specification**—details of the XML message format, message header content, and recommended use of certain XML features.
- **XML DTD**—The XML definition of the ONIX product information message. The DTD consists of a number of linked text files. Together, they constitute a formal

```
<!DOCTYPE EAD PUBLIC "-//Society of American Archivists//DTD ead.dtd (Encoded
Archival Description (EAD))//EN"[
<!ENTITY cutspec Public  "-//University of California, Berkeley::Library//TEXT
(CU union table specifications)//EN"  "cutspec.sgm">
<!ENTITY hdr-cu-s-spcoll PUBLIC  "-//University of California, San
Diego::Mandeville Special Collections Library//TEXT (eadheader: name and
address)//EN"  "hdrcussp.sgm">
<!ENTITY tp-cu-s-spcoll PUBLIC "-//University of California, San
Diego::Mandeville Special Collections Library//TEXT (titlepage: name and
address)//EN"  "tpcussp.sgm">
<!ENTITY ucseal PUBLIC  "-//University of California, Berkeley::Library//NONSGML
(University of California seal)//EN"  NDATA GIF>]>

<?Pub Inc>
<ead>
<?Pub Caret>

<eadheader audience="internal"  langencoding="ISO 639" findaidstatus="unverified-full-draft">
<eadid type="SGML catalog">

PUBLIC  "-//University of California, San Diego::Mandeville Special Collections
Library//TEXT (US::CU-S::MSS 0401::Arthur Conan Doyle. Sign of the four.)//EN"
"MSS 0401.sgml"
</eadid><filedesc><titlestmt>
<titleproper>Arthur Conan Doyle Sign of the four</titleproper>
</titlestmt>

<publicationstmt>
&hdr-cu-s-spcoll;<date>&copy; 1997</date>
<p>The Regents of the University of California. All rights reserved.</p>
</publicationstmt></filedesc>

<profiledesc>
<creation>Machine-readable finding aid derived from database output.</creation>
<langusage>Description is in <language>English.</language></langusage>
</profiledesc>
</eadheader>

<frontmatter>
<titlepage>
<titleproper>Arthur Conan Doyle Sign of the four, 1890</titleproper>
<num>MSS 0401</num>
<publisher>Mandeville Special Collections Library<lb>GEISEL LIBRARY<lb><extptr
displaytype="present"  entityref="ucseal"><lb>UNIVERSITY OF CALIFORNIA, SAN DIEGO
<lb>La Jolla, CA  92093-0175</publisher>
<p>&copy; 1997 The Regents of the University of California. All rights reserved.</p>
<date>This file last updated: August 1997.</date>
</titlepage>
</frontmatter>

<findaid>
<archdesc language="en"  level="collection"  langmaterial="en">
<did>
<head>DESCRIPTIVE SUMMARY</head>
<unittitle label="Title">Arthur Conan Doyle. Sign of the four.,
<unitdate type="inclusive">1890</unitdate></unittitle>
<unitid label="Collection number">MSS 0401</unitid>

<physdesc label="Extent">0.10 linear feet (1 item (1 leaf) in one folder.)</physdesc>
```

```
<repository label="Repository"><corpname>Mandeville Special Collections Library,
Geisel Library, UC, San Diego</corpname><address><addressline>La Jolla, CA
92093-0175</addressline></address></repository>
<unitloc label="Shelf Location">For current information on the location of these
materials, please consult the Library's online catalog.</unitloc>
</did>
<admininfo>
<head>ADMINISTRATIVE INFORMATION</head>

<prefercite>
<head>Preferred Citation</head>
<p>Arthur Conan Doyle. Sign of the four., MSS 0401.  Mandeville Special
Collections Library, UCSD.</p>
</prefercite>

</admininfo>

<bioghist>
<head>BIOGRAPHY</head>
<p>British novelist and physician.</p>
</bioghist>

<scopecontent>
<head>SCOPE AND CONTENT</head>
<p>The first leaf of the manuscript of the Sherlock Holmes nove, with
holograph corrections and printer's notations.  Glued to backing. </p>
</scopecontent>
</archdesc>
</findaid>
<ref>http://roger.ucsd.edu/search/t?ucsd MSS 401 </ref>
</ead>
```

Figure 5.7. EAD encoded finding aid. EAD coding is in bold.

definition that allows standard XML software to parse, verify, and operate on the content of any correctly formulated ONIX product information message.

- **XML Schema**—The XML definition of the ONIX product information message is also available expressed in XML Schema Language, which is increasingly preferred over the DTD in some application environments.

- **Code lists**—ONIX code lists are available in a variety of forms. These lists control the values entered into certain ONIX elements—these are forms of controlled vocabulary.[19]

All of these are found on the EDItEUR Web site. For an example showing part of an ONIX record, see Figure 5.8.

```
<Product>
	<RecordReference>1234567890</RecordReference>
	<NotificationType>03</NotificationType>
	<ProductIdentifier>
		<ProductIDType>02</ProductIDType>
		<IDValue>0816016356</IDValue>
	</ProductIdentifier>
	<ProductForm>BB</ProductForm>
	<Title>
		<TitleType>01</TitleType>
		<TitleText textcase = “02”>British English, A to Zed</TitleText>
	</Title>
	<Contributor>
		<SequenceNumber>1</SequenceNumber>
		<ContributorRole>A01</ContributorRole>
		<PersonNameInverted>Schur, Norman W</PersonNameInverted>
		 <BiographicalNote>A Harvard graduate in Latin and Italian literature, Norman Schur attended the
		 University of Rome and the Sorbonne before returning to the United States to study law at Harvard
		 and Columbia Law Schools.  Now retired from legal practise, Mr Schur is a fluent speaker and writer
		 of both British and American English</BiographicalNote>
	</Contributor>
	<EditionTypeCode>REV</EditionTypeCode>
	<EditionNumber>3</EditionNumber>
	<Language>
		<LanguageRole>01</LanguageRole>
		<LanguageCode>eng</LanguageCode>
	</Language>
	<NumberOfPages>493</NumberOfPages>
	<BASICMainSubject>REF008000</BASICMainSubject>
	<AudienceCode>01</AudienceCode>
	<OtherText>
		<TextTypeCode>01</TextTypeCode>
		<Text>BRITISH ENGLISH, A TO ZED is the thoroughly updated, revised, and expanded third edition
		of Norman Schur's highly acclaimed transatlantic dictionary for English speakers.  First published as
		BRITISH SELF-TAUGHT and then as ENGLISH ENGLISH, this collection of Briticisms for Americans,
		and Americanisms for the British, is a scholarly yet witty lexicon, combining definitions with commentary
		on the most frequently used and some lesser known words and phrases.  Highly readable, it's a snip of
		a book, and one that sorts out – through comments in American – the “Queen's English” – confounding
		as it may seem.</Text>
	</OtherText>
	<Imprint>
		<ImprintName>Facts on File Publications</ImprintName>
	</Imprint>
	<Publisher>
		<PublishingRole>01</PublishingRole>
		<PublisherName>Facts on File Inc</PublisherName>
	</Publisher>
	<PublicationDate>1987</PublicationDate>
	<Measure>
		<MeasureTypeCode>01</MeasureTypeCode>
		<Measurement>9.25</Measurement>
		<MeasureUnitCode>in</MeasureUnitCode>
	</Measure>
		...
</product>
```


Figure 5.8. Part of an ONIX message. (Source: Editeur. ONIX for Books 2.1 revision 03. Available: http://www.editeur.org/onixfiles2.1/prodinf%202.1rev3.html.)

MARCXML Schema and MODS. In the mid-1990s, LC's Network Development and MARC Standards Office developed MARC-to-SGML DTDs that were converted to XML DTDs as technology evolved. There are two MARC DTDs: (1) MARC Bibliographic/Holdings/Community Information Record XML DTD and (2) MARC Authority/Classification Record XML DTD.[20] They define all the elements that can appear in a MARC record and specify how they will be tagged and represented with XML coding. A goal of development of the MARC DTDs was that MARC records should be translatable to XML automatically, and that an XML-encoded MARC record should be easily translated back to a MARC record. One of the features that makes this possible is that each field of an XML-encoded record contains all the tags, indicators, and subfield codes of the MARC field in addition to the contents of the field. But as XML DTDs have gone out of fashion in favor of XML schemas, the MARC DTDs essentially have been retired.

Two XML schemas have been developed by the LC Network Development and MARC Standards Office: a MARCXML Schema[21] and MODS (Metadata Object Description Schema).[22] The MARCXML Schema supports XML markup of full MARC 21 records, featuring lossless conversion to and from MARC 21 records, a conversion toolkit, and style sheets. It simply duplicates the MARC content designation structure in a native XML encoding format. For an example of a MARCXML-encoded record, see Figure 5.9.

MODS is an XML schema that is intended to be able to carry selected data from existing MARC 21 records in an XML environment. It is also used to create original metadata records. It includes a subset of MARC fields and uses language-based tags rather than numeric ones. For example, <title> is used rather than 245. In some cases there has been a regrouping of elements from the MARC 21 bibliographic format. Because it is only a subset of MARC, after records have been converted to MODS, the MODS records cannot be converted back to MARC 21 records without a loss of data. Version 3.3 of MODS was made available early in 2008. Because it has a high compatibility with MARC 21 records, and because it provides for richer and more structured data than is possible with the Dublin Core, MODS may eventually be preferred by libraries to the Dublin Core as a means of resource description in XML. For an example of a MODS bibliographic record, see Figure 7.5.

CONCLUSION

This chapter has discussed some of the ways of encoding metadata. An understanding of this coding and how it is accomplished is necessary to understand the information systems in place for the retrieval and

```
  <?xml version="1.0" encoding="UTF-8" ?>
- <collection xmlns="http://www.loc.gov/MARC21/slim">
- <record>
  <leader>01142cam 2200301 a 4500</leader>
  <controlfield tag="001">92005291</controlfield>
  <controlfield tag="003">DLC</controlfield>
  <controlfield tag="005">19930521155141.9</controlfield>
  <controlfield tag="008">920219s1993 caua j 000 0 eng</controlfield>
- <datafield tag="010" ind1="" ind2="">
  <subfield code="a">92005291</subfield>
    </datafield>
- <datafield tag="020" ind1="" ind2="">
  <subfield code="a">0152038655 :</subfield>
  <subfield code="c">$15.95</subfield>
    </datafield>
- <datafield tag="040" ind1="" ind2="">
  <subfield code="a">DLC</subfield>
  <subfield code="c">DLC</subfield>
  <subfield code="d">DLC</subfield>
    </datafield>
- <datafield tag="042" ind1="" ind2="">
  <subfield code="a">lcac</subfield>
    </datafield>
- <datafield tag="050" ind1="0" ind2="0">
  <subfield code="a">PS3537.A618</subfield>
  <subfield code="b">A88 1993</subfield>
    </datafield>
- <datafield tag="082" ind1="0" ind2="0">
  <subfield code="a">811/.52</subfield>
  <subfield code="2">20</subfield>
    </datafield>
- <datafield tag="100" ind1="1" ind2="">
  <subfield code="a">Sandburg, Carl,</subfield>
  <subfield code="d">1878-1967.</subfield>
    </datafield>
- <datafield tag="245" ind1="1" ind2="0">
  <subfield code="a">Arithmetic /</subfield>
  <subfield code="c">Carl Sandburg ; illustrated as an anamorphic adventure by Ted
    Rand.</subfield>
    </datafield>
- <datafield tag="250" ind1="" ind2="">
  <subfield code="a">1st ed.</subfield>
    </datafield>
- <datafield tag="260" ind1="" ind2="">
  <subfield code="a">San Diego :</subfield>
  <subfield code="b">Harcourt Brace Jovanovich,</subfield>
  <subfield code="c">c1993.</subfield>
    </datafield>
- <datafield tag="300" ind1="" ind2="">
  <subfield code="a">1 v. (unpaged) :</subfield>
  <subfield code="b">ill. (some col.) ;</subfield>
  <subfield code="c">26 cm.</subfield>
    </datafield>
```

```
- <datafield tag="500" ind1="" ind2="">
  <subfield code="a">One Mylar sheet included in pocket.</subfield>
    </datafield>
- <datafield tag="520" ind1="" ind2="">
  <subfield code="a">A poem about numbers and their characteristics. Features
    anamorphic, or distorted, drawings which can be restored to normal by viewing
    from a particular angle or by viewing the image's reflection in the provided Mylar
    cone.</subfield>
    </datafield>
- <datafield tag="650" ind1="" ind2="0">
  <subfield code="a">Arithmetic</subfield>
  <subfield code="x">Juvenile poetry.</subfield>
    </datafield>
- <datafield tag="650" ind1="" ind2="0">
  <subfield code="a">Children's poetry, American.</subfield>
    </datafield>
- <datafield tag="650" ind1="" ind2="1">
  <subfield code="a">Arithmetic</subfield>
  <subfield code="x">Poetry.</subfield>
    </datafield>
- <datafield tag="650" ind1="" ind2="1">
  <subfield code="a">American poetry.</subfield>
    </datafield>
- <datafield tag="650" ind1="" ind2="1">
  <subfield code="a">Visual perception.</subfield>
    </datafield>
- <datafield tag="700" ind1="1" ind2="">
  <subfield code="a">Rand, Ted,</subfield>
  <subfield code="e">ill.</subfield>
    </datafield>
    </record>
    </collection>
```


Figure 5.9. A MARCXML-encoded record. MARC 21 tags and content are in bold. (Source: Library of Congress, MARCXML Web pages. http://www.loc.gov/standards/marcxml//Sandburg/sandburg.xml.)

display of various kinds of metadata records. These systems are discussed in the next chapter. Then there are some separate standards for the creation of the content to be included in metadata records, and there are some standards that include both prescription of text and encoding in the same standard. These are discussed in Chapter 7.

NOTES

All URLs accessed September 2008.

1. Unicode, "Frequently Asked Questions: Basic Questions." Available: http://www.unicode.org/unicode/faq/basic_q.html.

2. This is a holdover from card catalog days when an additional card for the title proper was not made when the title was already the main entry. In most cases now, it functions as an indicator of whether a title is the main entry for the record (0 = yes; 1= no).

3. *American National Standard for Bibliographic Information Interchange: Draft* (New York: American National Standards Institute, 1984). Revision of ANSI Z39.2–1979.

4. *Information and Documentation—Format for Information Exchange,* 3rd ed. (Geneva, Switzerland: International Organization for Standardization, 1996). ISO 2709:1996(E).

5. Library of Congress, Network Development and MARC Standards Office, "MARC 21 Specifications for Record Structure, Character Sets, and Exchange Media: Character Sets and Encoding Options." Available: http://www.loc.gov/marc/specifications/speccharintro.html.

6. Gail Borden Public Library District, "Local Organizations and Officials." Available: http://innovative.gailborden.info:81/. Some information has been removed from Figure 5.5 for reasons of privacy.

7. IFLA Universal Bibliographic Control and International MARC Core Programme (UBCIM), "UNIMARC Manual: Bibliographic Format 1994." Available: http://www.ifla.org/VI/3/p1996-1/sec-uni.htm.

8. *Information Processing: Text and Office Systems: Standard Generalized Markup Language (SGML)* (Geneva, Switzerland: International Organization for Standardization, 1988). ISO 8879:1986/A1:1988(E).

9. W3C, "HTML." Available: http://www.w3.org/html/.

10. W3C, "XHTML™ 1.0: The Extensible HyperText Markup Language (Second Edition): A Reformulation of HTML 4 in XML 1.0. W3C Recommendation." Available: http://www.w3.org/TR/xhtml1/.

11. W3C, "HTML5: A vocabulary and associated APIs for HTML and XHTML." Available: http://www.w3.org/html/wg/html5/.

12. Danny Sullivan, "How to Use HTML Meta Tags," Search Engine Watch. Available: http://searchenginewatch.com/showPage.html?page=2167931.

13. W3C, "XML in 10 Points." Available: http://www.w3.org/XML/1999/XML-in-10-points.

14. W3C, "Introduction to XML Schemas." Available: http://www.w3schools.com/schema/schema_intro.asp.

15. Text Encoding Initiative, "The TEI Guidelines." Available: http://www.tei-c.org/Guidelines/.

16. Text Encoding Initiative, "TEI Lite." Available: http://www.tei-c.org/Guidelines/Customization/Lite/.

17. "EAD: Encoded Archival Description," Version 2002 Official Site, Library of Congress. Available: http://www.loc.gov/ead/.

18. Editeur, "ONIX for Books." Available: http://www.editeur.org/onix.html.

19. Ibid.

20. Library of Congress, Network Development and MARC Standards Office, "MARC in XML." Available: http://www.loc.gov/marc/marcxml.html.

21. Library of Congress, Network Development and MARC Standards Office, "MARCXML: MARC 21 XML Schema: Official Web Site." Available: http://www.loc.gov/standards/marcxml/.

22. Library of Congress, Network Development and MARC Standards Office, "MODS: Metadata Object Description Schema: Official Web Site." Available: http://www.loc.gov/standards/mods/.

SUGGESTED READINGS

Caplan, Priscilla. *Metadata Fundamentals for All Librarians.* Chicago: American Library Association, 2003. Chapter 2: "Syntax, Creation, and Storage."

"EAD: Encoded Archival Description." Version 2002 Official Site. Available: http://www.loc.gov/ead/.

Fritz, Deborah A., and Richard J. Fritz. *MARC21 for Everyone: A Practical Guide.* Chicago: American Library Association, 2003.

Furrie, Betty. *Understanding MARC Bibliographic: Machine-Readable Cataloging.* 7th ed. Library of Congress, Cataloging Distribution Service, 2003. Available: http://www.loc.gov/marc/umb.

Johnson, Bruce Chr. "XML and MARC: Which Is 'Right'?" *Cataloging & Classification Quarterly* 32, no. 1 (2001): 81–90.

Library of Congress, Network Development and MARC Standards Office. "MARC Standards." Available: http://www.loc.gov/marc/.

———. "MARCXML: MARC21 XML Schema." Available: http://www.loc.gov/standards/marcxml/.

"The MARC 21 Formats: Background and Principles." [Prepared by] MARBI in conjunction with Network Development and MARC Standards Office, Library of Congress. Washington, D.C.: Library of Congress, 1996. Available: http://lcweb.loc.gov/marc/96principl.html.

Taylor, Arlene G. *Introduction to Cataloging and Classification.* 10th ed., with the assistance of David P. Miller. Greenwood, Conn.: Libraries Unlimited, 2006. Chapter 3: "Encoding."

Text Encoding Initiative. "TEI Lite." Available: http://www.tei-c.org/Guidelines/Customization/Lite/index.xml.

W3C. "Extensible Markup Language." Available: http://www.w3.org/XML/.

———. "HTML." Available: http://www.w3.org/html/.

———. "HTML" Tutorial. Available: http://www.w3schools.com/html/.

———. "XML Tutorial." Available: http://www.w3schools.com/xml/.

Yee, Martha M., and Sara Shatford Layne. *Improving Online Public Access Catalogs.* Chicago: American Library Association, 1998. Chapter 3: "The Building Blocks: The Structure of Bibliographic and Authority Records."

CHAPTER 6

SYSTEMS AND SYSTEM DESIGN

This chapter provides an overview of some of the issues and problems in organizing information as they relate to information systems and system design. The retrieval tools described in Chapter 2 require an adequate system design to allow users to find information they seek. In order to ensure resource discovery, systems must be designed to store, retrieve, and display metadata in useful and logical ways. This chapter looks at system components that assist professionals to organize information and assist users to retrieve needed information resources; it also addresses innovations in system design and a range of other systems issues related to the information organization process. Some system design issues, many technical in nature, are not addressed here because they go beyond the scope of this book.

SYSTEMS

The *Dictionary of Computing* defines the term *system* as "anything we choose to regard (a) as a whole and (b) as comprising a set of related components.... In computing the word is freely used to refer to all kinds of combinations of hardware, software, data and other information, procedures, and human activities."[1] Therefore, managing systems may involve a single source of data handled through a single type of software or a more complex mixture of various data sources, pieces of hardware, and software components.

In information organization, the term *system* generally refers to what we call an *information system* or an *information retrieval system*. An information system performs three basic functions: *storage* (data organization), *retrieval* (based on queries), and *display* (the interface or presentation design). Each one of these functions is necessary and vital to the system, and the operation of each depends on the other two. System design decisions take into consideration all three of these functions. Data is stored in a system using a specific format that is suitable for containing the type of information being amassed. The data stored in the system is partitioned into logical groupings (e.g., in tables or indexes) based on the nature or function of that data. The groupings are based on how the individual pieces of data are encoded or tagged. For example, all of the creator metadata in the system is stored together in one index, and this metadata is identified by particular codes or tags such as <creator>, <author>, the 100 and 700 MARC field tags, and so on. To access the information, a user or another system formulates a search string for the system, which is converted to the query language used in the system in order to retrieve the data stored there. Quick retrieval is achieved through the indexing process. It allows the query to look at only the appropriate index(es), rather than trying to match the query to individual pieces of data in individual records, one record at a time. Once the data is retrieved, the proper presentation renders the raw data usable and understandable.

Among the institutions discussed in this book, libraries were the first to automate. Though the question "Why automate?" is rarely asked these days, Larry Milsap reminds us that libraries automated in order to:

- provide access to the complete catalog from multiple locations
- increase and improve access points
- increase and improve search capabilities
- eliminate or reduce inconsistencies and inaccuracies of card catalogs
- reduce the increasing problems and costs of maintaining card catalogs
- deal with pressures and influences for change[2]

With the move to automation came major changes in the ways libraries performed daily tasks and fulfilled their obligations to patrons. Archives, museums, and other cultural heritage institutions also embraced the use of information technology in making their information resources accessible to users. Today, the automation "revolution" is a thing of the past; the importance and prevalence of information technology in organizing processes and in institutions in general are just assumed. From yesterday's quills and typewriters to today's Web 2.0 applications, technology has been and will continue to be a vital part of information organization. This does not mean, however, that all of the problems of systems and organizing information have been resolved. Information professionals still have much work to do and it is unlikely that all the problems will be completely resolved before new questions come along.

Databases

One of the most basic tools used for organizing information is the *database.* According to *FOLDOC,* a database is "one or more large structured sets of persistent data, usually associated with software to update and query the data."[3] In other words, databases are organized collections of data. They provide the structure that underlies many of our information systems. A database is a set of records, each representing a specific entity, all constructed in the same way (with common attributes), and connected by relationships. The records may contain numeric information, text, or graphic representations.

Records are the basic components of a database. A record comprises data fields or data elements (such as author's name, stock number, employee's date of birth, etc.), which describe chosen attributes of an entity (a book, a product, an employee, or any other entity). A database *can* be represented in a paper format, but it is nearly always thought of as machine-readable data. Databases become necessary when there is too much information for humans to process and analyze by themselves. An everyday example to help clarify the basic components of a database is a checkbook. Each entity (transaction) has a record (a row in the checkbook). Each entity has attributes, such as a date, a check number, a payee, a transaction description, an amount, and the adjusted balance. In each column, there is a field for holding the value of each attribute. The attribute values identify, describe, and explain the entity and may indicate relationships between entities.[4]

Date	**Check #**	**Payee**	**Description**	**Amount**	**Balance**
1/17/09	332	American Library Association	Student Membership	$ 33.00	$ 795.34

Of course, most databases are more complex than this, but the checkbook example does contain all elements of the basic database structure. It should be noted that a variety of organizational methods may be used to manage the data stored inside a database, and these methods vary from system to system. A key feature of bibliographic databases is the use of indexes created to hold different types of information. For example, separate indexes may be created to track creator data, title data, subject data, and the like; the number and types of indexes that are created vary from system to system.

Today, most database applications are *relational databases.* These are databases designed using the entity-relationship model described in Chapter 4. In the relational database model, the collection of metadata typically found in a surrogate record is divided into parts (entities), which are held in various tables. These parts are linked to each other to form individual metadata displays that show how the various entities are related. Each individual piece of information is stored in only one place, reducing data redundancy, but it may be used in multiple displays. For example, an author's name may be stored only once in a table of names, but every display for each work written by that author includes the author's name. In the past, some systems were based on *hierarchical databases,* which used a traditional tree structure as the model for holding information. They consisted of one file composed of many records, which in turn were made up of numerous data fields. These databases tended to be rather inflexible and used more space as data was often repeated. Hierarchical structures are rarely used in today's information systems, and the ones that exist are being replaced primarily by relational models. Today, another option being explored is the creation of native *XML databases,* which process the data and tagging of that data in the same files.

Databases serve various functions. They may hold administrative data, a collection of images, or raw numerical data. They may contain surrogate records or hold the actual information resources of interest. They may be repositories of full-text articles or they might keep track of inventory and sales. The functions of databases can be divided into two categories: *reference databases* and *source databases.* Reference databases contain links or pointers to information sources held outside of the database, for example, a journal index containing information about the location and contents of articles that are stored elsewhere. Source databases contain the actual information sought, for example, a human resources database containing employee information. Databases created as information retrieval tools generally contain surrogate records. The retrieval tools described in Chapter 2 can all be held in computer databases, although bibliographies and finding aids are more likely to be displayed as text on paper or as electronic documents on the Web. Databases underlie almost all the tools that we use to organize information. Indexing and abstracting services, book sellers, museums, and libraries, to name a few, all rely on databases to hold the records of their inventories.

Bibliographic Networks

Bibliographic networks have as their main resource a huge database of catalog-type records. Access to the database is available for a price, and members of the network can contribute new records and download existing ones. Databases maintained by bibliographic networks are essentially online union catalogs. Bibliographic networks acquire many machine-readable cataloging records from the Library of Congress and other subscription sources. The databases also include cataloging records contributed by participating libraries. In either case, the records contain two kinds of information: (1) descriptive cataloging and subject/classification data, typically in the MARC 21 format; and (2) holdings information for libraries that have added specific items to their collections.

Bibliographic networks were organized in the 1970s to support library technical services operations through cooperative cataloging and computer-assisted card production. Although they have steadily expanded their activities, their continued emphasis on cooperative cataloging most clearly distinguishes them from other online information services that provide access to similar surrogate records. The Library of Congress MARC records, for example, are available online through other information services, but these do not offer online entry of original cataloging data, record editing, or other services that specifically support cataloging services.

The two major bibliographic networks discussed here are OCLC and Auto-Graphics. Bibliographic networks differ in their administrative structures and customer bases. OCLC (formerly known as the Online Computer Library Center, and before that as the Ohio Computer Library Center) is the largest and most comprehensive bibliographic network, which operates as an international, nonprofit membership organization. Auto-Graphics (formerly known A-G Canada, and before that as ISM/LIS, which grew out of UTLAS at the University of Toronto) operates as a for-profit company. Both are general-purpose bibliographic networks that are available to libraries of all types and sizes. Another bibliographic network, Research Libraries Information Network (RLIN), was specifically created to meet the special needs of research institutions, but in 2006, it merged with OCLC and is no longer a separate entity. OCLC offers services to libraries all over the world with a database of more than 100 million records; it is used in 112 countries and contains records in over 470 languages. Auto-Graphics is used mostly in Canada, with some customers in the United States; it has a database of over 20 million records. OCLC encourages participation through regional networks that act as its authorized agents. More than 60,000 libraries or other institutions worldwide are OCLC members. Customers may access these bibliographic network databases through web interfaces. Although it is typical for organizations to subscribe to a single bibliographic network, some libraries in the past used both RLIN and OCLC for different purposes or types of materials.

Bibliographic network databases are specifically designed to automate cataloging and allow for record sharing. If existing cataloging copy is available, it is displayed in the full MARC format, or in OCLC it can alternatively be displayed in Dublin Core format. A record editor can be used to move, change, delete, or otherwise edit individual field values to meet local cataloging requirements (called *copy cataloging*). If no cataloging copy is available, a cataloger may create a new record (called *original cataloging*). To facilitate cataloging decisions and promote consistency, bibliographic networks provide online access to the Library of Congress Name Authority and Subject Authority files. Each network has an Interlibrary Loan (ILL) subsystem, which is an obvious use of a union catalog. A variety of retrospective conversion products are offered as well.

Integrated Library Systems (ILSs)

Another type of system in use in libraries is the *Integrated Library System* (ILS). The ILS is more than just an online public access catalog (OPAC); it is a fully integrated, data, management system that includes multiple modules to perform different functions. Its purpose is to incorporate the functionality of five or six separate database tools into one integrated system, all using the same database. The greatest benefit comes from information-sharing among the various modules, reducing duplication of data and effort. An ILS may have modules to support acquisitions, cataloging, authority control, circulation, digital object management, serials management, interlibrary loan, public access (the OPAC), course reserves, and system management. This system may also be known as an Integrated Library Management System (ILMS), Library Management Support System (LMSS), or sometimes as a Library Housekeeping System (LHS) particularly in the United Kingdom.

History of the ILS

Before the first ILS appeared on the scene, computers were already being used to organize information. As mentioned in Chapter 2, computers were used in catalog production in the 1960s and 1970s to produce book and microform catalogs. At that time, computers were not the desktop machines we think of today, but were instead large mainframe systems that were run in batch mode. A quick search in the computer was not possible;

jobs (e.g., queries) were sent in batches and often the results were not available until the next day. Record formats were defined locally, as the MARC standard was still in its infancy. It was not until the late 1970s that minicomputers, which could provide some online access to information, began appearing in libraries.[5] In order to have online catalogs, there had to be a convergence of computing power, mass storage, low costs, software that could handle large files, and the files themselves in electronic format.[6]

The first automated library systems were created in the 1970s. Many of these commercially produced products were *turnkey systems*. A turnkey system is a computer system customized to include all the hardware and software necessary for a particular function or application. Often these products were developed to handle only one specific type of function, such as circulation. Then as more vendors got into the library automation business (increasing competition), additional modules were created to expand system functionality. Numerous systems failed, but by the 1980s, a second generation of online catalogs began to appear with increased search capabilities.[7] In recent years, some vendors have focused on certain types of libraries and have tailored their systems to meet specialized needs. A number of early systems were created as in-house products, but by the end of the twentieth century, most of those systems had been replaced by commercially developed packages. The Library of Congress (LC) was one of the last holdouts before it announced in 1999 that it would replace its 30-year-old in-house computer systems with the commercially produced Voyager system (produced by Endeavor at that time, but now an Ex Libris product). A major reason that LC replaced its homegrown approach (which consisted of seven separate record systems) was that data in an ILS can be shared among the different modules.

ILS Developments

In the last 20 years, there have been tremendous improvements in Integrated Library Systems. Although many of these developments have centered around the OPAC, others have affected the entire system. Some of the major developments included: the creation of Web-PACs (web-accessible catalogs); the move to graphical user interfaces (GUI); widespread implementation of client-server architecture; the use of industry-standard relational databases; support for Unicode to enable the use of multiple scripts and multiple languages; implementation of self-service features; personalized interfaces; and the creation of authentication mechanisms for remote users.[8]

Over the years, ILS vendors have continued to innovate. They have developed, either as ILS modules or as add-ons to the system, packages for digital object management, collection management, license and rights management, and search and discovery. Of these new products, the innovations in resource discovery tools (or discovery interfaces) have received the most attention in the past few years. Marshall Breeding states:

> Reacting to the need for libraries to compete with other web destinations, much product development industry energy focused on development and marketing of new web-based interfaces. The battle is on to deliver interfaces that showcase faceted browsing, relevance-ranked results, end user rating or tagging, and visual navigation—all standard fare in commercial web interfaces.[9]

Some of these resource discovery tools were created by companies outside of the ILS vendor marketplace (such as Endeca[10] or AquaBrowser[11]), while others were created by the vendors themselves (such as Encore by Innovative Interfaces[12] and Primo by Ex Libris[13]). Most of these products profess to work with *all* major ILS systems and to use XML encoding to combine information from MARC records, user tags, Web-based data, and other sources in one seamless interface.

In recent years, a growing interest in open source software (OSS) has led to the development of a few viable open-source ILS systems for libraries (such as Koha[14] and Evergreen[15]). Compared to the commercial products in the ILS marketplace, the number of open source systems is still rather small, but it is predicted that OSS ILSs may gain greater market share in the near future. Breeding states, "The success of early adopters' implementations has already diminished skepticism. Many indicators suggest that open source ILS contracts will displace larger percentages of traditional licensing models in each subsequent year."[16] This also may be affected by the decreasing number of options available in the library automation marketplace. In 1990, there were approximately 40 companies providing library automation software solutions; in 2008, because of a large number of mergers and buyouts, only about half are still in the business. For more information about current trends in integrated library systems, see the April 1st issue of *Library Journal*, which contains a review of the ILS marketplace each year.

Development of Online Public Access Catalogs (OPACs)

The online public access catalog is probably the most familiar ILS module and is the one most in need of system design attention, due to its use by people who do not have in-depth training in OPAC use. Charles Hildreth states, "The online public access catalog is the first major development that brings the benefits of automation directly to the user as a means of expanded access to library collections and as a means of organizing and presenting bibliographic information for effective self-services."[17] The OPAC has been a focus of system design research for many years. System design issues are examined below after looking at the developmental stages of the OPAC.

The evolution of the OPAC is often described in terms of *generations.* The first generation of OPACs appeared in the early 1980s as crude finding lists, often based on circulation system records[18] or simple MARC records, perhaps with a circulation, serials, or acquisitions module added on.[19] Based on card catalogs and early online retrieval systems, their searching capabilities were limited generally to authors and titles, using only left-anchored searching (i.e., all searches must be based on the first word or text string starting at the left). For example, in left-anchored searching the title *Organization of Information* must be searched starting with the word *organization,* and it will not be found by a search on the word *information.* The interface of first generation OPACS was menu-based and fairly primitive. These early systems had no subject access or reference structures. First generation OPACs were little more than poor imitations of print catalogs. Some systems were programmed to respond to commands in which a code (e.g., *a:* for author, *t:* for title, etc.) was to be followed by an exact string of characters that would be matched against the system's internal index. In some others, derived key searching was supported (i.e., taking parts of names and/or titles to create a search string).[20]

In many early systems, the display of search results was by the "last in, first out" principle (i.e., the last records entered into the system were those listed first in the display). These first generation systems were highly intolerant of user mistakes. There was little or no browsing, and little or no keyword searching with or without Boolean operators. Access points were limited only to those that were available in the card catalog. First generation OPACs were primarily book finding lists and worked best for known-item searching.[21]

With designers learning from the problems of the first generation, the second generation of OPACs in the late 1980s showed major improvements. This generation was marked by significantly improved user interfaces. Keyword searching, with its use of Boolean operators, was introduced, thus increasing the number of access points available for searching. This meant that searches were no longer required to be exact word or phrase, left-anchored searches; words could now be matched, even if they were in the middle of a text string. Also greatly enhancing the searching process were truncation and wildcard support, browsing capabilities (including index term browsing), use of full MARC records, interactive search refinement, and subject access to items. Second-generation OPACs also provided greater manipulation of search results and provided better help systems with more informative error messages[22] (although there is still a lot of work to be done in this area).

Through the early stages of the second generation of OPACs, the characteristics distinguishing each generation are fairly clear. As we move beyond the second generation, however, there are differences in how the profession refers to the more recent developments in OPACs. Some consider the systems that are currently in use (WebPACs with GUI interfaces, Z39.50 compliant systems, etc.) to be third-generation OPACs. Others describe the third generation as catalogs that are still in experimental stages. Hildreth acknowledges the improvements made in catalogs during the 1990s, but refers to these improved catalogs as *E^3 OPACs,* rather than as third generation. The E^3 OPAC (a phrase that never really caught on) is so named because it is *enhanced* in functionality and usability, *expanded* in indexing, data records, and collection coverage, and *extended* through linkages and networks, acting as a gateway to additional collections. It is marked by an improved, more intuitive graphical user interface.

Hildreth believes the improvements will continue. He describes an *upcoming* generation of OPACs (the third according to him) as accepting natural language query expressions, where the user can search in his/her own words. They will have automatic term conversion/matching aids (spelling correction, intelligent stemming, synonym tables) and closest, best-match retrieval as opposed to today's systems, which require an exact match for an item to be retrieved as possibly relevant. His third generation OPAC will provide ranked retrieval output and relevance feedback methods. These OPACs will be full-collection access tools with expanded scope and coverage.[23]

Since 2006 or so, discussions have shifted away from how the current OPACs can be improved to boisterous discussions (some would say rants and/or diatribes) about how the current generation of OPACs are inadequate (actually the language they use is a bit more colorful than that) and how massive changes are needed immediately.[24] The question now is how to design a *next generation catalog*. These discussions, which are primarily taking place on various blogs, forums, and discussion lists (such as the futurelib wiki[25] and the NGC4LIB mailing list[26]) are mostly focused on determining just what the future OPAC should be and what it should do in this increasingly Web-based, "Google-philic" information environment. Some suggestions for next generation catalogs include:

- creating a simpler interface, similar to Google or Amazon.com
- providing faceted browsing (such as is found in North Carolina State University Library's Endeca-powered OPAC)[27]

- providing access to more than just surrogate records (e.g., full-text documents, digital objects, and other original materials)
- increasing interactivity and allowing user input, similar to Web 2.0 applications where users review, rank, recommend, or tag information resources (such as can be done at the University of Pennsylvania Libraries' Penn Tags,[28] the University of Rochester Library's eXtensible Catalog,[29] and Library Thing)[30]
- radically changing the platform, making OPACs more blog-like (such as appears at Casey Bisson's Scriblio).[31]

This is an exciting area where information organization and information technology intersect. This is a period of transition and it is expected that these lively discussions will continue for the foreseeable future. Stay tuned for further developments.

SYSTEM DESIGN

Organization of Information and System Design

At times, it is unclear where the process of organizing information ends and where system design begins. In a display of metadata records from a retrieval tool, both aspects come together to present to the user the information sought. This set of results combines features of the organizing process (standard punctuation, forms of headings, etc.) and features of system design (labels, screen layout, etc.) in the presentation of the metadata. When the metadata is clear, understandable, easily retrieved, and well presented, the user usually does not notice system design or organizing elements. It is only when there are problems or confusion that these elements are discussed.

In the print world, system design was not separate from the process of creating surrogate records. Panizzi's rules included principles for what information to include in surrogate records and also standards for placing those records into a cohesive catalog. Cutter's rules included record-creation rules that emphasized collocation (i.e., placing those records in logical juxtaposition with each other) and also included a section of filing rules (i.e., Cutter's design for the card catalog). Each edition of rules that has come from the American Library Association has assumed the system design of a card catalog. Standards for the creation of bibliographies and indexes often assume a print format, generally in book form.

Of course, the term *system design* was not used for the process of deciding how print tools would be arranged and laid out. The same people who created surrogate records also controlled the display of those records. They did not think of themselves as system designers. Yet some print tools were and still are quite sophisticated finding and collocation systems. They could be sophisticated because the designers knew the contents of the surrogate records intimately. As the tools became automated though, the task of design was taken on by people who understood computers, but often had little or no knowledge of the contents of the records that would make up the system. System design is a necessity for the retrieval of organized information, whether it is or is not done by the same people who create surrogate records. It can be a design that simply displays, in no particular order, every record that contains a certain keyword. Or it can be a design that displays records in a sophisticated way to show relationships among records and among works, as well as responding to requested search words.

System design research can be divided into two categories: technology-focused research and user-centered research. These two categories are not mutually exclusive. There are overlapping concerns and interconnections between the two (e.g., the system's search functionality and the user's information-seeking behavior have important connections). Users' needs and search behavior *should* influence the design of the technological systems we use (whether they do or not is another issue). While this book is not an appropriate forum for a treatise on information retrieval and information-seeking behavior, it is helpful to start with the basic underlying assumption that users approach retrieval tools with an information need. How they meet that need is greatly affected by the characteristics of the system they encounter.

Searching Methods

According to Hildreth, two basic approaches to searching, *querying* and *browsing*, can be subdivided into more specific methods. Querying can be *phrase matching* or *keyword matching*.[32] Phrase matching is matching a particular search string to the exact text located in records in the system (or more precisely, to particular indexes created by the system). This type of query demands that the words of the string be found together in the same order as given in the search query. It does not allow for the terms or strings to be found in various fields (or indexes). Allowing the terms to be separated is a characteristic of the second type of query. Keyword searching involves matching discrete words to the system's indexes, often using Boolean operators or proximity formulations to combine them. Keywords may be matched against terms that occur in more than one field or index.

Browsing, too, can be divided into two subcategories. Presequenced, linear, system-based browsing allows users to scan lists of terms, headings, or brief titles to find topics or items of interest. This is the more structured approach, using the system's internal organization of the data to guide browsing activities. Hildreth's second type of browsing is nonlinear and multidirectional. This is browsing that is more serendipitous. It is unstructured. It uses or can use hypertext links to navigate between various items and may be more exploratory or seemingly more random. In recent years, the phrase *faceted browsing* has come into use; it refers to system-based browsing that exploits various types of data found in metadata records. This type of browsing is discussed further below.

While querying is useful when the users know exactly what they want (i.e., known-item searching), browsing in many cases may be a preferable alternative to retrieving hundreds of records in response to a query. For example, if a user is looking for an item by an author with the last name *Shaw,* but only has an initial *L* for the forename, a browsing approach will put the searcher into an index of all personal names with the surname *Shaw,* at the point where the L-forenames would begin. From that point, the user may scan names either before or after the name entered. If this listing contains, in addition to the name, the entire authoritative heading for the author, including dates and the number of records associated with that name, then the user can more easily determine which name represents the *L Shaw* sought. A subject browsing option would provide the user with a list of subjects that surround the word that was input as the search. In cases where the user is unsure of what is wanted, or when the user does not know the exact string used in the system to describe what is sought, browsing may provide a more manageable approach to meeting the user's information need.

Retrieval Models

Despite the presence of browsing in retrieval tools, our current systems are mostly oriented toward exact-match queries, in which the exact specifications of the query must be satisfied by the document representation in order to create a match. In order for a system to work fairly well, users must have a good idea of what they are looking for. This is an all-or-nothing approach. It is precise and rigid, purely mechanistic, and the burden is placed on users, not on the system. If there is no exact match, then nothing is retrieved.

However, other models do exist. For example, probabilistic retrieval is based on term weighting (which is based on word frequency). Probabilistic systems return results that match the query to some degree and are displayed in the order of decreasing similarity. Such models have been the subjects of research for many years. They represent attempts to find ways around the limitations of exact-match, Boolean-based retrieval. Such retrieval models are not without criticism. They do not take into account information-seeking behaviors such as browsing or exploratory searching, which are not query-based. In the best of all possible systems, a variety of search options and retrieval techniques would be available.

Over the years, many researchers and practitioners have made suggestions for improving online retrieval systems, but the creators of these systems have seemingly not paid attention to many of the suggestions. Evidence of this comes from two articles by Christine Borgman. In 1986 she wrote an article titled, "Why Are Online Catalogs Hard to Use?"[33] A decade later she wrote another article, "Why Are Online Catalogs *Still* Hard to Use?"[34] Borgman says that OPACs are still hard to use because their design still does not reflect an understanding of user searching behavior. She suggests that a long-term goal of system designers should be to design intuitive systems that require a minimum of instruction. Instruction has often been touted as the way around inadequate system design, but in this age of remote access, where instruction may not be available, one has to agree with Borgman: "Good training is not a substitute for good system design."[35]

Standardization and Systems

David Thomas mentions that a user's need for standardized description has not been acknowledged in online systems, leading to a loss of familiarity for the user.[36] Standardization was a key feature of the card catalog. Users who were familiar with one catalog could apply the same knowledge and skills to other catalogs they encountered with a minimum of difficulty. Standardization, however, does not happen overnight. It takes time to develop. The lack of standardization today is reminiscent of a century ago, when catalogs contained cards of varying sizes (e.g., 2 × 5 inches, 2 × 10 inches, 3 × 5 inches, etc.) and the information placed on cards lacked a standard order. Standardization came when Melvil Dewey's 7.5 × 12.5 centimeter catalog cabinets won out over other sizes.[37] In the library cataloging community, throughout the latter part of the twentieth century, there were calls for standard interfaces for online catalogs. As Martha Yee stated, "The lack of standardization across OPACs can make it difficult for catalogue users to apply their knowledge of one OPAC to searching another OPAC in a different library."[38]

Today, there are still no real standards, just broad guidelines and suggestions. Due to the competitive nature of vendors in the OPAC marketplace, a standard interface is unlikely to occur anytime soon. Vendors develop new features, and each vendor places different levels of importance on different aspects of its system design. Some have different internal organization schemes; some have different search capabilities. Vendors try to develop the most appealing interface, search features, and modules in order to gain a greater market share. This competition contributes to the lack of standardization in system design, but then again, it may be contributing to long-term system innovations and progress. This may be a question of finding the right balance between standardization and market forces. Online indexes, too, have a great deal of variety and little standardization. This is a continuation of a long history of lack of standardization in print indexes. It seems that commercial enterprises have little interest in standardizing.

Some areas in which standardization has been recommended include:

- display
- basic search queries
- treatment of initial articles
- use of Boolean operators, proximity, and truncation
- punctuation

These are discussed below.

Display

One of the key areas in which the lack of standardization is most apparent is in system displays. Displays can be divided into two categories: (1) the display of sets of retrieved results, and (2) the display of metadata in surrogate records. Both of these incorporate issues of screen layout and design.

Display of Retrieved Results. The first concern in the display issue is whether the initial search results appear as a list of individual records or as a list of headings displayed first before the actual records are presented for viewing. An example may help clarify the problem here. Some systems, in response to a search for an author with the surname *Benson,* display all Bensons in the system, alphabetized by forename. One can browse through this list and find the appropriate heading before having lists of works to sift through. Other systems return results that are lists of works related to each Benson without one knowing first how many Bensons there are. One is required to page through the list of both authors *and* titles instead of being able to browse the list of names first.

The second concern in display of results is the order in which results are shown. As mentioned earlier in this chapter, first-generation catalogs often worked on the "last in, first out" principle. As systems matured, they began to display responses to specific searches, such as those for author or title, in alphabetical order sorted by a certain field. In catalogs and indexes, the primary access point[39] (the author in most cases) was usually chosen as the field by which responses would be arranged. However, results of less specific searches, such as keyword, were sometimes displayed in reverse chronological order—using date of publication or date of record creation or entry—or in order of relevance as defined by that particular system. As systems have become more sophisticated, more control of the display has been given to the user. In most systems, users can specify, from a short predefined list of options, how they wish search results to be sorted. However, such sorting may still present problems. For example, if one chooses to have results sorted by author, then the primary access point is displayed in the sorted list, but that access point may not be the author that the user is interested in (e.g., not the Benson who is a second or later author of an information resource).

In recent years, some institutions have added *discovery interfaces,* such as Endeca[40] or AquaBrowser,[41] to their information systems, which allow *faceted browsing.* Faceted browsing relies on the metadata indexes created by the system in order to provide new and interesting ways of grouping search results. Instead of simply putting a keyword into a search box and retrieving a large randomly returned set of results, faceted browsing systems cluster the results based on certain aspects of the data (i.e., facets), such as subject matter, format, genre, language, classification number, region, time period, author, and so on. By clustering the results according to these facets, users have the ability to narrow the set to only the most pertinent results without having to scroll through page after page of results ranked by system-defined relevance.

Display of Records. When dealing with the display of individual records several questions must be addressed. These include: Does the display provide an appropriate amount of information? Which fields should be displayed? What labels should be used? Will patrons be able to view the information on a single screen? In what order should the information appear?

The type of information contained in catalog records is guided by long-established and sometimes elaborate rules. However, in local situations many records may be either longer (e.g., addition of contents notes, reviews, etc.) or shorter (e.g., minimal level records) than the common standard. Information contained in index records is quite variable. Each commercial index has its own standard for inclusion of information in records. Differences may include length of citation, abbreviations, inclusion of abstracts, and precoordinated or postcoordinated controlled vocabulary (or no controlled vocabulary).

In the case of MARC records, some data that a cataloger includes in a record often goes unseen by the public (e.g., many pieces of coded information). In a good system design, coded information could be programmed to be displayed or to be searched in meaningful ways, but neither of these options is universally available. Indexes use their own encoding schemes, perhaps MARC-based or perhaps internally created. They display records in a variety of ways, often allowing the user some control over the types and amount of information they see. Other kinds of metadata have no typical ways of being displayed.

There are often multiple levels of display in an online catalog. There may be a one-or two-line version, a brief display, and a full display. Although *full* seldom means that all information in a record is displayed, some systems do allow the display of the entire MARC record, complete with MARC tagging, to the public. The default display, when only one record is retrieved in response to a query or after a user has selected a record to view from a list, is often a brief view. The default display, however, is different from system to system. The amount and kinds of information omitted from a full record to make a brief display also differ from system to system. Allyson Carlyle and Traci Timmons surveyed 122 Web-based catalogs and determined that personal author, title, and publication fields are almost always displayed in default single-records, but other fields are displayed less frequently, and the ones that are displayed are treated inconsistently (e.g., title fields sometimes include statements of responsibility, but sometimes do not).[42] Thomas notes that users find only a small number of fields useful; so there should be guidelines for selecting the most-needed fields for display.[43] Once employed, these guidelines could also help to reduce screen clutter.

The labeling of metadata in records also varies from system to system, and there are differences in the terminology used for labeling. Often, records for serials suffer from labeling problems more than do records for monographs. The holdings information can be confusing for the user even with the most explicit labels available. In addition, the need for labeling metadata at all has been questioned. Labels can be confusing and do not necessarily cover everything in a field. For example, in the MARC format, the 245 field, usually labeled *Title,* also contains the statement of responsibility (i.e., persons or corporate bodies responsible for the intellectual contents of an information resource). Thomas points out that although many assert the need for labels, there is no empirical evidence that labeled displays are superior.[44] One could assume, then, that using unlabeled displays (e.g., using the ISBD format as seen in Figures 7.1–7.3) would cause few or no problems for users, and the need for brief records could be eliminated. However, labels and brief displays persist.

One difficulty with brief displays is that what is included in them is inconsistent from system to system. Some delete all notes, which can cause confusion, while some keep only the first note. Notes are designed to give information that clarifies data given in earlier areas of the description. Without the notes, users may be misled by the information that is given. In some systems, subject headings are not presented in the initial display. Some brief displays show no statements of responsibility or added entries. If a user has searched for a secondary author or other contributor, the brief display may not mention that person or corporate body, especially when the statement of responsibility is not included in the title area. This can cause confusion if the user does not understand that the label *Author* may only be used for the first-named person or body responsible for the item. One cannot approach a new system expecting that the metadata presented in the display will be the same as seen in the last system used.

In addition to differences in record display, the user is often faced with major differences in the order of lists of retrieved results. If the list is chronological, it may be in ascending order or in descending order. If the list is supposed to be alphabetical, there are numerous ways a computer can be programmed for alphabetical order, affected by punctuation, spacing, and other such factors. Numerical order is likewise unpredictable; not to mention the problem of whether numbers come before or after letters. These and other issues are discussed in Appendix C: Arrangement of Metadata Displays.

Display Guidelines. These different approaches to both types of displays (i.e., display of retrieved results and display of records) have led some to work toward guidelines for standardizing displays. A task force of the International Federation of Library Associations and Institutions (IFLA) in 1999 issued guidelines to assist libraries in designing or redesigning their OPACs. The guidelines consist of 37 principles based on the objectives of the catalog and the types of searches that users conduct.

> The guidelines recommend a standard set of display defaults, defined as features that should be provided for users who have not selected other options, including users who want to begin searching right away without much instruction.... The goal for the display defaults recommended is ease of use, defined as the provision of as

> much power as possible with as little training as possible. If such defaults were widely implemented, users would benefit by being able to transfer catalogue use skills acquired in one library to many other libraries.[45]

The efforts of the IFLA task force and many researchers have been focused on the users' need for powerful, but easy-to-use search tools. While this goal is noble, there was nothing to guarantee that system vendors would comply with any of the suggestions and guidelines. As of yet, neither the 1999 IFLA guidelines, nor three decades of OPAC display research appear to have made much impact on the system design of integrated library systems; the only force that seems to hold any sway with vendors is the pursuit of greater market share.

Basic Search Queries

When approaching an unfamiliar information system, users must determine in which ways they can search. Author, title, subject, and keyword searches are found in most current retrieval tools. Many OPACs also allow call number searches. In some systems, the user may be offered searches that are less common, such as combined name/title, standard number, or journal title searches. While some search types may be fairly typical among systems, the ways in which systems are indexed are anything but consistent. To illustrate, consider some of the following questions that might arise as a user begins a search. Are all authors (primary and secondary; personal and corporate) included in the same author index? How are authors searched? If keyword searching is available, which fields are searched? Can the records be searched for form or genre headings? How can users find works by *and* about an author? These are only a few of the questions a user might ask when beginning a new search. Due to the lack of standardization, the answers vary from system to system.

Users may or may not be able to choose whether an author search is interpreted by the system as an exact match, browse, or keyword search. Users may not understand there are differences among these searches. For efficiency, a user must know how the system searches a particular string. If a search for *Smith, William* is entered, will the system search for that word string exactly, no more and no less (i.e., an exact match search)? Will it search for any entry beginning with that exact word string (i.e., a browse search)? Will it search any author-related field that contains both *William* and *Smith,* returning results for *Barney, William Smith* and *William, Jonathan Smith* (i.e., a keyword search)? In these examples, if a user wishes to see a record for a particular *William Smith,* whose middle names and/or dates are not known or remembered, then an exact match or a keyword match probably will not be satisfactory. Browsing is the only efficient solution. Unfortunately, users may not understand the differences in these types of searches and the system may not make these choices discernable or even available.

The results of keyword searching are determined by the fields that are searched in the system. Some systems have generic keyword searches that search almost every field of a record (or rather, a general keyword index is created by the system). In others, choices can be made as to the type of keyword search desired. There may be separate buttons or pull-down menus so users can specify the types of keyword searches they want (e.g., subject keyword, title keyword, author keyword, etc). The fields to be included in these different types of keyword indexes vary from system to system. For example, some subject keyword indexes contain terms from subject heading fields, contents notes, and title fields, while others include only subject heading fields. Although note fields may contain subject-laden terminology, system designers almost never include them as fields to be searched for subject keywords.

Form and genre searching is relatively new and it is hoped that users will find this concept easy to understand. If users are interested in autobiographies or in specialized dictionaries, it is helpful for them to include the form or genre in the search. Few systems, so far, allow searching by form/genre, but as more metadata schemas incorporate the concept, the need for this type of search increases. For certain materials, like those used in the art and visual resources community, searches by form/genre are often essential to successful retrieval. In some systems, form/genre searching is not available, but form/genre browsing is becoming more available to users through the use of discovery interfaces (such as AquaBrowser, Encore, or Endeca) with various retrieval tools.

Over the years, it has become apparent that not all users understand the differences among searching by author, title, or subject. This was discovered when card catalogs changed from the strict dictionary form to the divided catalog form. Users were especially confused by looking for persons *as authors* in the author drawers and looking for works *about* those same persons in the subject drawers. This problem was alleviated in some card catalogs by placing all works by and about persons in a *name* catalog. Very few online systems have allowed this solution, however. Users have to know that to find works about a person, one has to do a subject search, but to find works by a person, one has to do an author search. Or they may search by keyword, but the results list is then a mixture of works by and about the person, along with anything else that might be retrieved from the database.

Other searching considerations include choosing the collection or the library branch to search. Users also should be aware of the search limits available in the system (e.g., narrowing search results using language, date, format, etc.). As is true of most of the choices discussed here, these are handled differently from system to system.

Initial Articles

Another example of the lack of consistency among systems is the handling of initial articles (*a, an, the,* and their equivalents in other languages). In many systems, there are instructions to omit initial articles when entering a search string. Users tend to follow this advice, *if* the instruction is noticeable and *if* it can be seen from the search box. If a search still includes the initial article, the system may:

- return a message that the user received no hits and no other information is included at all.
- provide the user with a message to remove the article and try again.
- treat an initial article differently depending on whether it is a keyword, browse, or exact word search.
- eliminate the article without notifying the user and perform the search.

The last possibility in the bulleted list may be good for most searches, but there are times when the article (or what appears to be an article) is needed for the search to be successful (e.g., a book titled *A is for Apple*).

Truncation, Boolean Operators, and Proximity

Other examples of the lack of standardization are found in the manner in which systems handle truncation, Boolean operators, and proximity. Users need to know if there is automatic right-truncation and, if not, which truncation symbol is to be used. Automatic right-hand truncation happens when a user inputs a search word or string, and the system returns everything that begins with that word or string. For example, a search for *catalog* retrieves not only records for *catalog* but also records with the terms: *catalogs, catalogues, cataloging, cataloguing, cataloged, catalogued, cataloger, cataloguer, catalogers, cataloguers,* and so forth. If right-hand truncation is not automatic, a symbol must be used to indicate that right-hand truncation is desired in a search. The symbol may be a pound sign (#) or an asterisk (*) or a dollar sign ($) or any other of a number of characters. For example, in the search mentioned above, the search may need to be formulated as "catalog#" in order to bring about the same results. The use of truncation might also change depending on the type of search conducted. For example, in a single system, title searches and author searches may always use automatic truncation, but in keyword searches the user may need to input a specific truncation symbol.

Use of Boolean logic is far from consistent among systems. Most allow more than one word per command or search, but the ways in which multiple terms are treated can vary considerably. If default Boolean is used, the default may be *AND* or it may be *OR*. Most online catalogs, for example, treat a search with multiple terms as if the operator *AND* has been inserted between them. That is, all terms in the search must be present in a record for that record to be retrieved. Many search engines, though, treat such a search as if *OR* has been inserted between terms. That is, each record retrieved contains at least one of the terms, but not necessarily all the terms. When Boolean operators are *expressly* inserted, a user must know the order in which operations are carried out. For example, in a search for "catalogs OR indexes AND libraries," most systems execute the operators from left to right (i.e., records with either one of the terms *catalogs* or *indexes,* combined with the word *libraries*). Some online retrieval systems, however, may search for records with the term *catalogs* OR records containing both *indexes* and *libraries.* The best solution would be to use nesting to ensure that the execution will be carried out as desired: "(catalogs OR indexes) AND libraries"—although this may be beyond the knowledge of many users. Adding to the confusion, Boolean operators may be allowed in some types of searches, but not in others.

Users also need to know if proximity formulations are supported, and if so, how specific the formulations are. Proximity formulations are often used in indexes and some search engines, but less often in library catalogs. The degree of sophistication in formulation may range from a simple NEAR or ADJ (adjacent) to an indication of the distance allowed to appear between terms (e.g., *w2* or *w/2*—meaning within two words).

Punctuation

Punctuation can be a source of great confusion for users. When approaching a new system, there are a number of questions that need to be asked. They include: Are quotation marks used to indicate exact phrases? Are diacritical marks used and understood? For example, are the accent marks in *résumé* necessary, and if, so how are they to be entered? Should all punctuation be stripped from the query, and if not, which symbols can be used and which ones must be deleted? Are there filing rules or conventions based on punctuation that will thwart a user's ability to find desired search results? For example, are *meta-data* and *metadata* filed next to each other in a list of results or are they separated in the list because of the hyphen?

Removing punctuation from a string of text in order to provide better potential for matches is called *normalization*. Data normalization often occurs when the system indexes metadata records as they are entered into the database. Normalization is intended to allow better matching because users are not always precise in the placement of such marks as diacritics and commas. However, depending upon the algorithm used for normalization, results may be different from system to system.

A telling example of how the lack of standardization can affect users comes from an article by J. H. Bowman, who looked at how the ampersand (&) and the hyphen (-) are treated in various online catalogs.[46] Bowman found that the symbols were treated quite differently in various systems. The hyphen affected searching and the system's indexing in at least six different ways. In some systems, it was treated like a space. In others, it was treated as if it were a null character (i.e., nothing there, not even a space, thereby bringing the two pieces of the hyphenated word together into one word). Some systems treated it as both a null character and as a space (which meant the terms were indexed at least twice). Some viewed the hyphen simply as a hyphen, while one used the hyphen as a Boolean *NOT* (i.e., the hyphen as a minus sign). In one system, the hyphen invalidated the search altogether. In addition, Bowman found that the hyphen was sometimes processed differently in keyword searches than it was in phrase matching queries. The ampersand, too, had a variety of treatments. It was seen as an ampersand, as a Boolean *AND*, as a search string terminator, and as a null character. Besides the obvious effects that these different treatments have on the arrangement of results lists (and on the frustration levels of users scrolling through long lists of results), they can also have an impact on federated searching.

Federated Searching and Z39.50

Federated searching, also known as *meta-searching*, is the ability to search and retrieve results from multiple sources of information while using only a single, common interface. It features an all-inclusive overlay (one-search box) to multiple systems, which may include catalogs, indexes, databases, and other electronic resources. William Frost states:

> Metasearching (a.k.a. federated searching or broadcast searching) is considered by some to be the next evolutionary step of database searching. Proponents believe that novice users, such as undergraduates, are baffled by the number of databases they have to choose from and need one common interface to meet all their research needs. A common interface, they claim, could wean novice searchers from using the Internet as their primary source for research.[47]

Federated searching is a developing technology and the vocabulary has not, as of yet, been standardized. The meta-searching interface may be referred to as: a common-user interface, an integrated interface, a standardized interface, or simply as a meta-database. Wendi Arant and Leila Payne give the following three conceptual models for meta-searching:

- a single interface that masks multiple databases and platforms
- a single, monster database with all sorts of data
- some combination of the two[48]

While it appears that users may indeed desire this type of searching as a means of streamlining the research process, there are some downsides to consider. Federated searching functionality is limited to the level of the lowest common denominator. That is, if very sophisticated searching is available in System A but not in System B, then the searching that can be done from the more sophisticated System A is limited to the searching allowable in System B. In addition, precision may be greatly reduced because authority control of names and subject terms may or may not be implemented in all of the information sources being searched, or the types of controlled vocabulary may differ completely. Frost states that, in addition to these reasons, reliance on meta-searching prevents students and other users from developing a better understanding of the multiple, diverse, specialized resources available to them and how to take advantage of the different systems.[49]

Steps toward resolving problems in federated searching were once centered on the use of the Z39.50 protocol when it seemed as though all library-related searching would be done through the OPAC. This idea is somewhat passé today. The OPAC is no longer most users' first stop when looking for information resources. Discussions of federated searching, now, seem to be focused either on a meta-search engine (i.e., a search engine that searches multiple search engines) or on an interface superimposed on an integrated library system. In the latter, a single search box (found on the library's Web site) is the interface not only to the online catalog, but also to numerous databases, electronic resources, and indexes made available by the institution. Although Z39.50 is probably not going to be at the center of federated searching in the future, it continues to play a role in how some integrated library systems interact with each other today.

Z39.50

The Z39.50 communication protocol is a national standard developed by the National Information Standards Organization (NISO). Z39.50 (the number assigned to the first version of this standard) began as an attempt to get diverse library systems to communicate and share bibliographic information. The protocol establishes how one computer (the client) can query another computer (the server) and transfer search results from one to the other. The Z39.50 protocol comprises three components: (1) an abstract model of information retrieval activities, (2) a language consisting of syntax and semantics for information retrieval, and (3) a prescription for encoding search queries and retrieved results for transmission over a network.[50] The abstract information retrieval model, not tied to any specific design, allows it to interact with many information retrieval systems. Its fundamental components are the query, the database, records, results sets, and retrieval records. The standard's language allows the abstract conceptual model to be shared and understood among diverse systems. The creators of Z39.50 developed standard semantics to express queries. Attribute sets are used to define the types of qualifiers available for a search term. The combination of attribute types and values provides the way to express specifically the semantic intention of the query and to communicate what is expected of the server.

In simple terms, using the Z39.50 protocol, one system translates a set of local commands into a set of universal commands that are then sent to another computer. The second system translates the universal commands into equivalent commands for the second system. The results are then returned to the first computer in the same fashion. If two institutions both have Z39.50 clients installed, OPAC users in one institution can search the catalog of the other institution using the commands of the local system with the results display looking like the display used in the local system. Like federated searching, Z39.50 limits the searching of various catalogs to the lowest common denominator. The sophisticated programming of one system cannot be passed through Z39.50 to the other system. In addition to attribute sets, the Z39.50 protocol uses profiles to ensure interoperability:

> Profiles in Z39.50 tend to be used in order to gather particular suites of attributes, record syntaxes, and other factors together in order to meet the needs of a particular community, whether that be subject, area, or application based. Profiles span a wide range of task areas, including a profile for the geospatial community, one for government information, one for the cultural heritage sector, and others. These profiles are often developed within the community with a requirement for them.[51]

Individual communities may create more than one profile. For example, there are several library application profiles. One of the most recognized is the Bath profile *(The Bath Profile: An International Z39.50 Specification for Library Applications and Resource Discovery),* currently in its second release.[52] In fact, it was the basis for NISO Standard *Z39.89: The U.S. National Z39.50 Profile for Library Applications.*[53]

Although Z39.50 has been proven to be a useful protocol for communicating among information retrieval systems, developers are exploring new ways to perform the same tasks through updated processes. LC is now overseeing a new standard called *Search/Retrieval via URL* (SRU). SRU is a standard XML search protocol for Internet search queries that uses the Contextual Query Language (CQL), a standard syntax for representing queries.[54] It incorporates many of the ideas found in Z39.50 (i.e., it attempts to preserve many of the intellectual contributions that Z39.50 has accumulated in the last several decades); so, it can be viewed as an update or modernization of that protocol.

User-Centered System Design

Christine Borgman stated that one of the reasons that online catalogs were hard to use was that the designers did not take into account users' needs. Anna Schulze states, "Most information professionals would agree that user-centered design makes an important contribution to high quality information systems. However, there is no general agreement about how to define the term *user-centered design* or how to best implement user-centered design strategies in the development of systems and services."[55] She goes on to say that user-centered design, depending on the situation, may refer to enhancing system performance to deliver better results; creating a design for particular users, since one size does not fit all; or understanding the user through continual user input into the design process. The three keys to user-centered design are (1) observation and analysis of users at work, (2) assistance from relevant aspects of design theory, and (3) iterative testing with users.[56] These are processes that have been incorporated into the field of information architecture, which is associated with designing and structuring Web spaces. Andrew Dillon states, "conducting user-centered design does require specific skills and does involve methods and practices that shape designs in desirable ways. Information Architecture just happens to be a much better term for user-centered design and the creation of usable information spaces."[57]

Universal Design

A specific type of user-centered design is the idea of universal design. Sharon Farb states, "the goal of universal design is to accommodate the widest spectrum of users, which in turn increases commercial success."[58] Without attention to universal design, systems present multiple barriers to people with disabilities. For example, GUI interfaces, multicolumn layout, and Web sites with frames may not be readable by users of speech and Braille devices; the computer mouse may not be operable for people with visual or certain orthopedic difficulties; audio cues cannot be heard by people with hearing loss; screen colors may obscure text for people with color blindness and for others with visual impairment; blinking cursors and flashing text may be detrimental to people with photosensitive epilepsy; and workstations may be inaccessible to people in wheelchairs. Farb advocates implementing universal design from the outset of a system design project to create products usable by all individuals, some of whom may encounter barriers in accessing information with the current level of technology implemented in many information systems.[59]

Multiple Languages/Scripts

User-centered design also is needed to assist people whose native languages and writing scripts vary from the ones used by the majority of users. Much material is available, particularly in research institutions, in multiple languages and scripts. Ever since library catalogers stopped handwriting catalog cards, there has been a problem producing records in such non-Roman languages as Japanese, Arabic, Chinese, Korean, Persian

Hebrew, Yiddish (collectively known as JACKPHY languages), Greek, Russian, and others. Romanization was developed as a way to write metadata in Roman characters and be able to interfile the records with those in English and other Roman-alphabet languages. However, a majority of native speakers of non-Roman languages have found it difficult or impossible to read the Romanized records or to search for what they need. As a result, extensive non-Roman language collections have been underutilized.

For more than two decades, records created in bibliographic networks have included vernacular characters or scripts (first for Chinese, Japanese, and Korean, and gradually adding others) along with the Romanized data, but systems have not been able to display the vernacular to the public. With the Unicode standard, some systems now have the ability to display records in many character sets.[60] Each character in every modern written language is represented with a 16-bit unit of encoding with no duplication. Users in countries where the Roman alphabet is predominant also need special software to be able to search using the other character sets in addition to seeing vernacular displays of records.

Other Aids for Users

Many recommendations for improving system design to benefit users have been made over the years. One of particular importance to users is that of spelling correction. It has been proposed that spell-check programs should be incorporated into the search process. Many systems now include normalization of search strings, which eliminates the need for users to input punctuation. However, research has shown that users often make spelling errors.[61] When users receive no results due to misspelled search words, they may walk away thinking the retrieval tool does not contain the information they were seeking. Some systems already assist with this. For example, Google asks a user who types in the word "excercise" if the user really meant to search "exercise" instead (although on the Web, there are many hits for the misspelled word "excercise"). Other systems, such as those used in the airline industry, use sound-based codes so that names that sound alike but are spelled differently can be found easily. It has been suggested that such codes could be incorporated into information retrieval system design, along with dictionaries of alternative (e.g., American/British) spellings.

There have also been suggestions that making more use of MARC coding could improve systems. For example, the MARC fixed field (field 008) has coded information that is used in some systems to limit searches. Type-of-record codes (e.g., indicating sound recordings, serials, visual materials, etc.) are already used in a number of systems. In addition, the fixed field gives information as to whether the information resource being represented contains an index or bibliographical information, whether it is fiction or a biography, what the predominant language is, in which country it was published, its date of publication, and other such coded data. For example, a searcher might wish to find everything written by a prolific author that is not fiction. Good system design should be able to accommodate such a search. In addition to use of the fixed field, use of certain other MARC fields and subfields could enhance a system. For example, subfield codes in subject fields could be used to make indexes of geographic areas or form/genre terms. The 043 field, which contains encoded geographic information concerning the place covered by the content of the information resource, and the 045 field, its chronological equivalent, could also be used effectively.

Other recommendations to improve system design for users have addressed some of the following issues:

- In many systems, there are too few error messages, which are needed to help users understand their mistakes. Sometimes terminology used in error messages is not defined.
- Help screens are not always clear. And often the help system does not explain how to start or to refine a search.
- When users retrieve no hits or too many hits, instructions are needed to guide the user in how to increase or reduce results.
- *Stopword* lists (lists of words that are so common that they are of no use when searching) differ from system to system. They differ in application (e.g., stopwords that apply only at the beginning of a search string vs. stopwords that apply anywhere in the search string) and in which terms are used as stopwords (e.g., "committee" is a stopword in one system, but not another).

Authority Control Integration

Authority control is a mechanism for creating consistency in online systems and for allowing greater precision and better recall in searching.[62] Precision is enhanced by the use of standardized forms of names, while recall is improved by the system of references created. In order for authority control to be successful, authority work must be consistent and thorough. These days, in an integrated library system, authority records are linked to bibliographic records to ensure collocation of records that all relate to the same name, uniform title, or subject heading. These linkages may be one-to-one (e.g., an author who is associated with one information resource), or they may be one-to-many (e.g., a single author who has written several titles), or they may be many-to-one (e.g., linking more than one author to a single information resource). In subject headings, it is less common to find a one-to-one relationship as there are usually several or many works on the same topic. For a graphic representation of the relationship between bibliographic and authority records, see Figure 6.1. The figure shows the many-to-one and one-to-many relationships between authority records and bibliographic records.

The way this system linkage works, in simple terms, is this: Each name and subject access point (and some of the title access points) in a bibliographic record has an authority record. Each authority record may be linked to as many bibliographic records as are appropriate, and each bibliographic record may be linked to as many authority records as are appropriate. In the schematic representation in Figure 6.1, there are lines from

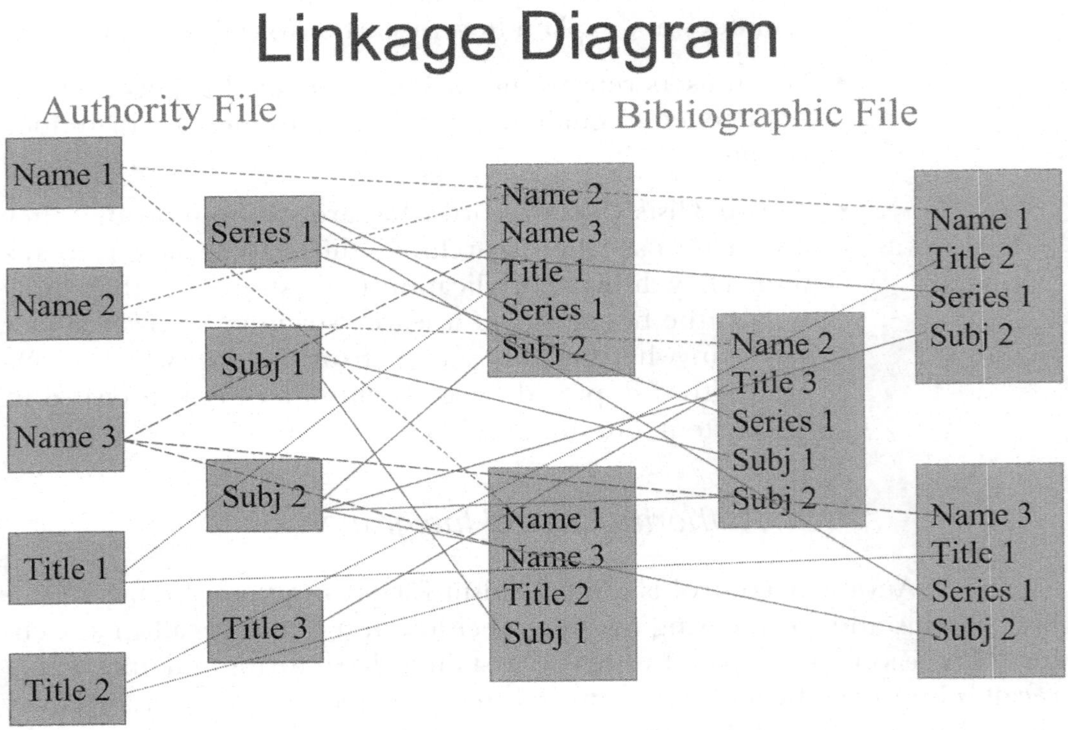

Figure 6.1. Schematic representation of Authority File/Bibliographic File linkage.

the authority records in the first two columns to the associated names, titles, or subjects in the records in the two right columns. In a system design there are links (sometime called *pointers*) from each authority record to each bibliographic record that uses the name, title, or subject in that authority record (e.g., a bibliographic record number for a record associated with an author could be used as a pointer in the authority record for the author). There would also be links in each bibliographic record back to the multiple authority records that represent all the names, titles, and subjects for that record. The result is that if a user searches for an unused subject term, the authority record presents a reference to the authorized subject term used. Then when the user requests records for the used term (usually by clicking on a hyperlink in the display), all the bibliographic records using that term are displayed. Going in the other direction, if a user has found a bibliographic record that looks promising and wants more on that subject, the link from the subject back to the subject authority record allows the system to return all of the bibliographic records that use that subject.

Because authority work on names and controlled subject vocabulary is expensive, time-consuming, human-based work, keyword searching is often touted as being a sufficient method for retrieving information resources. However, research has shown that keyword searching may result in false drops (i.e., irrelevant retrievals) because the word retrieved has a different meaning from the intended meaning and also may result in loss of recall because synonyms or near-synonyms were not retrieved with the word sought. In addition, Tina Gross and Arlene G. Taylor recently found that nearly one-third of keyword searches could fail if the authorized subject terminology is not included in the bibliographic records in the catalog, because the only place some keywords are found in some records is in the subject heading fields.[63] Users need to know, when searching, whether or not there are authority-controlled names and titles and controlled vocabulary, because, if not, users will have to think of all synonyms, related terms, and different forms of a name on their own.

Related to the need to know whether there are authority-controlled names and subject terms, users need to know whether subject relationships are available to help them to browse a subject area, to broaden or narrow searches, and to look at related topics. In the area of subject searching there have been suggestions that keyword searches be matched against both free text terms and controlled vocabulary, and that system additions be made to assist users in taking advantage of the power of controlled vocabulary. For example, the development of ways to show subject relationships in such indexes as MEDLINE could be incorporated into other retrieval tools. Tree structures, in which broader and narrower terms are shown in hierarchical relationships, have been shown to be quite useful and effective. Another example comes from commercial indexes, which often provide the ability to "explode a search." This allows a user to take advantage of the relationships among terms that are built into a controlled vocabulary. An exploded search is one in which the vocabulary term chosen is searched along with all of its narrower terms. Some systems search only the first level of narrower terms, while others search for narrower terms several levels further down in the hierarchy.

Another improvement to subject access might be to enhance subject terms with classification captions and terminology. Experimental systems have shown the viability of this approach. A notable one is the Cheshire II system created by Ray Larson and others.[64] In this system, words from the classification schedules that match the classification notation on the surrogate record are brought together with subject headings, with subject-related title words and subject-related terms from other parts of a surrogate record to create "subject clusters." Searching a cluster allows more accurate system responses than does searching each heading one by one. Others have suggested that user tags could work well to supplement the subject headings as well. At this time, the effect of user tags on subject retrieval is not clear, but it is an area where research will continue as more and more Web 2.0 applications are incorporated into traditional system designs.

CONCLUSION

This chapter has discussed systems and system design as they relate to information organization. In the days of paper indexes and card catalogs, organizers were also the designers of the systems. Perhaps a goal today would be for organizers and system designers to become so conversant in each other's languages and knowledge that each could step into the other's position with ease (or, more realistically, at least have a conversation about what is needed). Sophisticated design is wasted if the metadata that the system presents is inadequate, and sophisticated metadata is wasted if the system design is lacking.

Information professionals have provided guidelines and suggestions for interface design and for the display of results and records. Researchers and practitioners have long aimed at resolving some of the problems that users encounter in retrieval systems. There are large bodies of research on information-seeking behavior, user needs, the importance of subject access, and various retrieval methods. Some of the problems we see today could be eliminated if vendors would accept the guidelines and suggestions created by information organizations, professionals, and researchers. After 40 years of using automated systems in organizing information, it is unfortunate that we must continue to ask the question: "Why are systems still hard to use?" There are ways to institute standard features in all systems so that users can develop a lasting familiarity with retrieval tools, but that will not detract from the ability of vendors to create innovative and competitive products for the marketplace. In order for users to get the most benefit from the information tools available, organizers and system designers must work closely together. This seems to be happening in the development and use of information discovery tools and interfaces. They are allowing users to discover, browse, and explore resources in our collections. These tools show great promise in making accessible some resources that may have been hidden in traditional displays of retrieval results. Although there has been much progress in system design and in communication between organizers and designers, there is still a long way to go.

NOTES

All URLs accessed September 2008.

1. *A Dictionary of Computing*, 4th ed. (Oxford; New York: Oxford University Press, 1996), pp. 489–490.

2. Larry Milsap, "A History of the Online Catalog in North America," in *Technical Services Management, 1965–1990: A Quarter Century of Change, A Look to the Future: A Festschrift for Kathryn Luther Henderson*, eds. Linda C. Smith and Ruth C. Carter (Binghamton, N.Y.: Haworth Press, 1996), pp. 79–91.

3. Denis Howe, ed., "FOLDOC: Free On-line Dictionary of Computing." Available: http://foldoc.org/.

4. M. Jay Norton, "Knowledge Discovery in Databases," *Library Trends* 48, no. 1 (Summer 1999): 9–21.

5. Lucy A. Tedd, "OPACs through the Ages," *Library Review* 43, no. 4 (1994): 27–37.

6. Milsap, "A History of the Online Catalog," p. 79.

7. Ibid., pp. 85–86.

8. John Akeroyd and Andrew Cox, "Integrated Library Management Systems: Overview," *Vine*, no. 115 (2000): 3–10.

9. Marshall Breeding, "Automation System Marketplace 2007: An Industry Redefined," *Library Journal* 132, no. 6 (April 1, 2007): 36.

10. Endeca Technologies, "Endeca for Libraries." Available: http://endeca.com/byIndustry/media/libraries.html.

11. Medialab Solutions, "AquaBrowser." Available: http://www.aquabrowser.com/.

12. Innovative Interfaces, "Encore." Available: http://www.encoreforlibraries.com/main.html.

13. ExLibris, "Primo." Available: http://www.exlibrisgroup.com/category/PrimoOverview.

14. Koha. Available: http://www.koha.org/.

15. Evergreen. Available: http://open-ils.org/.

16. Marshall Breeding, "Automation System Marketplace 2008: Opportunity Out of Turmoil," *Library Journal* 133, no. 6 (April 1, 2008): 32.

17. Charles R. Hildreth, "Online Catalog Design Models: Are We Moving in the Right Direction? A Report Submitted to Council on Library Resources August, 1995." Available: http://myweb.cwpost.liu.edu/childret/clr-opac.html.

18. Akeroyd and Cox, "Integrated Library Management Systems," p. 3.

19. Mary K. Bolin, "Catalog Design, Catalog Maintenance, Catalog Governance," *Library Collections, Acquisitions, & Technical Services* 24 (2000): 53–63.

20. An example is a title search for *Home for the Holidays*. In OCLC, the derived search would be hom,fo,th,h. This is based on the prescribed "formula" for title searching of 3,2,2,1. That means the first three letters of the first non-stopword in the title, followed by the first two letters of the second word (whether stopword or not), and so on.

21. Tedd, "OPACs through the Ages," p. 28.

22. Hildreth, "Online Catalog Design Models."

23. Ibid.

24. See: Karen G. Schneider, "How OPACs Suck, Part 1: Relevance Rank (Or the Lack of It)," in "ALA TechSource." Available: http://www.techsource.

ala.org/blog/2006/03/how-opacs-suck-part-1-relevance-rank-or-the-lack-of-it.html; Karen G. Schneider, "How OPACs Suck, Part 2: The Checklist of Shame," in "ALA TechSource." Available: http://www.techsource.ala.org/blog/2006/04/how-opacs-suck-part-2-the-checklist-of-shame.html; Karen G. Schneider, "Unsucking the OPAC: One Man's Noble Efforts," in "ALA TechSource." Available: http://www.techsource.ala.org/blog/2006/12/unsucking-the-opac-one-mans-noble-efforts.html.

25. "Futurelib wiki." Available: http://futurelib.pbwiki.com/.

26. Archives of NGC4LIB@LISTSERV.ND.EDU: Next generation catalogs for libraries. Available: http://listserv.nd.edu/archives/ngc4lib.html.

27. North Carolina State University Libraries Catalog. Available: http://www.lib.ncsu.edu/catalog/.

28. University of Pennsylvania Libraries, "Penn Tags." Available: http://tags.library.upenn.edu/.

29. The Extensible Catalog project, University of Rochester, Rush Rhees Library. Available: http://www.extensiblecatalog.org/.

30. Library Thing. Available: http://www.librarything.com/.

31. Scriblio. Available: http://about.scriblio.net/.

32. Hildreth, "Online Catalog Design Models."

33. Christine L. Borgman, "Why Are Online Catalogs Hard to Use? Lessons Learned from Information Retrieval Studies," *Journal of the American Society for Information Science* 37, no. 6 (June 1986): 387–400.

34. Christine L. Borgman, "Why Are Online Catalogs *Still* Hard to Use?" *Journal of the American Society for Information Science* 47, no. 7 (July 1996): 493–503.

35. Ibid., p. 501.

36. David Thomas, "The Effect of Interface Design on Item Selection in an Online Catalog," *Library Resources & Technical Services* 45, no. 1 (January 2001): 20–45.

37. This was reinforced by the Library of Congress selling its cataloging on "3 × 5" cards. The size of the Library of Congress cards actually was, and continued to be, 7.5 cm × 12.5 cm, but the United States did not change to the metric system as Dewey believed was imminent. The size was just under 3 in. × 5 in., and the cards came to be called "3 × 5" cards.

38. Martha M. Yee, "Guidelines for OPAC displays: 1999," in *From Catalog to Gateway: Charting a Course for Future Access: Briefings from the ALCTS Catalog Form and Function Committee,* ed. Bill Sleeman and Pamela Bluh (Chicago: Association for Collections & Technical Services, American Library Association, 2005) p. 83. Also available: http://www.pitt.edu/~agtaylor/ala/papers/YeeOPACGuidelines.pdf.

39. For more information on primary access point, see Chapter 8.

40. Endeca Technologies, "Endeca for Libraries." Available: http://endeca.com/byIndustry/media/libraries.html.

41. Medialab Solutions, "AquaBrowser." Available: http://www.aquabrowser.com/.

42. Allyson Carlyle and Traci Timmons, "Default Record Displays in Web-Based Catalogs," *Library Quarterly* 72, no. 2 (April 2002): 179–204.

43. Thomas, "The Effect of Interface Design," pp. 42–44.

44. Ibid., p. 32.

45. Yee, "Guidelines for OPAC displays," p. 84.

46. J. H. Bowman, "The Catalog as Barrier to Retrieval—Part 1: Hyphens and Ampersands in Titles," *Cataloging & Classification Quarterly* 29, no. 4 (2000): 39–60.

47. William F. Frost, "Back Talk: Do We Want or Need Metasearching?" *Library Journal* 129, no. 6 (April 1, 2006): 68.

48. Wendi Arant and Leila Payne, "The Common User Interface in Academic Libraries: Myth or Reality?" *Library Hi Tech* 19, no. 1 (2001): 63–76.

49. Frost, "Back Talk: Do We Want or Need Metasearching?," p. 68.

50. William E. Moen, "Resource Discovery Using Z39.50: Promise and Reality," in *Proceedings of the Bicentennial Conference on Bibliographic Control for the New Millennium, November 15–17, 2000* (Washington, D.C.: Library of Congress Cataloging Distribution Service, 2001). Also available: http://www.loc.gov/catdir/bibcontrol/moen_paper.html.

51. Paul Miller, "Z39.50 for All," *Ariadne* 21 (September 20, 1999). Available: http://www.ariadne.ac.uk/issue21/z3950/.

52. Bath Profile Maintenance Agency, Library and Archives Canada, "The Bath Profile: An International Z39.50 Specification for Library Applications and Resource Discovery." Release 2.0. Available: http://www.collectionscanada.gc.ca/bath/tp-bath2-e.htm.

53. NISO, *Z39.89: The U.S. National Z39.50 Profile for Library Applications: An American Standard* (Bethesda, Md.: NISO Press, 2003).

54. Library of Congress, "SRU: Search/Retrieval via URL: SRU (the protocol), CQL (query language), ZeeRex (service description)." Available: http://www.loc.gov/standards/sru/.

55. Anna Noakes Schulze, "User-Centered Design for Information Professionals," *Journal of Education for Library and Information Science* 42, no. 2 (Spring 2001): 116.

56. Ibid.

57. Andrew Dillon, "Information Architecture in JASIST: Just Where Did We Come From?" *Journal of the American Society for Information Science and Technology* 53, no. 10 (2002): 822. Also available: http://www.gslis.utexas.edu/~adillon/Journals/IA%20ASIST%20intro.pdf.

58. Sharon Farb, "Universal Design and the Americans with Disabilities Act: Not all Systems Are Created Equal—How Systems Design Can Expand Information Access: 2000," in *From Catalog to Gateway: Charting a Course for Future Access: Briefings from the ALCTS Catalog Form and Function Committee,* ed. Bill Sleeman and Pamela Bluh (Chicago: Association for Collections & Technical Services, American Library Association, 2005) p. 100. Also available: http://www.pitt.edu/~agtaylor/ala/papers/FarbUniversalDesign.pdf.

59. Ibid.

60. Unicode, Unicode Consortium Home Page. Available: http://www.unicode.org/. For more about Unicode, see Chapter 5.

61. Arlene G. Taylor, "Authority Files in Online Catalogs: An Investigation of Their Value," *Cataloging & Classification Quarterly* 4 (Spring 1984): 1–17.

62. For more information on authority control, see Chapter 8.

63. Tina Gross and Arlene G. Taylor, "What Have We Got to Lose? The Effect of Controlled Vocabulary on Keyword Searching Results," *College & Research Libraries* 66, no. 3 (May 2005): 212–230.

64. Ray R. Larson, Jerome McDonough, Paul O'Leary, and Lucy Kuntz, "Cheshire II: Designing a Next-Generation Online Catalog," *Journal of the American Society for Information Science* 47, no. 7 (July 1996): 555–567.

SUGGESTED READINGS

Akeroyd, John, and Andrew Cox. "Integrated Library Management Systems: Overview." *Vine* 115 (2000): 3–10.

Allen, Sharon. *Beginning Relational Data Modeling.* 2nd ed. Berkeley, Calif.: Apress, 2005.

Bates, Marcia J. "The Design of Browsing and Berrypicking Techniques for the Online Search Interface." *Online Review* 13, no. 5 (October 1989): 407–424.

Beheshti, Jamshid. "The Evolving OPAC." *Cataloging & Classification Quarterly* 24, no. 1/2 (1997): 163–185.

Bilal, Dania. *Automating Media Centers and Small Libraries: A Microcomputer-Based Approach.* Greenwood Village, Colo.: Libraries Unlimited, 2002. Chapter 10: "Future OPACs."

Borgman, Christine L. "Why Are Online Catalogs *Still* Hard to Use?" *Journal of the American Society for Information Science* 47, no. 7 (July 1996): 493–503.

Breeding, Marshall. "Automation System Marketplace." *Library Journal.* April 1st issue each year.

———. Library Technology Guides. Available: http://www.librarytechnology.org/.

———. "Next Generation Catalogs." *Library Technology Reports: Expert Guides to Library Systems and Services* 43, no 4 (July/August 2007): 1–42.

Carlyle, Allyson. "Fulfilling the Second Objective in the Online Catalog: Schemes for Organizing Author and Work Records into Usable Displays." *Library Resources & Technical Services* 41, no. 2 (April 1997): 79–100.

Drabenstott, Karen M., and Marjorie S. Weller. "Failure Analysis of Subject Searches in a Test of a New Design for Subject Access to Online

Catalogs." *Journal of the American Society for Information Science* 47, no. 7 (July 1996): 519–537.

Elmasri, Ramez. *Fundamentals of Database Systems.* Boston: Pearson/Addison Wesley, 2007.

Farb, Sharon. "Universal Design and the Americans with Disabilities Act: Not All Systems Are Created Equal—How Systems Design Can Expand Information Access: 2000," in *From Catalog to Gateway: Charting a Course for Future Access: Briefings from the ALCTS Catalog Form and Function Committee,* ed. Bill Sleeman and Pamela Bluh. Chicago: Association for Collections & Technical Services, American Library Association, 2005, pp. 99–106. Also available: http://www.pitt.edu/~agtaylor/ala/papers/FarbUniversalDesign.pdf.

Hagler, Ronald. *The Bibliographic Record and Information Technology.* 3rd ed. Chicago: American Library Association, 1997. Chapter 4: "File Structure and Access Strategy."

Hildreth, Charles R. "The Use and Understanding of Keyword Searching in a University Online Catalog." *Information Technology and Libraries* 16, no. 2 (June 1997): 52–62.

Jacsó, Péter, and F. W. Lancaster. *Build Your Own Database.* Chicago: American Library Association, 1999. Chapter 1: "What is a Database?," Chapter 2: "Database Content," and Chapter 3: "Quality and Usability Factors."

Kochtanek, Thomas, and Joseph Matthews. *Library Information Systems: From Library Automation to Distributed Information Access Solutions.* Westport, Conn.: Libraries Unlimited, 2002.

Larson, Ray R. "Classification Clustering, Probabilistic Information Retrieval, and the Online Catalog." *Library Quarterly* 6, no. 2 (April 1991): 133–173.

Larson, Ray R., Jerome McDonough, Paul O'Leary, and Lucy Kuntz. "Cheshire II: Designing a Next-Generation Online Catalog." *Journal of the American Society for Information Science* 47, no. 7 (July 1996): 555–567.

Moen, William E. "Resource Discovery Using Z39.50: Promise and Reality." In *Proceedings of the Bicentennial Conference on Bibliographic Control for the New Millennium, November 15–17, 2000.* Washington, D.C.: Library of

Congress Cataloging Distribution Service, 2001, pp. 185–206. Also available: http://lcweb.loc.gov/catdir/bibcontrol/moen_paper.html.

Olson, Hope A., and John J. Boll. *Subject Analysis in Online Catalogs.* 2nd ed. Englewood, Colo.: Libraries Unlimited, 2001. Chapter 10: "User-System Interfaces" and Chapter 11: "Evaluation of Subject Retrieval in Online Catalogs."

The oss4lib Community. "oss4lib: Open Source Systems for Libraries." Available: http://www.oss4lib.org/.

Powell, Gavin. *Beginning XML Databases.* Indianapolis: Wiley, 2007.

Schulze, Anna Noakes. "User-Centered Design for Information Professionals." *Journal of Education for Library and Information Science* 42, no. 2 (Spring 2001): 116–122.

Taylor, Arlene G. *Introduction to Cataloging and Classification.* 10th ed., with the assistance of David P. Miller. Westport, Conn.: Libraries Unlimited, 2006. Chapter 19: "Processing Centers, Networking, and Cooperative Programs" and Chapter 20: "Catalog Management."

Wilson, Katie. *Computers in Libraries: An Introduction for Library Technicians.* New York: Hawthorn Information Press, 2006.

Yee, Martha M. "Guidelines for OPAC Displays: 1999." In *From Catalog to Gateway: Charting a Course for Future Access: Briefings from the ALCTS Catalog Form and Function Committee,* ed. Bill Sleeman and Pamela Bluh. Chicago: Association for Collections & Technical Services, American Library Association, 2005, pp. 83–90. Also available: http://www.pitt.edu/~agtaylor/ala/papers/YeeOPACGuidelines.pdf.

Yee, Martha M. and Sara Shatford Layne. *Improving Online Public Access Catalogs.* Chicago: American Library Association, 1998. Chapter 1: "Objectives of the Catalog" and Chapter 2: "Interfaces."

CHAPTER 7

METADATA: DESCRIPTION

Loosely speaking, there are three parts to creating metadata for an information resource: (1) providing a description of the information resource along with other information necessary for management, preservation, and structure of the resource, (2) providing for access to this description, and (3) encoding (i.e., providing the syntax of the metadata). Chapter 4 gives a general introduction to providing metadata, and encoding is discussed in Chapter 5. This chapter discusses metadata description, and Chapters 8, 9, 10, and 11 discuss various types of access to metadata and how such access may be provided.

In libraries, *bibliographic record* is the name that has been applied to the description of tangible information resources (e.g., books, sound recordings, etc.) for many years. Even though it has been applied to records created for motion pictures, sound recordings, computer files, and the like, the word *bibliographic* has continued to have a stigma arising from *biblio-*, meaning book. At times, the term *surrogate record* has been used instead. A surrogate stands in place of someone or something else. The term can be used for a record representing any kind of information resource in any kind of information retrieval system. In this and following chapters, *surrogate record* is used to mean the description and access content of a metadata record.

Some definitions are in order before discussing the creation of surrogate records. A *surrogate record* is a presentation of the characteristics of an information resource. The characteristics include both descriptive data and access points. The record stands in place of (i.e., is a surrogate for) the information resource in information retrieval systems such as catalogs, indexes, bibliographies, and search engines. An *information resource* is an instance of recorded information (e.g., a book, article, videocassette, online video, set of Web pages, sound recording, electronic journal, etc.). *Descriptive data* is data derived from an information resource and used to describe it, such as its title, associated names, edition or version, date of publication, extent, and notes identifying other pertinent features. In metadata records, a particular piece of descriptive data may be referred to as the *content* or *value* assigned to an *element*. An *access point* is any term (word, heading, etc.) in a surrogate record that is used to retrieve that record. Access points are often singled out from the descriptive data and are placed under authority control (see discussion in Chapter 8).

A file of surrogate records serves as a filter to keep a user from having to search through myriad irrelevant full texts. Surrogate records must be distinctive enough that no record can be confused with the record for any other information resource. A surrogate record's most important function is to assist the user in evaluating the possibility that the information resource it represents will be useful and contains information that the user wishes to explore further. Surrogate record descriptions are most helpful when they are predictable in both form and content. Adherence to standards ensures such predictability. Some of the existing standards are discussed below.

UNITS TO BE DESCRIBED

First, it is necessary to decide what is to be described. Traditions have been established in the library world as to what constitutes a "catalogable unit" when dealing with tangible resources. The principle, greatly simplified, has been that one physical resource is a catalogable unit with the caveat that resources that follow one another in succession and have the same title also may be a single unit. For example, this book is a single catalogable unit. Volume 1 of *The Works of Shakespeare in Two Volumes* is probably not a catalogable unit; but volumes 1 and 2 together are considered to be a single unit. Resources that come in a set with the same overarching title (although each can also have its own title) also may be called a unit. For example, *Great Books of the Western World* is a set where each volume has its own, often famous, author and title. It might be cataloged as a single unit with multiple volumes, or each volume might be cataloged as a unit.

Electronic resources have thrown this tradition into chaos. It can be very difficult to determine what is a *resource* in the electronic environment. It could be a university's home page and everything linked to it, for example, or it could be the grading policy of one department. It is going to take more time to sort through this; it may be that, given the ease of access to Web pages, a surrogate record can be created for any piece of information that someone determines needs metadata.

Finite versus Continuing Resources

One of the ways of determining the unit to be described has been to divide the world of information resources into two groups: (1) those that are complete or have a predetermined conclusion and (2) those that are ongoing—that is, those which will have additions made to them without a predetermined end in sight. For many years, these were called *monographs* and *serials,* and distinguishing between them has plagued libraries for decades. The monograph versus serial distinction has been used to set up working departments in most large academic libraries. In some cases, technical services units have been divided so that separate cataloging and acquisitions departments handle monographs, while serials departments handle both the acquisition and cataloging of serials. Other technical services units have been divided into acquisitions and cataloging, but with each of those departments being further divided into serials and monographs sections.

A new concept in the 2002 revision of AACR2R is *continuing resource,* defined as "a bibliographic resource that is issued over time with no predetermined conclusion. Continuing resources include serials and ongoing integrating resources."[1] An *integrating resource* is defined as "a bibliographic resource that is added to or changed by means of updates that do not remain discrete and are integrated into the whole."[2] This expresses the nature of many Web resources (e.g., online scholarly journals that store articles in a single cumulating database, as well as continually changing Web sites of all kinds) and has the added advantage of including traditional looseleaf print publications, which were in limbo in the past division of monograph versus serial.

Most ILSs (Integrated Library Systems) have separate modules for serials management. *Serial* was defined in AACR2R prior to the 2002 revision as: "A publication in any medium issued in successive parts bearing numeric or chronological designations and intended to be continued indefinitely."[3] This was quite limiting, and the reality is that most ILS serial modules are designed to handle anything that needs to be received and checked in over a period of time. This can include multiple-volume sets, unnumbered series, and looseleaf updates, none of which were included in AACR2R's previous definition of *serial.* The current definition is a bit better: "a continuing resource issued in a succession of discrete parts, usually bearing numbering, that has no predetermined conclusion."[4] However, this still does not encompass the whole range of ongoing resources, resulting in the need for the new concepts of *continuing resources* and *integrating resources.*

FRBR's Entities

Another problem in determining the unit to be described, also an issue for decades, is whether organizers should describe a *work* or an *item.* This problem was the source of debates between Seymour Lubetzky and Michael Gorman before the adoption of AACR2, which came down firmly on the side of describing the item, whereas Lubetzky believed that AACR1 had described the work. IFLA took on the challenge of identifying whether to describe works or items, and issued its report—*Functional Requirements for Bibliographic Records* (FRBR)—in 1998.[5] It offers the four entities of *work, expression, manifestation,* and *item.* FRBR also discusses entities that can be responsible for the existence of works—*person* and *corporate body* (with *family* added later)—and entities that can be subjects of works—*concept, object, event,* and *place.* These are discussed in other chapters.

The top level, *work,* is the one that essentially exists only in the mind of the creator. It is the distinct intellectual or artistic creation; an abstract entity, with no single material object one can point to. It is recognized through individual *expressions* of the work. Examples of *works* include Shakespeare's *Romeo and Juliet,* Mozart's *The Magic Flute,* and Michelangelo's *David.*

The second level, *expression,* is the realization of a work in alphanumeric, musical, or choreographic notation; sound; image; object; movement; among others; or a combination of such forms. An expression is "the specific intellectual or artistic form that a *work* takes each time it is 'realized.'"[6] It, too, is an intangible abstract entity (i.e., you cannot touch or buy a textual expression; only the physical item that contains it). Imagine the words of this book floating in the air before they are manifested on a computer screen or on a piece or paper. That would be an expression. There can be more than one expression of a single work. For example, for a work of Franz Schubert, expressions can be the composer's score, or a performance by the Amadeus Quartet, or a performance by the Cleveland Quartet. For this book (i.e., *The Organization of Information*), expressions might be the texts (i.e., the words, the order of presentation, etc.) that make up the first edition, the second edition, and the Chinese translation of the second edition.

The third level, *manifestation,* is a way of giving a physical embodiment to any one of the expressions of a work (although "physical" should be interpreted loosely here, as it might consist of electronic impulses in a computer, for example). It is the situation in which the same content is reproduced, even though the format may be different. In an example using *The New York Times,* a particular issue of the newspaper could have various manifestations—for example, print on paper, print on microfilm, or as a reproduction on CD-ROM. Another example might be for the expression of a school's grading policy. It might have manifestations as an HTML document, a word-processed file version, a PDF version, or a printout of one of these.

The fourth level, *item,* is the one used to define a single exemplar of a manifestation and is usually the same as the manifestation itself. As a rule, exemplars are identical to each other, but occasionally they can be different in interesting ways. For example, there might be a damaged copy, a copy autographed by the author, or a copy bound by a library's rebinding department.[7]

At this point in history, the unit that is usually chosen to be described is the *manifestation,* although in the case of something like a rare book, the *item* is described explicitly. Although metadata elements specifically related to the work and expression levels are included in surrogate records (usually as access points), some people have asked whether separate *work* and *expression* records should be created in addition to manifestation records. It is hypothesized that such descriptions could be invaluable aids in the retrieval of particular resources sought by users. They could also produce practical results such as allowing a user to place a hold on a work at the expression level if there is no reason to request a particular manifestation (e.g., the British edition is as useful to the patron as the American edition). Some have also suggested that in the future, the information now found in bibliographic records might be presented in some new form. For the time being, however, surrogate records are still the culmination of the process of description.

CREATION OF SURROGATE RECORDS

Once the unit to be described has been determined, a surrogate record is created by selecting important pieces of data (e.g., title, author, date, etc.) from the information resource, determining certain characteristics about the resource (e.g., size, terms of availability), and then placing those pieces of information in a certain order, usually dictated by a set of rules or conventions for description. These rules or conventions (i.e., *content standards*) are created by different communities, so that those communities can describe appropriately the information resources for which they are responsible. Content standards serve as style manuals for metadata, identifying the elements to be included, providing definitions of each element, and sometimes providing rules for exactly what information to include in a description, for the structure of that information, and occasionally for its punctuation and order.

Several of today's metadata schemas are outgrowths of rules that were known as bibliographic schemas or "cataloging rules." Such rules were essentially content standards, first for the content of records in print retrieval tools, and later for records to be entered into online systems. As online retrieval tools came into being, separate standards for the encoding of surrogate records were developed to be used to create online records. The conceptual pieces necessary for online records are, then, (1) elements (identification of which pieces of information are to be included), (2) content (which may be prescribed with formatting instructions or may be just loosely described in the standard), and (3) syntax (expressed as an encoding format or a markup language). A standard may dictate defined elements only (e.g., Dublin Core), content only (e.g., AACR2R), or syntax only (e.g., XML DTDs). Some metadata standards have been created that combine the conceptual pieces in different ways. TEI Headers, for example, specify what elements are required, dictate the content and form of those elements, and specify the XML syntax.

An information resource's properties may be described using community-specific or schema-associated rules. Discussed here are several examples of metadata from different communities. The emphasis in this chapter is on the content component of each schema discussed, including the elements required by each for description of information resources. The surrogate record creation standards and instructional tools discussed are:

- **Bibliographic and General Metadata Schemas**
  - *International Standard Bibliographic Description* (ISBD)
  - *Anglo-American Cataloguing Rules, Second Edition, 2002 revision* (AACR2R), with updates issued in 2003, 2004, and 2005
  - Dublin Core (DC)
  - Metadata Object Description Schema (MODS)
- **Domain-Specific Metadata Schemas**
  - *General International Standard Archival Description* (ISAD(G))

  - *Describing Archives: A Content Standard* (DACS)
  - Encoded Archival Description (EAD)
  - TEI (Text Encoding Initiative) Headers
  - FGDC (Federal Geographic Data Committee) *Content Standard for Digital Geospatial Metadata* (CSDGM)
  - VRA (Visual Resources Association) Core
  - *Categories for the Description of Works of Art* (CDWA)
  - *Cataloging Cultural Objects* (CCO)
  - ONIX (Online Information eXchange)
- **Other Surrogate Record Types**
  - Index and bibliography records
  - On-the-fly records

Bibliographic and General Metadata Schemas

Content standards in the library field were developed long before encoding standards and continue to exist as separate tools. Examples of such content standards discussed here are ISBD and AACR2. As the need for metadata for other communities, especially for electronic resources in those communities, became apparent in the mid-1990s, the Dublin Core was conceived and developed as a general-purpose schema. And MODS is the most recently developed general-purpose schema.

International Standard Bibliographic Description (ISBD)

The *International Standard Bibliographic Description* (ISBD)[8] was designed in the early 1970s to facilitate the international exchange of cataloging records by standardizing the elements to be used in the description, assigning an order to these elements, and specifying a system of symbols to be used in punctuating the elements. Actually, there have been several ISBDs based upon format of the information resource to be described.[9] The one discussed here is the consolidated version, published in 2007. Previously there were separate ISBDs for monographs, rare (antiquarian) materials, serials, continuing resources, cartographic materials, electronic resources, non-book materials, and printed music. The current version is called the "Preliminary Consolidated Edition," which, according to the IFLA ISBD Web site, has superseded the individual ISBDs. It is to be reviewed again in 2009.

When the ISBD was adopted as an international standard, it was expected that national cataloging agencies would incorporate it into their national cataloging rules. It has been widely adopted for use in many countries and incorporated into several sets of national cataloging rules, including the *Anglo-American Cataloguing Rules, Second Edition,* (AACR2R), which is discussed in more detail below.

ISBD requires that an information resource be totally identified by the description, independent of any access points. It contains eight areas:

- **Area 1**—Title and statement of responsibility
- **Area 2**—Edition
- **Area 3**—Material or type of resource specific details
- **Area 4**—Publication, production, distribution, etc.
- **Area 5**—Physical description
- **Area 6**—Series
- **Area 7**—Notes
- **Area 8**—Resource identifier and terms of availability

There are two things especially to remember when using ISBD for creating surrogate records. First, ISBD punctuation is prescribed, and it precedes and predicts the data element that comes next. For example, a space-slash-space in Area 1 says that the statement of responsibility is coming next. Second, each area contains more than one element, so the order of data is prescribed. For example, in Area 1 the prescription for content and punctuation is:

Title [GMD] : subtitle / 1st statement of responsibility ; 2nd statement of responsibility.

It can be seen that the prescribed punctuation is both preceded and followed by a space.

Area 1 contains the main title (called the *title proper*) assigned to the information resource by persons responsible for its existence. There may be more than one title (e.g., same title in two languages, subtitle, etc.), and there may be other information necessary to the understanding of the title (e.g., information about the place and date of a conference, etc.). Following the title proper and preceding any other sub-elements of the title element is the optional element, *general material designation* (GMD). The GMD indicates the class of material to which the resource belongs. The *statement of responsibility* element of Area 1 contains the names of persons or corporate bodies that are responsible for intellectual content of information resources, but not those responsible for presentation and packaging. For example, the name of the artist performing on a music CD would be included here, but not the name of the company that produced the CD. An example of Area 1 for a sound recording might look like this:

Army of me [sound recording] : remixes and covers / Björk.

Area 2 contains a statement about the version of the information resource represented in the surrogate record being created. It might be a new edition of a work, a new version of a software package, or a version of a work that is put out for a particular geographic area (e.g., the city edition of a newspaper that serves a region). Area 2 also may contain a statement of responsibility, this one relating only to the resource being described (e.g., a person who has worked on the edition in hand but did not work on earlier editions). For example:

6th ed. / revised by Richard L. DeGowin.

Area 3 contains data that are unique to a particular class of resource. For example, in describing serials, it is important to identify the date and the volume number of the first issue of the serial. An important point is that Area 3 is used only for some types of works, and this is determined by a specific implementation of ISBD in a particular national code. ISBD itself currently gives rules and examples only for mathematical data for cartographic resources, music format statements for notated music, and numbering and dates for serials. An example from a serial might be:

Vol. 1, no. 1 (Fall 1980)-

Area 4 contains the name of the publisher, producer, and/or distributor that is responsible for the issuing and release activities associated with the information resource, along with the geographic location of the publisher, producer, or distributor. There may be more than one such name and/or location. An important, broadly applicable element in this area is the date of public appearance of the resource. Area 4 is also used for data having to do with physical manufacture of a resource. Such data is given separately from the production data if manufacturing is the work of a separate entity. For example:

New Haven : Yale University Press, 2008.

Area 5 contains a physical description of an information resource that is in tangible form. The physical description includes the extent of the item given in terms of what kind of item it is (e.g., 2 sound discs, 365 p., 4 videocassettes, etc.), the dimensions of the item (often height, but also sometimes width, diameter, etc.), and other physical details such as information about illustrations or about material from which an object is made. This area, in general, is not meant for description of remote electronic resources, although sometimes an extent such as "3 maps" may be known and given, and some kinds of "other" details may be provided. For example, information about illustrations and whether or not they are in color could be important descriptive information about some electronic resources. Area 5 is also used to describe *accompanying material,* which is a physically separable part of the resource that is issued (or intended to be issued) at the same time. For example:

xxxiii, 535 p. : ill., maps ; 25 cm. + 1 answer book.

Area 6 contains the title of a larger bibliographic resource of which the information resource is part. This might be a series, sub-series, or multi-part monographic work. A series can be a group of separate works that are related in subject or form and/or are published by the same entity (e.g., *Library Science Text Series*). There may also be information other than the title: a larger bibliographic resource title can have the same kinds of additional title information as does the title proper in Area 1; and a larger resource may have statements of responsibility that relate only to the larger resource. If a series has an ISSN (International Standard Serial Number), it may appear in Area 6. Numbering of the resource within the larger resource set is also given in Area 6. For example:

(Historical preservation series ; v. 2).

Area 7 contains notes relating to the information resource being described. Notes may, to name a few, describe the nature, scope, or artistic form of the work; give the language of the text; identify the source of the title if there is no chief source of information; or explain relationships of this work to others. This is the most free-form of the areas. For example:

Includes index.

Originally published by Henmar Press as individual pieces; original copyright dates: 1960, 1977.

Area 8 contains a number that is accepted as a resource identifier, defined as a designation assigned by a publisher or a number recognized as an international standard—at the moment only the ISBN (International Standard Book Number) or the ISSN. The area may be repeated if more than one identifier is considered to be important to users. The area also contains information about the terms of availability of the information resource (e.g., it is free to members but others must pay, or it is unavailable to the public for a certain number of years, etc.). For example:

9780205430826 (pbk.)

Finally, we should say a few words about the formats that ISBD records take. In the ISBD standard, each area is to be set off from the next area by a point-space-dash-space or by the starting of a new line or paragraph. British practice in creating printed catalogs has been to have the areas follow one after another; but American practice has been to create cards and other printed catalogs by having Areas 1, 5, 7, and 8 each begin a new paragraph, and if there is more than one note in Area 7, each note begins a new paragraph. (Figures 7.1 through 7.3 are formatted using American practice.) In AACR2, both British and American formats are accepted. In most instances, at this time, format is a moot point, because the data created using rules based on ISBD are placed into MARC records. Displays that are based on these records seldom use the catalog card format. They are much more likely to have labels (e.g., TITLE: for Area 1).

Anglo-American Cataloguing Rules, Second Edition, 2002 Revision (AACR2R)

The descriptive part of *Anglo-American Cataloguing Rules, Second Edition, 2002 Revision*[10] is based on ISBD. (The access part of AACR2 is based on the Paris Principles; see discussion in Chapter 8.) After a general descriptive chapter in AACR2, other descriptive chapters cover different kinds of materials or patterns of publication:

- books, pamphlets, printed sheets—chapter 2
- cartographic materials—chapter 3
- manuscripts (including manuscript collections)—chapter 4
- music—chapter 5
- sound recordings—chapter 6
- motion pictures and videorecordings—chapter 7
- graphic materials—chapter 8
- electronic resources—chapter 9
- three-dimensional artifacts and realia—chapter 10
- microforms—chapter 11
- continuing resources—chapter 12

Rules are numbered so that the numbers of the ISBD areas follow the chapter number. Here is an example of ISBD areas as rules in chapter 5 of AACR2:

- rule 5.1—Title and statement of responsibility area
- rule 5.2—Edition area
- rule 5.3—Musical presentation statement [Material specific details area]
- rule 5.4—Publication, distribution, etc., area
- [rule 5.5 and so on]

An example of the same rule in more than one chapter is:

- rule 1.1B—general title proper
- rule 2.1B—book title proper
- rule 3.1B—map title proper
- rule 4.1B—manuscript title proper
- [rule 5.1B and so on]

Each chapter prescribes a chief source of information, from which much of the information is to be taken. For example, the chief source of information for a book is its title page. The chief source is preferred when the elements vary on or in various parts of the same information resource (e.g., if the title on the sound recording label is different from that on the container, then the one on the label is preferred).

Following ISBD, a GMD (general material designation) in Area 1 (title and statement of responsibility area) indicates the class of item being described (e.g., electronic resource, motion picture, sound recording, etc.). In this example: **American women artists [slide] : the twentieth century**, "[slide]" is the GMD. In practice, some classes of items are not given a GMD in accord with the policy of the Library of Congress (LC). For example, [cartographic material], [text], and [music] are in AACR2's GMD list but are not used by LC. This kind of information is given in the *Library of Congress Rule Interpretations* (LCRI).[11] Implementation of AACR2 in the United States is dominated by the Library of Congress, and anyone using this set of rules should also consult the decisions about how LC catalogers interpret and apply AACR2, as found in the LCRIs.

In AACR2, Area 3 [material (or type of publication) specific details] is used only for maps, printed music, and serials. Some examples of the wording that may be used in Area 3 for each of the three types of information resources are:

- **map:** Scale 1:24,000 ; Polyconic proj.
- **printed music:** Score and set of parts
- **serial:** Vol. 1, no. 1 (Jan. 1997)-

AACR2 itself prescribes three levels of description. The first level includes the minimum elements required to meet the standard. It is most likely to be used in small libraries, although LC catalogs serials at this level, adding a few elements that go beyond the first level's baseline set. The second level is the level used by LC for most cataloging. The third level includes every possible relevant element in the rules. It is used only in cataloging such things as rare items. See Figures 7.1, 7.2, and 7.3. (These figures are shown in ISBD format.)

There is one additional interpretation of AACR2 that should be mentioned. The Program for Cooperative Cataloging (PCC), which operates out of LC but is a cooperative group of catalogers from many places, has defined a set of Core Records (slightly different for different types of materials).[12] The Core Records present the minimal standard for what to include in nationally acceptable AACR2 records. The description part of the

Wireless personal communications / edited by Theodore S. Rappaport. – Kluwer Academic Publishers, 1997.

xii, 225 p. – (The Kluwer international series in engineering and computer science ; SECS 242).

"Papers in this book were originally presented at the 7th Virginia Tech/MPRG Symposium on Wireless Personal Communications held June 11-13, [1997], in Blacksburg, Virginia."

Includes bibliographical references and index.

ISBN: 0-7923-8017-7.

Figure 7.1. AACR2 first-level description.

Wireless personal communications : improving capacity, services, and reliability / edited by Theodore S. Rappaport. – Boston : Kluwer Academic Publishers, 1997.

xii, 225 p. : ill. ; 24 cm. – (The Kluwer international series in engineering and computer science ; SECS 424).

"Papers in this book were originally presented at the 7th Virginia Tech/MPRG Symposium on Wireless Personal Communications held June 11-13, [1997], in Blacksburg, Virginia."

Includes bibliographical references and index.

ISBN: 0-7923-8017-7.

Figure 7.2. AACR2 second-level description.

The works of the late Right Honorable Joseph Addison, Esq. : with a complete index. – Birmingham : printed by John Baskerville, for J. and R. Tonson ... London, 1761.

4 v. : ill., port. ; 30 cm. (4to).

Vol. 1: xxv, [3], 537, [5], 415-525 (i.e. 415-537), [5] p., [4] leaves of plates; v. 2: [8], 538, [14] p.; v. 3: 579, [13] p.; v. 4: 555, [13] p. Last leaves of v. 2 and 4 blank. Page 537 of last numbered section of v. 1 misnumbered 525.

References: Gaskell, P. J. Baskerville 17.

Contents: v. 1. Preface. Poems on several occasions. Rosamond. An essay on Virgil's Georgics. Cato. The drummer, or, The haunted house. Poemata. Dialogues upon the usefulness of ancient medals – v. 2. Remarks on several parts of Italy, &c. The Tatler. The Spectator, no. 1-89 – v. 3. The Spectator, no. 90-505 – v. 4. The Spectator, no. 507-600. The guardian. The Lover. The present state of the war, and the necessity of an augmentation, considered. The Whig-examiner. The Free-holder. Of the Christian religion.

LC copy: In v. 1 leaves Zzzz2-3 incorrectly bound before Zzz1. Vol. 2 lacks the blank at the end.

Figure 7.3. AACR2 third-level description. (Source: *Bibliographic Description of Rare Books.* Washington, D.C.: Office for Descriptive Cataloging Policy Processing Services, Library of Congress, 1981, p. 55.)

Core Record calls for complete description in Areas 1 through 6 and 8 and for some of the notes in Area 7. It is considered a *minimal* standard because it prescribes many fewer access points than does the full AACR2.

An additional source of description rules based on ISBD is *The Concise AACR2* by Michael Gorman.[13] It cannot be called a *standard* because it is a work of personal authorship and has not been adopted as official by any group. However, it is based on AACR2R and provides a way of applying much of ISBD without complicated rules or esoteric examples. It is especially useful for small libraries.

AACR2 is to be replaced in the near future by *RDA: Resource Description and Access,* which is scheduled to be published in 2009, but which will not be implemented immediately.[14] AACR2 has been criticized for inadequate rules for today's resources that often consist of multiple types of material, including Web-based resources. RDA is attempting to create a global approach to describing information resources, built upon the Anglo-American cataloging traditions, the conceptual models of FRBR (discussed above), *Functional Requirements for Authority Data* (FRAD),[15] and international cataloging principles.[16] RDA is intended to be a set of guidelines for the creation of descriptive metadata content, whether packaged as a bibliographic record, an authority record, or some other structure. It will not dictate data storage or display conventions. Rather, it is intended to provide guidelines for recording data that reflect the attributes and relationships associated with the entities described in FRBR and FRAD. Guidelines for implementing RDA in specific record syntaxes (such as ISBD, MARC 21, or Dublin Core) will be given in appendices. The current plan calls for two groups of sections: the first will focus on recording the attributes of each of the FRBR entities, and the second will focus on recording relationships between these entities.

The Dublin Core (DC)

The Dublin Core[17] (shortened form of Dublin Core Metadata Element Set—named for its first workshop, held in 1995 in Dublin, Ohio) was created in order to have an internationally agreed-upon set of metadata elements that could be completed by the creators of electronic documents. Participants in the workshops and conferences that have developed DC are experts from many different fields (e.g., publishers, computer specialists, librarians, software producers, text-markup experts, etc.). Therefore, it is a cross-domain standard and can be the basis for metadata for any type of resource in any field. It has been approved as ANSI/NISO Standard Z39.85–2007,[18] and ISO standard 15836.[19] It is used internationally, and a number of application profiles have been developed for specific domain applications that use the basic DC as a starting point.

The Dublin Core Metadata Initiative (DCMI)[20] oversees the development of implementations of the standard. DC has been implemented using HTML for a number of years. Templates have been developed that anyone can use to fill in the DC elements.[21] Such templates can be filled in and previewed, and then HTML-formatted data can be returned to the user's screen to be copied and pasted into a document header. More recently, DC has been implemented using XML. A document giving guidelines for implementing Dublin Core in XML can be found at the DCMI Web site.[22] Recommendations for expressing DC metadata using RDF are also provided.[23]

The DC Metadata Element Set[24] consists of 15 elements that can be divided into three groups:

- Elements related to the content of the resource
    - **Title**—the name of the information resource
    - **Subject**—the topic(s) of the content of the resource; use of controlled vocabularies and formal classification schemes is encouraged
    - **Description**—a textual statement of the content of the resource; could be an abstract, a table of contents, or free-text account
    - **Source**—information about a related resource from which the present one is derived in whole or in part; recommended best practice is to use a string or number from a formal identification system to identify the referenced resource
    - **Language**—an indication of the language of the intellectual content (text) of the resource; recommended best practice is to use the language tags defined in RFC 4646[25]
    - **Relation**—a reference to a related resource along with its relationship to the present source, such as a work that the described resource is a version of, is based on, or is referenced by; as with Source, recommended best practice is to use a string or number from a formal identification system to identify the referenced resource
    - **Coverage**—an identification of spatial location (i.e., a physical region), temporal period (note that this

element is for the time period of the subject of the resource, while the Date element below is for the date of creation of the resource), or jurisdiction (e.g., a named administrative entity); both spatial and temporal characteristics should be taken from a controlled list such as the *Thesaurus of Geographic Names* (TGN),[26] or geographic area should be spelled out, and date should be in a standard form such as YYYY-MM-DD

- Elements related to the resource when viewed as intellectual property

    - **Creator**—the name of the person or organization primarily responsible for creating the intellectual content of the resource (e.g., author, artist, composer, etc.)

    - **Publisher**—the name of the entity responsible for making the resource available (e.g., person, publishing house, university or one of its departments, other corporate body, etc.)

    - **Contributor**—the name of a person or organization that has made significant intellectual contributions to the content of the resource, but one that is secondary to the name in the Creator element (e.g., editor, illustrator, etc.)

    - **Rights**—a statement, link, or identifier that gives information about rights held in and over the resource (e.g., statement about property rights associated with the resource, including intellectual property rights)

- Elements related mainly to the issue of resource-as-an-instance

    - **Date**—the date of an event in the lifecycle of the resource (such as its creation date, availability date, or date of revision); it is recommended that the W3CDTF profile of ISO 8601 (Date and Time Formats) be used, especially YYYY-MM-DD as the form for a date[27]

    - **Type**—a designation of the nature or genre of the content of the resource (e.g., home page, poem, technical report, dictionary, etc.); recommended best practice is to select a value from a controlled vocabulary such as the DCMI Type Vocabulary[28]

- **Format**—a designation of the physical medium, file format, or dimensions of the resource, such as the size and duration of the resource; recommended best practice is to select a value from a controlled vocabulary such as the MIME Media Types[29]
- **Identifier**—a string or number that uniquely identifies the resource (e.g., URI, URL, DOI, or ISBN); recommended best practice is to conform to a formal identification system

From the above elements, Creator, Contributor, and Subject are access point elements, covered in Chapters 8, 10, and 11.

General principles for DC, when it was established, were: (1) the core set can be extended with further elements needed by a particular community; (2) all elements are optional; (3) all elements are repeatable; and (4) any element may be modified by qualifiers. The form of the content of each element is not prescribed. See Figure 7.4 for an example of a DC record.

For a time there were two camps among the DCMI community, each with strong advocates. The Minimalist camp wanted just the fifteen elements with no qualifiers. The Qualifiers camp insisted that subelements are both useful and necessary. In a sense, both have won. The NISO standard is just the basic elements, but qualifiers are accepted parts of the implementations.[30] There are two broad classes of qualifiers now used. *Element Refinement* qualifiers make the meaning of an element narrower or more specific. *Encoding Scheme* qualifiers identify schemes that aid in the interpretation of an element value. Table 7.1 shows some of the DC elements, with qualifiers that apply to each element shown under one of the two types of qualifiers.[31] These qualifiers have all been either approved or recommended.

Dublin Core is used worldwide. Different implementations organize resources ranging from simple cataloging of Web sites to metadata for government information in Australia. It has been used in catalogs, databases, and digital library applications. Among these, as noted already, is OCLC with an implementation in its WorldCat database. Catalogers using this system can view and download records encoded with MARC or encoded with an HTML or XML/RDF implementation of DC. A number of application profiles based on DC are in existence. An example is the *Library Application Profile*.[32] It is made up of the 15 DC elements plus an additional three elements from other namespaces: Audience, Edition, and Location.

Title	TPOT, technical processing online tools
Title.alternative	TPOT
Title.alternative	Technical processing online tools
Identifier.URI	http://tpot.ucsd.edu/
Type.AACR2-gmd	[electronic resource].
Type.Note	Web site primarily in HTML format
Contributor.namePersonal	Janczyn, George J.
Contributor.nameCorporate	UCSD Libraries.
Coverage.spatial.MARC21-gac	n-us-ca
Creator.namePersonal	
Date.issued.MARC21-Date	1994-9999
Description.note	Title from home page (viewed Jan. 19, 1999).
Description.note	Produced and managed by George J. Janczyn.
Description.note	"Serving the technical services departments of the UCSD Libraries since January 1994."
Description	Presents Technical Processing Online Tools (TPOT), serving the Library Technical Services departments of the University of California at San Diego. Provides links to TPOT news and information and to information about cataloging, acquisitions, special collections, training resources, and Innopac. Also offers access to a search utility and to information about the Library of Congress, the Online Computer Library Center (OCLC), the Internet, and Melvyl.
Format.IMT	
Language.ISO639-2	eng
Publisher	University of California, San Diego,
Publisher.place	[La Jolla, Calif. :
Relation.requires	Mode of access: Internet via World Wide Web.
Rights	
Source.URI	
Subject.class.DDC	021.65
Subject.class.DDC	025.02
Subject.class.DDC	025.3
Subject.nameCorporate.LCSH	UCSD Libraries.
Subject.topical.LCSH	Technical services (Libraries)
Subject.topical.LCSH	Cataloging.
Subject.topical	Library information networks.

Figure 7.4. Dublin Core record. (Source: OCLC WorldCat as viewed in Connexion, record number 33959367.)

DCMES Element	Element Refinement(s)	Encoding Scheme(s)
Title	Alternative	-
Subject	-	LCSH MeSH DDC LCC UDC
Description	Table Of Contents Abstract	-
Date	Created Valid Available Issued Modified Date Accepted Date Copyrighted Date Submitted	DCMI Period W3C-DTF
Type	-	DCMI Type Vocabulary
Relation	Is Version Of Has Version Is Replaced By Replaces Is Required By Requires Is Part Of Has Part Is Referenced By References Is Format Of Has Format Conforms To	URI
Coverage	Spatial	DCMI Point ISO 3166 DCMI Box TGN
	Temporal	DCMI Period W3C-DTF

Table 7.1. Some elements of the Dublin Core shown with possible qualifiers (refinements and/or encoding schemes).

Metadata Object Description Schema (MODS)

MODS was discussed in Chapter 5 as an encoding standard. It is actually a hybrid metadata schema that incorporates both encoding rules and a set of named elements. It was developed by the Library of Congress's Network Development and MARC Standards Office in consultation with other experts.[33] MODS provides an alternative "between a very simple metadata format with a minimum of fields and no or little substructure (for example, Dublin Core) and a very detailed format with many data elements having various structural complexities such as MARC21."[34] It is richer than Dublin Core but simpler than the MARC format. Its development as an XML standard means that its language-based tags can be understood by any English-speaking person; although as with all language-based tagging, international use by non-English readers is problematic.

When MODS was designed, it was decided that some MARC elements would be combined into a single MODS element and some MARC fields would be dropped altogether. In addition some MARC elements recur in more than one element as subelements. For example, *name, identifier,* and *titleInfo* can be used as both elements and subelements with the same definition for each. *Name,* for example, can be the primary name associated with the resource, or it can be a name associated with a related information resource.[35]

MODS has top-level elements followed by subelements. The 20 top-level elements are:

titleInfo	abstract	identifier
name	tableOfContents	location
typeOfResource	targetAudience	accessCondition
genre	note	part
originInfo	subject	extension
language	classification	recordInfo
physicalDescription	relatedItem	

An example of subelements follows, showing the subelements under *originInfo:*

place	dateCaptured	dateOther
publisher	dateValid	edition
dateIssued	dateModified	issuance (continuing, monographic)
dateCreated	copyrightDate	frequency

MODS was made available officially in June 2002, and experimentation and implementation have proceeded since then. In January 2008, MODS Version 3.3 was released. The MODS Implementation Registry enumerates many projects that are using MODS.[36] For example, the National Library of Australia's Australian National Bibliographic Database Metadata Project[37] has collected metadata records through the Open Archives Initiative Protocol for Metadata Harvesting (OAI-PMH) and other means. MODS has been used to transform the harvested Dublin Core descriptions into MARC records that can then be added to the National Library of Australia's "Libraries Australia Search Service." (See Figure 7.5 for a sample MODS record.)

Domain-Specific Metadata Schemas

Many metadata schemas have been developed by different communities to be used in specific situations for specialized resources. They support description that allows for details needed by users searching for resources in a particular domain. Only a few are given here as examples.

General International Standard Archival Description (ISAD(G))

The ISAD(G)[38] standard gives guidance for archival description. As with ISBD, the intention is that it be used with national standards or as a basis to develop national standards. It is designed to facilitate the creation of archival descriptions that "identify and explain the context and content of archival material in order to promote its accessibility."[39] Although much information is acquired and recorded at every stage of the management of archival resources, the ISAD rules are for description of materials starting at the point that it has been decided to preserve and control them. The rules in the standard do not explain how to describe special materials such as sound recordings, maps, and so on. Manuals that already exist for such materials are expected to be consulted as needed.

There are 26 elements identified in ISAD. Each has rules that include the name of the element, a statement of the purpose of the element in a description, the rules that apply to the element, and examples, if possible. The elements are organized into seven areas of descriptive information:

- **Identity Statement Area**—includes information essential to identify the unit being described
- **Context Area**—includes information about the origin and custody of the unit being described
- **Content and Structure Area**—includes information about the subject matter and the arrangement of the unit being described

```
- <mods:mods xmlns:mods="http://www.loc.gov/mods/">
  - <mods:titleInfo>
      <mods:title>Campbell County, Wyoming /</mods:title>
    </mods:titleInfo>
  - <mods:name type="corporate">
      <mods:namePart>Campbell County Chamber of
        Commerce</mods:namePart>
    </mods:name>
    <mods:typeOfResource>cartographic</mods:typeOfResource>
    <mods:genre authority="marc">map</mods:genre>
  - <mods:originInfo>
    - <mods:place>
        <mods:code authority="marc">wyu</mods:code>
        <mods:text>[Gillette, Wyo.]</mods:text>
      </mods:place>
      <mods:publisher>Campbell County Chamber of
        Commerce</mods:publisher>
      <mods:dateIssued>[1982?]</mods:dateIssued>
      <mods:dateIssued encoding="marc">1982</mods:dateIssued>
      <mods:issuance>monographic</mods:issuance>
    </mods:originInfo>
    <mods:language authority="iso639-2b">eng</mods:language>
  - <mods:physicalDescription>
      <mods:extent>1 map ; 33 x 15 cm.</mods:extent>
    </mods:physicalDescription>
    <mods:note type="statement of responsibility">this map reproduced by
      Campbell County Chamber of Commerce.</mods:note>
    <mods:note>In lower right corner: Kintzels-Casper.</mods:note>
  - <mods:subject>
    - <mods:cartographics>
        <mods:scale>Scale [ca. 1:510,000].</mods:scale>
      </mods:cartographics>
    </mods:subject>
  - <mods:subject authority="lcsh">
      <mods:geographic>Campbell County (Wyo.)</mods:geographic>
      <mods:topic>Maps</mods:topic>
    </mods:subject>
    <mods:classification authority="lcc">G4263.C3 1982
      .C3</mods:classification>
    <mods:identifier type="lccn">83691515</mods:identifier>
  - <mods:recordInfo>
      <mods:recordContentSource>DLC</mods:recordContentSource>
      <mods:recordCreationDate
        encoding="marc">830222</mods:recordCreationDate>
      <mods:recordChangeDate
        encoding="iso8601">19830426000000.0</mods:recordChangeDate
        >
      <mods:recordIdentifier>5466714</mods:recordIdentifier>
    </mods:recordInfo>
  </mods:mods>
```


Figure 7.5. MODS record. (Source: Library of Congress. MARC/XML Web pages.)

- **Condition of Access and Use Area**—includes information about the availability of the unit being described
- **Allied Materials Area**—includes information about other information resources that have an important relationship to the unit being described
- **Note Area**—includes information that cannot be accommodated into any of the other areas
- **Description Control Area**—includes information about the preparation of the archival description (e.g., by whom, when, how, when revised, etc.)

Only a few of the elements are considered essential for international exchange of descriptive information:

- **Reference code**—code made up of standardized country code, repository code, and local repository specific numbers
- **Title**—concise title conveying authorship, subject matter, and form of material
- **Creator**—originator of a particular collection
- **Date(s)**—dates of creation or subject matter, depending upon the nature of the unit being described
- **Extent of the unit of description**—statement of the bulk, quantity, or size
- **Level of description**—statement of the grouping being described (e.g., fonds or sub-fonds; series, sub-series, file, or item)

The standard does not dictate the encoding that is to be used, although there has been much cooperation with the development of the EAD DTD (see below).

Describing Archives: A Content Standard (DACS)

DACS[40] is a standard for the description of archival materials that has been accepted by most of the U.S. archival community. It replaces *Archives, Personal Papers, and Manuscripts* (APPM),[41] a content standard that was based on AACR2 and was used by the archival community as a standard for the creation of MARC catalog records. (AACR2 has only a skeleton chapter for manuscripts and itself acknowledges the need for other content standards to be used for archival descriptions.) DACS is based on the international standard for archives, ISAD(G), and can be used to create any type or level of description of archival and manuscript materials, including catalog records and full finding aids.[42]

DACS has three parts—one for describing archival materials, one for describing creators, and one for forms of names. The latter two parts are discussed in Chapter 8 of this text. The first chapter of DACS discusses levels of description, "from basic collection-level accession records to fully encoded, multilevel finding aids."[43] Chapters 2–8 present rules for the 25 elements of archival description. These are:

2. **Identity Elements**
   - Reference Code
   - Name and Location of Repository
   - Title
   - Date
   - Extent
   - Name of Creator(s)
   - Administrative/Biographical History
3. **Content and Structure Elements**
   - Scope and Content
   - System of Arrangement
4. **Conditions of Access and Use Elements**
   - Conditions Governing Access
   - Physical Access
   - Technical Access
   - Conditions Governing Reproduction and Use
   - Languages and Scripts of the Material
   - Finding Aids
5. **Acquisition and Appraisal Elements**
   - Custodial History
   - Immediate Source of Acquisition
   - Appraisal, Destruction, and Scheduling Information
   - Accruals (i.e., anticipated additions to the unit being described)

6. **Related Materials Elements**
   - Existence and Location of Originals
   - Existence and Location of Copies
   - Related Archival Materials
   - Publication Note
7. **Notes Elements**
   - Notes
8. **Description Control Elements**
   - Description Control

There are some major differences between describing archival materials and library resources. Aside from focusing on collection-level descriptions, archival materials usually do not have official titles, so the archivist must assign one. Guidelines are given for creating archivist-supplied titles. Archives generally contain materials that have not been published. If a collection is published, the published version is no longer archival material. Archival materials do not have series as defined in the library community; archival series are another concept entirely. In archival collections, a *series* is a logical group of files, books, correspondence, or other sets of documents. This concept is discussed in Chapter 1 of this text. Although DACS is a content standard separate from any particular method of output, it does give examples encoded both with EAD and with MARC 21.

Encoded Archival Description (EAD)

The *EAD Version 2002,*[44] discussed as an XML DTD and schema in Chapter 5, was created specifically to encode finding aids. Its design principles state: "EAD is a data structure and not a data content standard. It does not prescribe how one formulates the data that appears in any given data element—that is the role of external national or international data content standards."[45] Guidelines for finding aids are already in existence (e.g., ISAD(G) and DACS discussed above), so EAD does not need to contain prescriptions for content. However, it has a header that is based heavily on the TEI Header (see below). The header is meta-metadata, that is, metadata about the metadata in the rest of the EAD record. In many instances archival collections have been cataloged using DACS/MARC instead of, or in addition to, finding aids being created.

TEI (Text Encoding Initiative) Headers

As discussed in Chapter 5, TEI was originally an SGML DTD (now available as an XML schema) that was created in order to provide a way of encoding old, literary, and/or scholarly texts so that encoded versions could be exchanged easily. It is suggested in guidelines that one needs to customize TEI to get the best from it. A specific popular customization that is used by a core constituency is *TEI Lite.*[46]

One part of TEI is the TEI Header, created so that there is metadata as part of the text file. A strong motivation for the creation of a standard for the TEI Header was to provide a source of information for cataloging. TEI creators collaborated with library catalogers for the *file description* <fileDesc> element of the header. They wanted the mapping from TEI to a catalog record and vice versa to be as simple as possible. The standard TEI Header requires many of the same elements as does ISBD; therefore, the header content greatly resembles library cataloging.

The TEI Header has four sections, only one of which is required. The four sections are: *file description, encoding description, profile description,* and *revision description.* The *file description* is required and contains a bibliographic description of the text. It includes, for example, the title statement; author(s); publication statement; and the source description, which is a description of the original source from which the electronic text was derived. The *encoding description* explains what rules or editorial decisions were used in transcribing the text (e.g., how quotations and spelling variations were treated, information about the tags used in the document, etc.). The *profile description* has information characterizing various descriptive aspects of a text and contains what AACR2 calls added access points (e.g., names other than authors). It also contains language information, subject terminology, and classification notation(s). The *revision description* contains a record of every change that has been made to the text, including when each change was made and by whom. The form of the content that is entered into the fields is not dictated in the guidelines for TEI Headers. For an example of a TEI Header, refer back to Figure 5.6.

FGDC (Federal Geographic Data Committee) Content Standard for Digital Geospatial Metadata (CSDGM)

The title of this standard is *Content Standard for Digital Geospatial Metadata* (CSDGM),[47] but it has also been familiarly known as the FGDC metadata standard. It was mandated in 1994 when Congress passed the Paperwork

Reduction Act, and the Office of Management and Budget directed all U.S. federal agencies to create and to make publicly available metadata on their information holdings, with the directive that each agency should document all new geospatial data it collects or produces. The standard aims to provide a common set of terminology and definitions for metadata about digital geospatial data.

The FGDC standard consists of identification and definitions of elements; it does not dictate content layout or an encoding scheme, although it does provide "information about the values that are to be provided for the data elements."[48] Like the standards already discussed, it provides a way for users to learn what resources are available, whether the resources will meet their specific needs, where to find the data, and how to access the data. Version 2.0 of the standard was published in mid-1998. It has the following sections:

- identification information
- data quality information
- spatial data organization information
- spatial reference information
- entity and attribute information
- distribution information
- metadata reference information
- citation information
- time period information
- contact information

Within each of the sections, elements are listed. For example, within the section "Metadata Reference Information" the elements listed begin with: (1) date, (2) review date, (3) future review date, (4) contact, (5) standard name, (6) standard version, and so forth. Nearly all elements specify that they are "free text."

Like the standards already discussed, this one has application profiles that extend the base standard by adding elements to meet specific requirements. An example FGDC-endorsed profile of the CSDGM is the "Metadata Profile for Shoreline Data."[49] Also, like other standards, encoding using XML is recommended. The FGDC has a page giving a number of software tools available to support metadata development, some of which produce output in XML or MARCXML.[50]

Finally, it should be mentioned that there has been activity attempting to harmonize the FGDC Metadata Standard with ISO Metadata Standard 19115 for geographic information. At this writing, agreement has not been reached.[51]

VRA (Visual Resources Association) Core

According to the VRA Core[52] Web site, "the element set provides a categorical organization for the description of works of visual culture as well as the images that document them."[53] Version 4.0 of the VRA Core was released in 2007. Three documents make up this version: an introduction, an element outline, and the element descriptions with tagging examples. The element description document includes the names of the categories, each followed by a definition, information about attributes and sub-elements, recommendations for use of controlled vocabularies or standardized lists, and mappings to the previous version of the VRA Core Categories, the *Categories for the Description of Works of Art* (CDWA) (see below), and the Dublin Core elements. A VRA Core 4.0 XML Schema was developed along with Core 4.0, and in the document of element descriptions, examples are given encoded with XML. There are 19 basic categories:

- **work, collection or image**—identifies the record as being for a work (a physical or created object or an event), for an image (a visual surrogate of a work), or for a collection (an aggregate of work or image records)

- **agent**—identifies the names of entities that have contributed to the design, creation, or production of the work or image (may have subelements for personal name, corporate name, family name, culture, role, attribution; use of authority files recommended)

- **culturalContext**—identifies a culture, people, or country from which a work, image, or collection originates or with which it has been associated (use of controlled terms recommended)

- **date**—identifies date(s) associated with appearance of the work or image (the type of date attribute may be creation, design, production, alteration, restoration, etc., and subelements are for earliest date and latest date; use of standard date presentations recommended)

- **description**—note about the work, image, or collection that may include comments, description, interpretation, and any other information not recorded in other elements
- **inscription**—identifies marks or written words added to the object either at its production or in its later history (subelements may identify author, position, and type of text)
- **location**—identifies geographic location and/or a specific site location of the work or image (attributes by type may be owner, former site, creation site, discovery site, former repository, etc.; use of controlled terms recommended)
- **material**—identifies the substance that composes a work or image; often the material(s) used for the work, e.g., paper and ink, bronze, etc. (use of *Art & Architecture Thesaurus* [AAT][54] terms recommended)
- **measurements**—identifies the size, shape, scale, dimensions, or format of the work or image (attributes include types of dimensions, format, resolution, etc.)
- **relation**—identifies a related work or image and the relationship that exists between the work or image and the related work or image (includes a lengthy list of recommended relationships for the relationship type attribute, e.g., partOf, modelFor, mateOf, copyAfter, etc.)
- **rights**—identifies copyright information, intellectual property statements, or other information needed for rights management
- **source**—identifies the source of the information recorded about the work or image (e.g., a bibliographic citation to a book that describes the work or image)
- **stateEdition**—identifies the number or name of a state, edition, or impression of a work that exists in more than one form (attributes identify the number of known states, editions, or impressions and which one this is)
- **stylePeriod**—identifies a defined style, historical period, group, movement, etc., characteristics of which appear in the work or image (use of AAT terms recommended)

- **subject**—gives terms or phrases that describe or interpret the work or image and that represent what it depicts or expresses (use of controlled terms recommended)
- **technique**—identifies the processes, techniques, or methods used in making or altering the work or image (use of *AAT* terms recommended)
- **textref**—gives identification values derived from textual references (e.g., catalog number) that are not associated with a particular repository or other location
- **title**—the identifying phrase given to the work or image (use of data content rules for titles of works of art recommended)
- **worktype**—identifies the specific type of work, image, or collection being described (use of *AAT* terms recommended)

Guidelines for description using the VRA Core are included in *Cataloguing Cultural Objects: A Guide to Describing Cultural Works and Their Images*[55] (see below).

Categories for the Description of Works of Art (CDWA)

Categories for the Description of Works of Art (CDWA) is another metadata element set that, like the VRA Core, is used for describing and accessing information about works of art, architecture, other material culture, and related images.[56] CDWA comprises 512 categories and subcategories. Of these, 36 categories and subcategories are considered *core*—that is, the ones required to describe a work in a unique and unambiguous way. The CDWA core categories[57] are divided into six groupings based on their purpose or focus:

- For the object, architecture, or group
- For related textual references authority
- For creator identification authority
- For place/location authority
- For generic concept authority
- For subject authority

The core categories under the first group are:

- Catalog Level
- Object/Work Type
- Classification Term
- Title or Name
- Measurements Description
- Materials and Techniques Description
- Creator Description
- Creator Identity
- Creator Role
- Creation Date
    - Earliest Date
    - Latest Date
- Subject Matter Indexing Terms
- Current Location Repository Name/Geographic Location
- Current Repository Numbers

The remaining core categories are for access and authority control and are discussed in Chapter 8.

CDWA, like VRA Core, recommends encoding records with XML and has developed an XML schema called "CDWA Lite." CDWA Lite records are intended for repositories using the Open Archives Initiative Protocol for Metadata Harvesting (OAI-PMH).

Cataloging Cultural Objects (CCO)

Cataloging Cultural Objects (CCO),[58] like the VRA Core and CDWA, is designed for communities that describe works of art, architecture, cultural artifacts, and images of these things. While the VRA Core and CDWA provide lists and descriptions of elements or categories for metadata element sets, CCO is a content standard that, like AACR2 and DACS, prescribes the data values and defines the order, syntax, and form in which the values are to be entered into a data structure. CCO concentrates on principles of good cataloging and documentation, not on rigid rules. Catalogers are expected to make informed judgments.

CCO is divided into three parts. Part one, *General Guidelines,* deals with such issues as what unit is being cataloged, what is a work and what is an image, relationships between works and images, specificity and exhaustivity of cataloging, and several different kinds of relationships that may be delineated. Although CCO does not discuss administrative and technical metadata, part one includes a discussion of database design issues and what may be needed for such design. Lastly, part one discusses authority files and controlled vocabularies.

Part two of CCO, *Elements,* is divided into chapters on: object naming; creator information; physical characteristics; stylistic, cultural, and chronological information; location and geography; subject; class; description; and, view information. Each chapter has discussion of the concept, the rules for the elements covered by that chapter, and ways for presenting the data for display and indexing.

Part three of CCO covers authorities for personal and corporate names, geographic places, concepts, and subjects. These are discussed further in Chapters 8 and 10 of this text.

ONIX (ONline Information eXchange)

The publishing world has been developing standards that can be used for description of publications by their publishers. ONIX (ONline Information eXchange) for Books,[59] now available in Release 2.1, was discussed in the encoding standards chapter as an XML DTD. It is maintained by EDItEUR jointly with several book industry and user groups. It includes a data dictionary that defines the content of the elements. The elements allow a publisher to present online the information that was previously contained on book jackets and in publishing brochures and catalogs—information such as synopses, quotations from reviews, author biographies, intended audience, and so on. As mentioned in Chapter 5, ONIX uses XML to transmit ONIX messages. A mapping to MARC[60] allows consideration of using ONIX data in library catalogs. There are also projects that link MARC records in catalogs to ONIX data held in XML-encoded databases.

A partnership between EDItEUR and NISO has been responsible for the production of ONIX for Serials, a family of XML formats for information about serial products and subscription information.[61] SPS (Serials Products and Subscriptions), SOH (Serials Online Holdings), and SRN (Serials Release Notification) are three formats in the ONIX for Serials group that are currently being worked on, the latest update at this writing being June 2008. The ONIX Serials Coverage Statement is an XML structure for use in the three formats.

Other Surrogate Record Types

Index and Bibliography Records

At the moment, there is no official standard for the descriptive content of index records. An ANSI standard Z39.4–1984, subtitled "Basic Criteria for Indexes,"[62] has no mention of the data to be included in the description of an item. The National Information Standards Organization (NISO) tried to update this standard, but committees could not come to agreement with the American Society of Indexers, and so Z39.4 was withdrawn in 1996. In 1997 NISO issued a technical report TR-02, *Guidelines for Indexes and Related Information Retrieval Devices,* by James Anderson to help fill the void.[63]

Creators of indexes each have their own standards for information to be included in an index record. Agencies like H. W. Wilson that publish several different indexes in different subject areas have some consistency from index to index. Electronic index records tend to include more information than do paper versions. As in OPACs, electronic index records tend to have labels, which are not included in paper versions. (For an example of a labeled index record, refer back to Figure 2.3.)

There are two separate standards for bibliographic references, ISO 690 and ISO 690-2,[64] guiding the content that is to be included in entries in bibliographies. Revision of these two documents is in process. A new document is currently being developed as an ISO Technical Report and will replace both standards with up-to-date guidance on creating bibliographic references and citations for a wide range of information resources, both tangible and electronic.[65]

On-the-Fly Records

On-the-fly records are those created electronically for immediate use; such records may be created solely for display at the moment and then immediately disappear, or they may be created to be stored in a search engine index for a very short time. In some catalogs that have Web interfaces, the MARC records are converted to HTML-encoded records on the fly. That is, when a user puts in a search, a listing of authors, titles, and/or dates is returned to the screen. If the user then clicks, for example, on number 4 in the list, that MARC record is quickly put through the HTML converter that has been written for that catalog so that it can be displayed on the screen. These records display much of the same descriptive content that is found in the MARC records from which they are derived.

Search engines produce another kind of on-the-fly record. The information that is included in the results display depends upon what has been stored in the search engine's database after collection by the engine's agent or spider. Search engine surrogate records all include a hyperlinked URL. The rest of the record may consist of only the title of a document, or it may also include the first several lines of the text from the Web page (and some search engines even provide thumbnail images of the Web pages in results sets). Other pieces of information sometimes included are: a description taken from metadata at the head of the Web page (although the vast majority of Web pages still do not contain such metadata, and most search engines ignore it if it has been created), the size of the page or file, a relevance ranking calculated by the search engine, and/or a date (often the date the page or file was loaded into its server). The search engine Google gives a phrase from the contents of the page or file that includes the word or words the user put into the search. On-the-fly search engine surrogate records may or may not be helpful in the evaluation of whether or not the information resource they represent will be useful to the user. If the information resource has a title and the title is indicative of content, then the on-the-fly record is more useful than the record with no title. It is often necessary to look at the resource itself in order to learn what it is about and why it was retrieved in response to the search (see Figure 7.6).

CONCLUSION

From the preceding descriptions, one can see that the creation of surrogate records is somewhat dependent upon the community for which the records are being created. Some communities have long-standing standards. The library community's standard has the longest traditions, being based upon principles that have been developing for centuries. Other communities have recognized the library's long experience and have patterned their guidelines for creation of surrogate records after the ISBD standard. The creators of TEI Headers, the Dublin Core, VRA Core, CDWA, CCO, and others have included librarians, along with other people with organizing experience in their planning committees.

Results 1 - 10 **of about** 406,000 **for** Michael Gorman.

Michael Gorman
Homepage of the Dean of Library Services at California State University Fresno and nominee for the 2005 Presidency of the American Library Association ...
mg.csufresno.edu/ - 18k - Cached - Similar pages

Michael Gorman
Michael Gorman has been Dean of Library Services at the Henry Madden Library, California State University, Fresno since 1988. From 1977 to 1988 he worked at ...
mg.csufresno.edu/biography.htm - 17k - Cached - Similar pages

Michael Gorman (librarian) - Wikipedia, the free encyclopedia
Michael Gorman (born 1941) is a British librarian. He grew up in London, England and gained an interest in libraries in part through his experiences at the ...
en.wikipedia.org/wiki/**Michael_Gorman**_(librarian) - 36k - Cached - Similar pages

Mike **Gorman** - Wikipedia, the free encyclopedia
Michael "Mike" **Gorman** (born December 14, 1943, in Dorchester, Massachusetts) is a television play-by-play commentator for the Boston Celtics basketball team ...
en.wikipedia.org/wiki/Mike_**Gorman** - 20k - Cached - Similar pages

Michael Gorman -Britannica Blog
Michael Gorman was Dean of Library Services at the Henry Madden Library, California State University, Fresno, from 1988 to 2007. He previously worked at the ...
www.britannica.com/blogs/author/m**gorman** - 29k - Cached - Similar pages

Web 2.0: The Sleep of Reason, Part I -Britannica Blog
When I read **Michael Gorman**'s two-part blog post (yes, I said blog post; if that isn't ... Clay Shirky says: Over at the Britannica weblog, **Michael Gorman**, ...
www.britannica.com/blogs/2007/06/web-20-the-sleep-of-reason-part-i/ - 120k - Cached - Similar pages
More results from www.britannica.com »

www.MichaelGorman.net
The Blog of Writer & Director **Michael Gorman**. Topics of discussion range from Film, TV, Videogames, to politics and religion. Expect to see movie reviews ...
www.**michaelgorman**.net/ - 63k - Cached - Similar pages

Michael Gorman - Oregon Fishing Guide, McKenzie River fishing ...
McKenzie River fishing guide and Rogue River fishing guide specialist, fly fishing Oregon McKenzie River trout and Rogue River steelhead.
www.**gorman**flyfishing.com/ - Similar pages

BackTalk: Revenge of the Blog People! - 2/15/2005 - Library Journal
Feb 15, 2005 ... By **Michael Gorman** -- Library Journal, 2/15/2005 ... **Michael Gorman**, president-elect of the American Library Association, is Dean of Library ...
www.libraryjournal.com/article/CA502009.html - Similar pages

mike **gorman**
Michael Gorman. My Links · Lakewood · Home · Insight · Basketball · Flip Cup · Athens · Rules .
Michael Gorman Lakewood, Ohio ...
www.geocities.com/m2f2g2/ - 8k - Cached - Similar pages

Figure 7.6. Typical on-the-fly records in which it is often not possible to be certain whether the concept(s) or person sought is actually in the resource that is represented by the record. In this example, results 1–3, 5, and 9 are for the librarian Michael Gorman. The other five probably are not the same person; although the data given are not absolutely clear for all. (Source: http://www.google.com/search for "Michael Gorman" on June 1, 2008.)

This chapter has addressed the descriptive part of metadata, which we have called *surrogate records*. In discussion of the value of surrogate records, it was mentioned that surrogate record descriptions are most helpful when they are predictable in both form and content. The standards to prescribe form of content are ISBD, AACR2, DACS, and CCO. ISBD came to its prescription after years of experience with variant practices that brought an understanding of the value of predictability. AACR2 then followed ISBD. DACS and CCO authors studied AACR2 before creating their standards, and some resemblances can be seen, although needs of the specific communities differed from those of the library community that developed AACR2. The remaining standards discussed rarely prescribe form of content, although they prescribe and define elements. Perhaps experience with the large quantities of metadata records that have long existed in the library and archival communities, and more recently in the art and museum communities, will lead some creators of metadata to reevaluate their need for prescribed content. The next chapter addresses access and authority control, which is accepted as a necessity in the library and archival communities, and is highly recommended in the art and museum communities, but has barely been considered in the other communities.

NOTES

All URLs accessed September 2008.

1. *Anglo-American Cataloguing Rules, Second Edition, 2002 Revision* (AACR2R) prepared under the direction of the Joint Steering Committee for Revision of AACR (Ottawa: Canadian Library Association; Chicago: American Library Association, 2002, looseleaf, with updates), p. D-2. Also available in Cataloger's Desktop, by subscription.

2. Ibid., p. D-4.

3. *Anglo-American Cataloguing Rules, Second Edition, 1998 Revision* (Ottawa: Canadian Library Association; Chicago: American Library Association, 1998), p. 622.

4. AACR2R2002, p. D-7.

5. International Federation of Library Associations and Institutions, IFLA Study Group, *Functional Requirements for Bibliographic Records: Final Report* (München: Saur, 1998). Also available: http://www.ifla.org/VII/s13/frbr/frbr.pdf or http://www.ifla.org/VII/s13/frbr/frbr.htm.

6. International Federation of Library Associations and Institutions. IFLA Study Group, *Functional Requirements for Bibliographic Records,* p. 18.

7. For more about FRBR see: Arlene G. Taylor, "An Introduction to Functional Requirements for Bibliographic Records (FRBR)," in *Understanding FRBR: What It Is and How It Will Affect Our Retrieval Tools,* edited by Arlene G. Taylor (Westport, Conn.: Libraries Unlimited, 2007), pp. 1–19; and Robert L. Maxwell, *FRBR: A Guide for the Perplexed* (Chicago: American Library Association, 2008).

8. *International Standard Bibliographic Description* (ISBD), Recommended by the ISBD Review Group, approved by the Standing Committee of the IFLA Cataloguing Section, Preliminary consolidated ed. (München: K. G. Saur, 2007). Also available: http://www.ifla.org/VII/s13/pubs/cat-isbd.htm.

9. International Federation of Library Associations and Institutions, "Family of superseded ISBDs." Available: http://www.ifla.org/VI/3/nd1/isbdlist.htm.

10. AACR2R (see note 1 above).

11. *Library of Congress Rule Interpretations,* 2nd ed. (Washington, D.C.: Cataloging Distribution Service, Library of Congress, 1990- , looseleaf, with updates). Also available on Cataloger's Desktop, by subscription.

12. Program for Cooperative Cataloging, "Introduction to the Program for Co-operative Cataloging BIBCO Core Record Standards." Available: http://www.loc.gov/catdir/pcc/bibco/coreintro.html; "Chart of PCC BIBCO Core Record Standards." Available: http://www.loc.gov/catdir/pcc/bibco/core2002.html.

13. Michael Gorman, *The Concise AACR2,* 4th ed. (Chicago: American Library Association, 2004). [Based on *AACR2R* 2002 Revision, 2004 Update.]

14. Joint Steering Committee for Development of RDA, "Overview." Available: http://www.collectionscanada.gc.ca/jsc/index.html.

15. International Federation of Library Associations and Institutions, Working Group on FRANAR, "Functional Requirements for Authority Data: A Conceptual Model." Available: http://www.ifla.org/VII/d4/franar-conceptual-model-2ndreview.pdf.

16. International Federation of Library Associations and Institutions, Meeting of Experts on an International Cataloguing Code. "Statement of

International Cataloguing Principles," April 10, 2008 version. Available: http://www.ifla.org/VII/s13/icc/imeicc-statement_of_principles-2008.pdf.

17. Dublin Core Metadata Initiative, "Dublin Core Metadata Element Set," Version 1.1. Available: http://dublincore.org/documents/dces/.

18. *The Dublin Core Metadata Element Set,* ANSI/NISO Z39.85–2007 (Bethesda, Md.: NISO Press, 2007).

19. *Information and documentation—The Dublin Core metadata element set,* ISO 15836:2003.

20. Dublin Core Metadata Initiative. Available: http://dublincore.org/.

21. One such template is the Distributed Systems Technology's Reg Demo metadata editor. Available: http://www.metadata.net/cgi-bin/reg/demo.cgi; another is North Carolina Exploring Cultural Heritage Online (ECHO), "North Carolina Dublin Core Template." Available: http://www.ncecho.org/ncdc/template.html.

22. Andy Powell, Pete Johnston, "Guidelines for Implementing Dublin Core in XML." Dublin Core Metadata Initiative. Available: http://dublin core.org/documents/dc-xml-guidelines/.

23. Mikael Nilsson, Andy Powell, Pete Johnston, and Ambjörn Naeve, "Expressing Dublin Core metadata using the Resource Description Framework (RDF)," Dublin Core Metadata Initiative. Available: http://dublincore.org/documents/dc-rdf/.

24. Dublin Core Metadata Initiative, "Dublin Core Metadata Element Set."

25. "RFC4646: Tags for Identifying Languages." Available: http://rfc.net/rfc4646.html or http://www.faqs.org/rfcs/rfc4646.html.

26. "Thesaurus of Geographic Names Online," The Getty. Available: http://www.getty.edu/research/tools/vocabulary/tgn/index.html.

27. Misha Wolf and Charles Wicksteed, "Date and Time Formats," W3C. Available: http://www.w3.org/TR/NOTE-datetime.

28. Dublin Core Metadata Initiative, "DCMI Type Vocabulary." Available: http://dublincore.org/documents/dcmi-type-vocabulary/.

29. Internet Assigned Numbers Authority, "MIME Media Types." Available: http://www.iana.org/assignments/media-types/.

30. Dublin Core Metadata Initiative, "Using Dublin Core – Dublin Core Qualifiers." Available: http://dublincore.org/documents/usageguide/qualifiers.shtml.

31. Ibid.

32. Robina Clayphan, Rebecca Guenther, "Library Application Profile," Dublin Core Metadata Initiative. Available: http://dublincore.org/documents/library-application-profile/.

33. Library of Congress, Network Development and MARC Standards Office, "MODS: Metadata Object Description Schema: Official Web Site." Available: http://www.loc.gov/standards/mods/.

34. Rebecca S. Guenther, "MODS: The Metadata Object Description Schema," *Portal: Libraries and the Academy* 3, no. 1 (2003): 139.

35. Ibid., p. 140.

36. Library of Congress, Network Development and MARC Standards Office, "MODS Implementation Registry." Available: http://www.loc.gov/standards/mods/registry.php.

37. National Library of Australia, "The Australian National Bibliographic Database." Available: http://www.nla.gov.au/librariesaustralia/databases.html#nbd.

38. *ISAD(G): General International Standard Archival Description.* Adopted by the Committee on Descriptive Standards, Stockholm, Sweden, September 19–22, 1999, 2nd ed. (Ottawa: International Council on Archives, 2000). Also available: http://www.icacds.org.uk/eng/ISAD(G).pdf.

39. Ibid., p. 7.

40. *Describing Archives: A Content Standard* (DACS) (Chicago: Society of American Archivists, 2004).

41. Steven L. Hensen, comp., *Archives, Personal Papers, and Manuscripts: A Cataloging Manual for Archival Repositories, Historical Societies, and Manuscript Libraries,* 2nd ed. (Chicago: Society of American Archivists, 1989).

42. DACS, p. vii.

43. DACS, p. 7.

44. "EAD: Encoded Archival Description," Version 2002 Official Site, Library of Congress. Available: http://www.loc.gov/ead/.

45. "Design Principles for Enhancement to EAD (December 2002)," Library of Congress. Available: http://www.loc.gov/ead/eaddesgn.html.

46. Text Encoding Initiative, "TEI Lite." Available: http://www.tei-c.org/Guidelines/Customization/Lite/.

47. Federal Geographic Data Committee (FGDC), "Content Standard for Digital Geospatial Metadata," Version 2.0, 1998. Available: http://www.fgdc.gov/standards/projects/FGDC-standards-projects/metadata/base-metadata/.

48. Ibid.

49. FGDC, "Metadata Profile for Shoreline Data." Available: http://www.fgdc.gov/standards/projects/FGDC-standards-projects/metadata/shoreline-metadata/index_html.

50. FGDC, "Geospatial Metadata Tools." Available: http://www.fgdc.gov/metadata/geospatial-metadata-tools.

51. FGDC, "FGDC/ISO Metadata Standard Harmonization." Available: http://www.fgdc.gov/metadata/us-national-profile-iso19115/archive/.

52. Visual Resources Association, Data Standards Committee, "VRA Core 4.0." Available: http://www.vraweb.org/projects/vracore4/index.html.

53. Visual Resources Association, Data Standards Committee, "VRA Core 4.0 Introduction." Available: http://www.vraweb.org/projects/vracore4/VRA_Core4_Intro.pdf.

54. "Art & Architecture Thesaurus Online," The Getty. Available: http://www.getty.edu/research/conducting_research/vocabularies/aat/.

55. Murtha Baca, Patricia Harpring, Elisa Lanzi, Linda McRae, and Ann Whiteside, on behalf of the Visual Resources Association, *Cataloguing Cultural Objects: A Guide to Describing Cultural Works and Their Images* (Chicago: American Library Association, 2006). Partial availability on the Web: http://www.vraweb.org/ccoweb/cco/index.html.

56. "Categories for the Description of Works of Art," edited by Murtha Baca and Patricia Harpring, The Getty. Available: http://www.getty.edu/research/conducting_research/standards/cdwa/.

57. "Categories for the Description of Works of Art: Overview of Categories," edited by Murtha Baca and Patricia Harpring, The Getty. Available: http://www.getty.edu/research/conducting_research/standards/cdwa/categories.html.

58. Baca, et al., *Cataloging Cultural Objects.*

59. EDItEUR, "ONIX for Books." Available: http://www.editeur.org/onix.html.

60. Library of Congress, Network Development and MARC Standards Office, "ONIX to MARC 21 Mapping." Available: http://www.loc.gov/marc/onix2marc.html.

61. EDItEUR, "ONIX for Serials." Available: http://www.editeur.org/onix serials.html.

62. *American National Standard for Library and Information Sciences and Related Publishing Practices—Basic Criteria for Indexes, ANSI Z39.4–1984* (New York: American National Standards Institute, 1984).

63. James D. Anderson, *Guidelines for Indexes and Related Information Retrieval Devices* (Bethesda, Md.: NISO Press, 1997).

64. *Information and Documentation—Bibliographic References—Content, Form and Structure,* ISO 690, 2nd ed. (Geneva, Switzerland: International Organization for Standardization, 1987); *Information and Documentation—Bibliographic References—Part 2: Electronic Documents or Parts Therof,* ISO 690-2 (Geneva, Switzerland: International Organization for Standardization, 1997).

65. ISO Project 690, "Information and Documentation—References and Citations to Published Materials." Available: http://www.collectionscanada.gc.ca/iso/tc46sc9/docs/sc9n378.pdf.

SUGGESTED READINGS

ALA/ALCTS/CCS Committee on Cataloging: Description and Access. Task Force on Metadata and the Cataloging Rules. "Final Report," June 3, 1998. Available: http://www.libraries.psu.edu/tas/jca/ccda/tf-tei2.html.

Baca, Murtha. "A Picture Is Worth a Thousand Words: Metadata for Art Objects and Their Visual Surrogates." In *Cataloging the Web: Metadata, AACR, and MARC 21,* edited by Wayne Jones, et al. Lanham, Md.: Scarecrow Press, 2002, pp. 131–138.

Baca, Murtha, Patricia Harpring, Elisa Lanzi, Linda McRae, and Ann Whiteside. *Cataloguing Cultural Objects: A Guide to Describing Cultural Works and Their Images.* Chicago: American Library Association, 2006. Partial availability on the Web: http://www.vraweb.org/ccoweb/cco/index.html.

Caplan, Priscilla. *Metadata Fundamentals for All Librarians.* Chicago: American Library Association, 2003. Part II: "Metadata Schemes."

Denton, William. "FRBR and the History of Cataloging." In *Understanding FRBR: What It Is and How It Will Affect Our Retrieval Tools,* edited by Arlene G. Taylor. Westport, Conn.: Libraries Unlimited, 2007, pp. 35–57.

Describing Archives: A Content Standard (DACS). Chicago: Society of American Archivists, 2004.

Dublin Core Metadata Initiative. Available: http://dublincore.org/.

"EAD: Encoded Archival Description" Version 2002 Official Site. Library of Congress. Available: http://www.loc.gov/ead/.

Federal Geographic Data Committee (FGDC). "Content Standard for Digital Geospatial Metadata." Version 2.0, 1998. Available: http://www.fgdc.gov/standards/projects/FGDC-standards-projects/metadata/base-metadata.

Fox, Michael J., and Peter Wilkerson. *Introduction to Archival Organization and Description: Access to Cultural Heritage.* Los Angeles: The Getty Information Institute, 1998. Section entitled "Standards."

Gorman, Michael. *The Concise AACR2.* 4th ed. Chicago: American Library Association, 2004.

Guenther, Rebecca S. "MODS: The Metadata Object Description Schema." *Portal: Libraries and the Academy* 3, no. 1 (2003): 137–150.

Hillmann, Diane. "Using Dublin Core." Dublin Core Metadata Initiative. Available: http://dublincore.org/documents/usageguide/

Hsieh-Yee, Ingrid. *Organizing Audiovisual and Electronic Resources for Access: A Cataloging Guide.* 2nd ed. Westport, Conn.: Libraries Unlimited, 2006.

International Federation of Library Associations and Institutions. "Digital Libraries: Metadata Resources." Available: http://www.ifla.org/II/meta data.htm.

International Federation of Library Associations and Institutions. IFLA Study Group. *Functional Requirements for Bibliographic Records: Final Report.* München: Saur, 1998. Also available: http://www.ifla.org/VII/s13/frbr/frbr.pdf or http://www.ifla.org/VII/s13/frbr/frbr.htm.

International Standard Bibliographic Description (ISBD). Recommended by the ISBD Review Group approved by the Standing Committee of the IFLA Cataloguing Section. Preliminary consolidated ed. München: K. G. Saur, 2007. Also available: http://www.ifla.org/VII/s13/pubs/cat-isbd.htm.

Intner, Sheila S., Susan S. Lazinger, and Jean Weihs. *Metadata and Its Impact on Libraries.* Westport, Conn.: Libraries Unlimited, 2006. Chapter 2: "Metadata Schemas and Their Relationships to Particular Communities."

Intner, Sheila S., and Jean Weihs. *Standard Cataloging for School and Public Libraries.* 4th ed. Westport, Conn.: Libraries Unlimited, 2007. Chapter 4: "Description."

Maxwell, Robert L. *FRBR: A Guide for the Perplexed.* Chicago: American Library Association, 2008.

Program for Cooperative Cataloging. "Introduction to the Program for Cooperative Cataloging BIBCO Core Record Standards." Available: http://www.loc.gov/catdir/pcc/bibco/coreintro.html.

Svenonius, Elaine. *The Intellectual Foundation of Information Organization.* Cambridge, Mass.: The MIT Press, 2000. Chapter 7: "Document Languages."

Taylor, Arlene G. *Introduction to Cataloging and Classification.* 10th ed., with the assistance of David P. Miller. Westport, Conn.: Libraries Unlimited, 2006. Chapter 4: "Description."

———. "An Introduction to Functional Requirements for Bibliographic Records (FRBR)." In *Understanding FRBR: What It Is and How It Will Affect Our Retrieval Tools,* edited by Arlene G. Taylor. Westport, Conn.: Libraries Unlimited, 2007, pp. 1–19.

Tillett, Barbara B. "Problems and Solutions in Cataloging Electronic Resources." *International Cataloguing and Bibliographic Control* 29, no. 1 (January/March 2000): 14–15.

Visual Resources Association, Data Standards Committee. "VRA Core 4.0." Available: http://www.vraweb.org/projects/vracore4/index.html.

CHAPTER 8

METADATA: ACCESS AND AUTHORITY CONTROL

The issues addressed in this chapter are expressed in the following questions: How are resources (including information resources, surrogate records, names, concepts, etc.) made available to users? How do access points affect collocation? How can identification of relationships among entities be used to assist users in finding what they need? How does authority control affect collocation? How can persons or entities with the same name be distinguished from each other? How can variant names that represent the same entity be brought together? How can all expressions and manifestations of the same work be brought together? What standards and tools are available to assist with the processes of providing access and authority control?

ACCESS

In most online systems keyword searching is available. If a user knows exactly what words or names have been used in a description, then keyword searching is successful. But users who do not know exact words or names have to guess. This is sometimes successful and sometimes not. An alternative to relying on keyword searching is to have specific access points (i.e., names, titles, subjects, etc., chosen by a cataloger or indexer and placed in particular fields in a record) provided in surrogate records. Most words in the English language have more than one meaning, and most meanings have more than one word (discussed further in Chapter 10). Many research studies have shown that different users do not think of the same word(s) to express a concept; authors do not necessarily use the same word(s) to write about a concept; authors do not necessarily retain the same name or same form of name throughout their writing careers; many different people have the same name; corporate bodies do not necessarily use the same name or form of name in their documents, nor are they known by the same form of name by everyone; many different corporate bodies have the same acronym; and titles of works that are reproduced, edited, or adapted are not always the same in the original and the new version. For all of these reasons and more, the library world, followed by the archival world and, more recently, the art world, came to the realization that bibliographic records need access points (one of which is often designated as the *main* or *primary* one), and these access points need to be expressed consistently from record to record when several different records use the same word or name as an access point.

The rest of the metadata world has also begun to see a need for access points either with consistent form from record to record or with links to resources that identify a person, corporate body, concept, and so forth, uniquely. Much energy in the last two decades was spent on determining what descriptive metadata is needed for particular forms of information resources, and on how these descriptions can be encoded for display. As metadata accumulates to the massive numbers that library catalogs have been dealing with, the need for attention to problems of access to all this metadata becomes more apparent.

BIBLIOGRAPHIC RELATIONSHIPS

Few information resources exist in total isolation. The majority have various kinds of relationships to other resources. An information resource may have a creator who has also created other resources. It may have the same publisher or be in the same series as other items. It may originate in an institution where a research project has produced multiple reports concerning the same research data. It may be a manifestation of the same work but in a different format or medium. It may have intellectual content that is the same or similar to that of another resource, or it may be an adaptation. It may be a commentary on another work. It may be a supplement to something else or follow it in a sequential manner. It may be a part of a larger work, or conversely, it may be an entity that contains a number of smaller works within it. It may be a performance of a work that also appears in written form.

Successful document retrieval relies on having such relationships identified, at least implicitly, and retrieval is improved when such relationships are made explicit. Information retrieval systems operate on the perception that a user interested in one item may very well be interested in others that are related to it. When relationships are merely described (e.g., mentioned in a note)—or not even described—the user might discover those relationships only by chance. Access points can make relationships explicit. Library cataloging has provided rules for such access points at least since Lubetzky identified principles upon which the Paris Principles (1961) were based. However, research to formally identify and categorize relationships began only in the 1980s. Barbara Tillett researched and presented a taxonomy of bibliographic relationships:[1]

- **Equivalence relationships**—found in exact copies of the same manifestation of a work; include copies, issues, facsimiles, reprints, photocopies, microforms, audiotapes of sound recordings on disc (if same content), and other such reproductions
- **Derivative relationships**—found in modifications based on particular manifestations; include editions, revisions, adaptations, changes of genre (e.g., dramatization of a novel), new works based on style or thematic content of other works, and the like
- **Descriptive relationships**—found in description, criticism, evaluation, or review of a work; include book reviews, annotated editions, commentaries, critiques, and the like
- **Whole-part relationships**—found in a component part of a larger work or in the relationship between a work and each of its various parts; include selections from anthologies or collections, articles from journals, maps in atlases, series that have independent works within them, and the like
- **Accompanying relationships**—found in bibliographic manifestations that are created for the purpose of complementing particular works; they can complement equally, or one work can be the principal or predominant item; include text with supplements (e.g., teacher's manual for a textbook), software manuals or help programs, concordances, indexes, parts of a kit, and the like
- **Sequential relationships**—found in bibliographic manifestations that continue or precede other manifestations; include successive titles of a serial, sequels and prequels of a movie, parts in a numbered series, and the like

- **Shared characteristic relationships**—found in any works that coincidentally share characteristics in common, such as common authors, titles, subjects, language, country of publication, and the like

Following upon Tillett's research, other researchers have used empirical research to refine definitions and further delineate ways in which such relationships could be explicitly linked in retrieval tools.[2] For example, Richard Smiraglia presented the following taxonomy of Tillett's derivative relationships:[3]

- **Simultaneous derivations**—works published in two editions nearly simultaneously, such as a British edition and a North American edition of the same work; may have different titles, different sizes, or other differing characteristics
- **Successive derivations**—works revised one or more times and issued anew with statements indicating revision, as well as manifestations issued successively that may not have revision statements
- **Translations**—manifestations of a work presented in languages other than the original
- **Amplifications**—original works that have added to them such things as illustrations, musical settings, commentaries, and the like
- **Extractions**—manifestations of works in smaller forms such as abridgments, condensations, excerpts, and the like
- **Adaptations**—manifestations that modify original works, such as simplifications, screenplays, librettos, arrangements of musical works, and the like
- **Performances**—sound or visual recordings of works, each of which may differ in such things as tone, amplification, interpretation, and the like

Making such relationships explicit requires formalized rules for creating what Elaine Svenonius calls a *work language,* requiring a *work ID* and, possibly, such connecting devices as references.[4] This, of course, requires a consistent definition of *work,* which has eluded organizers and researchers until recently.[5] The *Anglo-American Cataloguing Rules* (AACR) has provided a work language for many years, although somewhat flawed and inconsistent because of the problems with definitions. It has also had difficulty with conceptualization of function for things such as references vs. added entries. The *AACR* work ID in most cases is an author-title combination, but in cases where author is not easily determined or is diffuse, the work ID is title. Both kinds of ID require qualifiers to be added to make relationships explicit, and references are required to bring together variant forms of names of authors and titles.

An attempt by the International Federation of Library Associations and Institutions (IFLA) to formalize the definition of *work* and the direct relationships to it of *expression, manifestation,* and *item* (i.e., as defined in *Functional Requirements for Bibliographic Records* [FRBR]) is discussed in Chapters 4 and 7. Going beyond that first group of entities, FRBR identifies a group of entities that can be responsible for the first group of entities—this second group comprising *person* and *corporate body,* with *family* added to this group later by the *Functional Requirements for Authority Data* (FRAD).[6] A third group identifies entities that can be considered to be subjects of the first group of entities—this third group comprising all entities from the first two groups plus *concept, object, event,* and *place.* FRBR identifies major types of relationships that operate between instances of the same entity type and between instances of different entity types. Research continues on ways to use FRBR for logical display of works and their relationships in online catalogs.[7]

AUTHORITY CONTROL

Authority control is the result of the process of maintaining consistency in the verbal form used to represent an access point and the further process of showing the relationships among names, works, and subjects. It is also the result of the process of doing authority work with or without the necessity of choosing one form of name or title or one subject term to be the "authorized" selection. If every variant name, title, or term is given equal status, then one form is chosen for default display. Whether or not an authorized form is chosen to represent the name, title, or term, a searcher may use any of the forms in the authority record to gain access to information resources related to the name, title, or subject. The process called *authority control* was so named because it was thought necessary to determine an authorized form for every entity known by variant forms. For example, the English form of Confucius' name has been determined by the Library of Congress to be the authoritative form, and the names given to this person in many other languages, including his Chinese name for himself, have been relegated to positions of unauthorized forms that act as references to the authorized name.

As the world of information becomes more global, many have recognized that different forms of a name (e.g., in different languages, etc.) can be used for access. In addition, the concepts of *authority* and *control* in a culture with an emphasis on individualism are not readily welcomed, and the words have negative connotations for many people. Efforts were made by Taylor and others a few years ago to begin using the phrase *access control* instead of *authority control*. But *access control* has come to mean a computer operating system feature that controls the access that certain categories of users have to files and to functions. (It has also come into use in some airports to name the function of determining who may enter a country.) We have not yet found better terminology.

Goals for authority control are to assist users:

- to find a creator, a place, a subject or other entity using the searcher's vocabulary (e.g., find books by Hans Christian Andersen, even if he used H.C. Andersen on the title page; find documents about *swimsuits* using the search term *bathing suits* or even *bikinis*)
- to identify (e.g., find the Michael Gorman who is a librarian, not the one who is an architect)
- to collocate (e.g., bring together related information resources, related corporate bodies, etc.) regardless of terminology used
- to aid in evaluating or selecting (e.g., Is Vincent Willem van Gogh the same person as the artist, Vincent van Gogh? Is the use of *bridge* in a search limited to the card game, or will I also get resources about structures across rivers or about dental work?)
- to provide synonyms and syndetic structure to aid in subject searching or to provide variant forms of name for persons, families, bodies, or works.

Authority control is needed for collocation—for bringing together everything related to a person, family, corporate body, place, or work, regardless of what name has been used for one of those entities. One has only to look at some Web sites that do not have authority control to see that there is value in collocation of forms of name. For example, a search for *Gorman, Michael* in the Books category at Amazon.com in April 2008 resulted in the following first 14 out of 995 results (sorted by Amazon's default arrangement of results—relevance):

1. *Apostle of the Crucified Lord: A Theological Introduction to Paul and His Letters* by Michael J. Gorman (Paperback—Feb 2004)
2. *Ethical and Environmental Challenges to Engineering* by Michael E. Gorman, Matthew M. Mehalik, Patricia Werhane (Paperback—Nov 15, 1999)

3. – 7. [Five more titles by Michael J. Gorman, published in 2003, 2007, 1998, 1982, and 2005, respectively]
8. *Real Men Don't Say Splendid: A Lexicon of Unmanliness (Keepsake Series)* by Michael Gorman (Hardcover—Jun 1, 2007)
9. *Cruciformity: Paul's Narrative Spirituality of the Cross* by Michael J. Gorman (Paperback—Jul 2001)
10. *Buckminster Fuller: Designing for Mobility* by Michael John Gorman (Hardcover—Sep 12, 2005)
11. *The Concise Aacr2: 1998 Revision* by Michael Gorman (Paperback—Oct 1999) [In the Amazon entry, the acronym for AACR does, in fact, have only the first "A" capitalized. The current 4th ed. of this work, published in 2004, is number 79 in the list.]
12. *The Enduring Library: Technology, Tradition, and the Quest for Balance* by Michael Gorman (Paperback—Mar 2003)
13. *Michael Harrington—speaking American* by Robert A. Gorman (Hardcover—1995)
14. *Our Enduring Values: Librarianship in the 21st Century* by Michael Gorman (Paperback—Jun 9, 2000)

One can see that 3 of the first 14 are for the librarian, Michael Gorman, but we know that there are a number of titles by him that might be among the remaining 981 items. In addition, number 13 is not even for someone named Michael Gorman. A search for *Gorman, Michael* in the catalog of the Library of Congress (LC) on the same day yielded:

#	*Hits*	*Headings*
[1]	2	Gorman, Michael
[2]	2	Gorman, Michael, 1895–1970
[3]	31	Gorman, Michael, 1941–
[4]	4	Gorman, Michael, 1944–
[5]	2	Gorman, Michael, 1948–
[6]	2	Gorman, Michael, 1952–
[7]	1	Gorman, Michael, 1959–
[8]	1	Gorman, Michael, 1965–
[9]	1	Gorman, Michael A., 1948–
[10]	4	Gorman, Michael E., 1952–
[11]	7	Gorman, Michael J., 1955–
[12]	2	Gorman, Michael James, 1856– [from old catalog]
[13]	1	Gorman, Michael John
		and so on

One may not know from this list which is the librarian, but once it is determined to be number 3, then all titles relating to that person are found together, and it is not necessary to look at any of the other entries.

Authority Work

In order to have authority control it is necessary for someone to do authority work, which requires that someone identify all variants for a name or title of a work and make the necessary decisions about which variants represent the same names, which should be the authorized form, and which should be references. Most systems still require the choice of one form as the heading. The entries from the LC catalog shown above are called *headings*. Current practice dictates the establishment of a heading for each name or title that is intended to be an access point. The term *heading* comes from print catalog days when each access point was printed at the top (head) of the copy of the surrogate record and was called the heading for the record (see Figure 8.1). In the online world *heading* has come to mean the exact string of characters of the authorized form of the access point as it appears in the authority record. It no longer appears at the head of each record in an online tool, although sometimes it is at the head (or side) of a list of records in a catalog display (see Figure 8.2).

The process of authority work involves more than determining the authorized form, however. It includes identification of relationships of all variant names and titles to their corresponding authorized forms. It then involves the process of documenting, in an authority record, the work done along with the decisions made. An authority record is a compilation of metadata about a person, a family, a corporate body, a place, a work, or a subject. It includes evidence of all the decisions made and all the relationships among variants that have been identified.

```
           Calorie guide to brand names and
              basic foods
641.10
Kra     Krause, Barbara.
           Calorie guide to brand names and basic
         foods / by Barbara Krause. -- New York :
         Penguin Books, 1996. -- 262 p. -- ISBN
         0-451-18524-2

           1. Calories (Food).  2. Food--Caloric
        content--Tables.  I. Title.
```

Figure 8.1. Catalog card showing the title placed at the top of the record as the heading for the card.

#	Name Heading	Name: Main Author, Creator, etc.	Full Title	Date
☐ [1]	Gorman, Michael, 1941-		Anglo-American cataloguing rules / prepared by the American Library Association ... [et al.] ; edited by Michael Gorman & Paul W. Winkler.	1978
	SELECT TITLE FOR HOLDINGS INFORMATION			
☐ [2]	Gorman, Michael, 1941-		Anglo-American cataloguing rules / prepared by the American Library Association ... [et al.] ; edited by Michael Gorman and Paul W. Winkler.	1978
	SELECT TITLE FOR HOLDINGS INFORMATION			
☐ [3]	Gorman, Michael, 1941-		Anglo-American cataloguing rules / prepared under the direction of the Joint Steering Committee for Revision of AACR, a committee of the American Library Association, the Australian Committee on Cataloguing, the British Library, the Canadian Committee on	1998
	SELECT TITLE FOR HOLDINGS INFORMATION			
☐ [4]	Gorman, Michael, 1941-		Anglo-American cataloguing rules / prepared under the direction of the Joint Steering Committee for Revision of AACR, a committee of the American Library Association, the Australian Committee on Cataloguing, the British Library, the Canadian Committee on	1988
	SELECT TITLE FOR HOLDINGS INFORMATION			
☐ [5]	Gorman, Michael, 1941-		Anglo-American cataloguing rules, second edition. Chapter 9, Computer files (draft revision) / edited for the Joint Steering Committee for the Revision of AACR by Michael Gorman.	1987
	ACCESS: Jefferson or Adams Bldg General or Area Studies Reading Rms		CALL NUMBER: Z695.615 .A46 1987	
☐ [6]	Gorman, Michael, 1941-		Californien : Henry Madden and the German travelers in America / edited by Michael Gorman.	1991
	ACCESS: Jefferson or Adams Bldg General or Area Studies Reading Rms		CALL NUMBER: F861 .C255 1991	

Figure 8.2. Screen from the Library of Congress Online Catalog, showing the "heading" ***Gorman, Michael, 1941-*** **in the left-hand box under the word "Name Heading." (Source: http://catalog.loc.gov/.)**

Thinking in terms of global or international access allows the possibility for authority records to contain all variant forms for an entity, without designating one as the "right" (authorized) one. In any case, a search for any one of the variants for an entity should retrieve all metadata records associated with the entity. In the process of authority work, even though there may be a desire to provide more global access by not designating one of the variants as the authorized one, it is still necessary to go through the process of creating a heading in particular locales so that one form can be designated for default display for cases where a user does not wish to designate a preference. Doing authority work in concert with many other people is very helpful, saving hours of work for individual catalogers. One such cooperative project is NACO, the Name Authority Cooperative Program of the PCC (Program for Cooperative Cataloging), which is mentioned in Chapter 7 with respect to its Core Record. Participants in NACO follow a common set of standards and guidelines when creating or updating authority records so that consistency is maintained in this large shared authority file.[8]

Authority Files

Authority records are accumulated into an authority file or files, which are separate files from the bibliographic file; although files of metadata for information resources are often linked with the authority files that contain metadata for names, works, and subjects. If linked, references from authority records can be displayed to users in the results of their searches of the bibliographic file.

In earlier chapters we said that metadata models are built on the proposition that resources are made up of entities that have properties or attributes, and those attributes have values (refer back to Figure 4.1). Occasionally, the value of a property is another resource or entity, which then itself has attributes which have values. With authority control we maintain control over the values. In Figure 8.3, which is an altered version of Figure 4.1, we have *value-spaces* preceding the actual values that have been assigned to these particular properties. One traditional name for a value-space is *authority file.* The LCNAF in this figure is the Library of Congress Name Authority File. The other two value-spaces are for subject headings and classification and are discussed in later chapters. Several different value-spaces or authority files exist for the purpose of name control. Discussed in this chapter are: the Library of Congress Name Authority File (LCNAF), the Getty Vocabulary tools (i.e., *Union List of Artist Names* [ULAN], *Thesaurus of Geographic Names* [TGN], and *Art & Architecture Thesaurus* [AAT]), and Encoded Archival Context (EAC).

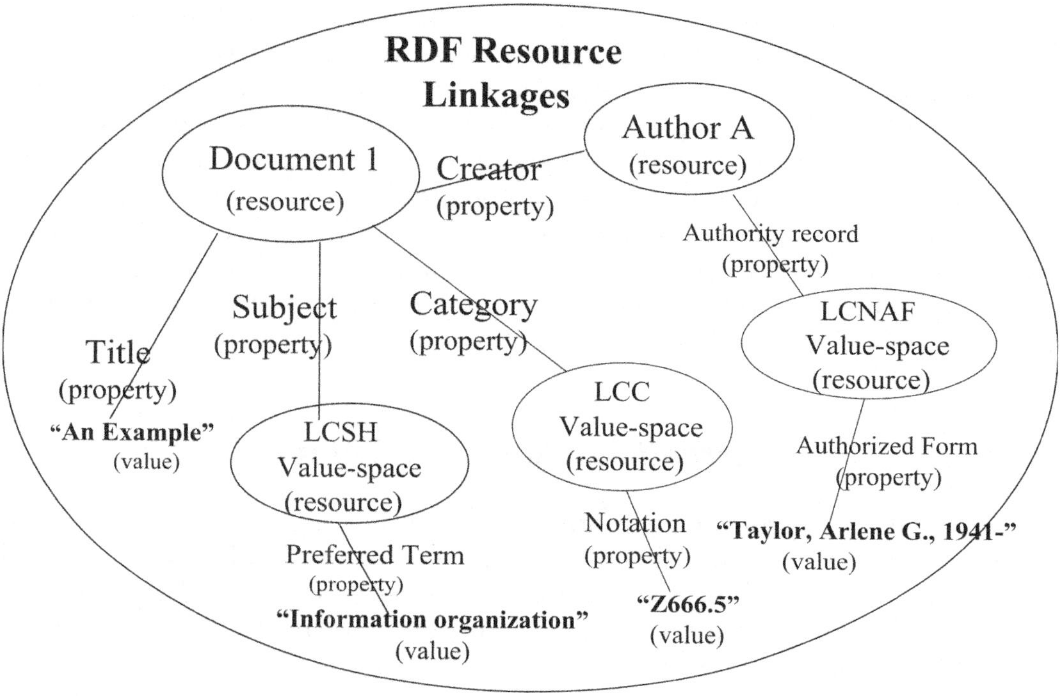

Figure 8.3. Illustration of values found in the value-spaces of a controlled vocabulary, a classification scheme, and an authority file.

A research project in this area that ended in 2003 was called InterParty.[9] Even though it has not yet produced an active namespace, it had some interesting characteristics that are thought provoking for anyone contemplating future uses of authority files. The project defined *party* as any one of the disparate types of identities responsible for creation of intellectual property or content (e.g., authors, composers, performers, producers, directors, publishers, libraries). The project brought together people from the book industry, music recording industry, rights management, libraries, the technology community, and the identifier community. InterParty looked at the fact that databases containing metadata about people and organizations already exist and identify parties in their own context (e.g., publisher databases of authors, editors, etc.; music industry databases of composers, directors, etc.; library authority files of authors, editors, composers, etc.). The existing databases are independent of one another, follow different approaches to identification, and involve different schemas and formats. For example, one music industry database might have recordings of John Williams, the composer, while another has recordings of John Williams the classical guitarist who formed the group Sky. Each of the publishers would have data files with information about its particular John Williams—some of it proprietary information, but some of it not. InterParty suggested that such databases could be linked with a common functional goal of unique identification and disambiguation of parties. Each database would agree to make available common non-confidential metadata. InterParty would add a new layer of links that could give messages such as "Person X in Namespace A is the same [or not the same] as Person Y in Namespace B." The owner of Namespace B would then need to verify such an assertion by agreeing or disputing. This research has not been implemented, but it has interesting implications for the possible future linking of value-spaces.

International Authority Control

Work is proceeding toward international authority control. We do not yet know exactly how this will happen. New structures always come incrementally, and at the beginning of such a process it is not usually possible to make the mental leap to envision the eventual construct. One possibility is that all forms of name could be accumulated on one authority record, with none chosen as *the* one that must be used. Each form would be identified by language. If there were several variant forms in one language, one of them would be designated as preferred for that language. A default display could be whichever form is most appropriate for users in a particular setting. A search for any one of the forms would retrieve records related to the entity represented by the record. A difficulty with this scenario is the immense size of records that would be produced for many names. Authority records already can have multiple forms of name even in one language; addition of multiple forms in each of multiple languages could result in very large records, indeed (see Figure 8.4).

Instead of one large international authority file, Barbara Tillett has suggested several models for a Virtual International Authority File (VIAF).[10] Some test projects use a distributed model. National bibliographic agencies have independent authority files that can be searched using a standard protocol like Z39.50. When a record for a name or title is not found in the local file, the system uses Z39.50 to search other national authority files, and if the name or title is found, the record can be imported to the local file. Another model is that of a union authority file to which participants could contribute as they wished. This model has the limitations of lengthy records already described and would also lend itself to less consistent information unless there were strict standards and checks. A variation of the union file model is a virtual union authority file. Records would remain in the national files but would be linked to a centralized server that would harvest metadata from the national files. Records for the same entity would be linked at the central

Rec stat	c	**Entered**	19800501	**Replaced**	20021127134340.0		
Type	z	**Upd status**	a	**Enc lvl**	n	**Source**	
Roman	|	**Ref status**	a	**Mod rec**		**Name use**	a
Govt agn	|	**Auth status**	a	**Subj**	a	**Subj use**	a
Series	n	**Auth/ref**	a	**Geo subd**	n	**Ser use**	b
Ser num	n	**Name**	a	**Subdiv tp**	n	**Rules**	c

010		n 80050515
040		DLC ‡c DLC ‡d DLC ‡d NIC ‡d DLC
100	0_	Confucius
400	0_	Konfuzius
400	0_	K'oeng Foe-tse
400	0_	Kung-foo-tsze
400	0_	Kung-Kew
400	0_	Kong-Fou-Tze
400	1_	K'ung, Ch'iu
400	0_	Kwan-Foo-Tze
400	0_	Kung-tse
400	0_	Konfut͡s͡ius
400	0_	Konfut͡s͡iĭ
400	1_	K'ung, Fu-tzu
400	0_	K'ung Fu-tzu
400	0_	Kongja
400	0_	Khong Tju
400	0_	Kōshi
400	0_	K'ung-tzu
400	0_	Kung Fu
400	0_	Kungfutse
400	0_	Confucio
400	0_	Kongzi
400	0_	Khongčhū
670		Jakobs, P. M. Kritik an Lin Piao und Konfuzius, c1983: ‡b t.p. (Konfuzius)
670		Konfut͡s͡iĭ, 1993: ‡b t.p. verso (551-479 B.C.)
670		His Gespräche (Lun yü), 1910: ‡b t.p. (Kungfutse)
670		Gómez Farías, A. Confucio y Martín Fierro, c1986.
670		Konfut͡s͡iĭ, 2001.

Figure 8.4. Authority record for a name that has variants in each of several languages. (Source: OCLC Connexion, Authorities, record number 432385.)

server and refreshed regularly. Maintenance of records would continue to be done in the separate files. Projects to test these models are under way.[11]

International authority control requires standards, and there are several that may be used to good advantage. In the international library community, IFLA has issued *Guidelines for Authority Records and References,* now in its second edition,[12] and the process of approving FRAD[13] is ongoing. The Z39.50 protocol makes it possible to retrieve and display authority records on the Internet. This enables the sharing of authority records for the same entities in different languages, and forms of heading in any particular language can be verified by experts in that language. The IFLA Working Group on Transnational Exchange of Authority Data looked at the possibility of an International Standard Authority Data Number (ISADN). At this writing the ISADN is on hold because of potential expense of maintaining such a system.[14] The OAI (Open Archive Initiative) also shows promise.[15] OAI promotes a protocol (Open Archives Initiative Protocol for Metadata Harvesting, or OAI-PMH) that defines a mechanism for harvesting XML-formatted metadata. It is intentionally simple with the intent of being easier and less costly to implement than Z39.50.

MODELS AND STANDARDS FOR AUTHORITY CONTROL

As mentioned in Chapter 7, the creation of metadata in a broad sense requires description of the information resource, attention to access points for the description, and encoding of the entire surrogate record content. Encoding is discussed in Chapter 5, and Chapter 7 addresses description. The next step after description is the selection of access points that enable the consistent and predictable retrieval of surrogate records. In order to have names, titles, and subjects both collocated and differentiated, the access points need to be brought under authority control.

General Bibliographic Models and Standards

A number of models and standards address the issues of access and authority control to varying degrees. First we discuss some general bibliographic models and standards followed by discussion of standards that exist for archives and for the art and museum communities. The general models are:

- *Functional Requirements for Bibliographic Records* (FRBR)
- *Functional Requirements for Authority Data* (FRAD)

The general standards are:

- *Anglo-American Cataloguing Rules, Second Edition, 2002 Revision* (AACR2R), with updates issued in 2003, 2004, and 2005
- *Statement of International Cataloguing Principles* and *RDA: Resource Description and Access*
- Dublin Core Agents
- Metadata Authority Description Schema (MADS)

Functional Requirements for Bibliographic Records (FRBR)

After identifying Group 1 entities (*work, expression, manifestation,* and *item*), and discussing what is needed to describe them, FRBR addresses Group 2 and Group 3 entities, both of which are important in the process of finding Group 1 entities. Group 2 entities are *person* and *corporate body* and FRBR says that these are responsible for the existence or care of the Group 1 entities. Group 3 entities comprise all Group 1 and Group 2 entities in addition to *concept, object, event,* and *place.* Any Group 3 entity may be the subject of any Group 1 entity. FRBR describes in detail relationships between the Group 1 and Group 2 and 3 entities, and some attributes for the Group 2 and 3 entities are given. It is fairly clear that the Group 2 and Group 3 entities are meant to be access points, but the FRBR model does not describe how those entities and relationships are reflected in access points in bibliographic records, nor does it delineate how a cataloger is to determine the form of name or heading that is to be used for these entities.[16] The task of turning Group 2 entities into access points was assigned to the IFLA Working Group on Functional Requirements and Numbering of Authority Records (FRANAR),[17] which has devised the *Functional Requirements for Authority Data* (FRAD).[18] Work on Group 3 entities is being completed by the Working Group on Functional Requirements for Subject Authority Records (FRSAR).[19]

Functional Requirements for Authority Data (FRAD)

FRAD, like FRBR, is a conceptual model. Its purpose is to provide a framework for functional requirements for the authority data necessary to support authority control both locally and internationally. FRAD, like FRBR, is centered around users, aiming to place in authority records the data that is required by the users of those records. Users of authority records are defined to be both the authority record creators and the end users who benefit both from authority information being available to them as reference tools and from improved retrieval tools that contain controlled access points with reference structures. Four user tasks are identified: *find, identify, contextualize,* and *justify*. The tasks *find* and *identify* are the same as in FRBR. The tasks *contextualize* and *justify* clearly are meant to apply to authority record creators, not to end users. *Contextualize* means to place in context or to clarify relationships; *justify* means to document one's reason for choosing the form of name on which a controlled access point is based.

The FRAD model, as mentioned already, has added the entity *family* to FRBR's Group 2 entities. In addition, FRAD has added five entities needed for a complete model of authority control: *name, identifier, controlled access point, rules,* and *agency*. These may be defined as follows:

- **Name**—the word, character, group of words, or character string that a FRBR entity is known by.
- **Identifier**—anything that uniquely identifies an entity, such as a number, a code, a word or phrase, a logo, or other such device.
- **Controlled access point**—a name, term, code, and the like, that is designated in a bibliographic record, authority record, or reference record as a character string to be used for retrieval.
- **Rules**—a set of instructions for formulating controlled access points.
- **Agency**—an organization that has responsibility for applying rules to the construction and/or modification of controlled access points.

FRAD uses entity-relationship modeling techniques to show all the relationships between and among the entities of the model.

FRBR identifies some attributes for each of the entities in its model. FRAD adds many attributes of its own. For example, the attributes listed in FRAD for *person* are listed below; the ones with asterisks have been added by FRAD.

- Dates associated with the person
- Title of person
- Other designation associated with the person
- Gender*

- Place of birth*
- Place of death*
- Country*
- Place of residence*
- Affiliation*
- Address*
- Language of person*
- Field of activity*
- Profession/occupation*
- Bibliography/history*

FRAD has an extensive relationships section, providing discussion of (1) relationships that operate at a generic level between the entity types, (2) relationships that are commonly shown in the reference structure of the authority record, and (3) relationships between one controlled access point and another.[20] For example, the following table illustrates relationships between entity types:[21]

Entity Type	Sample Relationship Types
Person → Person	▪ pseudonymous relationship ▪ attributive relationship ▪ collaborative relationship ▪ sibling relationship ▪ parent/child relationship
Person → Family	▪ membership relationship
Person → Corporate Body	▪ membership relationship
Family → Family	▪ genealogical relationship
Corporate Body → Corporate Body	▪ hierarchical relationship ▪ sequential relationship
Work → Work	▪ equivalence relationship ▪ derivative relationship ▪ descriptive relationship ▪ whole/part relationship ▪ accompanying relationship (part-to-part) ▪ sequential relationship ▪ shared characteristic relationship

Part II of FRAD delineates, in some detail, the practice of providing authority data in the world today—mostly within the library sector, although brief mention is made of the art/museum and archives communities.

Anglo-American Cataloguing Rules, Second Edition, 2002 Revision (AACR2R)

The principles that underlie access points in AACR2 are based upon the Paris Principles, which were accepted internationally at the International Conference on Cataloguing Principles, held in Paris in 1961.[22] Names, titles, and name/title combinations are the candidates for access points. AACR2 calls for access points for persons, corporate bodies, geographic names, and titles, as well as combinations of names and titles. Some specific access points called for by AACR2 include collaborators, editors and compilers, corporate bodies, titles (including titles of series), related works, and sometimes translators and illustrators. However, these are fairly book-oriented choices, reflecting the origins of AACR2. In fact many access points are for performers, choreographers, programmers, and cartographers, among others.

Primary Access Point. According to the Paris Principles, one of the access points is selected to be the primary access point. The Paris Principles call this the *main entry* and say that it must be a *full entry*. Full entry comes from the days of print catalogs. With print catalogs (i.e., card, book, and COM catalogs) it is necessary to place as many copies of the same surrogate record into the catalog as there are access points. Let us say that a record has the following access points: Author, Joint author, Corporate body, Subject 1, Subject 2, Title, Series title. In such a case there would need to be seven instances of the same surrogate record in the catalog—one filed alphabetically in each of the places where the Author, Joint author, and so forth, would appear (see Figure 8.5). The access point is at the top or head of the copy of the surrogate record in each instance.

Returning to the concept of full entry, in the days of handwritten and typed catalog entries, and later in book catalogs especially, it was often necessary to save time and space by having only one copy of the surrogate record created as a full entry (i.e., containing a complete set of all elements of the record as provided by the cataloger). The rest of the entries were abbreviated. The Paris Principles stated that the place where the full entry should be filed is the alphabetical location of the primary access point or main entry. Soon it became customary to refer to the full entry as the main entry.

```
JC178  Paine, Thomas, 1737-1809.
.B7      Common sense, by Thomas Paine.
1976   Cutchogue, N.Y., Buccaneer Books, c1976.
         129 p., ill., 22 cm.

         "Epistle to Quakers": p. 117-129.


  1. United States--Politics and Government--
1775-1783.  2. Monarchy.  I. Paine, Thomas.
Epistle to Quakers.  II. Epistle to Quakers.
III. Title
```

```
         Epistle to Quakers.

JC178  Paine, Thomas, 1737-1809.
.B7      Common sense. Buccaneer Books, c1976.
1976
         129 p.
```

Figure 8.5. Example of a main entry card and an abbreviated version of the main entry card. The top card is the main entry card and is also what one might call the *full entry*. The primary access point for this record is *Paine, Thomas, 1737-1809.* The bottom card is an abbreviated version of the main entry card with one of the added entries typed at the top of the card. This example would require that six cards be filed into the card catalog—one full entry at the alphabetical position for the primary access point, and one brief version for each of the five added entries.

Use of *main entry* to mean both *full entry* and *primary access point* causes great confusion today. Print catalogs have long since given up the practice of having one full entry and several abbreviated copies of each surrogate record. Instead, as the technology of photocopying and then computer-printed cards became commonplace, every entry became a duplicate of the full entry. The difference among the copies was that each copy had as its top line one of the chosen access points.

The concept of full entry is definitely not applicable in Online Public Access Catalogs (OPACs). In an OPAC there is only one copy of the complete metadata record. In response to a particular user request, that record is displayed on the screen. In the OPAC environment, *main entry* can refer only to the access point that is the main or primary one. In much of the literature that calls for doing away with the main entry, the argument is that we no longer have systems where only one copy of a record has all the information. Others understand the current meaning of main entry as the primary access point, but some in this second group also argue against the concept. Others argue forcefully for keeping the main entry concept.

Main Entry Controversy. Controversy over main entry (in the sense of primary access point) is more than three decades old. In 1978 Seymour Lubetzky and Michael Gorman disagreed quite publicly at a conference on the emergence of AACR2.[23] AACR2's introduction included the observation that the concept of main entry might have outlived its time. However, there had not been enough time to research the idea, and so the concept was included in AACR2. It stated that a library that wished to could choose access points without designating one as the main one. Lubetzky, whose principles underlie the Paris Principles, argued that this was a step backward instead of forward. Gorman believed that the time had come to make the distinction only when necessary to cite one work on the record for another work, a situation which he guessed would happen "less than 1 percent" of the time.[24] Research, however, has shown this estimate to be quite low. Richard Smiraglia found that approximately 50 percent of a sample of works had derivative relationships.[25] As explained earlier, derivative relationships exist when one work is derived from another (e.g., editions, translations, adaptations, performances, etc.). A derivative work requires a note or access point in its metadata to cite or refer to the work from which it has been derived.

Controversy raged again on the discussion list for the International Conference on AACR[26] in the fall of 1997. Martha Yee, a former student of Lubetzky, took up his cause in defense of the main entry. Some contributors suggested that system design can accomplish the same objectives.[27] Among the recommendations from the conference, however, none mentioned main entry.

The Joint Steering Committee for Development of RDA (formerly called Joint Steering Committee for Revision of AACR) is currently engaged in the process of creating a replacement for AACR (called *RDA: Resource Description and Access*).[28] One part of the plan for RDA is a thorough reworking of AACR2, chapter 21, "Choice of Access Points."[29] Among the planned revisions is a restatement of the rules for choice of entry in terms of the relationships among the entities that are presented in FRBR.[30] The reader should watch this rapidly developing work.

Justification for Choice of Primary Access Point. In Chapter 2, Cutter's "objects" of a catalog were quoted. Paraphrased, they are:

- to enable a person to find a book when author, title, or subject is known
- to show what the library has by a given author, on a given subject, or in a given kind of literature
- to assist in the choice of a book as to its edition or as to its character

In many ways, choosing a primary access point is a way to carry out Cutter's objectives. Reasons given for a need for a primary access point include the following:

- to provide a standard citation form in order to
  - show relationships between works and among expressions and manifestations of a work
  - identify works about other works
  - identify works contained in larger works
- to provide subarrangement under subjects (and as a corollary, to provide a way to subarrange items under classification number) in order to
  - show prolific authors in a field
  - bring together manifestations of a work
- to provide for collocation of all manifestations of a work, even though the work may be published with different titles (e.g., translations), or editions of a work may be written by different authors
- to assure a judgment of the most important and most predictable access point in situations where reduction of cataloging time has been mandated (especially where number of required access points has been reduced, as in the Core Record)

Let us briefly discuss each of these justifications.

Citation. First, choice of a primary access point is necessary every time someone cites a work in a document or lists it in a bibliography. That is, there is only going to be one entry for the work being cited, and the citer has to put something first: the first author, the editor, the title, or some other choice. Thus the concept of primary access point is put into practice with great frequency, but people usually do not recognize that every time they create an entry in a bibliography they choose a primary access point. Style

Visual Materials	Rec Stat	c	Entered	19950511	Replaced	20020712					
Type	g	ELvl	7	Srce		Audn		Ctrl		Lang	eng
BLvl	m	Form		GPub		Time	---	MRec		Ctry	xxu
Desc	a	TMat	m	Tech	l	DtSt	s	Dates	1994,		

007		m ‡b r ‡d c ‡e b ‡f a ‡g a ‡h f ‡i s
010		95-506926
040		DLC ‡e amim ‡c DLC ‡d OCLCQ
017		PA742-443 ‡b U.S. Copyright Office
043		n-us-ny
050	00	CGC 1381-1386 (ref print)
245	00	Nobody's fool / ‡c a Scott Rudin/Cinehous production ; directed and written by Robert Benton ; produced by Scott Rudin and Arlene Donovan.
257		U.S.
260		United States : ‡b Paramount Pictures : ‡b Capella International, ‡c 1994.
300		12 reels of 12 on 6 (ca. 9950 ft.) : ‡b sd., col. ; ‡c 35 mm. ref print.
500		Paramount Pictures Corporation. DCR 1994; PUB 11Oct94; REG 7Feb95; PA742-443.
508		Associate producer, Scott Ferguson ; music, Howard Shore.
511	1	Paul Newman, Jessica Tandy, Gene Saks, Bruce Willis, Melanie Griffith, Dylan Walsh, Pruitt Taylor Vince, Josef Sommer, Alexander Goodwin.
520		In this affectionate story of small town life in upstate New York, Sully, a fitfully employed 60-year-old construction worker, is a cheerful curmudgeon who seems to have missed all his chances and made nothing of his life. However, it becomes apparent that Sully, despite his best efforts to be a n'er-do-well, is an important and beloved member of his family and his community. He is, as he says, somebody's father, somebody's grandfather, somebody's friend.
500		Part of summary from Variety, 12-12-94.
500		**From the novel by Richard Russo.**
500		Sources used: Variety, 12-12-94.
650	0	Fathers and sons ‡v Drama.
650	0	Family ‡v Drama.
650	0	City and town life ‡z New York (State) ‡v Drama.
655	7	Features. ‡2 mim
655	7	Adaptations. ‡2 mim
700	1	Benton, Robert, ‡e direction, ‡e writing.
700	1	Newman, Paul, ‡d 1925- ‡e cast.
700	1	Tandy, Jessica, ‡e cast.
700	1	Saks, Gene, ‡d 1921- ‡e cast.
700	1	Willis, Bruce, ‡d 1955- ‡e cast.
700	1	Griffith, Melanie, ‡d 1957- ‡e cast.
700	**1**	**Russo, Richard, ‡d 1949- ‡t Nobody's fool.**
710	2	Copyright Collection (Library of Congress) ‡5 DLC

Figure 8.6. Metadata record for a work based on another work with an access point constructed using the primary access point and the title of the original work. (Source: OCLC Connexion, WorldCat, record number 32544834.)

manuals give suggestions for this choice, but the style manuals differ from each other, so predictability is lost.

Within a surrogate record for one work, it is often necessary to refer to another related work. This happens, as mentioned already, when one is describing a work that is based on another work (e.g., a screenplay based on a novel), when one work is a version of another work (e.g., a new edition of a work where the new edition is written by a new author), or other such cases (see one example in Figure 8.6). In these cases it is important to refer to the related work in a note in the surrogate record for the work being described. In addition to the note, the cataloger provides a controlled access point made up of the primary access point and title of the work being cited.

A second kind of instance that requires reference to another work is when the intellectual content of the work for which a surrogate record is being made has as its subject another work (e.g., a criticism of a literary work). In this case one of the subject headings in the surrogate record is the primary access point followed by the title of the work that is being discussed (see Figure 8.7).

Books **Rec Stat** a   **Entered** 19950601   **Replaced** 19951101

Type	a	**ELvl**		**Srce**		**Audn**		**Ctrl**		**Lang**	eng
BLvl	m	**Form**		**Conf**	0	**Biog**		**MRec**		**Ctry**	nju
		Cont	b	**GPub**		**LitF**	0	**Indx**	0		
Desc	a	**Ills**	a	**Fest**	0	**DtSt**	s	**Dates**	1995,		

010   95-68761
040   DLC ‡c DLC
020   0878917527
050 00 PS3537.A426 ‡b C3285 1995
082 00 813/.54 ‡2 20
100 1 Holzman, Robert S.
245 10 J.D. Salinger's The catcher in the rye / ‡c text by Robert S. Holzman, Gary L. Perkins ; illustrations by Karen Pica.
246 18 Catcher in the rye
260   Piscataway, N.J. : ‡b Research & Education Association, ‡c c1995.
300   v, 113, [1] p. : ‡b ill. ; ‡c 21 cm.
440 0 MAXnotes
504   Includes bibliographical references (p. [114]).
600 10 Salinger, J. D. ‡q (Jerome David), ‡d 1919- ‡t Catcher in the rye ‡x Examinations ‡x Study guides.
700 1 Perkins, Gary L.

Figure 8.7. Metadata record for a work that is about another work; the record contains a subject heading that consists of the primary access point and the title of the work that is the subject of the work represented by this record. (Source: OCLC Connexion, WorldCat, record number 33406432.)

A third situation that requires a citation to another work occurs when the work being described is one of the following:

- a work that is part of a larger work (e.g., a volume in a series or set) (see Figure 8.8)
- a work published with one or two other works (e.g., a collection)
- a work that contains a smaller work within it (e.g., a critique and analysis of a musical composition contains the composition)
- a work that contains one or more previously published works in addition to the main one being described (see Figure 8.9)

Books	Rec Stat c			Entered	19950605	Replaced	20020525				
Type	a	ELvl		Srce	d	Audn		Ctrl		Lang	eng
BLvl	m	Form		Conf	0	Biog		MRec		Ctry	nyu
		Cont		GPub		LitF	1	Indx	0		
Desc	a	Ills		Fest	0	DtSt	s	Dates	1995,		

010		95-77866
040		MdHyP ‡c DLC ‡d FIT ‡d OCL ‡d OCLCQ
020		0679441018 : ‡c $25.00
042		lccopycat
050	00	PS3568.I265 ‡b M46 1995
082	00	813/.54 ‡2 20
100	1_	Rice, Anne, ‡d 1941-
245	10	**Memnoch the Devil / ‡c Anne Rice.**
250		1st ed.
260		New York : ‡b Knopf, ‡c 1995.
300		353 p. ; ‡c 25 cm.
490	1	**The vampire chronicles** ; ‡v **[5th bk.]**
520		A vampire is offered work by both God and the Devil. He is Lestat, a man of action who just bumped off a billionaire for smuggling cocaine. The job interviews yield quite a bit of information on his prospective employers, including why God expelled the Devil from Paradise at the time of the Creation. It appears the Devil was against God's scheme to make suffering a regular part of life.
650	0	Vampires ‡v Fiction.
650	0	Lestat (Fictitious character) ‡v Fiction.
655	7	Horror tales. ‡2 gsafd
800	1_	**Rice, Anne, ‡d 1941- ‡t Vampire chronicles ; ‡v 5th bk.**

Figure 8.8. Metadata record for a work that is part of a larger work. Anne Rice's *Memnoch the Devil* is the fifth book in her series called *Vampire Chronicles.* The added entry, consisting of primary access point and title of the series, allows collocation of the series with the author's individual titles. (Source: OCLC Connexion, WorldCat, record number 32683203.)

Books		**Rec Stat**	c	**Entered**	19970307	**Replaced**	20020801				
Type	a	**ELvl**	I	**Srce**	d	**Audn**		**Ctrl**		**Lang**	eng
BLvl	m	**Form**		**Conf**	0	**Biog**		**MRec**		**Ctry**	nyu
		Cont		**GPub**		**LitF**	0	**Indx**	0		
Desc	a	**Ills**		**Fest**	0	**DtSt**	s	**Dates**	1835,		

040 NJL ‡c NJL ‡d OCLCQ
092 211.5 ‡b P14
100 1 Paine, Thomas, ‡d 1737-1809.
245 14 The theological works of Thomas Paine : ‡b the most complete edition ever published.
260 New York : ‡b George H. Evans, ‡c 1835.
300 xiv, [7]-384 p. ; ‡c 22 cm.
500 "The age of reason": p. [7]-159.
501 With: Miscellaneous letters and essays on various subjects / by Thomas Paine. Granville, Middletown, N.J. : G.H. Evans, 1844, and 2 other works.
650 0 Deism.
650 0 Rationalism.
700 12 Paine, Thomas, ‡d 1737-1809. ‡t Age of reason.
740 02 Age of reason.

Figure 8.9. Metadata record for a work that contains a smaller work within it. The work being described contains four works of Thomas Paine. One is considered to be a major work and is given an added entry consisting of the primary access point and the title. (Source: OCLC Connexion, WorldCat, record number 36504265.)

Subarrangement. The second justification for primary access point is for sorting search results. If primary access points have been chosen, then the results of a subject search can be displayed in the order of the primary access points, which, in a large percentage of cases, would be the name of the author or first-named author. Besides being a logical way to display subject search results, this allows users to determine the authors who write most in a particular field so that those authors' names can be searched in other retrieval tools. Arrangement by primary access point under subject headings also serves to collocate editions of works on the same subject.

Collocation. Primary access points also provide a way to collocate (i.e., bring together) all derivations of the same work. If there are several manifestations of a work—a translation, an illustrated version, a microform copy, an audio version, and so on—choosing the same primary access point for them means that in most retrieval tools they will be displayed together. Of course it is helpful, when all do not have the same title, to have a *uniform title* so that the manifestations will not only be displayed under the same primary access point, but will also be displayed together among all the search results under that access point (see Figure 8.10).

Collocation is an important outcome of the practice of choosing primary access points. This access point has proved to be, so far, the only way

Books **Rec Stat**	c			**Entered**	19980317			**Replaced**	20030109		
Type	a	**ELvl**	I	**Srce**	d	**Audn**		**Ctrl**		**Lang**	spa
BLvl	m	**Form**		**Conf**	0	**Biog**		**MRec**		**Ctry**	sp
		Cont	b	**GPub**		**LitF**	0	**Indx**	0		
Desc	a	**Ills**		**Fest**	0	**DtSt**	s	**Dates**	1997,		

040		ZQP ‡c ZQP ‡d NVC ‡d OCLCQ
020		8440670508 : ‡c $14.95
041	1	spa ‡h eng
090		PR2794.R7 ‡b F3x 1997
100	1_	**Shakespeare, William, ‡d 1564-1616.**
240	10	**Romeo and Juliet. ‡l Spanish**
245	10	**Romeo y Julieta** / ‡c William Shakespeare ; [traducción: Jaime Navarra Farré].
250		1. ed.
260		Barcelona, España : ‡b Ediciones B, S.A./Grupo Zeta, ‡c c1997.
300		167 p. ; ‡c 18 cm.
440	0	VIB ; ‡v 193/8
500		Translation of: Romeo and Juliet.
504		Includes bibliographical references (p. 161-167).
600	10	Shakespeare, William, ‡d 1564-1616 ‡x Translations into Spanish.
650	0	English drama (Tragedy) ‡y Early modern and Elizabethan, 1500-1600 ‡x Translations into Spanish.
650	0	Married people ‡z Italy ‡z Verona ‡v Drama.
650	0	Family ‡z Italy ‡z Verona ‡v Drama.
655	7	Tragedies. ‡2 gsafd
700	12	Shakespeare, William, ‡d 1564-1616. ‡t Romeo and Juliet. ‡l Spanish.
700	1_	Navarra Farré, Jaime.

Books **Rec Stat**	n			**Entered**	19951128			**Replaced**	19951128		
Type	a	**ELvl**	I	**Srce**	d	**Audn**		**Ctrl**		**Lang**	eng
BLvl	m	**Form**		**Conf**	0	**Biog**		**MRec**		**Ctry**	cou
		Cont		**GPub**		**LitF**	0	**Indx**	0		
Desc	a	**Ills**		**Fest**	0	**DtSt**	s	**Dates**	1994,		

040		IBA ‡c IBA
090		PR2831.A2 ‡b B4
100	1_	**Shakespeare, William, ‡d 1564-1616.**
240	10	**Romeo and Juliet**
245	14	**The tragedy of Romeo and Juliet** / ‡c by William Shakespeare. Edited by Richard and Joan Bell.
260		Boulder, CO : ‡b Armado and Moth, ‡c 1994.
300		96 p. ; ‡c 22 cm. + ‡e director's script (96 p. ; 28 cm.)
500		Title on cover: "Mr. William Shakespeares The Tragedie of Romeo and Ivliet. Published according to the True Originall Copies."
500		Actor's script and director's script include preface, notes, and glossary.
700	1	Bell, Richard. ‡4 edt
700	1_	Bell, Joan. ‡4 edt

Figure 8.10. Two metadata records showing two manifestations of a work—one that is a Spanish translation, and one with the original, but out-of-favor title. Each has a primary access point and uniform title that allows them to be collocated despite the different titles. (Source: OCLC Connexion, WorldCat, record numbers 38735799 and 33812768.)

to collocate all manifestations of a work, including instances when manifestations have different titles, and editions have different authors. A number of people on the discussion list for the international AACR2 conference[31] indicated that technology could accomplish this function. At the time of implementation of RDA, there will be potential for system design to take advantage of new ways for identifying works and their expressions and manifestations. Until this or something like it is determined, implemented, and made the norm for catalog display, primary access point is still the best way we have to provide collocation.

Judgment of Most Important. Finally, when times are tough and full surrogate records cannot be made, and when brief records have to be created for some information resources, choice of a primary access point ensures that at least the most important and most predictable access point will be created. The Program for Cooperative Cataloging (PCC) Core Record, mentioned in the preceding chapter, calls for the primary access point and perhaps one other name or title access point to be made and brought under authority control.

AACR2 Principles for Choosing Primary Access Point. AACR2 is made up of many rules that seem unfathomable to the uninitiated. However, they are based upon principles that can be laid out in much the same order as the rules themselves. First, most works are created by a single individual, in which case primary access point is the name of the person (or surrogate for the name, e.g., pseudonym). If the author is unknown and is unidentified in any way, then primary access point is the title. (*Note:* "Unidentified in any way" means that there is not even a phrase such as "Author of Little Nell" as a statement of responsibility.) Other works are created by multiple persons (or corporate bodies, families, or some combination of these), whose responsibility may be either *synchronous* or *asynchronous.*[32]

When responsibility is *synchronous,* it means that all persons or bodies made the *same kind* of contribution to the creation of the work, in which case primary access point is the *principal* responsible party, if one is identified. Under AACR2, if no responsible party is identified as the principal one, the first of two or three equally represented responsible parties is chosen as the main entry. If there are more than three responsible parties, and no one party is identified as having principal responsibility, the primary access point is the title.

When responsibility is *asynchronous,* it means that the responsible parties have made *different kinds* of contributions to the existence of the work. Basically, there are three kinds of asynchronous responsibility: (1) responsibility has varied over time, resulting in modifications of works (e.g., work of original author is revised or rewritten by a later author); (2) responsibility has varied during the creation of a completely new work (e.g., artist and writer); or (3) the work emanates from a corporate body, but is written by a person or persons.

When responsibility has varied over time, the primary access point is the original author unless it is clear that a later author has greater responsibility. For example, translations are works in which the work originally written by one person is put into another language by another person. Some revisions are works in which the work of an original person may have updates and additional comments written by another person.

On the other hand, there are situations in which a later author has greater responsibility. For example, in an adaptation, the idea contained in the work is that of the original author but all the words of this particular version are those of a new author (e.g., Shakespeare's plays completely rewritten as stories for children). Also, some revisions have so much updating and change that they are really the work of the new author. In these and cases like them, the primary access point should be the later author.

When responsibility has varied during the creation of a new work, the primary access point is the party deemed to have made the most important contribution. For example, many works are the result of the work of an artist and a writer. One criterion is whether the work was a collaboration. If so, it should be entered under the one named first, unless the other is given prominence by wording or layout. However, in a work that gathers together works of an artist, if a writer has added only short captions for the works, the artist should be the primary access point. On the other hand, if the work was first completed by the writer and then had illustrations added by the artist, the writer is clearly the one with primary responsibility.

When responsibility involves a corporate body, both the Paris Principles and AACR2 list situations when corporate body is to be main entry (AACR2's list is longer), and in the remainder of cases the primary access point is to be a person or the title. Main entry, according to the Paris Principles, should be a corporate body when the work is the expression of the corporate thought or activity of the body (e.g., official reports, rules and regulations, manifestos, etc.) or when the wording of the title and the nature of the work imply that the corporate body is collectively responsible for the content (e.g., serials whose titles consist of a generic term like *Bulletin* preceded or followed by a corporate body name, if they include some account of the activities of the body).

The concept of *corporate author* has been a matter of international controversy. Some traditions have declared that corporate bodies cannot be authors (i.e., only humans can be authors). When a new edition of AACR was being discussed in the late 1970s, a compromise solution was agreed upon. Its essence was that even though a corporate body is not an author in a real sense, there are times when a corporate body is so tied to a document (e.g., an annual report, a committee report, a musical performance that goes beyond mere performance) that the body must be chosen as the primary access point.

Some instances when title is primary access point have been mentioned in the preceding discussion, but it is useful to have all of these listed together. According to AACR2, the primary access point should be title when:

- a work is truly anonymous (*Note:* This does not include works that use a phrase for an author.)
- a work has more than three responsible parties and none is singled out as having had primary responsibility
- a work that compiles the work of several authors has been produced under editorial direction
- a work has a corporate body involved, but the rules for corporate bodies require a title primary access point instead
- a work is accepted as sacred scripture by a religious body.

Additional Access Points. In a catalog record, a primary access point is not enough to ensure that users will be able to retrieve the information they need. Additional access points must supplement the primary access point. In all the cases just discussed, every responsible party and title that has been considered to be a candidate for primary access point should be an access point (even if it is not chosen as the primary one). In the library cataloging world, non-primary access points are called *added entries.*

A hold-over in AACR2 from card catalog days is that if there are four or more parties responsible for the same kind of activity (e.g., authorship or editorship) in creating a work, an added entry is made only for the first one listed. (This rule was meant to save space in the card catalog.) This practice of making access points for all responsible parties only if there are fewer than four is a questionable one in today's information environment and is currently being examined for possible change in RDA.[33] Information resources often are created jointly by four or more persons. In the current electronic environment, where space is not an issue, following the so-called *Rule of Three* is unnecessary.

When access points are made for every responsible party, it is not necessary for a user to have to guess which one has been chosen to be the primary access point or even to understand what that choice is all about. The usefulness of choosing a primary access point is to be able to display results of searches in a logical and collocated fashion, not to require a user to understand it. If our systems do not provide logical displays, the fault lies with the system design.

The following section discusses the principles involved in heading creation for names and titles. Headings for subject concepts are discussed in Chapter 10.

Headings for Access Points. As mentioned already, headings are maintained in authority files, which are collections of authority records. Each authority record identifies the form of name or title that has been selected as "authoritative" according to the rules. It lists many of the variant forms of name or variant forms of title that are associated with the authorized form. It identifies sources of information about the variant forms of name or title or about the person or body or work represented by the name or title (see Figure 8.11).

The library world has had authority control for the longest time, and therefore its principles are given below as an example. AACR2 does not have a section for authority control, per se, but its chapters 22–25, on form of heading for personal, geographic, and corporate names, and uniform titles,

Rec stat	c	Entered	19810716	Replaced	20000204164435.0		
Type	z	Upd status	a	Enc lvl	n	Source	
Roman	|	Ref status	a	Mod rec		Name use	a
Govt agn	|	Auth status	a	Subj	a	Subj use	a
Series	n	Auth/ref	a	Geo subd	n	Ser use	b
Ser num	n	Name	a	Subdiv tp	n	Rules	c

010 n 81073496 ‡z n 82138607
040 DLC ‡c DLC ‡d DLC
100 0 Diana, ‡c Princess of Wales, ‡d 1961-1997
400 1 Spencer, Diana Frances, ‡c Lady, ‡d 1961-1997
400 0 Di, ‡c Lady, ‡d 1961-1997
400 0 Dayānā, ‡c Princess of Wales, ‡d 1961-1997
670 Dunlop, J. Charles and Diana, a royal romance, c1981 (subj.) ‡b p. 6, etc. (Lady Diana Frances Spencer; b. July 1, 1961)
670 Leete-Hodge, L. The Country Life book of the royal wedding, 1981: ‡b table of contents (Diana, Princess of Wales)
670 Carretier, M.-P. Lady Di chez elle, c1987.
670 The Washington post, Aug. 31, 1997 ‡b (Diana d. Aug. 31, 1997 from a fatal car accident)
670 al-Mūsād qatala Dayānā ... 1998- : ‡b v. 1, t.p. (Dayānā)

Figure 8.11. An authority record showing the "authoritative" heading for Princess Diana (in bold) and three variant forms of her name (in 400 fields). (Source: OCLC Connexion, Authorities, record number 618798.)

explain how headings are constructed and brought together with references from other names or titles and other forms of name or title representing the same entity. In the plan for RDA mentioned above, rules from these chapters will become the core of a new group of sections called "Recording Attributes." An appendix will contain instructions on designating relationships in authority records.[34]

In the process of creating headings for *names* one must make at least one of three choices, and often must make all three: (1) choice of which name to use, (2) choice of which form of that name to use, (3) choice of format. In the third choice there are two decisions to be made: (a) which part of the name will be used as the entry word; and (b) what additions need to be made to the name to distinguish it from the same or similar names.

In the process of creating headings for *titles,* it is necessary to: (1) choose which title will be used, and (2) decide upon the arrangement of the title and whether it is to be followed by distinguishing attributes such as language and date. AACR2 follows certain principles in its rules for making these decisions. These principles are presented in the following subsections.

Principles for Choice and Form of Heading of Personal Name. Choice of which name to use is required in cases where a person has used different names, not including differently shortened forms of part(s) of a name. The first principle is to use the latest name of a person if the person's name has been changed. Examples:

- Chris Wallace changed to Notorious B.I.G.—use Notorious B.I.G.
- Sarah Ferguson married and became the Duchess of York—use Duchess of York, that is, York, Sarah Mountbatten-Windsor, Duchess of

The second principle is to use the predominant name of a person who is known by more than one name. (A nickname is considered to be a different name, not a shortened form of the same name.) Examples:

- Bill Clinton is also known as William Jefferson Clinton—use Bill Clinton
- Mildred Zaharias was known in professional golf as Babe Zaharias—use Babe Zaharias

The third principle is for persons who use pseudonyms. One should use the pseudonym if only one pseudonym is always used with all works. However, if the same writer used different names for separate bibliographic identities, one should use each of the names and create a separate authority record for each bibliographic identity. Different bibliographic identities are represented if a person has used one name for one kind of work and has used another name for another kind of work. Examples:

- Ford H. M. Hueffer wrote all his works as Ford Madox Ford—use only the pseudonym

- Carolyn Heilbrun wrote literary criticism using her own name but used the pseudonym Amanda Cross for her mystery novels—use both names

However, if the writer is contemporary (i.e., still living or died after 1900) and uses more than one pseudonym or a real name and one or more pseudonyms, one should use each one for the works that are created using that name. Examples:

- Molly Keane and M. J. Farrell are the same person but the names are used with separate works—use both names

- Stephen King and Richard Bachman are the same person—use both names

Once the *name* has been chosen, one then determines which *form* of that name will be used. There may be variants in fullness, language, and spelling. Any of these may be affected by country of residence or activity. The overriding principle is that the form of name used by a person in his or her country of residence or activity is the form that is to be used.

When a person has used names of variant fullness, one should use the form most commonly found. For example, one should choose C. S. Lewis over Clive Staples Lewis. If no form predominates, one should choose the latest form. If in doubt, one should use fullest form. However, the form used in the person's country of residence or activity takes precedence. Even though the English-speaking world produces Hans Christian Andersen's works using the full form of name, during his lifetime in his country he preferred H. C. Andersen; so that is the form that should be chosen for the heading.

When there are variants in language one should use the form used by the person in his or her own country of residence or activity. Variants in spelling call for using the new spelling if there has been an official change in orthography. Otherwise, the predominant spelling should be used. Variants in transliteration of names written in a non-Roman script are either Romanized according to an adopted Romanization table, or if well known, a predominant English form may be used. For example, the Arabic name Qaddafi, can also be transliterated as Gadafi, Gadhafi, Kaddafi, Kadhafi, and Qadhafi, among others. The predominant spelling seems to be Qaddafi.

The structure of a personal name in a controlled access point is usually the family name (or surname), followed by forenames, and often followed by dates of birth and/or death. In cases where a person does not have a family name or surname, the entry word is the person's first forename. A good common sense methodology is to use as entry word the part of the name that would be the entry word in a telephone book in the person's country of residence or activity.[35] For example, in Brazil the entry word is the last part of a compound surname; in Argentina the entry word is the first part of a compound surname; in Iceland the entry word is the given name (forename) because the last names of persons in Iceland are patronymics, not family names (i.e., a person's last name is the given name of one's parent [often father, but sometimes mother] with either *son* or *dottir* attached to it). If a person has a known preference for the entry word to be used, then the person's preference takes precedence (e.g., a person with an unhyphenated compound surname in English that would ordinarily be entered under the last part may prefer entry under the first part).

Persons who are known only by their given names include royalty, persons of religious vocations, pop stars, and the like. In some cases the name consists only of one name followed by distinguishing additions; or, as in the case of royalty, there may be several names. When there is only one name (e.g., Aristotle), that name is obviously going to be the entry word, but there will likely be distinguishing additions.

In order to distinguish an author from others with the same name, additions to the heading may be necessary. The most common ones are birth and/or death dates and full forenames added in parentheses. For example, the name of H. C. Andersen would be followed by full forenames and dates: **Andersen, H. C. (Hans Christian), 1805–1875.** The Library of Congress has as its policy to add birth and/or death dates and full forenames when they are known at the time of creating the heading for the name, and to add death dates when they become known, even if there is not yet a conflict with an identical name.

Principles for Choice and Form of Heading of Corporate Name. Corporate names differ from personal names in that a corporate name change may signal what is really a new corporate body. And corporate bodies can merge with another body, split into two or more bodies, or absorb another body, among other changes. The rules for choice of corporate names in AACR2 reflect practice more than they do principle. According to the rules, one is to create a new heading and a separate authority record for each name change. This eliminates the necessity of determining whether a name change signals a new body with a new purpose or is simply a name change, perhaps for political or other such reasons. Then each heading is to be used as the access point on surrogate records for information resources that were created during the time the body had that name.

Each authority record contains a connection to the preceding name of the body or bodies and to the following name. For example, the American Society for Information Science and Technology (ASIST) once had the name American Documentation Institute; in 1968 the American Documentation Institute changed its name to American Society for Information Science; and in 2000 the name was changed again to American Society for Information Science & Technology. A properly constructed catalog would have references from each of the second two names to its preceding one as well as references from each of the first two names to the name following it (see Figure 8.12). Practice once included the entire history of name

---

American Documentation Institute

search also under later name

American Society for Information Science

American Society for Information Science

search also under earlier name

American Documentation Institute

American Society for Information Science

search also under later name

American Society for Information Science & Technology

American Society for Information Science & Technology

search also under earlier name

American Society for Information Science

Figure 8.12. References necessary in order to connect all three names of an organization.

changes of a corporate body in one record, but the great amount of work involved dictated an abandonment of the practice in the United States.

Publications of corporate bodies often have more than one form of the body's name on the same information resource. There can be an abbreviation, an acronym, a shortened form, or a popular name in addition to the official name. If a variant is not an official name change, one is to use the predominant name. For example, the conventional name Westminster Abbey would be chosen over the official name Collegiate Church of St. Peter in Westminster. If the name is for an international body, and the name is in more than one language, AACR2 calls for choosing the English form if there is one. It is hoped that with the move to international authority control a new principle would be to choose the name in whichever language is best for the users of the catalog, which is the principle stated in the Paris Principles.

In creating a heading for a corporate body, the general principle is to use the most common form of the name written in direct order as it appears on publications of the body. However, some corporate bodies are part of or subordinate to other corporate bodies (e.g., the Cataloging and Classification Section is subordinate to the Association for Library Collections & Technical Services of the American Library Association). If the body is a government, religious, or other subordinate body, the principle is that the heading for the subordinate body is its own name *if* that name is distinctive and can stand alone; otherwise, the body's name is added as a subheading to the name of the higher body (e.g., in the heading, **Association for Library Collections & Technical Services. Cataloging and Classification Section,** the name of the section cannot stand alone; it must be identified by the body in which it is a section). For many government bodies this means that the first word of the heading is the name of the jurisdiction, which is usually the geographic name of the area governed (e.g., **United States. Federal Bureau of Investigation**). Under AACR2 rules for jurisdictional names, names are all in English if there is an English form, but according to the Paris Principles, geographic names for governments are to be in the language suitable to the users of the catalog.

Principles for Choice and Arrangement of Uniform Title. *Uniform titles* are titles that have been chosen for a work (or an expression) so that all manifestations will be collocated under the same primary access point when multiple varying titles have been used for the work over time or in different languages (e.g., *Hamlet, Hamlet a tragedy, Hamlet Prince of Denmark, William Shakespeare's Hamlet, Amleto principe di Danimarca,* etc.). Uniform titles are created when works have more than one manifestation and need to have title resolution. They are also created when a work is made into a new work in a different form, which often has a different title. There needs to be a way to bring these two works together in the retrieval tool (e.g., the film *Gettysburg* based on the novel *The Killer Angels* by Michael Shaara). Uniform titles have been used for many years in the creation of bibliographic records for music. It has taken much longer for them to be accepted as useful in other situations, although the Library of Congress has long used uniform titles to subarrange and collocate the large number of records that fall under a famous prolific author such as Shakespeare or Mark Twain.

Use of the principle of uniform title requires an understanding of what constitutes a work. As mentioned earlier, a number of individuals have done research in this area,[36] and IFLA has created FRBR.[37] Research is proceeding on systems that might implement the FRBR model. Meanwhile, the rules in AACR2 reflect some inconsistency of interpretation.

The general principle for uniform titles is that if manifestations of a work appear under various titles, one must be chosen, and the original title in the original language is preferred unless another title in the same language has become better known. In the case of simultaneous publication of different titles, the choice should be the title of the edition published in the home country of the responsible party. With publication on the Web it remains to be seen how the issue of variant titles will play out. Uniform titles also serve to *differentiate* identical titles of different works. This is especially needed when title is the primary access point. For example, different serials often have identical titles (e.g., *The Times* is a popular newspaper title that needs to be differentiated by city).

Basically, the words of a uniform title are in direct order as they appear on at least one manifestation of a work. In the United States initial articles are omitted because in the MARC 21 fields where uniform title is placed in a subfield "t" (e.g., 6xx and 7xx fields) following the primary access point for the work being cited, there is no allowance for skipping over initial articles in the process of arranging uniform titles for display. Thus, for a criticism written about Dickens's *The Pickwick Papers,* the uniform title in the $t subfield would be *Pickwick Papers* so that it would be displayed with other titles beginning with *P* rather than those beginning with *T.* This would appear in the MARC record as:

600 10 $a Dickens, Charles, $d 1812-1870. $t Pickwick papers.

There are three main cases where additions to uniform titles may be needed: (1) for conflict resolution, (2) for language identification, and (3) to show parts of a work. An example of conflict resolution is:

Scarlet letter (Choreographic work : Graham).

This is clearly not the famous novel *The Scarlet Letter.* An example of language identification is:

Nome della rosa. English.

This would bring the English translation, *The Name of the Rose,* together with its Italian original. An example of a uniform title showing a part of a work is:

Paradise lost. Book 4.

Music uniform titles can be made for all these reasons, and in addition, they are used to organize the works of composers. Such works often do not have distinctive titles, and the same work often has a variety of titles (e.g., *Beethoven's Fifth Symphony* may be titled *Beethoven's Fifth, Symphony no. 5,* or *The Fifth Symphony,* to name a few). Uniform titles provide a way to organize collections of concertos, quartets, symphonies, and the like. An example of a music uniform title is:

Mozart, Wolfgang Amadeus, 1756–1791. Concertos, flute, harp, orchestra, K. 299, C major.

Uniform titles are also used for some types of collections in AACR2. The theory behind this is dubious, but it seems to be necessary for the purpose of displaying all works of a particular kind together if their titles proper are not distinctive (see Figure 8.13). Thus the record for a work called *Selected works of William Shakespeare* would display with the record for the title *Some works of Shakespeare,* if both had the uniform title **Selections.** Some uniform titles used in this way are:

Works.

Laws, etc.

Novels.

Statement of International Cataloguing Principles and RDA: Resource Description and Access

The *Statement of International Cataloguing Principles,*[38] still in draft form, but on its way through a formal adoption process, is an attempt by IFLA to adapt the Paris Principles to provide guidelines that are applicable to the online library catalogs of today as well as to the retrieval tools of the future. The process consisted of a series of IFLA Meetings of Experts on an International Cataloguing Code (IME ICC), the fifth and last of which was held

Books	Rec Stat c		Entered 19961204		Replaced 20020618						
Type	a	ELvl	I	Srce	d	Audn		Ctrl		Lang	eng
BLvl	m	Form		Conf	0	Biog		MRec		Ctry	nyu
		Cont		GPub		LitF	1	Indx	0		
Desc	a	Ills		Fest	0	DtSt	s	Dates	1885,		

040 NOC ‡c NOC ‡d OCL ‡d OCLCQ
090 PR4652 ‡b 1885
100 1_ Eliot, George, ‡d 1819-1880.
240 10 Novels. ‡k Selections

245 10 **Adam Bede ; ‡b Silas Marner, the weaver of Raveloe ; Impressions of Theophrastus Such** / ‡c by George Eliot.
246 3 Adam Bede ; Silas Marner, the weaver of Raveloe ; Impressions of Theophrastus Such
250 [Library ed.].
260 New York : ‡b J.B. Alden, ‡c 1885.
300 484, 167, 148 p. ; ‡c 21 cm.
700 12 Eliot, George, ‡d 1819-1880. ‡t Silas Marner.
700 12 Eliot, George, ‡d 1819-1880. ‡t Theophrastus Such.
740 02 Silas Marner.
740 02 Impressions of Theophrastus Such.

Books	Rec Stat c		Entered 19940825		Replaced 20000801						
Type	a	ELvl		Srce		Audn		Ctrl		Lang	eng
BLvl	m	Form		Conf	0	Biog		MRec		Ctry	nyu
		Cont		GPub		LitF	1	Indx	0		
Desc	a	Ills		Fest	0	DtSt	s	Dates	1995,		

010 94-24675
040 DLC ‡c DLC ‡d OCL
020 0517122235
043 e-uk-en
050 00 PR4652 ‡b 1995
082 00 823/.8 ‡2 20
100 1_ Eliot, George, ‡d 1819-1880.
240 10 Novels. ‡k Selections

245 10 **George Eliot, selected works.**
260 New York : ‡b Gramercy Books ; ‡a Avenel, N.J. : ‡b Distributed by Random House Value Pub., ‡c 1995.
300 xii, 820 p. ; ‡c 24 cm.
505 0 **Silas Marner -- The lifted veil -- Brother Jacob -- Middlemarch.**
651 0 England ‡x Social life and customs ‡y 19th century ‡v Fiction.
740 01 Selected works.

Figure 8.13. Two metadata records for two works that pull together different groupings of George Eliot's novels. The uniform title, *Novels. Selections,* allows these two works to be displayed together under the primary access point: *Eliot, George.* (Source: OCLC Connexion, WorldCat, record numbers 36033332 and 31134215.)

in 2007.[39] These new principles broaden the Paris Principles from covering primarily textual works to covering all types of materials, and in addition to choice and form of entry covered by the Paris Principles, these new principles cover all aspects of bibliographic and authority records used in library catalogs. They are built on the conceptual models of FRBR and FRAD in addition to cataloging traditions from the past (e.g., Cutter, Ranganathan, Lubetzky).

The draft principles echo FRBR's user tasks in the "functions of the catalogue": to find resources in a collection, to identify a resource or agent, to select a resource that is appropriate, to acquire or obtain access to an item, and to navigate a catalog. The draft states that the "highest principle for the construction of cataloguing codes should be the convenience of the users of the catalogue."[40]

The most extensive section of the draft principles is called "Access Points." Access points may be controlled or uncontrolled, the latter being such things as the *title proper* or *keywords* found anywhere in a bibliographic record. Names and titles needed for consistency in locating resources should be normalized, with variant forms used as references. The principles discuss choice of access points but do not mention *primary access point* or *main entry*. They suggest that the titles of works and expressions should be controlled, as well as the names of the creators of works. Corporate bodies may be considered to be creators if works are expressions of the collective thought or activity of the body or if the wording of the title, in combination with the nature of the work, clearly indicates that the corporate body is responsible for the content.

There are a number of principles for the normalized or authorized headings for entities chosen as controlled access points. These include:[41]

- Names (and the forms of those names) should be the ones found predominantly on manifestations or should be well-accepted conventional names.
- If needed, further identifying characteristics should be added to distinguish the entity from others with the same name.
- If variant forms, that are not representations of different personas, are found in manifestations or references sources, preference is given first to a commonly known or conventional name, but finally to an official name if a commonly known or conventional name is not found.
- Successive different names for a corporate body that are more than minor variations are treated as names of new entities connected with references to earlier/later names.

- When names or titles have been expressed in several languages, preference is given to a form on a manifestation in the original language and script; but if that language or script is not used in the catalog, the heading may be based on forms found on manifestations or in reference sources in languages or scripts best suited to the users of the catalog.

- In all cases, variant forms not selected as the authorized heading for an entity should be included in the authority record to be used as references or alternate display forms.

- Names of persons or families that consist of several words should be arranged in the order that follows the conventions of the country and language that is most associated with that person or family.

- Corporate names should be given in direct order unless they are part of a jurisdiction or the name implies subordination, in which case the authorized form should begin with the name of the jurisdiction or the superior body.

- A name for a work/expression may be a title that can stand alone, a name/title combination, or a title with qualifiers added. The preferred work/expression title should be the title most frequently found in manifestations of the work in the original language, or second, the title found in reference sources, or third, the title most frequently found on manifestations.

These principles are quite similar to those of AACR2 but with subtle differences. The creators of RDA include the following statement in the RDA "Objectives and Principles": "The JSC has affirmed the role of the IME-ICC draft *Statement of International Cataloguing Principles* as the basis for the cataloguing principles used throughout RDA."[42] In the proposed structure of RDA, the sections that seem to be most relevant to access and authority control are "Section 3: Recording attributes of person, family, and corporate body" and "Section 6: Recording relationships to persons, families, and corporate bodies associated with a resource."[43] The sections on recording attributes and relationships of works, expressions, manifestations, and items, will, presumably deal with what is now the concept of uniform title. The reader should check the *RDA* Web site often for the most current information.

Dublin Core Agents

Another project, being conducted by the Dublin Core community, has recognized the need for *agent records* to complement and be linked to metadata records for information resources. The term *agent* is being used to refer to creators, contributors, and publishers. The DCMI Agents Working Group[44] is working toward developing functional requirements for describing agents. They wish to identify existing conventions for agent description, one of which is the InterParty project described above. They will develop a recommendation for an agent element set and will then provide input to the DCMI Architecture working group on ways to link resource description records to agent records. The work, begun in 1998, is progressing very slowly at this writing.

Metadata Authority Description Schema (MADS)

MADS is an XML schema for an authority element set that may be used to provide metadata about agents (people, organizations), events, and terms (topics, geographic names, genres, etc.).[45] MADS was created to serve as a companion to the Metadata Object Description Schema (MODS) described in Chapter 7. It is intended to be a simpler way to encode authority data than the MARC 21 Authority Format. Each MADS record has one element, called "<authority>", that contains the authoritative form of the name or term covered by the record. The record may have any number of elements labeled <related> and/or <variant>. Each of these top-level elements can have one or more of the following descriptor elements: name, titleInfo, topic, temporal, genre, geographic, hierarchicalGeographic, occupation. Additional miscellaneous elements that might be added to a MADS record are: note, affiliation, URL, identifier, fieldOfActivity, extension, recordInfo (i.e., the meta-metadata for the record). A MADS record can be as basic or extensive as required and can be customized according to the level of description desired for the type of collection in which it is intended to be used.

Standards for Archives

Although the archival community has long-recognized the need for controlled access points, it has been relatively recently that they have created standards that provide consistency within the archival community. The standards addressed in this section are:

- *International Standard Archival Authority Record for Corporate Bodies, Persons, and Families* (ISAAR (CPF))
- Encoded Archival Context (EAC)
- *Describing Archives: A Content Standard* (DACS)

International Standard Archival Authority Record for Corporate Bodies, Persons, and Families (ISAAR (CPF))

In 1996 the International Council on Archives published the *International Standard Archival Authority Record for Corporate Bodies, Persons and Families* (ISAAR (CPF)), with a second edition following in 2004.[46] ISAAR (CPF) provides guidance on creating archival authority records for corporate bodies, persons, and families who have created and maintained the records, documents, and other resources that comprise archives. The precept behind this work is that the creation of separate descriptions of creators of archival collections, that are then linked to descriptions of those collections (e.g., finding aids, Web pages), provides an efficient means of capturing and managing the contextual information that is vital to the discovery, use, and understanding of archival collections. The second edition has increased consistency with related international standards such as the IFLA standard for authority records, ISAD(G) (discussed in Chapter 7), and the Encoded Archival Context (EAC) standard for machine readable interchange of ISAAR-compliant data.

The bulk of ISAAR (CPF) consists of a listing of elements needed for an authority record. A purpose is given for each element, followed by the rule for transcribing it and examples of its application. Elements are divided into four areas:

- **Identity area**—includes type of entity; authorized form(s) of name; parallel forms of name; standardized forms of name according to other rules; other forms of name; and identifiers for corporate bodies
- **Description area**—includes dates of existence; history; places; legal status; functions, occupations, and activities; mandates/sources of authority; internal structures/genealogy; and general context

- **Relationships area**—includes names/identifiers of related corporate bodies, persons, or families; category of relationship; description of relationship; and dates of the relationship
- **Control area**—includes authority record identifier; institution identifiers; rules and/or conventions; status; level of detail; dates of creation, revision, or deletion; languages and scripts; sources; and maintenance notes.

Encoded Archival Context (EAC)

There is now an archival standard for encoding the data in archival authority records called Encoded Archival Context (EAC).[47] EAC, like EAD (described in Chapter 7), uses XML for encoding; but while EAD describes archival collections, EAC describes the creators of archival collections. EAC records do more than just control all the different forms of name used by a person or corporate body. According to Daniel Pitti, they also describe "their essential functions, activities, and characteristics, and the dates and places they were active."[48] Pitti goes on to explain that creator descriptions facilitate interpretation of archival records in addition to facilitating access. Understanding the lives and work of people and groups who created the archival collections is essential to understanding the archival records that are the byproducts of those lives and activities. In other words, EAC records attempt to place creators in context.

Data encoded with EAC is intended for use in federated database applications and collaborative research across a broad range of domains, including prosopographical research (i.e., research that identifies and relates a group of persons or characters within a particular historical or literary context) and genealogical studies. The designers intend that intellectual content of EAC records comply with the ISAAR (CPF). EAC is also complementary to the UNIMARC/Authorities format, combining library authority records and archival authority records, which give information both about the creator and the context of creation of archival material.

Describing Archives: A Content Standard (DACS)

DACS is a standard that has been accepted and used by the U.S. archival community in the way that AACR2 is used by the library community. DACS has three parts—one for describing archival materials, one for describing creators, and one for forms of names. The first part is discussed in Chapter 7. The introduction to the second part again emphasizes, as does EAC, that in order to understand archival materials completely, one must have some knowledge of the context in which they were created. The three steps required for establishing such a context are:[49]

- identifying the persons, families, and corporate bodies that played important roles in the creation of the materials
- assembling biographical information about the individuals and families and collecting historical data about the corporate bodies, including their structure, functions, and relationships
- providing standardized forms of the names of the persons, families, and corporate bodies in order to facilitate retrieval.

Chapter 9 in DACS covers the first point, and chapter 10 provides guidance for the second point. Chapter 11, at the end of Part II, describes the elements of an archival authority record. Chapters 12–14, in Part III of DACS, cover the construction of the forms of names for persons and families, geographic entities, and corporate bodies, respectively.

Standards for Art and Museums

The art community has recently begun to address the need for control of names and titles in descriptions of objects. The Getty Art Museum has created a set of controlled vocabulary tools[50] including one for terminology in the fields of art and architecture, one for artist names (including biographical information as well as variations in names), one for geographic names (including vernacular and historical names, coordinates, and place types), and one for concept information. They have also created standards that provide for consistency within the art/museum community. The standards addressed in this section are:

- *Cataloging Cultural Objects* (CCO)
- *Categories for the Description of Works of Art* (CDWA)
- VRA (Visual Resources Association) Core

Cataloging Cultural Objects (CCO)

Cataloging Cultural Objects (CCO)[51] is discussed in Chapter 7 as being a content standard rather than a prescription of metadata elements.

The authors of CCO believe that authority control is especially critical in the online environment. They recommend using authority files for certain metadata elements. Part three of CCO covers guidelines for the elements that the authors believe are the most important to be controlled: personal and corporate names, geographic places, concepts, and subjects. Each of these four kinds of entities is discussed separately, with sections under each group for introductory material, "Editorial Rules," and "Presentation of the Data." The first three are discussed here. Subject authority (i.e., use of the AAT) is discussed in Chapter 10.

Personal and corporate names are discussed together and cover artists, architects, studios, architectural firms, patrons, repositories, and "other persons or corporate bodies related to particular works."[52] Elements that are recommended for name authority records are:

- Names (preferred, alternates, and variants)
- Note
- Display Biography
- Birth Date (Start Date for corporate bodies)
- Death Date (End Date for corporate bodies)
- Nationality (National Affiliation for corporate bodies)
- Life Roles (Functions for corporate bodies)
- Gender (not applicable for corporate bodies)
- Date of Earliest Activity
- Date of Latest Activity
- Place/Location
- Related People and Corporate Bodies
- Relationship Type
- Events
- Sources
- Record Type (Person or Corporate Body)

Some of the elements are free-text fields, others are suggested to have prescribed formatting (e.g., date fields should use the ISO standard for dates), and controlled vocabulary is recommended for others.

The geographic place authority section covers places that are both physical features and administrative geographic entities. Geographic place terms are used primarily for the location of works, but are also used in authority records for personal and corporate names. Recommended elements for geographic place authority records are:

- Names (preferred, alternates, and variants)
- Broader Context
- Place Type
- Coordinates
- Note
- Related Places
- Relationship Type
- Dates
- Sources

Some elements are controlled, some are free-text, and for "Coordinates" and "Dates," especially, it is recommended that consistent formatting be used.

Concept authority includes terminology needed for describing works or images that is not included in the other authorities (i.e., not names of persons, organizations, geographic places, events, and not subjects). Concepts may describe the type of work (e.g., painting), its material (e.g., canvas), activities associated with a work (e.g., oil painting (technique)), its style (e.g., Art Nouveau), the role of the creator or other persons (e.g., painters (artists)), and other attributes or various abstract concepts (e.g., contrast). Recommended elements for concept authority records are:

- Terms (preferred, alternates, and variants)
- Qualifier
- Broader Context
- Note
- Dates
- Related Concepts
- Relationship Type
- Sources

Concept authority records, in particular, are created in such a way that the terms in them can be displayed in a hierarchical arrangement.

CCO lists a number of sources for authority files for names, geographic places, and concepts. Among the most important in the world of art, architecture, and museums are the Getty Vocabularies:[53] *The Union List of Artist Names* (ULAN), *The Getty Thesaurus of Geographic Names* (TGN), and *The Art & Architecture Thesaurus* (AAT).

In addition to its emphasis on authority control for some fields, CCO puts a premium on identifying relationships between works.[54] CCO distinguishes between intrinsic and extrinsic relationships. An *intrinsic relationship* is one that is essential to identification of the work being cataloged. Whole-Part relationships, for example, are intrinsic. Examples of whole-part relationships include architectural complexes (e.g., the statues atop a building described separately from the building), manuscripts (e.g., the illustrations described separately from the text), triptychs (e.g., separate description of one panel of an altarpiece of three panels), works in collections, and items in a series. An *extrinsic relationship* is one that is informative but not essential. Examples of extrinsic relationships include a work copied after another, a preparatory sketch or model, a work referenced within another work (e.g., a famous painting on the wall behind the main object in another painting), or two works that are intended to be seen together (e.g., separate portraits of a husband and wife). CCO emphasizes displaying relationships in a way that is clear to the user. Attention is given to the concept of database design and to the display of relationships when designing and constructing databases.[55]

Categories for the Description of Works of Art (CDWA)

Categories for the Description of Works of Art (CDWA)[56] is discussed in Chapter 7 as an element set for describing and accessing works of art, architecture, and other material culture. Fifteen of the 36 core categories of CDWA are listed in Chapter 7. The remaining 21 are listed here, divided into five groupings as organized by CDWA for authority data:

For Related Textual References Authority

- Brief Citation
- Full Citation

For Creator Identification Authority

- Name
- Source

- Display Biography
- Birth Date
- Death Date
- Nationality/Culture/Race
- Life Roles

For Place/Location Authority

- Place Name
- Source
- Place Type
- Broader Context

For Generic Concept Authority

- Term
- Source
- Broader Context
- Scope Note
- Source

For Subject Authority

- Subject Name
- Source
- Broader Context

These elements are much like the ones listed in CCO. CDWA also recommends maintaining separate authority files for visual works, textual materials, persons/corporate bodies, locations/places, generic concepts, and subjects so that such information is recorded once and then linked to all appropriate work records.

VRA (Visual Resources Association) Core

The VRA Core[57] was discussed in Chapter 7 as an "element set [that] provides a categorical organization for the description of works of visual culture as well as the images that document them."[58] The 19 individual metadata elements of the VRA Core were listed in the previous chapter (in alphabetical order, except for the first element), along with suggestions as to which elements could take their values from an authority file or controlled vocabulary list.

VRA Core, like CCO, emphasizes relationships in its implementation, but it puts more emphasis on *images* of works than does CCO. The three primary types of relationships between records in VRA Core 4.0 are: work to work; image to work; and image or work to collection. The VRA Core introduction document explains that in order to give meaning to an image record, it is necessary to show its relationship to the work from which it was derived. The link is made via the *Relation* element, and the nature of the relationship is defined by the *type* attribute. A work may have several images associated with it, or an image may represent more than one work; such multiple relationships should be identified. In VRA Core, *collection* is defined as an aggregate of work or image records. Therefore, it may be necessary to show image-to-collection relationships or work-to-collection relationships as well.

SEMANTIC WEB

People working on the Semantic Web also have been working on the idea of creating *entity metadata* for people and corporate bodies so that these can be linked with metadata for the information resources with which they are associated. In the language of the Semantic Web, resources (including everything from documents to people to corporate bodies to schemas) have properties and properties have values. In this vision every resource has a unique identifier (e.g., URI) that can lead to the entity metadata that exists for the resource. The value of the property of *creator* can be the URI for a person. If this access point, then, is attached to every resource related to the same creator, there will be collocation, regardless of form of name used by a person in a particular document.

CONCLUSION

This chapter has discussed the creation of name and title access points for surrogate records. The massive amounts of data dealt with in libraries, archives, and museums for art, architecture, and cultural objects have led to the development of the concept of authority control. Searchers for information need to be able to find works related to specific persons, corporate bodies, places, or other works. As the number of names and titles increases to a critical mass, the ability to find specific names and titles and sort them out from similar and identical ones becomes very difficult without authority control. The building of the Semantic Web can be enhanced by linking authority files with biographical dictionaries, telephone directories, and official Web sites for named entities, as well as with the information resources created by those entities.

Most information resources have a subject or multiple subjects. It is often the subject content that is sought by users of retrieval tools. The next three chapters address the myriad ways of providing access to subject content.

NOTES

All URLs accessed September 2008.

1. Barbara B. Tillett, "A Taxonomy of Bibliographic Relationships," *Library Resources & Technical Services* 30, no. 2 (April 1991): 156.

2. For more in-depth treatments of bibliographic relationships, see: Elaine Svenonius, *The Intellectual Foundation of Information Organization* (Cambridge, Mass.: The MIT Press, 2001), pp. 98–106; and Richard P. Smiraglia, *The Nature of "A Work": Implications for the Organization of Knowledge* (Lanham, Md.: Scarecrow Press, 2001), pp. 35–52.

3. Smiraglia, *The Nature of "A Work,"* p. 42.

4. Svenonius, *The Intellectual Foundation of Information Organization,* pp. 95–97.

5. Martha M. Yee, "What Is a work?" [four-part series published in *Cataloging & Classification Quarterly* 19, nos. 1–2 (1994), and 20, nos. 1–2 (1995)]; Smiraglia, *The Nature of "A Work"*; International Federation of Library Associations and Institutions, IFLA Study Group, *Functional Requirements for Bibliographic Records: Final Report* (München: Saur, 1998). Also available: http://www.ifla.org/VII/s13/frbr/frbr.pdf or http://www.ifla.org/VII/s13/frbr/frbr.htm.

6. International Federation of Library Associations and Institutions, Working Group on FRANAR, "Functional Requirements for Authority Data: A Conceptual Model." Available: http://www.ifla.org/VII/d4/franar-conceptual-model-2ndreview.pdf.

7. For example, see the FRBR Web site of the OCLC Office of Research: "OCLC Research Activities and IFLA's *Functional Requirements*

for Bibliographic Records." OCLC, 2002. Available: http://www.oclc.org/research/projects/frbr/.

8. Program for Cooperative Cataloging, "NACO: Name Authority Cooperative Program of the PCC." Available: http://www.loc.gov/catdir/pcc/naco/nacopara.html.

9. Andrew MacEwan, "Project InterParty: From Library Authority Files to E-Commerce," *Cataloging & Classification Quarterly* 39, no. 1/2 (2004): 429–442; also published in *Authority Control in Organizing and Accessing Information: Definition and International Experience,* edited by Arlene G. Taylor and Barbara B. Tillett (New York: Haworth Information Press, 2004), p. 429–442.

10. Barbara Tillett, "Authority Control: State of the Art and New Perspectives," *Cataloging & Classification Quarterly* 38, no. 3/4 (2004): 23–42; also published in *Authority Control in Organizing and Accessing Information: Definition and International Experience,* edited by Arlene G. Taylor and Barbara B. Tillett (New York: Haworth Information Press, 2004), pp. 23–42.

11. See, for example: OCLC, "VIAF: The Virtual International Authority File." Available: http://www.oclc.org/research/projects/viaf/.

12. International Federation of Library Associations and Institutions, *Guidelines for Authority Records and References,* 2nd ed. (München: K. G. Saur, 2001). Also available: http://www.ifla.org/VII/s13/garr/.

13. International Federation of Library Associations and Institutions, Working Group on FRANAR, "Functional Requirements for Authority Data."

14. IFLA Cataloging Section, "Annual Report 2006." Available: www.ifla.org/VII/s13/annual/s13-AnnualReport2006.pdf

15. Open Archives Initiative [home page]. Available: http://www.openarchives.org/.

16. For more about FRBR see: Arlene G. Taylor, "An Introduction to Functional Requirements for Bibliographic Records (FRBR)," in *Understanding FRBR: What It Is and How It Will Affect Our Retrieval Tools,* edited by Arlene G. Taylor (Westport, Conn.: Libraries Unlimited, 2007), pp. 1–19; and Robert L. Maxwell, *FRBR: A Guide for the Perplexed* (Chicago: American Library Association, 2008).

17. International Federation of Library Associations and Institutions, Working Group on FRANAR. Available: http://www.ifla.org/VII/d4/wg-franar.htm.

18. International Federation of Library Associations and Institutions. Working Group on FRANAR, *Functional Requirements for Authority Data.*

19. International Federation of Library Associations and Institutions, Working Group on Functional Requirements for Subject Authority Records (FRSAR). Available: http://www.ifla.org/VII/s29/wgfrsar.htm.

20. FRAD, pp. 30–49.

21. Source of table: FRAD, pp. 31–32.

22. International Conference on Cataloguing Principles (Paris: 1961). *Report* (London, International Federation of Library Associations, 1963), pp. 91–96. Also available in: *Library Resources & Technical Services* 6 (1962), pp. 162–167; and *Statement of Principles Adopted at the International Conference on Cataloguing Principles, Paris, October, 1961,* annotated ed., with commentary and examples by Eva Verona (London, IFLA Committee on Cataloguing, 1971); and A. H. Chaplin and Dorothy Anderson, eds. *Report/International Conference on Cataloguing Principles, Paris, 9th–18th October 1961* (London: IFLA International Office for UBC, 1981).

23. Doris Hargrett Clack, ed., *The Making of a Code: The Issues Underlying AACR2* (Chicago: American Library Association, 1980).

24. Michael Gorman, "AACR2: Main Themes," in Clack, *The Making of a Code,* p. 46.

25. Richard P. Smiraglia, "Authority Control and the Extent of Derivative Bibliographic Relationships" (PhD diss., University of Chicago, 1992).

26. Joint Steering Committee for Revision of Anglo-American Cataloguing Rules, "Discussion List Archives," in "International Conference on the Principles and Future Development of AACR." Available: http://www.nlc-bnc.ca/jsc/intlconf.html.

27. See Chapter 5 for more about system design.

28. Joint Steering Committee for Development of RDA, "Overview." Available: http://www.collectionscanada.gc.ca/jsc/index.html.

29. Joint Steering Committee for Development of RDA, "A New Organization for RDA." Available: http://www.collectionscanada.gc.ca/jsc/rda-new-org.html.

30. International Federation of Library Associations and Institutions, IFLA Study Group, *Functional Requirements for Bibliographic Records.*

31. Joint Steering Committee for Revision of Anglo-American Cataloguing Rules, "Discussion List Archives" in "International Conference on the Principles and Future Development of AACR."

32. See also Wesley Simonton and Marilyn Jones McClaskey, *AACR2 and the Catalog: Theory, Structure, Changes* (Littleton, Colo.: Libraries Unlimited, 1981).

33. ALA/ALCTS/CCS, Committee on Cataloging: Description and Access, Task Force on the Rule of Three, "Report." Available: http://www.libraries.psu.edu/tas/jca/ccda/tf-r3b.html.

34. Joint Steering Committee for Development of RDA, "RDA: Resource Description and Access: Prospectus." Available: http://www.collectionscanada.gc.ca/jsc/rdaprospectus.html.

35. In AACR2, p. 391, a footnote says that the authoritative alphabetic lists are to be lists of the "who's who" type, *not* telephone directories or similar compilations. However, given the ease of access to telephone directories, but not to more formal sources, for most catalogers, and given the similarity of result, this author can see no reason why AACR2 maintains this restriction.

36. Smiraglia, *The Nature of "A Work."*

37. International Federation of Library Associations and Institutions, IFLA Study Group, *Functional Requirements for Bibliographic Records.*

38. International Federation of Library Associations and Institutions, Meeting of Experts on an International Cataloguing Code, "Statement of International Cataloguing Principles," April 10, 2008 version. Available: http://www.ifla.org/VII/s13/icc/imeicc-statement_of_principles-2008.pdf.

39. IFLA, Cataloguing Section, "IME-ICC." Available: http://www.ifla.org/VII/s13/index.htm#IME-ICC.

40. IFLA, Meeting of Experts on an International Cataloguing Code. "Statement of International Cataloguing Principles" [found in section called "1. Scope"].

41. Ibid. [found in section called "6. Authority Records"].

42. Joint Steering Committee for Development of RDA, "Draft Statement of Objectives and Principles for RDA," p. 3. Available: http://www.collectionscanada.gc.ca/jsc/docs/5rda-objectivesrev2.pdf.

43. Joint Steering Committee for Development of RDA, "RDA—Resource Description and Access: Prospectus," pp. 4–6.

44. DCMI Agents Working Group, Dublin Core Metadata Initiative. Available: http://www.dublincore.org/groups/agents/.

45. Library of Congress' Network Development and MARC Standards Office, "MADS: Metadata Authority Description Schema, Official Web Site." Available: http://www.loc.gov/standards/mads/.

46. International Council on Archives, *International Standard Archival Authority Record for Corporate Bodies, Persons, and Families* (ISAAR (CPF)), 2nd ed. (Paris: International Council on Archives, 2004). News announcement available: http://www.ica.org/en/node/696.

47. Encoded Archival Context (EAC). Available: http://www.library.yale.edu/eac/.

48. Daniel V. Pitti, "Creator Description: Encoded Archival Context," *Cataloging & Classification Quarterly* 39, no. 1/2 (2004): 201–226; also published in *Authority Control in Organizing and Accessing Information: Definition and International Experience,* edited by Arlene G. Taylor and Barbara B. Tillett. New York: Haworth Information Press, 2004, pp. 201–226.

49. *Describing Archives: A Content Standard* (DACS). Chicago: Society of American Archivists, 2004, p. 85.

50. The Getty, "Learn About the Getty Vocabularies." Available: http://www.getty.edu/research/conducting_research/vocabularies/.

51. Murtha Baca, Patricia Harpring, Elisa Lanzi, Linda McRae, and Ann Whiteside, on behalf of the Visual Resources Association, *Cataloging Cultural Objects: A Guide to Describing Cultural Works and Their Images* (Chicago: American Library Association, 2006). Partial availability on the Web: http://www.vraweb.org/ccoweb/cco/index.html [cited hereinafter as CCO].

52. CCO, p. 279.

53. The Getty, "Learn About the Getty Vocabularies."

54. CCO, pp. 13–19.

55. CCO, pp. 20–27.

56. "Categories for the Description of Works of Art," edited by Murtha Baca and Patricia Harpring. The Getty. Available: http://www.getty.edu/research/conducting_research/standards/cdwa/.

57. Visual Resources Association, Data Standards Committee, "VRA Core 4.0." Available: http://www.vraweb.org/projects/vracore4/index.html.

58. Visual Resources Association, Data Standards Committee, "VRA Core 4.0 Introduction." Available: http://www.vraweb.org/projects/vracore4/VRA_Core4_Intro.pdf.

SUGGESTED READINGS

Chan, Lois Mai, with the assistance of Theodora L. Hodges. *Cataloging and Classification: An Introduction.* 3rd ed. Lanham, Md.: Scarecrow Press, 2007. Chapter 4: "Choice of Access Points," Chapter 5: "Name Authority Control and Forms of Headings and Uniform Titles," and Chapter 6: "References."

The Getty. "Learn About the Getty Vocabularies." Available: http://www.getty.edu/research/tools/vocabulary/.

Hagler, Ronald. *The Bibliographic Record and Information Technology.* 3rd ed. Chicago: American Library Association, 1997. Chapter 3: "Access Points" and Chapter 6: "Controlled-Vocabulary Name Access Points."

Hsieh-Yee, Ingrid. *Organizing Audiovisual and Electronic Resources for Access: A Cataloging Guide.* 2nd ed. Westport, Conn.: Libraries Unlimited, 2006.

International Federation of Library Associations and Institutions. IFLA Study Group. *Functional Requirements for Bibliographic Records: Final Report.* München: Saur, 1998. Also available: http://www.ifla.org/VII/s13/frbr/frbr.pdf or http://www.ifla.org/VII/s13/frbr/frbr.htm.

International Federation of Library Associations and Institutions, Meeting of Experts on an International Cataloguing Code. "Statement of International Cataloguing Principles." April 10, 2008 version. Available: http://www.ifla.org/VII/s13/icc/imeicc-statement_of_principles-2008.pdf.

International Federation of Library Associations and Institutions. Working Group on FRANAR. "Functional Requirements for Authority Data: A Conceptual Model." Available: http://www.ifla.org/VII/d4/franar-conceptual-model-2ndreview.pdf.

Intner, Sheila S., and Jean Weihs. *Standard Cataloging for School and Public Libraries.* 4th ed. Westport, Conn.: Libraries Unlimited, 2007. Chapter 5: "Access."

Maxwell, Robert L. *FRBR: A Guide for the Perplexed.* Chicago: American Library Association, 2008.

Patton, Glenn E. "An Introduction to Functional Requirements for Authority Data (FRAD)" and "Understanding the Relationship between FRBR and FRAD." In *Understanding FRBR: What It Is and How It Will Affect Our Retrieval Tools,* edited by Arlene G. Taylor. Westport, Conn.: Libraries Unlimited, 2007, pp. 21–33.

Pitti, Daniel V. "Creator Description: Encoded Archival Context." *Cataloging & Classification Quarterly* 39, no. 1/2 (2004): 201–226; also published in *Authority Control in Organizing and Accessing Information: Definition and International Experience,* edited by Arlene G. Taylor and Barbara B. Tillett. New York: Haworth Information Press, 2004, pp. 201–226.

Smiraglia, Richard P. "Bibliographic Families and Superworks." In *Understanding FRBR: What It Is and How It Will Affect Our Retrieval Tools,* edited by Arlene G. Taylor. Westport, Conn.: Libraries Unlimited, 2007, pp. 73–86.

———. *The Nature of "A Work": Implications for the Organization of Knowledge.* Lanham, Md.: Scarecrow Press, 2001, pp. 35–52.

Svenonius, Elaine. *The Intellectual Foundation of Information Organization.* Cambridge, Mass.: The MIT Press, 2000. Chapter 3: "Bibliographic Entities" and Chapter 6: "Work Languages."

Taylor, Arlene G. *Introduction to Cataloging and Classification.* 10th ed. with the assistance of David P. Miller. Westport, Conn.: Libraries Unlimited, 2006. Chapter 6: "Choice of Access Points," Chapter 7: "Form of Headings for Names and Titles," and Chapter 8: "Authority Control."

———. "An Introduction to Functional Requirements for Bibliographic Records (FRBR)." In *Understanding FRBR: What It Is and How It Will Affect Our Retrieval Tools,* edited by Arlene G. Taylor. Westport, Conn.: Libraries Unlimited, 2007, pp. 1–19. [Other articles in this volume include discussions of FRAD, history of FRBR, research on FRBR, bibliographic families, and discussions of FRBR in relation to RDA, archival materials, art/architecture/material culture, cartographic materials, music, and serials.]

Tillett, Barbara B. "Authority Control: State of the Art and New Perspectives." *Cataloging & Classification Quarterly* 38, no. 3/4 (2004): 23–42; also published in *Authority Control in Organizing and Accessing Information: Definition and International Experience,* edited by Arlene G. Taylor and Barbara B. Tillett. New York: Haworth Information Press, 2004, pp. 23–42.

———. "Bibliographic Relationships." In *Relationships in the Organization of Knowledge,* edited by Carole A. Bean and Rebecca Green. Dordrecht: Kluwer Academic Publishers, 2001, pp. 9–35.

Vellucci, Sherry L. "Metadata and Authority Control." *Library Resources & Technical Services* 44, no. 1 (January 2000): 33–43.

Wilson, Patrick. "The Catalog as Access Mechanism: Background and Concepts." In *Foundations of Cataloging: A Sourcebook,* edited by Michael Carpenter and Elaine Svenonius. Littleton, Colo.: Libraries Unlimited, 1985, pp. 253–268.

CHAPTER 9

SUBJECT ANALYSIS

Historically, subject access has been one of the most challenging aspects of organizing information. Even with the most traditional information resources, determining and identifying what an item is about can be difficult and time-consuming. With non-textual, imaginative, or complex materials, the process can be even more demanding. Despite the difficulties and costs associated with subject analysis, information professionals still see the value inherent in identifying precisely an item's subject matter (often referred to as *aboutness* in the library and information science literature), and then carefully choosing the most suitable terms and symbols from a subject language to represent the item's aboutness in its surrogate record.

In recent years, with advances in search engine technology and the high costs of original cataloging, the necessity for subject analysis has been questioned. Some have suggested that information resources no longer need to be analyzed because when users are searching for information, computers (through automatic indexing) can identify some documents relevant to users' needs (although not all), and therefore the time and money spent on humans performing subject analysis could be diverted to other activities such as digitization projects. Others have suggested that computers can analyze documents and assign classification numbers and/or descriptors from a list of controlled vocabulary terms. However, given the interest in ontologies and taxonomies to support the development of the Semantic Web, it appears that, despite the improvements in search engines and the recent development of user tagging, many information professionals are reluctant to turn over all subject analysis activities to machines. There is still a desire for controlled approaches to subject access. Why is there still reluctance? Despite myriad advances, the available technology thus far is not up to the tasks of subject analysis. Machines are not yet good at identifying the aboutness of information resources and they still cannot assign controlled vocabulary and classification with any satisfactory degree of accuracy. While a computer can determine what words are used in a document and the frequency of those words, at this time it cannot understand the multifaceted or nuanced concepts represented by those words. Even the most sophisticated algorithms cannot replace the human mind for its efficiency in understanding the deeper meanings of texts and being able to represent those meanings through the use of subject languages. In 2008, the Working Group on the Future of Bibliographic Control, a group organized by the Library of Congress to examine the role of cataloging in the twenty-first century, reaffirmed the importance and need for this human-centric task: "Subject analysis—including analyzing content and creating and applying subject headings and classification numbers—is a core function of cataloging; although expensive, it is nonetheless critical."[1]

In libraries and indexing environments, it is still necessary for humans to determine what an information resource is about and which concepts are to be represented in the surrogate record for that resource. This approach, however, also has its share of problems. While researchers in library and information science have been prolific in exploring the usefulness and limitations of subject languages (i.e., classification schemes and controlled vocabularies), they have produced very little on how to actually determine aboutness. Ironically, the task most dependent on humans is the one least explored. Consequently, many catalogers and indexers have only had instruction in the application of various controlled vocabularies and not in the process of determining aboutness. This can lead to difficulties, especially when the topic of the resource is not self-evident or the resource has several meanings or purposes. Those who lack an understanding of the multiple components and approaches to determining aboutness may not identify key concepts and consequently may omit useful controlled vocabulary terms when describing an item. Over the years, a number of writers have pointed out that aboutness is more than just the words used by the author; determining aboutness may also involve determining the author's purpose, thinking about who may use the resource and for what purposes, considering what questions the document may answer, and various other aspects. F. W. Lancaster goes so far as to say that the same item could be described in various ways in different institutions, and that it *should* be, if the intended users would be interested in the resource for different reasons.[2] Due to concerns related to costs and interoperability, most libraries and indexing services focus their subject analysis activities on the most visible and universal aspects of an item's aboutness, rather than attempting to describe all possible uses of the item or all possible interpretations or meanings.

Several questions are addressed in this chapter. They include: What is subject analysis? What are some of the difficulties associated with the subject analysis process? How is the process performed? What bibliographic features are useful in the determination of aboutness? How is subject content determined for nontextual materials?

WHAT IS SUBJECT ANALYSIS?

Subject analysis is the part of the metadata creation process that identifies and articulates the subject matter of the information resource being described. The process includes: (1) conducting a conceptual analysis to determine what the item is about, (2) describing the aboutness in a written statement, and (3) using that aboutness statement to assign controlled vocabulary terms and/or classification notations. The first step, the *conceptual analysis,* is an examination of the intellectual or creative contents of an information resource to understand what the item is *about* and what the item *is* (i.e., its form or genre). In the second step, an *aboutness statement* is written. This may be a single sentence or a short paragraph describing and summarizing one's understanding of the aboutness, the form/genre, and the relationships among the important subject concepts. The aboutness statement is used to identify the terms or concepts to be searched in the controlled vocabulary. The statement can also help the cataloger to construct a rudimentary hierarchy to get a better understanding of how the concepts fit together and how they might fit into a scheme of classification. The third and final step entails translating the aboutness statement into the specific symbols and/or terminology found in the subject languages employed. For example, in the third step, one would assign appropriate, authorized terms found in *Library of Congress Subject Headings* (LCSH), *Sears Subject Headings, Art & Architecture Thesaurus* (AAT), or another such list, and/or classification notation(s) from *Dewey Decimal Classification* (DDC), *Library of Congress Classification* (LCC), *Universal Decimal Classification* (UDC), or another classification scheme.

Throughout this process, the goals are not only to identify the intellectual and creative contents of information resources, but also to ensure that individual information resources are carefully and purposefully positioned within a collection. In other words, subject analysis is performed to provide users with subject access to information, to collocate information resources of a like nature, and to provide a logical location for similar tangible information resources on the shelves. Subject analysis helps to alleviate retrieval problems associated with keywords and natural language through the predictable use of controlled terminology and symbols. Ultimately, the goal is to save the users' time by providing an intellectual framework for finding similar resources together. If we look at Cutter's "objects" once again, we see that he considered subject access to be an important function of a catalog. Not only did he want a user to be able to find a known work on a certain subject, but also he wanted a user to be able to find all the works that the library could offer on a particular subject. Subject analysis enables this to happen.

CHALLENGES IN SUBJECT ANALYSIS

Determining what an information resource is about can be difficult, and not everyone agrees on how it should be done or even where the difficulties lie. Patrick Wilson has discussed many of the challenges in the conceptual analysis process. He believed that one difficulty was imposed upon us by Cutter's second "object," which states that a catalog should show what a library has on a given subject. Wilson suggested that it is problematic to take Cutter's statement to mean that there is an obvious subject in every information resource and that we should be able to identify it as *the* subject of the work.[3] Although some resources may have a single, easily determined subject, others may not be quite so clear; they may have several multi-faceted themes, with complex relationships among the subtopics. While the aboutness of a college textbook entitled *An Introduction to Sociology* is fairly straightforward to analyze and describe, another text such as *The History of Sociology in the Nineteenth Century* is a bit more complex, and a third text, *Comparing Methods in Sociological Research in Panama, Peru, and Spain,* is even more so. All three are about sociology *per se,* but the second text is more specifically about the origins and development of sociology in the nineteenth century; it was written from a historical perspective, while not being *about* history. This distinction has a certain subtlety that is learned through education in our present-day Western tradition; in other places and other times, history would have been considered the subject of anything historical regardless of the specific topic. The third item is a more complex subject that involves not only the discipline of sociology but also a specific aspect of it, that is, *research.* The information resource, however, is not just about sociological research; it compares the methods used in sociological research in three different locations. This item involves a discipline, a subtopic, several geographic locations, and a comparative relationship (and possibly a chronological element and other content characteristics that are not evident from the title). While this item is more complex than the first (*An Introduction to Sociology*), still it is a relatively simple item to analyze. With the burgeoning relationships among various fields, topics, and ideas in this increasingly interdisciplinary world, the result can be some very challenging materials to analyze. Consequently, this increased level of complexity may affect one's ability to understand certain items and to articulate what they are about. For example, a highly technical dissertation may be more difficult to analyze than a work of popular science, and a complex literary analysis that demonstrates the confluence of social, religious, and economic factors in altering the portrayal of wealthy families in eighteenth-century English fiction is considerably more difficult to analyze than a book introducing, let's say, a new diet regimen.

Cultural Differences

There are numerous other factors that influence the conceptual analysis process. Some are related to the nature of the resource being analyzed and others are related to the persons who perform the analysis. An understanding of the place of one's culture as well as one's education in determining subject matter is important. George Lakoff has written about the research of Brent Berlin and Paul Kay on the understanding of color depending upon one's language. They found that there are eleven basic color categories in English, but in some other languages there are fewer categories. In languages that have only two basic color terms, the terms are the equivalent of *black* and *white,* or *cool* and *warm.*[4] When persons doing subject analysis have grown up in different cultures with different languages, they often cannot comprehend reality in the same way, which influences their perceptions of aboutness. D. W. Langridge provides another example when he comments upon the unconscious effect that must occur in the mind of a person accustomed to the former arrangement of the library in the People's University of China (now Renmin University of China), where all knowledge was divided into three groups: theory of knowledge, knowledge of the class struggle, and knowledge of the productive struggle.[5] Although differences among Western cultures are perhaps not quite so dissimilar as those between Western and non-Western cultures, indexers and catalogers can expect to see things differently depending upon such things as education, language, and cultural background.

Consistency

Another challenge associated with the subject analysis process is consistency. Evidence of the difficulty in consistently determining and articulating aboutness is found in a number of studies in which people have been asked to list terminology that they would use to search for specific items. For example, in a 1954 study by Oliver Lilley, 340 students looked at six books and suggested an average of 62 different terms that could be used to search for each book.[6] In a 1992 study, Lourdes Collantes found "an average of 25.6 [topical] names per object or concept."[7] Please note: *this is not a failure of controlled vocabulary*. It is a failure of individuals to come up with the same natural language terms to describe the item or to determine the same aboutness from a document. There is evidence that catalogers using the same controlled vocabulary and the same rules for applying it will produce consistent subject headings, as long as they have the same understanding of the aboutness of the item to draw upon.[8]

Langridge believes that inconsistencies in subject analysis are the result of confusing what an item is about with the purpose of an item, that is, mixing up *what is it for* with *what it is about*.[9] Langridge thinks that if those questions remain clear and separate, then determining the aboutness of an item should be fairly easy. Even if one does not agree with his assessment that determining aboutness can be straightforward, his question "What is it for?" provides a valuable insight into the conceptual analysis process. For example, Richard W. Unger's *The Art of Medieval Technology: Images of Noah the Shipbuilder*[10] appears at first glance to be about Noah and the Ark. However, upon examining the author's purpose, the table of contents, and the captions with the illustrations, one learns that the work is really about changes in the techniques used in shipbuilding during the Middle Ages, as documented through medieval religious art, noting that artists' depictions of Noah building the Ark changed as the technology and shipbuilding techniques advanced through the centuries.

Another example is found in the sociology texts mentioned earlier. In our culture, we consider the subject of the textbooks *The History of Sociology in the Nineteenth Century* and *An Introduction to Sociology* to be the same, that is, sociology. One resource, however, is written from the perspective of history. The two resources convey different types of information, and their purposes, perspectives, and/or forms affect our understanding of the aboutness. A user looking for one of these treatments would likely not be satisfied with the other. Addressing the item's form, the author's point of view, or the question "What is it for?" helps us to separate and distinguish among different treatments of the same subject. Addressing these types of issues, however, does not solve all of the challenges in the subject analysis process.

Nontextual Information

Determining the topics of nontextual information resources is even less clear-cut than the process for textual ones. For visual resources, several levels of conceptual analysis are possible. In 1939, art historian Erwin Panofsky identified three levels of meaning in works of art.[11]

1. **The primary or natural subject matter:** this is the pre-iconographic or "factual" level in which objects and events are identified (e.g., this is a painting of 13 long-haired men in robes gathered around a long table for dinner).
2. **The secondary or conventional subject matter:** this is the iconographic level, in which some cultural knowledge of themes and concepts manifested in stories, images, and allegory is needed (e.g., this is not *just* an image of 13 men gathered for dinner, it is a representation of the Lord's supper).
3. **The intrinsic meaning or content:** this is the iconological level, in which the work is interpreted, based on an understanding of the "basic attitudes of a nation, a period, a class, a religious or philosophical persuasion—unconsciously qualified by one personality [the artist] and condensed into one work"[12] (e.g., this painting is Leonardo da Vinci's *Last Supper* from 1498, a mural in the Convent of Santa Maria delle Grazie in Milan, Italy. It depicts the internal confusion of the twelve disciples after Jesus announced one of them would betray him—each one wondering if it would be him). Meaning on this level depends upon an understanding of the two previous levels. This level requires a sophisticated understanding of world cultures, symbolism, and the significance of the work and its context in art history.

Seventy years later, Panofsky's categories are still useful in understanding the ways the content of visual images can be analyzed. With art works it is certainly easiest to describe the item at the first level, that is, to enumerate objects and scenes represented rather than literary themes or intrinsic meaning. In some cases, it may be possible to identify a subject concept (e.g., a depiction of a battle scene), but also to determine from a work's title a specific instance of the concept (e.g., the Battle of Gettysburg). Sara Shatford Layne relates Panofsky's first level of meaning to the *of-ness* of the item (i.e., what this is an image of) and his second level to *aboutness;* she states that the third level cannot be used to analyze visual images with any degree of consistency.[13] With musical works, it is even harder to identify concepts or to enumerate what themes and topics are being represented. If one wants *true* conceptual analysis of nontextual information resources, such analysis would be at the interpretive thematic level. It is fairly easy to describe how objects look, but identification of intrinsic meaning or iconological significance for any nontextual information resources requires special study and training.

Exhaustivity

When examining documents for subject content, one must have a clear idea about the level of exhaustivity that is required. Exhaustivity is the number of concepts that will be considered in the analysis. The number of concepts included in the analysis will often be guided by local policy. A. G. Brown identifies two basic degrees of exhaustivity: *summarization* and *depth indexing*.[14] Summarization identifies only a dominant, overall subject of the item, recognizing only concepts embodied in the main theme. Depth indexing aims to extract all the main concepts addressed in an item, recognizing subtopics and lesser themes.

In library cataloging, subject analysis has traditionally been carried out at the summarization level, reserving depth indexing for other enterprises such as periodical indexes. That is, in the cataloging of books and serials in libraries, the cataloger generally attempts to find the one overall subject concept that encompasses the whole item. Depth indexing has traditionally been reserved for parts of items (e.g., articles in journals, chapters in books) and has usually been done by commercial indexing enterprises. In the case of an electronic serial such as the *Journal of Statistics Education,*[15] the subject at the summarization level can be no more in depth than *statistics education,* even though the subjects of individual articles are much more specific. There is no reason, however, that whole items cannot be indexed more exhaustively. At the summarization level, *Proceedings of the OCLC Internet Cataloging Colloquium*[16] would be about cataloging of Internet resources (see Figure 9.1). A look at the table of contents, however, shows the various other concepts that might be included if this resource were indexed at a more granular level of exhaustivity, such as classification of the Internet, metadata, search engines, and the like.

It should be pointed out that many books have extensive back-of-the-book indexes, and this has been one of the justifications for subject cataloging at the summarization level. That is, there is a difference in degree between *document retrieval* and *information retrieval* (see Figure 9.2). Summarization allows for document retrieval, after which many users consult the document's internal index (which, for electronic resources, may mean conducting a word search on the text) to retrieve the relevant information they need from the document. Depth indexing, however, allows retrieval at a much more specific level, even to the retrieval of sections or paragraphs in a document.

InterCAT
A Catalog of Internet Resources

Proceedings of the OCLC Internet Cataloging Colloquium

San Antonio, Texas
January 19, 1996

Introduction

Field Reports

- The "Ambivalent" Library, Mark Watson, University of Oregon
- Does It Really Matter?: The Choice of Format, Order of Note Fields, and Specifics of 856, Jackie Shieh, University of Virginia Library
- Access Information on the Internet: A Feasibility Study of MARC Formats and AACR2, Amanda Xu, MIT Libraries

Position Papers

- Using Library Classification Schemes for Internet Resources, Diane Vizine-Goetz, OCLC
- Cyberstacks, Gerry McKiernan, Iowa State University
- The Traditional Library and the National Information Infrastructure, Vianne T. Sha, Timothy B. Patrick, Thomas R. Kochtanek, University of Missouri-Columbia
- Access to Networked Documents: Catalogs? Search Engines? Both? Arlene G. Taylor and Patrice Clemson, University of Pittsburgh
- Catalogers and the Creation of Metadata Systems : A Collaborative Vision at the University of Michigan, Kevin Butterfield, University of Michigan
- Modifying Cataloging Practice and OCLC Infrastructure for Effective Organization of Internet Resources, Ingrid Hsieh-Yee, Catholic University of America

ISBN 1-55653-219-9

Figure 9.1. Web page table of contents for the proceedings of a conference in which the papers are about many different subtopics of the main theme. (Source: http://digitalarchive.oclc.org/da/ViewObject.jsp?objid=0000003889.)

Exhaustivity affects both precision and recall in retrieval. *Precision* is the measurement of how many of the documents retrieved are relevant. *Recall* is the measurement of how many of the relevant documents in a system are actually retrieved. Depth indexing is likely to increase precision because more specific terminology is used. Summarization is likely to increase

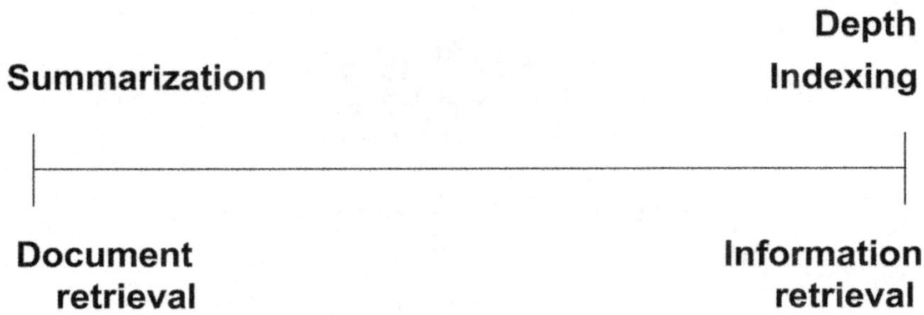

Figure 9.2. Illustration of the concept that summarization leads to document retrieval and depth indexing leads to information retrieval. The line moves gradually from summarization to depth indexing, and it is possible to have a subject analysis system that is between the two extremes.

recall because the search terms are broader and more sweeping in their application of terminology.

The summarization approach is very useful in retrieving tangible resources (e.g., CD-ROMs, DVDs, print journals, etc.). As we do more and more indexing of intangible electronic resources (e.g., Web sites, PDF files, etc.), we will have to think more carefully about summarization versus depth indexing. Search engines do the ultimate depth indexing. Often, the occurrence of a word anywhere in a Web site means that the Web site will be retrieved by a search on that word, whether or not the word reflects any topics actually covered in the information resource. However, because this retrieval approach is based on matching specific strings of characters, rather than searching for the concepts signified by those strings, depth indexing increases recall while greatly decreasing precision.

In addition to deciding the level of exhaustivity, we also face the problem of deciding what is an analyzable unit.[17] As already stated, traditionally, whole items have been analyzable units in libraries, collections have been analyzable units in archives, and articles in journals have been analyzable units for commercial indexing enterprises (along with individual poems, stories, or essays published in collections). In digital libraries and on the Internet there is, so far, no definition for an analyzable unit. Should it be the whole electronic journal or individual issues of that journal? Should it be the whole Web site (i.e., a homepage along with all links located and controlled at that site) or individual pieces of a Web site (one page on a particular topic)? Should it be a single image or an entire collection of 500 images scanned for a digital library project, or some combination of both? Once we have decided what is being described, we will have to rethink whether our users need summarization-level subject headings or depth indexing vocabulary for the analyzable units.

Objectivity

The challenges addressed above (levels of complexity, difficulty, consistency, etc.) raise questions as to whether the subject analysis process can be an objective or impartial one. For example, some find it much easier to analyze resources about topics with which they are already familiar or those they simply enjoy; some find it difficult to analyze resources they dislike or disagree with on a philosophical, moral, social, religious, or political basis. Information professionals are expected to remain objective and impartial in all of their work-related activities, but is this realistic? Daniel N. Joudrey found that 75% of the LIS students who participated in his study of aboutness determination questioned the validity of the author's premise in least one of the three information resources they were analyzing.[18] Is this surprising? Information professionals (and LIS students) are only human after all. While information professionals are expected to remain neutral, there is a human tendency to judge the information that we encounter, whether it is a bad first impression from cover art or lasting doubts about authors' evidence to support their claims. With some controversial resources or resources representing an opposing point of view, judgments and preconceptions may be unavoidable. In such cases, it is important to be aware of and to acknowledge one's biases, prejudices, and beliefs when conducting the conceptual analysis, and to seek the opinions of others when needed.

Those with vastly different understandings of the world might vehemently disagree as to how objective the subject analysis process is or can be. While some with a more positivist, empirical view of the world might believe that there is an innate, identifiable aboutness in each information resource just waiting to be discovered, others with a more constructivist understanding may view the process as one that can only be performed through the lens of the analyst's own background, knowledge, culture, responsibilities, and even mood. In other words, they see conceptual analysis as a highly subjective, interpretive process that is dependent on human skills of observation, interpretation, and analysis. Whatever one's epistemological orientation, the work of subject analysis must be done in order to provide subject access to information resources in a systematic, deliberate fashion. Consequently, information professionals often forego long philosophical debates over the nature of reality, aboutness, and subject determination, and just do the task—with an understanding that we should attempt to keep our biases in check as much as possible while performing the process.

Differences in Methods Used

As stated earlier, not everyone agrees on how to approach the determination of aboutness, so there is no single process that is used by everyone. Over the years, various methods have been offered. Some were simply lists of bibliographic features that could be consulted, whereas others provided questions and concepts to consider while examining the resource. Some view the process as comprising two activities, while others believe there are three or four discrete steps. Some do not think of the process in terms of steps at all. In this section, some of the most familiar and useful approaches to determining aboutness are discussed.

Langridge's Approach

Langridge views the subject analysis process as a series of discrete activities.[19] He also stresses that the conceptual analysis must be performed independently from any particular classification scheme or controlled vocabulary, and that the analysis should be written down so as to avoid muddled notions of aboutness.[20] In addition to examining the various parts of the text, he states that the cataloger or indexer must keep three basic questions in mind in order to determine the aboutness of an information resource. Those questions are:

- What is it?
- What is it for?
- What is it about?[21]

According to Langridge, the first question is answered by one of the fundamental forms (or categories) of knowledge. In other words, the indexer must ask: Is it history? Is it science? Is it philosophy? Langridge identifies twelve distinct forms of knowledge: philosophy, natural science, technology, human science, social practice, history, moral knowledge, religion, art, criticism, personal experience, and prolegomena (logic, mathematics, grammar—the foundations of knowledge). The second question looks at the purpose of the document. Why was it created? How might it be used? Looking at disciplines may help to answer the second question. Is it for a specific audience? Is this book on cows meant for a veterinarian? Is it for a zoologist? Is it for a dairy farmer? Is it for a child? These reflect four different perspectives that might affect our understanding of the aboutness. Langridge sees disciplines as ever-evolving areas of interest or specialization falling under the twelve forms of knowledge. A topic (or multiple topics) is the answer to the third question. Topics are the everyday phenomena that we perceive, that is, concepts, objects, places, events, and so on. Langridge points out that topics are not specific to any one form of knowledge or discipline. For example, the topic *clothing* can appear in any number of disciplines or sub-disciplines, such as clothing design, clothing manufacturing, home economics, or social or religious customs. Langridge, in his approach to subject analysis, also includes some other characteristics as part of the process, such as examining the nature of the text (bibliographic structures and mediums) and the nature of the thought (point of view, type of writing, audience, intellectual level, etc.).

Wilson's Approaches

Wilson has described four methods that one may use to come to an understanding of what a work is about.[22] Wilson did not name these methods himself; the authors have supplied the names used here. The first might be called the *Purposive Method*. In this approach, one tries to determine the author's aim or purpose in creating the information resource. If the creator gives a statement of purpose, then we may presume to know what the work is about. But some creators give no such statement, others seem to aim at several things at once, and others provide multiple statements indicating different purposes or objectives in each.

Wilson's second method of deciding what a work is about might be called the *Figure-Ground Method*. Using this method, one tries to determine a central figure that stands out from the background of the rest of the information resource. However, what stands out depends on the observer of the resource as well as on its creator. What catches one's interest is not necessarily the same from person to person, and may not even be constant for the same person a few weeks later. Education, background knowledge, intellectual interests, and initial assumptions about the information resource can also influence what stands out.

Wilson's third method is the *Objective Method* (which is, by the way, the method used in most attempts at automated conceptual analysis). One tries to be objective by "counting" references to various items to determine which ones vastly outnumber the others. Unfortunately, an item constantly referred to in the resource might be a background item (e.g., Germany in a work about World War II). This method is also difficult because a primary concept might be signified by different words throughout the item. For this method to be successful, the cataloger or indexer must understand that the variously expressed concepts are related. It is also possible that the concept that is central to the aboutness might not be expressed concretely in the text. Wilson gives the example of a work being about a person's political career, but those words are never used in the work. Collantes found that when people were asked to read abstracts and then write down subject words or phrases that they believed conveyed the meaning in the abstracts, eight percent of the readers used words that did not appear anywhere in the abstract.[23]

The last of Wilson's methods is the *Cohesion Method,* an approach that looks at the unity of the content. When using this method, one tries to determine what holds the work together, what content has been included, and what has been left out of the treatment of the topic. Again, the observer of the information resource has to be objective, and one has to know quite a lot about the subject in order to know what was omitted. In addition, there may be several ways in which the work can appear to be unified; and creators do not always reach the ideal of a completely unified presentation.

Use-based Approaches

Over the years, a number of other approaches to subject analysis have been discussed in the LIS literature. Some can be described as *Use-based* approaches. The main idea is that aboutness can be determined by looking at how a resource could be used or what questions a resource could answer. Lancaster, concerned about users and how the item might be used, suggests asking three questions to determine aboutness:

- What is it about?
- Why has it been added to our collection?
- What aspects will our users be interested in?[24]

Concerns about use, purpose, or patrons' interests, while informative, will not suffice as the only approach to aboutness determination because the cataloger is being asked to perform an impossible task: to predict all of the possible (present and future) uses for a document. No matter how skilled one may be, this approach amounts to little more than guessing why an information resource may be needed. Therein lie the difficulties associated with use-based approaches to aboutness. This is not to say that asking how a document could be used has no place in aboutness determination. On the contrary, it is a very important question; it just cannot be the *only* question.

As this discussion indicates, there seems to be no one correct way to determine aboutness. One can use any or all of these methods, but the different methods will not necessarily lead to the same result. If they give the same result, as they often could, it would appear that the subject has been identified. However, a single person might arrive at three or four different subjects using different methods, and several persons might arrive at different results using the same method. In the following section, the authors provide an approach to conceptual analysis that takes into account some of the important components described above, along with some insights from Joudrey's recent dissertation research on the topic.

CONCEPTUAL ANALYSIS PROCESS

Conceptual analysis comprises three interconnected components: an examination of the physical item (or the display of an electronic item), an examination of the intellectual or creative content, and numerous simultaneously performed stages of aboutness determination. In the following sections, each of these components is addressed.[25]

Item Examination

The conceptual analysis process begins with an examination of the information resource, particularly its bibliographic features and visual elements. Similar to the process of descriptive cataloging, in which both content and carrier are considered when creating metadata, the conceptual analysis of an information resource requires an examination of both the intellectual content and the physical item (if the resource is in tangible form). The examination starts with the parts of the item that stand out. In many instances this begins with the information resources themselves, but in other instances it begins with accompanying materials (e.g., manuals, containers, inserts from CD-ROM cases, labels, etc.). Somewhat different techniques have to be used for information resources that contain text versus those that contain nontextual information. Concentrating first on the textual resources, the following parts should be considered:

- **Cover, Jacket, or Container:** Generally, the cover (or jacket or container) is the first thing one sees when examining a physical item. It kicks off the input process. Without even realizing it, the cover gives a first impression of the item. For that reason alone, this source must be considered. This may be where the title information and the author's name are first encountered (which may or may not be identical to the information found on the title page or other chief source of information). In addition to basic information about title and author, one may encounter a great deal of visual information from this source. Whether this information is helpful or not depends upon many factors. A cover may be explicitly designed to include meaningful imagery or it may be designed simply to catch the eye; its illustrations may be subtle, symbolic, literal, apparently random, or simply a clever marketing strategy. While there are no guarantees that this information will be useful, it should be considered an important potential source of aboutness data.

- **Title and Subtitle:** A title can be helpful in giving an immediate impression of the topic of a document, but titles can also be misleading. Occasionally, more than one form of title or subtitle may be found on an information resource. The title of the Web page *Proceedings of the OCLC Internet Cataloging Colloquium*[26] is quite straightforward (see Figure 9.1). On the other hand, the title *A Compendium of Tiddlywinks Perversions*[27] is not so clear, and is not assisted by its other title information, *Alleghany Airlines Book Club Presents.* Another example, *What the Thunder Said,*[28] turns out to be a Web site devoted to the life and works of T. S. Eliot.

- **Table of Contents:** A list of contents can help to clarify the main topic and identify subtopics. It can be especially helpful for items that are collections of articles, papers, reports, and the like, by different authors. The table of contents for the *Proceedings of the OCLC Internet Cataloging Colloquium*[29] shows the variety of specific topics covered as well as different levels of specificity (see Figure 9.1). Individual chapter titles, like titles proper, are not always helpful or clear. Some authors prefer to use ironic, tongue-in-cheek, or cryptic chapter titles; so the table of contents is only one of the sources consulted during the conceptual analysis.

- **Introduction or equivalent:** Introductions, prefaces, and/or introductory essays may contain some of the most useful, concrete, and straightforward aboutness data in the entire text. Unfortunately, these bibliographic features are not always present in information resources. Often, an introduction is an aid in determining the author's overall purpose or objective in writing the text (as suggested by Wilson[30]) and may also serve to indicate an author's point of view or perspective on the topic (as recommended by Langridge[31]). The introduction to *JGarden: The Japanese Garden Database,* for example, explains that this is not just descriptions of the gardens, but draws upon literature, paintings, images, etc., to provide information "on the history, construction, materiality, people, language, patterns, and processes by which these gardens were constructed."[32]

- **Illustrations, Diagrams, Tables, and Their Captions:** Illustrations and their captions are particularly important in assessing the subjects in fields such as art, where in many cases, illustrations make up the vast majority of the content and therefore must be examined in order to determine aboutness. The captions for illustrations often are quite descriptive of subject content. In some items, however, the illustrations may provide little helpful aboutness information or may even be distracting.

- **Other Bibliographic Features:** Some catalogers and indexers also consult dedications and acknowledgements, hyperlinks, abstracts (if present), and index terms. These elements may confirm or contradict impressions gained from examining the title, table of contents, introduction, and so on. Similar to Wilson's objective method, a back-of-the-book index can show what topics are given the most attention by showing the number of pages devoted to each;[33] what it does not provide, however, is context to show how the topics are related.[34]

- **The Text:** In addition to examining the bibliographic and visual features, the text itself should be examined to get a more complete understanding of the item. In looking through the text, one may encounter helpful information in the introductory sections, opening paragraphs, conclusions, chapter summaries, and the bolded section headings throughout the item. Section headings, if used, can provide a quick overview of the content found in individual sections of a chapter. There are several approaches that may be taken to examining the text, the most common being *skimming*. Skimming allows the cataloger to get a sense quickly of what the creator has written and of the topics covered in the document. This process can be used to help reinforce, refine, or refute emerging aboutness assumptions. In addition to skimming, some may choose occasionally to sample paragraphs or to read longer passages when needed. While examining the text, some may choose to work in a linear fashion from the beginning to the end of the item, while others may choose to focus only on the beginning *and* the end of the information resource, under the assumption that the richest aboutness data will be found in the introductory and concluding chapters. Still others may flip randomly through an item stopping only at what catches the eye. Individuals must find the approach that works best for them and best for the resource they are examining at that moment. No single approach will work for every item equally well every time.

- **Nontextual Information:** For tangible nontextual information resources, one has to examine the object, picture, or other representation itself. Some nontextual resources are manufactured commercially and include accompanying materials such as boxes with text, booklets, instruction sheets, labels, and so on. Electronic nontangible information resources that are basically pictures or other forms of artistic work quite often have captions that explain something about them in text form. For individual works or objects with no accompanying text, however, one must examine the items themselves, and translating ideas into words can be difficult, if not impossible, without special training or education.

Content Examination

During the examination of the physical item, one must also be concerned with various aspects of the intellectual and creative contents of the resource. In this section, identifying concepts of interest, important content characteristics useful in aboutness determination, and some content examination strategies are addressed.

Identification of Concepts

Different types of concepts can be used as subjects of information resources, including: topics, several types of names (e.g., persons, corporate bodies, geographic areas, etc.), and time periods.

Topics Used as Subject Concepts. Most people think of topical terms when asked to identify the subject of an item. A topic can represent a principle object of attention or a theme running through an information resource. Topics can be concrete or abstract. Ideas, objects, phenomena, activities, processes, structures, groups, substances, and more, can be the topics of works. In short, an information resource can be about anything imaginable.

Names Used as Subject Concepts. In the process of determining what a document is about, it may be found that the subject, or one aspect of the subject, is a person, a corporate body, a geographic area, or some other named entity.

- **Persons.** An individual person, living or dead, can be the topic of a Web site, book, or other information resource. It may be primarily biographical or it may cover aspects of a person's career (e.g., the aforementioned site dedicated to T. S. Eliot). Such a work is also, in a sense, about one representative of a group of persons (e.g., literary writers). The Library of Congress, in applying the *Library of Congress Subject Headings* (LCSH), for example, has the policy of making a subject heading for the group, as well as for the person, on the assumption that if an information seeker wants to learn about *literary writers,* then a site about one such person may be of use. A work can be about deities, biblical figures, legendary and fictitious characters, or named animals as well.

- **Corporate Bodies.** A corporate body is an organization or group of persons who are identified by a name and who act as an entity. A corporate body may be the subject of an information resource about an organization, a musical group, a company, a legislative body, a church group, a vessel, and so forth, (e.g., a book may be about Exxon-Mobil, The Beatles, or the Cambridge Public Library). There are also entities whose names resemble corporate bodies, but they are not. Sometimes such bodies have the same name as the building they work in. This is often true of churches, for example, and then one has to be certain whether the building or the corporate group is the topic of the work.

- **Geographic Names.** Geographic names can take different roles in the determination of subject content. In some cases, a document may actually be about a specific place, (e.g., a work about the history of Brookline, Massachusetts).

However, much of the time, a work is not about the place *per se,* but the geographic location provides a context for the topical content, as in a work about the projects and life of architect Julia Morgan, who did virtually all of her work in California. Falling between these extremes is the case where the geographic area is the topic of the topic. An example is the exhibition catalog, *"A Sweet Foretaste of Heaven": Artists in the White Mountains, 1830–1930.*[35] The exhibition consisted of landscape paintings of the White Mountains of New Hampshire.

- **Other Named Entities.** Some named entities resemble both corporate names and geographic names, but are neither. Entities such as named buildings, structures, cemeteries, bridges, and archaeological sites fall into this category. An example is the subject heading, **Megiddo (Extinct city),** which is used to represent the archaeological site.

Chronological Elements. The time period can be an important aspect of the subject content of information resources. Time periods limit the coverage of the topic and therefore dictate content in subtle ways. For example, information resources about computer access to information in the 1970s will not be likely to include information about the World Wide Web or about XML. Time can be expressed in a number of ways. Named periods (e.g., World War II) and styles (e.g., Renaissance) often act as surrogates to chronology. These are of particular importance in the fields of art, architecture, music, and literature, but they have not been particularly well handled by controlled vocabularies or by the MARC format. Only specific dates or date ranges are usually treated as separate chronological elements, because named periods and styles generally have been treated as topical information.

Content Characteristics

Just as topics, names, and chronological elements are important to understanding the aboutness of information resources, so are some additional characteristics that are related to the content and some that are related to the author. These characteristics include what Langridge discussed as "the nature of the text" and "the nature of the thought."[36] According to Langridge:

> There remain a number of very important characteristics requiring identification which have always been treated

> as part of the process of subject analysis. I shall refer to these as formal characteristics to distinguish them from the real subject features. Though none of these formal elements alters the subject of a document, some of them can make a considerable difference to its treatment or presentation.[37]

For some information resources, a few of these content characteristics may be relevant in the conceptual analysis process, but with other resources, perhaps none will be useful at all. Like so many other factors in the conceptual analysis process, it will depend on the nature of the resource being analyzed. The following characteristics should be considered if they are applicable.

Research Methods. Although this characteristic will not be appropriate for most popular or creative works, some academic research materials, scientific articles, technical reports, and the like might benefit from considering the methods used by the author to examine the issue, the hypothesis, or the research questions being addressed in the information resource. This characteristic might be useful in helping one to better understand the aboutness, the form, and the level of the work, as well as the means the author used to reach his or her conclusions. It also may be particularly useful in the indexing of scientific datasets, papers, and articles.

Point of View. Except for Langridge, point of view is rarely mentioned in discussions of the conceptual analysis process. Although not all resources have a specialized or identifiable point of view, some of them are written from a particular perspective, which could be of special interest to some users and could be anathema to others. This content characteristic can be helpful when analyzing some types of information resources and necessary when describing those works from a particular viewpoint. For items that may be controversial in some fashion (e.g., political works, religious works, cultural treatises, works on sexuality, gender, age, socio-economic levels, etc.), the point of view may be an important piece of metadata that will help the users to find, identify, and select the information resources that they need. This content characteristic, however, is rarely if ever translated into controlled vocabulary terms or classification notations; instead, it may be addressed in summary statements or abstracts.

Language, Tone, Audience, and Intellectual Level. These four characteristics are addressed together because they are in many ways interrelated. The relationships among them are multi-faceted and myriad. For example, the language chosen by the author helps to set the tone of the work. The language and tone used are shaped by the intellectual level that the author is striving for and the author's intended audience for the work. In examining the work, the language and tone are particularly helpful in understanding the audience and intellectual level (e.g., whether it is an academic or a popular work). While none of these directly affects aboutness, they may help to establish some context for understanding the information resource as a whole.

These characteristics may also affect the item examination process. The indexer or cataloger may need to treat a scholarly, intellectual work differently than a popular work, (e.g., a scholarly resource may need more exploration of the content, more reading of the introduction and conclusion, and more time to complete the analysis than does a work of popular culture). Of those writing on aboutness determination, few address these issues. Langridge addresses one of the four—*audience*—in his discussion of "form of thought." Audience may also appear as the answer to his conceptual analysis question: *What is it for?*[38] Joudrey found that 92% of the participants in his qualitative study of aboutness were concerned with audience. Although the study participants found *audience* helpful in the aboutness determination process, some were reluctant to include the concept in their final descriptions of the resource. He notes, "the participants included audience [in their aboutness statements] when the book was written for and directed toward one particular audience, and they excluded the concept when the item could appeal to multiple audiences or a more general audience."[39]

Language and tone are almost never addressed in the subject analysis process; audience and intellectual level are sometimes addressed in form/genre headings (e.g., **Children's films**) and in subject subdivisions for juvenile materials (e.g., **Self-acceptance—Juvenile fiction**). Sometimes, audience appears in other places in metadata descriptions (e.g., the *Audience* element in the application profile for the Dublin Core education community and in the 008 field in MARC bibliographic records).

Form and Genre. The final characteristic to consider in the conceptual analysis process is the form of the information resource being analyzed or the form of important parts of that information resource. *Form* is not strictly a subject feature. It is a concept that has been associated with subject analysis from the inception of the idea that books could be entered in catalogs and placed on shelves according to the category to which they belonged. Early categories included such forms as encyclopedias, biographies, and histories, as well as subjects such as chemistry and religion. Later, as subject headings evolved to mean what an item is about instead of a category to which the book belonged, the idea of *form* remained as part of the subject analysis process. Because it was often difficult to separate the idea of *form* from *aboutness,* as in the case of *history* (which seems to incorporate elements of both), the concept of *form* has only recently begun to be treated differently in surrogate records.

In an effort to aid in the process of separating form from subject, the Subject Analysis Committee (SAC) of the American Library Association (ALA) devised a definition for form. The appropriate ALA bodies officially approved the definition in January 1993:

> Form data are those terms and phrases that designate specific kinds or genres of materials. Materials designated with these terms or phrases may be determined by an examination of:
>
> - their physical character (e.g., videocassettes, photographs, maps, broadsides)
> - the particular type of data that they contain (e.g., bibliographies, questionnaires, statistics)
> - the arrangement of information within them (e.g., diaries, outlines, indexes)
> - the style, technique, purpose, or intended audience (e.g., drama, romances, cartoons, commercials, popular works) or a combination of the above (e.g., scores)
>
> A single term may be modified by other terms, in which case the whole phrase is considered to be form data (e.g., aerial photographs, French dictionaries, conversation and phrase books, wind ensemble suites, telephone directories, vellum bound books, science fiction).[40]

Separating form from subject has become increasingly important as the organizing world has become more attuned to organizing information that is not in textual form. In the discipline of music, identifying form has always been critical and has been accommodated by treating it as subject. Now more users are looking for other kinds of information forms (e.g., chalk drawings, digital maps, sculpture reproductions, etc.). By separating form from subject, it is possible to take advantage of system design to allow searching for forms of information resources. Some metadata schemas have elements that are defined specifically for this concept (e.g., *Type* and *Format* in the Dublin Core; *worktype* and *material* in the VRA Core).

Content Examination Strategies

As discussed earlier, different approaches to identifying relevant aboutness data may be used by different catalogers or indexers, or by the same cataloger with different resources or on different days. Some may use Langridge's questions, while others may use one or more of Wilson's approaches, and still others may use no organized method at all. Answering a series of questions, either formally or informally, can help one go through the subject analysis process quickly. A sample set of questions and an example of the process is found in Appendix A.

Joudrey found in his aboutness determination research that LIS students with no previous experience or coursework in organizing information mostly used the same approaches to conceptual analysis. The most commonly used approaches are three of the four described by Wilson: *the Purposive Method, the Figure-Ground Method,* and *the Objective Method.* The participants rejected some of the other strategies described in the LIS literature by either using them infrequently (or not at all) or by stating that they were not approaches they had considered or they would consider. For example, although the participants explored the author's purpose in writing a document, on the whole they did not consider how patrons would use the documents, what questions the documents would answer, or how someone would search for the documents. Based on Joudrey's research, it appears that 40 years ago, Patrick Wilson got it right.[41] Joudrey concludes:

> Because of the interpretive nature of all of the processes that the participants used (and those that they did not use), it is recommended that each content examination strategy should be used in conjunction with other strategies. Wilson was accurate when he stated that each of the approaches that he described was *a* method, and not *the* method, to analyze aboutness. No one approach to the content was observed in isolation, nor should they be used in isolation. Similar to conducting good qualitative research, the content examination strategies need be triangulated. Getting as many perspectives as possible on the items is the best strategy for determining aboutness.[42]

Stages in Aboutness Determination

In an attempt to better understand what happens during the conceptual analysis process, Joudrey analyzed the activities that were being performed while his study participants were attempting to determine what the information resources were about. While the physical items were being examined and the participants were considering things like the author's purpose and what topics were mentioned most often, they were also advancing through a number of simultaneous stages. The researcher has categorized the stages as: the input process, assumption making, the revision process, sense making, and stopping.

The conceptual analysis process begins with an input phase in which data is collected by encountering content in some form or manner (seeing, noticing, envisioning, etc.). This may occur through simple visual examination, more in-depth exploration of general content, or through seeking specific desired chunks of data. Shortly after the input process begins (in some cases as early as viewing the cover), a second process begins in which assumptions about the item's aboutness begin to be made. These assumptions may be about macro-level, micro-level, or chapter-level aboutness, or they may be about other characteristics of the item. These assumptions then undergo a revision process, in which assumptions are refined, reinforced, and/or refuted. Concurrently with the input, assumption making, and revision processes, the multi-faceted process of sense making begins.[43] This entails a number of individual activities, including finding context, interpreting, comparing, and reasoning. After the first moments of the input process, all of these other processes are performed simultaneously and continuously until an understanding of the item's aboutness is reached. The final process centers on how and when one decides to stop the examination of the item.[44]

NEXT STEPS IN SUBJECT ANALYSIS

Once the conceptual analysis is complete, it can be very helpful to write an aboutness statement that begins, "This information resource is about. . . ." It may be one or two sentences or it may be a short paragraph. As Langridge states, the conceptual analysis should be written down to avoid muddled notions of aboutness.[45] It helps the cataloger or indexer to keep track of all of the major concepts and to relate them to each other. Depending on the degree of exhaustivity that is being followed, the concepts included may be limited to the main idea of the entire work or to all of the major subtopics found in the resource. Once the aboutness statement is complete, the aboutness concepts identified must be translated into the subject languages being used.

The cataloger or indexer then identifies the key concepts and chooses terms from the aboutness statement to be searched in the controlled vocabulary. Specific rules for using controlled vocabularies are found in their introductions, as well as, in some cases, manuals that accompany them. In order to translate an aboutness statement into classification notations, it is necessary to understand the hierarchy or the facets of the classification scheme that is to be used. If a hierarchical scheme is used, it is helpful to determine the discipline into which the information resource falls. For example, a history of Spain is usually considered to fall within the discipline of history and the sub-discipline of European history, while a history of chemistry is generally thought to fall within the broad area of the sciences, specifically in the discipline of chemistry. Creating a hierarchical string for discipline, sub-discipline, topic within discipline, accompanied by concepts of treatment, place, time, and form is helpful in translating the aboutness into a hierarchical classification. Using a faceted classification is much like choosing subject terms from a controlled vocabulary that precoordinates several terms into a subject heading string. Notations for separate facets must be found in the classification and then must be put together according to the rules for the scheme.

CONCLUSION

This chapter has discussed the nature of *subject* and the process of determining the aboutness of information resources. Determining aboutness must precede the use of the specific subject access tools employed for assigning controlled vocabulary and classification notations. Before being able to make the best use of the specific tools, it is helpful to understand controlled vocabularies and classification schemes in general. The following two chapters address these issues.

NOTES

All URLs accessed September 2008.

1. Working Group on the Future of Bibliographic Control, "On the Record: Report of the Library of Congress Working Group on the Future of Bibliographic Control," Library of Congress. Available: http://www.loc.gov/bibliographic-future/news/lcwg-ontherecord-jan08-final.pdf.

2. F. W. Lancaster, *Indexing and Abstracting in Theory and Practice,* 3rd ed. (Champaign: University of Illinois, Graduate School of Library and Information Science, 2003), p. 9.

3. Patrick Wilson, "Subjects and the Sense of Position," in *Two Kinds of Power: An Essay on Bibliographical Control* (Berkeley: University of California Press, 1968), pp. 69–92. Also reprinted in *Theory of Subject Analysis: A Sourcebook,* eds. Lois Mai Chan, Phyllis A. Richmond, and Elaine Svenonius (Littleton, Colo.: Libraries Unlimited, 1985), pp. 309–320.

4. George Lakoff, *Women, Fire, and Dangerous Things: What Categories Reveal about the Mind* (Chicago: University of Chicago Press, 1987), pp. 24–26.

5. D. W. Langridge, *Subject Analysis: Principles and Procedures* (London: Bowker-Saur, 1989), p. 4.

6. Oliver L. Lilley, "Evaluation of the Subject Catalog: Criticisms and a Proposal," *American Documentation* 5, no. 2 (1954): 41–60.

7. Lourdes Y. Collantes, "Agreement in Naming Objects and Concepts for Information Retrieval" (PhD diss., Rutgers University, 1992), p. 154.

8. For example: Regene C. Ross, Chair, Task Force on Copy Cataloging, *Report of the Task Force on Copy Cataloging,* May 12, 1993, cited by Thomas Mann, in "'Cataloging Must Change!' and Indexer Consistency Studies: Misreading the Evidence at Our Peril," *Cataloging & Classification Quarterly* 23, nos. 3/4 (1997): 37–38.

9. Langridge, *Subject Analysis,* p. 9.

10. Richard W. Unger, *The Art of Medieval Technology: Images of Noah the Shipbuilder* (New Brunswick, N.J.: Rutgers University Press, 1991).

11. Erwin Panofsky, *Studies in Iconology: Humanistic Themes in the Art of the Renaissance* (New York: Harper & Row, 1972), pp. 5–17.

12. Ibid., p. 7.

13. Sara Shatford [Layne], "Analyzing the subject of a picture: A theoretical approach," *Cataloging & Classification Quarterly* 6, no. 3 (1986): 45.

14. A. G. Brown, in collaboration with D. W. Langridge and J. Mills, *An Introduction to Subject Indexing,* 2nd ed. (London: Bingley, 1982), frames 48, 51.

15. Journal of Statistics Education. Available: http://www.amstat.org/publications/jse/.

16. OCLC Internet Cataloging Colloquium (1996: San Antonio, Tex.), *Proceedings of the OCLC Internet Cataloging Colloquium, San Antonio, Texas,*

January 19, 1996. Available: http://digitalarchive.oclc.org/da/ViewObject.jsp?objid=0000003889.

17. For more about what units are to be analyzed, see Chapter 7.

18. Daniel N. Joudrey, "Building Puzzles and Growing Pearls: A Qualitative Exploration of Determining Aboutness" (PhD diss., University of Pittsburgh, 2005), pp. 165–171.

19. Langridge, *Subject Analysis,* pp. 73–98, 136.

20. Ibid., p. 57.

21. Ibid., pp. 8–10.

22. Wilson, "Subjects and the Sense of Position," pp. 78–88.

23. Collantes, "Agreement in Naming Objects," p. 154.

24. Lancaster, *Indexing and Abstracting,* p. 9.

25. Some of this section appeared in an earlier form in Arlene G. Taylor, "Books and Other Bibliographic Materials," in *Guide to Indexing and Cataloging with the Art & Architecture Thesaurus,* eds. Toni Petersen and Patricia J. Barnett (New York: Oxford University Press, 1994), pp. 101–119 and in Daniel Joudrey's "Building Puzzles and Growing Pearls."

26. OCLC Internet Cataloging Colloquium (1996: San Antonio, Tex.), *Proceedings of the OCLC Internet Cataloging Colloquium.*

27. Sunshine, "A compendium of tiddlywinks perversions," North American Tiddlywinks Association. Available: http://www.tiddlywinks.org/how_to_play/rules/english/alleghany/.

28. Raymond Camden, "What the Thunder Said." Available: http://www.whatthethundersaid.org/.

29. OCLC Internet Cataloging Colloquium (1996: San Antonio, Tex.), *Proceedings of the OCLC Internet Cataloging Colloquium.*

30. Wilson, "Subjects and the Sense of Position," pp. 78–88.

31. Langridge, *Subject Analysis,* pp. 73–98, 136.

32. "JGarden: The Japanese Garden Database." Available: http://www.jgarden.org/.

33. Wilson, "Subjects and the Sense of Position," pp. 78–88.

34. Joudrey, "Building Puzzles," p. 127.

35. *"A Sweet Foretaste of Heaven": Artists in the White Mountains, 1830–1930,* with essays by Robert L. McGrath and Barbara J. MacAdam (Hanover, N.H.: Hood Museum of Art, 1988).

36. Langridge, *Subject Analysis,* pp. 55–57.

37. Ibid., p. 45.

38. Ibid.

39. Joudrey, "Building Puzzles," p. 198.

40. American Library Association, Association for Library Collections and Technical Services, Subject Analysis Committee, "Definition of Form Data." Available: http://www.pitt.edu/~agtaylor/ala/form-def.htm.

41. Joudrey, "Building Puzzles," pp. 357–360.

42. Ibid., p. 361.

43 This is *not* specifically referring to Brenda Dervin's Sense-Making research methodology, about which more information can be found at her Web site. Available: http://communication.sbs.ohio-state.edu/sense-making/.

44. Joudrey, "Building Puzzles," pp. 351–352.

45. Langridge, *Subject Analysis,* p. 57.

SUGGESTED READINGS

Bates, Marcia J. "Subject Access in Online Catalogs: A Design Model." *Journal of the American Society for Information Science* 37, no. 6 (1986): 357–376.

Cleveland, Donald B., and Ana D. Cleveland. *Introduction to Indexing and Abstracting.* 3rd ed. Englewood, Colo.: Libraries Unlimited, 2001. Chapter 4: "Vocabulary Control," Chapter 6: "The Indexing Process," and Chapter 7: "The Abstracting Process."

Dooley, Jackie M. "Subject Indexing in Context." *American Archivist* 55, no. 2 (Spring 1992): 344–354.

Joudrey, Daniel N. "Building Puzzles and Growing Pearls: A Qualitative Exploration of Determining Aboutness." PhD diss. Pittsburgh,

Pa.: University of Pittsburgh, 2005. Available: http://etd.library.pitt.edu/ETD/available/etd-12132005-155713/.

Lakoff, George. *Women, Fire, and Dangerous Things: What Categories Reveal about the Mind.* Chicago: University of Chicago Press, 1987. Part I: "Categories and Cognitive Models."

Lancaster, F. W. *Indexing and Abstracting in Theory and Practice.* 3rd ed. Champaign: University of Illinois, Graduate School of Library and Information Science, 2003.

———. *Vocabulary Control for Information Retrieval.* 2nd ed. Arlington, Va.: Information Resources Press, 1986. Chapter 1: "Why Vocabulary Control?"

Langridge, D. W. *Subject Analysis: Principles and Procedures.* London: Bowker-Saur, 1989. Chapter 5: "Summarization," Chapter 6: "Summarizing in Practice," and Appendix 2: "The Forms of Knowledge."

Pettee, Julia. "The Subject Approach to Books and the Development of the Dictionary Catalog." In *Theory of Subject Analysis: A Sourcebook,* edited by Lois Mai Chan, Phyllis A. Richmond, and Elaine Svenonius. Littleton, Colo.: Libraries Unlimited, 1985, pp. 94–98.

Taylor, Arlene G. *Introduction to Cataloging and Classification.* 10th ed., with the assistance of David P. Miller. Westport, Conn.: Libraries Unlimited, 2006. Chapter 9: "Subject Access to Library Materials."

———. "On the Subject of Subjects." *Journal of Academic Librarianship* 21, no. 6 (November 1995): 484–491.

Weinberg, Bella Hass. "Exhaustivity of Indexes: Books, Journals, and Electronic Full Text." *Key Words* 7, no. 5 (September/October 1999): 1, 6–19.

Wellish, Hans H. "Aboutness and Selection of Topics." *Key Words* 4, no. 2 (March/April 1996): 7–9.

Wilson, Patrick. *Two Kinds of Power: An Essay on Bibliographical Control.* Berkeley: University of California Press, 1968. Chapter 5: "Subjects and the Sense of Position." Reprinted in *Theory of Subject Analysis: A Sourcebook,* edited by Lois Mai Chan, Phyllis A. Richmond, and Elaine Svenonius. Littleton, Colo.: Libraries Unlimited, 1985, pp. 309–320.

CHAPTER 10

SYSTEMS FOR VOCABULARY CONTROL

In the electronic age, subject searching remains a vital approach to finding information resources. Users search catalogs, indexes, museum Web collections, and digital libraries to find resources that match their interests. In this increasingly Web-centric information environment, a search engine is often the first retrieval tool that users approach to find information about a topic they want to explore. Yet some users have become frustrated with the tens of thousands of results from keyword searches performed on the Internet. With the massive increase in availability of recorded information it has become more and more evident that keyword searching alone—the approach primarily used by search engines—will not suffice for all information retrieval tools in all information environments. One of the major reasons that problems occur is that when keywords are the focus of a search, myriad semantic difficulties can arise. Virtually every word in the English language has more than one meaning or sense, and many of those senses have more than one nuance; many words can be used as nouns, verbs, adjectives, and/or adverbs. Search systems that purport to allow the use of natural language cannot yet successfully distinguish among different meanings or various parts of speech in very large general systems, although some progress has been made in narrow subject areas.

In addition, there is evidence that people writing about the same concepts often do not use the same words to express them, and people searching for the same concept do not think of the same words to search for it. Many of the inter-indexer consistency studies in the second half of the twentieth century asked participants to think up words in their heads, not to take vocabulary from a list; therefore, although these studies have been used by some authors to "prove" that subject indexing is worth little because indexers are inconsistent, what the studies really showed was that people do not think of the same terms to express the same aboutness concepts. Thomas Mann has given an excellent analysis of some inter-indexer consistency studies that support these observations.[1] The clear implication is that controlled vocabulary—usually in the form of a list of authorized subject terms with their accompanying cross-references—is needed to reconcile all the various possible words that can be used to express a concept and to differentiate among all the possible meanings that can be attached to certain words.

In recent years however, it has also become clearer that controlled vocabularies are not necessarily appropriate for *all* information environments. Controlled vocabularies appear to work best in contained systems. It is only feasible to create, maintain, and apply them in systems such as indexes, databases, or catalogs, which rely on human expertise for success. A controlled approach to terminology does not and cannot work well for a large-scale, distributed system like the Internet, where no one is responsible for identifying the subjects of works and assigning authorized descriptors, and where the number of resources is enormous.

Several questions are addressed in this chapter. They include: How is subject content expressed verbally in metadata? How are controlled vocabularies structured? Is a controlled vocabulary necessary or can natural language approaches suffice in some environments? How do ontologies assist in identifying concepts? How are tagging and keyword searching used with subject content?

CONTROLLED VOCABULARIES

A *controlled vocabulary* is a list or database of subject terms in which all terms or phrases representing a concept are brought together. Often one of the terms or phrases is designated as the preferred term or authorized phrase to be used in metadata records in a retrieval tool. The terms that are not designated as preferred have references from them to the chosen terms or phrases, and relationships among the preferred terms are identified (e.g., broader terms, narrower terms, related terms, etc.). There may also be scope notes for the terms, creation dates, identifier codes, associated classification numbers, categories, and notes included in the term lists.

Controlled vocabularies roughly fall into three categories: (1) subject heading lists, (2) thesauri, and (3) ontologies. All three have certain similarities, but they are also different. First, we compare subject heading lists with thesauri. Subject heading lists have been created largely in library communities; thesauri have been created largely in indexing communities.

Both attempt to provide subject access to information resources by providing terminology that can be consistent and reliable rather than uncontrolled and unpredictable. Both choose preferred terms and make references from non-used terms. Both provide structural hierarchies so that terms are presented in relation to their broader terms, narrower terms, and related terms. There are also certain differences worth noting:

- Thesauri are made up of single terms and bound terms representing single concepts (often called *descriptors*). Bound terms occur when some concepts can only be represented by two or more words (e.g., Type A Personality; the words *type, A,* and *personality* cannot be separated without losing the meaning. The entire phrase is necessary for expressing the concept.). Subject heading lists tend to have phrases and other precoordinated terms in addition to single terms.

- Thesauri are more strictly hierarchical. Because they are made up of single terms, each term usually has only one broader term. The rules in the NISO *Guidelines for the Construction, Format, and Management of Monolingual Thesauri*[2] that have to do with identifying broader, narrower, and related terms are much easier to follow when working with a single-term system than when working with a system that includes phrases and compound headings.

- Thesauri are narrower in scope. They are usually made up of terms from one specific subject area. Subject heading lists tend to be more general in scope, covering a broad subject area or, indeed, the entire scope of knowledge.

- Thesauri are more likely to be multilingual than subject heading lists. Again, because single terms are used, equivalent terms in other languages are easier to find and maintain.

Ontologies, the third type of vocabulary, are similar to both subject heading lists and thesauri in bringing together all the variant ways of expressing a concept and in showing the relationships of a concept to broader, narrower, and related concepts. They are different, however, in that they do not select one term to be a preferred or authorized term. In the field of philosophy the term *ontology* has a long and respectable history meaning a systematic account of existence. More recently the term came to be used for the categories of things that may exist in a particular domain and to refer to the knowledge shared by persons working in a particular domain; in other words, it is a systematic account of the entities and their relationships found in a particular domain. At some point in the last decade, the word was adopted by the information science community to designate the building blocks that are used to help computers and humans share knowledge. Elin Jacob argues that an ontology, "constitutes a controlled vocabulary... only...if the standard concept of a controlled vocabulary is redefined."[3] The authors see no problem with the expansion of the definition of controlled vocabulary to include the kind of control that brings together concepts and shows relationships among them without designating one term as the authorized one. This is the same kind of redefinition that is taking place with authority control of names (discussed in Chapter 8). The different types of controlled vocabularies are described in more detail later in this chapter.

CONTROLLED VOCABULARY CHALLENGES

In the process of creating a controlled vocabulary there are certain difficulties that must be addressed. An understanding of these problems can enhance one's ability to use a particular existing controlled vocabulary.

Specific vs. General Terms

The level of specificity must be decided at the outset of establishing a controlled vocabulary. Various lists may have different thresholds for how specific the terminology will be. The heading *Cats* is not as specific as *Cat breeds. Cat breeds* is not as specific as *Siamese cats,* which in turn is not as specific as *Bluepoint Siamese cats.* In *Library of Congress Subject Headings* (LCSH), for example, the most specific term is *Siamese cat;* in *Sears List of Subject Headings (Sears),* the most specific term is *Cats,* although an instruction is given that, if needed, a term for a specific breed of cat may be created.

To some extent the decision on this matter is based on the types of users who are expected to search for headings from the list, and upon the nature of the information resources that are to be assigned terms from the list. If the collection has mainly general kinds of information, then *Cats* is probably sufficient, even to cover a few more specific items. If the users are children likely to be looking for general kinds of information, then again *Cats* is probably sufficient as the most specific level. A vocabulary used to describe a collection in a veterinary school, however, most likely will need to be more specific.

Synonymous Concepts

The English language rarely has absolutely true synonyms—that is, situations where two words mean the same thing and have no variations in nuance. However, there are multitudes of synonymous words and phrases that mean so close to the same thing that they can be interchanged for each other. Hans Wellish wrote, "Authors have, therefore, great freedom in the choice of terms and may use several words for the same concept, which may be admirable from the point of view of style, but would be disastrous when transferred unchanged to an index."[4] These are the terms that make keyword searching so problematic and frustrating.

In the creation of a controlled vocabulary it is necessary to identify all the synonymous and nearly synonymous terms that should be brought together under a single authorized term. For example, do the terms *attire, dress, outfits, clothes, garments,* and *clothing* all mean the same thing? If not exactly the same, or if they have different nuances, are the differences important enough to warrant separate vocabulary terms for them? Is there enough of a logical distinction among them that some information resources should be placed under the term *garments,* others under *clothing,* and still others under *clothes?* Would users (or indexers and catalogers) understand the distinctions among them? If not, then perhaps they should be treated as synonyms despite their slight differences. When making such a determination, one should take into account which term is best known to the intended users; but with regional, national, and international differences in English-language usage, a decision may have to be arbitrary.

Word Form for One-Word Terms

Words in English often have more than one form that can mean the same thing (e.g., *clothing* and *clothes*). Also, language evolves, and as it does, a concept has a tendency to be expressed first as two words, then as a hyphenated word, then as one word (e.g., *meta data, meta-data, metadata*). Sometimes all three forms appear in use at the same time. British and American spellings give us another case of word form difference (e.g., *catalogue* and *catalog*). Prefixes to a word can create a word with a different meaning, but in some cases, where the meaning is opposite, it would not make sense to use both terms in the controlled vocabulary because one of the concepts can never be discussed without the other (e.g., *armament* and *disarmament; equality* and *inequality*).

A major word form difference is singular versus plural. There is no rule on which form to use. Most of the time the plural has the broadest coverage (e.g., *videocassettes* rather than *videocassette*); but at times the singular is broader (e.g., the term *apple* can apply to both the fruit and the tree, while *apples* refers only to the fruit). Sometimes the singular and the plural forms of a word have different meanings (e.g., in LCSH, the term *art* refers specifically to visual art; the heading *arts* refers to a broader concept that includes visual arts, literature, and the performing arts).

Sequence and Form for Multiword Terms and Phrases

In some controlled vocabularies there are terms and phrases made up of two or more words. Some of these are modified nouns (e.g., *Environmental education*); others are phrases with conjunctions or prepositions (e.g., *Information theory in biology*); and a third group has qualifiers added in parentheses (see discussion below). A problem in constructing such terminology in a controlled way is being consistent in the order and form of the individual words used. For example, *Energy conservation* and *Conservation of energy resources* mean the same thing. The first phrase places the concept with other headings beginning with the word *energy;* the second phrase puts the concept with other topics having to do with conservation. If the list creates such phrases, it must be certain to have references from every possible construction of the phrase—referring from them to the construction that was chosen.

Some controlled vocabularies (notably LCSH) present some multiword terms and phrases in inverted order (e.g., *Education, Bilingual; Asylum, Right of*). Much of this was done in the past in order to collocate a group of headings on a broad concept with subconcepts arranged alphabetically below it. Thus, instead of *Bilingual education* being found in the Bs and *Higher education* being found in the Hs, both were found in the Es as *Education, Bilingual* and *Education, Higher.* Research has shown that few users think of such phrases in inverted order, but look for them in direct order. In LCSH few new inverted forms are being established, but already-established ones still exist. One therefore finds inconsistencies such as *Moral education* and *Medical education* juxtaposed with *Education, Humanistic* and *Education, Greek.*

Homographs and Homophones

Homographs are words that look the same but have very different meanings. *Mercury* can be a liquid metal, a planet, a car, or a Roman god; *bridge* can be a game, a structure spanning a chasm, a location on a ship, or a dental device, among other meanings. In a controlled vocabulary there must be some way to differentiate among the various meanings. Two common ways are either to use qualifiers to distinguish between the terms or to choose synonyms as the preferred terms.

Homographs may or may not be pronounced the same (e.g., *mare* pronounced as one syllable with a silent *e* is a mature female horse; *mare* pronounced as two syllables is a large, dark area on the moon [possibly derived from the Italian *mare,* meaning *sea*]). Traditionally, different pronunciations did not play a role in creating a controlled vocabulary, because the vocabulary was treated visually.

Homophones, which are words that are spelled differently but pronounced the same, have also been ignored in controlled vocabularies in a visual world (e.g., *moat* and *mote; fowl* and *foul*). Because what appears on computer screens is now quite regularly read aloud electronically to people with visual impairments, we need to give attention to pronunciations of homographs and to distinguishing among homophones.

Qualification of Terms

One of the ways of dealing with homographs is to add a qualifier to one or more of the meanings. For example, *Mercury* can be represented as *Mercury (Planet)* and *Mercury (Roman deity)*. Qualifiers are also used to differentiate usages of a word in different settings. For example:

Adultery (Aztec law)
Adultery (Jewish law)
Adultery (Yanzi law)

In addition qualifiers can be used to help identify the context of unfamiliar words. For example, the name *Yanzi* can be identified as *Yanzi (African people).*

Abbreviations and Acronyms

Traditionally, abbreviations and acronyms have either been spelled out or not depending upon the intended users of the controlled vocabulary and their expected knowledge. With a move to more global retrieval, one cannot assume a certain population. Under these circumstances it would probably be best to assume that abbreviations and acronyms should be spelled out. A few, however, have global recognition. An example is AIDS, the acronym for Acquired Immune Deficiency Syndrome (although in Spanish the acronym is SIDA, so in an international index even this acronym might need to be spelled out).

Popular vs. Technical Terms

When a concept can be represented by both technical and popular terminology, the creator of a controlled vocabulary must decide which will be used. For example, the National Library of Medicine's *Medical Subject Headings* (MeSH) uses *Neoplasms,* where LCSH uses *Cancer.* If the list is intended to be used for information resources that will be retrieved by a specialized audience only, then specialized terminology is justified. However, in a global information world, one can no longer be certain of a particular audience. Perhaps this is another area where the kind of authority control discussed in Chapter 8 should be put into use. With international authority control, technical terms and their equivalent popular terms could reside on the same record which could be activated by a search on any of the equivalent terms. This is, in fact, the approach used in many ontologies.

Subdivision of Terms

Subdivisions are used in controlled vocabularies that precoordinate terms. Among the uses of subdivisions are:

- to separate by form/genre (e.g., **Chemistry—Dictionaries**)
- to show treatment of only a part of the larger subject (e.g., **Merchant marine—Officers**)
- to show special aspects of the larger subject (e.g., **Merchant marine—Watch duty**)
- to show geographical or chronological limitations (e.g., **Architecture—Great Britain—19th century**)

PRECOORDINATION VS. POSTCOORDINATION

Index terms can be assigned either in a precoordinated fashion (i.e., the indexer constructs subject strings with main terms followed by subdivisions), or in a fashion that requires the searcher of the system to coordinate the terms (i.e., postcoordination). When terms are precoordinated in the controlled vocabulary or are precoordinated by the cataloger or indexer, some concepts, subconcepts, place names, time periods, and form concepts are put together in subject strings. This does not mean that all concepts used for indexing a particular item will be placed in the same subject string.

That happens only when the subject analysis system attempts to have each subject heading be coextensive with the aboutness statement of an item. In most precoordinated systems in use today, there are several precoordinated strings per surrogate record. In postcoordinated systems, each concept is entered into the surrogate record discretely, without stringing together subconcepts, place names, etc. Searchers, therefore, must combine terms in the search box using Boolean operators (e.g., AND, OR, NOT, etc.). Keyword searching is the ultimate form of postcoordinate indexing.

With the use of most controlled vocabularies, the searcher must still do some postcoordination, even if the cataloger or indexer has already precoordinated some concepts. It is a matter of degree. LCSH, for example, has no precoordinated terminology for the concept *dancers and musicians.* It is up to the user who wants a work covering this concept to search *dancers* AND *musicians* using Boolean logic, and then to determine which metadata records have both terms in their controlled vocabulary sections.

Postcoordination is sometimes confused with depth indexing, but these are very different concepts. Although it is often the case that the numerous discrete terms in a record that result from depth indexing are used in a postcoordinated system, depth indexing does not require the indexer to assign only single terms. There is nothing to keep a depth indexer from stringing together concepts with subconcepts or modifiers to make more meaningful precoordinated index terms. It depends on local indexing policies or rules associated with the particular controlled vocabulary being used.

GENERAL PRINCIPLES FOR CREATING CONTROLLED VOCABULARIES

There are some general principles that apply to creating controlled vocabularies. These are to be distinguished from principles that come into play when applying particular vocabulary terms. The general principles discussed here for creating vocabularies are *specificity, literary warrant,* and *direct entry.*

Specificity

Specificity is the level of semantic depth found in a particular controlled vocabulary. For example, LCSH has greater specificity in its established subject headings than does *Sears.* This is evident from the greater hierarchical depth in the concepts that are found in LCSH, and is made physically obvious by the relative size of the printed volumes. For example, the very specific *Canned raspberries* is found in LCSH; it is a narrower term found under *Canned berries,* which is a narrower term found under the broader heading *Canned fruit,* which in turn is a narrower term under *Canned foods.* In *Sears,* the choices are either: (1) *Canning and preserving,* which is used for canned foods, or (2) *Fruit—Preservation,* which seems to be more about the process of preserving fruit than a particular product. Subject heading lists and thesauri created for specific subject fields or disciplines, such as MeSH for the field of medicine, are even more specific in their headings than LCSH.

Literary Warrant

Controlled vocabulary lists tend to be created using the principle of *literary warrant.* This means that terminology is added to a subject heading list or thesaurus when a new concept shows up in the information resources that need organizing and therefore needs to have specific terminology assigned to it. This is often described as a "bottom-up" approach because existing resources are used to expand the controlled vocabulary. Usually, no attempt is made to add new terminology to a list until it is needed for use in metadata records; otherwise, the creators of the vocabulary would be predicting the future or basing new additions on what should be there, at least theoretically. In recent years, these "top-down" approaches to creating subject languages have fallen out of favor.

Direct Entry

Another principle of creating controlled vocabulary terms is that of *direct entry,* which states that a concept should be entered into the vocabulary using the term that names it, rather than treating that concept as a subdivision of a broader concept. For example, in LCSH there is currently a preference for a modified term to express a concept (e.g., *Railroad stations*) over the use of a broader term subdivided by a narrower term (e.g., *Railroads—Stations*).

GENERAL PRINCIPLES FOR APPLYING CONTROLLED VOCABULARY TERMS

The first step in applying controlled vocabulary takes place just after the cataloger or indexer determines the aboutness of an information resource. Once the nature of content is understood, and an aboutness statement has been written, choices must be made to determine which subject concepts are to be represented by the controlled vocabulary in the metadata record. Not every concept in an aboutness statement can be translated into the controlled vocabulary that has been chosen for use in a particular institution or situation. While controlled vocabularies are useful in describing key concepts, places, events, time periods, and objects (often in the form of nouns and various types of noun phrases), they are not always helpful in translating actions and relationships among those concepts. The indexer, therefore, must be familiar enough with the controlled vocabulary to know which ideas can be translated and which cannot.

In the aboutness statement, the most important concepts are selected as targeted searches in the controlled vocabulary. This may entail circling key words in the statement or compiling a list of terms. Translating these words into authorized descriptors or subject headings, however, may be more difficult than one might initially expect, especially when attempting to apply complex rules that may accompany the controlled vocabulary. In some cases, it may take a staggering effort to remain faithful to the aboutness of the resource, while following specific application rules in addition to following general principles of applying controlled vocabulary. In other cases, the indexer or cataloger may discover that there is no appropriate way to translate a particular concept into the vocabulary, or if it is possible, the translation no longer makes sense in the context of the resource being described.

The general principles discussed below are *specific entry* and *coextensive entry*. The number of terms assigned and what to do when the concept is not in the particular vocabulary are also discussed. Specific rules for individual controlled vocabularies are not addressed.

Specific Entry and Coextensive Entry

The principle of *specific entry* states that an aboutness concept should be assigned the most specific term that is available for that concept in the controlled vocabulary. An information resource about musicians should be entered under *musicians,* not under *performing artists,* or if it is about pianists, and that term is in the vocabulary, then the entry should be *pianists,* not *musicians.* However, if the vocabulary does not get as specific as *pianists,* or does not allow creation of such terms for specific categories of musicians, then the principle of specific entry calls for using *musicians* as the most specific entry from that vocabulary. Specific entry allows an experienced user to know when to stop searching for an appropriate controlled vocabulary term. One does not have to keep trying broader terms, unless no information is found under the most specific terms.

It should be noted that the concept of *specific entry* is not the same as the concept of *coextensive entry*. Coextensivity is the idea that the subject headings applied to an information resource will cover all, but no more than, the concepts or topics covered in that resource; it is about matching exactly the subject entries to the limits and scope of the aboutness of the information resource. In order to have coextensive entry using LCSH, for example, an information resource about crocheting potholders requires two specific entries: one for *crocheting* and another for *potholders*. There is no one specific heading to cover these two concepts together. In order to have just one heading that is coextensive with the subject of such a resource, the heading would have to be *crocheting potholders*, or *potholders—crocheting*, but these phrases are not used in LCSH.

It once was true that *specific entry* could be treated in a relative way. In a small collection there might be only one or two items about musicians, although there might be several items about performing artists that include musicians as one type of performing artist; for that collection, there might be a decision that *performing artists* would be the most specific heading used. Now that we are all essentially contributing to a global union catalog, however, we must follow the principle of specific entry in order for searching to be effective.[5] On the other hand, in recent years, some have called for including broader terms in catalog records to assist less-experienced catalog users navigate the system and find the resources that they need[6] (e.g., a record could include headings for both *Siamese cats* and *Cats*, even though the item focuses primarily on Siamese cats). Or, if we could break out of tradition and make references in our retrieval tools from specific subject headings to broader ones, then "too specific" would not have to be a concern.

Number of Terms Assigned

There should be no arbitrary limit on the number of terms or descriptors assigned. If the conceptual analysis has been done at the summarization level, then the number of terms given should be the number that is needed to express that summary. Likewise, if the conceptual analysis has been performed in depth, the number of terms necessary to cover all of the concepts should be allowed. This, however, is not always the case. Some information institutions have local policies that restrict the number of subject headings assigned to an information resource. While this *might* help to cut down on the time spent indexing, it does the users no favors. For example, if the local policy states, "No more than three descriptors are to be added to a record," but the information resource is about *four* specific, discrete concepts, which one is to be left out of the record? The time spent deciding what topics to omit might in fact be lengthier than the time spent adding a fourth subject term.

Concepts Not in Controlled Vocabulary

If a concept is not present in the controlled vocabulary, it should be represented temporarily by a more general concept, rather than simply adding unauthorized terms to the record (e.g., use *Artificial intelligence* until a new heading for machine discovery is established). The new concept should be proposed as a new addition to the subject list or thesaurus. And once (or *if*) the new concept is added to the vocabulary, a change in the metadata record should be made. This means that the cataloger or indexer should flag the record for updating; otherwise, it might be forgotten or lost among a sea of records.

INDEX TERMS FOR NAMES

Although the names for most topical concepts are handled by the controlled vocabulary list itself, a separate authority file generally controls most proper names. For example, the Library of Congress (LC) maintains a name authority file, called the NAF (Name Authority File), for names of persons, corporate bodies, geographic names of political entities, and titles of works.[7] Geographic names that are *not* political entities and other names such as names of archaeological sites are also controlled by LC, but as subject headings rather than as names. The art world also has name authority files: *Union List of Artist Names* (ULAN)[8] and *Thesaurus of Geographic Names* (TGN).[9] maintained by the Getty.

MECHANICS OF CONTROLLED VOCABULARIES

A traditional controlled vocabulary operates by choosing a preferred way of expressing a concept and then making certain that synonymous ways of expressing the concept will be connected to the preferred terminology. Traditionally, the nonused (or unauthorized) terminology appears in the controlled vocabulary listed under the preferred terminology and is often preceded by the abbreviation **UF** meaning *used for.* The unauthorized terms also appear in the list as entry words (or entry vocabulary) to act as pointers to the chosen terms (i.e., as a **Use** reference). For example, under the heading **Maintenance,** two unauthorized terms are listed.

Maintenance
UF Preventive maintenance
Upkeep

Elsewhere in the vocabulary, two reciprocal references are made at the place in the list where the unauthorized terms appear. For example:

Preventive maintenance
Use **Maintenance**
. . .
Upkeep
Use **Maintenance**

A traditional controlled vocabulary also keeps track of the hierarchical relationships of a concept. The preferred term (in boldface type) is shown in relationship to its broader term(s), narrower term(s), and related term(s), if any. These are often designated by the abbreviations **BT, NT,** and **RT,** respectively. In addition, see also notes (**SA**) may provide additional information about relationships with other headings. For example:

Maintenance
UF Preventive maintenance
Upkeep
BT Maintainability (Engineering)
RT Repairing
Service life (Engineering)
SA subdivision **Maintenance and repair** under kinds of objects, including machinery, vehicles, structures, etc., e.g. Automobiles—Maintenance and repair; Dwellings—Maintenance and repair
NT Buildings—Repair and reconstruction
Grounds maintenance

(This example is not exhaustive, but only illustrative.) These **BT, NT,** and **RT** relationships are reciprocal: under **Maintainability (Engineering),** the narrower term **Maintenance** would be listed. Under **Repairing,** the related term **Maintenance** would be listed, and under **Grounds maintenance,** the broader term **Maintenance** would be listed.

There are different kinds of hierarchical relationships that may be designated as simply broader and narrower terms in a general vocabulary, but which may be designated more specifically in some thesauri. These include: genus/species or class/class member relationships (e.g., the class *buildings* includes houses, apartment buildings, etc.); whole/part relationships (e.g., fingers are part of a hand); and generic topic/named example or instance relationships (e.g., San Francisco is an instance of a city). Likewise, there are different kinds of related-term relationships. A few include: one term needed in the definition of the other (e.g., stamps is needed in the definition of philately); meanings of two terms overlap, or two terms may be used interchangeably, yet are not synonyms (e.g., carpets and rugs); and linking of persons and their fields of endeavor (e.g., attorneys and law).

Relationships can also be expressed in ontologies. For example, the relationships shown in the general lexical ontology WordNet®[10] are the following:

- **Synonyms**—Terms that have the same, or nearly the same, meaning and often can be substituted for each other. A synonym is like the **UF** relationships and Use references in traditional controlled vocabularies.

- **Coordinate terms**—Terms that might be called siblings; they all have the same parent term. A coordinate term is *somewhat* similar to the **RT** relationships in traditional controlled vocabularies, although related terms in the same hierarchy are not articulated in many controlled vocabularies.

- **Hypernyms**—These are parent terms. It is a category comprising all of the instances that are "kinds of" the hypernym (e.g., *family* is a hypernym for *nuclear family, extended family, foster home,* etc.). A hypernym is like some **BT** relationships in traditional controlled vocabularies.

- **Hyponyms**—These designate child terms. A hyponym is a member of a class (e.g., *nuclear family* is a hyponym of the class *family*). A hyponym is like the **NT** relationships in traditional controlled vocabularies.

- **Holonyms** and **Meronyms**—A holonym is the name of the whole of which the meronym is a part. With a holonym, one has a whole that is made up of parts (e.g., a *family* has as its members: *children, parents, siblings,* etc.). With a meronym, one has a constituent part or a member of something (e.g., *sister* is a meronym of *family*). A holonym is like some **BT** relationships and a meronym is like some **NT** relationships in traditional controlled vocabularies.

- **Antonyms**—Terms that have opposite meanings (e.g., *hot* is an antonym of *cold*). Antonyms are not addressed in traditional controlled vocabularies.

Another example of ontological relationships comes from OWL: the Web Ontology Language,[11] a language used to build ontologies. Some relationships provided for in OWL are:

- **subClassOf**—x is a subset of the class y (e.g., the class *Mammals* is a subset of the class *Animals*)
- **oneOf**—the enumerated thing is an instance of the class (e.g., the continent *Asia* is one member of the class *Continents*)
- **equivalentClass**—two class descriptions have the same set of individuals (e.g., the class *U.S. President* is equivalent to the class *Principal Resident of White House*)
- **intersectionOf**—a class can belong to two other classes (e.g., the class *Student* can be both *Person* and *University Asset*)
- **disjointWith**—two classes have no individuals in common (e.g., the class *Cats* does not include any individuals of the class *Dogs*)

Most controlled vocabularies display all of the terms in alphabetical order with all of their relationships enumerated below the entry as seen in the **Maintenance** example above, but some also provide a hierarchical display of the vocabulary terms. In the latter, the terms are placed in juxtaposition to each other so that one can visualize broader and narrower relationships. Such lists are helpful in seeing where a term fits within an entire hierarchy, not just its relationship to the terms immediately above and below it. These are often called *tree structures,* an excellent example of which is the MeSH Tree Structures.[12] Hierarchical listings in Internet directories can resemble tree structures if shown as levels rather than being presented in a single string at the top of the screen.

TYPES OF CONTROLLED VOCABULARIES

As mentioned above, there are three types of controlled vocabularies being described in this chapter: *subject heading lists, thesauri,* and *ontologies.* Each are described further and examples are provided for each type below.

Subject Heading Lists

Among the best-known and most-used subject heading lists are *Library of Congress Subject Headings* (LCSH), *Sears List of Subject Headings (Sears),* and *Medical Subject Headings* (MeSH). A brief description of each follows, but more detailed descriptions can be found in other sources, some of which are suggested at the end of this chapter.

Library of Congress Subject Headings (LCSH)

Starting in 1988 with the eleventh edition, new print versions of LCSH have been produced once a year, currently as a five-volume set. LCSH is updated continuously, and a fully updated electronic version is available by subscription through *Classification Web*[13] and through the subject authority files accessible through OCLC and at the LC Web site. The goal of LCSH is to cover the world of knowledge; it is not restricted to any one subject domain. It is meant to be used by all kinds of libraries in many different kinds of settings, including countries other than the United States. In the subject cataloging process, LCSH is used in conjunction with the *Subject Cataloging Manual: Subject Headings* (SCM:SH).[14] This four-volume set of manuals gives the subject heading policies and practices employed at the Library of Congress, which is responsible for the maintenance of LCSH; the SCM:SH is an essential tool if one wishes to apply LCSH correctly. A sample from LCSH is shown as Figure 10.1. MARC-encoded authority records for two of the headings in Figure 10.1 are shown in Figure 10.2. (Note: MARC records from LC do not contain narrower terms.)

Sears List of Subject Headings (Sears)

Sears is still published in print form with a new single-volume edition coming out every few years.[15] It is also updated continuously, and updates are periodically available in electronic form. *Sears* is expected to be accessible online by 2009. This subject heading list is intended for small collections used by persons with general information needs. Its main users are

Hair
[GN193 (Physical Anthropology)]
[QL942 (Comparative anatomy)]
[QM488 (Human anatomy)]
UF Hairs
BT Body covering (Anatomy)
Head
RT Scalp
NT Beards
Bristles
Eyebrows
Eyelashes
Gray hair
Guard hair
Horsehair
Long hair
Molting
Mustaches
Sale of human hair
Sidelocks
Trichomes
Whiskers
Wigs
Wool
. . .
Hair--Coloring
USE Hair--Dyeing and bleaching
. . .
Hair--Dyeing and bleaching [R S D]
[TT973] [B L S D]
UF Coloring of hair
Hair--Bleaching
Hair--Coloring
Hair--Tinting
Tinting of hair
BT Bleaching
Hairdressing
. . .
Hair dyes (May Subd Geog)
[TP984 (Chemical technology)]
[TT969 (Hairdressing)]
UF Dyes and dyeing--Hair
Hair tints
Tints, Hair
BT Hair preparations

Hair dyes--Law and legislation (May Subd Geog)

Figure 10.1. Sample entries from *Library of Congress Subject Headings* (LCSH), as found in *Classification Web* (May 2008). Available: http://classweb.loc.gov (by subscription).

Rec stat c **Entered** 20030731 **Replaced** 200330912123452.0

Type	z	**Upd status**	a	**Enc lvl**	n	**Source**	
Roman	|	**Ref status**	b	**Mod rec**		**Name use**	b
Govt agn	|	**Auth status**	a	**Subj**	a	**Subj use**	a
Series	n	**Auth/ref**	a	**Geo subd**	|	**Ser use**	b
Ser num	n	**Name**	n	**Subdiv tp**	n	**Rules**	n

010 sh 85058305
040 DLC ‡c DLC ‡d DLC
053 GN193 ‡c Physical anthropology
053 QL942 ‡c Comparative anatomy
053 QM488 ‡c Human anatomy
150 Hair
450 Hairs
550 Body covering (Anatomy) ‡w g
550 Head ‡w g
550 Scalp

Rec stat c **Entered** 19860211 **Replaced** 19870903094434.7

Type	z	**Upd status**	a	**Enc lvl**	n	**Source**	
Roman	|	**Ref status**	b	**Mod rec**		**Name use**	b
Govt agn	|	**Auth status**	a	**Subj**	a	**Subj use**	a
Series	n	**Auth/ref**	a	**Geo subd**	i	**Ser use**	b
Ser num	n	**Name**	n	**Subdiv tp**	n	**Rules**	n

010 sh 85058317
040 DLC ‡c DLC ‡d DLC
053 TP984 ‡c Chemical technology
053 TT969 ‡c Hairdressing
150 Hair dyes
450 Dyes and dyeing ‡x Hair
450 Hair tints
450 Tints, Hair
550 Hair preparations ‡w g

Figure 10.2. Sample authority records for two of the headings shown in Figure 10.1. (Source: OCLC Connexion, Authorities, record numbers 02051217 and 02051346.)

school and small to medium-sized public libraries. For most of its existence *Sears* has followed the lead of LCSH in format and in terminology choices, although in the last few editions, *Sears* has taken the initiative to make changes that were later followed by LCSH. For example, the change of *Afro-American* to *African American* was made first by *Sears*. In its use of LCSH terminology, though, *Sears* has used only the more general terms and has not included the more specific terms or the ones geared for research audiences. In addition, *Sears* has fewer subdivisions. In 2008, a Spanish-language translation, *Sears*

Dyes and dyeing 646.6; 667; 746.6
SA types of dyes and types of dyeing
[to be added as needed]
BT **Color**
Pigments
...

Hair 612.7; 646.7
Use for general materials on hair as well as
for materials on hairdressing and haircutting.
UF Barbering
Coiffure
Haircutting
Hairdressing
Hairstyles
Hairstyling
BT **Head**
Personal Grooming
NT **Braids (Hairstyling)**
Wigs

Haircutting
USE **Hair**

Figure 10.3. Sample entry from *Sears List of Subject Headings (Sears),* 19th ed., 2008.

Lista de Encabezamientos de Materia, was published.[16] A sample from *Sears* is shown as Figure 10.3.

Medical Subject Headings (MeSH)

The National Library of Medicine (NLM) calls MeSH a thesaurus,[17] and in the sense that it provides a strict hierarchical structure and it is focused on a particular subject area, it is a thesaurus. But in the sense that it precoordinates phrases (e.g., *Sensitivity Training Groups; Life Change Events*), it is a subject heading list. It also has a subdivision list, which can be used with the single terms and phrases found in the main heading list. MeSH, which is updated annually, is used for providing subject access points on every bibliographic record created at the National Library of Medicine, whether it is for the MEDLINE database or the NLM catalog. As of 2008, the print version of MeSH is no longer produced; it is now an entirely electronic resource.[18] MeSH is provided free on the Web for all those who wish to use it. It can be searched through the MeSH Browser[19] or can be downloaded in either XML or ASCII format. A sample from MeSH is shown as Figure 10.4.

Sample entries of MeSH Descriptor Data:

MeSH Heading	Hair
Tree Number	A17.360
Annotation	abnormally pulling at one's hair = TRICHOTILLOMANIA; HAIR FOLLICLE is available
Scope Note	A filament-like structure consisting of a shaft which projects to the surface of the SKIN from a root which is softer than the shaft and lodges in the cavity of a HAIR FOLLICLE. It is found on most surfaces of the body.
Entry Term	Animal Fur
Entry Term	Fetal Hair
Entry Term	Hair, Fetal
Entry Term	Lanugo
Allowable Qualifiers	AB AH CH CY DE EM EN GD IM ME MI PA PH PP PS RA RE RI TR UL US VI
Online Note	use HAIR to search LANUGO 1966-78
History Note	LANUGO was see under HAIR 1963-78
Unique ID	D006197

MeSH Heading	Hair Dyes
Tree Number	D27.720.233.688
Tree Number	D27.720.269.430.430
Scope Note	Dyes used as cosmetics to change hair color either permanently or temporarily.
Entry Term	Coloring Agents, Hair
Entry Term	Dyes, Hair
Entry Term	Hair Colorants
Allowable Qualifiers	AE AN CH CL CS CT DU EC HI IP ME PD PK PO RE SD ST TO
Registry Number	0
Previous Indexing	Cosmetics (1966-1978)
Previous Indexing	Dyes (1966-1978)
Previous Indexing	Hair (1966-1978)
Previous Indexing	Hair Color (1976-1978)
History Note	91(79); was see under HAIR PREPARATIONS 1980-90; was see under COSMETICS 1979
Date of Entry	19780501
Unique ID	D006202

Sample entries of MeSH Tree Structures:

Integumentary System [A17]
- ➤ **Hair [A17.360]**
  - Eyebrows [A17.360.296]
  - Eyelashes [A17.360.421]
  - Hair Follicle [A17.360.710]
  - Wool [A17.360.855]
- Nails [A17.600]
- Skin [A17.815] +

Chemical Actions and Uses [D27]
- Specialty Uses of Chemicals [D27.720]
  - Cosmetics [D27.720.269]
    - Hair Preparations [D27.720.269.430]
      - ➤ **Hair Dyes [D27.720.269.430.430]**

Figure 10.4. Sample entries from National Library of Medicine "Medical Subject Headings." (Source: http://www.nlm.nih.gov/mesh/.)

Thesauri

Since the mid-twentieth century, numerous thesauri have been created for a vast number of different subject areas. Some thesauri are publicly available on the Web, but many are proprietary products of a particular institution or database, and cannot be accessed without a subscription. Some thesauri comprise terms from multiple disciplines, such as the *UNESCO Thesaurus*,[20] which covers education, culture, natural sciences, social and human sciences, communication and information, and the *Ethnographic Thesaurus*, designed to provide access to resources about folklore, ethnomusicology, cultural anthropology, and other related fields.[21] Other thesauri focus primarily on narrower subject areas, such as the *NASA Thesaurus*,[22] covering the aerospace industry, and the Institute of Electrical Engineers' *Inspec Thesaurus*.[23] In this section, two representative thesauri, the *Art & Architecture Thesaurus* and the *Thesaurus of ERIC Descriptors*, are described briefly.

Art & Architecture Thesaurus (AAT)

The *Art & Architecture Thesaurus* is intended to assist in verbal access to all kinds of cultural heritage information. Terms are provided for describing objects, textual materials, images, architecture, and material culture.[24] AAT is widely used in several communities: archives, libraries, museums, visual resources collections, and conservation agencies. It is arranged into seven facets (categories) that progress from the abstract to the concrete: Associated Concepts, Physical Attributes, Styles and Periods, Agents, Activities, Materials, and Objects. The facets are divided into one or more hierarchies. For example, the Physical Attributes facet is broken down into the following hierarchies: Attributes and Properties, Conditions and Effects, Design Elements, and Color; each of which may be broken down further into additional conceptual hierarchies or clusters of terms organized into tree structures of broader and narrower terms.

AAT is available as a searchable Web resource that provides full access to the preferred terms, alterative terms, and sources.[25] It can also be licensed in three formats for incorporation into local retrieval tools. It is available in XML, as relational tables, or as MARC authority records. The electronic version is constantly updated. Extensive online documentation is available to help the novice searcher. A Spanish-language version of AAT is currently in development. A sample from AAT is shown as Figure 10.5.

Art & Architecture Thesaurus

ID: 300013029

Record Type: concept

dye (colorant (material), <materials by function>, ... Materials)

Note: A colored substance that dissolves or is suspended in a liquid and imparts its color by staining or being absorbed, or by serving as a pigment.

Terms:

dye (preferred, C,U,D,English, American-P)
dyes (C,U,AD,English, American)
dyestuff (C,U,UF,English, American)
dyestuffs (C,U,UF,English, American)
colorant (dye) (C,U,D,French-P)
colorants (dye) (C,U,AD,French)
teinture (colorant) (C,U,UF,French)

Facet/Hierarchy Code: M.MT

Hierarchical Position:

Materials Facet
.... Materials
.... materials
.... <materials by function>
.... colorant (material)
.... dye

Related concepts:

activity/event needing/produced by is .... dyeing
.... (coloring, <additive and joining processes and techniques>, ... Processes and Techniques) [300053049]

...

ID: 300011814

Record Type: concept

hair (<hair and hair components>, <keratinous material>, ... Materials)

Note: The fibrous outgrowths of the skins of various animals, composed of the protein keratin, used with other fibers for making fabrics, as stuffing, and for making brushes.

Terms:

hair (preferred, C,U,D,English, American-P)
poil (C,U,D,French-P)

Facet/Hierarchy Code: M.MT

Hierarchical Position:

Materials Facet
.... Materials

.... materials
.... <materials by origin>
.... <biological materials
.... animal material
.... <keratinous material>
.... <hair and hair components>
.... hair

Related concepts:

activity/event needing/produced by is	hairstyling (<processes and techniques by material>, <processes and techniques by specific type>, ... Processes and Techniques) [300261971]
thing(s) needing context are	hairstyles (<accessories worn on the head>, <costume accessories worn>, ... Furnishings and Equipment) [300262903]

...

Figure 10.5. Sample entries from *Art & Architecture Thesaurus Browser* 2008. (Source: http://www.getty.edu/research/tools/vocabulary/aat/.)

Thesaurus of ERIC Descriptors

ERIC is an acronym for the Educational Resources Information Center, which is a national information system designed to provide access to a large body of education-related literature. Among the documents that ERIC indexes besides journal articles are descriptions and evaluations of programs, book reviews, research reports, curriculum and teaching guides, instructional materials, position papers, computer files, and resource materials. These materials are indexed using terms from the *Thesaurus of ERIC Descriptors*.[26]

The print version of the thesaurus, last published in 2001, consists of four parts: the main Alphabetical Display, the Rotated Display, the Hierarchical Display, and the Descriptor Group Display. The Alphabetical Display is like the display in LCSH, i.e., all of the terms in one alphabetical sequence. The Rotated Display provides an alphabetical index to every word in the thesaurus, including access to unused terms as well as main terms. The Hierarchical Display shows broader and narrower terms in their relationships to each other. The Descriptor Group Display offers a kind of table of contents by placing all descriptors into a set of broad categories.

The most current version of the thesaurus is available as an electronic product on the Web. Its interface allows both searching and browsing the thesaurus.[27] It displays the ERIC descriptors in alphabetical order as search results and in the browse interface. Within each record for each term,

Term:	**Color**
Record Type:	Main
Scope Note:	n/a
Category:	Science and Technology
Broader Terms:	n/a
Narrower Terms:	n/a
Related Terms:	Art; Color Planning; Contrast (2004); Dimensional Preference; Light; Painting (Visual Arts); Visual Environment; Visual Perception;
Used For:	Color Presentation (1969 1980); Hue;
Use Term:	n/a
Add Date:	10/08/1969
Postings:	690

Figure 10.6. Sample entry from the online *Thesaurus of ERIC Descriptors*, 2008. (Source: http://www.eric.ed.gov/.)

broader and narrower terms are hyperlinked, allowing users to explore the hierarchical relationships among terms. Conveniently, the interface also allows users to search for a descriptor in the ERIC index directly from that term's record. A sample of the online display of the ERIC thesaurus is shown as Figure 10.6.

Ontologies

Ontology is a word with many nuances, which is ironic considering the common purpose of the term. An *ontology* is an attempt to define the essence of a situation, domain, or conceptual framework. The broadest usage of the term is for a formal representation or specification of what is common sense or objective reality to a human being. An ontology may be as simple as a thesaurus with definitions, or it may be a more complex hierarchical taxonomy of concepts and categories or a technological solution for the semantics-based problems of information sharing. An ontology defines the nature of reality by identifying the concepts, entities, terms, and categories in a particular domain in order to model the relationships among them. It is created to keep conceptual and semantic ambiguity at a minimum in an information and technological environment. A formal ontology is useful for enhancing interoperability among systems in different knowledge domains or for creating intelligent agents that can perform certain tasks; both of which are goals of the Semantic Web.

There have been attempts to formalize both physical domains and activities (e.g., a robot vacuuming the floor) and abstract concepts (e.g., defining a knowledge domain for machine understandability and processing).

An ontology that will work for organizing and retrieving documents must formalize the reality of using language for communication. These are sometimes called *linguistic ontologies* and may include realities of grammar, semantics, syntax, and the like. The parts that deal with semantics may be called *lexicons* or *lexical dictionaries,* but as noted above they are also called *ontologies.* Natalya Noy and Deborah McGuinness point out that in the artificial intelligence literature, ontologies have been defined in many ways, some of which contradict each other.[28] Some definitions indicate a strong underpinning of categorization or classification; others emphasize vocabulary and definitions. This is still an evolving area that bears watching. An OWL Web Ontology Language document provides the following definition:

> An ontology defines the terms used to describe and represent an area of knowledge. Ontologies are used by people, databases, and applications that need to share domain information...Ontologies include computer-usable definitions of basic concepts in the domain and the relationships among them....They encode knowledge in a domain and also knowledge that spans domains. In this way, they make that knowledge reusable.[29]

The vision for the Semantic Web requires that terms have explicit meaning so that machines can automatically process information found on the Web. Ontologies providing such meaning are building blocks for the Semantic Web, to be used with XML, the XML Schema, RDF, and the RDF Schema. Ontologies are important if agents on the Web are to be able to search and/or merge information from diverse communities. This is because the same term may be used in different contexts with different meanings, and the same meaning may be represented by different terms in different contexts. In order to standardize the means for creating ontologies that can be used on the Web, the Web Ontology Working Group of the W3C developed the OWL Web Ontology Language.[30] It is, as it is named, a language for creating interoperable ontologies that can be extensions of RDF.

Ontologies have different degrees of structure. Some ontologies are taxonomies (i.e., classifications or hierarchical listings) of terminology of a particularly narrow subject area. Some are specifications of sets of conceptual characteristics. For example, metadata schemas are ontologies that specify elements to be used, what those elements mean, and what kinds of attributes and values those elements can have. Other ontologies appear to be categorized controlled vocabularies. These include semantic analysis of words, putting them into categories such as nouns, verbs, adjectives, and adverbs, as is done in WordNet®. This is in contrast to subject heading lists and thesauri that tend to give only noun forms of the terminology contained within them (along with modifiers in other than noun form).

WordNet® calls itself a "large lexical database of English" with nouns, verbs, adjectives and adverbs "grouped into sets of cognitive synonyms (synsets), each expressing a distinct concept. Synsets are interlinked by means of conceptual-semantic and lexical relations."[31] It allows four categories of words: nouns, adjectives, adverbs, and verbs. Relationships between words and their meanings are "many to many"; that is, some words have different meanings *(polysemy),* and some meanings have several different ways of being expressed *(synonyms).* A word can be placed into as many of the four categories as are appropriate, and in each category there can be as many different meanings (or senses) as are appropriate. For each sense, all synonyms are grouped together in *synsets,* and unlike thesauri, none of the synonyms is designated as the preferred term with all others designated as unused. At the main screen that shows all the senses (see Figure 10.7), one can click on links to reveal synset relationships, such as antonyms, hyponyms, hypernyms, and so on.

Another example of an ontology is the Unified Medical Language System (UMLS).[32] This system does not call itself an ontology, but it has many of the characteristics that distinguish ontologies from thesauri. The UMLS comprises three knowledge sources: a metathesaurus, a lexicon, and a semantic network. The metathesaurus pulls together terminology from more than 100 biomedical vocabularies and classifications, linking many different names for the same concepts, without designating one as a preferred term. The lexicon contains syntactic information for words (including verbs) that do not appear in the metathesaurus. The semantic network contains information about the categories to which the metathesaurus concepts have been assigned and describes the relationships among them. It can be seen, then, that the three parts together fit the definition of an ontology.

NATURAL LANGUAGE APPROACHES TO SUBJECTS

In addition to controlled approaches to subject terminology, there are also natural language or "uncontrolled" approaches. These uncontrolled approaches include the longstanding practices of Natural Language Processing (NLP) and keyword searching, as well as the fairly recent development of *tagging* (also known as *user tagging, social tagging,* or *social indexing*), which has been incorporated into some designs for current information tools.

WordNet Search - 3.0 - WordNet home page - Glossary - Help

Word to Search for: **HAIR**
Key: "S:" = Show Synset (semantic) relations, "W:" = Show Word (lexical) relations

Noun

- S: (n) **hair** (a covering for the body (or parts of it) consisting of a dense growth of threadlike structures (as on the human head); helps to prevent heat loss) "he combed his hair"; "each hair consists of layers of dead keratinized cells"
  - direct hyponym / full hyponym
    - + S: (n) coat, pelage (growth of hair or wool or fur covering the body of an animal)
    - + S: (n) guard hair (coarse hairs that form the outer fur and protect the underfur of certain mammals)
    - + S: (n) mane (long coarse hair growing from the crest of the animal's neck)
    - + S: (n) forelock, foretop (a lock of a horse's mane that grows forward between the ears
    - + S: (n) beard (hairy growth on or near the face of certain mammals)
    - + S: (n) body hair (short hair growing over a person's body)
    - + S: (n) down, pile (fine soft dense hair (as the fine short hair of cattle or deer or the wool of sheep or the undercoat of certain dogs))
    - + S: (n) mane, head of hair (growth of hair covering the scalp of a human being)
    - + S: (n) cowlick (a tuft of hair that grows in a different direction from the rest of the hair and usually will not lie flat)
    - + S: (n) hairdo, hairstyle, hair style, coiffure, coif (the arrangement of the hair (especially a woman's hair))
    - + S: (n) lock, curl, ringlet, whorl (a strand or cluster of hair)
    - + S: (n) facial hair (hair on the face (especially on the face of a man))

    ...
  - part meronym
  - substance meronym
  - direct hypernym / inherited hypernym / sister term
  - part holonym
  - derivationally related form

- S: (n) hair's-breadth, hairsbreadth, **hair**, whisker (a very small distance or space) "they escaped by a hair's-breadth"; "they lost the election by a whisker"
- S: (n) **hair**, fuzz, tomentum (filamentous hairlike growth on a plant) "peach fuzz"
- S: (n) **hair**, pilus (any of the cylindrical filaments characteristically growing from the epidermis of a mammal) "there is a hair in my soup"
- S: (n) haircloth, **hair** (cloth woven from horsehair or camelhair; used for upholstery or stiffening in garments)
- S: (n) **hair** (a filamentous projection or process on an organism)

Figure 10.7. Sample entry from WordNet® showing senses of the term *hair*. (Source: http://wordnet.princeton.edu/.)

Natural Language Processing (NLP)

Although there has been some work in computer processing of spoken words, most work has been done on the processing of written words. Therefore, in discussing Natural Language Processing (NLP), we are concentrating on written language processing. One goal of NLP is to be able to create information retrieval (IR) systems that can accomplish three things: (1) interpret users' information needs as expressed in free text; (2) represent the complete range of meaning conveyed in documents; and (3) "understand" when there is a match between the user's information need and all (and no more than) the documents that meet it. In order to do this, certain language problems have to be addressed:[33]

- English sentences are often incomplete descriptions of what they mean. For example, "The door opened" does not tell whether the door was opened by a person, the wind, or its own weight. If the next sentence is, "Susan walked in," then the implication is that Susan opened the door, although that may or not be the case.
- The same expression can mean different things in different contexts. For example, "Where's the water?" can mean that one is thirsty, or it can mean that one wants to know how to get to the beach.
- Natural language is constantly gaining new words, usages, expressions, and meanings. During the 1998 Olympics one could hear that "The United States has not yet medaled." Most people had not heard the word *medal* used as a verb before that. Another example is the creation and evolution of the word, *blog*, which descended from *web log* or *weblog* and can be used as both a noun and a verb.
- There are many ways to say the same thing. For example, "Mary registered for two summer courses" and "Mary signed up for two courses in the summer term" mean essentially the same thing. This problem applies not only to natural language sentences, but also to individual words, as discussed above as the challenges related to synonymous concepts.
- Sentences that are constructed identically can mean different things. In the two sentences, "Jennifer took the course with Professor Jones" and "Jennifer took the course with Mary," the first sentence indicates that the professor taught the course that Jennifer took. But the second could mean that Jennifer and Mary are both students and took a course together, or it could mean that Professor Mary Jones likes to be addressed by her first name. Such

ambiguities can often be sorted out through the context of surrounding sentences, but some cannot.

Elaine Rich and Kevin Knight identify the following steps as necessary for NLP:[34]

- **Morphological analysis**—separate components of words (e.g., prefixes, suffixes, possessive endings, etc.) and separate punctuation from words.
- **Syntactic analysis**—analyze the linear sequences of words to show how the words relate to each other; the computer converts the flat sequence of words into a structure. For those who learned to diagram sentences in grammar classes, diagramming is essentially what is done in this step.
- **Semantic analysis**—map individual words into appropriate places in the knowledge base; create a structure to indicate how the meanings of the individual words combine with each other (e.g., the sentence "She wants to print a Web page" indicates a wanting event in which *she* wants a printing event to occur wherein she must have access to a Web browser and a printer).
- **Discourse integration**—determine the meaning of an individual sentence in relation to the sentences that precede and follow it. For example, the meaning of pronouns such as *it, them,* and *her* can be given individual meanings only if what or who they refer to can be determined.
- **Pragmatic analysis**—reinterpret the structure that represents what was said to show what was actually meant. For example, the question "Do you have the time?" should not be answered with "*yes,*" but should be interpreted as a request to be told the time. In the case of an IR system, the result of such analysis should be a translation to a command to be executed by the system. If the system is asked a question such as "Do you have anything on artificial intelligence?" the response should be a list of sources on artificial intelligence, not the word "*yes.*"

Semantic analysis includes, as its first step, looking up individual words in an ontology to determine which of a word's meanings or nuances is meant in the sentence at hand. Such a resource must give not only definitions, but also must give semantic markers. For example, the word *at* requires a time or a location as its object. Identification of this fact is a semantic marker. Others might be: physical object, abstract concept, animate object, and so forth.

Keywords

One of the first approaches used by NLP researchers was the manipulation of keywords. The success of keyword searching depends upon at least two assumptions: (1) that authors writing about the same concepts will use the same words in their writings, and (2) that searchers will be able to guess what words those authors used for the concept. A 1993 study of journal articles in the pure sciences and social sciences looked at articles that shared common references.[35] An assumption was made that if articles shared common references they dealt with the same or a related subject. It was found that few articles with common references shared common keywords. Another study the same year reported difficulty in choosing keywords for a literature search due to the use of multiple terms representing the same concepts.[36]

Among other problems discovered with keyword searching were that not all related information was retrieved, and searches often led to the extraction of irrelevant materials. A synonym list approach was tried. Synonym lists were databases consisting of groupings of synonymous terms. When a keyword search was done, the synonym list was tapped to provide synonyms without the searcher having to be the one to think of all of them. This approach also failed for several reasons: the lists were not large or general enough; they were implemented in very small and specialized domains; the lists did not attempt any level of word role assignment (e.g., although one could substitute *aircraft* for *planes* and *big* for *large,* it was not possible to substitute *big aircraft* for *large planes* because the system had no knowledge of adjectives and nouns and which kinds of words could be used together to make a phrase).[37]

In IR systems that process full-text, the texts are analyzed and indexed when they are entered into the system and are retrieved through the use of keywords. Although full-text analysis retrieval systems are being marketed, many systems (e.g., distributed networks, the Web) cannot transmit the complete text of hundreds of documents in response to a search query and do not adequately address the semantic problems described above. Sujata Banerjee and Vibhu Mittal proposed an indexing system using keyword searching combined with a well-developed linguistic ontology, such as WordNet®, to address some of these issues.[38] Banerjee and Mittal have proposed the following model (enhanced by this book's authors): For each keyword query (e.g., *family crisis*) of an IR system, results of an exact match would be given first. If there were insufficient matches the system would prompt the user for other options. It could first substitute synonymous adjectives from WordNet® and then present a list to the user who would choose the combinations that make sense.[39] (The user would be involved also at each of the following stages.) Our example would yield the search terms: *household crisis, house crisis, home crisis,* and so forth. Then the system would substitute noun synonyms, resulting in a search for *family emergency.* The system would then drop adjectives, resulting in *crisis* being searched. Then the noun would be generalized to its hypernyms, resulting in: *family situation, family state of affairs, family juncture, family occasion.* Then the synonymous adjectives could be combined with the noun hypernyms, resulting in: *household situation, household state of affairs, home situation, home state of affairs,* and so forth. Also, the hyponyms of both noun and adjective could be searched, resulting in: *family challenge, family complication, family nightmare, foster home crisis, couple crisis, marriage crisis,* and so forth. Thus, there is potential for a very large lexical ontology, covering many fields of knowledge, to be used to enhance keyword searching of full-text documents (and possibly surrogate records) in IR systems that implement such tools. This, however, is not yet a common feature of most systems.

Tagging and Folksonomies

The latest venture into natural language approaches to the content of resources is *tagging.* Tagging is a populist approach to subject description; it is a process by which a distributed mass of users applies keywords to various types of Web-based resources for the purposes of collaborative information organization and retrieval. This activity occurs within a contained system such as a catalog or on a Web site that supports Web 2.0 interactive technologies. Tagging allows individual users to group similar resources together by using their own terms or labels, with few or no restrictions. The tags assigned to a resource can be based on:

- **subject** (e.g., cooking, Sigur_Ros, metadata, PattyGriffin);
- **form** (e.g., images, blogs, humor, gossip, recipes);
- **purpose** (e.g., reference, delivery, travel, howto);
- **time** (e.g., February, now, 2008, future);

- **tasks or status** (e.g., toRead, toDo, toSort, mine, own);
- **affective or critical reactions** (e.g., cool, fun, schlocky author, Questionable Literary Merit); or
- **myriad other reasons,** some of which may be unclear to others (e.g., I am morbid, woo woo, o, 5, zzzzzz).

The tags applied are then displayed in the form of an alphabetical list or as a tag cloud. Tag clouds are visual representations of all or only some of the tags assigned. In some systems, tag clouds display the tags used in the entire site, and in others, the tag clouds represent the tags of only one person or group. The tag cloud may look like a paragraph composed of individual words displayed in various font sizes—the font size representing the relative popularity of the tag. The larger the font is for a tag, the more that tag has been used in the system (see Figure 10.8). The individual tags in the cloud may be arranged alphabetically or ranked by the popularity of the tags, and in some systems, tags can be clustered into several mini-clouds. In other systems the tags may be displayed as a concept map laid out like a solar system, with one key concept found in the center and any number of satellites surrounding it.

Figure 10.8. A tag cloud compiled from the individually assigned tags for the second edition of *The Organization of Information* by Arlene G. Taylor. (Source: Library Thing. http://www.librarything.com/work/28622.)

Tagging may be applied in numerous domains to various types of resources. As long as a resource has a URL, it can be tagged. Tags may be used to label:

- Web bookmarks (e.g., Delicious);[40]
- digital images and videos (e.g., Flickr[41] and YouTube[42]);
- citations for scholarly articles (e.g., CiteULike[43] and Connotea[44]);
- products for sale (e.g., Amazon.com);[45]
- an individual's postings to a blog (e.g., Technorati);[46] and
- individual resources in online catalogs and other retrieval tools (e.g., Queens Library catalog,[47] Ann Arbor District Library catalog,[48] and the California State University Fresno library catalog[49]).

According to Thomas Vander Wal, "The value in this external tagging is derived from people using their own vocabulary and adding explicit meaning.... People are not so much categorizing, as providing a means to connect items... to provide their meaning in their own understanding."[50]

The aggregation of these tags created by a large number of individual users results in what is referred to as a *folksonomy* (a blend of *folks* and *taxonomy*). Thomas Gruber states that with folksonomies, "we now have an entirely new source of data for finding and organizing information: user participation.... Tags introduce distributed human intelligence into the system."[51] The implication is that if enough users tag enough resources, sufficient data can be aggregated to achieve stability, reliability, and consensus. In order for this data to be useful in augmenting current approaches to subject access, though, a critical mass of tags must be accumulated. The idea is that many tags applied to discrete resources by myriad individuals (who are tagging for countless reasons) will provide sufficient information to understand the nature of the resource and to allow us to take technological advantage of an inexpensive way to organize Web-accessible information resources. Without a sufficient volume of data, however, the benefits are limited. For example, one or two user tags assigned to a catalog record do not provide extra insight into the resource being described or reliable supplementary access points; but 200 tags, similar in purpose, can provide additional, useful, meaningful machine-derived subject access points for the record.

Tagging is an exciting development to some because it is an approach to subject metadata by the people, for the people—without restrictions, unfamiliar jargon, and complex application rules. Users can assign as many tags as they like and the terminology they use is their own. It can be done by non-experts, and it is primarily performed by volunteers. In other words, it is an inexpensive alternative to the traditional cataloging of Internet resources. While tagging may eventually provide added value to our current retrieval tools, there are also some drawbacks associated with user tagging. These problems are familiar to anyone who has ever performed a keyword search on the Internet or in another retrieval tool: no synonym and homograph control, no control of word forms (i.e., singular vs. plurals, etc.), impaired precision and recall, and no hierarchical and associative relationships identified. For example, science fiction can be represented by the tags *science fiction, sciencefiction, science_fiction, ScienceFiction, scifi, SciFi, sci-fi, fiction.sciencefiction, ciencia ficcion, sf, SF, sff,* and even *siensfixion* (if someone cannot spell correctly—or chooses not to). In other words, tagging lacks all of the benefits of controlled vocabularies. In addition, the tags assigned by some users may be so idiosyncratic or personal that they are of no real value to anyone else or may be misleading. Despite these shortcomings, tagging appears to be here to stay; the general populace has embraced it and besides being helpful, many find it fun to do. After more research into how tagging can be leveraged has been conducted, information professionals will need to find inexpensive ways of taking advantage of all of this user-generated metadata to supplement, augment, and enhance the expert-created subject metadata found in surrogate records (in the form of controlled vocabulary terms and classification notations).

CONCLUSION

This chapter has addressed verbal approaches to the provision of subject access to information resources. The process of determining what information resources are about was addressed in the preceding chapter as a crucial first step in providing subject access. In the provision of verbal subject approaches, the determination of aboutness is followed by translation of that aboutness into index terms, usually controlled vocabulary. Controlled vocabularies all have to deal with issues and problems during their construction; understanding these issues contributes to making the best use of the vocabulary, as does understanding the general principles of application. Subject heading lists, thesauri, and ontologies make up three kinds of controlled vocabularies in use today. Subject heading lists created by libraries were the first to appear. Thesauri are more strictly hierarchical and, for the most part, are developed in subject-specific situations and/or commercial indexing services. Ontologies have evolved as a way to help humans and computers share knowledge about a particular knowledge domain. Ontologies have grown out of the computer science community and from Natural Language Processing (NLP), which holds promise for sophisticated keyword approaches. The latest addition to verbal approaches to subject access is the folksonomy, which is made up of user tags assigned to Web-based information resources. The next chapter is also concerned with subject access, but from the point of view of categorization and classification.

NOTES

All URLs accessed September 2008.

1. Thomas Mann, "'Cataloging Must Change!' and Indexer Consistency Studies: Misreading the Evidence at Our Peril," *Cataloging & Classification Quarterly* 23, nos. 3/4 (1997): 3–45.

2. National Information Standards Organization, *Guidelines for the Construction, Format, and Management of Monolingual Thesauri* (Bethesda, Md.: NISO Press, 1994). "ANSI/NISO Z39.19-1993."

3. Elin K. Jacob, "Ontologies and the Semantic Web," *Bulletin of the American Society for Information Science and Technology* 29, no. 4 (April/May 2003): 22. Available: http://www.asis.org/Bulletin/Apr-03/BulletinAprMay03.pdf.

4. Hans H. Wellish, "Aboutness and Selection of Topics," *Key Words* 4, no. 2 (March/April 1996): 9.

5. Mann, " 'Cataloging Must Change!' " pp. 9–10.

6. Working Group on the Future of Bibliographic Control, "On the Record: Report of the Library of Congress Working Group on the Future of Bibliographic Control," Library of Congress. Available: http://www.loc.gov/bibliographic-future/news/lcwg-ontherecord-jan08-final.pdf.

7. Library of Congress, "Library of Congress Authorities." Available: http://authorities.loc.gov/.

8. The Getty, "Union List of Artist Names Online." Available: http://www.getty.edu/research/conducting_research/vocabularies/ulan.

9. The Getty, "Getty Thesaurus of Geographic Names Online." Available: http://www.getty.edu/research/conducting_research/vocabularies/tgn.

10. Cognitive Science Laboratory, Princeton University, "WordNet®—A Lexical Database for English." Available: http://wordnet.princeton.edu/.

11. W3C, "OWL Web Ontology Language Overview." Available: http://www.w3.org/TR/owl-features/.

12. National Library of Medicine, "MeSH Tree Structures—2008." Available: http://www.nlm.nih.gov/mesh/MBrowser.html (click on "Navigate from tree top").

13. Library of Congress, "Classification Web." Available (by subscription): http://classweb.loc.gov/.

14. *Subject Cataloging Manual: Subject Headings,* prepared by The Cataloging Policy and Support Office, Library of Congress, 5th ed. (Washington, D.C.: Cataloging Distribution Service, Library of Congress, 1996). Also available in *Cataloger's Desktop* by subscription.

15. *Sears List of Subject Headings,* 19th ed. Joseph Miller, ed. (New York: H. W. Wilson, 2007).

16. *Sears Lista de Encabezamientos de Materia,* Iván E. Calimano, ed. (New York: H.W. Wilson, 2008).

17. National Library of Medicine, "Fact Sheet: Medical Subject Headings (MeSH®)." Available: http://www.nlm.nih.gov/pubs/factsheets/mesh.html.

18. National Library of Medicine, "Medical Subject Headings." Available: http://www.nlm.nih.gov/mesh/.

19. National Library of Medicine, "Medical Subject Headings Browser." Available: http://www.nlm.nih.gov/mesh/MBrowser.html.

20. UNESCO, "UNESCO Thesaurus." Available: http://databases.unesco.org/thesaurus/.

21. The American Folklore Society, "Ethnographic Thesaurus." Available: http://et.afsnet.org/.

22. NASA, "The NASA Thesaurus." Available: http://www.sti.nasa.gov/thesfrm1.htm.

23. Institution of Electrical Engineers, *Inspec Thesaurus* (London: Institution of Electrical Engineers, 2007).

24. The Getty, "Art & Architecture Thesaurus Online: About the AAT." Available: http://www.getty.edu/research/conducting_research/vocabularies/aat/about.html.

25. The Getty, "The Art & Architecture Thesaurus Online." Available: http://www.getty.edu/research/conducting_research/vocabularies/aat.

26. Educational Resources Information Center (ERIC), *Thesaurus of ERIC Descriptors,* 14th ed. (Phoenix, Ariz.: Oryx Press, 2001).

27. ERIC Educational Resources Information Center, "Search & Browse the Thesaurus." Available: http://www.eric.ed.gov/searchthesaurus/.

28. Natalya Fridman Noy and Deborah L. McGuinness, "Ontology Development 101: A Guide to Creating Your First Ontology" (Knowledge Systems Laboratory, Stanford University, 2000), p. 3. Available: http://www.ksl.stanford.edu/people/dlm/papers/ontology-tutorial-noy-mcguinness.pdf.

29. W3C, "Web Ontology Language (OWL) Use Cases and Requirements." Available: http://www.w3.org/TR/webont-req/.

30. W3C, "OWL Web Ontology Language Overview." Available: http://www.w3.org/TR/owl-features/.

31. Cognitive Science Laboratory, Princeton University, "WordNet®—A Lexical Database for English." Available: http://wordnet.princeton.edu/.

32. National Library of Medicine, "Unified Medical Language System (UMLS®)." Available: http://www.nlm.nih.gov/research/umls/.

33. Elaine Rich and Kevin Knight, *Artificial Intelligence,* 2nd ed. (New York: McGraw-Hill, 1991), pp. 377–379.

34. Ibid., pp. 379–380.

35. S. N. Ali, "Subject Relationship Between Articles Determined by Co-occurrence of Keywords in Citing and Cited Titles," *Journal of Information Science* 19, no. 3 (1993): 225–231.

36. R. B. Bush, "A Bibliography of Monographic Works on Biomaterials and Biocompatibility," *Journal of Applied Biomaterials* 4, no. 2 (1993): 195–209.

37. Sujata Banerjee and Vibhu O. Mittal, "On the Use of Linguistic Ontologies for Accessing and Indexing Distributed Digital Libraries," in *Digital Libraries '94: Proceedings of the First Annual Conference on the Theory and Practice*

of Digital Libraries, June 19–21, 1994, College Station, Texas. Available: http://www.hpl.hp.com/personal/Sujata_Banerjee/pubs.html.

38. Banerjee and Mittal, "On the Use of Linguistic Ontologies."

39. Ibid.

40. Delicious Social Bookmarking. Available: http://delicious.com/.

41. Flickr. Available: http://www.flickr.com/.

42. YouTube. Available: http://www.youtube.com/.

43. CiteULike. Available: http://www.citeulike.com/.

44. Connatea. Available: http://www.connotea.org/.

45. Amazon.com. Available: http://www.amazon.com/.

46. Technorati. Available: http://www.technorati.com/.

47. Queens Library catalog. Available: http://aqua.queenslibrary.org/.

48. Ann Arbor District Library catalog. Available: http://www.aadl.org/catalog/.

49. California State University, Fresno, Henry Madden Library catalog. Available: http://www.csufresno.edu/library/.

50. Thomas Vander Wal, "Folksonomy Coinage and Definition." Available: http://vanderwal.net/folksonomy.html.

51. Thomas Gruber, "Ontology of Folksonomy: A Mash-Up of Apples and Oranges," *International Journal on Semantic Web and Information Systems* 3, no. 1 (2007): 3–4. Available: http://tomgruber.org/writing/ontology-of-folksonomy.htm.

SUGGESTED READINGS

Banerjee, Sujata, and Vibhu O. Mittal. "On the Use of Linguistic Ontologies for Accessing and Indexing Distributed Digital Libraries." In *Digital Libraries '94: Proceedings of the First Annual Conference on the Theory and Practice of Digital Libraries, June 19–21, 1994, College Station, Texas.* Available: http://www.hpl.hp.com/personal/Sujata_Banerjee/pubs.html.

Berman, Sanford. *Joy of Cataloging.* Phoenix, Ariz.: Oryx Press, 1981.

Chan, Lois Mai. *Library of Congress Subject Headings: Principles and Applications.* 4th ed. Westport, Conn.: Libraries Unlimited, 2006.

Cleveland, Donald B., and Ana D. Cleveland. *Introduction to Indexing and Abstracting.* 3rd ed. Englewood, Colo.: Libraries Unlimited, 2001. Chapter 8: "Indexing and Abstracting a Document" and Chapter 11: "Indexing Special Subject Areas and Formats."

"ERIC's Indexing and Retrieval: 2001 Update" and "Thesaurus Construction and Format." In *Thesaurus of ERIC Descriptors,* edited by James E. Houston. 14th ed. Phoenix, Ariz.: Oryx Press, 2001, pp. xiv–xxxi.

The Getty. "Art & Architecture Thesaurus Online: About the AAT." Available: http://www.getty.edu/research/conducting-research/vocabularies/aat/about.html.

Harris, Mary Dee. *Introduction to Natural Language Processing.* Reston, Va.: Reston, 1985.

Jacob, Elin K. "Ontologies and the Semantic Web." *Bulletin of the American Society for Information Science and Technology* 29, no. 4 (April/May 2003): 19–22. Available: http://www.asis.org/Bulletin/Apr-03/BulletinAprMay03.pdf.

Lancaster, F. W. *Indexing and Abstracting in Theory and Practice.* 3rd ed. Champaign: University of Illinois, Graduate School of Library and Information Science, 2003. Chapter 2: "Indexing Principles," Chapter 4: "Precoordinate Indexes," Chapter 5: "Consistency of Indexing," Chapter 6: "Quality of Indexing," Chapter 16: "Indexing and the Internet," and Chapter 17: "The Future of Indexing and Abstracting."

Mann, Thomas. *The Oxford Guide to Library Research.* New York: Oxford University Press, 2005. Chapter 4: "Subject Headings and Indexes to Journal Articles," and Chapter 5: "Keyword Searches."

Miller, Joseph, ed. *Sears List of Subject Headings.* 19th ed. New York: H. W. Wilson, 2007. "Principles of the Sears List of Subject Headings," pp. xv–xxix.

National Library of Medicine. "Fact Sheet: Medical Subject Headings (MeSH®)." Available: http://www.nlm.nih.gov/pubs/factsheets/mesh.html.

———. "Fact Sheet: UMLS® Metathesaurus®." Available: http://www.nlm.nih.gov/pubs/factsheets/umlsmeta.html.

———."Introduction to MeSH-2008." Available: http://www.nlm.nih.gov/mesh/introduction2008.html.

Noy, Natalya F., and Deborah L. McGuinness. *Ontology Development 101: A Guide to Creating Your First Ontology.* Knowledge Systems Laboratory, Stanford University, 2000. Available: http://www.ksl.stanford.edu/people/dlm/papers/ontology-tutorial-noy-mcguinness-abstract.html.

Olson, Hope A., and John J. Boll. *Subject Analysis in Online Catalogs.* 2nd ed. Englewood, Colo.: Libraries Unlimited, 2001.

Rich, Elaine, and Kevin Knight. *Artificial Intelligence.* 2nd ed. New York: McGraw-Hill, 1991.

Svenonius, Elaine. *The Intellectual Foundation of Information Organization.* Cambridge, Mass.: The MIT Press, 2000.

Taylor, Arlene G. *Introduction to Cataloging and Classification.* 10th ed., with the assistance of David P. Miller. Westport, Conn.: Libraries Unlimited, 2006. Chapter 10: "Verbal Subject Access," Chapter 11: "*Library of Congress Subject Headings* (LCSH)," Chapter 12: "*Sears List of Subject Headings (Sears),*" and Chapter 13: "Other Types of Verbal Access."

CHAPTER 11

SYSTEMS FOR CATEGORIZATION

Chapter 10 discusses methods of providing subject access using words or tags. Another type of subject access is provided through categories. Both approaches attempt to translate the aboutness of information resources into an artificial subject language and to bring together like items, but each approach does this in a different way. When using verbal techniques, topical words or tags are assigned to a resource; in systems for categorization, a resource is placed into the most suitable group available. These groupings, which may or may not be represented by notations or symbols, are often based on disciplines or broad forms of knowledge.

Categorization has a much longer history than that of controlled vocabularies. Philosophers have tried to categorize knowledge for many centuries. Classification is a form of categorization, but over the last two centuries, classification (particularly bibliographic classification) has come to be associated with assigning some kind of notation to physical information resources; this is reinforced by the tendency of many to confound the ideas of classification notations and call numbers. (Call numbers are not addressed in this chapter. For more information about call numbers, see Appendix B.) In the thinking of some, the connection to categorization has been lost. However, the categories devised by philosophers in past centuries are the bases for the major classification schemes still in use today.

Classification theory has not received as much attention in the United States as it has in other places around the world such as India, Great Britain, and some other European countries. There has been a tendency in the United States to see classification only as a location device for the arrangement of physical items upon a shelf (exemplified by the phrase, "mark 'em and park 'em"). Nevertheless, there is great potential for categorizing electronic resources. This chapter addresses this potential along with the following questions: What are categories, classifications, and taxonomies? How do humans categorize? How is subject content expressed symbolically in metadata records? What conflicts arise in the application of classification to information resources? What is the role of automatic classification in organizing information?

WHAT ARE CATEGORIES, CLASSIFICATIONS, AND TAXONOMIES?

The concepts *classification* and *categorization* are often used interchangeably, but are they the same? The answer is not clear. This question is further complicated by the recent resurgence of the term *taxonomy* for systems of categorization that are used on the Web and in intranet systems. Before moving on to various approaches to grouping similar items or ideas, it may be helpful to attempt to discuss and distinguish among the terms *categorization, classification,* and *taxonomy.*

According to the Oxford English Dictionary Online (OED), *categorization* is "to place in a category or categories; to classify." It defines *category* as "a term . . . given to certain general classes of terms, things, or notions; a class, or division, in any general scheme of classification." The OED states that *classification* is "the action of classifying or arranging in classes, according to common characteristics or affinities; a systematic distribution, allocation, or arrangement in a class or classes." It defines *class* as "a number of . . . things possessing common attributes, and grouped together under a general . . . name."[1] Merriam-Webster defines *classification* as the "systematic arrangement in groups or categories according to established criteria."[2] Ultimately, neither source helps to distinguish between the two concepts.

This lack of clarity is not confined only to dictionaries. The two words, *classification* and *categorization,* are sometimes used interchangeably in the literature. Some, however, are more rigorous in their use of the terms. Classification has specific connotations in libraries; thus, over the years some distinctions have been made. In general, categorization is considered to be broader and more abstract than classification, that is, categorization is a cognitive function that is used to group concepts, rather than a structured process used to systematically arrange physical items. Categorization can be seen as amorphous or less well-defined grouping; whereas classification can be viewed as a comprehensive hierarchical structure for organizing information resources on linear shelves. Elin Jacob points out that in the

LIS field the term *classification* can have several senses. It "is used to refer to three distinct but related concepts: a system of classes, ordered according to a predetermined set of principles and used to organize a set of entities; a group or class in a classification system; and the process of assigning entities to classes in a classification system."[3] Jacob also compares *categorization* and *classification:*

> Although systems of classification and categorization are both mechanisms for establishing order through the grouping of related phenomena, fundamental differences between them influence how that order is effected—differences that do make a difference in the information contexts established by each of these systems. While traditional classification is rigorous in that it mandates that an entity either is or is not a member of a particular class, the process of categorization is flexible and creative and draws nonbinding associations between entities—associations that are based not on a set of predetermined principles but on the simple recognition of similarities that exist across a set of entities.[4]

Commenting on a 1977 conference paper by P. A. Studer,[5] Christopher Dent also attempts to distinguish between the terms classification and categorization to countermand the lack of precision found in the LIS literature:

> In my view *classification* is an artificial (synthetic, non-fundamental) process by which we organize things for presentation or later access. It involves the arbitrary creation of a group of classes, which have explicit definitions and may be arranged in a hierarchy. In other words, a class is strictly defined and once inhabited the inhabitants can be enumerated. *Categorization,* on the other hand is a natural process in the sense that humans do it as part of their cognitive fundament. It is, like Studer reports, an act of simplification to make apprehension and comprehension of the environment more efficient. Categories spring up out of necessity and because they are designed to replace the details of definition are themselves resistant to definition.[6]

To put it more succinctly, he concludes, a class "is a defined grouping of entities in which the members fulfill the definition of the class and can be listed" and a category "is a cognitive label applied to a non-enumerable grouping of entities wherein membership is determined by typicality amongst the members and not some overarching definition."[7] While few are as precise as Dent or Jacob in differentiating between the two concepts, the authors feel these distinctions are helpful in understanding the discussions of categories and classes that follow.

Complicating this discussion is the renewed popularity of the term *taxonomy.* Definitions of taxonomy abound in the literature, and some of those definitions contradict each other. Amy Warner says that the terms *taxonomies, thesauri,* and *classification systems* are synonyms. They are "organized lists of words and phrases, or notation systems, that are used to initially tag content, and then to find it through navigation or search."[8] She states that definitions of these terms are currently in flux, and hopes that definitions will soon be standardized. Similar confusion is indicated in the *Montague Institute Review:*

> Taxonomies have recently emerged from the quiet backwaters of biology, book indexing, and library science into the corporate limelight. They are supposed to be the silver bullets that will help users find the needle in the intranet haystack, reduce "friction" in electronic commerce, facilitate scientific research, and promote global collaboration. But before this can happen, practitioners need to dispel the myths and confusion, created in part by the multi-disciplinary nature of the task and the hype surrounding content management technologies.[9]

The article continues by saying that the confusion begins with definitions and gives the following very broad definition: "A taxonomy is a system for naming and organizing things into groups that share similar characteristics."[10] These definitions do not include the necessity for hierarchy, but Thomas Wason says that, "A taxonomy is a controlled vocabulary of terms and or phrases...an orderly classification of information according to presumed natural relationships....The most typical form of a taxonomy is a hierarchy."[11] F. W. Lancaster, in decrying the "rediscovery of wheels" he sees in today's "new" concepts says:

> My biggest complaint, however, is the fact that the noun *classification* has virtually been replaced by (shudder!)

> *taxonomy,* (double shudder!!) *ontology,* or even (triple shudder!!!) *taxonomized set of terms.* The way these terms are defined in recent articles clearly shows that they are used synonymously with *classification scheme.*[12]

The word *taxonomy* comes from the Greek *taxis* (arrangement, order) and *nomos* (law). Taxonomies have existed in the strict, hierarchical world of science since Aristotle, in *Historia Animalium,* created a taxonomy of the animal kingdom. The most famous scientific taxonomy, however, is Linnaeus's *Systema Naturae,* a classification of plants and animals from 1735. The taxonomies being constructed today for use in intranets, though, do not necessarily follow such strict rules, nor are they always hierarchical. What they do seem to have in common is categories. Therefore, the discussions of categorization in this chapter are also applicable to taxonomies.

Lists of taxonomies that one finds on the Web often include traditional classification schemes, subject heading lists, folksonomies, ontologies, and Internet directories and gateways, as well as subject-specific tools that actually call themselves taxonomies. Examples of the last are the Taxonomy of Educational Technology[13] and GRIN Taxonomy[14] from the Germplasm Resources Information Network. A number of taxonomies are proprietary to the organizations that created them and are under copyright, so they may not be freely used in other situations.

THEORY OF CATEGORIZATION

It was mentioned in Chapter 1 that human beings seem to have a basic drive to organize and that children begin to categorize early in their development. For example, it is essential that children learn to distinguish between things that are and are not edible. At later stages, children begin to categorize toys and other objects by color, shape, purpose, or their own notions of value. Adults have a great need for categories, too. Categories abound in daily life—from the grocery store to the office to our homes. Most people, although they may not even realize it, categorize the various items found in their homes and offices every day; for example, few would place their forks and knives in the living room because eating utensils are associated with kitchen items—not with couches, bookcases, or photos of grandma.

Theories of categories go back at least as far as the ancient Greeks. For example, the ancient philosopher and mathematician Pythagoras categorized the cycle of life as consisting of birth, growth, decay, death, absorption, and metamorphosis. Later, Empedocles placed every physical thing into one of four elements: earth, air, fire, and water. The most influential discussion of categories comes from Aristotle and his attempt to organize the objects and ideas of the world.

The Rise and Fall of the Classical Theory of Categories

The roots of contemporary classification systems can be traced back to Aristotle's "classical theory of categories." The word *category* comes from the Greek *kategorein* meaning "to accuse, to assert, to predicate."[15] Aristotle's theory reflected this definition; his categories were 10 states of being or 10 things that can be expressed about an object or an idea. His categories include: Substance, Quantity, Quality, Relation, Place, Time, Position, State, Action, and Affection.[16] Aristotle's theory placed objects or ideas into the same category based on what they have in common. This approach went unchallenged until the mid-twentieth century because, as George Lakoff says, categories were thought to be well understood. Until then, a category was considered to be an abstract container with strict binary membership, that is, things belonged either inside or outside of the container; there were no grey or fuzzy areas. Categories were also defined as mutually exclusive groups, that is, things could belong to one and only one category, and the shared, common attributes of the group members were what defined the category.[17] This narrow view of categories, however, began to change about 60 years ago.

Cracks in the Classical Theory

A brief history of the research of the second half of the twentieth century will serve to illuminate the process of categorizing and its relationship to classification. This history is summarized from Lakoff's *Women, Fire, and Dangerous Things: What Categories Reveal about the Mind.*[18] Cracks began to appear in the classical theory of categories in 1953, when Ludwig Wittgenstein showed that a category like *game* does not fit the classical mold. This category has no single collection of common properties. For example, a game may be for education, amusement, or competition, and it may involve luck or skill. The category also has no fixed boundary, because new kinds of games such as video games and interactive computer games can be added to it. Wittgenstein proposed that since there is no one attribute that is common to all games, *family resemblances* (a complex network of similarities and relationships) unite games into what we call a category. Just as members of a family have similarities, so do games.

J. L. Austin, in a paper published in 1961, extended Wittgenstein's analysis to the study of words. He wondered why we call different things by the same name (e.g., foot of a mountain, foot of a list, person's foot). Should not *mountain, list,* and *person* be in the same category if they all have a foot? But there are times when words do belong in the same category even though they share no common properties (e.g., *ball, bat,* and *umpire* can all go into the category *baseball*). Austin, like Wittgenstein, helped to show that traditional views of categories were inadequate.

Lotfi Zadeh contributed *fuzzy set theory* to the chipping away of the classical theory of categories. He noted that some categories are well defined while others are not. One either is or is not a member of a club, but whether one is tall or not depends to some extent upon the observer. The category *tall* is graded—one may be neither clearly tall nor clearly short; and a short person, looking at someone of medium height, might say that the person is tall. In 1965, Zadeh devised a form of set theory to include gradations of membership in categories.

Floyd Lounsbury's studies of Native American kinship systems also chipped away at the classical theory. He found that among various groups, the same name (category) is used to express the kinship relationships of several different types of relatives. For example, in one group, uncles, great-uncles, and nephews on one's mother's side of the family are all called by the same word. (Perhaps they find it strange that in the dominant culture there are no verbal distinctions between maternal uncles, paternal uncles, or uncles by marriage.) The challenge to classical theory is that what seem to be definite and distinct categories in one culture and language are not the same categories in another culture and language.

Brent Berlin and Paul Kay (also mentioned in the preceding chapter) published their work on color in 1969. They found that there could be anywhere from 2 to 11 expressions for the basic colors in different languages. (In recent years, some have identified a twelfth basic color in various languages, but the color is not always the same!)[19] Although most people around the world can physiologically perceive and conceptually differentiate all of the 11 to 12 basic colors, depending on their language, they may not be able to express all of them as separate words. For example, in traditional Welsh, the word *glas* was used for blue, but also for some shades of green and grey. Again, it is shown that language and culture play a major role in the establishment of categories. Paul Kay and Chad McDaniel in 1978 described some follow-up research on colors. They drew on work that had been done in neurophysiology to conclude that human biology influences perception of color. They drew on fuzzy set theory to determine that in all cultures that have fewer than 11 basic colors, *cold* colors always include green, blue, and black, whereas *warm* colors always include red, orange, yellow, and white.

Thus, color categories are not quite as arbitrary as some might infer from the Berlin/Kay studies.

Roger Brown began the study of basic-level categories. His work published in 1965 observed that there is a first level at which children learn categories (e.g., *flower,* for any variety of flower). Yet, there are many names that can be used for such categories; some are more specific (e.g., *rose, daffodil*) and some more general (e.g., *plant*). Brown considered the children's level to be the "natural" level, whereas the more specific and general levels were viewed as "achievements of the imagination." Brent Berlin and associates, in research on naming plants and animals published from 1969 to 1977, also showed that there seems to be a universal level at which humans name things, and for plants and animals it is more likely to be at the genus level (e.g., *oak,* not *tree* and not *Sawtooth oak;* although this might not hold true for someone with experience only in an urban culture or for someone whose training has led to a more precisely honed level). It can be suggested that certain basic levels of categories have to do with being human and are the same across cultures.

Prototype Theory

The major crack in the classical theory of categories came when Eleanor Rosch developed *prototype theory* with her work between 1973 and 1981. She theorized that if, as classical theory states, categories are defined only by properties that all members share, then no members should be better examples of the category than any other members. She further theorized that if categories are defined only by properties that all members share, then categories should be independent of the humans doing the categorizing. She found that, contrary to classical theory, categories *do* have best examples (i.e., *prototypes*). For example, Rosch found in her research that people thought that *robin* was a better example of *bird* than was *ostrich.* And she found that human capacities *do* play a role in categorization (e.g., for someone 5 feet tall, there are many more tall people in the world than there are for someone 6 feet tall). This is related to Zadeh's *fuzzy set theory* mentioned earlier. *Ad hoc* categories also figure in here. Ad hoc categories are those that are made up on the spur of the moment. Different people will put different things into a category such as "camping gear" depending upon their experience, where they are going, how they will camp, and so forth.

Because the most widely used classification schemes in the United States are based upon the classical theory of categories, classifiers using them are sometimes quite frustrated to find that they have a subject concept that does not fit neatly into one of the categories. For example, multi-faceted, cross-disciplinary information resources cannot easily be accommodated by the structure and rigidity of classical categories. These classifiers are often relieved to learn that classical theory has major cracks; so it is not unusual to run into non-prototypes and fuzzy sets.

BIBLIOGRAPHIC CLASSIFICATION

Classification, as noted earlier, is a structured system of categories used to collocate similar ideas or objects. One particular type of classification is *bibliographic classification,* which came into being for the purpose of arranging and retrieving information resources, and later became used for arranging metadata records in library catalogs and other information retrieval tools. Bibliographic classification schemes (henceforth referred to as *classification schemes* or *classifications*) in the form that we know them are relatively new in the history of information organization. Early depositories of recorded information usually had some arrangement: title, broad subject, chronology, author, order of acquisition, or size. At the Alexandrian library, Callimachus's *Pinakes* had at least 10 broad categories (or main classes). Arrangement within the classes tended to be by author. This seemed to be a model for arrangement of catalogs and bibliographies into the Early Middle Ages.

During the High Middle Ages when monastery libraries became the keepers of books, there was little need for classification because libraries were so small. In the Late Middle Ages, the universities that developed began to divide their books according to the Trivium (Grammar, Rhetoric, Logic) and the Quadrivium (Arithmetic, Music, Geometry, Astronomy), the seven subjects taught in the medieval university. But within the seven classes, the books had fixed shelf locations.

Starting in the sixteenth century, librarians devised many different classification schemes. Often these were based upon philosophers' systems of knowledge. However, none caught on, and fixed locations continued to predominate. With the rapid growth of libraries in the nineteenth century, librarians felt a need for better arrangement so that the content of the collections would be more apparent to users. Philosopher Francis Bacon in the early seventeenth century had divided knowledge into three basic "faculties": history (natural, civil, literary, ecclesiastical); philosophy (including theology); and works of imagination (poetry, fables, etc.). This scheme had widespread influence, and numerous classification schemes were based upon it. The most famous was that of Thomas Jefferson, who classified his own library before he eventually sold it to the Library of Congress as the basis of a new collection in 1815.

Some history of the development of specific classification schemes in the nineteenth and twentieth centuries is discussed in Chapter 3 and need not be repeated in full here. Very briefly, in 1876 Melvil Dewey published his *Dewey Decimal Classification* (DDC), and shortly thereafter, Charles Cutter began work on his *Expansive Classification* (EC). Otlet and LaFontaine began development of the *Universal Decimal Classification* (UDC) in 1895, based on the fifth edition of DDC. At the beginning of the twentieth century, the Library of Congress created its own classification (LCC), based loosely on the main class outline of Cutter's *Expansive Classification*. S. R. Ranganathan created his *Colon Classification* (CC) in the early 1930s and adapted the word *facet* as a term to indicate the various subparts of the whole classification.

While classification is mostly associated with arranging tangible items on shelves, it is also a useful way to divide large databases. It offers an alternative to alphabetical subdivision. And if several databases choose the same classification scheme, it is possible to enable subject searching across systems. Classification can also be used as a switching language among different languages. The notations of a classification are not language specific, and therefore the meanings of the notations can be given in whatever language is appropriate for the setting. For the DDC, for example, translations into a number of languages either already exist or are being worked on, including: Arabic, French, Greek, Hebrew, Italian, Persian, Russian, and Spanish. The UDC is also multilingual; there are full editions in English, French, German, Japanese, Russian, and eight other languages. The LCC has not yet moved in a multilingual direction.

Hierarchical, Enumerative, and Faceted Classifications

As all of the schemes mentioned above were devised before anyone challenged the classical theory of categories, these schemes are firmly based in *hierarchical* arrangements (even the faceted *Colon Classification* is hierarchical at its top level and within its individual sub-categories). Hierarchical schemes begin with broad, top-level categories, which branch into any number of subordinate levels, moving from the general to the specific (creating the familiar tree structure associated with hierarchies). For example, DDC starts with 10 main classes, divides each of those into 10 divisions (creating 100 divisions), divides each of the divisions into 10 sections (1,000 sections), divides each of those into 10 subsections (10,000), and so on into potential infinity (see Figure 11.1).

The same classification schemes are also *enumerative*. Enumerative schemes attempt to assign a designation for every subject concept (both single and composite) needed in the system. All schemes have elements that are enumerative, but some have much more than others. LCC is much more enumerative than DDC (see Figure 11.2) because it attempts to list a notation for every possible topic (or to allow for alphabetical arrangement of unlisted

DEWEY DECIMAL CLASSIFICATION
22nd edition

The Ten Main Classes

000	Computer science, information & general works
100	Philosophy & psychology
200	Religion
300	Social sciences
400	Language
500	Science
600	Technology
700	Arts & recreation
800	Literature
900	History & geography

The Hundred Divisions

. . .

600	**Technology**
600	Technology
610	Medicine & health
620	Engineering
630	Agriculture
640	Home & family management
650	Management & public relations
660	Chemical engineering
670	Manufacturing
680	Manufacture for specific uses
690	Building & construction

. . .

Detailed hierarchy for 646.724

600	Technology
640	Home & family management
646	Sewing, clothing, management of personal and family life
646.7	Management of personal and family life
646.72	Care of hair, face, skin, nails
646.724	**Care of hair** Including care of beard, shaving; dyeing, hairweaving, permanent waving, relaxing Class here barbering, haircutting, hairdressing hairstyling
646.7247	Braiding

Figure 11.1. Illustration of hierarchical arrangement in the *Dewey Decimal Classification* (DDC). (Source: WebDewey through OCLC Connexion.)

LIBRARY OF CONGRESS CLASSIFICATION

A – General Works
B – Philosophy. Psychology. Religion
C – Auxiliary Sciences of History
D – History: General and Old World
E – History: America
F – History: America
. . .
S – Agriculture
T – Technology

TT1-999	Handicrafts. Arts and crafts
	Including mechanic trades

TT950-979	Hairdressing, barbering, beauty culture, cosmetology, etc.
	Including beauty shop practice
TT950	Periodicals, societies, collections, etc.
TT951	Dictionaries and encyclopedias
	Documents
	United States
TT952	General works
TT953.A-.W	States, A-W
TT954.A-Z	Other Countries, A-Z
	. . .
TT960	Barbers' manuals
TT963	Hair styles for men
TT964	Shaving
	. . .
TT970	Haircutting (General)
	Cf. TT960 Barber's manuals
TT971	Study and teaching
	Hairdressing for women
TT972	General works
TT973	Hair tinting and bleaching
	Hairwork
TT975	Braids, wigs, toupees, etc.
TT976	Ornaments, jewelry, etc.
TT977	Recipes for barbers (for hair preparations)
TT979	Catalogs of equipment and supplies

Figure 11.2. Illustration of the hierarchical and enumerative arrangement of the *Library of Congress Classification* (LCC). (Source: Classification Web: http://classweb.loc.gov/by subscription.)

topics), whereas DDC lists some basic numbers, but allows for more complex numbers to be constructed through the use of tables. UDC, originally based on DDC, was hierarchical and enumerative at its base when it was designed; it has now developed into a scheme that is somewhat closer to what is called a *faceted* scheme through the addition of number-building techniques.

Faceted classification, like hierarchical/enumerative schemes, attempts to include all possible subjects, but it does not do this by creating a singular place in a hierarchy for each topic (with its own specified number). Faceted classification is made up of many discrete topics. It is an attempt to divide the universe of knowledge into its component parts, and then to gather those parts into individual categories or facets. Within each facet, the topics are assigned an individual notation. When the cataloger assigns a classification notation to an information resource, the notations assigned to each subtopic in the resource are identified and then strung together, in the appropriate order, to create a multi-dimensional classification. If one thinks of each of the faces of a cut and polished diamond as a facet of the whole, one can picture a classification notation that has small notations standing for subparts of the whole topic, which are pieced together to create a complete classification notation. This concept of faceted classification was named first by Ranganathan in his explanation of his *Colon Classification.* CC provides lists of symbols for single concepts, with rules for combining them into complex concepts. This approach is also referred to as *analytico-synthetic* classification, because the classification is established through an analysis of topics into component parts and then notation is synthesized from those parts.

Ranganathan posited five fundamental categories that can be used to illustrate the facets of a subject. They are:

- **Personality (P)**—the focal or most specific subject;
- **Material** or **Matter (M)**—a component;
- **Energy (E)**—an activity, operation, or process;
- **Space (S)**—a specific or generic place or location; and
- **Time (T)**—a chronological period, a year, a season, etc.

Using the first letters of the five words, this is often referred to as the PMEST formula. For example, "the design of wooden furniture in eighteenth-century America" has all five facets. Furniture is the focal subject, or personality; wood is the material facet; design is an activity and so constitutes the energy facet; the space is America; and the time is the eighteenth century. If each facet has a specific notation (e.g., let's say P28 for furniture, M16 for wood, etc.), then these notations can be strung together according to the rules of the system.

Both CC and UDC use punctuation marks and symbols between the notations as *facet indicators*. These help to identify the relationships among the facets. In the earliest versions of the scheme, CC used the colon (:) in significant positions; thus the name of the scheme. By the middle of the twentieth century, Ranganathan realized that a more elaborate system of facet indicators was needed to avoid confusion, and additional pieces of punctuation were adopted for this purpose. The typically long and complex notations created in faceted schemes are not easy to use for arranging physical information resources on shelves. However, in online retrieval systems they have the potential to be quite helpful, as each facet may be searched independently.

LCC has limited faceting capabilities. There are tables of geographic areas in some schedules, for example, that can be used to build notations that show place. Many of the table numbers, however, are literally mathematically added to a number in the schedule; the resulting notation does not show the geographic area as a separate facet. Only the geographic area notations that are "cutter numbers," consisting of the first letter of the geographic area name and one or more numerical digits, are recognizable as facets.

DDC has many faceting capabilities and gains more with each new edition. There are currently six tables that can be used at various places in the classification. The notations from the tables are appended to the end of the notation from the schedules so that the facet is intact. In some cases, the end of the schedule notation and the beginning of the table notation are not demarcated; but most of the time the table notation is preceded by the digit 0 or 1. For information about DDC and LCC *call numbers* (combinations of classification notations and cutter numbers [i.e., specific notations that represent the primary access point]), see Appendix B.

Major Bibliographic Classification Schemes

The major bibliographic classification schemes (i.e., DDC, LCC, UDC) have certain components in common. These have been outlined by Hope Olson and John Boll as follows:

- A verbal description, topic by topic, of the things and concepts that can be represented in or by the scheme.
- An arrangement of these verbal descriptions in classed or logical order that is intended to permit a meaningful arrangement of topics and that will be convenient to users.
- A notation that appears alongside each verbal description, which is used to represent it and which shows

the order. The entire group of verbal descriptions and notations form the schedules.

- References within the schedules to guide the classifier and the searcher in different aspects of a desired topic or to other related topics (like the related term references in alphabetical lists).
- An alphabetical index of terms used in the schedules, and of synonyms of those terms, that leads to the notations.
- Instructions for use. General instructions (with examples) are usually to be found at the beginning of the scheme, and instructions relating to particular parts of the schedules are, or should be, given in the parts to which they relate.
- An organization that will ensure that the classification scheme is maintained, that is, revised and republished. This is external to the scheme, but an important factor in evaluating its comparative usefulness.[20]

In addition to the schedules mentioned in the third point above, the schemes include tables, which are independent listings of notations for concepts that can be appended or added to the notations from the schedules. The tables comprise listings of such concepts as form/genre, geographic area, chronological periods, and language. In addition to the instructions in the schemes themselves, these major bibliographic classifications have separate manuals that give further instructions and examples. Manuals can be written by the organizations responsible for the maintenance of the schemes, by independent parties, or by both.

Traugott Koch has suggested that there are four broad varieties of classification schemes:

- **Universal schemes**—examples include the Dewey Decimal Classification (DDC), the Universal Decimal Classification (UDC), and the Library of Congress Classification (LCC);
- **National general schemes**—universal in subject coverage but usually designed for use in a single country. Examples include the Nederlandse Basisclassificatie (BC) and the Sveriges Allmäma Biblioteksförening (SAB);

- **Subject specific schemes**—designed for use by a particular subject community. Examples include Iconclass for art resources and the National Library of Medicine (NLM) scheme for medicine and Engineering Information (Ei) for engineering subjects;
- **Home-grown schemes**—schemes devised for use in a particular service. An example from the Internet is the "ontology" developed for the Yahoo! search service.[21]

At Koch's Web site there is a description of each of the major schemes he mentions. Koch also has created a useful list of many classification systems, as well as controlled vocabularies, available on the Web.[22] In addition, there are a number of homegrown schemes in print that are interesting and useful in particular contexts. One example is *A Classification System for Libraries of Judaica,* now in its third edition.[23] It is kept up-to-date by people who use it. For example, after the publication of the third edition, a synagogue librarian created a Holocaust expansion that is posted on the home page of the authors of the third edition.[24]

Many classifications have not been mentioned in this chapter, as we have focused only on the major bibliographic classification schemes. More has been written about each of the classifications mentioned, as well as others not mentioned. Suggestions for further reading about various classification schemes (and, in some cases, manuals for applying them) are found at the end of this chapter.

CLASSIFICATION CONCEPTS

A number of classification concepts and issues affect the use of classification schemes. Some of these apply to the schemes regardless of how they are going to be used (e.g., as a way of arranging physical information resources; as a way of identifying subject content in metadata; as a way of organizing and/or presenting virtual information resources; etc.). Others are issues particularly in the use of classification as a device for arranging physical items. The following sections are arranged from general to specific.

Broad vs. Close Classification

Broad classification is classification that uses only the main classes and divisions of a scheme and perhaps only one or two levels of subdivisions. *Close classification* is classification that uses all the minute subdivisions that are available for very specific subjects. This is somewhat like the specific versus general issue in controlled vocabularies. When beginning to use a classification scheme it is necessary to decide whether to use only the top levels of the scheme or whether to use the scheme at the deepest level possible (or something in between).

One issue here is that if the intent of using the scheme is to collocate topics, then broad versus close may depend upon the size of the collection that is being classified. If the collection is very large, then using only the top levels of the scheme means that very large numbers of information resources, or the surrogate records for them, will be collocated at the same notation. On the other hand, if the collection is very small, then using close classification may mean that most notations are assigned to only one or two resources, with the result that collocation is minimal (unless one is using a scheme like DDC where one can drop digits off the end of the notation to get to the next broader level of the concept being sought).

It should be noted that what is considered close classification for a small collection may be broad classification for a large collection. That is, for a small collection, DDC's 612.1, meaning the concept of *blood and circulation* in medicine, is a very specific level; but in a medical collection there may be a thousand or more information resources on blood and circulation, and for that collection, close classification would mean going to, for example 612.112 *white corpuscles.*

Another issue has to do with the globalization of information organization. Even if a collection in a particular place is small, its metadata may be combined with that of many collections, producing a mega-collection. If some of the metadata has been created using close classification, and some has been created using broad classification, the combined effect will be confusing and less helpful. It may be necessary in today's world to use the closest classification available in the scheme being used. This is problematic in some institutions where the classification is used for arranging physical items. Close classification often produces very long notations, which sometimes have to be placed on very small items. Michael Gorman has suggested that this problem be solved by using shorter notations for *call numbers* but using close classification for the purposes of intellectual retrieval.[25] (See discussion of call numbers in Appendix B.) This, of course, is objected to in many quarters because of the extra cost of providing two notations; but there is a cost to the user who is trying to retrieve information when classification is not usable for collocating topics.

Classification of Knowledge vs. Classification of a Particular Collection

Classification of knowledge is the concept that a classification system can be created that will encompass all knowledge that exists. DDC began as a classification of knowledge (at least Western knowledge as understood by Melvil Dewey). Classification of a particular collection is the concept that a classification system should only be devised for the information resources that are being added to collections, using the concept of *literary warrant.* Literary warrant is the name applied to the concept that new notations are created for a classification scheme and new terms are added to a controlled vocabulary only when information resources actually exist that are about a new concept. (See also comments on literary warrant in Chapter 10.) LCC began as a classification of a particular collection.

Even though DDC began as a classification of knowledge, it has been forced to use literary warrant for updates and revisions. Some areas of knowledge that have developed in the twentieth century need significantly more space in the scheme than originally given, if indeed they existed and were given any at all (e.g., computer science). Dewey devoted a whole division to the artificial waterways called *canals,* but the concept has been moved to allow expansion of other areas such as engineering; canals are no longer being given the attention they were given in Dewey's day. And this is one value of the approach taken by LCC. The alphabet has 26 letters. In most places in LCC letters are doubled, and in the last revisions letters have been tripled, giving the potential for up to 1,352 divisions versus the 100 available to DDC. LCC has not come close to using this amount of space.

It can be seen that if a scheme has been devised using literary warrant, it can be more flexible than one devised on the basis of classification of knowledge. This issue may come down to preference as to the logical approach of a classification of knowledge versus the practical approach of a classification of what is being studied, created, or written about at the present time.

Integrity of Numbers vs. Keeping Pace with Knowledge

Integrity of numbers is the concept that in the creation and maintenance of a classification scheme, a notation, once assigned, should always retain the same meaning and should never be used with another meaning. *Keeping pace with knowledge* is the concept that in the creation and maintenance of a classification scheme, it is recognized that knowledge changes, and therefore it is necessary to be able to move concepts, insert new concepts, and to change meanings of numbers.

Melvil Dewey was a strong advocate of the integrity of numbers. He did not want the users of his system ever to have to change a number on an item because the number's meaning had been changed in the classification. He wanted new concepts to be assigned to new numbers. As the twentieth century went forward, however, it became impossible to keep pace with new knowledge without sometimes changing the older notations. For example, in the field of mathematics the understanding of the field changed with new research. So it became necessary to change Dewey's arrangement of the basic sections of mathematics, with the following result:

DDC 1st edition	*DDC 22nd edition*
510 Mathematics	510 Mathematics
511 Arithmetic	511 General principles of mathematics
512 Algebra	512 Algebra
513 Geometry	513 Arithmetic
514 Trigonometry	514 Topology
515 Conic sections	515 Analysis
516 Analytical geometry	516 Geometry
517 Calculus	517 [Unassigned]
518 Quaternions	518 Numerical analysis [formerly 515]
519 Probabilities	519 Probabilities and applied mathematics

Such changing of meanings of numbers always involves soul searching on the part of classifiers. As cost is an ever-present issue, there is a desire not to have to change notations because this can be expensive. On the other hand, if changes are not made, then the digits 513 would mean both *geometry* and *arithmetic,* and consequently, collocation would be compromised. In such a scenario, both searching for classification in the catalog and browsing the shelves could confuse the user. On the other hand, it has been argued that leaving the older materials in the older numbers accurately reflects their contents, while newer materials reflect the new thinking that prompted the change in the scheme. This only works if the different schemes are kept separate both in arranging and in searching.

At the level of the classification scheme itself, notation and structural changes also involve soul searching on the part of those designing and maintaining the classification. They worry about the impact of changes on those applying the system, but they must update the classification periodically, or it will become irrelevant and out of date, and consequently the scheme will not continue to serve its purpose. If it is flexible enough, updates can be accomplished by inserting new notations. LCC, for example, accomplishes most of its updating in this fashion. If the scheme is less flexible, as with DDC, some inserting can be done, but sometimes the meanings of numbers must also be changed.

It was mentioned earlier that some classification issues are general, but others are issues for the use of classification for arranging physical items. *Integrity of numbers* versus *keeping pace with knowledge* is an issue that has both general and physical implications and gives us a transition into the issues regarding physical entities. In this case, reclassification of physical items when meanings of numbers have been changed is an expensive process. In most collections complete reclassification is not done. Instead there often is some kind of process set up to reclassify items as they are used. Items needing reclassification are taken care of as they are returned after the first use after a number's meaning has changed. Or sometimes, all of the items affected by a change of numbers in a whole section of the scheme are reclassified on a project basis. Changing only some of a collection, of course, ignores the use of classification as a search key in an online system. Searching a system where certain notations bring up surrogate records for information resources on different subjects is not satisfactory.

Fixed vs. Relative Location

The term *fixed location* signifies a set place where a physical information resource will always be found or to which it will be returned after having been removed for use. A fixed location identifier can be an accession number; or a designation made up of room number, stack number, shelf number, position on shelf; or other such designations. The term *relative location* is used to mean that an information resource will be or might be in a different place each time it is reshelved; that is, it is reshelved relative to what else has been acquired, taken out, returned, and so forth, while it was out for use. The method for accomplishing this is usually a *call number* with the top line or two being a classification notation. (See discussion of call numbers in Appendix B.)

Fixed location is often used for the purpose of saving space. If fixed location is used, space does not have to be left at the end of each shelf for potential new acquisitions in a particular area of the classification. This is particularly useful for remote storage facilities where space must be saved. Relative location, however, is desirable in a situation where users have access to the stacks and can browse (see discussion of closed versus open stacks below). It is often argued that the cost of fixed location is much less than that of relative location. If classification notations do not have to be assigned, and if space can be used to the fullest, then cost of fixed location is less to the agency involved. However, especially in libraries, the cost is passed on to the user who loses the collocation provided by classification and the serendipity of being able to browse in the stacks.

Closed vs. Open Stacks

Closed stacks is the name given to the situation where information resource storage areas are accessible only to the staff of the library, archives, or other place that houses information resources. *Open stacks* is the name given to the opposite situation where patrons of the facility have the right to go into the storage areas themselves. In closed stack situations users must call for items at a desk and then wait for them to be retrieved and delivered. This eliminates any possibility of what is called *browsing* in the stacks. Browsing is a process of looking, usually based on subject, at all the items in a particular area of the stacks, or in a listing in an online retrieval tool, in order to find, often by serendipity, the items that best suit the needs of those browsing. In a closed stacks situation one can browse only in the catalog—not always an easy process, depending upon the system design.

In cases where remote storage is used for older and less-used materials, compact shelving is often used. This means that in order to make the most efficient use of space, items are shelved using every inch of shelf space, usually with fixed locations. In such situations the storage areas are closed. A number of large research libraries have had closed stacks for a long time. There are various reasons for this, including tradition, vandalism, and precedence of certain classes of users over others. In such libraries, a proposal to stop classifying resurfaces every so often. The question asked is, "Why classify if readers cannot browse?" Such a proposal includes data about how costs will be lowered if classification is stopped. However, classification is a major form of subject access, and if browsing of the stacks is not allowed, then browsing of the classification listing in the catalog becomes even more important. Reference librarians often use classification to assist users in finding subject-related material.[26]

In archives, the storage areas are almost always closed. This hardly matters as far as classification goes because classification has not been found to be particularly useful for archives in any case. A collection of records can have individual pieces that are on diverse subjects, and dividing and separating these out to classify would violate the principle of *respect des fonds*. It is conceivable that whole collections could be classified, but usually the classification in such a case would be so broad as to be nearly meaningless.

Location Device vs. Collocation Device

Another controversy surrounding classification is that of whether classification serves as a collocation device or whether it is simply a location device. A *location device* is a number or other designation on an item to tell where it is located physically. It can be, among other designators, an accession number, a physical location number, or a call number. A *collocation device* is a number or other designation on an item used to place it next to (i.e., collocate with) other items that are like it. It is usually a classification notation.

Those responsible for the costs of organizing collections tend to take the location device view. They believe that any call number is fine as long as the notation placed on the physical item matches the notation in the surrogate record for the item. The argument is that if the notations on item and record match, the user will be able to find the item. However, this assumes that the subject headings are sufficient for finding subject-related material in a catalog. Thomas Mann, cited above, and others have shown that both subject headings and classification are required for the most effective retrieval of subject-related material.[27]

It is not clear whether the same notation is adequate to serve both the collocation and the location functions. Gorman, as mentioned above, has suggested that a fully detailed classification be assigned for the purpose of collocation, while a shortened version of it be used for a location device.[28] (This would not really be helpful in the case of LCC, because most notations, even for complex subjects, are relatively short.) In most of the United States, one classification notation has served for both collocation and location for many decades. In some other places, especially where classified catalogs are used, the functions of collocation and location have been served by different notations for decades.

A recent point for discussion has been the classification of Internet resources. Cost managers often believe that classification is mainly for location, and because Internet resources have location devices in the form of URLs, no classification is needed. However, from the viewpoint of the user, classification can be an effective means of organizing Internet information resources for subject retrieval (see discussion below).

Classification of Serials vs. Alphabetical Order of Serials

Serials are sometimes called *journals* or *magazines.* A *serial* may be defined as a publication issued in successive parts (regularly or irregularly) that is intended to continue indefinitely. Classification of serials means that a classification notation is assigned to a serial, and this classification notation is placed on each bound volume and/or each issue of that serial. Alphabetical order of serials means that the serials are placed in order on shelves or in a listing according to the alphabetical order of the titles of the serials. The concerns involved in the classification/alphabetical order dilemma apply to runs of printed serials. Serials now produced only on the Internet bring us questions and problems, but classification is not yet one of these.

With serials it is sometimes quite difficult to discern the intended title because of its placement (e.g., following a corporate body name that is in larger type than the title). In addition, serials are apt to change titles, sometimes several times. They also can merge or split, and can be absorbed by another serial, all of which result in title changes. This is one of the most persuasive arguments against alphabetical order of serials. What to do with runs of serials when there has been a title change is not a resolved issue. Some institutions move the whole run and place at the alphabetical position of the old title(s) a "dummy block" that gives the new title. It is argued in this situation that users will expect to find all of that serial together in spite of the title change. Other institutions divide the serial at the point of the new title. It is argued here that when a title changes, it does so because of a change of emphasis in the serial; therefore, the two runs are almost like two different serials.

Classification of serials provides a solution to the title change dilemma. The new title can be given the same classification as the old. It also has the advantage of allowing the serial to be placed with monographs on the same subject; this is beneficial for browsing purposes. However, classification requires two look-ups. That is, a user comes to the collection with a citation to an article in a journal. If the serial collection is classified, the user must look for the journal title in the catalog, note its call number, and then go to the stacks to find that call number. If serials are placed alphabetically, the user goes to the serials stacks with the citation and finds the journal title. Classification also requires more cataloging/indexing time and thus seems to cost more, although the maintenance of title changes in an alphabetically arranged situation may offset some of the cost that would be incurred by classifying.

One other consideration is the arrangement of serials in a special library. Many such libraries are subject area specific. In some of these situations, most of the serials are on the same or closely related subjects, which could mean that their classification notations would be very near each other, resulting in a semi-alphabetical order. Such libraries often choose alphabetical arrangement in the first place. The actual arrangement of serials in all libraries in the United States is about 50 percent alphabetical and 50 percent classified.

Classification of Monographic Series (Classified Separately vs. Classified as a Set)

A *monograph* is a complete bibliographic unit or information resource. It is often a single work, but may also be one work or more than one work issued in successive parts; but unlike a serial, it is not intended to be continued indefinitely. A work intended to be complete in, let's say,

28 volumes, is a monograph. A *monographic series* is a hybrid of monograph and serial. In a monographic series each work that is issued as a part of the series is a monograph, but is identified as one work in the series. The series itself may or may not be intended to be continued indefinitely. For example, the *Library and Information Science Text Series* published by Libraries Unlimited, continues to have new works added to it as appropriate works are identified by the publisher.

The difficulty with classification of monographic series is whether to classify each work in the series separately with a specific notation representing its particular subject matter, or to treat the series as if it were a multivolume monograph and give all parts of the series the same (usually broad) classification notation representing the subject matter of the entire series. Classification of the series as a set results in the loss of collocation of the specific subjects contained in each of the works.

On the other hand, especially in public libraries, classification of the series as a set may meet with resounding approval by the users. There are readers who wish to go through a series one by one and find it satisfactory to have them classified together. It is obviously the intention of some publishers that some series be shelved together, especially those series that are bound alike. In some cases the situation is handled by acquiring duplicates, and then classifying one with the set and the other in its specific subject area. The cost of doing this usually is not supported, however, and sometimes cost is the deciding factor for classifying a series as a set; it is cheaper to slap on an already-conceived classification notation than to do the subject analysis necessary for specific classification.

SYSTEMS FOR CATEGORIZATION AND THE INTERNET

Despite improvements in recent years, not everyone is satisfied by the quality of search engines. Some dissatisfaction is related to the inability of search engines to search for concepts rather than for character strings; some is related to information overload; and some is related to less-than-obvious relevance ranking. Whether the issue is that search engines are inadequate in successfully locating scholarly information,[29] that search engines cannot distinguish between homographs or recognize synonyms,[30] or that search engines "inundate users with irrelevant results,"[31] many users and information professionals agree that there is substantial room for improvement. One suggestion for improvement has been the possible use of categories or classification to improve the retrieval and display of Internet resources.

Although classification has an obvious role in organizing tangible resources, the role that classification can play in organizing Internet resources is less well understood. In some subject gateways and directories, hierarchical or faceted classifications have been used without classification notation (this may be better understood, if referred to as *categorization*). In some directories, actual classification schemes (with notation) have been used to organize Internet resources. Another approach used is document clustering. *Clustering* is an automated sorting technique used by a few search engines to group similar results together based on content (and a variety of other factors), which can then be used to display the search results. All three of these techniques are attempts to address some dissatisfaction with Internet search engines.

Categories and Taxonomies on the Web

Categorization or taxonomy (the terminology seems to depend upon the site) is readily apparent on the Web. On a commercial site like Amazon.com,[32] the taxonomy is found directly on the homepage. An information architect created this taxonomy to provide shoppers with a quick, user-friendly set of links to the main Amazon divisions in order to improve navigation and the overall experience of the site, as well as the ability to find and purchase merchandise quickly and efficiently; the following main headings/categories are provided:

- Books
- Movies, Music & Games
- Digital Downloads
- Electronics & Computers
- Home & Garden
- Grocery
- Toys, Kids & Baby
- Apparel, Shoes & Jewelry
- Health & Beauty
- Sports & Outdoors
- Tools, Auto & Industrial

The second level of hierarchy contains a more extensive set of headings. Taking *Books* as an example, the second level includes: Best Books, Popular Features, and a long list of topics, forms, and genres such as Arts & Photography, Audiobooks, Biographies & Memoirs, Business & Investing, Children's Books, and so on. Although an Amazon-specific search engine is also provided, the taxonomy offers users, who may not know what they want, an option to browse (or "window shop"). The difficulty with the taxonomy at some commercial sites is the overwhelming size of the overall collection (i.e., the inventory), and the shallowness of the hierarchies employed. Even at the deepest, most specific levels of the taxonomy, there still may be too many resources to browse and the user still may need to conduct a keyword search.

Taxonomies also are used by non-commercial sites, such as the Fairfax County (Virginia) government's "Human Services Resource Guide"[33] and the National Center for Biotechnology Information's Entrez database.[34] But, perhaps, the most well-known example of using categorization on the Internet is the Yahoo! directory,[35] where Web sites are placed into categories created by Yahoo! indexers, and the categories can be browsed in hierarchical fashion. However, the hierarchies are not true hierarchies in the sense that they represent actual genus/species relationships. In other words, the categories at the second hierarchical level are not necessarily a type or kind of the broader concept at the first level, nor are the subcategories at the second level necessarily at equivalent levels of specificity with each other. For example, under *Recreation & Sports* one finds the following subcategories:

- Automotive
- Aviation
- Chats and Forums
- Events
- Gambling
- Games
- Hobbies
- Jobs and Employment
- [and so on]

These are interfiled with references for:

- Amusement and Theme Parks (categorized under *Entertainment*)

- Booksellers (categorized under Business and Economy > Shopping and Services > Books > Bookstores)
- Cooking (categorized under Society and Culture > Food and Drink)
- Dance (categorized under Arts > Performing Arts)
- Fitness (categorized under *Health*)
- [and so on]

In comparing the terms in the list, one can see that *Automotive* and *Aviation* might be seen as kinds of *Recreation,* but *Chats and Forums* and *Events* are about recreation, and *Jobs and Employment* identifies opportunities in the recreation and leisure field. Under *Automotive,* there is a top category of *Makes and Models,* followed by a group called *Additional Categories:*

- Accessories
- Alternative fuel vehicles
- British cars
- Buyer's Guides
- Charitable Vehicle Donation
- Chats and Forums
- Classic Cars
- Clubs and Organizations
- [and so on]

These are interfiled with references for:

- Auto-free Transportation (categorized under *Recreation > Travel > Transportation*)
- Booksellers (categorized under Business and Economy > Shopping and Services > Books > Bookstores)
- Buses (categorized under Recreation > Travel > Transportation)
- Business to Business (categorized under Business and Economy)

- Car Art (categorized under Arts: Visual Arts)
- Classifieds (categorized under Business and Economy > Shopping and Services > Automotive)
- [and so on]

The category *Accessories* is not at the same level of specificity as *British cars* or *Classic Cars. Buyer's Guides, Chats and Forums,* and *Clubs and Organizations* are not kinds of *Automotive;* they are entities that concern themselves with the topic. The references for *Auto-free Transportation* and *Classifieds* appear to have strayed somewhat from the broader concept of *Recreation,* just one level above.

Some see it as unfortunate that Yahoo! chose not to take advantage of an already-existing classification or at least use basic principles of classification to structure their site. The subcategories under each level of the hierarchy cannot all be viewed on a single screen, and as more categories are added and the lists grow longer, users are more and more dependent upon the words chosen to represent the categories. Thus, all of the problems associated with keywords need to be addressed. An already-existing classification has several advantages: it provides consistent levels in a hierarchy; it is kept up-to-date through consultation with many users; and it may be well known to many users. On the other hand, as the popularity of directories has waned, few users are clamoring for new Internet gateways, let alone ones organized by DDC or LCC.

Classification on the Internet

Classifying Web sites could assist with browsing Internet resources and with narrowing or broadening subject searches. It could also provide context for individual search results that could possibly appear in more than one field of knowledge or discipline. For example, the concept *children* can be in relation to psychology, religion, education, language, medicine, art, parenting, and so forth. Classification could show which context applies to the returned results. In addition, on the Internet, an information resource can be placed into as many categories as are appropriate. If a work discusses *children* in relation to both education and art, it can be placed in both categories. What one would have, then, is essentially a classified catalog in electronic form.

Around the turn of the twenty-first century, several portals or subject gateways on the Internet used a classification scheme for organization. In response, Gerry McKiernan created a list of known sites that used classification schemes or subject headings to organize resources. His list, a site called *Beyond Bookmarks,*[36] unfortunately is out-of-date (not having been updated since 2001), and no known successor has appeared. There are few examples of current Web sites that use some form of bibliographic classification to organize their resources. CyberDewey[37] (which obviously uses the DDC to organize its resources) was one of the first, and it is still a good structural example, but its content has not been updated recently, so it contains many broken links and out-of-date references. A more current example is the Web site for the Queensland, Australia, Department of Education, Training, and the Arts, which allows users to browse public government documents and links to other Web sites by using broad Dewey Decimal class numbers.[38] Another is E-Ref, from Bloomsburg University's Harvey A. Andruss Library, which uses LCC to organize a small collection of online reference works.[39] On the site, the classification is divided into broad letter and number ranges. For example:

P: Communication, Language (General)
PA-PD: Greek, Latin, Celtic, & Romanic Languages
PE1—PE1599: English Language Etymology, Grammar, Thesauri
PE1600—PE9999: English Language Abbreviations & Acronyms, Collective Nouns, Dictionaries
PF-PM: German, Eastern European, & Asian Languages
PN: Journalism, Literature, Performing Arts
PQ-PZ: National literatures: American, British

On the **P** Web page, the following metadata record is found:

Title: Omniglot[40]
Provider: Omniglot
Subject Heading/s: Writing.
LC Class: P211
Reference Category: Guides
Description: "This website provides a guide to over 200 different alphabets, syllabaries and other writing systems, including a few you will find nowhere else. It also contains details of many of the languages written with those writing systems and links to a wide range of language-related resources, such as fonts, online dictionaries and online language courses."[41]

In order to provide multi-faceted subject access to users, the record is not only placed in the broad P class, but also it contains a subject heading, a more specific class number, an annotation describing the resource, and a link to the resource itself.

Clustering Search Results

Some researchers believe that search satisfaction and effectiveness could be improved if classification techniques were applied to search engines.[42] The use of classification in conjunction with search engines is not a new idea. In the late 1990s and early 2000s, Northern Light, a free and publicly available search engine, used document-clustering techniques to divide search results into broad subject categories. While it did not work directly with a formal classification system, Northern Light used document clustering to improve the user's ability to navigate though results sets. At the time, Northern Light was the only major search engine to use these techniques for displaying results. By 2001, Northern Light had stopped offering a public Web search engine, instead focusing on commercial enterprises.[43] Since then, research has continued on automatic classification techniques, and other clustering search engines have been developed, including Kartoo[44] and Grokker,[45] which feature concept maps to display their results, and Clusty,[46] which provides individual page results along with a list of categories to help users sharpen or focus their search results.

All of these projects use document-clustering techniques to achieve these navigable, user-friendly results sets. What is *document clustering*? According to Srividhya Subramanian and Keith Shafer, clustering is a computer science approach to classifying documents in a collection, based on the contents of the entire collection. They state, "It explores collection relationships by computing the similarity between every pair of documents in the collection. Using the similarity information, clustering attempts to divide a collection of documents into groups (clusters)."[47] As a result, documents in the same clusters are more similar than documents in different clusters. Because these techniques are automated, they are not without errors (e.g., some odd pairings can occur), but overall, the technology is becoming more sophisticated and can provide impressive results.

Another automatic classification tool comes from the Scorpion project at OCLC, which attempts to assign actual classification notation to Internet resources through document clustering techniques. When cataloging Web resources through OCLC Connexion, one can request a classification number to be assigned automatically to the metadata record. Software developed by OCLC researchers analyzes the text of the Web site, compares the text to the headings and notes found in the DDC schedules and index, and then assigns classification numbers based on the comparisons. The software suggests one or more possible DDC numbers, which the cataloger may use or reject as appropriate. Scorpion software is available for licensing on its Web site.[48]

The last approach to organizing electronic documents that we will mention is that of *artificial neural networks* (ANNs), complex computer systems inspired by the architecture of the human nervous system, and often described as computing systems that can learn on their own. Artificial neural networks have been used in a variety of applications such as pattern and handwriting recognition. One of the many functions that an ANN can perform is the clustering and classification of documents, which results in a widespread application called a *self-organizing map* (SOM). An SOM, based on the work of Teuvo Kohonen,[49] is a browsing tool, which at first may look like a flow chart, a constellation diagram, or a set of local voting district boundaries.[50] SOM clustering can bring related items together allowing for browsing by subject area.

> The SOM is quite a unique kind of neural network in the sense that it constructs a topology preserving mapping from the high-dimensional space onto map units in such a way that relative distances between data points are preserved. The map units, or neurons, usually form a two-dimensional regular lattice where the location of a map unit carries semantic information. The SOM can thus serve as a clustering tool of high-dimensional data. Because of its typical two-dimensional shape, it is also easy to visualize.[51]

Researchers at the Neural Networks Research Centre of the Helsinki University of Technology have developed an exploratory full-text information retrieval method and browsing tool called the WEBSOM,[52] which uses ANNs to categorize automatically a variety of Web documents. The result is a map that provides visual representation of a collection of documents or other kinds of information. Not only are similar documents clustered together, but the map also uses proximity to represent the relationship among subjects. The size of an area in the map corresponds to the frequencies of word occurrence in the document set (see Figure 11.3).

CONCLUSION

This chapter has addressed categorization and classification as a way to provide subject access to information resources. One of the most important factors in information retrieval is to have resources and metadata

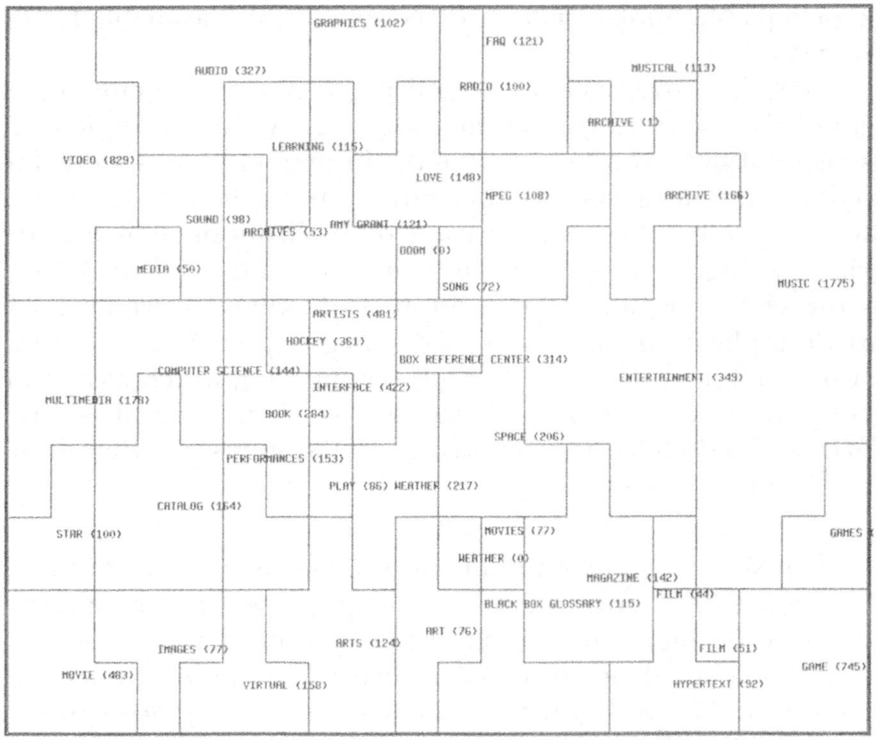

Figure 11.3. Example of use of Artificial Neural Network principles to provide visual representation of the subject matter in a collection of documents. This SOM clusters words in an "entertainment" document set.

records arranged and displayed in a logical fashion. Classification often plays a major role in this arrangement and display. Familiarity with the history of categories and the basics of classification theory can be helpful in understanding and using the classification schemes employed today. Arrangement of classification schemes (i.e., hierarchical, enumerative, and faceted) is based in classification theory. Specific classifications are numerous and run from universal schemes to homegrown schemes. Regardless of which scheme is used, there are classification concepts and controversies that must be addressed in the application of any scheme. Some concepts apply to physical resources, while others apply both to physical and intangible resources. A number of sites that organize Internet resources are using categories, classifications (often called taxonomies in this environment), or clustering techniques. Automatic techniques are growing in number and in sophistication. The future holds great potential for the expanded use of document clustering and ANNs for the automatic categorization of documents, especially using these techniques to produce user-friendly visualizations of topics and relationships among those topics.

NOTES

All URLs accessed September 2008.

1. Oxford English Dictionary Online. Available by subscription only at: http://dictionary.oed.com.

2. Merriam-Webster Online Search. Available: http://www.merriam-webster.com/.

3. Elin K. Jacob, "Classification and Categorization: A Difference That Makes a Difference," *Library Trends* 52, no. 3 (Winter 2004): 522.

4. Ibid., p. 527.

5. P. A. Studer, "Classification as a General Systems Construct," in *Information management in the 1980's: Proceedings of the [40th] ASIS Annual Meeting, Chicago, Illinois, September 26–October 1, 1977,* edited by B. M. Fry & C. A. Shepherd (White Plains, N.Y.: Knowledge Industry for American Society for Information Science, 1977), p. 67 and microfiche nos. 8–9, pp. G6–A9.

6. Christopher J. Dent, "Old Stuff: Classification v Categorization," in "Glacial Erratics." Available: http://www.burningchrome.com/~cdent/mt/archives/000401.html.

7. Ibid.

8. Amy J. Warner, "A Taxonomy Primer." Available: http://www.ischool.utexas.edu/~i385e/readings/Warner-aTaxonomyPrimer.html.

9. "Ten Taxonomy Myths," *Montague Institute Review* (November 2002; updated April 29, 2003). Available: http://www.montague.com/review/myths.html.

10. Ibid.

11. Thomas D. Wason, "Dr. Tom's Taxonomy Guide: Description, Use and Selections," IMS Global Learning Consortium, Inc. Available: http://www.twason.com/drtomtaxonomiesguide.html.

12. F. W. Lancaster, *Indexing and Abstracting in Theory and Practice,* 3rd ed. (Champaign: University of Illinois, Graduate School of Library and Information Science, 2003), p. xiii.

13. Bertram C. Bruce and James A. Levin, "Educational Technology: Media for Inquiry, Communication, Construction, and Expression," *Journal of Educational Computing Research* 17, no. 1 (1997): 79–102. Also available: http://www.isrl.uiuc.edu/~chip/pubs/taxonomy/taxonomy.pdf.

14. Agricultural Research Service, "GRIN Taxonomy for Plants." Available: http://www.ars-grin.gov/cgi-bin/npgs/html/index.pl.

15. Douglas Harper, "Online Etymology Dictionary." Available: http://www.etymonline.com/index.php?term=category.

16. Aristotle, *Categories,* translated by E. M. Edghill (Adelaide, South Australia: eBooks@Adelaide, University of Adelaide Library, 2007), section 4. Available: http://etext.library.adelaide.edu.au/a/aristotle/categories/ and http://www.classicallibrary.org/aristotle/categories/index.htm.

17. George Lakoff, *Women, Fire, and Dangerous Things: What Categories Reveal about the Mind* (Chicago: University of Chicago Press, 1987), p. 6.

18. Ibid., pp. 16–57.

19. Stephen L. Zegura, "Genes, Opsins, Neurons, and Color Categories: Closing the Gaps," in *Color Categories in Thought and Language,* edited by C. L. Hardin and Luisa Maffi (Cambridge; New York: Cambridge University Press, 1997), p. 289.

20. Hope A. Olson and John J. Boll, *Subject Analysis in Online Catalogs,* 2nd ed. (Englewood, Colo.: Libraries Unlimited, 2001), pp. 155–156.

21. Traugott Koch and Michael Day, "The Role of Classification Schemes in Internet Resource Description and Discovery: Executive Summary." Available: http://www.ukoln.ac.uk/metadata/desire/classification/class_su.htm.

22. Traugott Koch, "Controlled Vocabularies, Thesauri and Classification Systems Available in the WWW. DC Subject." Available: http://www.mpdl.mpg.de/staff/tkoch/publ/subject-help.html.

23. David H. Elazar and Daniel J. Elazar, *A Classification System for Libraries of Judaica,* 3rd ed., with the assistance of Rachel K. Glasser and Rita C. Frischer (Northvale, N.J.: Jason Aronson, 1997). Home page for this work is available: http://www.geocities.com/Athens/Acropolis/6527/class.html.

24. Carylyn Gwyn Moser, "Elazar Classification System Holocaust Expansion." Available: http://www.geocities.com/Athens/Acropolis/6527/holocaust.html.

25. Michael Gorman, "The Longer the Number, the Smaller the Spine; or, Up and Down with Melvil and Elsie," *American Libraries* 12, no. 8 (September 1981): 498–499.

26. Thomas Mann, *The Oxford Guide to Library Research,* 3rd ed. (New York: Oxford University Press, 2005).

27. Ibid.

28. Gorman, "The Longer the Number," pp. 498–499.

29. Heidi Frank, "Cataloging the World Wide Web: Organizing the Internet for Distance Learners," *Journal of Business & Finance Librarianship* 7, no. 2/3 (2002): 36.

30. David Ellis and Ana Vasconcelos, "Ranganathan and the Net: Using Facet Analysis to Search and Organise the World Wide Web," *Aslib Proceedings* 51, no. 1 (1999): 8.

31. Christine Jenkins, Mike Jackson, Peter Burden, and Jon Wallis, "Automatic Classification of Web Resources Using Java and Dewey Decimal Classification," *Computer Networks and ISDN Systems* 30 (1998): 646.

32. Amazon.com. Available: http://www.amazon.com/.

33. Fairfax County, Va., "Human Services Resource Guide, Taxonomy Classification List." Available: http://www.fairfaxcounty.gov/rim/taxonomylist.asp.

34. National Center for Biotechnology Information. "The NCBI Entrez Taxonomy Homepage." Available: http://www.ncbi.nlm.nih.gov/sites/entrez?db=taxonomy.

35. Yahoo! Available: http://dir.yahoo.com/.

36. Gerry McKiernan, "Beyond Bookmarks: Schemes for Organizing the Web." Available: http://www.public.iastate.edu/~CYBERSTACKS/CTW.htm.

37. David Mundie, "CyberDewey." Available: http://library.tedankara.k12.tr/dewey/index.html.

38. Queensland Department of Education, Training and the Arts, "Subject Directory using Dewey Classification." Available: http://education.qld.gov.au/search/dewey.html.

39. Bloomsburg University's Harvey A. Andruss Library, "E-Ref: Electronic Reference." Available: http://icrc.bloomu.edu/icrc/lc.php.

40. Simon Ager, "Omniglot: Writing Systems & Languages of the World." Available: http://www.omniglot.com/writing/index.htm.

41. Bloomsburg University's Harvey A. Andruss Library, "E-Ref: Electronic Reference: P - P9999: Communication, Language (General)." Available: http://icrc.bloomu.edu/icrc/searchlc.php?top=P&bottom=P9999&name=Communication,+Language+(General).

42. Young Mee Chung and Young-Hee Noh, "Developing a Specialized Directory System by Automatically Classifying Web Documents," *Journal of Information Science* 29, no. 2 (2003): p. 118.

43. Northern Light. Available: http://www.northernlight.com.

44. Kartoo: Visual Meta Search Engine. Available: http://www.kartoo.com/.

45. Grokker: Enterprise Search Management. Available: http://www.grokker.com/.

46. Clusty: the Clustering Search Engine. Available: http://clusty.com/.

47. Srividhya Subramanian and Keith E. Shafer, "Clustering," OCLC. Available: http://digitalarchive.oclc.org/da/ViewObjectMain.jsp?objid=0000003409.

48. OCLC Scorpion Software. Available: http://www.oclc.org/research/software/scorpion/.

49. Teuvo Kohonen, *Self-Organizing Maps*, 3rd ed. (New York: Springer-Verlag, 2001).

50. Jeremy Douglass, "Self-Organizing Maps: A Tourist's Guide to Neural Network (re)Presentation(s)." Available: http://www.english.ucsb.edu/grad/student-pages/jdouglass/coursework/hyperliterature/soms/.

51. Petri Hodju and Jokko Halme, "Self-Organizing Map" in "Neural Networks Information Homepage." Available: http://koti.mbnet.fi/~phodju/nenet/SelfOrganizingMap/General.html.

52. Teuvo Kohonen, "WEBSOM: Self-Organizing Maps for Internet Exploration." Available: http://websom.hut.fi/websom/.

SUGGESTED READINGS

Classification in General

Bowker, Geoffrey C., and Susan Leigh Star. *Sorting Things Out: Classification and Its Consequences*. Cambridge, Mass.: MIT Press, 1999. Introduction:

"To Classify Is Human," Chapter 9: "Categorical Work and Boundary Infrastructures: Enriching Theories of Classification," and Chapter 10: "Why Classifications Matter."

Broughton, Vanda. "The Need for a Faceted Classification as the Basis of All Methods of Information Retrieval." *Aslib Proceedings: New Information Perspectives* 58, no. 1/2 (2006): 49–72.

Classification Research Group. "The Need for a Faceted Classification as the Basis of All Methods of Information Retrieval." In *Theory of Subject Analysis: A Sourcebook,* edited by Lois Mai Chan, Phyllis A. Richmond, and Elaine Svenonius. Littleton, Colo.: Libraries Unlimited, 1985, pp. 154–167.

Chan, Lois Mai, with the assistance of Theodora L. Hodges. *Cataloging and Classification: An Introduction.* 3rd ed. Lanham, Md.: Scarecrow Press, 2007. Chapter 11: "General Principles of Classification."

Gorman, Michael. "The Longer the Number, the Smaller the Spine; or, Up and Down with Melvil and Elsie." *American Libraries* 12, no. 8 (September 1981): 498–499.

Hunter, Eric J. *Classification Made Simple.* 2nd ed. Aldershot, England; Brookfield, Vt.: Gower, 2002.

Intner, Sheila S., and Jean Weihs. *Standard Cataloging for School and Public Libraries.* 4th ed. Westport, Conn.: Libraries Unlimited, 2007. Chapter 9: "Classification Systems."

Lakoff, George. *Women, Fire, and Dangerous Things: What Categories Reveal about the Mind.* Chicago: University of Chicago Press, 1987. Chapter 1: "The Importance of Categorization."

Langridge, D. W. *Classification: Its Kinds, Elements, Systems, and Applications.* London: Bowker-Saur, 1992.

Leise, Fred. "Using Faceted Classification to Assist Indexing." *Key Words* 9, no. 6 (November/December 2001): 178–179.

Mann, Thomas. *The Oxford Guide to Library Research,* 3rd ed. New York: Oxford University Press, 2005. Chapter 3: "Systematic Browsing, Scanning, and Use of Classified Bookstacks."

———. *Doing Research at the Library of Congress: A Guide to Subject Searching in a Closed Stacks Library.* Washington, D.C.: Library of Congress, Humanities and Social Sciences Division, 1994.

Marcella, Rita, and Arthur Maltby, eds. *The Future of Classification.* Aldershot, England; Brookfield, Vt.: Gower, 2000. Chapter 1: Eric Hunter. "Do We Still Need Classification?"

Olson, Hope A., and John J. Boll. *Subject Analysis in Online Catalogs.* 2nd ed. Englewood, Colo.: Libraries Unlimited, 2001. Chapter 7: "Bibliographic Classification."

Soergel, Dagobert. "The Rise of Ontologies or the Reinvention of Classification." *Journal of the American Society for Information Science* 50, no. 12 (October 1999): 1119–1120.

Taylor, Arlene G. *Introduction to Cataloging and Classification.* 10th ed., with the assistance of David P. Miller. Westport, Conn.: Libraries Unlimited, 2006. Chapter 14: "Classification of Library Materials."

Specific Classification Schemes

Dewey Decimal Classification

Chan, Lois Mai, and Joan S. Mitchell. *Dewey Decimal Classification: Principles and Application.* 3rd ed. Dublin, Ohio: OCLC, 2003.

Dewey Decimal Classification Homepage. Available: http://www.oclc.org/dewey/.

Foskett, A. C. *The Subject Approach to Information.* 5th ed. London: Library Association Publishing, 1996. Chapter 17: "The Dewey Decimal Classification."

Olson, Hope A., and John J. Boll. *Subject Analysis in Online Catalogs.* 2nd ed. Englewood, Colo.: Libraries Unlimited, 2001. Chapter 8: "Online Catalogs and the Dewey Decimal and Library of Congress Classifications."

Taylor, Arlene G. *Introduction to Cataloging and Classification.* 10th ed., with the assistance of David P. Miller. Westport, Conn.: Libraries Unlimited, 2006. Chapter 15: "Decimal Classification."

Universal Decimal Classification

Foskett, A. C. *The Subject Approach to Information.* 5th ed. London: Library Association Publishing, 1996. Chapter 18: "The Universal Decimal Classification."

Taylor, Arlene G. *Introduction to Cataloging and Classification.* 10th ed., with the assistance of David P. Miller. Westport, Conn.: Libraries Unlimited, 2006. Chapter 15: "Decimal Classification."

UDC Consortium. "About Universal Decimal Classification and the UDC Consortium." Available: http://www.udcc.org/about.htm.

LC Classification

Chan, Lois Mai. *A Guide to the Library of Congress Classification.* 5th ed. Englewood, Colo.: Libraries Unlimited, 1999.

Foskett, A. C. *The Subject Approach to Information.* 5th ed. London: Library Association Publishing, 1996. Chapter 22: "The Library of Congress Classification."

Library of Congress Cataloging and Acquisitions. "Classification." Available: http://www.loc.gov/aba/cataloging/classification/.

Olson, Hope A., and John J. Boll. *Subject Analysis in Online Catalogs.* 2nd ed. Englewood, Colo.: Libraries Unlimited, 2001. Chapter 8: "Online Catalogs and the Dewey Decimal and Library of Congress Classifications."

Taylor, Arlene G. *Introduction to Cataloging and Classification.* 10th ed., with the assistance of David P. Miller. Westport, Conn.: Libraries Unlimited, 2006. Chapter 16: "Library of Congress Classification (LCC)."

Colon Classification

Foskett, A. C. *The Subject Approach to Information.* 5th ed. London: Library Association Publishing, 1996. Chapter 21: "The Colon Classification."

Ranganathan, S. R. *Prolegomena to Library Classification.* 3rd ed. London: Asia Publishing House, 1967.

Steckel, Mike. "Ranganathan for IAs: An Introduction to the Thought of S.R. Ranganathan for Information Architects." *Boxes and Arrows* (October 7, 2002). Available: http://www.boxesandarrows.com/view/ranganathan_for_ias.

Other Classification Schemes

Foskett, A. C. *The Subject Approach to Information.* 5th ed. London: Library Association Publishing, 1996. Chapter 19: "The Bibliographic Classification" and Chapter 20: "The Broad System of Ordering."

Hearst, Marti A. "Interfaces for Searching the Web." *Scientific American* 276, no. 3 (March 1997): 68–72. Also available: http://people.ischool.berkeley.edu/~hearst/papers/sciam/0397hearst.html.

Taylor, Arlene G. *Introduction to Cataloging and Classification.* 10th ed., with the assistance of David P. Miller. Westport, Conn.: Libraries Unlimited, 2006. Chapter 18: "Other Classification Systems."

Taxonomies, Categories, and Classification and the Internet

Anderson, James A. *An Introduction to Neural Networks.* Cambridge, Mass.: MIT Press, 1995, pp. vii–xi, 1–15.

Bertolucci, Katherine. "Happiness Is Taxonomy: Four Structures for Snoopy." *Information Outlook* 7, no. 3 (March 2003): 36–44.

Chen, Hao, and Susan Dumais. "Bringing Order to the Web: Automatically Categorizing Search Results." Microsoft Research Publications, 2000. Available: http://research.microsoft.com/~sdumais/chi00.pdf.

Koch, Traugott, and Michael Day. "The Role of Classification Schemes in Internet Resource Description and Discovery." Available: http://www.ukoln.ac.uk/metadata/desire/classification/class_ti.htm.

Kohonen, Teuvo. *Self-Organizing Maps.* 3rd ed. Berlin, N.Y.: Springer-Verlag, 2001.

McKiernan, Gerry. "Beyond Bookmarks: Schemes for Organizing the Web." Available: http://www.public.iastate.edu/~CYBERSTACKS/CTW.html.

Nash, Lisa, and Aaron Press. "Taxonomies: Structuring Today's Knowledge Management Systems." *Information About Information Briefing* 4, no. 26 (July 18, 2001): 1–18.

Vizine-Goetz, Diane. "Using Library Classification Schemes for Internet Resources." Available: http://staff.oclc.org/~vizine/Intercat/vizine-goetz.htm.

"What Is a Neural Network?" NeuroDimension, Inc., 2002. Available: http://www.nd.com/welcome/whatisnn.htm.

CONCLUSION

In the preceding chapters we have discussed the past and present of information organization. Organizing has been going on, we suspect, since the first appearance of humans, because it seems to be such an innate need. Even some nonhuman animals, birds, and insects are organizers (e.g., ants have highly organized societies with certain responsibilities assigned to various individuals). The organization of information among humans began as soon as language developed sufficiently for information to be passed from person to person. In oral traditions information was organized in people's minds, and, in recorded information traditions, ways of identifying information resources were developed at least as early as clay tablets.

Current retrieval tools, including bibliographies, catalogs, indexes, finding aids, museum registers, databases, and search engines, represent the highest state of progress in information organization that humans have achieved so far. These tools are far from perfect, though, and there is much room for organizers to improve metadata and for system designers to provide more helpful retrievals and more logical displays. Development of seamless interfaces among these tools, which once was seen only as a possibility, has become a necessity; more work in this area has to be done.

Arrival at this current state of organization has taken centuries. Progress in the Western world was given impetus by printing with moveable type, but even then, movement toward bibliographic control was slow as printing moved through the stage of imitating manuscript production to the stage of creating new type fonts just for printing. We are experiencing a similar stage now as we use computers to imitate our previous print culture. Alan Kay, the first person to conceive of the laptop computer, has said that the computer revolution has not yet begun:

> The printing press was invented in the middle of the 15th century, yet it took 100 years before a book was considered dangerous enough to be banned, 150 years before science was invented, almost 200 years before a new kind of political essay was invented, and more than 300 years

> before a country with an invented political system (the US) could be argued into existence via the press and a citizenry that could understand the arguments. Schooling and general literacy were also fruits of the press, and also took many centuries to become established. The commercial computer is now about 50 years old and is still imitating the paper culture that came before it, just as the printing press did with the manuscript culture it gradually replaced. No media revolution can be said to have happened without a general establishment of "literacy": fluent "reading" and "writing" at the highest level of ideas that the medium can represent. With computers we are so far from that fluent literacy—or even understanding what that literacy should resemble—that we could claim that the computer revolution hasn't even started.[1]

Although it seems that much has happened in the 10-plus years since Kay said this, we still have not accomplished the literacy of which he spoke. Therefore, we cannot know what organized information will look like in another 50 years or even 25 years. We believe, however, that the principles of organization that have developed over the last several hundred centuries will not be thrown out but will continue to evolve into the organizing principles of the future.

NOTE

1. Alan Kay, "The Computer Revolution Hasn't Happened Yet," lecture in the SCS Distinguished Lecture Series, presented at Carnegie Mellon University, April 29, 1998.

APPENDIX A: AN APPROACH TO SUBJECT ANALYSIS

A way to use the subject analysis concepts presented in Chapter 9 is to follow the outline presented below. It attempts to take the analyst through the most commonly used features of a work, to address the concepts that are most helpful in determining aboutness, and to consider some questions that might help to make the process less vague. It is followed by an example providing subject analysis of a popular Web site.

I. Analyze the information resource

A. Identify the overall discipline, branch of knowledge, or subject area in which the work fits. Consider the intended audience and the purpose of the information resource (e.g., why the resource was created, what it accomplishes, what questions it might answer, and for whom).

B. Identify the important topics or concepts in the information resource. Look for frequently mentioned topics or ideas in the following:

1. Title and subtitle.

2. Table of contents, chapter titles, section headings, or equivalents.

3. Preface and/or introduction, first chapter, etc.

4. Illustrations and their captions.

5. Conclusion (e.g., last chapter, section, etc.).

C. Identify names used as subject concepts.

D. Identify role(s) of any geographic name(s) present.

E. Identify chronological elements.

F. Identify form or genre of the resource being analyzed.

II. Construct an aboutness statement

A. Describe what the information resource is about.

B. Review the resource again. Look for support of your ideas. Refine the sentence as needed.

C. Identify terms from the aboutness statement to be searched in the controlled vocabulary.

D. Sketch out a rudimentary hierarchy (discipline/sub-discipline/concept/topic, etc.) into which the aboutness concepts fall.

III. Translate the aboutness into controlled vocabulary

A. Search the chosen terms in the controlled vocabulary. Translate the terms into the specific headings or descriptors used in the controlled vocabulary list.

B. Using the hierarchy as a guide, search the classification for the most appropriate class(es) to describe the resource's aboutness. Convert the aboutness into specific classification notation(s).

C. Review your choices and compare to similar items.

EXAMPLE

The summarization-level analysis of the Web site *JGarden: The Japanese Garden Database* (see Figures A.1, A.2, and A.3) created and maintained by Robert Cheetham, might proceed as follows:

I. Analyze the information resource

A. Identify the overall discipline, branch of knowledge, or subject area into which the work fits. Consider the intended audience and the purpose of the information resource.

This work falls in the arts, particularly in the area of landscaping or garden design. It is for a general audience. The

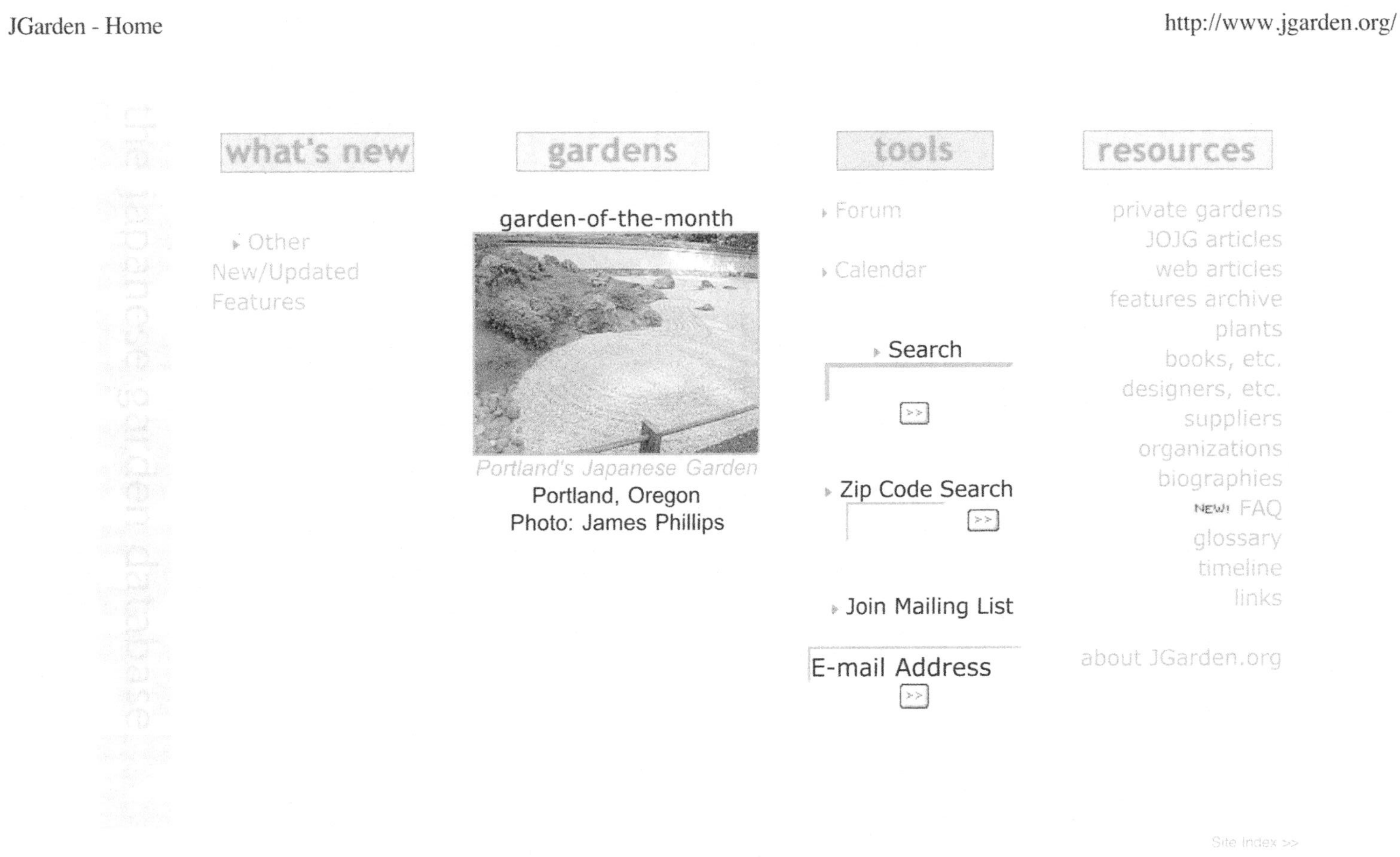

Figure A.1 Homepage for *JGarden: The Japanese Garden Database.* (Source: http://www.jgarden.org/.)

gardens tools resources

About JGarden

The Japanese Garden Database is intended as a repository of information on the historical and contemporary gardens of Japan as well as the gardens located outside Japan that have been inspired by the culture. It is a non-profit, educational web site that seeks to provide information on a selection of outstanding examples of garden art found in Japan while juxtaposing a diversity of media related to them. This juxtaposition is intended to bring about fresh insight to a body of discourse that can often be mired in romanticized and exoticized notions of Asia and the cultures therein.

For further information about the site, please refer to the following pages:

- How to support JGarden
- Linking to JGarden
- Copyright information
- Contact JGarden
- Content Submissions
- Suggestions

JGarden.org Background

What you see on the screen is now the fifth iteration of the site. In some ways it is the closest to what I had originally conceived. What began simply as a proof-of-concept for a more comprehensive multimedia reference work on the gardens of Japan, this web site has since taken on a life of its own. Many of the changes have also come about due to changing technology. For the past several years the World Wide Web has transformed itself about every twelve months and to both push myself and to keep the site fresh, I have done my best to keep up.

Since Josiah Condor's *Landscape Gardening in Japan* (1912) and particularly in the post-World War II era, the gardens of Japan have received a great deal of attention in both popular and professional design literature. A small number of gardens have become almost iconic. The *karesansui* garden of Ryoanji, the shrine at Ise and the Katsura and Shugakuin imperial villas are ubiquitous in writings from Walter Gropius to John Cage.

However, with a few exceptions, discussion of the gardens of Japan has tended to be generic and superficial, often grouping them into an amorphous category called 'Japanese gardens' devoid of the social, historical and cultural context within which they were constructed. The language barrier coupled with a persistent romanticization of the 'mysterious, enigmatic Orient' often encouraged by the Japanese themselves, has contributed to this situation.

In recent years important contributions have been made by David Slawson, Marc Treib, Norris Brock Johnson, Loraine Kuck, Mitchell Bring, Josse Wayembergh, Gunter Nitschke and others to ameliorate this condition. To this list must be added translations of the work of Itoh Teiji, Yoshikawa Isao and Mori Osamu as well as the educational efforts of the late Nakane Kinsaku toward the training of young, Western landscape architects in the design principles behind the gardens of Japan.

This site was originally proposed as an interactive, multimedia reference work on the gardens of Japan that would support these other efforts, providing comprehensive visual and textual information on the history, construction, materiality, people, language, patterns and processes by which these gardens were constructed. The database was to be organized in a hypertext-based, non-linear fashion that would be both flexible and open-ended. It was to be directed at professionals in the field of landscape architecture and garden history but was also to be made available to the general public through the internet.

I have changed some of my ideas since then. It's still based on hypertext, but I am no longer attempting to be comprehensive or exhaustive. Nor will I attempt to define what I mean by the gardens of Japan. It is also not my intention to simply present digital versions of the plans, sections and verbal descriptions given by others. Rather I hope to provide a few examples of a few gardens and bring a diversity of media into juxtaposition. Removing the material from the printed book, arranging it non-linearly and disseminating it to a wider audience has value in itself; but this project is intended to go beyond this; I want to draw on other kinds of information including literature, paintings, images and mappings in an accretive process that brings about a thickening of the cultural imagination vis a vis the gardens.

The objective of the project is to include text and still images of the selected gardens constructed prior to the 20th century. The information is arranged as 'pages' or 'documents' that are organized and cross-referenced through in-line hyperlinks. The information is be loosely arranged in bodies of data including: gardens, plants, poetry and literature, and reference materials such as glossaries, bibliographies, and media galleries. The material is retrievable through clickable maps, time lines, and alphabetical lists. The organization is deliberately designed to allow multiple entrees to any given page. I hope this approach will resist closure of a given inquiry. The user creates her own path through the information.

What began as a proof-of-concept for a more comprehensive multimedia reference work, this site has been transformed multiple times since its inception in 1996 but it remains committed to its purpose as a non-profit, educational project aimed at raising awareness of Japanese gardens.

search

--Entire Site-- >>

shop

Contemplative Gardens
Messervy, Julie Moir and Abell, Sam (photographer)
[JGarden Bibliography]

browse

gardens
tools
JOJG articles NEW!
web articles
features archive
plants
books, etc.
designers
suppliers
organizations
biographies
glossary
timeline
links

jgarden news

Keep up with JGarden changes and news!

Subscribe to our monthly newsletter:

E-mail Address >>

©1996-2002, Robert Cheetham; ©2008 Japanese Garden Research Network, Inc.

contact us site map privacy search --Entire Site-- >>

Figure A.2 Introductory page from *JGarden: The Japanese Garden Database.* (Source: http://www.jgarden.org/about.asp.)

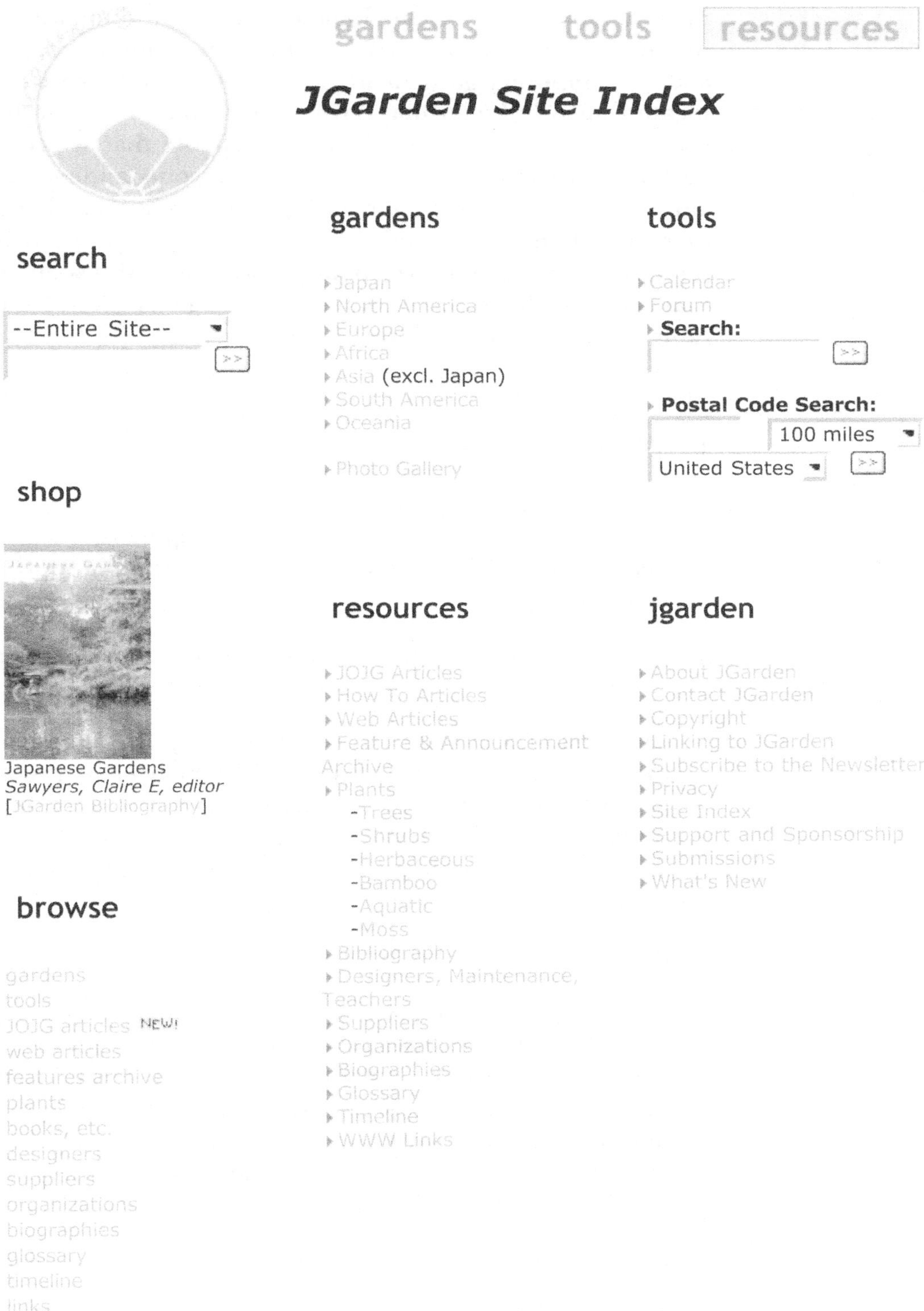

Figure A.3 Site index for *JGarden: The Japanese Garden Database.* (Source: http://www.jgarden.org/site_index.asp.)

introduction states, "The Japanese Garden Database is intended as a repository of information on the historical and contemporary gardens of Japan as well as the gardens located outside Japan that have been inspired by the culture. It is a non-profit, educational web site that seeks to provide information on a selection of outstanding examples of garden art found in Japan while juxtaposing a diversity of media related to them. This juxtaposition is intended to bring about fresh insight to a body of discourse that can often be mired in romanticized and exoticized notions of Asia and the cultures therein."

B. Identify concepts in:

1. Title and subtitle.

   The Japanese Garden Database
   Note that the title contains the words *Japanese, Garden,* and *Database.* (Does this Web site fit the definition of a *database?*)

2. Table of contents, chapter titles, section headings, or equivalents.

   The headings include: private gardens, JOJG (Journal of Japanese Gardening) articles, Web articles, features archive, plants, books, designers, suppliers, organizations, biographies, FAQ, glossary, timeline, and links. Some of these are helpful for subject aboutness; some are not.

3. Preface, introduction, and/or first chapter.

   The introduction equivalent is the AboutJGarden.org page. It frequently uses several terms such as gardens, plants, designers, and Japanese. Note that it states that the site was originally intended for professionals in the field of landscape architecture and garden history, but has been broadened to be made available to the general public through the Internet.

4. Illustrations and their captions.

   Note that illustrations are of various gardens, some at varying times of year, and that there are also topo-

graphical and location maps. However, these do not constitute a large proportion of the work

5. Conclusion (e.g., last chapter, section, etc.).

   None in this resource.

C. Identify names used as subject concepts.

The personal names involved are names of garden designers. There are too many to include at the summarization level. A few corporate names are given in lists, such as lists of organizations or lists of related sites; the work is not about these corporate bodies, however.

D. Identify role(s) of any geographic name(s) present.

The geographic area Japan provides the context for the topic of this work. The work is not about Japan, but the gardens discussed are of a type originally designed in Japan. Only *some* of the individual gardens discussed in this site actually are in Japan.

E. Identify chronological elements.

The time-periods involved here are from several centuries B.C.E. to the present, much too long a time to be meaningful in a subject heading string.

F. Identify form of the resource being analyzed.

This resource consists of many different kinds of information: text, pictures, maps, and the like. Note that the word database is included in the subtitle, but the entire work is not a database. Much of the resource comprises internal Web pages and links to outside resources. A larger portion of this resource is dedicated to lists of articles about Japanese gardens (i.e., a bibliography).

II. Construct an aboutness statement.

A. Describe what the resource is about.

This resource is about the history and design of Japanese-style gardens (as a concept) and also the history and design of major Japanese-style gardens in Japan and around the

world. Much of the resource contains text and images of gardens, but large portions comprise a bibliography of resources related to the topic and a database of important Japanese-style gardens.

B. Review the resource again. Look for support of your ideas. Refine the sentence as needed.

C. Identify terms from the aboutness statement to be searched in the controlled vocabulary.

Japan, Japanese, Japanese-style

Gardens

History, Historic

Design

Database

Bibliography

D. Sketch out a rudimentary hierarchy (discipline/subdiscipline/concept/topic, etc.) into which the aboutness concepts fall.

Arts / design / landscaping / gardens / Japanese

III. Translate the aboutness into controlled vocabulary

A. Search the chosen terms in the controlled vocabulary. Translate the terms into specific headings from the controlled vocabulary list.

LCSH:

Gardens, Japanese—History

Gardens, Japanese—Design

Historic gardens—Japan

Gardens, Japanese—Bibliography

Gardens, Japanese—Databases

B. Using the hierarchy as a guide, search the classification for the most appropriate class(es) to described the resource's aboutness. Convert the aboutness into specific classification notation(s).

LC Classification: SB466.J3
Dewey Decimal Classification: 712.0952

C. Review your choices and compare to similar items.

How did you do? Does this resource fit with others around it? Would you search for it using these words? If you searched using these words, would you be happy with this item?

APPENDIX B: ARRANGEMENT OF PHYSICAL INFORMATION RESOURCES IN LIBRARIES

Arrangement of physical information resources has been of concern to information centers for centuries. Clay tablets, papyrus scrolls, parchment, and eventually paper resources all had to be arranged. In the twentieth century, various new media (e.g., films, photographs, sound recordings, etc.) appeared, needing eventually to be arranged. Since the early 1980s, there has been concern about arrangement of electronic resources contained in physical packaging (e.g., CD-ROMs, videodiscs, music CDs, etc.).

Physical information resources are often arranged by *call number.* A call number is a notation on an information resource that matches the same notation in the metadata record. It is the number used to "call" for an item in closed stacks—thus, the source of the name *call number.* A call number usually consists of at least two lines on a label placed on the outside of the packaging. The top line is usually a classification notation. With long notations, the classification notation may continue onto a second line. The next line is usually a *cutter number.*

Cutter numbers were devised by Charles A. Cutter more than a century ago for the purpose of creating a logical subarrangement of resources under classification notations. In most instances, the most logical subarrangement is alphabetical by the primary access point, whether it is an author, creator, or a title. In essence, cuttering alphabetizes all of the works that fall under the same classification notation. Cutter devised a table in which letters of the alphabet were listed in one column and equivalent numerals were listed in an adjoining column (see Figure B.1).[1]

Using the following example from "F" in Cutter's table,

Fonti	684
Fontr	685
Foo	686

a Cutter number for an author named Fontrain might be F685d. The small "d" is a *work mark* assigned to help keep the works of a particular author

CUTTER-SANBORN Three-Figure Author Table (SWANSON-SWIFT REVISION)

Goetz	611	Goun	711	Greene J	811	Guald	911
Gof	612	Goup	712	Greene S	812	Gualt	912
Gog	613	Gour	713	Greenh	813	Guan	913
Goh	614	Gourd	714	Greenl	814	Guar	914
Goi	615	Gourg	715	Greeno	815	Guari	915
Gois	616	Gouri	716	Greenw	816	Guarn	916
Gol	617	Gous	717	Gref	817	Guas	917
Gold	618	Gout	718	Greg	818	Guat	918
Goldi	619	Gouv	719	Gregg	819	Guaz	919
Goldo	621	Gov	721	Gregori	821	Gub	921
Golds	622	Gow	722	Gregory	822	Gud	922
Goldsc	623	Gower	723	Gregory M	823	Gudm	923
Goldsm	624	Goy	724	Grei	824	Gue	924
Gole	625	Goz	725	Grel	825	Guel	925
Goli	626	Gr	726	Gren	826	Guen	926
Golo	627	Grab	727	Greni	827	Gueno	927
Golov	628	Graber	728	Grenv	828	Guep	928
Golt	629	Grac	729	Grep	829	Guer	929
Gom	631	Graci	731	Gres	831	Guere	931
Gombe	632	Grad	732	Gress	832	Gueri	932
Gome	633	Grado	733	Gresw	833	Guern	933
Gomm	634	Grae	734	Gret	834	Guerr	934
Gon	635	Graes	735	Gretto	835	Guerri	935
Gond	636	Graf	736	Greu	836	Gues	936
Gondi	637	Graft	737	Grev	837	Guet	937
Gone	638	Grah	738	Grevi	838	Gueu	938
Gonn	639	Graham G	739	Grevy	839	Guev	939
Gont	641	Graham M	741	Grew	841	Guf	941
Gonz	642	Graham S	742	Grey	842	Gug	942
Gonzal	643	Grai	743	Grey G	843	Gui	943
Goo	644	Gral	744	Grey M	844	Guib	944
Gooc	645	Gram	745	Grey S	845	Guic	945
Good	646	Grammo	746	Gri	846	Guid	946
Goodc	647	Gramo	747	Grid	847	Guidi	947
Goodel	648	Gran	748	Grie	848	Guido	948
Gooden	649	Granc	749	Grif	849	Guie	949
Goodf	651	Grand	751	Griffin	851	Guig	951
Goodh	652	Grandes	752	Griffin M	852	Guij	952
Goodm	653	Grandi	753	Griffith	853	Guil	953
Goodr	654	Grandm	754	Griffith M	854	Guild	954
Goodrich M	655	Grandv	755	Griffiths	855	Guild M	955
Goodw	656	Grane	756	Grifo	856	Guile	956
Goodwin M	657	Grang	757	Grig	857	Guill	957
Goody	658	Granger	758	Gril	858	Guille	958
Gook	659	Grani	759	Grillo	859	Guilli	959
Gor	661	Grant	761	Grim	861	Guillo	961
Gordon	662	Grant H	762	Grime	862	Guillot	962
Gordon G	663	Grant S	763	Grimk	863	Guim	963
Gordon M	664	Grantl	764	Grimm	864	Guin	964
Gordon S	665	Granv	765	Grimo	865	Guir	965
Gore	666	Grap	766	Grin	866	Guis	966
Gorg	667	Gras	767	Grinf	867	Guise	967
Gorh	668	Grass	768	Grinn	868	Guit	968
Gori	669	Grassi	769	Gris	869	Guiz	969
Gorm	671	Grat	771	Grisw	871	Gul	971
Goro	672	Grati	772	Griv	872	Gulg	972
Gorr	673	Gratt	773	Gro	873	Gull	973
Gors	674	Grau	774	Groc	874	Gum	974
Gort	675	Grav	775	Grol	875	Gun	975
Gos	676	Graves	776	Gron	876	Gunn	976
Goss	677	Gravi	777	Gros	877	Gunt	977
Gosse	678	Grav	778	Gross	878	Gur	978

Figure B.1. Part of a page from a Cutter table.

who writes on the same subject in alphabetical order. The work mark usually stands for the first word (that is not an article) of the title of the work; although for biographies, the work is usually *cuttered* for the name of the person the work is about, and the work mark stands for the last name of the author of the biography. This kind of Cutter number is most often used with *Dewey Decimal Classification* (DDC) notations.

Library of Congress Classification (LCC) also uses cutter numbers (with a small "c") (see Figure B.2). LC borrowed Charles Cutter's idea, but created its own table that takes only a few lines.[2] With LCC, a third line for a call number is often the date. (Dates are usually used in DDC call numbers only for another edition of a work for which an institution already has an edition.) Examples of call numbers are:

DDC	**LCC**
378.4	QE22.D25
F685d	S65
	1997

There are also alphabetical arrangements, accession order arrangements (i.e., numbers assigned to items in the order in which they arrive), and fixed location arrangements for physical information resources. In public and school libraries, in particular, fiction is often grouped together, subarranged in alphabetical order by author (sometimes with a prefix indicating *fiction,* such as "F" or "Fic"). Other uses for alphabetical order include arrangements of biographies and serials. Biographies may be arranged in alphabetical order by the last name of the person the biography is about (sometimes with "B" as a prefix indicating *biography*). And, as discussed in Chapter 11, serials are often arranged in alphabetical order by title. Accession order arrangements may be used for materials waiting to be cataloged, and sometimes for backlogs that are more "permanent." They may also be used for fixed location settings, such as remote storage.

In most institutions there is more than one sequence of the classification scheme or other arrangement used (e.g., more than one A–Z sequence, if using LCC, or more than one 000–999 sequence, if using DDC) There is often a reference collection, for example, that gathers together information resources from all parts of the classification scheme. In some libraries, the prefix "R" or "Ref" is used to indicate an item's inclusion in the reference collection. These are kept separately from regular circulating collections. In academic libraries there are often collections of reserve items for use for certain courses. In many libraries some kinds of information resources are separated by format. Microforms, DVDs, sound recordings, and the like, are arranged in their own groups with their own sequences. This is often for housing and preservation purposes. Some media centers have tried to interfile all formats in classification order, but the idea has never really caught on.

LC Cutter Table

(1)	After initial *vowels*								
	for the second letter:	b	d	l-m	n	p	r	s-t	u-y
	use number:	2	3	4	5	6	7	8	9
(2)	After initial letter *S*								
	for the second letter:	a	ch	e	h-i	m-p	t	u	w-z
	use number:	2	3	4	5	6	7	8	9
(3)	After initial letters *Qu*								
	for the second [i.e. next] letter:	a	e	i	o	r	t	y	
	use number:	3	4	5	6	7	8	9	
	For initial letters *Qa-Qt*, use: **2-29**								
(4)	After other initial *consonants*								
	for the second letter:	a	e	i	o	r	u	y	
	use number:	3	4	5	6	7	8	9	
(5)	For *expansion*								
	for the letter:	a-d	e-h	i-l	m-o	p-s	t-v	w-z	
	use number:	3	4	5	6	7	8	9	

The following examples show cutters that would be used if entries already shelflisted conform to the table [above]. In most cases, cutters must be adjusted to file an entry correctly and to allow room for later entries.

Vowels		**S**		**Q**		**Consonants**	
IBM	.I26	Sadron	.S23	*Qadduri	.Q23	Campbell	.C36
Idaho	.I33	*Scanlon	.S29	*Qiao	.Q27	Ceccaldi	.C43
*Ilardo	.I4	Schreiber	.S37	Quade	.Q33	*Chertok	.C48
*Import	.I48	*Shillingburg	.S53	Queiroz	.Q45	*Clark	.C58
Inman	.I56	*Singer	.S57	Quinn	.Q56	Cobblestone	.C63
Ipswich	.I67	Stinson	.S75	Quorum	.Q67	Cryer	.C79
*Ito	.I87	Suranyi	.S87	Qutub	.Q88	Cuellar	.C84
*Ivy	.I94	*Symposium	.S96	*Qvortrup	.Q97	Cymbal	.C96

*These cutters reflect the adjustments made to allow for a range of letters on the table, e.g., **l-m**, or for letters not explicitly stated, e.g., **h** after an initial consonant.

Figure B.2. Cutter table used with the *Library of Congress Classification.*

NOTES

1. The various editions of the Cutter tables (including the Cutter-Sanborn tables) are available from Libraries Unlimited, Inc.

2. For more explanation of call numbers, see Arlene G. Taylor, *Introduction to Cataloging and Classification,* 10th ed., with the assistance of David P. Miller (Westport, Conn.: Libraries Unlimited, 2006), pp. 448–455.

APPENDIX C: ARRANGEMENT OF METADATA DISPLAYS

For most of the twentieth century, catalogs were in card, book, or microform formats. In card catalogs, the order of surrogate records was by a filing arrangement achieved by humans. Persons doing the filing had rules to follow that would lead to an arrangement that was deemed to be conducive to helping users find what they were looking for. In early book catalogs, the same was true because book catalogs often were made from cards or slips created by catalogers and placed in order by filers.

As computers entered the picture, book and then microform catalogs began to be created in electronic databases where the actual filing was done according to computer algorithms. Finally, Online Public Access Catalogs (OPACs) came into use. The records were stored sequentially or randomly within the computer, but in order to display the results of a search to a user, the subset of records retrieved had to be arranged and then displayed on the screen in some order. Early computer algorithms dictated an order of characters: sometimes numerals preceded letters, sometimes not; and there was (and still is) great difficulty in even displaying diacritical marks, let alone arranging them to display in some meaningful order.

Search results in OPACs and other electronic databases continue to be arranged on screen by computer algorithm. A few systems have been developed to make use of MARC tags and subfield codes to create more logical arrangements. Whatever the algorithm, no computer can make up for a typographical error the way a filer can. In a card catalog, an alert filer would see a *typo* such as *Salve rebellions* and file it properly as *Slave rebellions*. In a computer, which would see *salve* as a properly spelled word in any spelling checker, the title with the typo would be arranged before all other entries for the correctly spelled title. Intervening between *Salve* and *Slave* would be *Scarlet letter, Search for sanity, Silent world,* and many hundreds of other titles. (Note: retrieval of known items is much more difficult when a typographical error is involved.)

FILING HISTORY

Charles A. Cutter included filing rules in his cataloging code, in addition to his rules for description, name headings, and subject headings.[1] There have been separate filing codes, not connected with cataloging rules, ever since Cutter. Earlier filing codes reflected the influence of the classified catalog. They presorted catalog entries into categories. For example, entries beginning with the word *orange* were sorted into: personal names—separating single surname entries (e.g., Orange, Carolyn) from compound surname entries (e.g., Orange-Keysville, James); geographic entities (e.g., Orange County (Calif.)); corporate bodies (e.g., Orange and Rockland Utilities, Inc.); subject headings—separating the fruit (e.g., Orange peel) from the color (e.g., Orange azalea); and titles (e.g., *Orange Bear reader*). Even though the rules were for *dictionary* catalogs, the categories were to be filed one after another instead of being interfiled alphabetically. The earlier codes also reflected the many variant local practices that existed. The 1942 *A.L.A. Rules for Filing Catalog Cards*[2] had many rules with two or three correct alternatives for a particular filing dilemma. One library could use rules 1.a. and 2.b., while another library could use rules 1.b. and 2.a. Both could claim to be following the American Library Association (ALA) filing rules. Users going from one library to another had to learn new filing rules for each catalog.

By the mid-1960s frustration with the rules had peaked. People in ALA decided to create a consistent code of filing rules derived from one basic principle. The resulting 1968 *ALA Rules for Filing Catalog Cards*[3] recommended straight alphabetical order, but there were exceptions. For example, personal surname entries (for single surnames only) were to be arranged before other entries beginning with the same word (e.g., Love, Harold G. was filed before *Love and beauty*). Also, a filer had to spell out numerals and abbreviations in the language of the item and then file the card in the place where the spelled-out form would go in the catalog (e.g., *1984* was filed as *Nineteen eighty-four*).

In 1980 ALA again published a code of filing rules,[4] and this time they were so different that they were not identified as a third edition. They called for straightforward filing according to principles, but still, alphabetical order was not absolute. A brief review of these rules serves to highlight some of the problems that keep people from finding what they want in computer displays, especially when a displayed set takes up more than one or two screens.

GENERAL RULES FOR ARRANGEMENT

Traditional arrangement in catalogs is *word-by-word.* This means that everything beginning with a particular word should precede other entries beginning with a word that has the same beginning letters as the first word (e.g., New York files before Newark). Not all information retrieval tools use this arrangement. Some encyclopedias and dictionaries, for example, use *letter-by-letter* arrangement. The difference is that in word-by-word arrangement, a space between words is treated according to the principle: "nothing files before something." That is, a space is "nothing," and it should be filed before a character, which is "something." According to the *ALA Filing Rules,* spaces, dashes, hyphens, diagonal slashes, and periods are all considered to be "nothing." Arrangements using the letter-by-letter approach ignore spaces and some of the punctuation marks just mentioned, and the entry files as if it is all run together into one word (e.g., New York is treated as Newyork and follows Newark). A longer example may assist in clarifying the distinction:

Word-by-Word	**Letter-by-Letter**
A book about myself	A book about myself
Book bytes	Bookbinding
Book-making (Betting)	Book bytes
Book of bells	Booker T. Washington
Book reports	Booker, William, 1905–
Bookbinding	Bookfinder
Booker T. Washington	Bookkeeping made simple
Booker, William, 1905–	Book-making (Betting)
Bookfinder	Book of bells
Bookkeeping made simple	Book reports
Books that changed the world	Booksellers and bookselling
Booksellers and bookselling	Books that changed the world

Another principle of arrangement is that numerals precede letters. Formerly, numerals were filed as spoken and spelled out, for example,

Twenty-four dramatic cases...
24 ways to...
XXIVth Congress of...

However, in the 1980 filing rules the difficulties of mentally spelling out *24* in French, German, Russian, and so on, for both filers and users were recognized. Numerals were to go first, but in numerical order, and Roman numerals filed with Arabic numerals. Thus, *1/2* (the fraction) was to file before *1* (the first integer). But computers have difficulty with this. The computer sees *1/2* as *one-slash-two,* not *one-half.* In the following example one can see that numerical order for a computer is based upon an arrangement of numerals by whatever is the first digit, then the second digit, and so on, rather than by the value of the number, and Roman numerals are seen as letters:

Manual Filing	**Machine Arrangement**
6 concerti grossi	10 times a poem
9 to 5	1984
10 times a poem	6 concerti grossi
XIXth century drawings	9 to 5
90 days to a better heart	90 days to a better heart
1984	XIXth century drawings

Among other principles of manual filing are: letters in the English alphabet precede letters of nonroman alphabets; an ampersand (&) may be ignored, or optionally, may be spelled out in its language equivalent; and punctuation, nonalphabetic signs, and symbols are ignored. Computers generally treat these the same way except that they cannot follow the option of spelling out ampersands in their language equivalents. Ampersands are problematic for retrieval because a user who has heard a title, but has not seen it, does not know whether *and* is spelled out or represented by an ampersand, and usually does not know to try the other way if one way does not work. Recently, catalogers have often made additional title access points for the spelled-out form when ampersands or numerals have been used in titles.

FILING/DISPLAY DILEMMAS

There are quite a few situations that cannot be resolved by human intellect as was done in the past. It seems impossible to program computers to handle all these situations so that the outcome is logical. For example, when titles are transcribed from chief sources of information in the process of creating metadata, the title is taken character by character as it appears. This results in some titles that begin with or contain the same words appearing to a computer to contain different words. Names beginning with prefixes, for example, are sometimes written with a space following the prefix (e.g., De Gaulle and DeGaulle). Another case arises from words that began as two words and are in the process of becoming one word (e.g., *on line, on-line,* and *online*). Here is another case where a user, having heard a title spoken, would not know which way to look for it.

Another spacing problem comes from punctuation marks. As mentioned above, the *ALA Filing Rules* says that spaces, dashes, hyphens, diagonal slashes, and periods are all considered to be "nothing." However, this is not true in all computer systems. Such marks might be replaced by a space, or they might not even be replaced by a space, resulting in words being run together inappropriately (e.g., "surrogate/metadata records" might become "surrogatemetadata records").

Computers also have difficulty with abbreviations. A human or a natural language processing system can tell whether *Co.* means *County* or *Company;* whether *St.* means *Street* or *Saint;* whether *Dr.* means *Doctor* or *Drive.* Most systems cannot tell the difference, however, and arrangement is simply done by the letters that are there. A retrieval challenge is that even if users know the titles they are searching for word-for-word, if they have only heard the titles and have not seen them, they do not know if certain words are abbreviated or spelled out.

Dates in subject headings present yet another challenge. In traditional manual practice, dates are to be arranged in chronological order. With *Library of Congress Subject Headings (LCSH),* however, some dates are preceded by a verbal phrase identifying a name for the particular period of time. These headings can be placed in chronological order by a human, but a computer cannot see *1775–1783* until it has arranged *Revolution* preceding or following all other numerals. For example:

Dates (Manual Filing)	**Dates (Machine Arrangement)**
United States—History—Revolution, 1775–1783	United States—History—1800–
United States—History—1800–	United States—History—1801–1809
United States—History—1801–1809	United States—History—1900–
United States—History—War of 1812	United States—History—1945–
United States—History—Civil War, 1861–1865	United States—History—Civil War, 1861–1865
United States—History—1900–	United States—History—Revolution, 1775–1783
United States—History—1945–	United States—History—War of 1812

Some machine systems place numerals after letters, but in any case the letters would be together and the numerals would be together. How many users know that in a long list of time periods for the history of a country, the named periods come last or the dates alone come last?

Initials and acronyms present yet another arrangement and retrieval challenge. If they are written with periods or spaces between them, they are filed as if each letter is a word (e.g., *A B C* files as if the first word is *A,* the second is *B* and the third word is *C;* while *ABC* files as a single word). For example:

A.A.
A.A.U.W.
A apple pie
A B C programs
AAA
Aabel, Marie
Abacus calculating
ABCs of collecting

Users are at a loss to know whether periods or spaces have been used. This kind of situation requires the assistance of someone to add access points both with and without spaces.

The final arrangement problem to be discussed here is the one surrounding initial articles and elisions. Articles (*a, an, the,* and their equivalents in other languages) that come at the beginning of a heading are supposed to be ignored in filing. This can only happen in all languages if the system is using an encoding scheme like MARC, wherein a human can give in an indicator the number of characters that the computer should ignore before beginning the arrangement order. Even in the MARC format there is no provision for indicating articles for every possible title access point. In MARC 21, for example, uniform titles and titles in subfield *t* of several access point fields do not have indicators for articles. In addition, if a system is programmed to give access to subtitles, those beginning with articles will be arranged under the articles.

A system cannot just have a stopword list of all articles in all languages. First, some articles are ordinary words in other languages (e.g., the German *die*). Second, if the article is part of a proper name, it should be arranged under the article. For example:

Los angeles custodios *[title in A]*
Los Angeles in fiction *[title in L]*
Los Angeles Bar Association *[corporate body in L]*

Elisions (substitution of an apostrophe for a letter or letters when running two words together, e.g., *they'll* for *they will*) present a similar problem, especially when they begin a heading. In the following example an elided article begins the heading:

> L'enfant abandonee *[title in E]*
> L'Enfant, Edouard *[person in L]*

The main concern in the issues discussed above is that in online systems, when searchers retrieve responses that take more than two screens to display, they have to understand the arrangement. If they think that responses are in alphabetical order, and if they expect, for example, an acronym to be at the beginning of the listing, they might not even go to the screen that actually has the entry. Although arrangement is done by the computer system, some programming can be done by humans to enable displays to be more predictable.

Arrangement of retrieved metadata in response to a search is still evolving. The first online catalogs were automated card catalogs, but they lacked the sophisticated filing arrangements that could be accomplished in card catalogs. Display of search results has had many improvements, but problems still abound. An appropriate display is highly dependent upon system design, as discussed in Chapter 5.

NOTES

1. Charles A. Cutter, *Rules for a Dictionary Catalog,* 4th ed. (Washington, D.C.: Government Printing Office, 1904; reprint, London: The Library Association, 1962), p. 12.

2. *A.L.A. Rules for Filing Catalog Cards* (Chicago: American Library Association, 1942).

3. *ALA Rules for Filing Catalog Cards,* 2nd ed. (Chicago: American Library Association, 1968).

4. *ALA Filing Rules* (Chicago: American Library Association, 1980).

GLOSSARY

AACR2 ***(Anglo-American Cataloguing Rules, 2nd ed.).*** A set of rules, published in 1978, for producing the descriptive and name-and-title access points part of a surrogate record for an information resource; the creation of these rules was the result of collaboration among representatives from Canada, Great Britain, and the United States.

AACR2R ***(Anglo-American Cataloguing Rules, Second Edition, [various] Revisions).*** Revisions of AACR2; rules monitored by the Joint Steering Committee (JSC) for AACR, made up of representatives from Australia, Canada, Great Britain, and the United States. The JSC operated with continuous revision after 1988.

AAT ***(Art & Architecture Thesaurus).*** A thesaurus of terms in hierarchical arrangement that cover content and materials in the disciplines of art and architecture.

Aboutness. The subject of an information resource. *See also* **Subject analysis.**

Aboutness statement. A single sentence or a short paragraph describing and summarizing one's understanding of a resource's aboutness, the form/genre, and the relationships among the important subject concepts. The aboutness statement is used to identify the terms or concepts to be searched in the controlled vocabulary. The statement can also help the cataloger to construct a rudimentary hierarchy to get a better understanding of how the concepts fit together and how they might fit into a scheme of classification.

Access point. Any word or phrase used to obtain information from a retrieval tool or other organized system; in cataloging and indexing, *access points* are specific names, titles, and subjects chosen by the cataloger or indexer, when creating a surrogate/metadata record, to allow for the retrieval of the record. *See also* **Added entry; Primary access point.**

Accession number. A notation assigned to an information resource that is unique to the resource; the notations are often based upon the order in which information resources are acquired.

Accession record. In archives and museums, a record that contains basic information about the acquisition of a collection or object. It may include an identification number, information about the donor, any associations, provenance, any information needed for insurance purposes, and so forth. The accession record becomes the basis for one or more files that help provide organization of the museum's content, or in archives, is the basis for the finding aid.

Added entry. Any access point in a metadata record other than the primary access point.

Agent (Dublin Core). Creators, contributors, and publishers of information resources.

Agent (Internet). *See* **Spider.**

A-G Canada. *See* **Auto-Graphics.**

Aggregation. Collection of publications in electronic form (also called *aggregator database* or *aggregator*). Aggregations come in many forms (e.g., publisher-based aggregations in which all the journals in the collection are from one publisher; subject-based aggregations that usually include publications from numerous publishers but that share the same broad subject; vendor-based aggregations in which full-text publications can be accessed through vendors who have aggregated journals of many publishers).

Alphabetical catalog. Catalog in which the surrogate records are arranged or displayed in the order of the alphabet that is used in the institution that houses the catalog.

Alphabetico-classed catalog. Catalog in which subject categories are used for arrangement of surrogate records; broad categories are subdivided by narrower categories that are placed alphabetically within each broad category.

Analytical entry. An entry made for each of the works in a volume, as opposed to making only one entry for the entire volume.

Analytico-synthetic classification. *See* **Faceted classification.**

ANN (Artificial Neural Network). *See* **Artificial neural network.**

Annotation. A brief note indicating the subject matter or commenting on the usefulness of information in a particular information resource.

ANSI (American National Standards Institute). A body that takes responsibility for establishing voluntary industry standards; works closely with NISO (q.v.).

Application profile. Document that describes a community's recommended best practices for metadata creation; a formal way to declare which elements from which namespaces are used in a particular application or project or by a particular community.

APPM ***(Archives, Personal Papers, and Manuscripts).*** A standard based on AACR2R for the description of archival materials; has been accepted as a standard by most of the archival community. Now largely replaced by *Describing Archives: A Content Standard* (DACS) (q.v.).

Archival description. The process of establishing intellectual control over the holdings of an archives through the preparation of finding aids.

Archival series. A logical group of files, books, correspondence, or other such set.

Archives. Organization that preserves records of enduring value that document activities of organizations or persons and are accumulated in the course of daily activities.

Arrangement. The placing of entities in a certain order (e.g., alphabetical, by classification, by size, etc.). In card catalogs, this activity was called filing.

Art & Architecture Thesaurus. *See* **AAT.**

Artificial neural network (ANN). A computer system inspired by the architecture of the human biological nervous system.

ASCII (American Standard Code for Information Interchange). A standard code that assigns specific bit patterns to letters, numbers, and symbols;

used for exchange of textual data in instances where programs are incompatible, because ASCII can be read almost universally by any computing machine.

Asynchronous responsibility. The situation in which the persons or corporate bodies involved in the creation of an information resource have made different kinds of contributions to the creation of the work (e.g., author and illustrator; performer, conductor, choreographer, and producer; etc.).

Attribute. In metadata, a property or an element of an information resource, such as title, creator, subject, and so on; in searching, a characteristic of a search query.

Author. A person who is responsible for all or some of the intellectual content of a text. *See also* **Creator.**

Author entry. The place in a retrieval tool where a surrogate record beginning with the name of the creator of an information resource may be found.

Author/title access point. Access point that includes both the author and the title of a work in the construction of a single access point.

Authority control. The result of the process of maintaining consistency of forms of headings and the further process of showing relationships among headings—all for the purpose of collocation. Following this process means that headings in surrogate records are consistent with the character strings for those headings established in the authority file. One form may be identified as the authorized one to be used as a heading, with the others designated as references; or every variant name, title, or term may be given equal status, with one form chosen for default display. In either case a searcher may use any of the forms to gain access to information resources related to the name, title, or subject. *See also* **Authority work.**

Authority file. A collection of authority records.

Authority record. A compilation of metadata about a person, a family, a corporate body, a place, a work, or a subject; it includes all the decisions made and all the relationships among variants that have been identified in the process of authority work.

Authority work. The process of determining and maintaining the form of a name, title, or subject concept to be used in creating access points. In the name and title areas, the process includes identifying all variant names or titles and relating the variants to the name or title forms chosen to be access points. In some cases it may also include relating names and/or titles to each other. In the verbal subject area, the process includes identifying and maintaining relationships among terms—relationships such as synonyms, broader terms, narrower terms, and related terms.

Auto-Graphics. A computer-based bibliographic network offering its database and services to a variety of Canadian libraries and also to a few libraries in the northeastern United States; formerly Utlas International, which became ISM/LIS, and then A-G Canada.

A–Z index. *See* **Back-of-the-book index.**

Back-of-the-book index. An alphabetical list of entries for the major subjects, authors, and works referred to in an information resource. Each entry is accompanied by references or pointers (e.g., page numbers) to the locations in the resource that contain information about that entry. On the Web, similar indexes may be referred to as *A–Z indexes,* with direct links to the Web pages that contain information about the entries.

Bibliographic control. The process of describing items in the bibliographic universe and then providing name, title, and subject access to the descriptions, resulting in records that serve as surrogates for the actual items of recorded information. Bibliographic control further requires that surrogate records be placed into retrieval systems where they act as pointers to the actual information resources. *See also* **Information Organization.**

Bibliographic data. Information gathered in the process of creating bibliographic records.

Bibliographic database. A collection of bibliographic records held in the format of a database (q.v.).

Bibliographic network. A corporate entity that has as its main resource a bibliographic database; access to the database is available for a price, and members of the network can contribute new records and download existing ones.

Bibliographic record. Full descriptive and access information for an information resource; later terms used for descriptions of information resources are *surrogate record* and *metadata.*

Bibliographic tool. *See* **Retrieval tool.**

Bibliographic universe. A concept that encompasses all instances of recorded information.

Bibliographic utility. *See* **Bibliographic network.**

Bibliography. A list of information resources; bibliographies bring together lists of sources based on subject matter, on authors, by time periods, and the like.

Book catalog. Catalog in which surrogate records are printed on pages that are bound into book form.

Boolean operators. The terms AND, OR, and NOT as used to construct search topics through *postcoordinate indexing* (q.v.).

Boolean searching. The process of searching with individual index terms or keywords that are linked with Boolean operators (either using actual operators, or using a system where operators are implied if not specified).

Broad classification. A method of applying a classification scheme that uses only the main classes and divisions of a scheme and perhaps only one or two levels of subdivisions. *See also* **Close classification.**

Broader term (BT). A term one level up from the term being examined in a listing where terms for subject concepts have been organized into relationships that are hierarchical. *See also* **Narrower term; Related term.**

Browsing. A process of looking, usually based on subject, at all the items in a particular area of the stacks in order to find, often by serendipity, the items that best suit the needs of the person who is browsing. In online systems, browsing is the process of looking at all the surrogate records that are displayed under a certain subject, in a particular classification, or under a certain name or title.

Call number. A notation on an information resource that matches the same notation in the surrogate/metadata record; it is the number used to "call" for an item in a closed stack library—thus the source of the name *call number.*

Card catalog. Catalog in which surrogate records are written, typed, or printed on cards (usually measuring 3 by 5 inches) that are placed in file drawers in a particular order (usually alphabetical or classified order).

Catalog. Retrieval tool that provides access to individual items within collections of information resources (e.g., physical entities such as books, videos, and CDs in a library; artists' works in an art museum; Web pages on the Internet; etc.).

Catalog gateway. *See* **Gateway.**

Catalog record. *See* **Surrogate record.**

Cataloger. Person in an archives, a library, a museum, or other such organization who creates surrogate records for the information resources collected by the organization and who works to maintain the system through which those surrogate records are made available to users; the person may also be an independent contractor. *See also* **Indexer.**

Cataloging. The acts of creating surrogate records for information resources by describing the resources, choosing appropriate access points, and maintaining the system through which the records are made available. Such work done in nonprofit agencies is usually called *cataloging,* while such work done for commercial enterprises is usually called *indexing.*

***Cataloging Cultural Objects* (CCO).** A content standard for communities that describe works of art, architecture, cultural artifacts, and images. It prescribes the data values and defines the order, syntax, and form in which the values are to be entered into a data structure.

***Categories for the Description of Works of Art* (CDWA).** A metadata element set that is used for describing and accessing information about works of art, architecture, other material culture, and related images.

Categorization. The cognitive function that involves grouping together like entities, concepts, objects, resources, and so on.

Category. A cognitive label applied to a group of like entities.

CD-ROM (Compact Disc–Read Only Memory). A computer storage medium that is "read" with a laser beam.

Character-by-character filing. *See* **Letter-by-letter filing.**

Checksum. A value computed for a block of data, based on the contents of the block; used to detect corruption of the data.

Chief source of information. The location from which much of the information is to be taken that is used to create the descriptive part of a surrogate record (e.g., title page of a book, title screen of a motion picture, label on a sound recording tape or disc).

CIP (Cataloging-in-Publication). A program in which cataloging is provided by an authorized agency to the publisher or producer of an information resource so that the cataloging can be issued with the information resource; ordinarily the phrase is applied in the case of cataloging provided by the Library of Congress to the publishers of books.

Classical theory of categorization. Theory based on Aristotle's theory that categories contain entities or concepts based on what they have in common and that categories are like containers with things either in or out of the container.

Classification. The placing of subjects into categories; in organization of information, classification is the process of determining where an information resource fits into a given hierarchy and often then assigning the notation associated with the appropriate level of the hierarchy to the information resource and to its surrogate.

Classification notation. A set of numbers, letters, symbols, or a combination of these that is assigned to a certain level of hierarchy or to a certain concept in a classification scheme.

Classification schedule. A listing of the hierarchy of a classification scheme along with the notation for each level.

Classification scheme. A specification of a systematic organization of knowledge. *See also* **Taxonomy.**

Classification table. Supplementary part of a classification scheme in which notations are assigned for concepts that can be applied in conjunction with many different topical subjects. Tables commonly exist for geographic locations, time periods, standard subdivisions (e.g., dictionaries, theory, serial publications, historical treatment, etc.), ethnic and national groups, and the like.

Classified catalog. Catalog in which surrogate records for the main part of the catalog are arranged or displayed in the order of the classification scheme used in the institution that houses the catalog.

Close classification. Classification that uses all the minute subdivisions that are available in a particular classification for very specific subjects. *See also* **Broad classification.**

Closed stacks. The name given to the situation where information resource storage areas are accessible only to the staff of the library, archives, or other place that houses information resources. *See also* **Open stacks.**

Clustering. An automated sorting technique used by retrieval tools to group similar search results together based on content (and a variety of other factors), which can then be used to display the results.

Code (as a noun). (1) A set of rules. (2) A specific designation in an encoding standard that defines and limits the kinds of data that can be stored at that point.

Code (as a verb). The process of assigning the appropriate specified designations of an encoding standard.

Codification. The process of creating sets of rules to govern such things as the making of surrogate records.

Coextensive subject entry. A subject heading or a set of headings that covers all, but no more than, the concepts or topics covered in the information resource.

Collation. A statement of details about the pagination, illustrations, and size of a book. The concept as applied to other types of resources is called *physical description.*

Collocation. The bringing together of records and/or information resources that are related in some way (e.g., same author, same work [different titles or different editions], same subject, etc.).

Collocation device. A number or other designation on an item used to place it next to (i.e., collocate with) other items that are like it.

Colon Classification. Classification scheme devised by S. R. Ranganathan in the early 1930s; it was the first fully faceted classification scheme.

Colophon. A set of data at the end of a resource that gives varying kinds of bibliographic data. It might give information usually found on a title page, and, in items after the invention of printing with moveable type, it gives such information as date of printing, printer, typeface used, and the like.

Command searching. The process of searching in which a "code" (e.g., "a" or "au" for "author," "t" or "ti" for "title," etc.) is followed by an exact string of characters that are matched against the system's internal index.

Computer Output Microform (COM) catalog. Catalog in which surrogate records are produced on either microfiche or microfilm and require a microform reader in order to be able to use them.

Conceptual analysis. An examination of the intellectual or creative contents of an information resource to understand what the item is about and what the item is (i.e., its form and/or genre).

Container architecture. A model for pulling together distinct packages of metadata, which are related to the same information resource, into a single container. This conceptual model allows different communities to create, maintain, and share their metadata.

Content. The intellectual information transmitted in or by an information resource or metadata; content is distinguished from the encoding, packaging, or framework used for transmission.

Content Standard for Digital Geospatial Metadata (CSDGM). A specification that provides a common set of terminology and definitions for metadata about digital geospatial data. *See also* **FGDC (Federal Geographic Data Committee) metadata standard.**

Continuing resource. A work that is issued in parts, sometimes as separate entities, and sometimes with new information integrated into the existing information resource. *See also* **Integrating resource; Serial (as opposed to "monographic") work.**

Contract cataloging. An institution's use of a contractual relationship with a person or agency to provide surrogate records that represent the institution's acquisitions for its collection. *See also* **Outsourcing.**

Controlled vocabulary. A list or database of terms in which all terms or phrases representing a concept are brought together. Often a preferred term or phrase is designated for use in surrogate records in a retrieval tool; the terms not to be used have references from them to the chosen term or phrase, and relationships (e.g., broader terms, narrower terms, related terms, etc.) among used terms are identified. There may also be scope notes to explain the terms and there may be hierarchical listings.

Cooperative cataloging. The working together of independent institutions to create cataloging that can be shared with others.

Copy cataloging. The process of adapting for use in a catalog a copy of the original cataloging created by another library. *See also* **Original cataloging.**

Core Record. Standard set by the Program for Cooperative Cataloging (PCC) that presents the minimum requirements for elements to be included in a nationally acceptable AACR2 record.

Corporate body. A group of persons who have a group name and who act as an entity.

Crawler. *See* **Spider.**

Creator. Person who is responsible for the intellectual content of an information resource.

Cross reference. *See* **Reference.**

Crosswalks. Visual instruments for showing equivalent values in two or more schemes; for example, a crosswalk could be used to show which element in one metadata standard matches a particular element in another standard, or it could be used to show which classification notation in, say, DDC, is equivalent to a notation in LCC.

Cutter number. A designation that has the purpose of alphabetizing all works that have exactly the same classification notation; named for Charles Ammi Cutter, who devised such a scheme. *See also* **Call number.**

DACS. *See Describing Archives: A Content Standard.*

Data. Unprocessed information, which may be in the form of numbers (binary data, numerical data sets), text (facts, information without context), images, etc.

Data administration. *See* **Records management.**

Data modeling. The process of designing a system for managing office and administrative records; the process involves developing a conceptual model of an activity in a particular setting, followed by a logical model that includes much more detail, which is then translated into a physical data model that can be implemented as a database management system.

Database. A set of records that are all constructed in the same way and are often connected by relationship links; the structure underlying retrieval tools.

Database index. A retrieval tool that provides access to the analyzed contents of information resources (e.g., articles in journals, short stories in collections, papers in conference proceedings, reviews, reports, etc.). A database index contains electronically accessible and searchable entries that provide descriptive and administrative metadata, as well as descriptor terms (and, in some instances, classification notation) to represent the aboutness. May be referred to as a *journal index* or a *periodical index. See also* **Index.**

DDC ***(Dewey Decimal Classification)***. *See* ***Dewey Decimal Classification.***

Depth indexing. Indexing that extracts all the main concepts dealt with in an information resource, recognizing many subtopics and subthemes. *See also* **Exhaustivity; Summarization.**

Describing Archives: A Content Standard (**DACS**). A content standard for archival description. It may be used with EAD-encoded finding aids and MARC records that describe finding aids. It has largely replaced APPM. *See also* **APPM; Archival description.**

Description. *See* **Descriptive data.**

Descriptive cataloging. The process of providing the descriptive data and access points (other than subject) for surrogate records that are to be part of a catalog.

Descriptive data. Data that describes an information resource, such as its title, its associated names, its edition, its date of publication, its extent, and notes identifying pertinent features.

Descriptor. Subject concept term, representing a single concept, usually found in thesauri and used in indexes. *See also* **Subject heading.**

***Dewey Decimal Classification* (DDC).** Classification devised by Melvil Dewey in 1876; it divides the world of knowledge hierarchically into 10 divisions, which are in turn divided into ten sections, and so on, using the ten digits of the Arabic numeral system. DDC is enumerative but with many faceting capabilities, especially in its later editions.

Diacritic. Modifying mark over, under, or through a character to indicate that pronunciation is different from that of the character without the diacritic.

Dictionary catalog. Catalog in which surrogate records are arranged in alphabetical order by access point, intermixing name, title, and subject access points.

Digital library. A collection of information resources in digital form that are selected, brought together, organized, preserved, and to which access is provided over digital networks for a particular community of users.

Direct entry. A principle in the *formulation* of controlled vocabularies that stipulates the entry of a concept directly under the term that names it, rather than as a subdivision of a broader concept (e.g., Child rearing, *not* Children—Development and guidance). *See also* **Specific entry.**

Divided catalog. Catalog in which surrogate records are arranged or displayed in separate files or displays, separated by name access points, title access points, and subject access points.

Document. An information resource; often associated in people's minds with text and illustrations having been produced on paper, but increasingly associated with a video, a music disc, a computer file, or other such manifestation.

Document retrieval vs. Information retrieval. A dichotomy that is created by the level of exhaustivity used in subject indexing; summarization allows for retrieval of a document which can, itself, then be searched for relevant information, whereas depth indexing allows for retrieval of information at a much more specific level than the whole document.

Domain. (1) A sphere of knowledge, influence, or activity. (2) In networking, a group of computers whose host names share a common name (i.e., the domain name).

DTD (Document Type Definition). An SGML or XML application; defines the structure of a particular type of document.

Dublin Core (shortened form of Dublin Core Metadata Element Set). An internationally agreed-upon set of elements that can be completed by the creator of an electronic document in order to create a metadata record for the document; the 15 elements are broad and generic and therefore can be used to describe a wide range of resources.

EAC (Encoded Archival Context). An XML schema created to encode metadata about the parties (persons, corporate bodies, etc.) involved in the creation of archival materials and to put those parties into historical, geographical, and chronological context.

EAD (Encoded Archival Description). An XML schema created specifically to encode finding aids.

EAD Header. Descriptive data about the metadata in the rest of the EAD record. It is based heavily on the TEI Header.

Edition. Specific manifestation of the intellectual content (work, expression) found in an information resource.

Electronic resource. Information resource that requires the use of a computer to access its intellectual contents.

Element. An individual category or field that holds an individual piece of description of an information resource; typical metadata elements include title, creator, creation date, subject identification, and the like.

Encoding. The setting off of each part of a record so that the part can be displayed in certain positions according to the wishes of those creating a display mechanism, and so that certain parts of a record can be searchable.

Entity. (1) A *thing* (resource, person, name, address, etc.); used in an entity-relationship model. (2) A term used in the field of organization of information to indicate an item; both *entity* and *item* are used in order to avoid using *book* or other such specific designation.

Entity-relationship model. Data analysis method used to describe the requirements and assumptions in the system. These models comprise three components: entities are the *things* about which information is sought, attributes are the data collected about the things, and relationships provide the structure for relating things within the system. FRBR is based on this type of modeling.

Entry. The place in a print retrieval tool where a surrogate record is found.

Entry word. The first word of a *heading* (q.v.).

Enumerative classification. A subject concept arrangement that attempts to assign a designation for every subject concept (both single and composite) needed in the system.

ERIC thesaurus. A commonly used name for the *Thesaurus of ERIC Descriptors,* a thesaurus for indexing and searching documents indexed by the Educational Resources Information Center.

Exemplar. A typical or standard model or example.

Exhaustivity. The number of concepts that will be considered in the process of providing subject analysis; two basic degrees of exhaustivity are *depth indexing* and *summarization.*

Expansive classification. A scheme in which a set of coordinated schedules gives successive development possibilities from very simple (broad) to very detailed (close) subdivisions. Charles A. Cutter, in the late 1800s, created a classification scheme that he named *Expansive Classification.*

Expression. Level in describing works where the work takes a specific artistic or intellectual form each time that it is brought into existence; an intangible, abstract entity that is made tangible in a *manifestation.*

Extensibility (metadata). The ability to use additional metadata elements and qualifiers to adapt to the specific needs of a community or project. *See also* **Qualifier.**

Facet. (1) A fundamental aspect, feature, or characteristic used in describing a topic, object, or idea. (2) Any of the definable segments that make up a subject.

Facet indicator. A symbol, letter, or number used to signify a facet or category. For example, in *Colon Classification,* a period (full stop) is used to indicate the space facet (i.e., geographic characteristic) in classification notations.

Faceted browsing. A feature in information systems that allows the searcher to browse retrieved metadata by various categories established in the metadata record such as resource type, date, form, subject, place, etc.

Faceted classification. A subject concept arrangement that has small notations standing for subparts of the whole topic, which, when strung together, usually in prescribed sequence, create a complete classification notation for a multipart concept.

Federated searching. The ability to search and retrieve results from multiple sources of information while using only a single, common interface. It features an all-inclusive search box for multiple systems, which may include catalogs, indexes, databases, and other electronic resources. Also known as *meta-searching.*

FGDC (Federal Geographic Data Committee) metadata standard. Provides a common set of terminology and definitions for metadata about geospatial data (e.g., maps) that are in digital form. *See also* **Content Standard for Digital Geospatial Metadata (CSDGM).**

Field. A separately designated part of an encoded record; it may contain one or more subfields.

Filing. The process of placing paper records (e.g., catalog cards, acquisition forms, etc.) in order, usually in drawers.

Finding aid. A long, inventory-like description of an archival collection; it describes a whole collection rather than individual pieces of the collection. A shorter surrogate record may be made for the finding aid.

Fixed field. A field of an encoded record that is always the same length from record to record.

Fixed location. A set place where a physical information resource will always be found or to which it will be returned after having been removed for use.

Flexibility (metadata). The ability to include as much or as little detail as needed in one's metadata.

Folksonomy. The aggregation of the tags created by a large number of individual users. The term is a blend of *folks* and *taxonomy. See also* **Tagging.**

Functional Requirements for Authority Data **(FRAD).** A conceptual model that describes the need for and the uses of authority-controlled data by information professionals and information seekers.

Functional Requirements for Bibliographic Records **(FRBR).** A conceptual model (entity-relationship model) that identifies various entities found in the bibliographic universe, attributes associated with those entities, relationships among the entities, uses of bibliographic data by information seekers, and the relationships between the attributes and the uses of bibliographic data.

Full entry. *See* **Main entry (record).**

Fuzzy set theory of categorization. A theory that holds that some categories are not well defined and sometimes depend upon the observer, rather than upon a definition (e.g., people under five feet tall think the category of "tall people" is larger than do people over six feet tall).

Gateway. A computer system or a Web location that provides access to many different databases or other resources through the same interface.

General International Standard Archival Description **(ISAD (G)).** An international content standard for archival description. It is used with national standards or as a basis for developing national standards for archival description. It is a foundation for *Describing Archives: A Content Standard. See also* **Archival description.**

GILS (Government [or Global] Information Locator Service) record. Metadata that describes the information holdings of a U.S. federal agency.

GMD (General Material Designation). In an AACR2 record, an indication of the class of item being described (e.g., art original, electronic resource, motion picture, etc.).

Granularity. In metadata description, the level and depth at which information resources are described; in database design, a measure of the size or number of segments into which memory is divided.

GUI (Graphical User Interface). A computer interface that uses icons and other such graphics to make a screen more intuitive for users.

Heading. (1) An access point printed at the top (head) of a copy of a surrogate record or at the top of a listing of related works in an online retrieval tool. (2) The exact string of characters of the authorized form of an access point as it appears in the authority record.

Hierarchical classification. A subject concept arrangement that follows the classical theory of categorization, creating categories from general to specific. *See also* **Taxonomy.**

Hierarchy. An arrangement by which categories are grouped in such a way that a concept (e.g., class or discipline) is subdivided into subconcepts of an equal level of specificity, each of those subconcepts are further subdivided into subcategories, and so on. In science, for example, living organisms are in the hierarchy: phylum, class, order, family, genus, species.

HTML (HyperText Markup Language). A scheme for encoding text, pictures, and the like, so that they can be displayed using various programs because the coding is totally made up of ASCII text.

HTTP (HyperText Transfer Protocol). The part of a URL that lets the system's browser know that a Web page is being sought; the protocol itself defines how messages are formatted and is the protocol most often used to transfer information from World Wide Web servers to system browsers.

Hyperlink. An electronic connection between two separate pieces of information: it may be between two Web pages, between two parts of an electronic information resource, between text and an image, and so forth.

Hypertext. Document in which words, pictures, references, and the like, may be linked to other locations or documents so that clicking on one of the links takes a person to related information.

IFLA (International Federation of Library Associations and Institutions). International organization for the promotion of library standards and the sharing of ideas and research.

ILL (Interlibrary loan). The process of acquiring a physical information resource or a copy of it from a library that owns it by a library that does not own it.

ILS (Integrated Library System). Computer system that includes various modules to perform different functions while sharing access to the same database.

Imprint. The information in a textual publication that tells where it was published, who published it, and when it was published.

Index. A bibliographic tool that provides access to the analyzed contents of information resources (e.g., articles in a journal, short stories in a collection, papers in a conference proceeding, etc.). Back-of-the-book indexes provide access to the analyzed contents of one work.

Indexer. A person who determines access points (usually subject terms, but also sometimes authors or titles) that are needed in order to make surrogate records available to searchers; an indexer also may create surrogate records. Indexers often are employed by for-profit organizations. *See also* **Cataloger.**

Indexing. The process of creating surrogate records, especially the access points, for information resources; such work done in commercial enterprises is often called *indexing,* while similar work done in nonprofit agencies is usually called *cataloging.*

Indexing language. A rule-based means for choosing and structuring terms, either controlled or noncontrolled, that can assist in providing access to an information resource.

Indexing vocabulary. *See* **Controlled vocabulary.**

Indicators. In the MARC encoding standards, indicators for a field contain coded information that is needed for interpreting or supplementing data in the field.

Information. The communication or reception of knowledge; organized data. *See also* **Data; Knowledge.**

Information architecture. A methodology for planning, designing, building, organizing, and maintaining an information system (usually associated with systems on the Web).

Information organization. The process of describing information resources and providing name, title, and subject access to the descriptions, resulting in records that serve as surrogates for the actual items of recorded information and in resources that are logically arranged. Also referred to as *Bibliographic control* or *Organization of information. See also* **Bibliographic control.**

Information package. *See* **Information resource.**

Information resource. An instance of recorded information (e.g., book, article, video, Internet document or set of "pages," sound recording, electronic journal, etc.). *See also* **Item; Work.**

Information retrieval vs. Document retrieval. *See* **Document retrieval vs. Information retrieval.**

Integrating resource. In AACR2R (2002 revision), a bibliographic resource that is added to or changed by means of updates that are integrated into the whole resource (includes updating loose-leafs and updating Web sites).

Interface design. The part of a system design that controls the interaction between the computer and the user.

Interlibrary Loan. *See* **ILL.**

International Standard Archival Authority Record for Corporate Bodies, Persons, and Families **(ISAAR (CPF)).** A content standard that provides guidance on creating archival authority records for corporate bodies, persons, and families who have created and maintained the records, documents, and other resources that comprise archives.

Internet. A global network comprised of thousands of interconnected computer networks; it allows access to such services as electronic mail, remote login, file transfer services, and the World Wide Web; the networks all use TCP/IP (Transmission Control Protocol/Internet Protocol).

Interoperability. The compatibility of two or more systems such that they can exchange information and data and can use the exchanged information and data without any special manipulation.

Inventory. A tool whose purpose is to provide a record of what is owned.

ISAAR (CPF). *See* ***International Standard Archival Authority Record for Corporate Bodies, Persons, and Families.***

ISAD (G). *See* ***General International Standard Archival Description.***

ISBD ***(International Standard Bibliographic Description).*** A standard that was designed in the early 1970s to facilitate the international exchange of cataloging records by standardizing the elements to be used in the description, assigning an order to those elements, and specifying a system of symbols to be used in punctuating the elements.

ISBN (International Standard Book Number). A number that is accepted as an international standard for a unique number for a monographic item.

ISM/LIS (Information Systems Management/Library Information Services). *See* **Auto-Graphics.**

ISO (International Standards Organization). A corporate body that oversees the creation and approval of standards.

ISSN (International Standard Serial Number). A number that is accepted as an international standard for a unique number for a serial.

Item (as opposed to "work"). One copy of a manifestation of a work, focusing on the packaging of an information resource rather than its intellectual contents.

Keyword. A term that is chosen, either from actual text or from a searcher's head, that is considered to be a "key" to finding certain information.

Keyword searching. The use of one or more keywords as the intellectual content of a search command.

Knowledge. What exists in the mind (rather than in any stored form) of an individual who has studied a subject, understands it, and perhaps has added to it through research or other means; a combination of information, context, and experience.

Knowledge management. The attempt to capture, evaluate, store, and reuse what the employees of an organization know.

Knowledge Organization System (KOS). A generic term for all types of schemes for organizing information, including classification schemes, categories, authority files, subject headings, thesauri, and ontologies.

Known-item searching. Searching for a specific name, title, or subject within a retrieval tool to retrieve a particular information resource.

LCRIs ***(Library of Congress Rule Interpretations).*** A collection of the decisions that have been made by the Library of Congress's Cataloging Policy and Support Office as to how catalogers at the Library of Congress will interpret and apply AACR2.

LCSH. *See* ***Library of Congress Subject Headings.***

Letter-by-letter filing. An arrangement of entries in a retrieval tool in which spaces and some punctuation marks are ignored so that an entry files as if it is all run together into one word (e.g., "New York" is treated as "Newyork" and follows "Newark"). *See also* **Word-by-word filing.**

Library of Congress Classification **(LCC).** Classification scheme created by the Library of Congress beginning in the late 1890s; it divides the world of knowledge hierarchically into categories using letters of the English alphabet and then using Arabic numerals for further subdivisions. LCC is basically an enumerative scheme, allowing only a limited amount of faceting.

Library of Congress Rule Interpretations. *See* **LCRIs.**

Library of Congress Subject Headings **(LCSH).** A list of terms to be used as controlled vocabulary for subject headings created by the Library of Congress and used by any agency that wishes to provide controlled subject access to surrogate records.

Literary warrant. The concept that new notations are created for a classification scheme and new terms are added to a controlled vocabulary only when information resources actually exist about new concepts.

Location device. A number or other designation on an item to tell where it is physically located.

MADS (Metadata Authority Description Schema). An XML schema for an authority data element set that has been particularly developed for library applications.

Main entry (access point). *See* **Primary access point.**

Main entry (record). A copy of the surrogate record that contains a complete set of all elements of the record as provided by the cataloger.

Manifestation. Any one of the formats in which one of the expressions of a work can be found.

Manuscripts. Papers created by an individual (not organizational papers); original handwritten or typed documents that usually exist in single copies (unless they have been carbon-copied or photocopied).

MARC (Machine-Readable Cataloging). A standard prescribing codes that precede and identify specific elements of a catalog record, allowing the record to be "read" by machine and thus to be displayed in a fashion designed to make the record intelligible to users.

MARC 21. A MARC standard agreed upon and adopted by Canada and the United States; MARC 21 represents a consolidation of USMARC and CAN/MARC, previous national MARC schemes for the two countries. MARC 21 has been adopted by Great Britain and Germany, and is being considered for adoption by others.

Markup language. A scheme that allows the tagging and describing of individual structural elements of text for the purpose of digital storage, appropriate layout display, and retrieval of individual components.

***Medical Subject Headings* (MeSH®).** A list of terms to be used as controlled vocabulary for subject headings created by the National Library of Medicine and used by any agency that wishes to provide controlled subject access to surrogate records in the field of medicine.

Menu searching. A process of searching that allows one to navigate by making choices, not by giving commands.

Metadata. An encoded description of an information resource (e.g., an AACR2 record encoded with MARC, a Dublin Core record, etc.); the purpose of metadata is to provide a level of data at which choices can be made as to which information resources one wishes to view or search, without having to search massive amounts of irrelevant full text. *See also* **Surrogate record.**

Metalanguage. A language for describing markup languages.

Meta-metadata. Data describing metadata (e.g., administrative data used to track metadata).

Meta-searching. *See* **Federated searching.**

Meta tag. A tag in the header of an HTML document that contains **Metadata.**

METS (Metadata Encoding and Transmission Standard). A standard for encoding descriptive, administrative, and structural metadata for objects in a digital library.

Model. An abbreviated description of a complex entity or process used to explain or demonstrate the entity or process.

MODS (Metadata Object Description Schema). A schema for a bibliographic element set that has been particularly developed for library applications; a subset of MARC expressed in XML.

Monographic (as opposed to "serial") work. A complete bibliographic unit or information resource. It is often a single work, but may also be one work or more than one work issued in successive parts; but unlike serials, it is not intended to be continued indefinitely.

Museum accession record. A record used as a surrogate for an object acquired by a museum; it contains many kinds of information about the object, such as its provenance, financial history, location in the museum, historical significance, and the like.

Museum registration. *See* **Registration.**

Namespace. A collection of element type and attribute names; the collection (i.e., namespace) is identified by a unique name (i.e., a URI). In a traditional namespace, each name must be unique within that namespace; however, the same name can be used in more than one namespace with different meanings. An XML namespace identifies each element type or attribute name uniquely by a two-part name that includes the URI of its XML namespace and its local name.

Narrower term (NT). A term one level down from the term being considered in a listing where terms for subject concepts have been organized into relationships that are hierarchical. *See also* **Broader term; Related term.**

***National Union Catalog* (NUC).** A publication of the Library of Congress that cumulated cataloging records from many libraries and indicated by "NUC symbol" those libraries that owned a particular item.

Natural language. The language used by a person when expressing a concept about which information is desired.

Natural language processing (NLP). Computer analysis of written or spoken language in order to interpret meaning in a way that can allow the computer to "understand" and "respond."

Neural network. *See* **Artificial neural network (ANN).**

NISO (National Information Standards Organization). A corporate body that oversees the creation and approval of standards to be used in information processing; an American counterpart to ISO (q.v.).

NLP (Natural language processing). *See* **Natural language processing.**

Nonbook materials. Terminology used for any information resources that are not text in book form.

Notation. A representation in a system, such as a classification system, with a set of marks, usually consisting of letters, numbers, and/or symbols.

OCLC (Online Computer Library Center). A bibliographic network, based in Dublin, Ohio, that is the largest and most comprehensive bibliographic network in the world.

OCLC Connexion. A Web-based interface to OCLC's database; it began as CORC, a system that helped libraries provide access to Web resources.

ONIX International (ONline Information eXchange). The book industry standard for representing and communicating product information in e-format; designed to carry the kind of information traditionally carried on jacket covers and, optionally, also to carry excerpts, book reviews, cover images, author photos, and the like.

Online catalog. Catalog in which surrogate records are encoded for computer display and are stored on a local or remote server; arrangement within the server is irrelevant to the user, as arrangement is created in response to a query.

Online index. An index in which surrogate records for the analyzed contents of information resources are encoded for computer display and are stored on a local or remote server.

On-the-fly record. A record created electronically for an information resource between the request by a searcher and the display of responses.

Ontology. In the field of artificial intelligence, a formal representation of what, to a human, is common sense; in metadata and on the Web, a formal representation of language that identifies specific terms, usually from a defined subject area, and lays out the relationships that exist between the terms.

OPAC (Online Public Access Catalog). *See* **Online catalog.**

Open stacks. The name given to the situation where patrons of a facility have the right to go into the storage areas themselves. *See also* **Closed stacks.**

Organization of information. *See* **Bibliographic control; Information organization.**

Organization of knowledge. *See* **Bibliographic control; Information organization.**

Organize. To perform the process of forming unity and arranging separate parts into a whole that functions as an integrated unit.

Original cataloging. Cataloging in which a surrogate/metadata record for an information resource is created wholly by a cataloger without the use of cataloging data for the resource that may have been created by someone else first. *See also* **Copy cataloging.**

Original order. The order in which records in an archival collection were originally kept when they were in active use.

Outsourcing. A management technique whereby some activities, formerly conducted in-house, are contracted out for completion by a contracting agency; technical services operations are sometimes outsourced. *See also* **Contract cataloging.**

Paris Principles. The conventional name of the Statement of Principles agreed upon by attendees at the International Conference on Cataloguing Principles in Paris, October 9–18, 1961.

Pathfinder. A subject bibliography that uses a systematic approach to lead a user to find the resources a library has available on a specific topic;

a pathfinder may be in print or online, and the resources listed may be physical or digital.

PCC (Program for Cooperative Cataloging). An international cooperative program coordinated jointly by the Library of Congress and participants around the world; effort is aimed at expanding access to collections through useful, timely, cost-effective cataloging that meets internationally accepted standards.

Portals. Transactional Internet gateways targeted to a specific audience.

Postcoordinate indexing. The assigning of single concept terms from a controlled vocabulary to surrogate records so that the searcher of the system is required to coordinate the terms through such techniques as Boolean searching.

Precision. The measurement of how many of the documents retrieved are relevant.

Precoordinate indexing. The assigning of subject terms to surrogate records in such a way that some concepts, subconcepts, place names, time periods, and form concepts are put together in subject strings, and searchers of the system do not have to coordinate these particular terms themselves.

Primary access point. Access point that is chosen as the main or primary one; often referred to as *main entry* in the library and archival worlds.

Property. (1) In metadata, an element or attribute of an information resource, such as the title, the description, or the creator of the resource. (2) In legal terms, it designates ownership or proprietorship, as in *intellectual property.*

Protocol. A standard set of rules that determines how computers communicate with each other across networks (e.g., HTTP and Z39.50 are protocols); it describes the format that a message must take and the way in which computers must exchange a message.

Prototype theory of categorization. The theory that categories have prototypes (i.e., best examples; for example, most people think a robin is a better example of a bird than is an ostrich).

Provenance. The origin or ownership trail of an archival document or collection, or of a museum object. In the case of an archival collection the origin may be an organization, office, or person that created, received, or accumulated and used the item or the records in the collection. In the case of a museum object, the origin may be a person, family, or other prior owner of the object, or it may be an archaeological expedition, or it may be the location where a natural history specimen was found. In the case of an art work, the provenance may be the prior owners of the art.

Proximity (in searching). The concept of *nearness* of search terms to one another in a text.

Publisher. The person or corporate body responsible for issuing information resources to make them available for public use.

Qualifier. A refinement to a metadata element to either sharpen the focus of the element or to identify a controlled vocabulary from which the value has been supplied. *See also* **Extensibility (Metadata).**

RDA: Resource Description and Access. A content standard being developed to replace AACR2. It is scheduled to be published in 2009.

RDF (Resource Description Framework). An infrastructure that enables the encoding, exchange, and reuse of structured metadata; it uses XML as the means for exchanging and processing the metadata. RDF is based on the premise that resources have properties, properties have values, some values can be other resources with their own properties and values, and all these relationships can be linked within the framework.

Recall. The measurement of how many of the relevant documents in a system are actually retrieved.

Record. *See* **Bibliographic record; Metadata; Surrogate record.**

Records management. The process of maintaining records for an organization; it includes such functions as making decisions about what records should be created, saving necessary records, establishing effective systems for retrieval of records, and archiving important records for posterity.

Reference (cross reference). An instruction in a retrieval tool that directs a user to another place in the tool.

Register (accession log). One of the control tools for a museum; it functions like a catalog with a number of additional kinds of access points (e.g., donor, style, provenance, etc.).

Registration. The process of creating a surrogate record that uniquely identifies an object belonging to a museum; the records form the register (or catalog) for the museum.

Related term (RT). A term at the same level of specificity or bearing a non-hierarchical relationship to another term in a listing where terms for subject concepts have been organized into relationships that are hierarchical. *See also* **Broader term; Narrower term.**

Relational database. A database in which records are structured in such a way that information is not all stored in the same file; files for different kinds of information are created (e.g., a bibliographic file, a personal name file, a corporate name file, a subject file, a classification file, etc.); records in the bibliographic file contain pointers to records in the other files and vice versa. A relational database structure conserves storage space, allows for faster searching, and allows for easier modification of records. Pointers establish "relationships" among records.

Relative location. The situation in which an information resource will be or might be in a different place each time it is reshelved because it is shelved in relation (usually classificatory) to entities already shelved.

Relevance. A measure of how pertinent retrieval results are to particular queries or user needs. This concept is defined and calculated quite differently among various information retrieval systems.

Reprint. A new printing of an item either by photographic methods or by resetting unchanged text.

Resource. *See* **Information Resource.**

Resource Description and Access. *See* ***RDA.***

Resource discovery. The process of locating, accessing, retrieving, and bringing together relevant information from widely distributed networks.

Respect des fonds. The principle that states that archival materials created and/or collected together should be kept together, in their original order without mixing in records or materials from other creators or collections. *See also* **Original order; Provenance.**

Retrieval tool. Device such as a catalog, an index, a search engine, and the like, created for use as an information retrieval system.

Retrospective conversion. The process of changing information in eye-readable surrogate records into machine-readable form.

RLIN (Research Libraries Information Network). A bibliographic network that was particularly aimed at academic/research libraries and was especially important for special collections. It has now been absorbed by OCLC.

Robot (Internet). *See* **Spider.**

Schedule. *See* **Classification schedule.**

Schema. (1) A set of metadata elements created by a particular community or for a particular type of resource. (2) A document or piece of code that controls a set of terms in another document or piece of code; similar in function to a master checklist.

Scope note. A statement delimiting the meaning and associative relations of a subject heading, index term, or classification notation.

Search engine. A computerized retrieval tool that, in general, matches keywords input by a user to words found in documents of the site being searched; the more sophisticated search engines may allow other than keyword searching.

Sears List of Subject Headings (Sears). A controlled vocabulary of terms and phrases that is used mostly in small libraries to provide subject access to information resources available from those libraries.

Semantic Web. An extension of the current Web in which the meaning of information is well defined through metadata and ontologies. Its intent is to allow computers to "understand" what is meant by the character strings that make up words and phrases; if a computer is able to understand the meaning, then a human's request for information and services can be responded to with much more precision.

Semantics. The meaning of a string of characters, as opposed to the syntax, which dictates the structure, independent of meaning.

Serial record file. A group of records that contains information about receipt of specific issues of serials or other continuing resources.

Serial (as opposed to "monographic") work. A publication issued in successive parts (regularly or irregularly) that is intended to continue indefinitely. *See also* **Continuing resource; Integrating resource.**

Series. A group of separate works that are related in subject or form and are published by the same entity.

Series (archives). A logically grouped set of files, books, correspondence, or other such set.

SGML (Standard Generalized Markup Language). An international standard for document markup for machine readability.

Shelflist. Originally, a list of physical information resources owned by an institution in the order in which they appeared on the shelves of the institution in which they were housed; with time, the meaning has developed to indicate classification order display of surrogate records for information resources, which now allows for intangible as well as physical information resources.

Shelving. The process of placing physical information resources on shelves in the order of the arrangement of their call numbers or other notations that indicate their appropriate locations.

Social Indexing and Social Tagging. *See* **Tagging.**

Specific entry. A principle observed in *application* of controlled vocabularies, by which a cataloger and/or an indexer assigns to an information resource the most precise term available in the controlled vocabulary (or allowed to be created by the rules of the vocabulary), rather than assigning some broader heading. *See also* **Direct entry; Specificity.**

Specificity. The level of subject analysis that is addressed by a particular controlled vocabulary (e.g., LCSH has greater specificity in its established headings than does *Sears,* as, for example, in the greater depth of subdivisions that are established under main headings by LCSH). *See also* **Specific entry.**

Spider. An automated Internet program that gathers content from Web pages (storing URLs and indexing keywords, links, and text) for inclusion in a search engine; may also be referred to as *crawler, Web crawler, agent,* or *robot.*

SRU (Search/Retrieval via URL). A standard XML search protocol for Internet search queries that uses the Contextual Query Language (CQL), a standard syntax for representing queries.

Stopword list. A list of words *not* included in, or filtered out of, retrieval tools.

Standard. Something established by authority or custom as a model or example; in the information field, standards are approved by national and/or international bodies after discussion and voting by representatives.

Structure. Arrangement in a definite pattern of the parts of a whole.

Subfield. A separately designated segment of a field in an encoded record.

Subject access. The provision to users of the means of locating information using subject terminology and/or classification notations.

Subject analysis. The part of indexing or cataloging that deals with the conceptual analysis of an information resource; the translation of that conceptual analysis into a framework for a particular classification, subject heading, or indexing system; and then using the framework to assign specific notations or terminology to the information resource and its surrogate record.

Subject authority file. A record of choices made in the development of a controlled vocabulary. The authority file contains such things as justification for the choice of one synonym over another; references from unused synonyms or near-synonyms; references for broader terms, narrower terms, and related terms; scope notes; citations for references used; and the like. *See also* **Subject heading list.**

Subject cataloging. The process of providing subject analysis, including subject headings and classification notations, when creating catalog records for archives, libraries, museums, and the like.

Subject entry. The place in a retrieval tool where a surrogate record containing a particular controlled vocabulary term is found.

Subject heading. Subject concept term or phrase found in a subject heading list and used in catalog records; sometimes used in indexes. *See also* **Descriptor.**

Subject heading list. A list of authorized controlled vocabulary terms or phrases together with any references, scope notes, and subdivisions associated with each term or phrase. *See also* **Subject authority file; Thesaurus.**

Subject indexing. The process of determining the aboutness of an information resource and determining appropriate subject terminology to express the aboutness in an indexing language.

Subject subdivision. A method of precoordinating subject headings by using terms or phrases following main concepts to show special treatment of a subject.

Summarization. Indexing that identifies only a dominant, overall subject of an information resource, recognizing only concepts embodied in the main theme. *See also* **Depth indexing; Exhaustivity.**

Surrogate record. A presentation of the characteristics (e.g., title, creator, physical description if appropriate, date of creation, subject[s], etc.) of an information resource. *See also* **Metadata.**

Switching language. A mediation language used to establish equivalencies between or among different subject indexing languages or classification schemes.

Synchronous responsibility. The situation in which all persons or corporate bodies involved in the creation of an information resource have made the same kind of contribution to the creation of the work (e.g., joint authors).

Syndetic structure. The system of controlled vocabulary with all its references as used in a catalog or other retrieval tool.

Synonym. A term with the same meaning as another term; often, in controlled vocabularies, used for a term that has nearly the same meaning as well as for a term that has the same meaning.

Syntax. The arrangement of parts or elements so that they become constituents of a connected or orderly system; metadata's syntax is described by its encoding schema (e.g., MARC, XML), just as a language's syntax is described by its grammar.

System design. The specification of the working relations among all parts of a system; important design concepts include small testable components, user-friendly operation, and attractive functionality.

Table. *See* **Classification table.**

Tag. (1) A number, set of letters, certain set of punctuation marks, and so forth, that designates the kind of field in an encoding standard. (2) In Web 2.0 applications, a keyword assigned to a resource by a user.

Tagging. A populist approach to subject description. It is a process by which a distributed mass of users applies keywords to various types of Web-based resources for the purposes of collaborative information organization and retrieval. Tagging allows individual users to group similar resources together by using their own terms or labels, with few or no restrictions. Also referred to as *user tagging, social tagging,* and *social indexing.*

Taxonomy. A classification, usually in a restricted subject field, that is arranged to show presumed natural relationships. *See also* **Classification scheme.**

Technical metadata. Metadata that describes the "physical characteristics," origins, and lifecycles of digital resources; it is key to the preservation of the resource for future use. Basic technical information is needed in order to understand the nature of the information resource, the software and hardware environments in which it was created, and what is needed to make the resource accessible to users.

Technical services. The group of activities in an institution that involves acquiring, organizing, housing, maintaining, and conserving collections and automating these activities. In some places circulating collections is also considered to be a technical service.

TEI (Text Encoding Initiative). Refers to both the corporate organization with that name and to the encoding standard created by that group. The encoding standard was originally intended for the encoding of literary texts, although it has expanded to be used for other types of texts, as well.

TEI Header. A set of encoded metadata at the beginning of a TEI document that describes the document, its contents, and its origins.

Thesaurus. A list of authorized controlled vocabulary terms representing single concepts together with any references, scope notes, and subdivisions associated with each term, and organized so that the relationships between concepts are made explicit. *See also* **Subject heading list.**

Title entry. The place in a retrieval tool where a surrogate record containing the name of an information resource may be found.

Tracing. On printed surrogate records (e.g., catalog cards, records in book catalogs), the set of name, title, and subject access points, other than the primary access point, that appear at the bottom of the record and are used to "trace" the additional copies of the surrogate record.

Triple (RDF). This is the model used to structure RDF statements. A triple consists of a subject (a resource), a predicate (a property), and an object (a value).

UBC (Universal Bibliographic Control). *See* **Universal Bibliographic Control.**

UCS (Universal Character Set). ISO standard for encoded representation of characters in computers; has the purpose of including all characters in all written languages of the world.

UDC ***(Universal Decimal Classification).*** *See* ***Universal Decimal Classification.***

Unicode. An American industry counterpart to UCS, which permits computers to be able to handle the large number of character sets used in various languages. Both UCS and Unicode provide a unique number for every character to be used regardless of platform or format; a number of countries have adopted it as their national format.

Uniform title. A title chosen for a work so that all manifestations will be displayed together under the same primary access point and also will be displayed together among all the entries for that access point. Uniform titles also are used to distinguish between and among different works that have the same title. The concept is referred to as *work/expression name* in the new *Statement of International Cataloguing Principles.*

UNIMARC (UNIversal MARC). Originally conceived as a conversion format, in which capacity it requires that each national agency create a translator to change records from UNIMARC to the particular national format and vice versa; some countries have adopted it as their national format.

Union catalog. A catalog that represents the holdings of more than one institution or collection.

Universal Bibliographic Control. The concept that it will someday be possible to have access to surrogate records for all the world's important information resources.

***Universal Decimal Classification* (UDC).** A classification devised by Otlet and LaFontaine in the late 1890s. It was originally based on DDC, but has evolved into a much more faceted scheme than DDC.

URI (Uniform Resource Identifier). A way (such as use of a name or number) used on the Web to identify things such as people, corporations, books, abstract concepts, or network-accessible things; not limited to things that have network locations.

URL (Uniform Resource Locator). One form of URI: the address of an information resource on the Internet; it indicates what protocol to use (e.g., "http," "telnet") and then gives the IP address or the domain name where the resource is located: most often server address, directory path, and file name.

User tagging. *See* **Tagging.**

USMARC (United States MARC). The version of MARC used in the United States until it was superseded by MARC 21.

USNAF (United States Name Authority File). A file housed at the Library of Congress (LC), containing not only the authority records created by LC and its cooperating U.S. contributors, but also records contributed from Australia, Canada, Great Britain, and others.

Utlas International. *See* **Auto-Graphics.**

Value. A specific name of an attribute (or property) of a resource; for example, the value of an *author* attribute might be "Jane Smith," or the value of a *subject* attribute might be "Information organization."

Value-spaces. A set of values established for a particular metadata element or data type. *See also* **Authority file; Controlled vocabulary.**

Variable field. A field of an encoded record that can be as long or as short as the data to be placed into that field.

Vocabulary control. The process of creating and using a controlled vocabulary (q.v.).

VRA (Visual Resources Association) Core. A set of guidelines for describing visual documents depicting works of art, architecture, and artifacts or structures from material, popular, and folk culture.

Web. Short for World Wide Web (WWW); a nonlinear, multimedia, flexible system to provide information resources on the Internet and to gain access to such resources; based on hypertext and HTTP.

Web 2.0. The trend in Web technology that emphasizes collaboration among users and interactivity between users and content. Examples of Web 2.0 features include rating resources, reviews, and tagging (q.v.).

Web crawler. *See* **Spider.**

WLN (Western Library Network). Formerly a bibliographic network that served western North America; its software was used in Australia, Canada, and other places; now absorbed by OCLC.

Word-by-word filing. An arrangement of terms in a retrieval tool in such a way that spaces between words take precedence over any letter that may follow (e.g., "New York" appears before "Newark"). *See also* **Letter-by-letter filing.**

Work (as opposed to "item"). A distinct intellectual or artistic creation; an abstract instance of content or ideas, regardless of the packaging in which the content or ideas may be expressed.

Work/expression name. *See* **Uniform title.**

Work mark. A designation added to a cutter number, in a call number, that usually stands for the first word, not an article, of the title of the entity, but may stand for other entities, such as the name of a biographee, depending upon the circumstances.

Wrapper. In programming or in an encoding scheme (e.g., XML), a code or element that can have subcodes or subelements nested within it.

WWW (World Wide Web). *See* **Web.**

XML (eXtensible Markup Language). A subset of SGML, designed specifically for Web documents, that omits some features of SGML and includes a few additional features (e.g., a method for reading non-ASCII text); it allows designers to create their own customized tags, thus overcoming many of the limitations of HTML.

XML Schema. A definition, like the Document Type Definition (DTD), that provides the constraints of XML document instances and provides a mechanism for their validation. Unlike a DTD, an XML Schema is expressed in XML syntax itself, and follows XML rules. Moreover, XML Schemas support namespaces, inheritance, and are capable of defining data types.

Z39. The standards section of ANSI/NISO that is devoted to libraries, information science, and publishing.

Z39.50. A national standard that provides for the exchange of information, such as surrogate records or full text, between otherwise noncompatible computer systems.

Z39.50 protocol. A standard applications-level tool that allows one computer to query another computer and transfer search results without the user having to know the search commands of the remote computer.

SELECTED BIBLIOGRAPHY

Akeroyd, John, and Andrew Cox. "Integrated Library Management Systems: Overview." *Vine* 115 (2000): 3–10.

ALA/ALCTS/CCS Committee on Cataloging: Description and Access. Task Force on Metadata and the Cataloging Rules. "Final Report." Available: http://www.libraries.psu.edu/tas/jca/ccda/tf-tei2.html.

Allen, Sharon. *Beginning Relational Data Modeling.* 2nd ed. Berkeley, Calif.: Apress, 2005.

Anderson, James A. *An Introduction to Neural Networks.* Cambridge, Mass.: MIT Press, 1995.

Anglo-American Cataloguing Rules, Second Edition, 2002 Revision, prepared under the direction of the Joint Steering Committee for Revision of AACR. Ottawa: Canadian Library Association; Chicago: American Library Association, 2002.

Arms, William Y. *Digital Libraries.* Cambridge, Mass.: MIT Press, 2000.

Atherton, Jay. "From Life Cycle to Continuum: Some Thoughts on the Records Management–Archives Relationship." *Archivaria* 21 (Winter 1985–1986): 43–51.

Baca, Murtha. "A Picture Is Worth a Thousand Words: Metadata for Art Objects and Their Visual Surrogates." In *Cataloging the Web: Metadata, AACR, and MARC 21,* edited by Wayne Jones, et al. Lanham, Md.: Scarecrow Press, 2002, pp. 131–138.

Baca, Murtha, ed. *Introduction to Metadata.* 2nd ed. Los Angeles, Calif.: Getty Research Institute, 2008.

Baca, Murtha, Patricia Harpring, Elisa Lanzi, Linda McRae, and Ann Whiteside. *Cataloguing Cultural Objects: A Guide to Describing Cultural Works and*

Their Images. Chicago: American Library Association, 2006. Partial availability on the Web: http://www.vraweb.org/ccoweb/cco/index.html.

Baker, Nicholson. "Discards." *New Yorker* 70, no. 7 (April 4, 1994): 64–86.

Banerjee, Sujata, and Vibhu O. Mittal. "On the Use of Linguistic Ontologies for Accessing and Indexing Distributed Digital Libraries." In *Digital Libraries '94: Proceedings of the First Annual Conference on the Theory and Practice of Digital Libraries, June 19–21, 1994, College Station, Texas.* Available: http://www.hpl.hp.com/personal/Sujata_Banerjee/pubs.html.

Bates, Marcia J. "The Design of Browsing and Berrypicking Techniques for the Online Search Interface." *Online Review* 13, no. 5 (October 1989): 407–424.

———. "Subject Access in Online Catalogs: A Design Model." *Journal of the American Society for Information Science* 37, no. 6 (1986): 357–376.

Bearman, David. "Functional Requirements for Collections Management Systems." *Archival Informatics Technical Report* 1, no. 3 (Fall 1987): 1–87.

Beheshti, Jamshid. "The Evolving OPAC." *Cataloging & Classification Quarterly* 24, no. 1/2 (1997): 163–185.

Berman, Sanford. *Joy of Cataloging*. Phoenix, Ariz.: Oryx Press, 1981.

Berner, Richard C. "Historical Development of Archival Theory and Practices in the United States." *Midwestern Archivist* 7, no. 2 (1982): 103–117.

Berners-Lee, Tim, James Hendler, and Ora Lassila. "The Semantic Web." *Scientific American* 284, no. 5 (May 2001): 34–38, 40–43. Also available: http://www.sciam.com/article.cfm?id=the-semantic-web.

Bertolucci, Katherine. "Happiness Is Taxonomy: Four Structures for Snoopy." *Information Outlook* 7, no. 3 (March 2003): 36–44.

Bhatt, G. D. "Knowledge Management in Organizations: Examining the Interactions Between Technologies, Techniques, and People." *Journal of Knowledge Management* 5, no. 1 (2001): 68–75.

Bierbaum, Esther Green. "Records and Access: Museum Registration and Library Cataloging." *Cataloging & Classification Quarterly* 9, no. 1 (1988): 97–111.

Bilal, Dania. *Automating Media Centers and Small Libraries: A Microcomputer-Based Approach.* Greenwood Village, Colo.: Libraries Unlimited, 2002.

Borgman, Christine L. *From Gutenberg to the Global Information Infrastructure: Access to Information in the Networked World.* Cambridge, Mass.: MIT Press, 2000.

———. "Why Are Online Catalogs Hard to Use? Lessons Learned from Information Retrieval Studies." *Journal of the American Society for Information Science* 37, no. 6 (June 1986): 387–400.

———. "Why Are Online Catalogs *Still* Hard to Use?" *Journal of the American Society for Information Science* 47, no. 7 (July 1996): 493–503.

Bowker, Geoffrey C., and Susan Leigh Star. *Sorting Things Out: Classification and Its Consequences.* Cambridge, Mass.: MIT Press, 1999.

Breeding, Marshall. "Automation System Marketplace." *Library Journal.* April 1st issue each year.

———. Library Technology Guides. Available: http://www.librarytechnology.org/.

———. "Next Generation Catalogs." *Library Technology Reports: Expert Guides to Library Systems and Services* 43, no 4 (July/August 2007): 1–42.

Broughton, Vanda. "The Need for a Faceted Classification as the Basis of All Methods of Information Retrieval." *Aslib Proceedings: New Information Perspectives* 58, no. 1/2 (2006): 49–72.

Buck, Rebecca A., and Jean Allman Gilmore, eds. *The New Museum Registration Methods.* Washington, D.C.: American Association of Museums, 1998.

Buckland, Michael K. "What is a 'Document'?" *Journal of the American Society for Information Science* 48, no. 9 (September 1997): 804–809. Also available: http://people.ischool.berkeley.edu/~buckland/whatdoc.html.

Burke, Frank G. "Archives: Organization and Description." In *World Encyclopedia of Library and Information Services.* 3rd ed. Chicago: American Library Association, 1993, pp. 63–68.

Bush, Vannevar. "As We May Think." *Atlantic Monthly* 176 (July 1945): 101–108. Also available: http://www.theatlantic.com/doc/194507/bush.

Caplan, Priscilla. *Metadata Fundamentals for All Librarians.* Chicago: American Library Association, 2003.

Carlyle, Allyson. "Fulfilling the Second Objective in the Online Catalog: Schemes for Organizing Author and Work Records into Usable Displays." *Library Resources & Technical Services* 41, no. 2 (April 1997): 79–100.

Carlyle, Allyson, and Traci Timmons. "Default Record Displays in Web-Based Catalogs." *Library Quarterly* 72, no. 2 (April 2002): 179–204.

Carpenter, Michael. "The Original 73 Rules of the British Museum: A Preliminary Analysis." *Cataloging & Classification Quarterly* 35, no. 1/2 (2002): 23–36.

"Categories for the Description of Works of Art," edited by Murtha Baca and Patricia Harpring. The Getty. Available: http://www.getty.edu/research/conducting_research/standards/cdwa/.

Chan, Lois Mai. *A Guide to the Library of Congress Classification.* 5th ed. Englewood, Colo.: Libraries Unlimited, 1999.

———. *Library of Congress Subject Headings: Principles and Applications.* 4th ed. Westport, Conn.: Libraries Unlimited, 2006.

Chan, Lois Mai, and Joan S. Mitchell. *Dewey Decimal Classification: Principles and Application.* 3rd ed. Dublin, Ohio: OCLC, 2003.

Chan, Lois Mai, with the assistance of Theodora L. Hodges. *Cataloging and Classification: An Introduction.* 3rd ed. Lanham, Md.: Scarecrow Press, 2007.

Chen, Hao, and Susan Dumais. "Bringing Order to the Web: Automatically Categorizing Search Results." Microsoft Research Publications, 2000. Available: http://research.microsoft.com/~sdumais/chi00.pdf.

Classification Research Group. "The Need for a Faceted Classification as the Basis of All Methods of Information Retrieval." In *Theory of Subject Analysis: A Sourcebook,* edited by Lois Mai Chan, Phyllis A. Richmond, and Elaine Svenonius. Littleton, Colo.: Libraries Unlimited, 1985, pp. 154–167.

Clayton, Mark. "Library Stacks? No, That's My Office." *Christian Science Monitor* (July 16, 2002). Also available: http://www.csmonitor.com/2002/0716/p16s01-lehl.html.

Cleveland, Donald B., and Ana D. Cleveland. *Introduction to Indexing and Abstracting.* 3rd ed. Englewood, Colo.: Libraries Unlimited, 2001.

Collantes, Lourdes Y. "Agreement in Naming Objects and Concepts for Information Retrieval." PhD diss. New Brunswick, N.J.: Rutgers University, 1992.

Crawford, Walt. "The Card Catalog and Other Digital Controversies: What's Obsolete and What's Not in the Age of Information." *American Libraries* 30, no. 1 (January 1999): 52–58.

Cutter, Charles A. *Rules for a Dictionary Catalog.* 4th ed. Washington, D.C.: Government Printing Office, 1904; Reprint, London: The Library Association, 1962.

Denton, William. "FRBR and the History of Cataloging." In *Understanding FRBR: What It Is and How It Will Affect Our Retrieval Tools,* edited by Arlene G. Taylor. Westport, Conn.: Libraries Unlimited, 2007.

Describing Archives: A Content Standard. Chicago: Society of American Archivists, 2004.

Dewey Decimal Classification Homepage. Available: http://www.oclc.org/dewey/.

Digital Library Technology Trends. Santa Clara, Calif.: Sun Microsystems, 2002.

Dillon, Andrew. "Information Architecture in JASIST: Just Where Did We Come From?" *Journal of the American Society for Information Science and Technology* 53, no. 10 (2002): 821–823. Also available: http://www.gslis.utexas.edu/~adillon/Journals/IA%20ASIST%20intro.pdf.

Dooley, Jackie M. "Subject Indexing in Context." *American Archivist* 55, no. 2 (Spring 1992): 344–354.

Drabenstott, Karen M., and Marjorie S. Weller. "Failure Analysis of Subject Searches in a Test of a New Design for Subject Access to Online Catalogs." *Journal of the American Society for Information Science* 47, no. 7 (July 1996): 519–537.

Dublin Core Metadata Initiative. Available: http://dublincore.org/.

Dunkin, Paul S. *Cataloging U.S.A.* Chicago: American Library Association, 1969.

"EAD: Encoded Archival Description." Version 2002 Official Site. Library of Congress. Available: http://www.loc.gov/ead/.

Ellis, Judith, ed. *Keeping Archives.* 2nd ed. Port Melbourne, Australia: Thorpe, in association with the Australian Society of Archivists, 1993.

Elmasri, Ramez. *Fundamentals of Database Systems.* Boston: Pearson/Addison Wesley, 2007.

"ERIC's Indexing and Retrieval: 2001 Update" and "Thesaurus Construction and Format." In *Thesaurus of ERIC Descriptors,* edited by James E. Houston. 14th ed. Phoenix, Ariz.: Oryx Press, 2001, pp. xiv–xxxi.

Farb, Sharon. "Universal Design and the Americans with Disabilities Act: Not All Systems Are Created Equal—How Systems Design Can Expand Information Access: 2000." In *From Catalog to Gateway: Charting a Course for Future Access: Briefings from the ALCTS Catalog Form and Function Committee,* edited by Bill Sleeman and Pamela Bluh. Chicago: Association for Collections & Technical Services, American Library Association, 2005, pp. 99–106. Also available: http://www.pitt.edu/~agtaylor/ala/papers/FarbUniversalDesign.pdf.

Federal Geographic Data Committee (FGDC). "Content Standard for Digital Geospatial Metadata." Version 2.0, 1998. Available: http://www.fgdc.gov/standards/projects/FGDC-standards-projects/metadata/base-metadata.

Federal Geographic Data Committee (FGDC). "What Are Metadata?" Available: http://www.fgdc.gov/metadata.

Fishbein, Meyer H. "Archives: Records Management and Records Appraisal." In *World Encyclopedia of Library and Information Services.* 3rd ed. Chicago: American Library Association, 1993, pp. 60–63.

Foskett, A. C. *The Subject Approach to Information.* 5th ed. London: Library Association Publishing, 1996.

Fox, Michael J., and Peter Wilkerson. *Introduction to Archival Organization and Description: Access to Cultural Heritage.* Los Angeles: The Getty Information Institute, 1998.

Fritz, Deborah A., and Richard J. Fritz. *MARC21 for Everyone: A Practical Guide.* Chicago: American Library Association, 2003.

Furrie, Betty. *Understanding MARC Bibliographic: Machine-Readable Cataloging.* 7th ed. Library of Congress, Cataloging Distribution Service, 2003. Available: http://www.loc.gov/marc/umb.

The Getty. "Art & Architecture Thesaurus Online: About the AAT." Available: http://www.getty.edu/research/conducting_research/vocabularies/aat/about.html.

The Getty. "Learn About the Getty Vacabularies." Available: http://www.getty.edu/research/conducting_research/vocabularies/.

Gilster, Paul. *Digital Literacy.* New York: Wiley, 1997.

Gladwell, Malcolm. "The Social Life of Paper: Looking for Method in the Mess." *The New Yorker* (March 25, 2002). Available: http://www.newyorker.com/archive/2002/03/25/020325crbo_books.

Gorman, Michael. *The Concise AACR2.* 4th ed. Chicago: American Library Association, 2004.

———. "The Longer the Number, the Smaller the Spine; or, Up and Down with Melvil and Elsie." *American Libraries* 12, no. 8 (September 1981): 498–499.

Gross, Tina, and Arlene G. Taylor. "What Have We Got to Lose? The Effect of Controlled Vocabulary on Keyword Searching Results." *College & Research Libraries,* 66, no. 3 (May 2005): 212–230.

Guenther, Rebecca S. "MODS: The Metadata Object Description Schema." *Portal: Libraries and the Academy* 3, no. 1 (2003): 137–150.

Hagler, Ronald. *The Bibliographic Record and Information Technology.* 3rd ed. Chicago: American Library Association, 1997.

Harris, Mary Dee. *Introduction to Natural Language Processing.* Reston, Va.: Reston, 1985.

Harris, Michael H. *History of Libraries in the Western World.* 4th ed. Metuchen, N.J.: Scarecrow Press, 1995.

Hearst, Marti A. "Interfaces for Searching the Web." *Scientific American* 276, no. 3 (March 1997): 68–72. Also available: http://people.ischool.berkeley.edu/~hearst/papers/sciam/0397hearst.html.

Hedden, Heather. *Indexing Specialties: Web Sites.* Medford, N.J.: Information Today, for The American Society of Indexers, 2007.

Hider, Philip, with Ross Harvey. *Organising Knowledge in a Global Society: Principles and Practice in Libraries and Information Centres.* Rev. ed. Wagga Wagga, NSW, Australia: Centre for Information Studies, Charles Sturt University, 2008.

Hildreth, Charles R. "Online Catalog Design Models: Are We Moving in the Right Direction? A Report Submitted to Council on Library Resources August, 1995." Available: http://myweb.cwpost.liu.edu/childret/clr-opac.html.

———. "The Use and Understanding of Keyword Searching in a University Online Catalog." *Information Technology and Libraries* 16, no. 2 (June 1997): 52–62.

Hillmann, Diane. "Using Dublin Core." Dublin Core Metadata Initiative. Available: http://dublincore.org/documents/usageguide/.

Hillmann, Diane, and Elaine L. Westbrooks, eds. *Metadata in Practice.* Chicago: American Library Association, 2004.

Hodge, Gail. *Systems of Knowledge for Digital Libraries: Beyond Traditional Authority Files.* Washington, D.C.: Digital Library Federation, Council on Library and Information Resources, 2000.

———. *Understanding Metadata.* Bethesda, Md.: National Information Standards Organization, 2004. Available: http://www.niso.org/publications/press/UnderstandingMetadata.pdf.

Hopkins, Judith. "The 1791 French Cataloging Code and the Origins of the Card Catalog." *Libraries & Culture* 27, no. 4 (Fall 1992): 378–404.

Hsieh-Yee, Ingrid. *Organizing Audiovisual and Electronic Resources for Access: A Cataloging Guide.* 2nd ed. Westport, Conn.: Libraries Unlimited, 2006.

Humbert, de Romans. *Regulations for the Operation of a Medieval Library.* St. Paul: Associates of the James Ford Bell Library, University of Minnesota, 1980.

Hunter, Eric J. *Classification Made Simple.* 2nd ed. Aldershot, Eng.; Brookfield, Vt.: Gower, 2002.

Ince, A. Nejat, Cem Evrendilek, Dag Wilhelmsen, and Fadil Gezer. *Planning and Architectural Design of Modern Command Control Communications and Information Systems: Military and Civilian Applications.* Boston: Kluwer Academic, 1997.

International Conference on Cataloguing Principles, Paris, 9th–18th October, 1961, *Report.* London, International Federation of Library Associations, 1963. Also available in: *Library Resources & Technical Services* 6 (1962), pp. 162–167; and *Statement of principles adopted at the International Conference on Cataloguing Principles, Paris, October, 1961,* annotated ed., with commentary and examples by Eva Verona. London, IFLA Committee on Cataloguing, 1971; and A. H. Chaplin and Dorothy Anderson, eds. *Report/International Conference on Cataloguing Principles, Paris, 9th–18th October 1961.* London: IFLA International Office for UBC, 1981.

International Federation of Library Associations and Institutions. "Digital Libraries: Metadata Resources." Available: http://www.ifla.org/II/metadata.htm.

International Federation of Library Associations and Institutions, IFLA Study Group. *Functional Requirements for Bibliographic Records: Final Report.* München: Saur, 1998. Also available: http://www.ifla.org/VII/s13/frbr/frbr.pdf or http://www.ifla.org/VII/s13/frbr/frbr.htm.

International Federation of Library Associations and Institutions, Meeting of Experts on an International Cataloguing Code. "Statement of International Cataloguing Principles." April 10, 2008 version. Available: http://www.ifla.org/VII/s13/icc/imeicc-statement_of_principles-2008.pdf.

International Federation of Library Associations and Institutions, Working Group on FRANAR. "Functional Requirements for Authority Data: A Conceptual Model." Available: http://www.ifla.org/VII/d4/franar-conceptual-model-2ndreview.pdf.

International Standard Bibliographic Description (ISBD). Recommended by the ISBD Review Group; approved by the Standing Committee of the IFLA Cataloguing Section. Preliminary consolidated ed. München: K. G. Saur, 2007. Also available: http://www.ifla.org/VII/s13/pubs/cat-isbd.htm.

Intner, Sheila, Susan S. Lazinger, and Jean Weihs. *Metadata and Its Impact on Libraries.* Westport, Conn.: Libraries Unlimited, 2006.

Intner, Sheila S., Sally C. Tseng, and Mary Lynette Larsgaard, eds. *Electronic Cataloging: AACR2 and Metadata for Serials and Monographs.* Binghamton, N.Y.: Haworth Information Press, 2003.

Intner, Sheila S., and Jean Weihs. *Standard Cataloging for School and Public Libraries.* 4th ed. Westport, Conn.: Libraries Unlimited, 2007.

ISAD(G): General International Standard Archival Description. Adopted by the Committee on Descriptive Standards, Stockholm, Sweden, September 19–22, 1999, 2nd ed. Ottawa: International Council on Archives, 2000. Also available: http://www.icacds.org.uk/eng/ISAD(G).pdf.

Jackson, Sidney L. *Libraries and Librarianship in the West: A Brief History.* New York: McGraw-Hill, 1974.

Jacob, Elin K. "Classification and Categorization: A Difference That Makes a Difference." *Library Trends* 52, no. 3 (Winter 2004): 515–540.

———. "Ontologies and the Semantic Web." *Bulletin of the American Society for Information Science and Technology* 29, no. 4 (April/May 2003): 19–22. Also available: http://www.asis.org/Bulletin/Apr-03/BulletinAprMay03.pdf.

Jacsó, Péter, and F. W. Lancaster. *Build Your Own Database.* Chicago: American Library Association, 1999.

Jewett, Charles Coffin. *On the Construction of Catalogues of Libraries, and Their Publication by Means of Separate, Stereotyped Titles.* 2nd ed. Washington, D.C.: Smithsonian Institution, 1853.

Johnson, Bruce Chr. "XML and MARC: Which Is 'Right'?" *Cataloging & Classification Quarterly* 32, no. 1 (2001): 81–90.

Jones, Wayne, Judith R. Ahronheim, and Josephine Crawford, eds. *Cataloging the Web: Metadata, AACR, and MARC 21.* (ALCTS Papers on Library

Technical Services and Collections, no. 10.) Lanham, Md.: Scarecrow Press, 2002.

Joudrey, Daniel N. "Building Puzzles and Growing Pearls: A Qualitative Exploration of Determining Aboutness." PhD diss. Pittsburgh, Pa.: University of Pittsburgh, 2005. Available: http://etd.library.pitt.edu/ETD/available/etd-12132005-155713/.

Koch, Traugott, and Michael Day. "The Role of Classification Schemes in Internet Resource Description and Discovery." Available: http://www.ukoln.ac.uk/metadata/desire/classification/class_ti.htm.

Kochtanek, Thomas, and Joseph Matthews. *Library Information Systems: From Library Automation to Distributed Information Access Solutions.* Westport, Conn.: Libraries Unlimited, 2002.

Kohonen, Teuvo. *Self-Organizing Maps.* 3rd ed. Berlin, N.Y.: Springer-Verlag, 2001.

Kwasnik, Barbara H. "How a Personal Document's Intended Use or Purpose Affects Its Classification in an Office." In *Proceedings of the 12th Annual International ACM SIGIR Conference on Research and Development in Information Retrieval.* New York: ACM, [1989], pp. 207–210.

Lakoff, George. *Women, Fire, and Dangerous Things: What Categories Reveal about the Mind.* Chicago: University of Chicago Press, 1987.

Lancaster, F. W. *Indexing and Abstracting in Theory and Practice.* 3rd ed. Champaign: University of Illinois, Graduate School of Library and Information Science, 2003.

———. *Vocabulary Control for Information Retrieval.* 2nd ed. Arlington, Va.: Information Resources Press, 1986.

———. "Whither Libraries? or Wither Libraries." *College & Research Libraries* 39, no. 5 (September 1978): 345–357; also reprinted in *College & Research Libraries* 50, no. 4 (July 1989): 406–419.

Langridge, D. W. *Classification: Its Kinds, Elements, Systems and Applications.* London: Bowker-Saur, 1992.

———. *Subject Analysis: Principles and Procedures.* London: Bowker-Saur, 1989.

Larson, Ray R. "Classification Clustering, Probabilistic Information Retrieval, and the Online Catalog." *Library Quarterly* 6, no. 2 (April 1991): 133–173.

Larson, Ray R., Jerome McDonough, Paul O'Leary, and Lucy Kuntz. "Cheshire II: Designing a Next-Generation Online Catalog." *Journal of the American Society for Information Science* 47, no. 7 (July 1996): 555–567.

Lazinger, Susan S. *Digital Preservation and Metadata: History, Theory, Practice.* Englewood, Colo.: Libraries Unlimited, 2001.

Leise, Fred. "Using Faceted Classification to Assist Indexing." *Key Words* 9, no. 6 (November/December 2001): 178–179.

Levy, David M. "Cataloging in the Digital Order." In *Digital Libraries '95: The Second Annual Conference on the Theory and Practice of Digital Libraries, June 11–13, 1995, Austin, Texas.* Available: http://www.csdl.tamu.edu/DL95/papers/levy/levy.html.

Library of Congress. "Manuscript Division Finding Aids Online." Available: http://www.loc.gov/rr/mss/f-aids/mssfa.html.

Library of Congress Cataloging and Acquisitions. "Classification." Available: http://www.loc.gov/aba/cataloging/classification/.

Library of Congress, Network Development and MARC Standards Office. "MARC Standards." Available: http://www.loc.gov/marc/.

———. "MARCXML: MARC21 XML Schema." Available: http://www.loc.gov/standards/marcxml/.

Lubetzky, Seymour. *Cataloging Rules and Principles; a Critique of the A.L.A. Rules for Entry and a Proposed Design for their Revision.* Washington, D.C.: Library of Congress, 1953.

Lynch, Clifford A. "The Battle to Define the Future of the Book in the Digital World." *First Monday* 6, no. 6 (June 2001). Available: http://www.firstmonday.org/issues/issue6_6/lynch/index.html.

———. "Future Developments in Metadata and Their Role in Access to Networked Information." In *Cataloging the Web: Metadata, AACR, and MARC 21,* edited by Wayne Jones, et al. Lanham, Md.: Scarecrow Press, 2002, pp. 183–187.

Mann, Thomas. *Doing Research at the Library of Congress: A Guide to Subject Searching in a Closed Stacks Library.* Washington, D.C.: Library of Congress, Humanities and Social Sciences Division, 1994.

———. *The Oxford Guide to Library Research.* 3rd ed. New York: Oxford University Press, 2005.

"The MARC 21 Formats: Background and Principles." [Prepared by] MARBI in conjunction with Network Development and MARC Standards Office, Library of Congress. Washington, D.C.: Library of Congress, 1996. Available: http://lcweb.loc.gov/marc/96principl.html.

Marcella, Rita, and Arthur Maltby, eds. *The Future of Classification.* Aldershot, Eng.; Brookfield, Vt.: Gower, 2000.

Markey, Karen. "The Online Library Catalog: Paradise Lost and Paradise Regained?" *D-Lib Magazine* 13, no. 1/2 (2007). Available: http://www.dlib.org/dlib/january07/markey/01markey.html.

Matthews, Joseph R. "The Value of Information: The Case of the Library Catalog." *Technical Services Quarterly* 19, no. 2 (2001): 1–16.

Maxwell, Robert L. *FRBR: A Guide for the Perplexed.* Chicago: American Library Association, 2008.

McKiernan, Gerry. "Beyond Bookmarks: Schemes for Organizing the Web." Available: http://www.public.iastate.edu/~CYBERSTACKS/CTW.htm.

"Metadata Standards, Crosswalks, and Standard Organizations." In "Cataloger's Toolbox." Memorial University of Newfoundland Libraries. Available: http://staff.library.mun.ca/staff/toolbox/standards.htm.

Miller, Fredric M. "Archival Description." In *Reference Services for Archives and Manuscripts,* edited by Laura B. Cohen. Binghamton, N.Y.: Haworth Press, 1997, pp. 55–66.

Miller, Joseph, ed. *Sears List of Subject Headings.* 19th ed. New York: H. W. Wilson, 2007. "Principles of the Sears List of Subject Headings," pp. xv–xxix.

Moen, William E. "Resource Discovery Using Z39.50: Promise and Reality." In *Proceedings of the Bicentennial Conference on Bibliographic Control for the*

New Millennium, November 15–17, 2000. Washington, D.C.: Library of Congress Cataloging Distribution Service, 2001, pp. 185–206. Also available: http://lcweb.loc.gov/catdir/bibcontrol/moen_paper.html.

Morville, Peter, and Louis Rosenfeld. *Information Architecture for the World Wide Web.* 3rd ed. Sebastopol, Calif.: O'Reilly, 2007.

Mullins, Craig. *Database Administration: The Complete Guide to Practices and Procedures.* Boston: Addison-Wesley, 2002.

Nash, Lisa, and Aaron Press. "Taxonomies: Structuring Today's Knowledge Management Systems." In *Information About Information Briefing* (Outsell, Inc.) 4, no. 26 (July 18, 2001): 1–18.

National Library of Medicine. "Fact Sheet: Medical Subject Headings (MeSH®)." Available: http://www.nlm.nih.gov/pubs/factsheets/mesh.html.

———. "Fact Sheet: UMLS® Metathesaurus®." Available: http://www.nlm.nih.gov/pubs/factsheets/umlsmeta.html.

———. "Introduction to MeSH–2008." Available: http://www.nlm.nih.gov/mesh/introduction2008.html.

Norris, Dorothy May. *A History of Cataloging and Cataloging Methods.* London: Grafton, 1939.

Noy, Natalya Fridman, and Deborah L. McGuinness. *Ontology Development 101: A Guide to Creating Your First Ontology.* Knowledge Systems Laboratory, Stanford University, 2000. Available: http://www.ksl.stanford.edu/people/dlm/papers/ontology-tutorial-noy-mcguinness-abstract.html.

OCLC. *Bibliographic Formats and Standards.* 4th ed. 2008. Available: http://www.oclc.org/bibformats/.

Oder, Norman. "Cataloging the Net: Can We Do It?" *Library Journal* 123, no. 16 (October 1, 1998): 47–51.

———. "Cataloging the Net: Two Years Later." *Library Journal* 125, no. 16 (October 1, 2000): 50–51.

Olson, Hope A., and John J. Boll. *Subject Analysis in Online Catalogs.* 2nd ed. Englewood, Colo.: Libraries Unlimited, 2001.

The oss4lib Community. "oss4lib: Open Source Systems for Libraries." Available: http://www.oss4lib.org/.

Osborn, Andrew D. "The Crisis in Cataloging." In *Foundations of Cataloging: A Sourcebook,* edited by Michael Carpenter and Elaine Svenonius. Littleton, Colo.: Libraries Unlimited, 1985, pp. 90–103. Originally published in *Library Quarterly* 11, no. 4 (October 1941): 393–411.

Patton, Glenn E. "An Introduction to Functional Requirements for Authority Data (FRAD)" and "Understanding the Relationship between FRBR and FRAD." In *Understanding FRBR: What It Is and How It Will Affect Our Retrieval Tools,* edited by Arlene G. Taylor. Westport, Conn.: Libraries Unlimited, 2007, pp. 21–33.

Petroski, Henry. *The Book on the Bookshelf.* New York: Knopf, 1999.

Pettee, Julia. "The Subject Approach to Books and the Development of the Dictionary Catalog." In *Theory of Subject Analysis: A Sourcebook,* edited by Lois Mai Chan, Phyllis A. Richmond, and Elaine Svenonius. Littleton, Colo.: Libraries Unlimited, 1985, pp. 94–98.

Pitti, Daniel V. "Creator Description: Encoded Archival Context." *Cataloging & Classification Quarterly* 39, no. 1/2 (2004): 201–226; also published in *Authority Control in Organizing and Accessing Information: Definition and International Experience,* edited by Arlene G. Taylor and Barbara B. Tillett. New York: Haworth Information Press, 2004, pp. 201–226.

Powell, Gavin. *Beginning XML Databases.* Indianapolis: Wiley, 2007.

Program for Cooperative Cataloging. "Introduction to the Program for Cooperative Cataloging BIBCO Core Record Standards." Available: http://www.loc.gov/catdir/pcc/bibco/coreintro.html.

Ranganathan, S. R. *Prolegomena to Library Classification.* 3rd ed. London: Asia Publishing House, 1967.

Reynolds, Dennis. *Library Automation: Issues and Applications.* New York: Bowker, 1985.

"Report of the Working Group on Standards for Archival Description." *American Archivist* 52, no. 4 (Fall 1989): 440–461.

Rich, Elaine, and Kevin Knight. *Artificial Intelligence.* 2nd ed. New York: McGraw-Hill, 1991.

Robins, David. "Information Architecture, Organizations, and Records Management." *Records and Information Management Report* 17, no. 3 (March 2001): 1–14.

Rogers, JoAnn V., and Jerry D. Saye. *Nonprint Cataloging for Multimedia Collections.* 2nd ed. Littleton, Colo.: Libraries Unlimited, 1987.

Rowley, Jennifer, and Richard Hartley. *Organizing Knowledge: An Introduction to Managing Access to Information.* 4th ed. Aldershot, Eng.; Burlington, Vt.: Ashgate, 2008.

Russell, Beth M. "Hidden Wisdom and Unseen Treasure: Revisiting Cataloging in Medieval Libraries." *Cataloging & Classification Quarterly* 26, no. 3 (1998): 21–30.

Sauperl, Alenka. *Subject Determination during the Cataloging Process.* Lanham, Md.: Scarecrow Press, 2002.

Schulze, Anna Noakes. "User-Centered Design for Information Professionals." *Journal of Education for Library and Information Science* 42, no. 2 (Spring 2001): 116–122.

Shatford, Sarah. "Analyzing the Subject of a Picture: A Theoretical Approach." *Cataloging & Classification Quarterly* 6, no. 3 (1986): 39–62.

Shepherd, Elizabeth, and Geoffrey Yeo. *Managing Records: A Handbook of Principles and Practice.* London: Facet Publishing, 2003.

Smalley, Joseph. "The French Cataloging Code of 1791: A Translation." *Library Quarterly* 61, no. 1 (January 1991): 1–14.

Smiraglia, Richard P. "Authority Control and the Extent of Derivative Bibliographic Relationships." PhD diss. Chicago: University of Chicago, 1992.

———. "Bibliographic Families and Superworks." In *Understanding FRBR: What It Is and How It Will Affect Our Retrieval Tools,* edited by Arlene G. Taylor. Westport, Conn.: Libraries Unlimited, 2007, pp. 73–86.

———, ed. *Metadata: A Cataloger's Primer.* New York: Haworth Information Press, 2005.

———. *The Nature of "A Work": Implications for the Organization of Knowledge.* Lanham, Md.: Scarecrow Press, 2001.

Smith, Sherry and Kari Kells. *Inside Indexing: The Decision-Making Process.* Bend, Ore.: Northwest Indexing Press, 2005. Available: http://www.insideindexing.com.

Snowden, Dave. "Complex Acts of Knowing: Paradox and Descriptive Self-Awareness." *Bulletin of the American Society for Information Science and Technology* 29, no. 4 (April/May 2003): 23–28. Available: http://www.asis.org/Bulletin/Apr-03/BulletinAprMay03.pdf. This version is extracted and condensed from one that first appeared in *Journal of Knowledge Management* 6, no. 2 (May 2003): 100–111.

Society of American Archivists, Committee on Finding Aids. *Inventories and Registers: A Handbook of Techniques and Examples.* Chicago: Society of American Archivists, 1976.

Soergel, Dagobert. "The Rise of Ontologies or the Reinvention of Classification." *Journal of the American Society for Information Science* 50, no. 12 (October 1999): 1119–1120.

Steckel, Mike. "Ranganathan for IAs: An Introduction to the Thought of S. R. Ranganathan for Information Architects." *Boxes and Arrows* (October 7, 2002). Available: http://www.boxesandarrows.com/archives/ranganathan_for_ias.php.

Stoll, Clifford. *Silicon Snake Oil: Second Thoughts on the Information Highway.* New York: Doubleday, 1995.

Strout, Ruth French. "The Development of the Catalog and Cataloging Codes." *Library Quarterly* 26, no. 4 (October 1956): 254–275.

Svenonius, Elaine. *The Intellectual Foundation of Information Organization.* Cambridge, Mass.: The MIT Press, 2000.

Taylor, Arlene G. "Cataloguing." In *World Encyclopedia of Library and Information Services.* 3rd ed. Chicago: American Library Association, 1993, pp. 177–181.

———. "The Information Universe: Will We Have Chaos or Control?" *American Libraries* 25, no. 7 (July/August 1994): 629–632.

———. *Introduction to Cataloging and Classification.* 10th ed., with the assistance of David P. Miller. Westport, Conn.: Libraries Unlimited, 2006.

———. "An Introduction to Functional Requirements for Bibliographic Records (FRBR)." In *Understanding FRBR: What It Is and How It Will Affect Our Retrieval Tools,* edited by Arlene G. Taylor. Westport, Conn.: Libraries Unlimited, 2007, pp. 1–19.

———. "On the Subject of Subjects." *Journal of Academic Librarianship* 21, no. 6 (November 1995): 484–491.

Taylor, Arlene G., ed. *Understanding FRBR: What It is and How It Will Affect Our Retrieval Tools.* Westport, Conn.: Libraries Unlimited, 2007.

Taylor, Arlene G., and Barbara Tillett, eds. *Authority Control in Organizing and Accessing Information: Definition and International Experience.* New York: Haworth Information Press, 2004.

Taylor, Arlene G., and Daniel N. Joudrey. "Cataloging." In *Encyclopedia of Library and Information Sciences.* 3rd ed., edited by Marcia J. Bates and Mary Niles Maack. New York: Taylor & Francis, 2009.

Text Encoding Initiative. "TEI Lite." Available: http://www.tei-c.org/Guidelines/Customization/Lite/index.xml.

Tillett, Barbara B. "Authority Control: State of the Art and New Perspectives." *Cataloging & Classification Quarterly* 38, no. 3/4 (2004): 23–42; also published in *Authority Control in Organizing and Accessing Information: Definition and International Experience,* edited by Arlene G. Taylor and Barbara B. Tillett. New York: Haworth Information Press, 2004, pp. 23–42.

———. "Bibliographic Relationships." In *Relationships in the Organization of Knowledge,* edited by Carole A. Bean and Rebecca Green. Dordrecht: Kluwer Academic Publishers, 2001, pp. 9–35.

———. "Problems and Solutions in Cataloging Electronic Resources." *International Cataloguing and Bibliographic Control* 29, no. 1 (January/March 2000): 14–15.

———. "A Taxonomy of Bibliographic Relationships." *Library Resources & Technical Services* 30, no. 2 (April 1991): 156.

UDC Consortium. "About Universal Decimal Classification and the UDC Consortium." Available: http://www.udcc.org/about.htm.

Vellucci, Sherry L. "Metadata and Authority Control." *Library Resources & Technical Services* 44, no. 1 (January 2000): 33–43.

Visual Resources Association, Data Standards Committee. "VRA Core, Version 4.0." Available: http://www.vraweb.org/projects/vracore4/index.html.

Vizine-Goetz, Diane. "Using Library Classification Schemes for Internet Resources." Available: http://staff.oclc.org/~vizine/Intercat/vizine-goetz.htm.

W3C. "Extensible Markup Language." Available: http://www.w3.org/XML/.

———. "HTML." Available: http://www.w3.org/html/.

———. "HTML Tutorial." Available: http://www.w3schools.com/html/.

———. "Semantic Web Activity." Available: http://www.w3.org/2001/sw/.

———. "XML Tutorial." Available: http://www.w3schools.com/xml/.

Wallace, Danny P. *Knowledge Management: Historical and Cross-disciplinary Themes.* Westport, Conn.: Libraries Unlimited, 2007.

Weinberg, Bella Hass. *Can You Recommend a Good Book on Indexing? Collected Reviews on the Organization of Information.* Medford, N.J.: Information Today, 1998.

———. "Exhaustivity of Indexes: Books, Journals, and Electronic Full Text." *Key Words* 7, no. 5 (September/October 1999): 1, 6–19.

Weldon, J. L. "A Career in Data Modeling." *Byte* 22, no. 6 (June 1997): 103–106.

Wellish, Hans H. "Aboutness and Selection of Topics." *Key Words* 4, no. 2 (March/April 1996): 7–9.

"What Is a Neural Network?" NeuroDimension, Inc., 2002. Available: http://www.nd.com/welcome/whatisnn.htm.

Wilson, Katie. *Computers in Libraries: An Introduction for Library Technicians.* New York: Hawthorn Information Press, 2006.

Wilson, Patrick. "The Catalog as Access Mechanism: Background and Concepts." In *Foundations of Cataloging: A Sourcebook,* edited by Michael Carpenter and Elaine Svenonius. Littleton, Colo.: Libraries Unlimited, 1985, pp. 253–268.

———. *Two Kinds of Power: An Essay on Bibliographical Control.* Berkeley: University of California Press, 1968.

Witty, Francis J. "The Beginnings of Indexing and Abstracting: Some Notes Towards a History of Indexing and Abstracting in Antiquity and the Middle Ages." *The Indexer* 8 (1973): 193–198.

Working Group on the Future of Bibliographic Control. "On the Record: Report of the Library of Congress Working Group on the Future of Bibliographic Control." Library of Congress. Available: http://www.loc.gov/bibliographic-future/news/lcwg-ontherecord-jan08-final.pdf.

Wyllys, R. E. "Information Architecture." Reading prepared for Information Technologies and the Information Profession, Graduate School of Library & Information Science, University of Texas at Austin, 2000. Last updated June 28, 2003. Available: http://www.ischool.utexas.edu/~wyllys/ITIPMaterials/InfoArchitecture.html.

Yee, Martha M. "Guidelines for OPAC Displays: 1999." In *From Catalog to Gateway: Charting a Course for Future Access: Briefings from the ALCTS Catalog Form and Function Committee,* edited by Bill Sleeman and Pamela Bluh. Chicago: Association for Collections & Technical Services, American Library Association, 2005, pp. 83–90. Also available: http://www.pitt.edu/~agtaylor/ala/papers/YeeOPACGuidelines.pdf.

Yee, Martha M., and Sara Shatford Layne. *Improving Online Public Access Catalogs.* Chicago: American Library Association, 1998.

Zeng, Marcia Lei, and Jian Qin. *Metadata.* New York: Neal-Schuman, 2008.

INDEX

About the Authors

ARLENE G. TAYLOR is professor emerita, School of Information Sciences, University of Pittsburgh, and author of several works on cataloging and classification and authority control. She has received ALA's Margaret Mann Citation in Cataloging and Classification and the ALA Highsmith Library Literature Award.

DANIEL N. JOUDREY is an assistant professor in the Graduate School of Library and Information Science, Simmons College, Boston, Massachusetts, where he teaches information organization, descriptive cataloging, subject cataloging, and classification. His research interests include aboutness determination, subject access to information, and cataloging education.

CPSIA information can be obtained at www.ICGtesting.com
Printed in the USA
LVOW03*1555080215

426179LV00023B/948/P

9 781591 585862